PROFESSIONAL RESPONSIBILITY STANDARDS, RULES & STATUTES

2016–2017 Abridged Edition

Selected and Edited

by

JOHN S. DZIENKOWSKI
Professor of Law & Dean John F. Sutton, Jr.
Chair in Lawyering and the Legal Process
University of Texas

WEST ACADEMIC PUBLISHING

444 Cedar Street, Suite 700
St. Paul, MN 55101
1-877-888-1330

Printed in the United States of America

ISBN: 978-1-63460-766-7

PREFACE

In recent years, the ABA, the states, and other entities have been active in the promulgation of standards, rules, and statutes that regulate lawyers' conduct. These sources of the law of professional responsibility have significantly affected the manner in which lawyers analyze problems in this area. Similarly, the existence of different formal sources of professional responsibility have altered the way in which lawyers and law students are taught about ethical problems. This pamphlet of Professional Responsibility Standards, Rules, and Statutes is designed to provide teachers and students with easy access to the important sources of professional responsibility.

Beginning with the 1995 edition of Professional Responsibility Standards Rules and Statutes, this book is now published in a full version and an abridged version. The full version will continue to include various sources of professional responsibility including standards for specialized areas of practice and standards for the organized regulation of the profession. The abridged edition will present the ABA versions of the codes governing lawyers and judges as well as several selected rules of procedure and evidence and selected rules from California and New York. The purpose of the two editions is to allow professors to choose which version best fits the class that they plan to teach. This preface will, however, cover materials in both versions.

The full version of Professional Responsibility Standards Rules and Statutes is organized into eight different parts: (1) Codes Regulating Lawyers' Conduct; (2) Code of Judicial Conduct; (3) Rules of Evidence and Procedure that Affect the Legal Profession; (4) Restatement (Third) of the Law Governing Lawyers; (5) Statutes that Affect the Legal Profession; (6) Standards for Specialized Areas of Practice; (7) Standards for the Organized Regulation of Lawyers, and (8) Prior Versions of the ABA Model Rules and the ABA Code of Judicial Conduct. The abridged edition includes the first three parts which focus on the ABA's pronouncements as well as the federal rules of evidence and procedure that influence the legal profession.

In February 2000, the ABA House of Delegates amended the Model Rules to reflect the revisions proposed by the Ethics 2000 Commission. In 2003, the ABA amended the Model Rules to reflect the work of the ABA Commission on Multijurisdictional Practice and the work of the Cheek Commission. In 2012 and 2013, the ABA House of Delegates has begun to amend the Model Rules in light of proposals made by the Ethics 20/20 Commission. Where appropriate, the annotations also contain the text of a prior draft of the Model Rules to illustrate a shift in the final ABA position. In light of the fact that the states have made significant modifications to the ABA's version of the Model Rules, it has become desirable to include a section on selected significant state modifications to the Model Rules. Both the full and abridged editions now contain the California and New York state materials.

Both the full and abridged versions include the ABA Model Code of Professional Conduct and the 1908 Canons, as well as the 2015 Code of Judicial Conduct. The unabridged version of this supplement will continue to reproduce the 2001 version of the Model Rules in the annotated format because many court opinions relied upon this language. The unabridged version of this supplement will continue to reproduce the 1990 Code of Judicial Conduct. The prior standards are included to facilitate study of the evolution of professional standards as well as cases and jurisdictions that rely on the prior rules. These two documents are contained in part eight of the unabridged edition.

The full edition contains the text of the sections in the Restatement of Law Governing Lawyers and selected Reporters Comments. This project plays a significant role in shaping the law of professional responsibility.

I welcome comments and suggestions on the materials contained in this edition. My E-mail address is jdzienkowski@law.utexas.edu.

The materials are current through May 2016, and this supplement will be updated annually to reflect new and amended statutes and rules.

JOHN S. DZIENKOWSKI

Austin, Texas
May 2016

TABLE OF CONTENTS

PROFESSIONAL RESPONSIBILITY STANDARDS, RULES & STATUTES

2016–2017 Abridged Edition

PART ONE

CODES AND STANDARDS REGULATING LAWYERS' CONDUCT

Table of Contents

Introduction

One of the traditional characteristics of a profession is the attempt to achieve self regulation. Throughout history, professions have enacted codes of conduct to assert control over their members. Various groups within the legal profession have similarly sought to exercise a degree of self regulation by enacting codes of conduct. This part includes several codes and standards which have attempted to regulate the conduct of all lawyers in their practice of law.

The first three codes contained in this section were promulgated by the American Bar Association (ABA), a national voluntary organization of lawyers. The ABA has assumed the primary responsibility for promulgating national ethical standards for the legal profession. In 1908, the ABA enacted 32 Canons of Professional Ethics. In 1969, it replaced the Canons with the Model Code of Professional Responsibility. In 1983, the Model Code was replaced with the Model Rules of Professional Conduct. The 1983 version was amended many times by the ABA House of Delegates until the year 2001. That version of the Model Rules is reproduced in the full version of this supplement in part eight.

In 1997, the ABA established an Ethics 2000 Committee to revise the Model Rules in light of developments in law and practice. The ABA House of Delegates adopted a series of revisions in February 2002 to reflect the Ethics 2000 project. In August 2002, the ABA adopted further changes to the Model Rules to reflect the work of the committee on multijurisdictional practice of law. In August 2003, the ABA amended Model Rules 1.6 and 1.13 to reflect the profession's concern for lawyer involvement in financial frauds.

In 2009, the ABA formed the Ethics 20/20 Commission that was charged with modernizing the Model Rules in light of changes in the legal professions around the world. The 20/20 Commission held many hearings and produced several working papers. However, in the end, the Commission produced only two rounds of relatively minor changes that the ABA House of Delegates adopted in 2012 and 2013. Thus, the

Ethics 2000 revision of the Model Rules adopted in 2002 and 2003 remains the basis for the current ABA code.

Although the ABA's codes of conduct have been influential in shaping the law of professional responsibility, they only have force as a body of rules with its voluntary members. However, the various states and the federal courts have looked to the ABA versions as a basis for regulating lawyers within the jurisdiction. Thus, the ABA's codes have been used as the basis for state and federal codes. With the Model Code, many states adopted the ABA version without many significant changes. However, with the ABA's promulgation of the Model Rules, the states have been less deferential. Many states have made significant modifications to the ABA version. Thus, this part includes a section on significant state modifications to the Model Rules.

A final series of documents in this part reflect a recent trend on the part of the ABA and the states to focus on lawyer professionalism as a basis for regulating lawyers' conduct. The origin of this movement was a study on professionalism commissioned by the ABA. The results of the study identified several reasons for the decline in lawyer professionalism and offered several suggestions to address this problem. The ABA Creed of Professionalism and the ABA Pledge of Professionalism illustrate attempts to implement the suggestions of the Commission on Professionalism. The Texas Creed on Professionalism provides a similar example of a state effort to address this problem. The ABA's Aspirational Goals on Lawyer Advertising provide a more concrete example of urging standards of professionalism in the communication of advertising to the general public.

2016 AMERICAN BAR ASSOCIATION MODEL RULES OF PROFESSIONAL CONDUCT

Annotated to Include Amendments Since February 2016

CONTENTS

PREAMBLE: A LAWYER'S RESPONSIBILITIES

[1] A lawyer, as a member of the legal profession, is a representative of clients, an officer of the legal system and a public citizen having special responsibility for the quality of justice.

[2] As a representative of clients, a lawyer performs various functions. As advisor, a lawyer provides a client with an informed understanding of the client's legal rights and obligations and explains their practical implications. As advocate, a lawyer zealously asserts the client's position under the rules of the adversary system. As negotiator, a lawyer seeks a result advantageous to the client but consistent with requirements of honest dealings with others. As an evaluator, a lawyer acts by examining a client's legal affairs and reporting about them to the client or to others.

[3] In addition to these representational functions, a lawyer may serve as a third-party neutral, a nonrepresentational role helping the parties to resolve a dispute or other matter. Some of these Rules apply directly to lawyers who are or have served as third-party neutrals. See, e.g., Rules 1.12 and 2.4. In addition, there are Rules that apply to lawyers who are not active in the practice of law or to practicing lawyers even when they are acting in a nonprofessional capacity. For example, a lawyer who commits fraud in the conduct of a business is subject to discipline for engaging in conduct involving dishonesty, fraud, deceit or misrepresentation. See Rule 8.4.

[4] In all professional functions a lawyer should be competent, prompt and diligent. A lawyer should maintain communication with a client concerning the representation. A lawyer should keep in confidence information relating to representation of a client except so far as disclosure is required or permitted by the Rules of Professional Conduct or other law.

[5] A lawyer's conduct should conform to the requirements of the law, both in professional service to clients and in the lawyer's business and personal affairs. A lawyer should use the law's procedures only for legitimate purposes and not to harass or intimidate others. A lawyer should demonstrate respect for the legal system and for those who serve it, including judges, other lawyers and public officials. While it is a lawyer's duty, when necessary, to challenge the rectitude of official action, it is also a lawyer's duty to uphold legal process.

[6] As a public citizen, a lawyer should seek improvement of the law, access to the legal system, the administration of justice and the quality of service rendered by the legal profession. As a member of a learned profession, a lawyer should cultivate knowledge of the law beyond its use for clients, employ that knowledge in reform of the law and work to strengthen legal education. In addition, a lawyer should further the public's understanding of and confidence in the rule of law and the justice system because legal institutions in a constitutional democracy depend on popular participation and support to maintain their authority. A lawyer should be mindful of deficiencies in the administration of justice and of the fact that the poor, and sometimes persons who are not poor, cannot afford adequate legal assistance. Therefore, all lawyers should devote professional time and resources and use civic influence to ensure equal access to our system of justice for all those who because of economic or social barriers cannot afford or secure adequate legal counsel. A lawyer should aid the legal profession in pursuing these objectives and should help the bar regulate itself in the public interest.

[7] Many of a lawyer's professional responsibilities are prescribed in the Rules of Professional Conduct, as well as substantive and procedural law. However, a lawyer is also guided by personal conscience and the approbation of professional peers. A lawyer should strive to attain the highest level of skill, to improve the law and the legal profession and to exemplify the legal profession's ideals of public service.

[8] A lawyer's responsibilities as a representative of clients, an officer of the legal system and a public citizen are usually harmonious. Thus, when an opposing party is well represented, a lawyer can be a zealous advocate on behalf of a client and at the same time assume that justice is being done. So also, a lawyer can be sure that preserving client confidences ordinarily serves the public interest because people are more likely to seek legal advice, and thereby heed their legal obligations, when they know their communications will be private.

[9] In the nature of law practice, however, conflicting responsibilities are encountered. Virtually all difficult ethical problems arise from conflict between a lawyer's responsibilities to clients, to the legal system and to the lawyer's own interest in remaining an ethical person while earning a satisfactory living. The Rules of Professional Conduct often prescribe terms for resolving such conflicts. Within the framework of these Rules, however, many difficult issues of professional discretion can arise. Such issues must be resolved through the exercise of sensitive professional and moral judgment guided by the basic principles underlying the Rules. These principles include the lawyer's obligation zealously to protect and pursue a client's legitimate interests, within the bounds of the law, while maintaining a professional, courteous and civil attitude toward all persons involved in the legal system.

[10] The legal profession is largely self-governing. Although other professions also have been granted powers of self-government, the legal profession is unique in this respect because of the close relationship between the profession and the processes of government and law enforcement. This connection is manifested in the fact that ultimate authority over the legal profession is vested largely in the courts.

[11] To the extent that lawyers meet the obligations of their professional calling, the occasion for government regulation is obviated. Self-regulation also helps maintain the legal profession's independence from government domination. An independent legal profession is an important force in preserving government under law, for abuse of legal authority is more readily challenged by a profession whose members are not dependent on government for the right to practice.

[12] The legal profession's relative autonomy carries with it special responsibilities of self-government. The profession has a responsibility to assure that its regulations are conceived in the public interest and not in furtherance of parochial or self-interested concerns of the bar. Every lawyer is responsible for observance of the Rules of Professional Conduct. A lawyer should also aid in securing their observance by other lawyers. Neglect of these responsibilities compromises the independence of the profession and the public interest which it serves.

[13] Lawyers play a vital role in the preservation of society. The fulfillment of this role requires an understanding by lawyers of their relationship to our legal system. The Rules of Professional Conduct, when properly applied, serve to define that relationship.

SCOPE

[14] The Rules of Professional Conduct are rules of reason. They should be interpreted with reference to the purposes of legal representation and of the law itself. Some of the Rules are imperatives, cast in the terms "shall" or "shall not." These define proper conduct for purposes of professional discipline. Others, generally cast in the term "may," are permissive and define areas under the Rules in which the lawyer has discretion to exercise professional judgment. No disciplinary action should be taken when the lawyer chooses not to act or acts within the bounds of such discretion. Other Rules define the nature of relationships between the lawyer and others. The Rules are thus partly obligatory and disciplinary and partly constitutive and descriptive in that they define a lawyer's professional role. Many of the Comments use the term "should." Comments do not add obligations to the Rules but provide guidance for practicing in compliance with the Rules.

[15] The Rules presuppose a larger legal context shaping the lawyer's role. That context includes court rules and statutes relating to matters of licensure, laws defining specific obligations of lawyers and substantive and procedural law in general. The Comments are sometimes used to alert lawyers to their responsibilities under such other law.

[16] Compliance with the Rules, as with all law in an open society, depends primarily upon understanding and voluntary compliance, secondarily upon reinforcement by peer and public opinion and finally, when necessary, upon enforcement through disciplinary proceedings. The Rules do not, however, exhaust the moral and ethical considerations that should inform a lawyer, for no worthwhile human activity can be completely defined by legal rules. The Rules simply provide a framework for the ethical practice of law.

[17] Furthermore, for purposes of determining the lawyer's authority and responsibility, principles of substantive law external to these Rules determine whether a client-lawyer relationship exists. Most of the duties flowing from the client-lawyer relationship attach only after the client has requested the lawyer to render legal services and the lawyer has agreed to do so. But there are some duties, such as that of confidentiality under Rule 1.6, that attach when the lawyer agrees to consider whether a client-lawyer relationship shall be established. See Rule 1.18. Whether a client-lawyer relationship exists for any specific purpose can depend on the circumstances and may be a question of fact.

[18] Under various legal provisions, including constitutional, statutory and common law, the responsibilities of government lawyers may include authority concerning legal matters that ordinarily reposes in the client in private client-lawyer relationships. For example, a lawyer for a government agency may have authority on behalf of the government to decide upon settlement or whether to appeal from an adverse judgment. Such authority in various respects is generally vested in the attorney general and the state's attorney in state government, and their federal counterparts, and the same may be true of other government law officers. Also, lawyers under the supervision of these officers may be authorized to represent several government agencies in intragovernmental legal controversies in circumstances where a private lawyer could not represent multiple private clients. These Rules do not abrogate any such authority.

[19] Failure to comply with an obligation or prohibition imposed by a Rule is a basis for invoking the disciplinary process. The Rules presuppose that disciplinary assessment of a lawyer's conduct will be made on the basis of the facts and circumstances as they existed at the time of the conduct in question and in recognition of the fact that a lawyer often has to act upon uncertain or incomplete evidence of the situation. Moreover, the Rules presuppose that whether or not discipline should be imposed for a violation, and the severity of a sanction, depend on all the circumstances, such as the willfulness and seriousness of the violation, extenuating factors and whether there have been previous violations.

[20] Violation of a Rule should not itself give rise to a cause of action against a lawyer nor should it create any presumption in such a case that a legal duty has been breached. In addition, violation of a Rule does not necessarily warrant any other nondisciplinary remedy, such as disqualification of a lawyer in pending litigation. The Rules are designed to provide guidance to lawyers and to provide a structure for regulating conduct through disciplinary agencies. They are not designed to be a basis for civil liability. Furthermore, the purpose of the Rules can be subverted when they are invoked by opposing parties as procedural weapons. The fact that a Rule is a just basis for a lawyer's self-assessment, or for sanctioning a lawyer under the administration of a disciplinary authority, does not imply that an antagonist in a collateral proceeding or transaction has standing to seek enforcement of the Rule. Nevertheless, since the Rules do establish standards of conduct by lawyers, a lawyer's violation of a Rule may be evidence of breach of the applicable standard of conduct.

[21] The Comment accompanying each Rule explains and illustrates the meaning and purpose of the Rule. The Preamble and this note on Scope provide general orientation. The Comments are intended as guides to interpretation, but the text of each Rule is authoritative.

CLIENT-LAWYER RELATIONSHIP

Rule 1.0 Terminology

(a) "Belief" or "believes" denotes that the person involved actually supposed the fact in question to be true. A person's belief may be inferred from circumstances.

(b) "Confirmed in writing," when used in reference to the informed consent of a person, denotes informed consent that is given in writing by the person or a writing that a lawyer promptly transmits to the person confirming an oral informed consent. See paragraph (e) for the definition of "informed consent." If it is not feasible to obtain or transmit the writing at the time the person gives informed consent, then the lawyer must obtain or transmit it within a reasonable time thereafter.

(c) "Firm" or "law firm" denotes a lawyer or lawyers in a law partnership, professional corporation, sole proprietorship or other association authorized to practice law; or lawyers employed in a legal services organization or the legal department of a corporation or other organization.

(d) "Fraud" or "fraudulent" denotes conduct that is fraudulent under the substantive or procedural law of the applicable jurisdiction and has a purpose to deceive.

(e) "Informed consent" denotes the agreement by a person to a proposed course of conduct after the lawyer has communicated adequate information and explanation about the material risks of and reasonably available alternatives to the proposed course of conduct.

(f) "Knowingly," "known," or "knows" denotes actual knowledge of the fact in question. A person's knowledge may be inferred from circumstances.

(g) "Partner" denotes a member of a partnership, a shareholder in a law firm organized as a professional corporation, or a member of an association authorized to practice law.

(h) "Reasonable" or "reasonably" when used in relation to conduct by a lawyer denotes the conduct of a reasonably prudent and competent lawyer.

(i) "Reasonable belief" or "reasonably believes" when used in reference to a lawyer denotes that the lawyer believes the matter in question and that the circumstances are such that the belief is reasonable.

(j) "Reasonably should know" when used in reference to a lawyer denotes that a lawyer of reasonable prudence and competence would ascertain the matter in question.

(k) "Screened" denotes the isolation of a lawyer from any participation in a matter through the timely imposition of procedures within a firm that are reasonably adequate under the circumstances to protect information that the isolated lawyer is obligated to protect under these Rules or other law.

(*l*) "Substantial" when used in reference to degree or extent denotes a material matter of clear and weighty importance.

(m) "Tribunal" denotes a court, an arbitrator in a binding arbitration proceeding or a legislative body, administrative agency or other body acting in an adjudicative capacity. A legislative body, administrative agency or other body acts in an adjudicative capacity when a neutral official, after the presentation of evidence or legal argument by a party or parties, will render a binding legal judgment directly affecting a party's interests in a particular matter.

***(n) "Writing" or "written" denotes a tangible or electronic record of a communication or representation, including handwriting, typewriting, printing, photostating, photography, audio or videorecording and electronic communications. A "signed" writing includes an electronic sound, symbol or process attached to or logically associated with a writing and executed or adopted by a person with the intent to sign the writing.**

COMMENT

Confirmed in Writing

[1] If it is not feasible to obtain or transmit a written confirmation at the time the client gives informed consent, then the lawyer must obtain or transmit it within a reasonable time thereafter. If a lawyer has obtained a client's informed consent, the lawyer may act in reliance on that consent so long as it is confirmed in writing within a reasonable time thereafter.

Firm

[2] Whether two or more lawyers constitute a firm within paragraph (c) can depend on the specific facts. For example, two practitioners who share office space and occasionally consult or assist each other ordinarily would not be regarded as constituting a firm. However, if they present themselves to the public in a way that suggests that they are a firm or conduct themselves as a firm, they should be regarded as a firm for purposes of the Rules. The terms of any formal agreement between associated lawyers are relevant in determining whether they are a firm, as is the fact that they have mutual access to information concerning the clients they serve. Furthermore, it is relevant in doubtful cases to consider the underlying purpose of the Rule that is involved. A group of lawyers could be regarded as a firm for purposes of the Rule that the same lawyer should not represent opposing parties in litigation, while it might not be so regarded for purposes of the Rule that information acquired by one lawyer is attributed to another.

[3] With respect to the law department of an organization, including the government, there is ordinarily no question that the members of the department constitute a firm within the meaning of the Rules of Professional Conduct. There can be uncertainty, however, as to the identity of the client. For example, it may not be clear whether the law department of a corporation represents a subsidiary or an

* In August 2012, the ABA House of Delegates amended this provision to change the word "e-mail" to "electronic communications."

affiliated corporation, as well as the corporation by which the members of the department are directly employed. A similar question can arise concerning an unincorporated association and its local affiliates.

[4] Similar questions can also arise with respect to lawyers in legal aid and legal services organizations. Depending upon the structure of the organization, the entire organization or different components of it may constitute a firm or firms for purposes of these Rules.

Fraud

[5] When used in these Rules, the terms "fraud" or "fraudulent" refer to conduct that is characterized as such under the substantive or procedural law of the applicable jurisdiction and has a purpose to deceive. This does not include merely negligent misrepresentation or negligent failure to apprise another of relevant information. For purposes of these Rules, it is not necessary that anyone has suffered damages or relied on the misrepresentation or failure to inform.

Informed Consent

[6] Many of the Rules of Professional Conduct require the lawyer to obtain the informed consent of a client or other person (e.g., a former client or, under certain circumstances, a prospective client) before accepting or continuing representation or pursuing a course of conduct. See, e.g., Rules 1.2(c), 1.6(a) and 1.7(b). The communication necessary to obtain such consent will vary according to the Rule involved and the circumstances giving rise to the need to obtain informed consent. The lawyer must make reasonable efforts to ensure that the client or other person possesses information reasonably adequate to make an informed decision. Ordinarily, this will require communication that includes a disclosure of the facts and circumstances giving rise to the situation, any explanation reasonably necessary to inform the client or other person of the material advantages and disadvantages of the proposed course of conduct and a discussion of the client's or other person's options and alternatives. In some circumstances it may be appropriate for a lawyer to advise a client or other person to seek the advice of other counsel. A lawyer need not inform a client or other person of facts or implications already known to the client or other person; nevertheless, a lawyer who does not personally inform the client or other person assumes the risk that the client or other person is inadequately informed and the consent is invalid. In determining whether the information and explanation provided are reasonably adequate, relevant factors include whether the client or other person is experienced in legal matters generally and in making decisions of the type involved, and whether the client or other person is independently represented by other counsel in giving the consent. Normally, such persons need less information and explanation than others, and generally a client or other person who is independently represented by other counsel in giving the consent should be assumed to have given informed consent.

[7] Obtaining informed consent will usually require an affirmative response by the client or other person. In general, a lawyer may not assume consent from a client's or other person's silence. Consent may be inferred, however, from the conduct of a client or other person who has reasonably adequate information about the matter. A number of Rules require that a person's consent be confirmed in writing. See Rules 1.7(b) and 1.9(a). For a definition of "writing" and "confirmed in writing," see paragraphs (n) and (b). Other Rules require that a client's consent be obtained in a writing signed by the client. See, e.g., Rules 1.8(a) and (g). For a definition of "signed," see paragraph (n).

Screened

[8] This definition applies to situations where screening of a personally disqualified lawyer is permitted to remove imputation of a conflict of interest under Rules 1.10, 1.11, 1.12 or 1.18.

*[9] The purpose of screening is to assure the affected parties that confidential information known by the personally disqualified lawyer remains protected. The personally disqualified lawyer should acknowledge the obligation not to communicate with any of the other lawyers in the firm with respect to the matter. Similarly, other lawyers in the firm who are working on the matter should be informed that the screening is in place and that they may not communicate with the personally disqualified lawyer with respect to the matter. Additional screening measures that are appropriate for the particular matter will

* In August 2012, the ABA House of Delegates amended this comment to change the word "materials" to the phrase "information, including information in electronic form."

depend on the circumstances. To implement, reinforce and remind all affected lawyers of the presence of the screening, it may be appropriate for the firm to undertake such procedures as a written undertaking by the screened lawyer to avoid any communication with other firm personnel and any contact with any firm files or other information, including information in electronic form, relating to the matter, written notice and instructions to all other firm personnel forbidding any communication with the screened lawyer relating to the matter, denial of access by the screened lawyer to firm files or other information, including information in electronic form, relating to the matter and periodic reminders of the screen to the screened lawyer and all other firm personnel.

[10] In order to be effective, screening measures must be implemented as soon as practical after a lawyer or law firm knows or reasonably should know that there is a need for screening.

Rule 1.1 Competence

A lawyer shall provide competent representation to a client. Competent representation requires the legal knowledge, skill, thoroughness and preparation reasonably necessary for the representation.

COMMENT

Legal Knowledge and Skill

[1] In determining whether a lawyer employs the requisite knowledge and skill in a particular matter, relevant factors include the relative complexity and specialized nature of the matter, the lawyer's general experience, the lawyer's training and experience in the field in question, the preparation and study the lawyer is able to give the matter and whether it is feasible to refer the matter to, or associate or consult with, a lawyer of established competence in the field in question. In many instances, the required proficiency is that of a general practitioner. Expertise in a particular field of law may be required in some circumstances.

[2] A lawyer need not necessarily have special training or prior experience to handle legal problems of a type with which the lawyer is unfamiliar. A newly admitted lawyer can be as competent as a practitioner with long experience. Some important legal skills, such as the analysis of precedent, the evaluation of evidence and legal drafting, are required in all legal problems. Perhaps the most fundamental legal skill consists of determining what kind of legal problems a situation may involve, a skill that necessarily transcends any particular specialized knowledge. A lawyer can provide adequate representation in a wholly novel field through necessary study. Competent representation can also be provided through the association of a lawyer of established competence in the field in question.

[3] In an emergency a lawyer may give advice or assistance in a matter in which the lawyer does not have the skill ordinarily required where referral to or consultation or association with another lawyer would be impractical. Even in an emergency, however, assistance should be limited to that reasonably necessary in the circumstances, for ill-considered action under emergency conditions can jeopardize the client's interest.

[4] A lawyer may accept representation where the requisite level of competence can be achieved by reasonable preparation. This applies as well to a lawyer who is appointed as counsel for an unrepresented person. See also Rule 6.2.

Thoroughness and Preparation

[5] Competent handling of a particular matter includes inquiry into and analysis of the factual and legal elements of the problem, and use of methods and procedures meeting the standards of competent practitioners. It also includes adequate preparation. The required attention and preparation are determined in part by what is at stake; major litigation and complex transactions ordinarily require more extensive treatment than matters of lesser complexity and consequence. An agreement between the lawyer and the client regarding the scope of the representation may limit the matters for which the lawyer is responsible. See Rule 1.2(c).

Retaining or Contracting With Other Lawyers*

[6] Before a lawyer retains or contracts with other lawyers outside the lawyer's own firm to provide or assist in the provision of legal services to a client, the lawyer should ordinarily obtain informed consent from the client and must reasonably believe that the other lawyers' services will contribute to the competent and ethical representation of the client. See also Rules 1.2 (allocation of authority), 1.4 (communication with client), 1.5(e) (fee sharing), 1.6 (confidentiality), and 5.5(a) (unauthorized practice of law). The reasonableness of the decision to retain or contract with other lawyers outside the lawyer's own firm will depend upon the circumstances, including the education, experience and reputation of the nonfirm lawyers; the nature of the services assigned to the nonfirm lawyers; and the legal protections, professional conduct rules, and ethical environments of the jurisdictions in which the services will be performed, particularly relating to confidential information.

[7] When lawyers from more than one law firm are providing legal services to the client on a particular matter, the lawyers ordinarily should consult with each other and the client about the scope of their respective representations and the allocation of responsibility among them. See Rule 1.2. When making allocations of responsibility in a matter pending before a tribunal, lawyers and parties may have additional obligations that are a matter of law beyond the scope of these Rules.

Maintaining Competence**

[8] To maintain the requisite knowledge and skill, a lawyer should keep abreast of changes in the law and its practice, including the benefits and risks associated with relevant technology, engage in continuing study and education and comply with all continuing legal education requirements to which the lawyer is subject.

Rule 1.2 Scope of Representation and Allocation of Authority Between Lawyer and Client

(a) Subject to paragraphs (c) and (d), a lawyer shall abide by a client's decisions concerning the objectives of representation and, as required by Rule 1.4, shall consult with the client as to the means by which they are to be pursued. A lawyer may take such action on behalf of the client as is impliedly authorized to carry out the representation. A lawyer shall abide by a client's decision whether to settle a matter. In a criminal case, the lawyer shall abide by the client's decision, after consultation with the lawyer, as to a plea to be entered, whether to waive jury trial and whether the client will testify.

(b) A lawyer's representation of a client, including representation by appointment, does not constitute an endorsement of the client's political, economic, social or moral views or activities.

(c) A lawyer may limit the scope of the representation if the limitation is reasonable under the circumstances and the client gives informed consent.

(d) A lawyer shall not counsel a client to engage, or assist a client, in conduct that the lawyer knows is criminal or fraudulent, but a lawyer may discuss the legal consequences of any proposed course of conduct with a client and may counsel or assist a client to make a good faith effort to determine the validity, scope, meaning or application of the law.

COMMENT

Allocation of Authority between Client and Lawyer

[1] Paragraph (a) confers upon the client the ultimate authority to determine the purposes to be served by legal representation, within the limits imposed by law and the lawyer's professional obligations.

* In August 2012, the ABA House of Delegates added new Comments 6 and 7 to address the issue of outsourcing of work to lawyers and nonlawyers outside of the law firm.

** In August 2012, the ABA House of Delegates renumbered Comment 6 as Comment 8 and added a clause to require lawyers to keep abreast of relevant technology.

The decisions specified in paragraph (a), such as whether to settle a civil matter, must also be made by the client. See Rule 1.4(a)(1) for the lawyer's duty to communicate with the client about such decisions. With respect to the means by which the client's objectives are to be pursued, the lawyer shall consult with the client as required by Rule 1.4(a)(2) and may take such action as is impliedly authorized to carry out the representation.

[2] On occasion, however, a lawyer and a client may disagree about the means to be used to accomplish the client's objectives. Clients normally defer to the special knowledge and skill of their lawyer with respect to the means to be used to accomplish their objectives, particularly with respect to technical, legal and tactical matters. Conversely, lawyers usually defer to the client regarding such questions as the expense to be incurred and concern for third persons who might be adversely affected. Because of the varied nature of the matters about which a lawyer and client might disagree and because the actions in question may implicate the interests of a tribunal or other persons, this Rule does not prescribe how such disagreements are to be resolved. Other law, however, may be applicable and should be consulted by the lawyer. The lawyer should also consult with the client and seek a mutually acceptable resolution of the disagreement. If such efforts are unavailing and the lawyer has a fundamental disagreement with the client, the lawyer may withdraw from the representation. See Rule 1.16(b)(4). Conversely, the client may resolve the disagreement by discharging the lawyer. See Rule 1.16(a)(3).

[3] At the outset of a representation, the client may authorize the lawyer to take specific action on the client's behalf without further consultation. Absent a material change in circumstances and subject to Rule 1.4, a lawyer may rely on such an advance authorization. The client may, however, revoke such authority at any time.

[4] In a case in which the client appears to be suffering diminished capacity, the lawyer's duty to abide by the client's decisions is to be guided by reference to Rule 1.14.

Independence from Client's Views or Activities

[5] Legal representation should not be denied to people who are unable to afford legal services, or whose cause is controversial or the subject of popular disapproval. By the same token, representing a client does not constitute approval of the client's views or activities.

Agreements Limiting Scope of Representation

[6] The scope of services to be provided by a lawyer may be limited by agreement with the client or by the terms under which the lawyer's services are made available to the client. When a lawyer has been retained by an insurer to represent an insured, for example, the representation may be limited to matters related to the insurance coverage. A limited representation may be appropriate because the client has limited objectives for the representation. In addition, the terms upon which representation is undertaken may exclude specific means that might otherwise be used to accomplish the client's objectives. Such limitations may exclude actions that the client thinks are too costly or that the lawyer regards as repugnant or imprudent.

[7] Although this Rule affords the lawyer and client substantial latitude to limit the representation, the limitation must be reasonable under the circumstances. If, for example, a client's objective is limited to securing general information about the law the client needs in order to handle a common and typically uncomplicated legal problem, the lawyer and client may agree that the lawyer's services will be limited to a brief telephone consultation. Such a limitation, however, would not be reasonable if the time allotted was not sufficient to yield advice upon which the client could rely. Although an agreement for a limited representation does not exempt a lawyer from the duty to provide competent representation, the limitation is a factor to be considered when determining the legal knowledge, skill, thoroughness and preparation reasonably necessary for the representation. See Rule 1.1.

[8] All agreements concerning a lawyer's representation of a client must accord with the Rules of Professional Conduct and other law. See, e.g., Rules 1.1, 1.8 and 5.6.

Criminal, Fraudulent and Prohibited Transactions

[9] Paragraph (d) prohibits a lawyer from knowingly counseling or assisting a client to commit a crime or fraud. This prohibition, however, does not preclude the lawyer from giving an honest opinion about the actual consequences that appear likely to result from a client's conduct. Nor does the fact that a client

uses advice in a course of action that is criminal or fraudulent of itself make a lawyer a party to the course of action. There is a critical distinction between presenting an analysis of legal aspects of questionable conduct and recommending the means by which a crime or fraud might be committed with impunity.

[10] When the client's course of action has already begun and is continuing, the lawyer's responsibility is especially delicate. The lawyer is required to avoid assisting the client, for example, by drafting or delivering documents that the lawyer knows are fraudulent or by suggesting how the wrongdoing might be concealed. A lawyer may not continue assisting a client in conduct that the lawyer originally supposed was legally proper but then discovers is criminal or fraudulent. The lawyer must, therefore, withdraw from the representation of the client in the matter. See Rule 1.16(a). In some cases, withdrawal alone might be insufficient. It may be necessary for the lawyer to give notice of the fact of withdrawal and to disaffirm any opinion, document, affirmation or the like. See Rule 4.1.

[11] Where the client is a fiduciary, the lawyer may be charged with special obligations in dealings with a beneficiary.

[12] Paragraph (d) applies whether or not the defrauded party is a party to the transaction. Hence, a lawyer must not participate in a transaction to effectuate criminal or fraudulent avoidance of tax liability. Paragraph (d) does not preclude undertaking a criminal defense incident to a general retainer for legal services to a lawful enterprise. The last clause of paragraph (d) recognizes that determining the validity or interpretation of a statute or regulation may require a course of action involving disobedience of the statute or regulation or of the interpretation placed upon it by governmental authorities.

[13] If a lawyer comes to know or reasonably should know that a client expects assistance not permitted by the Rules of Professional Conduct or other law or if the lawyer intends to act contrary to the client's instructions, the lawyer must consult with the client regarding the limitations on the lawyer's conduct. See Rule 1.4(a)(5).

Rule 1.3 Diligence

A lawyer shall act with reasonable diligence and promptness in representing a client.

COMMENT

[1] A lawyer should pursue a matter on behalf of a client despite opposition, obstruction or personal inconvenience to the lawyer, and take whatever lawful and ethical measures are required to vindicate a client's cause or endeavor. A lawyer must also act with commitment and dedication to the interests of the client and with zeal in advocacy upon the client's behalf. A lawyer is not bound, however, to press for every advantage that might be realized for a client. For example, a lawyer may have authority to exercise professional discretion in determining the means by which a matter should be pursued. See Rule 1.2. The lawyer's duty to act with reasonable diligence does not require the use of offensive tactics or preclude the treating of all persons involved in the legal process with courtesy and respect.

[2] A lawyer's work load must be controlled so that each matter can be handled competently.

[3] Perhaps no professional shortcoming is more widely resented than procrastination. A client's interests often can be adversely affected by the passage of time or the change of conditions; in extreme instances, as when a lawyer overlooks a statute of limitations, the client's legal position may be destroyed. Even when the client's interests are not affected in substance, however, unreasonable delay can cause a client needless anxiety and undermine confidence in the lawyer's trustworthiness. A lawyer's duty to act with reasonable promptness, however, does not preclude the lawyer from agreeing to a reasonable request for a postponement that will not prejudice the lawyer's client.

[4] Unless the relationship is terminated as provided in Rule 1.16, a lawyer should carry through to conclusion all matters undertaken for a client. If a lawyer's employment is limited to a specific matter, the relationship terminates when the matter has been resolved. If a lawyer has served a client over a substantial period in a variety of matters, the client sometimes may assume that the lawyer will continue to serve on a continuing basis unless the lawyer gives notice of withdrawal. Doubt about whether a client-lawyer relationship still exists should be clarified by the lawyer, preferably in writing, so that the client will not mistakenly suppose the lawyer is looking after the client's affairs when the lawyer has ceased to do so. For

example, if a lawyer has handled a judicial or administrative proceeding that produced a result adverse to the client and the lawyer and the client have not agreed that the lawyer will handle the matter on appeal, the lawyer must consult with the client about the possibility of appeal before relinquishing responsibility for the matter. See Rule 1.4(a)(2). Whether the lawyer is obligated to prosecute the appeal for the client depends on the scope of the representation the lawyer has agreed to provide to the client. See Rule 1.2.

[5] To prevent neglect of client matters in the event of a sole practitioner's death or disability, the duty of diligence may require that each sole practitioner prepare a plan, in conformity with applicable rules, that designates another competent lawyer to review client files, notify each client of the lawyer's death or disability, and determine whether there is a need for immediate protective action. Cf. Rule 28 of the American Bar Association Model Rules for Lawyer Disciplinary Enforcement (providing for court appointment of a lawyer to inventory files and take other protective action in absence of a plan providing for another lawyer to protect the interests of the clients of a deceased or disabled lawyer).

Rule 1.4 Communication

(a) A lawyer shall:

(1) promptly inform the client of any decision or circumstance with respect to which the client's informed consent, as defined in Rule 1.0(e), is required by these Rules;

(2) reasonably consult with the client about the means by which the client's objectives are to be accomplished;

(3) keep the client reasonably informed about the status of the matter;

(4) promptly comply with reasonable requests for information; and

(5) consult with the client about any relevant limitation on the lawyer's conduct when the lawyer knows that the client expects assistance not permitted by the Rules of Professional Conduct or other law.

(b) A lawyer shall explain a matter to the extent reasonably necessary to permit the client to make informed decisions regarding the representation.

COMMENT

[1] Reasonable communication between the lawyer and the client is necessary for the client effectively to participate in the representation.

Communicating with Client

[2] If these Rules require that a particular decision about the representation be made by the client, paragraph (a)(1) requires that the lawyer promptly consult with and secure the client's consent prior to taking action unless prior discussions with the client have resolved what action the client wants the lawyer to take. For example, a lawyer who receives from opposing counsel an offer of settlement in a civil controversy or a proffered plea bargain in a criminal case must promptly inform the client of its substance unless the client has previously indicated that the proposal will be acceptable or unacceptable or has authorized the lawyer to accept or to reject the offer. See Rule 1.2(a).

[3] Paragraph (a)(2) requires the lawyer to reasonably consult with the client about the means to be used to accomplish the client's objectives. In some situations—depending on both the importance of the action under consideration and the feasibility of consulting with the client—this duty will require consultation prior to taking action. In other circumstances, such as during a trial when an immediate decision must be made, the exigency of the situation may require the lawyer to act without prior consultation. In such cases the lawyer must nonetheless act reasonably to inform the client of actions the lawyer has taken on the client's behalf. Additionally, paragraph (a)(3) requires that the lawyer keep the client reasonably informed about the status of the matter, such as significant developments affecting the timing or the substance of the representation.

*[4] A lawyer's regular communication with clients will minimize the occasions on which a client will need to request information concerning the representation. When a client makes a reasonable request for information, however, paragraph (a)(4) requires prompt compliance with the request, or if a prompt response is not feasible, that the lawyer, or a member of the lawyer's staff, acknowledge receipt of the request and advise the client when a response may be expected. A lawyer should promptly respond to or acknowledge client communications.

Explaining Matters

[5] The client should have sufficient information to participate intelligently in decisions concerning the objectives of the representation and the means by which they are to be pursued, to the extent the client is willing and able to do so. Adequacy of communication depends in part on the kind of advice or assistance that is involved. For example, when there is time to explain a proposal made in a negotiation, the lawyer should review all important provisions with the client before proceeding to an agreement. In litigation a lawyer should explain the general strategy and prospects of success and ordinarily should consult the client on tactics that are likely to result in significant expense or to injure or coerce others. On the other hand, a lawyer ordinarily will not be expected to describe trial or negotiation strategy in detail. The guiding principle is that the lawyer should fulfill reasonable client expectations for information consistent with the duty to act in the client's best interests, and the client's overall requirements as to the character of representation. In certain circumstances, such as when a lawyer asks a client to consent to a representation affected by a conflict of interest, the client must give informed consent, as defined in Rule 1.0(e).

[6] Ordinarily, the information to be provided is that appropriate for a client who is a comprehending and responsible adult. However, fully informing the client according to this standard may be impracticable, for example, where the client is a child or suffers from diminished capacity. See Rule 1.14. When the client is an organization or group, it is often impossible or inappropriate to inform every one of its members about its legal affairs; ordinarily, the lawyer should address communications to the appropriate officials of the organization. See Rule 1.13. Where many routine matters are involved, a system of limited or occasional reporting may be arranged with the client.

Withholding Information

[7] In some circumstances, a lawyer may be justified in delaying transmission of information when the client would be likely to react imprudently to an immediate communication. Thus, a lawyer might withhold a psychiatric diagnosis of a client when the examining psychiatrist indicates that disclosure would harm the client. A lawyer may not withhold information to serve the lawyer's own interest or convenience or the interests or convenience of another person. Rules or court orders governing litigation may provide that information supplied to a lawyer may not be disclosed to the client. Rule 3.4(c) directs compliance with such rules or orders.

Rule 1.5 Fees

(a) A lawyer shall not make an agreement for, charge, or collect an unreasonable fee or an unreasonable amount for expenses. The factors to be considered in determining the reasonableness of a fee include the following:

(1) the time and labor required, the novelty and difficulty of the questions involved, and the skill requisite to perform the legal service properly;

(2) the likelihood, if apparent to the client, that the acceptance of the particular employment will preclude other employment by the lawyer;

(3) the fee customarily charged in the locality for similar legal services;

(4) the amount involved and the results obtained;

(5) the time limitations imposed by the client or by the circumstances;

* In August 2012, the ABA House of Delegates deleted a line referring to a duty to return or acknowledge client telephone calls and added a line referring to client communications.

(6) the nature and length of the professional relationship with the client;

(7) the experience, reputation, and ability of the lawyer or lawyers performing the services; and

(8) whether the fee is fixed or contingent.

(b) The scope of the representation and the basis or rate of the fee and expenses for which the client will be responsible shall be communicated to the client, preferably in writing, before or within a reasonable time after commencing the representation, except when the lawyer will charge a regularly represented client on the same basis or rate. Any changes in the basis or rate of the fee or expenses shall also be communicated to the client.

(c) A fee may be contingent on the outcome of the matter for which the service is rendered, except in a matter in which a contingent fee is prohibited by paragraph (d) or other law. A contingent fee agreement shall be in a writing signed by the client and shall state the method by which the fee is to be determined, including the percentage or percentages that shall accrue to the lawyer in the event of settlement, trial or appeal; litigation and other expenses to be deducted from the recovery; and whether such expenses are to be deducted before or after the contingent fee is calculated. The agreement must clearly notify the client of any expenses for which the client will be liable whether or not the client is the prevailing party. Upon conclusion of a contingent fee matter, the lawyer shall provide the client with a written statement stating the outcome of the matter and, if there is a recovery, showing the remittance to the client and the method of its determination.

(d) A lawyer shall not enter into an arrangement for, charge, or collect:

(1) any fee in a domestic relations matter, the payment or amount of which is contingent upon the securing of a divorce or upon the amount of alimony or support, or property settlement in lieu thereof; or

(2) a contingent fee for representing a defendant in a criminal case.

(e) A division of a fee between lawyers who are not in the same firm may be made only if:

(1) the division is in proportion to the services performed by each lawyer or each lawyer assumes joint responsibility for the representation;

(2) the client agrees to the arrangement, including the share each lawyer will receive, and the agreement is confirmed in writing; and

(3) the total fee is reasonable.

COMMENT

Reasonableness of Fee and Expenses

[1] Paragraph (a) requires that lawyers charge fees that are reasonable under the circumstances. The factors specified in (1) through (8) are not exclusive. Nor will each factor be relevant in each instance. Paragraph (a) also requires that expenses for which the client will be charged must be reasonable. A lawyer may seek reimbursement for the cost of services performed in-house, such as copying, or for other expenses incurred in-house, such as telephone charges, either by charging a reasonable amount to which the client has agreed in advance or by charging an amount that reasonably reflects the cost incurred by the lawyer.

Basis or Rate of Fee

[2] When the lawyer has regularly represented a client, they ordinarily will have evolved an understanding concerning the basis or rate of the fee and the expenses for which the client will be responsible. In a new client-lawyer relationship, however, an understanding as to fees and expenses must be promptly established. Generally, it is desirable to furnish the client with at least a simple memorandum or copy of the lawyer's customary fee arrangements that states the general nature of the legal services to be

provided, the basis, rate or total amount of the fee and whether and to what extent the client will be responsible for any costs, expenses or disbursements in the course of the representation. A written statement concerning the terms of the engagement reduces the possibility of misunderstanding.

[3] Contingent fees, like any other fees, are subject to the reasonableness standard of paragraph (a) of this Rule. In determining whether a particular contingent fee is reasonable, or whether it is reasonable to charge any form of contingent fee, a lawyer must consider the factors that are relevant under the circumstances. Applicable law may impose limitations on contingent fees, such as a ceiling on the percentage allowable, or may require a lawyer to offer clients an alternative basis for the fee. Applicable law also may apply to situations other than a contingent fee, for example, government regulations regarding fees in certain tax matters.

Terms of Payment

[4] A lawyer may require advance payment of a fee, but is obliged to return any unearned portion. See Rule 1.16(d). A lawyer may accept property in payment for services, such as an ownership interest in an enterprise, providing this does not involve acquisition of a proprietary interest in the cause of action or subject matter of the litigation contrary to Rule 1.8(i). However, a fee paid in property instead of money may be subject to the requirements of Rule 1.8(a) because such fees often have the essential qualities of a business transaction with the client.

[5] An agreement may not be made whose terms might induce the lawyer improperly to curtail services for the client or perform them in a way contrary to the client's interest. For example, a lawyer should not enter into an agreement whereby services are to be provided only up to a stated amount when it is foreseeable that more extensive services probably will be required, unless the situation is adequately explained to the client. Otherwise, the client might have to bargain for further assistance in the midst of a proceeding or transaction. However, it is proper to define the extent of services in light of the client's ability to pay. A lawyer should not exploit a fee arrangement based primarily on hourly charges by using wasteful procedures.

Prohibited Contingent Fees

[6] Paragraph (d) prohibits a lawyer from charging a contingent fee in a domestic relations matter when payment is contingent upon the securing of a divorce or upon the amount of alimony or support or property settlement to be obtained. This provision does not preclude a contract for a contingent fee for legal representation in connection with the recovery of post-judgment balances due under support, alimony or other financial orders because such contracts do not implicate the same policy concerns.

Division of Fee

[7] A division of fee is a single billing to a client covering the fee of two or more lawyers who are not in the same firm. A division of fee facilitates association of more than one lawyer in a matter in which neither alone could serve the client as well, and most often is used when the fee is contingent and the division is between a referring lawyer and a trial specialist. Paragraph (e) permits the lawyers to divide a fee either on the basis of the proportion of services they render or if each lawyer assumes responsibility for the representation as a whole. In addition, the client must agree to the arrangement, including the share that each lawyer is to receive, and the agreement must be confirmed in writing. Contingent fee agreements must be in a writing signed by the client and must otherwise comply with paragraph (c) of this Rule. Joint responsibility for the representation entails financial and ethical responsibility for the representation as if the lawyers were associated in a partnership. A lawyer should only refer a matter to a lawyer whom the referring lawyer reasonably believes is competent to handle the matter. See Rule 1.1.

[8] Paragraph (e) does not prohibit or regulate division of fees to be received in the future for work done when lawyers were previously associated in a law firm.

Disputes over Fees

[9] If a procedure has been established for resolution of fee disputes, such as an arbitration or mediation procedure established by the bar, the lawyer must comply with the procedure when it is mandatory, and, even when it is voluntary, the lawyer should conscientiously consider submitting to it. Law may prescribe a procedure for determining a lawyer's fee, for example, in representation of an executor or

administrator, a class or a person entitled to a reasonable fee as part of the measure of damages. The lawyer entitled to such a fee and a lawyer representing another party concerned with the fee should comply with the prescribed procedure.

Rule 1.6 Confidentiality of Information*

(a) A lawyer shall not reveal information relating to the representation of a client unless the client gives informed consent, the disclosure is impliedly authorized in order to carry out the representation or the disclosure is permitted by paragraph (b).

(b) A lawyer may reveal information relating to the representation of a client to the extent the lawyer reasonably believes necessary:

(1) to prevent reasonably certain death or substantial bodily harm;

(2) to prevent the client from committing a crime or fraud that is reasonably certain to result in substantial injury to the financial interests or property of another and in furtherance of which the client has used or is using the lawyer's services;

(3) to prevent, mitigate or rectify substantial injury to the financial interests or property of another that is reasonably certain to result or has resulted from the client's commission of a crime or fraud in furtherance of which the client has used the lawyer's services;

(4) to secure legal advice about the lawyer's compliance with these Rules;

(5) to establish a claim or defense on behalf of the lawyer in a controversy between the lawyer and the client, to establish a defense to a criminal charge or civil claim against the lawyer based upon conduct in which the client was involved, or to respond to allegations in any proceeding concerning the lawyer's representation of the client; or

(6) to comply with other law or a court order; or

(7) to detect and resolve conflicts of interest arising from the lawyer's change of employment or from changes in the composition or ownership of a firm, but only if the revealed information would not compromise the attorney-client privilege or otherwise prejudice the client.

(c) A lawyer shall make reasonable efforts to prevent the inadvertent or unauthorized disclosure of, or unauthorized access to, information relating to the representation of a client.

---

* In August 2003, the ABA House of Delegates modified Model Rule 1.6 by adding new (b)(2) and (b)(3) and modifying some corresponding comments. The original rule text read as follows:

(a) A lawyer shall not reveal information relating to the representation of a client unless the client gives informed consent, the disclosure is impliedly authorized in order to carry out the representation or the disclosure is permitted by paragraph (b).

(b) A lawyer may reveal information relating to the representation of a client to the extent the lawyer reasonably believes necessary:

(1) to prevent reasonably certain death or substantial bodily harm;

(2) to secure legal advice about the lawyer's compliance with these Rules;

(3) to establish a claim or defense on behalf of the lawyer in a controversy between the lawyer and the client, to establish a defense to a criminal charge or civil claim against the lawyer based upon conduct in which the client was involved, or to respond to allegations in any proceeding concerning the lawyer's representation of the client; or

(4) to comply with other law or a court order.

In August 2012, the ABA House of Delegates added a new (b)(7) and (c) to this rule.

COMMENT

[1] This Rule governs the disclosure by a lawyer of information relating to the representation of a client during the lawyer's representation of the client. See Rule 1.18 for the lawyer's duties with respect to information provided to the lawyer by a prospective client, Rule 1.9(c)(2) for the lawyer's duty not to reveal information relating to the lawyer's prior representation of a former client and Rules 1.8(b) and 1.9(c)(1) for the lawyer's duties with respect to the use of such information to the disadvantage of clients and former clients.

[2] A fundamental principle in the client-lawyer relationship is that, in the absence of the client's informed consent, the lawyer must not reveal information relating to the representation. See Rule 1.0(e) for the definition of informed consent. This contributes to the trust that is the hallmark of the client-lawyer relationship. The client is thereby encouraged to seek legal assistance and to communicate fully and frankly with the lawyer even as to embarrassing or legally damaging subject matter. The lawyer needs this information to represent the client effectively and, if necessary, to advise the client to refrain from wrongful conduct. Almost without exception, clients come to lawyers in order to determine their rights and what is, in the complex of laws and regulations, deemed to be legal and correct. Based upon experience, lawyers know that almost all clients follow the advice given, and the law is upheld.

[3] The principle of client-lawyer confidentiality is given effect by related bodies of law: the attorney-client privilege, the work product doctrine and the rule of confidentiality established in professional ethics. The attorney-client privilege and work-product doctrine apply in judicial and other proceedings in which a lawyer may be called as a witness or otherwise required to produce evidence concerning a client. The rule of client-lawyer confidentiality applies in situations other than those where evidence is sought from the lawyer through compulsion of law. The confidentiality rule, for example, applies not only to matters communicated in confidence by the client but also to all information relating to the representation, whatever its source. A lawyer may not disclose such information except as authorized or required by the Rules of Professional Conduct or other law. See also Scope.

[4] Paragraph (a) prohibits a lawyer from revealing information relating to the representation of a client. This prohibition also applies to disclosures by a lawyer that do not in themselves reveal protected information but could reasonably lead to the discovery of such information by a third person. A lawyer's use of a hypothetical to discuss issues relating to the representation is permissible so long as there is no reasonable likelihood that the listener will be able to ascertain the identity of the client or the situation involved.

Authorized Disclosure

[5] Except to the extent that the client's instructions or special circumstances limit that authority, a lawyer is impliedly authorized to make disclosures about a client when appropriate in carrying out the representation. In some situations, for example, a lawyer may be impliedly authorized to admit a fact that cannot properly be disputed or to make a disclosure that facilitates a satisfactory conclusion to a matter. Lawyers in a firm may, in the course of the firm's practice, disclose to each other information relating to a client of the firm, unless the client has instructed that particular information be confined to specified lawyers.

Disclosure Adverse to Client

[6] Although the public interest is usually best served by a strict rule requiring lawyers to preserve the confidentiality of information relating to the representation of their clients, the confidentiality rule is subject to limited exceptions. Paragraph (b)(1) recognizes the overriding value of life and physical integrity and permits disclosure reasonably necessary to prevent reasonably certain death or substantial bodily harm. Such harm is reasonably certain to occur if it will be suffered imminently or if there is a present and substantial threat that a person will suffer such harm at a later date if the lawyer fails to take action necessary to eliminate the threat. Thus, a lawyer who knows that a client has accidentally discharged toxic waste into a town's water supply may reveal this information to the authorities if there is a present and substantial risk that a person who drinks the water will contract a life-threatening or debilitating disease and the lawyer's disclosure is necessary to eliminate the threat or reduce the number of victims.

[7] Paragraph (b)(2) is a limited exception to the rule of confidentiality that permits the lawyer to reveal information to the extent necessary to enable affected persons or appropriate authorities to prevent the client from committing a crime or fraud, as defined in Rule 1.0(d), that is reasonably certain to result in substantial injury to the financial or property interests of another and in furtherance of which the client has used or is using the lawyer's services. Such a serious abuse of the client-lawyer relationship by the client forfeits the protection of this Rule. The client can, of course, prevent such disclosure by refraining from the wrongful conduct. Although paragraph (b)(2) does not require the lawyer to reveal the client's misconduct, the lawyer may not counsel or assist the client in conduct the lawyer knows is criminal or fraudulent. See Rule 1.2(d). See also Rule 1.16 with respect to the lawyer's obligation or right to withdraw from the representation of the client in such circumstances, and Rule 1.13(c), which permits the lawyer, where the client is an organization, to reveal information relating to the representation in limited circumstances.

[8] Paragraph (b)(3) addresses the situation in which the lawyer does not learn of the client's crime or fraud until after it has been consummated. Although the client no longer has the option of preventing disclosure by refraining from the wrongful conduct, there will be situations in which the loss suffered by the affected person can be prevented, rectified or mitigated. In such situations, the lawyer may disclose information relating to the representation to the extent necessary to enable the affected persons to prevent or mitigate reasonably certain losses or to attempt to recoup their losses. Paragraph (b)(3) does not apply when a person who has committed a crime or fraud thereafter employs a lawyer for representation concerning that offense.

[9] A lawyer's confidentiality obligations do not preclude a lawyer from securing confidential legal advice about the lawyer's personal responsibility to comply with these Rules. In most situations, disclosing information to secure such advice will be impliedly authorized for the lawyer to carry out the representation. Even when the disclosure is not impliedly authorized, paragraph (b)(4) permits such disclosure because of the importance of a lawyer's compliance with the Rules of Professional Conduct.

[10] Where a legal claim or disciplinary charge alleges complicity of the lawyer in a client's conduct or other misconduct of the lawyer involving representation of the client, the lawyer may respond to the extent the lawyer reasonably believes necessary to establish a defense. The same is true with respect to a claim involving the conduct or representation of a former client. Such a charge can arise in a civil, criminal, disciplinary or other proceeding and can be based on a wrong allegedly committed by the lawyer against the client or on a wrong alleged by a third person, for example, a person claiming to have been defrauded by the lawyer and client acting together. The lawyer's right to respond arises when an assertion of such complicity has been made. Paragraph (b)(5) does not require the lawyer to await the commencement of an action or proceeding that charges such complicity, so that the defense may be established by responding directly to a third party who has made such an assertion. The right to defend also applies, of course, where a proceeding has been commenced.

[11] A lawyer entitled to a fee is permitted by paragraph (b)(5) to prove the services rendered in an action to collect it. This aspect of the rule expresses the principle that the beneficiary of a fiduciary relationship may not exploit it to the detriment of the fiduciary.

[12] Other law may require that a lawyer disclose information about a client. Whether such a law supersedes Rule 1.6 is a question of law beyond the scope of these Rules. When disclosure of information relating to the representation appears to be required by other law, the lawyer must discuss the matter with the client to the extent required by Rule 1.4. If, however, the other law supersedes this Rule and requires disclosure, paragraph (b)(6) permits the lawyer to make such disclosures as are necessary to comply with the law.

Detection of Conflicts of Interest*

[13] Paragraph (b)(7) recognizes that lawyers in different firms may need to disclose limited information to each other to detect and resolve conflicts of interest, such as when a lawyer is considering an association with another firm, two or more firms are considering a merger, or a lawyer is considering the purchase of a law practice. See Rule 1.17, Comment [7]. Under these circumstances, lawyers and law firms

---

* In August 2012, the ABA House of Delegates added new Comments 13 and 14 and substantially expanded Comment 18 to reflect the changes made in the text of the rule. Other comments were renumbered to take account of these additions.

are permitted to disclose limited information, but only once substantive discussions regarding the new relationship have occurred. Any such disclosure should ordinarily include no more than the identity of the persons and entities involved in a matter, a brief summary of the general issues involved, and information about whether the matter has terminated. Even this limited information, however, should be disclosed only to the extent reasonably necessary to detect and resolve conflicts of interest that might arise from the possible new relationship. Moreover, the disclosure of any information is prohibited if it would compromise the attorney-client privilege or otherwise prejudice the client (e.g., the fact that a corporate client is seeking advice on a corporate takeover that has not been publicly announced; that a person has consulted a lawyer about the possibility of divorce before the person's intentions are known to the person's spouse; or that a person has consulted a lawyer about a criminal investigation that has not led to a public charge). Under those circumstances, paragraph (a) prohibits disclosure unless the client or former client gives informed consent. A lawyer's fiduciary duty to the lawyer's firm may also govern a lawyer's conduct when exploring an association with another firm and is beyond the scope of these Rules.

[14] Any information disclosed pursuant to paragraph (b)(7) may be used or further disclosed only to the extent necessary to detect and resolve conflicts of interest. Paragraph (b)(7) does not restrict the use of information acquired by means independent of any disclosure pursuant to paragraph (b)(7). Paragraph (b)(7) also does not affect the disclosure of information within a law firm when the disclosure is otherwise authorized, see Comment [5], such as when a lawyer in a firm discloses information to another lawyer in the same firm to detect and resolve conflicts of interest that could arise in connection with undertaking a new representation.

[15] A lawyer may be ordered to reveal information relating to the representation of a client by a court or by another tribunal or governmental entity claiming authority pursuant to other law to compel the disclosure. Absent informed consent of the client to do otherwise, the lawyer should assert on behalf of the client all nonfrivolous claims that the order is not authorized by other law or that the information sought is protected against disclosure by the attorney-client privilege or other applicable law. In the event of an adverse ruling, the lawyer must consult with the client about the possibility of appeal to the extent required by Rule 1.4. Unless review is sought, however, paragraph (b)(64) permits the lawyer to comply with the court's order.

[16] Paragraph (b) permits disclosure only to the extent the lawyer reasonably believes the disclosure is necessary to accomplish one of the purposes specified. Where practicable, the lawyer should first seek to persuade the client to take suitable action to obviate the need for disclosure. In any case, a disclosure adverse to the client's interest should be no greater than the lawyer reasonably believes necessary to accomplish the purpose. If the disclosure will be made in connection with a judicial proceeding, the disclosure should be made in a manner that limits access to the information to the tribunal or other persons having a need to know it and appropriate protective orders or other arrangements should be sought by the lawyer to the fullest extent practicable.

[17] Paragraph (b) permits but does not require the disclosure of information relating to a client's representation to accomplish the purposes specified in paragraphs (b)(1) through (b)(6). In exercising the discretion conferred by this Rule, the lawyer may consider such factors as the nature of the lawyer's relationship with the client and with those who might be injured by the client, the lawyer's own involvement in the transaction and factors that may extenuate the conduct in question. A lawyer's decision not to disclose as permitted by paragraph (b) does not violate this Rule. Disclosure may be required, however, by other Rules. Some Rules require disclosure only if such disclosure would be permitted by paragraph (b). See Rules 1.2(d), 4.1(b), 8.1 and 8.3. Rule 3.3, on the other hand, requires disclosure in some circumstances regardless of whether such disclosure is permitted by this Rule. See Rule 3.3(c).

Acting Competently to Preserve Confidentiality

[18] Paragraph (c) requires a lawyer to act competently to safeguard information relating to the representation of a client against unauthorized access by third parties and against inadvertent or unauthorized disclosure by the lawyer or other persons who are participating in the representation of the client or who are subject to the lawyer's supervision. See Rules 1.1, 5.1 and 5.3. The unauthorized access to, or the inadvertent or unauthorized disclosure of, information relating to the representation of a client does not constitute a violation of paragraph (c) if the lawyer has made reasonable efforts to prevent the access or

disclosure. Factors to be considered in determining the reasonableness of the lawyer's efforts include, but are not limited to, the sensitivity of the information, the likelihood of disclosure if additional safeguards are not employed, the cost of employing additional safeguards, the difficulty of implementing the safeguards, and the extent to which the safeguards adversely affect the lawyer's ability to represent clients (e.g., by making a device or important piece of software excessively difficult to use). A client may require the lawyer to implement special security measures not required by this Rule or may give informed consent to forgo security measures that would otherwise be required by this Rule. Whether a lawyer may be required to take additional steps to safeguard a client's information in order to comply with other law, such as state and federal laws that govern data privacy or that impose notification requirements upon the loss of, or unauthorized access to, electronic information, is beyond the scope of these Rules. For a lawyer's duties when sharing information with nonlawyers outside the lawyer's own firm, see Rule 5.3, Comments [3]–[4].

*[19] When transmitting a communication that includes information relating to the representation of a client, the lawyer must take reasonable precautions to prevent the information from coming into the hands of unintended recipients. This duty, however, does not require that the lawyer use special security measures if the method of communication affords a reasonable expectation of privacy. Special circumstances, however, may warrant special precautions. Factors to be considered in determining the reasonableness of the lawyer's expectation of confidentiality include the sensitivity of the information and the extent to which the privacy of the communication is protected by law or by a confidentiality agreement. A client may require the lawyer to implement special security measures not required by this Rule or may give informed consent to the use of a means of communication that would otherwise be prohibited by this Rule. Whether a lawyer may be required to take additional steps in order to comply with other law, such as state and federal laws that govern data privacy, is beyond the scope of these Rules.

Former Client

[20] The duty of confidentiality continues after the client-lawyer relationship has terminated. See Rule 1.9(c)(2). See Rule 1.9(c)(1) for the prohibition against using such information to the disadvantage of the former client.

Rule 1.7 Conflict of Interest: Current Clients

(a) Except as provided in paragraph (b), a lawyer shall not represent a client if the representation involves a concurrent conflict of interest. A concurrent conflict of interest exists if:

(1) the representation of one client will be directly adverse to another client; or

(2) there is a significant risk that the representation of one or more clients will be materially limited by the lawyer's responsibilities to another client, a former client or a third person or by a personal interest of the lawyer.

(b) Notwithstanding the existence of a concurrent conflict of interest under paragraph (a), a lawyer may represent a client if:

(1) the lawyer reasonably believes that the lawyer will be able to provide competent and diligent representation to each affected client;

(2) the representation is not prohibited by law;

(3) the representation does not involve the assertion of a claim by one client against another client represented by the lawyer in the same litigation or other proceeding before a tribunal; and

(4) each affected client gives informed consent, confirmed in writing.

* In August 2012, the ABA House of Delegates added the last line to renumbered Comment 19.

COMMENT

General Principles

[1] Loyalty and independent judgment are essential elements in the lawyer's relationship to a client. Concurrent conflicts of interest can arise from the lawyer's responsibilities to another client, a former client or a third person or from the lawyer's own interests. For specific Rules regarding certain concurrent conflicts of interest, see Rule 1.8. For former client conflicts of interest, see Rule 1.9. For conflicts of interest involving prospective clients, see Rule 1.18. For definitions of "informed consent" and "confirmed in writing," see Rule 1.0(e) and (b).

[2] Resolution of a conflict of interest problem under this Rule requires the lawyer to: 1) clearly identify the client or clients; 2) determine whether a conflict of interest exists; 3) decide whether the representation may be undertaken despite the existence of a conflict, i.e., whether the conflict is consentable; and 4) if so, consult with the clients affected under paragraph (a) and obtain their informed consent, confirmed in writing. The clients affected under paragraph (a) include both of the clients referred to in paragraph (a)(1) and the one or more clients whose representation might be materially limited under paragraph (a)(2).

[3] A conflict of interest may exist before representation is undertaken, in which event the representation must be declined, unless the lawyer obtains the informed consent of each client under the conditions of paragraph (b). To determine whether a conflict of interest exists, a lawyer should adopt reasonable procedures, appropriate for the size and type of firm and practice, to determine in both litigation and non-litigation matters the persons and issues involved. See also Comment to Rule 5.1. Ignorance caused by a failure to institute such procedures will not excuse a lawyer's violation of this Rule. As to whether a client-lawyer relationship exists or, having once been established, is continuing, see Comment to Rule 1.3 and Scope.

[4] If a conflict arises after representation has been undertaken, the lawyer ordinarily must withdraw from the representation, unless the lawyer has obtained the informed consent of the client under the conditions of paragraph (b). See Rule 1.16. Where more than one client is involved, whether the lawyer may continue to represent any of the clients is determined both by the lawyer's ability to comply with duties owed to the former client and by the lawyer's ability to represent adequately the remaining client or clients, given the lawyer's duties to the former client. See Rule 1.9. See also Comments [5] and [29].

[5] Unforeseeable developments, such as changes in corporate and other organizational affiliations or the addition or realignment of parties in litigation, might create conflicts in the midst of a representation, as when a company sued by the lawyer on behalf of one client is bought by another client represented by the lawyer in an unrelated matter. Depending on the circumstances, the lawyer may have the option to withdraw from one of the representations in order to avoid the conflict. The lawyer must seek court approval where necessary and take steps to minimize harm to the clients. See Rule 1.16. The lawyer must continue to protect the confidences of the client from whose representation the lawyer has withdrawn. See Rule 1.9(c).

Identifying Conflicts of Interest: Directly Adverse

[6] Loyalty to a current client prohibits undertaking representation directly adverse to that client without that client's informed consent. Thus, absent consent, a lawyer may not act as an advocate in one matter against a person the lawyer represents in some other matter, even when the matters are wholly unrelated. The client as to whom the representation is directly adverse is likely to feel betrayed, and the resulting damage to the client-lawyer relationship is likely to impair the lawyer's ability to represent the client effectively. In addition, the client on whose behalf the adverse representation is undertaken reasonably may fear that the lawyer will pursue that client's case less effectively out of deference to the other client, i.e., that the representation may be materially limited by the lawyer's interest in retaining the current client. Similarly, a directly adverse conflict may arise when a lawyer is required to cross-examine a client who appears as a witness in a lawsuit involving another client, as when the testimony will be damaging to the client who is represented in the lawsuit. On the other hand, simultaneous representation in unrelated matters of clients whose interests are only economically adverse, such as representation of competing economic enterprises in unrelated litigation, does not ordinarily constitute a conflict of interest and thus may not require consent of the respective clients.

[7] Directly adverse conflicts can also arise in transactional matters. For example, if a lawyer is asked to represent the seller of a business in negotiations with a buyer represented by the lawyer, not in the same transaction but in another, unrelated matter, the lawyer could not undertake the representation without the informed consent of each client.

Identifying Conflicts of Interest: Material Limitation

[8] Even where there is no direct adverseness, a conflict of interest exists if there is a significant risk that a lawyer's ability to consider, recommend or carry out an appropriate course of action for the client will be materially limited as a result of the lawyer's other responsibilities or interests. For example, a lawyer asked to represent several individuals seeking to form a joint venture is likely to be materially limited in the lawyer's ability to recommend or advocate all possible positions that each might take because of the lawyer's duty of loyalty to the others. The conflict in effect forecloses alternatives that would otherwise be available to the client. The mere possibility of subsequent harm does not itself require disclosure and consent. The critical questions are the likelihood that a difference in interests will eventuate and, if it does, whether it will materially interfere with the lawyer's independent professional judgment in considering alternatives or foreclose courses of action that reasonably should be pursued on behalf of the client.

Lawyer's Responsibilities to Former Clients and Other Third Persons

[9] In addition to conflicts with other current clients, a lawyer's duties of loyalty and independence may be materially limited by responsibilities to former clients under Rule 1.9 or by the lawyer's responsibilities to other persons, such as fiduciary duties arising from a lawyer's service as a trustee, executor or corporate director.

Personal Interest Conflicts

[10] The lawyer's own interests should not be permitted to have an adverse effect on representation of a client. For example, if the probity of a lawyer's own conduct in a transaction is in serious question, it may be difficult or impossible for the lawyer to give a client detached advice. Similarly, when a lawyer has discussions concerning possible employment with an opponent of the lawyer's client, or with a law firm representing the opponent, such discussions could materially limit the lawyer's representation of the client. In addition, a lawyer may not allow related business interests to affect representation, for example, by referring clients to an enterprise in which the lawyer has an undisclosed financial interest. See Rule 1.8 for specific Rules pertaining to a number of personal interest conflicts, including business transactions with clients. See also Rule 1.10 (personal interest conflicts under Rule 1.7 ordinarily are not imputed to other lawyers in a law firm).

[11] When lawyers representing different clients in the same matter or in substantially related matters are closely related by blood or marriage, there may be a significant risk that client confidences will be revealed and that the lawyer's family relationship will interfere with both loyalty and independent professional judgment. As a result, each client is entitled to know of the existence and implications of the relationship between the lawyers before the lawyer agrees to undertake the representation. Thus, a lawyer related to another lawyer, e.g., as parent, child, sibling or spouse, ordinarily may not represent a client in a matter where that lawyer is representing another party, unless each client gives informed consent. The disqualification arising from a close family relationship is personal and ordinarily is not imputed to members of firms with whom the lawyers are associated. See Rule 1.10.

[12] A lawyer is prohibited from engaging in sexual relationships with a client unless the sexual relationship predates the formation of the client-lawyer relationship. See Rule 1.8(j).

Interest of Person Paying for a Lawyer's Service

[13] A lawyer may be paid from a source other than the client, including a co-client, if the client is informed of that fact and consents and the arrangement does not compromise the lawyer's duty of loyalty or independent judgment to the client. See Rule 1.8(f). If acceptance of the payment from any other source presents a significant risk that the lawyer's representation of the client will be materially limited by the lawyer's own interest in accommodating the person paying the lawyer's fee or by the lawyer's responsibilities to a payer who is also a co-client, then the lawyer must comply with the requirements of paragraph (b) before accepting the representation, including determining whether the conflict is consentable and, if so, that the client has adequate information about the material risks of the representation.

Prohibited Representations

[14] Ordinarily, clients may consent to representation notwithstanding a conflict. However, as indicated in paragraph (b), some conflicts are nonconsentable, meaning that the lawyer involved cannot properly ask for such agreement or provide representation on the basis of the client's consent. When the lawyer is representing more than one client, the question of consentability must be resolved as to each client.

[15] Consentability is typically determined by considering whether the interests of the clients will be adequately protected if the clients are permitted to give their informed consent to representation burdened by a conflict of interest. Thus, under paragraph (b)(1), representation is prohibited if in the circumstances the lawyer cannot reasonably conclude that the lawyer will be able to provide competent and diligent representation. See Rule 1.1 (competence) and Rule 1.3 (diligence).

[16] Paragraph (b)(2) describes conflicts that are nonconsentable because the representation is prohibited by applicable law. For example, in some states substantive law provides that the same lawyer may not represent more than one defendant in a capital case, even with the consent of the clients, and under federal criminal statutes certain representations by a former government lawyer are prohibited, despite the informed consent of the former client. In addition, decisional law in some states limits the ability of a governmental client, such as a municipality, to consent to a conflict of interest.

[17] Paragraph (b)(3) describes conflicts that are nonconsentable because of the institutional interest in vigorous development of each client's position when the clients are aligned directly against each other in the same litigation or other proceeding before a tribunal. Whether clients are aligned directly against each other within the meaning of this paragraph requires examination of the context of the proceeding. Although this paragraph does not preclude a lawyer's multiple representation of adverse parties to a mediation (because mediation is not a proceeding before a "tribunal" under Rule 1.0(m)), such representation may be precluded by paragraph (b)(1).

Informed Consent

[18] Informed consent requires that each affected client be aware of the relevant circumstances and of the material and reasonably foreseeable ways that the conflict could have adverse effects on the interests of that client. See Rule 1.0(e) (informed consent). The information required depends on the nature of the conflict and the nature of the risks involved. When representation of multiple clients in a single matter is undertaken, the information must include the implications of the common representation, including possible effects on loyalty, confidentiality and the attorney-client privilege and the advantages and risks involved. See Comments [30] and [31] (effect of common representation on confidentiality).

[19] Under some circumstances it may be impossible to make the disclosure necessary to obtain consent. For example, when the lawyer represents different clients in related matters and one of the clients refuses to consent to the disclosure necessary to permit the other client to make an informed decision, the lawyer cannot properly ask the latter to consent. In some cases the alternative to common representation can be that each party may have to obtain separate representation with the possibility of incurring additional costs. These costs, along with the benefits of securing separate representation, are factors that may be considered by the affected client in determining whether common representation is in the client's interests.

Consent Confirmed in Writing

[20] Paragraph (b) requires the lawyer to obtain the informed consent of the client, confirmed in writing. Such a writing may consist of a document executed by the client or one that the lawyer promptly records and transmits to the client following an oral consent. See Rule 1.0(b). See also Rule 1.0(n) (writing includes electronic transmission). If it is not feasible to obtain or transmit the writing at the time the client gives informed consent, then the lawyer must obtain or transmit it within a reasonable time thereafter. See Rule 1.0(b). The requirement of a writing does not supplant the need in most cases for the lawyer to talk with the client, to explain the risks and advantages, if any, of representation burdened with a conflict of interest, as well as reasonably available alternatives, and to afford the client a reasonable opportunity to consider the risks and alternatives and to raise questions and concerns. Rather, the writing is required in order to impress upon clients the seriousness of the decision the client is being asked to make and to avoid disputes or ambiguities that might later occur in the absence of a writing.

Revoking Consent

[21] A client who has given consent to a conflict may revoke the consent and, like any other client, may terminate the lawyer's representation at any time. Whether revoking consent to the client's own representation precludes the lawyer from continuing to represent other clients depends on the circumstances, including the nature of the conflict, whether the client revoked consent because of a material change in circumstances, the reasonable expectations of the other clients and whether material detriment to the other clients or the lawyer would result.

Consent to Future Conflict

[22] Whether a lawyer may properly request a client to waive conflicts that might arise in the future is subject to the test of paragraph (b). The effectiveness of such waivers is generally determined by the extent to which the client reasonably understands the material risks that the waiver entails. The more comprehensive the explanation of the types of future representations that might arise and the actual and reasonably foreseeable adverse consequences of those representations, the greater the likelihood that the client will have the requisite understanding. Thus, if the client agrees to consent to a particular type of conflict with which the client is already familiar, then the consent ordinarily will be effective with regard to that type of conflict. If the consent is general and open-ended, then the consent ordinarily will be ineffective, because it is not reasonably likely that the client will have understood the material risks involved. On the other hand, if the client is an experienced user of the legal services involved and is reasonably informed regarding the risk that a conflict may arise, such consent is more likely to be effective, particularly if, e.g., the client is independently represented by other counsel in giving consent and the consent is limited to future conflicts unrelated to the subject of the representation. In any case, advance consent cannot be effective if the circumstances that materialize in the future are such as would make the conflict nonconsentable under paragraph (b).

Conflicts in Litigation

[23] Paragraph (b)(3) prohibits representation of opposing parties in the same litigation, regardless of the clients' consent. On the other hand, simultaneous representation of parties whose interests in litigation may conflict, such as coplaintiffs or codefendants, is governed by paragraph (a)(2). A conflict may exist by reason of substantial discrepancy in the parties' testimony, incompatibility in positions in relation to an opposing party or the fact that there are substantially different possibilities of settlement of the claims or liabilities in question. Such conflicts can arise in criminal cases as well as civil. The potential for conflict of interest in representing multiple defendants in a criminal case is so grave that ordinarily a lawyer should decline to represent more than one codefendant. On the other hand, common representation of persons having similar interests in civil litigation is proper if the requirements of paragraph (b) are met.

[24] Ordinarily a lawyer may take inconsistent legal positions in different tribunals at different times on behalf of different clients. The mere fact that advocating a legal position on behalf of one client might create precedent adverse to the interests of a client represented by the lawyer in an unrelated matter does not create a conflict of interest. A conflict of interest exists, however, if there is a significant risk that a lawyer's action on behalf of one client will materially limit the lawyer's effectiveness in representing another client in a different case; for example, when a decision favoring one client will create a precedent likely to seriously weaken the position taken on behalf of the other client. Factors relevant in determining whether the clients need to be advised of the risk include: where the cases are pending, whether the issue is substantive or procedural, the temporal relationship between the matters, the significance of the issue to the immediate and long-term interests of the clients involved and the clients' reasonable expectations in retaining the lawyer. If there is significant risk of material limitation, then absent informed consent of the affected clients, the lawyer must refuse one of the representations or withdraw from one or both matters.

[25] When a lawyer represents or seeks to represent a class of plaintiffs or defendants in a class-action lawsuit, unnamed members of the class are ordinarily not considered to be clients of the lawyer for purposes of applying paragraph (a)(1) of this Rule. Thus, the lawyer does not typically need to get the consent of such a person before representing a client suing the person in an unrelated matter. Similarly, a lawyer seeking to represent an opponent in a class action does not typically need the consent of an unnamed member of the class whom the lawyer represents in an unrelated matter.

Nonlitigation Conflicts

[26] Conflicts of interest under paragraphs (a)(1) and (a)(2) arise in contexts other than litigation. For a discussion of directly adverse conflicts in transactional matters, see Comment [7]. Relevant factors in determining whether there is significant potential for material limitation include the duration and intimacy of the lawyer's relationship with the client or clients involved, the functions being performed by the lawyer, the likelihood that disagreements will arise and the likely prejudice to the client from the conflict. The question is often one of proximity and degree. See Comment [8].

[27] For example, conflict questions may arise in estate planning and estate administration. A lawyer may be called upon to prepare wills for several family members, such as husband and wife, and, depending upon the circumstances, a conflict of interest may be present. In estate administration the identity of the client may be unclear under the law of a particular jurisdiction. Under one view, the client is the fiduciary; under another view the client is the estate or trust, including its beneficiaries. In order to comply with conflict of interest rules, the lawyer should make clear the lawyer's relationship to the parties involved.

[28] Whether a conflict is consentable depends on the circumstances. For example, a lawyer may not represent multiple parties to a negotiation whose interests are fundamentally antagonistic to each other, but common representation is permissible where the clients are generally aligned in interest even though there is some difference in interest among them. Thus, a lawyer may seek to establish or adjust a relationship between clients on an amicable and mutually advantageous basis; for example, in helping to organize a business in which two or more clients are entrepreneurs, working out the financial reorganization of an enterprise in which two or more clients have an interest or arranging a property distribution in settlement of an estate. The lawyer seeks to resolve potentially adverse interests by developing the parties' mutual interests. Otherwise, each party might have to obtain separate representation, with the possibility of incurring additional cost, complication or even litigation. Given these and other relevant factors, the clients may prefer that the lawyer act for all of them.

Special Considerations in Common Representation

[29] In considering whether to represent multiple clients in the same matter, a lawyer should be mindful that if the common representation fails because the potentially adverse interests cannot be reconciled, the result can be additional cost, embarrassment and recrimination. Ordinarily, the lawyer will be forced to withdraw from representing all of the clients if the common representation fails. In some situations, the risk of failure is so great that multiple representation is plainly impossible. For example, a lawyer cannot undertake common representation of clients where contentious litigation or negotiations between them are imminent or contemplated. Moreover, because the lawyer is required to be impartial between commonly represented clients, representation of multiple clients is improper when it is unlikely that impartiality can be maintained. Generally, if the relationship between the parties has already assumed antagonism, the possibility that the clients' interests can be adequately served by common representation is not very good. Other relevant factors are whether the lawyer subsequently will represent both parties on a continuing basis and whether the situation involves creating or terminating a relationship between the parties.

[30] A particularly important factor in determining the appropriateness of common representation is the effect on client-lawyer confidentiality and the attorney-client privilege. With regard to the attorney-client privilege, the prevailing rule is that, as between commonly represented clients, the privilege does not attach. Hence, it must be assumed that if litigation eventuates between the clients, the privilege will not protect any such communications, and the clients should be so advised.

[31] As to the duty of confidentiality, continued common representation will almost certainly be inadequate if one client asks the lawyer not to disclose to the other client information relevant to the common representation. This is so because the lawyer has an equal duty of loyalty to each client, and each client has the right to be informed of anything bearing on the representation that might affect that client's interests and the right to expect that the lawyer will use that information to that client's benefit. See Rule 1.4. The lawyer should, at the outset of the common representation and as part of the process of obtaining each client's informed consent, advise each client that information will be shared and that the lawyer will have to withdraw if one client decides that some matter material to the representation should be kept from the other. In limited circumstances, it may be appropriate for the lawyer to proceed with the representation

when the clients have agreed, after being properly informed, that the lawyer will keep certain information confidential. For example, the lawyer may reasonably conclude that failure to disclose one client's trade secrets to another client will not adversely affect representation involving a joint venture between the clients and agree to keep that information confidential with the informed consent of both clients.

[32] When seeking to establish or adjust a relationship between clients, the lawyer should make clear that the lawyer's role is not that of partisanship normally expected in other circumstances and, thus, that the clients may be required to assume greater responsibility for decisions than when each client is separately represented. Any limitations on the scope of the representation made necessary as a result of the common representation should be fully explained to the clients at the outset of the representation. See Rule 1.2(c).

[33] Subject to the above limitations, each client in the common representation has the right to loyal and diligent representation and the protection of Rule 1.9 concerning the obligations to a former client. The client also has the right to discharge the lawyer as stated in Rule 1.16.

Organizational Clients

[34] A lawyer who represents a corporation or other organization does not, by virtue of that representation, necessarily represent any constituent or affiliated organization, such as a parent or subsidiary. See Rule 1.13(a). Thus, the lawyer for an organization is not barred from accepting representation adverse to an affiliate in an unrelated matter, unless the circumstances are such that the affiliate should also be considered a client of the lawyer, there is an understanding between the lawyer and the organizational client that the lawyer will avoid representation adverse to the client's affiliates, or the lawyer's obligations to either the organizational client or the new client are likely to limit materially the lawyer's representation of the other client.

[35] A lawyer for a corporation or other organization who is also a member of its board of directors should determine whether the responsibilities of the two roles may conflict. The lawyer may be called on to advise the corporation in matters involving actions of the directors. Consideration should be given to the frequency with which such situations may arise, the potential intensity of the conflict, the effect of the lawyer's resignation from the board and the possibility of the corporation's obtaining legal advice from another lawyer in such situations. If there is material risk that the dual role will compromise the lawyer's independence of professional judgment, the lawyer should not serve as a director or should cease to act as the corporation's lawyer when conflicts of interest arise. The lawyer should advise the other members of the board that in some circumstances matters discussed at board meetings while the lawyer is present in the capacity of director might not be protected by the attorney-client privilege and that conflict of interest considerations might require the lawyer's recusal as a director or might require the lawyer and the lawyer's firm to decline representation of the corporation in a matter.

Rule 1.8 Conflict of Interest: Current Clients: Specific Rules

(a) A lawyer shall not enter into a business transaction with a client or knowingly acquire an ownership, possessory, security or other pecuniary interest adverse to a client unless:

(1) the transaction and terms on which the lawyer acquires the interest are fair and reasonable to the client and are fully disclosed and transmitted in writing in a manner that can be reasonably understood by the client;

(2) the client is advised in writing of the desirability of seeking and is given a reasonable opportunity to seek the advice of independent legal counsel on the transaction; and

(3) the client gives informed consent, in a writing signed by the client, to the essential terms of the transaction and the lawyer's role in the transaction, including whether the lawyer is representing the client in the transaction.

(b) A lawyer shall not use information relating to representation of a client to the disadvantage of the client unless the client gives informed consent, except as permitted or required by these Rules.

(c) A lawyer shall not solicit any substantial gift from a client, including a testamentary gift, or prepare on behalf of a client an instrument giving the lawyer or a person related to the lawyer any substantial gift unless the lawyer or other recipient of the gift is related to the client. For purposes of this paragraph, related persons include a spouse, child, grandchild, parent, grandparent or other relative or individual with whom the lawyer or the client maintains a close, familial relationship.

(d) Prior to the conclusion of representation of a client, a lawyer shall not make or negotiate an agreement giving the lawyer literary or media rights to a portrayal or account based in substantial part on information relating to the representation.

(e) A lawyer shall not provide financial assistance to a client in connection with pending or contemplated litigation, except that:

(1) a lawyer may advance court costs and expenses of litigation, the repayment of which may be contingent on the outcome of the matter; and

(2) a lawyer representing an indigent client may pay court costs and expenses of litigation on behalf of the client.

(f) A lawyer shall not accept compensation for representing a client from one other than the client unless:

(1) the client gives informed consent;

(2) there is no interference with the lawyer's independence of professional judgment or with the client-lawyer relationship; and

(3) information relating to representation of a client is protected as required by Rule 1.6.

(g) A lawyer who represents two or more clients shall not participate in making an aggregate settlement of the claims of or against the clients, or in a criminal case an aggregated agreement as to guilty or nolo contendere pleas, unless each client gives informed consent, in a writing signed by the client. The lawyer's disclosure shall include the existence and nature of all the claims or pleas involved and of the participation of each person in the settlement.

(h) A lawyer shall not:

(1) make an agreement prospectively limiting the lawyer's liability to a client for malpractice unless the client is independently represented in making the agreement; or

(2) settle a claim or potential claim for such liability with an unrepresented client or former client unless that person is advised in writing of the desirability of seeking and is given a reasonable opportunity to seek the advice of independent legal counsel in connection therewith.

(i) A lawyer shall not acquire a proprietary interest in the cause of action or subject matter of litigation the lawyer is conducting for a client, except that the lawyer may:

(1) acquire a lien authorized by law to secure the lawyer's fee or expenses; and

(2) contract with a client for a reasonable contingent fee in a civil case.

(j) A lawyer shall not have sexual relations with a client unless a consensual sexual relationship existed between them when the client-lawyer relationship commenced.

(k) While lawyers are associated in a firm, a prohibition in the foregoing paragraphs (a) through (i) that applies to any one of them shall apply to all of them.

COMMENT

Business Transactions between Client and Lawyer

[1] A lawyer's legal skill and training, together with the relationship of trust and confidence between lawyer and client, create the possibility of overreaching when the lawyer participates in a business, property or financial transaction with a client, for example, a loan or sales transaction or a lawyer investment on behalf of a client. The requirements of paragraph (a) must be met even when the transaction is not closely related to the subject matter of the representation, as when a lawyer drafting a will for a client learns that the client needs money for unrelated expenses and offers to make a loan to the client. The Rule applies to lawyers engaged in the sale of goods or services related to the practice of law, for example, the sale of title insurance or investment services to existing clients of the lawyer's legal practice. See Rule 5.7. It also applies to lawyers purchasing property from estates they represent. It does not apply to ordinary fee arrangements between client and lawyer, which are governed by Rule 1.5, although its requirements must be met when the lawyer accepts an interest in the client's business or other nonmonetary property as payment of all or part of a fee. In addition, the Rule does not apply to standard commercial transactions between the lawyer and the client for products or services that the client generally markets to others, for example, banking or brokerage services, medical services, products manufactured or distributed by the client, and utilities services. In such transactions, the lawyer has no advantage in dealing with the client, and the restrictions in paragraph (a) are unnecessary and impracticable.

[2] Paragraph (a)(1) requires that the transaction itself be fair to the client and that its essential terms be communicated to the client, in writing, in a manner that can be reasonably understood. Paragraph (a)(2) requires that the client also be advised, in writing, of the desirability of seeking the advice of independent legal counsel. It also requires that the client be given a reasonable opportunity to obtain such advice. Paragraph (a)(3) requires that the lawyer obtain the client's informed consent, in a writing signed by the client, both to the essential terms of the transaction and to the lawyer's role. When necessary, the lawyer should discuss both the material risks of the proposed transaction, including any risk presented by the lawyer's involvement, and the existence of reasonably available alternatives and should explain why the advice of independent legal counsel is desirable. See Rule 1.0(e) (definition of informed consent).

[3] The risk to a client is greatest when the client expects the lawyer to represent the client in the transaction itself or when the lawyer's financial interest otherwise poses a significant risk that the lawyer's representation of the client will be materially limited by the lawyer's financial interest in the transaction. Here the lawyer's role requires that the lawyer must comply, not only with the requirements of paragraph (a), but also with the requirements of Rule 1.7. Under that Rule, the lawyer must disclose the risks associated with the lawyer's dual role as both legal adviser and participant in the transaction, such as the risk that the lawyer will structure the transaction or give legal advice in a way that favors the lawyer's interests at the expense of the client. Moreover, the lawyer must obtain the client's informed consent. In some cases, the lawyer's interest may be such that Rule 1.7 will preclude the lawyer from seeking the client's consent to the transaction.

[4] If the client is independently represented in the transaction, paragraph (a)(2) of this Rule is inapplicable, and the paragraph (a)(1) requirement for full disclosure is satisfied either by a written disclosure by the lawyer involved in the transaction or by the client's independent counsel. The fact that the client was independently represented in the transaction is relevant in determining whether the agreement was fair and reasonable to the client as paragraph (a)(1) further requires.

Use of Information Related to Representation

[5] Use of information relating to the representation to the disadvantage of the client violates the lawyer's duty of loyalty. Paragraph (b) applies when the information is used to benefit either the lawyer or a third person, such as another client or business associate of the lawyer. For example, if a lawyer learns that a client intends to purchase and develop several parcels of land, the lawyer may not use that information to purchase one of the parcels in competition with the client or to recommend that another client make such a purchase. The Rule does not prohibit uses that do not disadvantage the client. For example, a lawyer who learns a government agency's interpretation of trade legislation during the representation of one client may properly use that information to benefit other clients. Paragraph (b) prohibits disadvantageous use of client information unless the client gives informed consent, except as permitted or required by these Rules. See Rules 1.2(d), 1.6, 1.9(c), 3.3, 4.1(b), 8.1 and 8.3.

Gifts to Lawyers

[6] A lawyer may accept a gift from a client, if the transaction meets general standards of fairness. For example, a simple gift such as a present given at a holiday or as a token of appreciation is permitted. If a client offers the lawyer a more substantial gift, paragraph (c) does not prohibit the lawyer from accepting it, although such a gift may be voidable by the client under the doctrine of undue influence, which treats client gifts as presumptively fraudulent. In any event, due to concerns about overreaching and imposition on clients, a lawyer may not suggest that a substantial gift be made to the lawyer or for the lawyer's benefit, except where the lawyer is related to the client as set forth in paragraph (c).

[7] If effectuation of a substantial gift requires preparing a legal instrument such as a will or conveyance, the client should have the detached advice that another lawyer can provide. The sole exception to this Rule is where the client is a relative of the donee.

[8] This Rule does not prohibit a lawyer from seeking to have the lawyer or a partner or associate of the lawyer named as executor of the client's estate or to another potentially lucrative fiduciary position. Nevertheless, such appointments will be subject to the general conflict of interest provision in Rule 1.7 when there is a significant risk that the lawyer's interest in obtaining the appointment will materially limit the lawyer's independent professional judgment in advising the client concerning the choice of an executor or other fiduciary. In obtaining the client's informed consent to the conflict, the lawyer should advise the client concerning the nature and extent of the lawyer's financial interest in the appointment, as well as the availability of alternative candidates for the position.

Literary Rights

[9] An agreement by which a lawyer acquires literary or media rights concerning the conduct of the representation creates a conflict between the interests of the client and the personal interests of the lawyer. Measures suitable in the representation of the client may detract from the publication value of an account of the representation. Paragraph (d) does not prohibit a lawyer representing a client in a transaction concerning literary property from agreeing that the lawyer's fee shall consist of a share in ownership in the property, if the arrangement conforms to Rule 1.5 and paragraphs (a) and (i).

Financial Assistance

[10] Lawyers may not subsidize lawsuits or administrative proceedings brought on behalf of their clients, including making or guaranteeing loans to their clients for living expenses, because to do so would encourage clients to pursue lawsuits that might not otherwise be brought and because such assistance gives lawyers too great a financial stake in the litigation. These dangers do not warrant a prohibition on a lawyer lending a client court costs and litigation expenses, including the expenses of medical examination and the costs of obtaining and presenting evidence, because these advances are virtually indistinguishable from contingent fees and help ensure access to the courts. Similarly, an exception allowing lawyers representing indigent clients to pay court costs and litigation expenses regardless of whether these funds will be repaid is warranted.

Person Paying for a Lawyer's Services

[11] Lawyers are frequently asked to represent a client under circumstances in which a third person will compensate the lawyer, in whole or in part. The third person might be a relative or friend, an indemnitor (such as a liability insurance company) or a co-client (such as a corporation sued along with one or more of its employees). Because third-party payers frequently have interests that differ from those of the client, including interests in minimizing the amount spent on the representation and in learning how the representation is progressing, lawyers are prohibited from accepting or continuing such representations unless the lawyer determines that there will be no interference with the lawyer's independent professional judgment and there is informed consent from the client. See also Rule 5.4(c) (prohibiting interference with a lawyer's professional judgment by one who recommends, employs or pays the lawyer to render legal services for another).

[12] Sometimes, it will be sufficient for the lawyer to obtain the client's informed consent regarding the fact of the payment and the identity of the third-party payer. If, however, the fee arrangement creates a conflict of interest for the lawyer, then the lawyer must comply with Rule. 1.7. The lawyer must also

conform to the requirements of Rule 1.6 concerning confidentiality. Under Rule 1.7(a), a conflict of interest exists if there is significant risk that the lawyer's representation of the client will be materially limited by the lawyer's own interest in the fee arrangement or by the lawyer's responsibilities to the third-party payer (for example, when the third-party payer is a co-client). Under Rule 1.7(b), the lawyer may accept or continue the representation with the informed consent of each affected client, unless the conflict is nonconsentable under that paragraph. Under Rule 1.7(b), the informed consent must be confirmed in writing.

Aggregate Settlements

[13] Differences in willingness to make or accept an offer of settlement are among the risks of common representation of multiple clients by a single lawyer. Under Rule 1.7, this is one of the risks that should be discussed before undertaking the representation, as part of the process of obtaining the clients' informed consent. In addition, Rule 1.2(a) protects each client's right to have the final say in deciding whether to accept or reject an offer of settlement and in deciding whether to enter a guilty or nolo contendere plea in a criminal case. The rule stated in this paragraph is a corollary of both these Rules and provides that, before any settlement offer or plea bargain is made or accepted on behalf of multiple clients, the lawyer must inform each of them about all the material terms of the settlement, including what the other clients will receive or pay if the settlement or plea offer is accepted. See also Rule 1.0(e) (definition of informed consent). Lawyers representing a class of plaintiffs or defendants, or those proceeding derivatively, may not have a full client-lawyer relationship with each member of the class; nevertheless, such lawyers must comply with applicable rules regulating notification of class members and other procedural requirements designed to ensure adequate protection of the entire class.

Limiting Liability and Settling Malpractice Claims

[14] Agreements prospectively limiting a lawyer's liability for malpractice are prohibited unless the client is independently represented in making the agreement because they are likely to undermine competent and diligent representation. Also, many clients are unable to evaluate the desirability of making such an agreement before a dispute has arisen, particularly if they are then represented by the lawyer seeking the agreement. This paragraph does not, however, prohibit a lawyer from entering into an agreement with the client to arbitrate legal malpractice claims, provided such agreements are enforceable and the client is fully informed of the scope and effect of the agreement. Nor does this paragraph limit the ability of lawyers to practice in the form of a limited-liability entity, where permitted by law, provided that each lawyer remains personally liable to the client for his or her own conduct and the firm complies with any conditions required by law, such as provisions requiring client notification or maintenance of adequate liability insurance. Nor does it prohibit an agreement in accordance with Rule 1.2 that defines the scope of the representation, although a definition of scope that makes the obligations of representation illusory will amount to an attempt to limit liability.

[15] Agreements settling a claim or a potential claim for malpractice are not prohibited by this Rule. Nevertheless, in view of the danger that a lawyer will take unfair advantage of an unrepresented client or former client, the lawyer must first advise such a person in writing of the appropriateness of independent representation in connection with such a settlement. In addition, the lawyer must give the client or former client a reasonable opportunity to find and consult independent counsel.

Acquiring Proprietary Interest in Litigation

[16] Paragraph (i) states the traditional general rule that lawyers are prohibited from acquiring a proprietary interest in litigation. Like paragraph (e), the general rule has its basis in common law champerty and maintenance and is designed to avoid giving the lawyer too great an interest in the representation. In addition, when the lawyer acquires an ownership interest in the subject of the representation, it will be more difficult for a client to discharge the lawyer if the client so desires. The Rule is subject to specific exceptions developed in decisional law and continued in these Rules. The exception for certain advances of the costs of litigation is set forth in paragraph (e). In addition, paragraph (i) sets forth exceptions for liens authorized by law to secure the lawyer's fees or expenses and contracts for reasonable contingent fees. The law of each jurisdiction determines which liens are authorized by law. These may include liens granted by statute, liens originating in common law and liens acquired by contract with the client. When a lawyer acquires by contract a security interest in property other than that recovered through the lawyer's efforts in the litigation, such an acquisition is a business or financial transaction with a client

and is governed by the requirements of paragraph (a). Contracts for contingent fees in civil cases are governed by Rule 1.5.

Client-Lawyer Sexual Relationships

[17] The relationship between lawyer and client is a fiduciary one in which the lawyer occupies the highest position of trust and confidence. The relationship is almost always unequal; thus, a sexual relationship between lawyer and client can involve unfair exploitation of the lawyer's fiduciary role, in violation of the lawyer's basic ethical obligation not to use the trust of the client to the client's disadvantage. In addition, such a relationship presents a significant danger that, because of the lawyer's emotional involvement, the lawyer will be unable to represent the client without impairment of the exercise of independent professional judgment. Moreover, a blurred line between the professional and personal relationships may make it difficult to predict to what extent client confidences will be protected by the attorney-client evidentiary privilege, since client confidences are protected by privilege only when they are imparted in the context of the client-lawyer relationship. Because of the significant danger of harm to client interests and because the client's own emotional involvement renders it unlikely that the client could give adequate informed consent, this Rule prohibits the lawyer from having sexual relations with a client regardless of whether the relationship is consensual and regardless of the absence of prejudice to the client.

[18] Sexual relationships that predate the client-lawyer relationship are not prohibited. Issues relating to the exploitation of the fiduciary relationship and client dependency are diminished when the sexual relationship existed prior to the commencement of the client-lawyer relationship. However, before proceeding with the representation in these circumstances, the lawyer should consider whether the lawyer's ability to represent the client will be materially limited by the relationship. See Rule 1.7(a)(2).

[19] When the client is an organization, paragraph (j) of this Rule prohibits a lawyer for the organization (whether inside counsel or outside counsel) from having a sexual relationship with a constituent of the organization who supervises, directs or regularly consults with that lawyer concerning the organization's legal matters.

Imputation of Prohibitions

[20] Under paragraph (k), a prohibition on conduct by an individual lawyer in paragraphs (a) through (i) also applies to all lawyers associated in a firm with the personally prohibited lawyer. For example, one lawyer in a firm may not enter into a business transaction with a client of another member of the firm without complying with paragraph (a), even if the first lawyer is not personally involved in the representation of the client. The prohibition set forth in paragraph (j) is personal and is not applied to associated lawyers.

Rule 1.9 Duties to Former Clients

(a) A lawyer who has formerly represented a client in a matter shall not thereafter represent another person in the same or a substantially related matter in which that person's interests are materially adverse to the interests of the former client unless the former client gives informed consent, confirmed in writing.

(b) A lawyer shall not knowingly represent a person in the same or a substantially related matter in which a firm with which the lawyer formerly was associated had previously represented a client

(1) whose interests are materially adverse to that person; and

(2) about whom the lawyer had acquired information protected by Rules 1.6 and 1.9(c) that is material to the matter;

unless the former client gives informed consent, confirmed in writing.

(c) A lawyer who has formerly represented a client in a matter or whose present or former firm has formerly represented a client in a matter shall not thereafter:

(1) use information relating to the representation to the disadvantage of the former client except as these Rules would permit or require with respect to a client, or when the information has become generally known; or

(2) reveal information relating to the representation except as these Rules would permit or require with respect to a client.

COMMENT

[1] After termination of a client-lawyer relationship, a lawyer has certain continuing duties with respect to confidentiality and conflicts of interest and thus may not represent another client except in conformity with this Rule. Under this Rule, for example, a lawyer could not properly seek to rescind on behalf of a new client a contract drafted on behalf of the former client. So also a lawyer who has prosecuted an accused person could not properly represent the accused in a subsequent civil action against the government concerning the same transaction. Nor could a lawyer who has represented multiple clients in a matter represent one of the clients against the others in the same or a substantially related matter after a dispute arose among the clients in that matter, unless all affected clients give informed consent. See Comment [9]. Current and former government lawyers must comply with this Rule to the extent required by Rule 1.11.

[2] The scope of a "matter" for purposes of this Rule depends on the facts of a particular situation or transaction. The lawyer's involvement in a matter can also be a question of degree. When a lawyer has been directly involved in a specific transaction, subsequent representation of other clients with materially adverse interests in that transaction clearly is prohibited. On the other hand, a lawyer who recurrently handled a type of problem for a former client is not precluded from later representing another client in a factually distinct problem of that type even though the subsequent representation involves a position adverse to the prior client. Similar considerations can apply to the reassignment of military lawyers between defense and prosecution functions within the same military jurisdictions. The underlying question is whether the lawyer was so involved in the matter that the subsequent representation can be justly regarded as a changing of sides in the matter in question.

[3] Matters are "substantially related" for purposes of this Rule if they involve the same transaction or legal dispute or if there otherwise is a substantial risk that confidential factual information as would normally have been obtained in the prior representation would materially advance the client's position in the subsequent matter. For example, a lawyer who has represented a businessperson and learned extensive private financial information about that person may not then represent that person's spouse in seeking a divorce. Similarly, a lawyer who has previously represented a client in securing environmental permits to build a shopping center would be precluded from representing neighbors seeking to oppose rezoning of the property on the basis of environmental considerations; however, the lawyer would not be precluded, on the grounds of substantial relationship, from defending a tenant of the completed shopping center in resisting eviction for nonpayment of rent. Information that has been disclosed to the public or to other parties adverse to the former client ordinarily will not be disqualifying. Information acquired in a prior representation may have been rendered obsolete by the passage of time, a circumstance that may be relevant in determining whether two representations are substantially related. In the case of an organizational client, general knowledge of the client's policies and practices ordinarily will not preclude a subsequent representation; on the other hand, knowledge of specific facts gained in a prior representation that are relevant to the matter in question ordinarily will preclude such a representation. A former client is not required to reveal the confidential information learned by the lawyer in order to establish a substantial risk that the lawyer has confidential information to use in the subsequent matter. A conclusion about the possession of such information may be based on the nature of the services the lawyer provided the former client and information that would in ordinary practice be learned by a lawyer providing such services.

Lawyers Moving Between Firms

[4] When lawyers have been associated within a firm but then end their association, the question of whether a lawyer should undertake representation is more complicated. There are several competing considerations. First, the client previously represented by the former firm must be reasonably assured that the principle of loyalty to the client is not compromised. Second, the rule should not be so broadly cast as to preclude other persons from having reasonable choice of legal counsel. Third, the rule should not

unreasonably hamper lawyers from forming new associations and taking on new clients after having left a previous association. In this connection, it should be recognized that today many lawyers practice in firms, that many lawyers to some degree limit their practice to one field or another, and that many move from one association to another several times in their careers. If the concept of imputation were applied with unqualified rigor, the result would be radical curtailment of the opportunity of lawyers to move from one practice setting to another and of the opportunity of clients to change counsel.

[5] Paragraph (b) operates to disqualify the lawyer only when the lawyer involved has actual knowledge of information protected by Rules 1.6 and 1.9(c). Thus, if a lawyer while with one firm acquired no knowledge or information relating to a particular client of the firm, and that lawyer later joined another firm, neither the lawyer individually nor the second firm is disqualified from representing another client in the same or a related matter even though the interests of the two clients conflict. See Rule 1.10(b) for the restrictions on a firm once a lawyer has terminated association with the firm.

[6] Application of paragraph (b) depends on a situation's particular facts, aided by inferences, deductions or working presumptions that reasonably may be made about the way in which lawyers work together. A lawyer may have general access to files of all clients of a law firm and may regularly participate in discussions of their affairs; it should be inferred that such a lawyer in fact is privy to all information about all the firm's clients. In contrast, another lawyer may have access to the files of only a limited number of clients and participate in discussions of the affairs of no other clients; in the absence of information to the contrary, it should be inferred that such a lawyer in fact is privy to information about the clients actually served but not those of other clients. In such an inquiry, the burden of proof should rest upon the firm whose disqualification is sought.

[7] Independent of the question of disqualification of a firm, a lawyer changing professional association has a continuing duty to preserve confidentiality of information about a client formerly represented. See Rules 1.6 and 1.9(c).

[8] Paragraph (c) provides that information acquired by the lawyer in the course of representing a client may not subsequently be used or revealed by the lawyer to the disadvantage of the client. However, the fact that a lawyer has once served a client does not preclude the lawyer from using generally known information about that client when later representing another client.

[9] The provisions of this Rule are for the protection of former clients and can be waived if the client gives informed consent, which consent must be confirmed in writing under paragraphs (a) and (b). See Rule 1.0(e). With regard to the effectiveness of an advance waiver, see Comment [22] to Rule 1.7. With regard to disqualification of a firm with which a lawyer is or was formerly associated, see Rule 1.10.

Rule 1.10 Imputation of Conflicts of Interest: General Rule*

(a) While lawyers are associated in a firm, none of them shall knowingly represent a client when any one of them practicing alone would be prohibited from doing so by Rules 1.7 or 1.9, unless

(1) the prohibition is based upon a personal interest of the disqualified lawyer and does not present a significant risk of materially limiting the representation of the client by the remaining lawyers in the firm; or

(2) the prohibition is based upon Rule 1.9(a), or (b), and arises out of the disqualified lawyer's association with a prior firm, and

* In February 2009, the ABA House of Delegates modified Model Rule 1.10(a) by adding the language in (a)(2). This amendment permits a law firm to screen a disqualified lawyer in order to avoid imputation of the screened lawyer's conflict to other attorneys in the firm. After the rule was adopted, critics noted that the February 2009 language did not limit the screening to the migratory lawyer context. Thus, several groups within the ABA proposed a housekeeping amendment, which was adopted by the house of Delegates in August 2009. In 1.10(a)(1), the word "prohibited" was replaced with the word, "disqualified." And, in 1.10(a)(2), a clause was added at the end of the first line: "and arises out of the disqualified lawyer's association with a prior firm."

(i) the disqualified lawyer is timely screened from any participation in the matter and is apportioned no part of the fee therefrom;

(ii) written notice is promptly given to any affected former client to enable the former client to ascertain compliance with the provisions of this Rule, which shall include a description of the screening procedures employed; a statement of the firm's and of the screened lawyer's compliance with these Rules; a statement that review may be available before a tribunal; and an agreement by the firm to respond promptly to any written inquiries or objections by the former client about the screening procedures; and

(iii) certifications of compliance with these Rules and with the screening procedures are provided to the former client by the screened lawyer and by a partner of the firm, at reasonable intervals upon the former client's written request and upon termination of the screening procedures.

(b) When a lawyer has terminated an association with a firm, the firm is not prohibited from thereafter representing a person with interests materially adverse to those of a client represented by the formerly associated lawyer and not currently represented by the firm, unless:

(1) the matter is the same or substantially related to that in which the formerly associated lawyer represented the client; and

(2) any lawyer remaining in the firm has information protected by Rules 1.6 and 1.9(c) that is material to the matter.

(c) A disqualification prescribed by this rule may be waived by the affected client under the conditions stated in Rule 1.7.

(d) The disqualification of lawyers associated in a firm with former or current government lawyers is governed by Rule 1.11.

COMMENT*

Definition of "Firm"

[1] For purposes of the Rules of Professional Conduct, the term "firm" denotes lawyers in a law partnership, professional corporation, sole proprietorship or other association authorized to practice law; or lawyers employed in a legal services organization or the legal department of a corporation or other organization. See Rule 1.0(c). Whether two or more lawyers constitute a firm within this definition can depend on the specific facts. See Rule 1.0, Comments [2]–[4].

Principles of Imputed Disqualification

[2] The rule of imputed disqualification stated in paragraph (a) gives effect to the principle of loyalty to the client as it applies to lawyers who practice in a law firm. Such situations can be considered from the premise that a firm of lawyers is essentially one lawyer for purposes of the rules governing loyalty to the client, or from the premise that each lawyer is vicariously bound by the obligation of loyalty owed by each lawyer with whom the lawyer is associated. Paragraph (a)(1) operates only among the lawyers currently associated in a firm. When a lawyer moves from one firm to another, the situation is governed by Rules 1.9(b) and 1.10(a)(2) and 1.10(b).

[3] The rule in paragraph (a) does not prohibit representation where neither questions of client loyalty nor protection of confidential information are presented. Where one lawyer in a firm could not effectively represent a given client because of strong political beliefs, for example, but that lawyer will do no work on the case and the personal beliefs of the lawyer will not materially limit the representation by others in the firm, the firm should not be disqualified. On the other hand, if an opposing party in a case were owned

---

* In February 2009, the ABA House of Delegates amended the comments to Model Rule 1.10. Comment 2 was modified to clarify references to (a)(1) and (a)(2) of Rule 1.10. Comments 7–10 are new and old Comments 7–8 are renumbered as 11 and 12.

by a lawyer in the law firm, and others in the firm would be materially limited in pursuing the matter because of loyalty to that lawyer, the personal disqualification of the lawyer would be imputed to all others in the firm.

[4] The rule in paragraph (a) also does not prohibit representation by others in the law firm where the person prohibited from involvement in a matter is a nonlawyer, such as a paralegal or legal secretary. Nor does paragraph (a) prohibit representation if the lawyer is prohibited from acting because of events before the person became a lawyer, for example, work that the person did while a law student. Such persons, however, ordinarily must be screened from any personal participation in the matter to avoid communication to others in the firm of confidential information that both the nonlawyers and the firm have a legal duty to protect. See Rules 1.0(k) and 5.3.

[5] Rule 1.10(b) operates to permit a law firm, under certain circumstances, to represent a person with interests directly adverse to those of a client represented by a lawyer who formerly was associated with the firm. The Rule applies regardless of when the formerly associated lawyer represented the client. However, the law firm may not represent a person with interests adverse to those of a present client of the firm, which would violate Rule 1.7. Moreover, the firm may not represent the person where the matter is the same or substantially related to that in which the formerly associated lawyer represented the client and any other lawyer currently in the firm has material information protected by Rules 1.6 and 1.9(c).

[6] Rule 1.10(c) removes imputation with the informed consent of the affected client or former client under the conditions stated in Rule 1.7. The conditions stated in Rule 1.7 require the lawyer to determine that the representation is not prohibited by Rule 1.7(b) and that each affected client or former client has given informed consent to the representation, confirmed in writing. In some cases, the risk may be so severe that the conflict may not be cured by client consent. For a discussion of the effectiveness of client waivers of conflicts that might arise in the future, see Rule 1.7, Comment [22]. For a definition of informed consent, see Rule 1.0(e).

[7] Rule 1.10(a)(2) similarly removes the imputation otherwise required by Rule 1.10(a), but unlike section (c), it does so without requiring that there be informed consent by the former client. Instead, it requires that the procedures laid out in sections (a)(2)(i)-(iii) be followed. A description of effective screening mechanisms appears in Rule 1.0(k). Lawyers should be aware, however, that, even where screening mechanisms have been adopted, tribunals may consider additional factors in ruling upon motions to disqualify a lawyer from pending litigation.

[8] Paragraph (a)(2)(i) does not prohibit the screened lawyer from receiving a salary or partnership share established by prior independent agreement, but that lawyer may not receive compensation directly related to the matter in which the lawyer is disqualified.

[9] The notice required by paragraph (a)(2)(ii) generally should include a description of the screened lawyer's prior representation and be given as soon as practicable after the need for screening becomes apparent. It also should include a statement by the screened lawyer and the firm that the client's material confidential information has not been disclosed or used in violation of the Rules. The notice is intended to enable the former client to evaluate and comment upon the effectiveness of the screening procedures.

[10] The certifications required by paragraph (a)(2)(iii) give the former client assurance that the client's material confidential information has not been disclosed or used inappropriately, either prior to timely implementation of a screen or thereafter. If compliance cannot be certified, the certificate must describe the failure to comply.

[11] Where a lawyer has joined a private firm after having represented the government, imputation is governed by Rule 1.11(b) and (c), not this Rule. Under Rule 1.11(d), where a lawyer represents the government after having served clients in private practice, nongovernmental employment or in another government agency, former-client conflicts are not imputed to government lawyers associated with the individually disqualified lawyer.

[12] Where a lawyer is prohibited from engaging in certain transactions under Rule 1.8, paragraph (k) of that Rule, and not this Rule, determines whether that prohibition also applies to other lawyers associated in a firm with the personally prohibited lawyer.

Rule 1.11 Special Conflicts of Interest for Former and Current Government Officers and Employees

(a) Except as law may otherwise expressly permit, a lawyer who has formerly served as a public officer or employee of the government:

(1) is subject to Rule 1.9(c); and

(2) shall not otherwise represent a client in connection with a matter in which the lawyer participated personally and substantially as a public officer or employee, unless the appropriate government agency gives its informed consent, confirmed in writing, to the representation.

(b) When a lawyer is disqualified from representation under paragraph (a), no lawyer in a firm with which that lawyer is associated may knowingly undertake or continue representation in such a matter unless:

(1) the disqualified lawyer is timely screened from any participation in the matter and is apportioned no part of the fee therefrom; and

(2) written notice is promptly given to the appropriate government agency to enable it to ascertain compliance with the provisions of this rule.

(c) Except as law may otherwise expressly permit, a lawyer having information that the lawyer knows is confidential government information about a person acquired when the lawyer was a public officer or employee, may not represent a private client whose interests are adverse to that person in a matter in which the information could be used to the material disadvantage of that person. As used in this Rule, the term "confidential government information" means information that has been obtained under governmental authority and which, at the time this Rule is applied, the government is prohibited by law from disclosing to the public or has a legal privilege not to disclose and which is not otherwise available to the public. A firm with which that lawyer is associated may undertake or continue representation in the matter only if the disqualified lawyer is timely screened from any participation in the matter and is apportioned no part of the fee therefrom.

(d) Except as law may otherwise expressly permit, a lawyer currently serving as a public officer or employee:

(1) is subject to Rules 1.7 and 1.9; and

(2) shall not:

(i) participate in a matter in which the lawyer participated personally and substantially while in private practice or nongovernmental employment, unless the appropriate government agency gives its informed consent, confirmed in writing; or

(ii) negotiate for private employment with any person who is involved as a party or as lawyer for a party in a matter in which the lawyer is participating personally and substantially, except that a lawyer serving as a law clerk to a judge, other adjudicative officer or arbitrator may negotiate for private employment as permitted by Rule 1.12(b) and subject to the conditions stated in Rule 1.12(b).

(e) As used in this Rule, the term "matter" includes:

(1) any judicial or other proceeding, application, request for a ruling or other determination, contract, claim, controversy, investigation, charge, accusation, arrest or other particular matter involving a specific party or parties, and

(2) any other matter covered by the conflict of interest rules of the appropriate government agency.

COMMENT

[1] A lawyer who has served or is currently serving as a public officer or employee is personally subject to the Rules of Professional Conduct, including the prohibition against concurrent conflicts of interest stated in Rule 1.7. In addition, such a lawyer may be subject to statutes and government regulations regarding conflict of interest. Such statutes and regulations may circumscribe the extent to which the government agency may give consent under this Rule. See Rule 1.0(e) for the definition of informed consent.

[2] Paragraphs (a)(1), (a)(2) and (d)(1) restate the obligations of an individual lawyer who has served or is currently serving as an officer or employee of the government toward a former government or private client. Rule 1.10 is not applicable to the conflicts of interest addressed by this Rule. Rather, paragraph (b) sets forth a special imputation rule for former government lawyers that provides for screening and notice. Because of the special problems raised by imputation within a government agency, paragraph (d) does not impute the conflicts of a lawyer currently serving as an officer or employee of the government to other associated government officers or employees, although ordinarily it will be prudent to screen such lawyers.

[3] Paragraphs (a)(2) and (d)(2) apply regardless of whether a lawyer is adverse to a former client and are thus designed not only to protect the former client, but also to prevent a lawyer from exploiting public office for the advantage of another client. For example, a lawyer who has pursued a claim on behalf of the government may not pursue the same claim on behalf of a later private client after the lawyer has left government service, except when authorized to do so by the government agency under paragraph (a). Similarly, a lawyer who has pursued a claim on behalf of a private client may not pursue the claim on behalf of the government, except when authorized to do so by paragraph (d). As with paragraphs (a)(1) and (d)(1), Rule 1.10 is not applicable to the conflicts of interest addressed by these paragraphs.

[4] This Rule represents a balancing of interests. On the one hand, where the successive clients are a government agency and another client, public or private, the risk exists that power or discretion vested in that agency might be used for the special benefit of the other client. A lawyer should not be in a position where benefit to the other client might affect performance of the lawyer's professional functions on behalf of the government. Also, unfair advantage could accrue to the other client by reason of access to confidential government information about the client's adversary obtainable only through the lawyer's government service. On the other hand, the rules governing lawyers presently or formerly employed by a government agency should not be so restrictive as to inhibit transfer of employment to and from the government. The government has a legitimate need to attract qualified lawyers as well as to maintain high ethical standards. Thus a former government lawyer is disqualified only from particular matters in which the lawyer participated personally and substantially. The provisions for screening and waiver in paragraph (b) are necessary to prevent the disqualification rule from imposing too severe a deterrent against entering public service. The limitation of disqualification in paragraphs (a)(2) and (d)(2) to matters involving a specific party or parties, rather than extending disqualification to all substantive issues on which the lawyer worked, serves a similar function.

[5] When a lawyer has been employed by one government agency and then moves to a second government agency, it may be appropriate to treat that second agency as another client for purposes of this Rule, as when a lawyer is employed by a city and subsequently is employed by a federal agency. However, because the conflict of interest is governed by paragraph (d), the latter agency is not required to screen the lawyer as paragraph (b) requires a law firm to do. The question of whether two government agencies should be regarded as the same or different clients for conflict of interest purposes is beyond the scope of these Rules. See Rule 1.13 Comment [6].

[6] Paragraphs (b) and (c) contemplate a screening arrangement. See Rule 1.0(k) (requirements for screening procedures). These paragraphs do not prohibit a lawyer from receiving a salary or partnership share established by prior independent agreement, but that lawyer may not receive compensation directly relating the lawyer's compensation to the fee in the matter in which the lawyer is disqualified.

[7] Notice, including a description of the screened lawyer's prior representation and of the screening procedures employed, generally should be given as soon as practicable after the need for screening becomes apparent.

[8] Paragraph (c) operates only when the lawyer in question has knowledge of the information, which means actual knowledge; it does not operate with respect to information that merely could be imputed to the lawyer.

[9] Paragraphs (a) and (d) do not prohibit a lawyer from jointly representing a private party and a government agency when doing so is permitted by Rule 1.7 and is not otherwise prohibited by law.

[10] For purposes of paragraph (e) of this Rule, a "matter" may continue in another form. In determining whether two particular matters are the same, the lawyer should consider the extent to which the matters involve the same basic facts, the same or related parties, and the time elapsed.

Rule 1.12 Former Judge, Arbitrator, Mediator, or Other Third-Party Neutral

(a) Except as stated in paragraph (d), a lawyer shall not represent anyone in connection with a matter in which the lawyer participated personally and substantially as a judge or other adjudicative officer or law clerk to such a person or as an arbitrator, mediator or other third-party neutral, unless all parties to the proceeding give informed consent, confirmed in writing.

(b) A lawyer shall not negotiate for employment with any person who is involved as a party or as lawyer for a party in a matter in which the lawyer is participating personally and substantially as a judge or other adjudicative officer or as an arbitrator, mediator or other third-party neutral. A lawyer serving as a law clerk to a judge or other adjudicative officer may negotiate for employment with a party or lawyer involved in a matter in which the clerk is participating personally and substantially, but only after the lawyer has notified the judge, or other adjudicative officer.

(c) If a lawyer is disqualified by paragraph (a), no lawyer in a firm with which that lawyer is associated may knowingly undertake or continue representation in the matter unless:

(1) the disqualified lawyer is timely screened from any participation in the matter and is apportioned no part of the fee therefrom; and

(2) written notice is promptly given to the parties and any appropriate tribunal to enable them to ascertain compliance with the provisions of this rule.

(d) An arbitrator selected as a partisan of a party in a multimember arbitration panel is not prohibited from subsequently representing that party.

COMMENT

[1] This Rule generally parallels Rule 1.11. The term "personally and substantially" signifies that a judge who was a member of a multimember court, and thereafter left judicial office to practice law, is not prohibited from representing a client in a matter pending in the court, but in which the former judge did not participate. So also the fact that a former judge exercised administrative responsibility in a court does not prevent the former judge from acting as a lawyer in a matter where the judge had previously exercised remote or incidental administrative responsibility that did not affect the merits. Compare the Comment to Rule 1.11. The term "adjudicative officer" includes such officials as judges pro tempore, referees, special masters, hearing officers and other parajudicial officers, and also lawyers who serve as part-time judges. Compliance Canons A(2), B(2) and C of the Model Code of Judicial Conduct provide that a part-time judge, judge pro tempore or retired judge recalled to active service, may not "act as a lawyer in any proceeding in which he served as a judge or in any other proceeding related thereto." Although phrased differently from this Rule, those Rules correspond in meaning.

[2] Like former judges, lawyers who have served as arbitrators, mediators or other third-party neutrals may be asked to represent a client in a matter in which the lawyer participated personally and

substantially. This Rule forbids such representation unless all of the parties to the proceedings give their informed consent, confirmed in writing. See Rule 1.0(e) and (b). Other law or codes of ethics governing third-party neutrals may impose more stringent standards of personal or imputed disqualification. See Rule 2.4.

[3] Although lawyers who serve as third-party neutrals do not have information concerning the parties that is protected under Rule 1.6, they typically owe the parties an obligation of confidentiality under law or codes of ethics governing third-party neutrals. Thus, paragraph (c) provides that conflicts of the personally disqualified lawyer will be imputed to other lawyers in a law firm unless the conditions of this paragraph are met.

[4] Requirements for screening procedures are stated in Rule 1.0(k). Paragraph (c)(1) does not prohibit the screened lawyer from receiving a salary or partnership share established by prior independent agreement, but that lawyer may not receive compensation directly related to the matter in which the lawyer is disqualified.

[5] Notice, including a description of the screened lawyer's prior representation and of the screening procedures employed, generally should be given as soon as practicable after the need for screening becomes apparent.

Rule 1.13 Organization as Client*

(a) A lawyer employed or retained by an organization represents the organization acting through its duly authorized constituents.

(b) If a lawyer for an organization knows that an officer, employee or other person associated with the organization is engaged in action, intends to act or refuses to act in a matter related to the representation that is a violation of a legal obligation to the organization, or a violation of law that reasonably might be imputed to the organization, and that is likely to result in substantial injury to the organization, then the lawyer shall proceed as is reasonably necessary in the best interest of the organization. Unless the lawyer reasonably believes that it is not necessary in the best interest of the organization

---

* In August 2003, the ABA House of Delegates modified Model Rule 1.13 to respond to the claims that the old rule did not permit lawyers to prevent corporate fraud which had a significant impact on their client's financial well being. The old rule text read as follows:

(a) A lawyer employed or retained by an organization represents the organization acting through its duly authorized constituents.

(b) If a lawyer for an organization knows that an officer, employee or other person associated with the organization is engaged in action, intends to act or refuses to act in a matter related to the representation that is a violation of a legal obligation to the organization, or a violation of law which reasonably might be imputed to the organization, and is likely to result in substantial injury to the organization, the lawyer shall proceed as is reasonably necessary in the best interest of the organization. In determining how to proceed, the lawyer shall give due consideration to the seriousness of the violation and its consequences, the scope and nature of the lawyer's representation, the responsibility in the organization and the apparent motivation of the person involved, the policies of the organization concerning such matters and any other relevant considerations. Any measures taken shall be designed to minimize disruption of the organization and the risk of revealing information relating to the representation to persons outside the organization. Such measures may include among others:

(1) asking for reconsideration of the matter;

(2) advising that a separate legal opinion on the matter be sought for presentation to appropriate authority in the organization; and

(3) referring the matter to higher authority in the organization, including, if warranted by the seriousness of the matter, referral to the highest authority that can act on behalf of the organization as determined by applicable law.

(c) If, despite the lawyer's efforts in accordance with paragraph (b), the highest authority that can act on behalf of the organization insists upon action, or a refusal to act, that is clearly a violation of law and is likely to result in substantial injury to the organization, the lawyer may resign in accordance with Rule 1.16.

(d) In dealing with an organization's directors, officers, employees, members, shareholders or other constituents, a lawyer shall explain the identity of the client when the lawyer knows or reasonably should know that the organization's interests are adverse to those of the constituents with whom the lawyer is dealing.

(e) A lawyer representing an organization may also represent any of its directors, officers, employees, members, shareholders or other constituents, subject to the provisions of Rule 1.7. If the organization's consent to the dual representation is required by Rule 1.7, the consent shall be given by an appropriate official of the organization other than the individual who is to be represented, or by the shareholders.

to do so, the lawyer shall refer the matter to higher authority in the organization, including, if warranted by the circumstances, to the highest authority that can act on behalf of the organization as determined by applicable law.

(c) Except as provided in paragraph (d), if,

(1) despite the lawyer's efforts in accordance with paragraph (b), the highest authority that can act on behalf of the organization insists upon or fails to address in a timely and appropriate manner an action, or a refusal to act, that is clearly a violation of law, and

(2) the lawyer reasonably believes that the violation is reasonably certain to result in substantial injury to the organization,

then the lawyer may reveal information relating to the representation whether or not Rule 1.6 permits such disclosure, but only if and to the extent the lawyer reasonably believes necessary to prevent substantial injury to the organization.

(d) Paragraph (c) shall not apply with respect to information relating to a lawyer's representation of an organization to investigate an alleged violation of law, or to defend the organization or an officer, employee or other constituent associated with the organization against a claim arising out of an alleged violation of law.

(e) A lawyer who reasonably believes that he or she has been discharged because of the lawyer's actions taken pursuant to paragraphs (b) or (c), or who withdraws under circumstances that require or permit the lawyer to take action under either of those paragraphs, shall proceed as the lawyer reasonably believes necessary to assure that the organization's highest authority is informed of the lawyer's discharge or withdrawal.

(f) In dealing with an organization's directors, officers, employees, members, shareholders or other constituents, a lawyer shall explain the identity of the client when the lawyer knows or reasonably should know that the organization's interests are adverse to those of the constituents with whom the lawyer is dealing.

(g) A lawyer representing an organization may also represent any of its directors, officers, employees, members, shareholders or other constituents, subject to the provisions of Rule 1.7. If the organization's consent to the dual representation is required by Rule 1.7, the consent shall be given by an appropriate official of the organization other than the individual who is to be represented, or by the shareholders.

COMMENT

The Entity as the Client

[1] An organizational client is a legal entity, but it cannot act except through its officers, directors, employees, shareholders and other constituents. Officers, directors, employees and shareholders are the constituents of the corporate organizational client. The duties defined in this Comment apply equally to unincorporated associations. "Other constituents" as used in this Comment means the positions equivalent to officers, directors, employees and shareholders held by persons acting for organizational clients that are not corporations.

[2] When one of the constituents of an organizational client communicates with the organization's lawyer in that person's organizational capacity, the communication is protected by Rule 1.6. Thus, by way of example, if an organizational client requests its lawyer to investigate allegations of wrongdoing, interviews made in the course of that investigation between the lawyer and the client's employees or other constituents are covered by Rule 1.6. This does not mean, however, that constituents of an organizational client are the clients of the lawyer. The lawyer may not disclose to such constituents information relating to the representation except for disclosures explicitly or impliedly authorized by the organizational client in order to carry out the representation or as otherwise permitted by Rule 1.6.

[3] When constituents of the organization make decisions for it, the decisions ordinarily must be accepted by the lawyer even if their utility or prudence is doubtful. Decisions concerning policy and operations, including ones entailing serious risk, are not as such in the lawyer's province. Paragraph (b) makes clear, however, that when the lawyer knows that the organization is likely to be substantially injured by action of an officer or other constituent that violates a legal obligation to the organization or is in violation of law that might be imputed to the organization, the lawyer must proceed as is reasonably necessary in the best interest of the organization. As defined in Rule 1.0(f), knowledge can be inferred from circumstances, and a lawyer cannot ignore the obvious.

[4] In determining how to proceed under paragraph (b), the lawyer should give due consideration to the seriousness of the violation and its consequences, the responsibility in the organization and the apparent motivation of the person involved, the policies of the organization concerning such matters, and any other relevant considerations. Ordinarily, referral to a higher authority would be necessary. In some circumstances, however, it may be appropriate for the lawyer to ask the constituent to reconsider the matter; for example, if the circumstances involve a constituent's innocent misunderstanding of law and subsequent acceptance of the lawyer's advice, the lawyer may reasonably conclude that the best interest of the organization does not require that the matter be referred to higher authority. If a constituent persists in conduct contrary to the lawyer's advice, it will be necessary for the lawyer to take steps to have the matter reviewed by a higher authority in the organization. If the matter is of sufficient seriousness and importance or urgency to the organization, referral to higher authority in the organization may be necessary even if the lawyer has not communicated with the constituent. Any measures taken should, to the extent practicable, minimize the risk of revealing information relating to the representation to persons outside the organization. Even in circumstances where a lawyer is not obligated by Rule 1.13 to proceed, a lawyer may bring to the attention of an organizational client, including its highest authority, matters that the lawyer reasonably believes to be of sufficient importance to warrant doing so in the best interest of the organization.

[5] Paragraph (b) also makes clear that when it is reasonably necessary to enable the organization to address the matter in a timely and appropriate manner, the lawyer must refer the matter to higher authority, including, if warranted by the circumstances, the highest authority that can act on behalf of the organization under applicable law. The organization's highest authority to whom a matter may be referred ordinarily will be the board of directors or similar governing body. However, applicable law may prescribe that under certain conditions the highest authority reposes elsewhere, for example, in the independent directors of a corporation.

Relation to Other Rules

[6] The authority and responsibility provided in this Rule are concurrent with the authority and responsibility provided in other Rules. In particular, this Rule does not limit or expand the lawyer's responsibility under Rules 1.6, 1.8, 1.16, 3.3 or 4.1. Paragraph (c) of this Rule supplements Rule 1.6(b) by providing an additional basis upon which the lawyer may reveal information relating to the representation, but does not modify, restrict, or limit the provisions of Rule 1.6(b)(1)–(6). Under paragraph (c) the lawyer may reveal such information only when the organization's highest authority insists upon or fails to address threatened or ongoing action that is clearly a violation of law, and then only to the extent the lawyer reasonably believes necessary to prevent reasonably certain substantial injury to the organization. It is not necessary that the lawyer's services be used in furtherance of the violation, but it is required that the matter be related to the lawyer's representation of the organization. If the lawyer's services are being used by an organization to further a crime or fraud by the organization, Rules 1.6(b)(2) and 1.6(b)(3) may permit the lawyer to disclose confidential information. In such circumstances Rule 1.2(d) may also be applicable, in which event, withdrawal from the representation under Rule 1.16(a)(1) may be required.

[7] Paragraph (d) makes clear that the authority of a lawyer to disclose information relating to a representation in circumstances described in paragraph (c) does not apply with respect to information relating to a lawyer's engagement by an organization to investigate an alleged violation of law or to defend the organization or an officer, employee or other person associated with the organization against a claim arising out of an alleged violation of law. This is necessary in order to enable organizational clients to enjoy the full benefits of legal counsel in conducting an investigation or defending against a claim.

[8] A lawyer who reasonably believes that he or she has been discharged because of the lawyer's actions taken pursuant to paragraph (b) or (c), or who withdraws in circumstances that require or permit the lawyer to take action under either of these paragraphs, must proceed as the lawyer reasonably believes necessary to assure that the organization's highest authority is informed of the lawyer's discharge or withdrawal.

Government Agency

[9] The duty defined in this Rule applies to governmental organizations. Defining precisely the identity of the client and prescribing the resulting obligations of such lawyers may be more difficult in the government context and is a matter beyond the scope of these Rules. See Scope [18]. Although in some circumstances the client may be a specific agency, it may also be a branch of government, such as the executive branch, or the government as a whole. For example, if the action or failure to act involves the head of a bureau, either the department of which the bureau is a part or the relevant branch of government may be the client for purposes of this Rule. Moreover, in a matter involving the conduct of government officials, a government lawyer may have authority under applicable law to question such conduct more extensively than that of a lawyer for a private organization in similar circumstances. Thus, when the client is a governmental organization, a different balance may be appropriate between maintaining confidentiality and assuring that the wrongful act is prevented or rectified, for public business is involved. In addition, duties of lawyers employed by the government or lawyers in military service may be defined by statutes and regulation. This Rule does not limit that authority. See Scope.

Clarifying the Lawyer's Role

[10] There are times when the organization's interest may be or become adverse to those of one or more of its constituents. In such circumstances the lawyer should advise any constituent, whose interest the lawyer finds adverse to that of the organization of the conflict or potential conflict of interest, that the lawyer cannot represent such constituent, and that such person may wish to obtain independent representation. Care must be taken to assure that the individual understands that, when there is such adversity of interest, the lawyer for the organization cannot provide legal representation for that constituent individual, and that discussions between the lawyer for the organization and the individual may not be privileged.

[11] Whether such a warning should be given by the lawyer for the organization to any constituent individual may turn on the facts of each case.

Dual Representation

[12] Paragraph (g) recognizes that a lawyer for an organization may also represent a principal officer or major shareholder.

Derivative Actions

[13] Under generally prevailing law, the shareholders or members of a corporation may bring suit to compel the directors to perform their legal obligations in the supervision of the organization. Members of unincorporated associations have essentially the same right. Such an action may be brought nominally by the organization, but usually is, in fact, a legal controversy over management of the organization.

[14] The question can arise whether counsel for the organization may defend such an action. The proposition that the organization is the lawyer's client does not alone resolve the issue. Most derivative actions are a normal incident of an organization's affairs, to be defended by the organization's lawyer like any other suit. However, if the claim involves serious charges of wrongdoing by those in control of the organization, a conflict may arise between the lawyer's duty to the organization and the lawyer's relationship with the board. In those circumstances, Rule 1.7 governs who should represent the directors and the organization.

Rule 1.14 Client with Diminished Capacity

(a) When a client's capacity to make adequately considered decisions in connection with a representation is diminished, whether because of minority, mental impairment or

for some other reason, the lawyer shall, as far as reasonably possible, maintain a normal client-lawyer relationship with the client.

(b) When the lawyer reasonably believes that the client has diminished capacity, is at risk of substantial physical, financial or other harm unless action is taken and cannot adequately act in the client's own interest, the lawyer may take reasonably necessary protective action, including consulting with individuals or entities that have the ability to take action to protect the client and, in appropriate cases, seeking the appointment of a guardian ad litem, conservator or guardian.

(c) Information relating to the representation of a client with diminished capacity is protected by Rule 1.6. When taking protective action pursuant to paragraph (b), the lawyer is impliedly authorized under Rule 1.6(a) to reveal information about the client, but only to the extent reasonably necessary to protect the client's interests.

COMMENT

[1] The normal client-lawyer relationship is based on the assumption that the client, when properly advised and assisted, is capable of making decisions about important matters. When the client is a minor or suffers from a diminished mental capacity, however, maintaining the ordinary client-lawyer relationship may not be possible in all respects. In particular, a severely incapacitated person may have no power to make legally binding decisions. Nevertheless, a client with diminished capacity often has the ability to understand, deliberate upon, and reach conclusions about matters affecting the client's own well-being. For example, children as young as five or six years of age, and certainly those of ten or twelve, are regarded as having opinions that are entitled to weight in legal proceedings concerning their custody. So also, it is recognized that some persons of advanced age can be quite capable of handling routine financial matters while needing special legal protection concerning major transactions.

[2] The fact that a client suffers a disability does not diminish the lawyer's obligation to treat the client with attention and respect. Even if the person has a legal representative, the lawyer should as far as possible accord the represented person the status of client, particularly in maintaining communication.

[3] The client may wish to have family members or other persons participate in discussions with the lawyer. When necessary to assist in the representation, the presence of such persons generally does not affect the applicability of the attorney-client evidentiary privilege. Nevertheless, the lawyer must keep the client's interests foremost and, except for protective action authorized under paragraph (b), must to look to the client, and not family members, to make decisions on the client's behalf.

[4] If a legal representative has already been appointed for the client, the lawyer should ordinarily look to the representative for decisions on behalf of the client. In matters involving a minor, whether the lawyer should look to the parents as natural guardians may depend on the type of proceeding or matter in which the lawyer is representing the minor. If the lawyer represents the guardian as distinct from the ward, and is aware that the guardian is acting adversely to the ward's interest, the lawyer may have an obligation to prevent or rectify the guardian's misconduct. See Rule 1.2(d).

Taking Protective Action

[5] If a lawyer reasonably believes that a client is at risk of substantial physical, financial or other harm unless action is taken, and that a normal client-lawyer relationship cannot be maintained as provided in paragraph (a) because the client lacks sufficient capacity to communicate or to make adequately considered decisions in connection with the representation, then paragraph (b) permits the lawyer to take protective measures deemed necessary. Such measures could include: consulting with family members, using a reconsideration period to permit clarification or improvement of circumstances, using voluntary surrogate decisionmaking tools such as durable powers of attorney or consulting with support groups, professional services, adult-protective agencies or other individuals or entities that have the ability to protect the client. In taking any protective action, the lawyer should be guided by such factors as the wishes and values of the client to the extent known, the client's best interests and the goals of intruding into the client's decisionmaking autonomy to the least extent feasible, maximizing client capacities and respecting the client's family and social connections.

[6] In determining the extent of the client's diminished capacity, the lawyer should consider and balance such factors as: the client's ability to articulate reasoning leading to a decision, variability of state of mind and ability to appreciate consequences of a decision; the substantive fairness of a decision; and the consistency of a decision with the known long-term commitments and values of the client. In appropriate circumstances, the lawyer may seek guidance from an appropriate diagnostician.

[7] If a legal representative has not been appointed, the lawyer should consider whether appointment of a guardian ad litem, conservator or guardian is necessary to protect the client's interests. Thus, if a client with diminished capacity has substantial property that should be sold for the client's benefit, effective completion of the transaction may require appointment of a legal representative. In addition, rules of procedure in litigation sometimes provide that minors or persons with diminished capacity must be represented by a guardian or next friend if they do not have a general guardian. In many circumstances, however, appointment of a legal representative may be more expensive or traumatic for the client than circumstances in fact require. Evaluation of such circumstances is a matter entrusted to the professional judgment of the lawyer. In considering alternatives, however, the lawyer should be aware of any law that requires the lawyer to advocate the least restrictive action on behalf of the client.

Disclosure of the Client's Condition

[8] Disclosure of the client's diminished capacity could adversely affect the client's interests. For example, raising the question of diminished capacity could, in some circumstances, lead to proceedings for involuntary commitment. Information relating to the representation is protected by Rule 1.6. Therefore, unless authorized to do so, the lawyer may not disclose such information. When taking protective action pursuant to paragraph (b), the lawyer is impliedly authorized to make the necessary disclosures, even when the client directs the lawyer to the contrary. Nevertheless, given the risks of disclosure, paragraph (c) limits what the lawyer may disclose in consulting with other individuals or entities or seeking the appointment of a legal representative. At the very least, the lawyer should determine whether it is likely that the person or entity consulted with will act adversely to the client's interests before discussing matters related to the client. The lawyer's position in such cases is an unavoidably difficult one.

Emergency Legal Assistance

[9] In an emergency where the health, safety or a financial interest of a person with seriously diminished capacity is threatened with imminent and irreparable harm, a lawyer may take legal action on behalf of such a person even though the person is unable to establish a client-lawyer relationship or to make or express considered judgments about the matter, when the person or another acting in good faith on that person's behalf has consulted with the lawyer. Even in such an emergency, however, the lawyer should not act unless the lawyer reasonably believes that the person has no other lawyer, agent or other representative available. The lawyer should take legal action on behalf of the person only to the extent reasonably necessary to maintain the status quo or otherwise avoid imminent and irreparable harm. A lawyer who undertakes to represent a person in such an exigent situation has the same duties under these Rules as the lawyer would with respect to a client.

[10] A lawyer who acts on behalf of a person with seriously diminished capacity in an emergency should keep the confidences of the person as if dealing with a client, disclosing them only to the extent necessary to accomplish the intended protective action. The lawyer should disclose to any tribunal involved and to any other counsel involved the nature of his or her relationship with the person. The lawyer should take steps to regularize the relationship or implement other protective solutions as soon as possible. Normally, a lawyer would not seek compensation for such emergency actions taken.

Rule 1.15 Safekeeping Property

(a) A lawyer shall hold property of clients or third persons that is in a lawyer's possession in connection with a representation separate from the lawyer's own property. Funds shall be kept in a separate account maintained in the state where the lawyer's office is situated, or elsewhere with the consent of the client or third person. Other property shall be identified as such and appropriately safeguarded. Complete records of such account funds and other property shall be kept by the lawyer and shall be preserved for a period of [five years] after termination of the representation.

(b) A lawyer may deposit the lawyer's own funds in a client trust account for the sole purpose of paying bank service charges on that account, but only in an amount necessary for that purpose.

(c) A lawyer shall deposit into a client trust account legal fees and expenses that have been paid in advance, to be withdrawn by the lawyer only as fees are earned or expenses incurred.

(d) Upon receiving funds or other property in which a client or third person has an interest, a lawyer shall promptly notify the client or third person. Except as stated in this rule or otherwise permitted by law or by agreement with the client, a lawyer shall promptly deliver to the client or third person any funds or other property that the client or third person is entitled to receive and, upon request by the client or third person, shall promptly render a full accounting regarding such property.

(e) When in the course of representation a lawyer is in possession of property in which two or more persons (one of whom may be the lawyer) claim interests, the property shall be kept separate by the lawyer until the dispute is resolved. The lawyer shall promptly distribute all portions of the property as to which the interests are not in dispute.

COMMENT

[1] A lawyer should hold property of others with the care required of a professional fiduciary. Securities should be kept in a safe deposit box, except when some other form of safekeeping is warranted by special circumstances. All property that is the property of clients or third persons, including prospective clients, must be kept separate from the lawyer's business and personal property and, if monies, in one or more trust accounts. Separate trust accounts may be warranted when administering estate monies or acting in similar fiduciary capacities. A lawyer should maintain on a current basis books and records in accordance with generally accepted accounting practice and comply with any recordkeeping rules established by law or court order. See, e.g., ABA Model Financial Recordkeeping Rule.

[2] While normally it is impermissible to commingle the lawyer's own funds with client funds, paragraph (b) provides that it is permissible when necessary to pay bank service charges on that account. Accurate records must be kept regarding which part of the funds are the lawyer's.

[3] Lawyers often receive funds from which the lawyer's fee will be paid. The lawyer is not required to remit to the client funds that the lawyer reasonably believes represent fees owed. However, a lawyer may not hold funds to coerce a client into accepting the lawyer's contention. The disputed portion of the funds must be kept in a trust account and the lawyer should suggest means for prompt resolution of the dispute, such as arbitration. The undisputed portion of the funds shall be promptly distributed.

[4] Paragraph (e) also recognizes that third parties may have lawful claims against specific funds or other property in a lawyer's custody, such as a client's creditor who has a lien on funds recovered in a personal injury action. A lawyer may have a duty under applicable law to protect such third-party claims against wrongful interference by the client. In such cases, when the third-party claim is not frivolous under applicable law, the lawyer must refuse to surrender the property to the client until the claims are resolved. A lawyer should not unilaterally assume to arbitrate a dispute between the client and the third party, but, when there are substantial grounds for dispute as to the person entitled to the funds, the lawyer may file an action to have a court resolve the dispute.

[5] The obligations of a lawyer under this Rule are independent of those arising from activity other than rendering legal services. For example, a lawyer who serves only as an escrow agent is governed by the applicable law relating to fiduciaries even though the lawyer does not render legal services in the transaction and is not governed by this Rule.

[6] A lawyers' fund for client protection provides a means through the collective efforts of the bar to reimburse persons who have lost money or property as a result of dishonest conduct of a lawyer. Where such a fund has been established, a lawyer must participate where it is mandatory, and, even when it is voluntary, the lawyer should participate.

Rule 1.16 Declining or Terminating Representation

(a) Except as stated in paragraph (c), a lawyer shall not represent a client or, where representation has commenced, shall withdraw from the representation of a client if:

(1) the representation will result in violation of the rules of professional conduct or other law;

(2) the lawyer's physical or mental condition materially impairs the lawyer's ability to represent the client; or

(3) the lawyer is discharged.

(b) Except as stated in paragraph (c), a lawyer may withdraw from representing a client if:

(1) withdrawal can be accomplished without material adverse effect on the interests of the client;

(2) the client persists in a course of action involving the lawyer's services that the lawyer reasonably believes is criminal or fraudulent;

(3) the client has used the lawyer's services to perpetrate a crime or fraud;

(4) the client insists upon taking action that the lawyer considers repugnant or with which the lawyer has a fundamental disagreement;

(5) the client fails substantially to fulfill an obligation to the lawyer regarding the lawyer's services and has been given reasonable warning that the lawyer will withdraw unless the obligation is fulfilled;

(6) the representation will result in an unreasonable financial burden on the lawyer or has been rendered unreasonably difficult by the client; or

(7) other good cause for withdrawal exists.

(c) A lawyer must comply with applicable law requiring notice to or permission of a tribunal when terminating a representation. When ordered to do so by a tribunal, a lawyer shall continue representation notwithstanding good cause for terminating the representation.

(d) Upon termination of representation, a lawyer shall take steps to the extent reasonably practicable to protect a client's interests, such as giving reasonable notice to the client, allowing time for employment of other counsel, surrendering papers and property to which the client is entitled and refunding any advance payment of fee or expense that has not been earned or incurred. The lawyer may retain papers relating to the client to the extent permitted by other law.

COMMENT

[1] A lawyer should not accept representation in a matter unless it can be performed competently, promptly, without improper conflict of interest and to completion. Ordinarily, a representation in a matter is completed when the agreed-upon assistance has been concluded. See Rules 1.2(c) and 6.5. See also Rule 1.3, Comment [4].

Mandatory Withdrawal

[2] A lawyer ordinarily must decline or withdraw from representation if the client demands that the lawyer engage in conduct that is illegal or violates the Rules of Professional Conduct or other law. The lawyer is not obliged to decline or withdraw simply because the client suggests such a course of conduct; a client may make such a suggestion in the hope that a lawyer will not be constrained by a professional obligation.

[3] When a lawyer has been appointed to represent a client, withdrawal ordinarily requires approval of the appointing authority. See also Rule 6.2. Similarly, court approval or notice to the court is often required by applicable law before a lawyer withdraws from pending litigation. Difficulty may be encountered if withdrawal is based on the client's demand that the lawyer engage in unprofessional conduct. The court may request an explanation for the withdrawal, while the lawyer may be bound to keep confidential the facts that would constitute such an explanation. The lawyer's statement that professional considerations require termination of the representation ordinarily should be accepted as sufficient. Lawyers should be mindful of their obligations to both clients and the court under Rules 1.6 and 3.3.

Discharge

[4] A client has a right to discharge a lawyer at any time, with or without cause, subject to liability for payment for the lawyer's services. Where future dispute about the withdrawal may be anticipated, it may be advisable to prepare a written statement reciting the circumstances.

[5] Whether a client can discharge appointed counsel may depend on applicable law. A client seeking to do so should be given a full explanation of the consequences. These consequences may include a decision by the appointing authority that appointment of successor counsel is unjustified, thus requiring self-representation by the client.

[6] If the client has severely diminished capacity, the client may lack the legal capacity to discharge the lawyer, and in any event the discharge may be seriously adverse to the client's interests. The lawyer should make special effort to help the client consider the consequences and may take reasonably necessary protective action as provided in Rule 1.14.

Optional Withdrawal

[7] A lawyer may withdraw from representation in some circumstances. The lawyer has the option to withdraw if it can be accomplished without material adverse effect on the client's interests. Withdrawal is also justified if the client persists in a course of action that the lawyer reasonably believes is criminal or fraudulent, for a lawyer is not required to be associated with such conduct even if the lawyer does not further it. Withdrawal is also permitted if the lawyer's services were misused in the past even if that would materially prejudice the client. The lawyer may also withdraw where the client insists on taking action that the lawyer considers repugnant or with which the lawyer has a fundamental disagreement.

[8] A lawyer may withdraw if the client refuses to abide by the terms of an agreement relating to the representation, such as an agreement concerning fees or court costs or an agreement limiting the objectives of the representation.

Assisting the Client upon Withdrawal

[9] Even if the lawyer has been unfairly discharged by the client, a lawyer must take all reasonable steps to mitigate the consequences to the client. The lawyer may retain papers as security for a fee only to the extent permitted by law. See Rule 1.15.

Rule 1.17 Sale of Law Practice

A lawyer or a law firm may sell or purchase a law practice, or an area of law practice, including good will, if the following conditions are satisfied:

(a) The seller ceases to engage in the private practice of law, or in the area of practice that has been sold, [in the geographic area] [in the jurisdiction] (a jurisdiction may elect either version) in which the practice has been conducted;

(b) The entire practice, or the entire area of practice, is sold to one or more lawyers or law firms;

(c) The seller gives written notice to each of the seller's clients regarding:

(1) the proposed sale;

(2) the client's right to retain other counsel or to take possession of the file; and

(3) the fact that the client's consent to the transfer of the client's files will be presumed if the client does not take any action or does not otherwise object within ninety (90) days of receipt of the notice.

If a client cannot be given notice, the representation of that client may be transferred to the purchaser only upon entry of an order so authorizing by a court having jurisdiction. The seller may disclose to the court in camera information relating to the representation only to the extent necessary to obtain an order authorizing the transfer of a file.

(d) The fees charged clients shall not be increased by reason of the sale.

COMMENT

[1] The practice of law is a profession, not merely a business. Clients are not commodities that can be purchased and sold at will. Pursuant to this Rule, when a lawyer or an entire firm ceases to practice, or ceases to practice in an area of law, and other lawyers or firms take over the representation, the selling lawyer or firm may obtain compensation for the reasonable value of the practice as may withdrawing partners of law firms. See Rules 5.4 and 5.6.

Termination of Practice by the Seller

[2] The requirement that all of the private practice, or all of an area of practice, be sold is satisfied if the seller in good faith makes the entire practice, or the area of practice, available for sale to the purchasers. The fact that a number of the seller's clients decide not to be represented by the purchasers but take their matters elsewhere, therefore, does not result in a violation. Return to private practice as a result of an unanticipated change in circumstances does not necessarily result in a violation. For example, a lawyer who has sold the practice to accept an appointment to judicial office does not violate the requirement that the sale be attendant to cessation of practice if the lawyer later resumes private practice upon being defeated in a contested or a retention election for the office or resigns from a judiciary position.

[3] The requirement that the seller cease to engage in the private practice of law does not prohibit employment as a lawyer on the staff of a public agency or a legal services entity that provides legal services to the poor, or as in-house counsel to a business.

[4] The Rule permits a sale of an entire practice attendant upon retirement from the private practice of law within the jurisdiction. Its provisions, therefore, accommodate the lawyer who sells the practice on the occasion of moving to another state. Some states are so large that a move from one locale therein to another is tantamount to leaving the jurisdiction in which the lawyer has engaged in the practice of law. To also accommodate lawyers so situated, states may permit the sale of the practice when the lawyer leaves the geographical area rather than the jurisdiction. The alternative desired should be indicated by selecting one of the two provided for in Rule 1.17(a).

[5] This Rule also permits a lawyer or law firm to sell an area of practice. If an area of practice is sold and the lawyer remains in the active practice of law, the lawyer must cease accepting any matters in the area of practice that has been sold, either as counsel or co-counsel or by assuming joint responsibility for a matter in connection with the division of a fee with another lawyer as would otherwise be permitted by Rule 1.5(e). For example, a lawyer with a substantial number of estate planning matters and a substantial number of probate administration cases may sell the estate planning portion of the practice but remain in the practice of law by concentrating on probate administration; however, that practitioner may not thereafter accept any estate planning matters. Although a lawyer who leaves a jurisdiction or geographical area typically would sell the entire practice, this Rule permits the lawyer to limit the sale to one or more areas of the practice, thereby preserving the lawyer's right to continue practice in the areas of the practice that were not sold.

Sale of Entire Practice or Entire Area of Practice

[6] The Rule requires that the seller's entire practice, or an entire area of practice, be sold. The prohibition against sale of less than an entire practice area protects those clients whose matters are less lucrative and who might find it difficult to secure other counsel if a sale could be limited to substantial fee-generating matters. The purchasers are required to undertake all client matters in the practice or practice

area, subject to client consent. This requirement is satisfied, however, even if a purchaser is unable to undertake a particular client matter because of a conflict of interest.

Client Confidences, Consent and Notice

*[7] Negotiations between seller and prospective purchaser prior to disclosure of information relating to a specific representation of an identifiable client no more violate the confidentiality provisions of Model Rule 1.6 than do preliminary discussions concerning the possible association of another lawyer or mergers between firms, with respect to which client consent is not required. See Rule 1.6(b)(7). Providing the purchaser access to detailed information relating to the representation, such as the client's file, however, requires client consent. The Rule provides that before such information can be disclosed by the seller to the purchaser the client must be given actual written notice of the contemplated sale, including the identity of the purchaser, and must be told that the decision to consent or make other arrangements must be made within 90 days. If nothing is heard from the client within that time, consent to the sale is presumed.

[8] A lawyer or law firm ceasing to practice cannot be required to remain in practice because some clients cannot be given actual notice of the proposed purchase. Since these clients cannot themselves consent to the purchase or direct any other disposition of their files, the Rule requires an order from a court having jurisdiction authorizing their transfer or other disposition. The Court can be expected to determine whether reasonable efforts to locate the client have been exhausted, and whether the absent client's legitimate interests will be served by authorizing the transfer of the file so that the purchaser may continue the representation. Preservation of client confidences requires that the petition for a court order be considered in camera. (A procedure by which such an order can be obtained needs to be established in jurisdictions in which it presently does not exist.)

[9] All elements of client autonomy, including the client's absolute right to discharge a lawyer and transfer the representation to another, survive the sale of the practice or area of practice.

Fee Arrangements Between Client and Purchaser

[10] The sale may not be financed by increases in fees charged the clients of the practice. Existing arrangements between the seller and the client as to fees and the scope of the work must be honored by the purchaser.

Other Applicable Ethical Standards

[11] Lawyers participating in the sale of a law practice or a practice area are subject to the ethical standards applicable to involving another lawyer in the representation of a client. These include, for example, the seller's obligation to exercise competence in identifying a purchaser qualified to assume the practice and the purchaser's obligation to undertake the representation competently (see Rule 1.1); the obligation to avoid disqualifying conflicts, and to secure the client's informed consent for those conflicts that can be agreed to (see Rule 1.7 regarding conflicts and Rule 1.0(e) for the definition of informed consent); and the obligation to protect information relating to the representation (see Rules 1.6 and 1.9).

[12] If approval of the substitution of the purchasing lawyer for the selling lawyer is required by the rules of any tribunal in which a matter is pending, such approval must be obtained before the matter can be included in the sale (see Rule 1.16).

Applicability of the Rule

[13] This Rule applies to the sale of a law practice of a deceased, disabled or disappeared lawyer. Thus, the seller may be represented by a non-lawyer representative not subject to these Rules. Since, however, no lawyer may participate in a sale of a law practice which does not conform to the requirements of this Rule, the representatives of the seller as well as the purchasing lawyer can be expected to see to it that they are met.

[14] Admission to or retirement from a law partnership or professional association, retirement plans and similar arrangements, and a sale of tangible assets of a law practice, do not constitute a sale or purchase governed by this Rule.

---

* In August 2012, the ABA House of Delegates amended Comment 7 to reflect the addition of new Rule 1.6(b)(7).

[15] This Rule does not apply to the transfers of legal representation between lawyers when such transfers are unrelated to the sale of a practice or an area of practice.

Rule 1.18 Duties to Prospective Client*

(a) A person who consults with a lawyer about the possibility of forming a client-lawyer relationship with respect to a matter is a prospective client.

(b) Even when no client-lawyer relationship ensues, a lawyer who has learned information from a prospective client shall not use or reveal that information, except as Rule 1.9 would permit with respect to information of a former client.

(c) A lawyer subject to paragraph (b) shall not represent a client with interests materially adverse to those of a prospective client in the same or a substantially related matter if the lawyer received information from the prospective client that could be significantly harmful to that person in the matter, except as provided in paragraph (d). If a lawyer is disqualified from representation under this paragraph, no lawyer in a firm with which that lawyer is associated may knowingly undertake or continue representation in such a matter, except as provided in paragraph (d).

(d) When the lawyer has received disqualifying information as defined in paragraph (c), representation is permissible if:

(1) both the affected client and the prospective client have given informed consent, confirmed in writing, or:

(2) the lawyer who received the information took reasonable measures to avoid exposure to more disqualifying information than was reasonably necessary to determine whether to represent the prospective client; and

(i) the disqualified lawyer is timely screened from any participation in the matter and is apportioned no part of the fee therefrom; and

(ii) written notice is promptly given to the prospective client.

COMMENT*

[1] Prospective clients, like clients, may disclose information to a lawyer, place documents or other property in the lawyer's custody, or rely on the lawyer's advice. A lawyer's consultations with a prospective client usually are limited in time and depth and leave both the prospective client and the lawyer free (and sometimes required) to proceed no further. Hence, prospective clients should receive some but not all of the protection afforded clients.

[2] A person becomes a prospective client by consulting with a lawyer about the possibility of forming a client-lawyer relationship with respect to a matter. Whether communications, including written, oral, or electronic communications, constitute a consultation depends on the circumstances. For example, a consultation is likely to have occurred if a lawyer, either in person or through the lawyer's advertising in any medium, specifically requests or invites the submission of information about a potential representation without clear and reasonably understandable warnings and cautionary statements that limit the lawyer's obligations, and a person provides information in response. See also Comment [4]. In contrast, a consultation does not occur if a person provides information to a lawyer in response to advertising that merely describes the lawyer's education, experience, areas of practice, and contact information, or provides legal information of general interest. Such a person communicates information unilaterally to a lawyer, without any reasonable expectation that the lawyer is willing to discuss the possibility of forming a client-lawyer

* In August 2012, the ABA House of Delegates amended Rule 1.18(a) and (b) to broaden the definition of a prospective client.

* In August 2012, the ABA House of Delegates amended Comments 1, 4, and 5 to reflect the change made in the text and substantially added to Comment 2.

relationship, and is thus not a "prospective client." Moreover, a person who communicates with a lawyer for the purpose of disqualifying the lawyer is not a "prospective client."

[3] It is often necessary for a prospective client to reveal information to the lawyer during an initial consultation prior to the decision about formation of a client-lawyer relationship. The lawyer often must learn such information to determine whether there is a conflict of interest with an existing client and whether the matter is one that the lawyer is willing to undertake. Paragraph (b) prohibits the lawyer from using or revealing that information, except as permitted by Rule 1.9, even if the client or lawyer decides not to proceed with the representation. The duty exists regardless of how brief the initial conference may be.

[4] In order to avoid acquiring disqualifying information from a prospective client, a lawyer considering whether or not to undertake a new matter should limit the initial consultation to only such information as reasonably appears necessary for that purpose. Where the information indicates that a conflict of interest or other reason for non-representation exists, the lawyer should so inform the prospective client or decline the representation. If the prospective client wishes to retain the lawyer, and if consent is possible under Rule 1.7, then consent from all affected present or former clients must be obtained before accepting the representation.

[5] A lawyer may condition a consultation with a prospective client on the person's informed consent that no information disclosed during the consultation will prohibit the lawyer from representing a different client in the matter. See Rule 1.0(e) for the definition of informed consent. If the agreement expressly so provides, the prospective client may also consent to the lawyer's subsequent use of information received from the prospective client.

[6] Even in the absence of an agreement, under paragraph (c), the lawyer is not prohibited from representing a client with interests adverse to those of the prospective client in the same or a substantially related matter unless the lawyer has received from the prospective client information that could be significantly harmful if used in the matter.

[7] Under paragraph (c), the prohibition in this Rule is imputed to other lawyers as provided in Rule 1.10, but, under paragraph (d)(1), imputation may be avoided if the lawyer obtains the informed consent, confirmed in writing, of both the prospective and affected clients. In the alternative, imputation may be avoided if the conditions of paragraph (d)(2) are met and all disqualified lawyers are timely screened and written notice is promptly given to the prospective client. See Rule 1.0(k) (requirements for screening procedures). Paragraph (d)(2)(i) does not prohibit the screened lawyer from receiving a salary or partnership share established by prior independent agreement, but that lawyer may not receive compensation directly related to the matter in which the lawyer is disqualified.

[8] Notice, including a general description of the subject matter about which the lawyer was consulted, and of the screening procedures employed, generally should be given as soon as practicable after the need for screening becomes apparent.

[9] For the duty of competence of a lawyer who gives assistance on the merits of a matter to a prospective client, see Rule 1.1. For a lawyer's duties when a prospective client entrusts valuables or papers to the lawyer's care, see Rule 1.15.

COUNSELOR

Rule 2.1 Advisor

In representing a client, a lawyer shall exercise independent professional judgment and render candid advice. In rendering advice, a lawyer may refer not only to law but to other considerations such as moral, economic, social and political factors, that may be relevant to the client's situation.

COMMENT

Scope of Advice

[1] A client is entitled to straightforward advice expressing the lawyer's honest assessment. Legal advice often involves unpleasant facts and alternatives that a client may be disinclined to confront. In presenting advice, a lawyer endeavors to sustain the client's morale and may put advice in as acceptable a form as honesty permits. However, a lawyer should not be deterred from giving candid advice by the prospect that the advice will be unpalatable to the client.

[2] Advice couched in narrow legal terms may be of little value to a client, especially where practical considerations, such as cost or effects on other people, are predominant. Purely technical legal advice, therefore, can sometimes be inadequate. It is proper for a lawyer to refer to relevant moral and ethical considerations in giving advice. Although a lawyer is not a moral advisor as such, moral and ethical considerations impinge upon most legal questions and may decisively influence how the law will be applied.

[3] A client may expressly or impliedly ask the lawyer for purely technical advice. When such a request is made by a client experienced in legal matters, the lawyer may accept it at face value. When such a request is made by a client inexperienced in legal matters, however, the lawyer's responsibility as advisor may include indicating that more may be involved than strictly legal considerations.

[4] Matters that go beyond strictly legal questions may also be in the domain of another profession. Family matters can involve problems within the professional competence of psychiatry, clinical psychology or social work; business matters can involve problems within the competence of the accounting profession or of financial specialists. Where consultation with a professional in another field is itself something a competent lawyer would recommend, the lawyer should make such a recommendation. At the same time, a lawyer's advice at its best often consists of recommending a course of action in the face of conflicting recommendations of experts.

Offering Advice

[5] In general, a lawyer is not expected to give advice until asked by the client. However, when a lawyer knows that a client proposes a course of action that is likely to result in substantial adverse legal consequences to the client, the lawyer's duty to the client under Rule 1.4 may require that the lawyer offer advice if the client's course of action is related to the representation. Similarly, when a matter is likely to involve litigation, it may be necessary under Rule 1.4 to inform the client of forms of dispute resolution that might constitute reasonable alternatives to litigation. A lawyer ordinarily has no duty to initiate investigation of a client's affairs or to give advice that the client has indicated is unwanted, but a lawyer may initiate advice to a client when doing so appears to be in the client's interest.

Rule 2.2 Intermediary

[Deleted 2002]

Rule 2.3 Evaluation for Use by Third Persons

(a) A lawyer may provide an evaluation of a matter affecting a client for the use of someone other than the client if the lawyer reasonably believes that making the evaluation is compatible with other aspects of the lawyer's relationship with the client.

(b) When the lawyer knows or reasonably should know that the evaluation is likely to affect the client's interests materially and adversely, the lawyer shall not provide the evaluation unless the client gives informed consent.

(c) Except as disclosure is authorized in connection with a report of an evaluation, information relating to the evaluation is otherwise protected by Rule 1.6.

COMMENT

Definition

[1] An evaluation may be performed at the client's direction or when impliedly authorized in order to carry out the representation. See Rule 1.2. Such an evaluation may be for the primary purpose of establishing information for the benefit of third parties; for example, an opinion concerning the title of property rendered at the behest of a vendor for the information of a prospective purchaser, or at the behest of a borrower for the information of a prospective lender. In some situations, the evaluation may be required by a government agency; for example, an opinion concerning the legality of the securities registered for sale under the securities laws. In other instances, the evaluation may be required by a third person, such as a purchaser of a business.

[2] A legal evaluation should be distinguished from an investigation of a person with whom the lawyer does not have a client-lawyer relationship. For example, a lawyer retained by a purchaser to analyze a vendor's title to property does not have a client-lawyer relationship with the vendor. So also, an investigation into a person's affairs by a government lawyer, or by special counsel by a government lawyer, or by special counsel employed by the government, is not an evaluation as that term is used in this Rule. The question is whether the lawyer is retained by the person whose affairs are being examined. When the lawyer is retained by that person, the general rules concerning loyalty to client and preservation of confidences apply, which is not the case if the lawyer is retained by someone else. For this reason, it is essential to identify the person by whom the lawyer is retained. This should be made clear not only to the person under examination, but also to others to whom the results are to be made available.

Duties Owed to Third Person and Client

[3] When the evaluation is intended for the information or use of a third person, a legal duty to that person may or may not arise. That legal question is beyond the scope of this Rule. However, since such an evaluation involves a departure from the normal client-lawyer relationship, careful analysis of the situation is required. The lawyer must be satisfied as a matter of professional judgment that making the evaluation is compatible with other functions undertaken in behalf of the client. For example, if the lawyer is acting as advocate in defending the client against charges of fraud, it would normally be incompatible with that responsibility for the lawyer to perform an evaluation for others concerning the same or a related transaction. Assuming no such impediment is apparent, however, the lawyer should advise the client of the implications of the evaluation, particularly the lawyer's responsibilities to third persons and the duty to disseminate the findings.

Access to and Disclosure of Information

[4] The quality of an evaluation depends on the freedom and extent of the investigation upon which it is based. Ordinarily a lawyer should have whatever latitude of investigation seems necessary as a matter of professional judgment. Under some circumstances, however, the terms of the evaluation may be limited. For example, certain issues or sources may be categorically excluded, or the scope of search may be limited by time constraints or the noncooperation of persons having relevant information. Any such limitations that are material to the evaluation should be described in the report. If after a lawyer has commenced an evaluation, the client refuses to comply with the terms upon which it was understood the evaluation was to have been made, the lawyer's obligations are determined by law, having reference to the terms of the client's agreement and the surrounding circumstances. In no circumstances is the lawyer permitted to knowingly make a false statement of material fact or law in providing an evaluation under this Rule. See Rule 4.1.

Obtaining Client's Informed Consent

[5] Information relating to an evaluation is protected by Rule 1.6. In many situations, providing an evaluation to a third party poses no significant risk to the client; thus, the lawyer may be impliedly authorized to disclose information to carry out the representation. See Rule 1.6(a). Where, however, it is reasonably likely that providing the evaluation will affect the client's interests materially and adversely, the lawyer must first obtain the client's consent after the client has been adequately informed concerning the important possible effects on the client's interests. See Rules 1.6(a) and 1.0(e).

Financial Auditors' Requests for Information

[6] When a question concerning the legal situation of a client arises at the instance of the client's financial auditor and the question is referred to the lawyer, the lawyer's response may be made in accordance with procedures recognized in the legal profession. Such a procedure is set forth in the American Bar Association Statement of Policy Regarding Lawyers' Responses to Auditors' Requests for Information, adopted in 1975.

Rule 2.4 Lawyer Serving as a Third-Party Neutral

(a) A lawyer serves as a third-party neutral when the lawyer assists two or more persons who are not clients of the lawyer to reach a resolution of a dispute or other matter that has arisen between them. Service as a third-party neutral may include service as an arbitrator, a mediator or in such other capacity as will enable the lawyer to assist the parties to resolve the matter.

(b) A lawyer serving as a third-party neutral shall inform unrepresented parties that the lawyer is not representing them. When the lawyer knows or reasonably should know that a party does not understand the lawyer's role in the matter, the lawyer shall explain the difference between the lawyer's role as a third-party neutral and a lawyer's role as one who represents a client.

COMMENT

[1] Alternative dispute resolution has become a substantial part of the civil justice system. Aside from representing clients in dispute-resolution processes, lawyers often serve as third-party neutrals. A third-party neutral is a person, such as a mediator, arbitrator, conciliator or evaluator, who assists the parties, represented or unrepresented, in the resolution of a dispute or in the arrangement of a transaction. Whether a third-party neutral serves primarily as a facilitator, evaluator or decisionmaker depends on the particular process that is either selected by the parties or mandated by a court.

[2] The role of a third-party neutral is not unique to lawyers, although, in some court-connected contexts, only lawyers are allowed to serve in this role or to handle certain types of cases. In performing this role, the lawyer may be subject to court rules or other law that apply either to third-party neutrals generally or to lawyers serving as third-party neutrals. Lawyer-neutrals may also be subject to various codes of ethics, such as the Code of Ethics for Arbitration in Commercial Disputes prepared by a joint committee of the American Bar Association and the American Arbitration Association or the Model Standards of Conduct for Mediators jointly prepared by the American Bar Association, the American Arbitration Association and the Society of Professionals in Dispute Resolution.

[3] Unlike nonlawyers who serve as third-party neutrals, lawyers serving in this role may experience unique problems as a result of differences between the role of a third-party neutral and a lawyer's service as a client representative. The potential for confusion is significant when the parties are unrepresented in the process. Thus, paragraph (b) requires a lawyer-neutral to inform unrepresented parties that the lawyer is not representing them. For some parties, particularly parties who frequently use dispute-resolution processes, this information will be sufficient. For others, particularly those who are using the process for the first time, more information will be required. Where appropriate, the lawyer should inform unrepresented parties of the important differences between the lawyer's role as third-party neutral and a lawyer's role as a client representative, including the inapplicability of the attorney-client evidentiary privilege. The extent of disclosure required under this paragraph will depend on the particular parties involved and the subject matter of the proceeding, as well as the particular features of the dispute-resolution process selected.

[4] A lawyer who serves as a third-party neutral subsequently may be asked to serve as a lawyer representing a client in the same matter. The conflicts of interest that arise for both the individual lawyer and the lawyer's law firm are addressed in Rule 1.12.

[5] Lawyers who represent clients in alternative dispute-resolution processes are governed by the Rules of Professional Conduct. When the dispute-resolution process takes place before a tribunal, as in

binding arbitration (see Rule 1.0(m)), the lawyer's duty of candor is governed by Rule 3.3. Otherwise, the lawyer's duty of candor toward both the third-party neutral and other parties is governed by Rule 4.1.

ADVOCATE

Rule 3.1 Meritorious Claims and Contentions

A lawyer shall not bring or defend a proceeding, or assert or controvert an issue therein, unless there is a basis in law and fact for doing so that is not frivolous, which includes a good faith argument for an extension, modification or reversal of existing law. A lawyer for the defendant in a criminal proceeding, or the respondent in a proceeding that could result in incarceration, may nevertheless so defend the proceeding as to require that every element of the case be established.

COMMENT

[1] The advocate has a duty to use legal procedure for the fullest benefit of the client's cause, but also a duty not to abuse legal procedure. The law, both procedural and substantive, establishes the limits within which an advocate may proceed. However, the law is not always clear and never is static. Accordingly, in determining the proper scope of advocacy, account must be taken of the law's ambiguities and potential for change.

[2] The filing of an action or defense or similar action taken for a client is not frivolous merely because the facts have not first been fully substantiated or because the lawyer expects to develop vital evidence only by discovery. What is required of lawyers, however, is that they inform themselves about the facts of their clients' cases and the applicable law and determine that they can make good faith arguments in support of their clients' positions. Such action is not frivolous even though the lawyer believes that the client's position ultimately will not prevail. The action is frivolous, however, if the lawyer is unable either to make a good faith argument on the merits of the action taken or to support the action taken by a good faith argument for an extension, modification or reversal of existing law.

[3] The lawyer's obligations under this Rule are subordinate to federal or state constitutional law that entitles a defendant in a criminal matter to the assistance of counsel in presenting a claim or contention that otherwise would be prohibited by this Rule.

Rule 3.2 Expediting Litigation

A lawyer shall make reasonable efforts to expedite litigation consistent with the interests of the client.

COMMENT

[1] Dilatory practices bring the administration of justice into disrepute. Although there will be occasions when a lawyer may properly seek a postponement for personal reasons, it is not proper for a lawyer to routinely fail to expedite litigation solely for the convenience of the advocates. Nor will a failure to expedite be reasonable if done for the purpose of frustrating an opposing party's attempt to obtain rightful redress or repose. It is not a justification that similar conduct is often tolerated by the bench and bar. The question is whether a competent lawyer acting in good faith would regard the course of action as having some substantial purpose other than delay. Realizing financial or other benefit from otherwise improper delay in litigation is not a legitimate interest of the client.

Rule 3.3 Candor Toward the Tribunal

(a) A lawyer shall not knowingly:

(1) make a false statement of fact or law to a tribunal or fail to correct a false statement of material fact or law previously made to the tribunal by the lawyer;

(2) fail to disclose to the tribunal legal authority in the controlling jurisdiction known to the lawyer to be directly adverse to the position of the client and not disclosed by opposing counsel; or

(3) offer evidence that the lawyer knows to be false. If a lawyer, the lawyer's client, or a witness called by the lawyer, has offered material evidence and the lawyer comes to know of its falsity, the lawyer shall take reasonable remedial measures, including, if necessary, disclosure to the tribunal. A lawyer may refuse to offer evidence, other than the testimony of a defendant in a criminal matter, that the lawyer reasonably believes is false.

(b) A lawyer who represents a client in an adjudicative proceeding and who knows that a person intends to engage, is engaging or has engaged in criminal or fraudulent conduct related to the proceeding shall take reasonable remedial measures, including, if necessary, disclosure to the tribunal.

(c) The duties stated in paragraphs (a) and (b) continue to the conclusion of the proceeding, and apply even if compliance requires disclosure of information otherwise protected by Rule 1.6.

(d) In an ex parte proceeding, a lawyer shall inform the tribunal of all material facts known to the lawyer that will enable the tribunal to make an informed decision, whether or not the facts are adverse.

COMMENT

[1] This Rule governs the conduct of a lawyer who is representing a client in the proceedings of a tribunal. See Rule 1.0(m) for the definition of "tribunal." It also applies when the lawyer is representing a client in an ancillary proceeding conducted pursuant to the tribunal's adjudicative authority, such as a deposition. Thus, for example, paragraph (a)(3) requires a lawyer to take reasonable remedial measures if the lawyer comes to know that a client who is testifying in a deposition has offered evidence that is false.

[2] This Rule sets forth the special duties of lawyers as officers of the court to avoid conduct that undermines the integrity of the adjudicative process. A lawyer acting as an advocate in an adjudicative proceeding has an obligation to present the client's case with persuasive force. Performance of that duty while maintaining confidences of the client, however, is qualified by the advocate's duty of candor to the tribunal. Consequently, although a lawyer in an adversary proceeding is not required to present an impartial exposition of the law or to vouch for the evidence submitted in a cause, the lawyer must not allow the tribunal to be misled by false statements of law or fact or evidence that the lawyer knows to be false.

Representations by a Lawyer

[3] An advocate is responsible for pleadings and other documents prepared for litigation, but is usually not required to have personal knowledge of matters asserted therein, for litigation documents ordinarily present assertions by the client, or by someone on the client's behalf, and not assertions by the lawyer. Compare Rule 3.1. However, an assertion purporting to be on the lawyer's own knowledge, as in an affidavit by the lawyer or in a statement in open court, may properly be made only when the lawyer knows the assertion is true or believes it to be true on the basis of a reasonably diligent inquiry. There are circumstances where failure to make a disclosure is the equivalent of an affirmative misrepresentation. The obligation prescribed in Rule 1.2(d) not to counsel a client to commit or assist the client in committing a fraud applies in litigation. Regarding compliance with Rule 1.2(d), see the Comment to that Rule. See also the Comment to Rule 8.4(b).

Legal Argument

[4] Legal argument based on a knowingly false representation of law constitutes dishonesty toward the tribunal. A lawyer is not required to make a disinterested exposition of the law, but must recognize the existence of pertinent legal authorities. Furthermore, as stated in paragraph (a)(2), an advocate has a duty to disclose directly adverse authority in the controlling jurisdiction that has not been disclosed by the opposing party. The underlying concept is that legal argument is a discussion seeking to determine the legal premises properly applicable to the case.

Offering Evidence

[5] Paragraph (a)(3) requires that the lawyer refuse to offer evidence that the lawyer knows to be false, regardless of the client's wishes. This duty is premised on the lawyer's obligation as an officer of the court to prevent the trier of fact from being misled by false evidence. A lawyer does not violate this Rule if the lawyer offers the evidence for the purpose of establishing its falsity.

[6] If a lawyer knows that the client intends to testify falsely or wants the lawyer to introduce false evidence, the lawyer should seek to persuade the client that the evidence should not be offered. If the persuasion is ineffective and the lawyer continues to represent the client, the lawyer must refuse to offer the false evidence. If only a portion of a witness's testimony will be false, the lawyer may call the witness to testify but may not elicit or otherwise permit the witness to present the testimony that the lawyer knows is false.

[7] The duties stated in paragraphs (a) and (b) apply to all lawyers, including defense counsel in criminal cases. In some jurisdictions, however, courts have required counsel to present the accused as a witness or to give a narrative statement if the accused so desires, even if counsel knows that the testimony or statement will be false. The obligation of the advocate under the Rules of Professional Conduct is subordinate to such requirements. See also Comment [9].

[8] The prohibition against offering false evidence only applies if the lawyer knows that the evidence is false. A lawyer's reasonable belief that evidence is false does not preclude its presentation to the trier of fact. A lawyer's knowledge that evidence is false, however, can be inferred from the circumstances. See Rule 1.0(f). Thus, although a lawyer should resolve doubts about the veracity of testimony or other evidence in favor of the client, the lawyer cannot ignore an obvious falsehood.

[9] Although paragraph (a)(3) only prohibits a lawyer from offering evidence the lawyer knows to be false, it permits the lawyer to refuse to offer testimony or other proof that the lawyer reasonably believes is false. Offering such proof may reflect adversely on the lawyer's ability to discriminate in the quality of evidence and thus impair the lawyer's effectiveness as an advocate. Because of the special protections historically provided criminal defendants, however, this Rule does not permit a lawyer to refuse to offer the testimony of such a client where the lawyer reasonably believes but does not know that the testimony will be false. Unless the lawyer knows the testimony will be false, the lawyer must honor the client's decision to testify. See also Comment [7].

Remedial Measures

[10] Having offered material evidence in the belief that it was true, a lawyer may subsequently come to know that the evidence is false. Or, a lawyer may be surprised when the lawyer's client, or another witness called by the lawyer, offers testimony the lawyer knows to be false, either during the lawyer's direct examination or in response to cross-examination by the opposing lawyer. In such situations or if the lawyer knows of the falsity of testimony elicited from the client during a deposition, the lawyer must take reasonable remedial measures. In such situations, the advocate's proper course is to remonstrate with the client confidentially, advise the client of the lawyer's duty of candor to the tribunal and seek the client's cooperation with respect to the withdrawal or correction of the false statements or evidence. If that fails, the advocate must take further remedial action. If withdrawal from the representation is not permitted or will not undo the effect of the false evidence, the advocate must make such disclosure to the tribunal as is reasonably necessary to remedy the situation, even if doing so requires the lawyer to reveal information that otherwise would be protected by Rule 1.6. It is for the tribunal then to determine what should be done—making a statement about the matter to the trier of fact, ordering a mistrial or perhaps nothing.

[11] The disclosure of a client's false testimony can result in grave consequences to the client, including not only a sense of betrayal but also loss of the case and perhaps a prosecution for perjury. But the alternative is that the lawyer cooperate in deceiving the court, thereby subverting the truth-finding process which the adversary system is designed to implement. See Rule 1.2(d). Furthermore, unless it is clearly understood that the lawyer will act upon the duty to disclose the existence of false evidence, the client can simply reject the lawyer's advice to reveal the false evidence and insist that the lawyer keep silent. Thus the client could in effect coerce the lawyer into being a party to fraud on the court.

Preserving Integrity of Adjudicative Process

[12] Lawyers have a special obligation to protect a tribunal against criminal or fraudulent conduct that undermines the integrity of the adjudicative process, such as bribing, intimidating or otherwise unlawfully communicating with a witness, juror, court official or other participant in the proceeding, unlawfully destroying or concealing documents or other evidence or failing to disclose information to the tribunal when required by law to do so. Thus, paragraph (b) requires a lawyer to take reasonable remedial measures, including disclosure if necessary, whenever the lawyer knows that a person, including the lawyer's client, intends to engage, is engaging or has engaged in criminal or fraudulent conduct related to the proceeding.

Duration of Obligation

[13] A practical time limit on the obligation to rectify false evidence or false statements of law and fact has to be established. The conclusion of the proceeding is a reasonably definite point for the termination of the obligation. A proceeding has concluded within the meaning of this Rule when a final judgment in the proceeding has been affirmed on appeal or the time for review has passed.

Ex Parte Proceedings

[14] Ordinarily, an advocate has the limited responsibility of presenting one side of the matters that a tribunal should consider in reaching a decision; the conflicting position is expected to be presented by the opposing party. However, in any ex parte proceeding, such as an application for a temporary restraining order, there is no balance of presentation by opposing advocates. The object of an ex parte proceeding is nevertheless to yield a substantially just result. The judge has an affirmative responsibility to accord the absent party just consideration. The lawyer for the represented party has the correlative duty to make disclosures of material facts known to the lawyer and that the lawyer reasonably believes are necessary to an informed decision.

Withdrawal

[15] Normally, a lawyer's compliance with the duty of candor imposed by this Rule does not require that the lawyer withdraw from the representation of a client whose interests will be or have been adversely affected by the lawyer's disclosure. The lawyer may, however, be required by Rule 1.16(a) to seek permission of the tribunal to withdraw if the lawyer's compliance with this Rule's duty of candor results in such an extreme deterioration of the client-lawyer relationship that the lawyer can no longer competently represent the client. Also see Rule 1.16(b) for the circumstances in which a lawyer will be permitted to seek a tribunal's permission to withdraw. In connection with a request for permission to withdraw that is premised on a client's misconduct, a lawyer may reveal information relating to the representation only to the extent reasonably necessary to comply with this Rule or as otherwise permitted by Rule 1.6.

Rule 3.4 Fairness to Opposing Party and Counsel

A lawyer shall not:

(a) unlawfully obstruct another party's access to evidence or unlawfully alter, destroy or conceal a document or other material having potential evidentiary value. A lawyer shall not counsel or assist another person to do any such act;

(b) falsify evidence, counsel or assist a witness to testify falsely, or offer an inducement to a witness that is prohibited by law;

(c) knowingly disobey an obligation under the rules of a tribunal, except for an open refusal based on an assertion that no valid obligation exists;

(d) in pretrial procedure, make a frivolous discovery request or fail to make reasonably diligent effort to comply with a legally proper discovery request by an opposing party;

(e) in trial, allude to any matter that the lawyer does not reasonably believe is relevant or that will not be supported by admissible evidence, assert personal knowledge of facts in issue except when testifying as a witness, or state a personal opinion as to the

justness of a cause, the credibility of a witness, the culpability of a civil litigant or the guilt or innocence of an accused; or

(f) request a person other than a client to refrain from voluntarily giving relevant information to another party unless:

(1) the person is a relative or an employee or other agent of a client; and

(2) the lawyer reasonably believes that the person's interests will not be adversely affected by refraining from giving such information.

COMMENT

[1] The procedure of the adversary system contemplates that the evidence in a case is to be marshalled competitively by the contending parties. Fair competition in the adversary system is secured by prohibitions against destruction or concealment of evidence, improperly influencing witnesses, obstructive tactics in discovery procedure, and the like.

[2] Documents and other items of evidence are often essential to establish a claim or defense. Subject to evidentiary privileges, the right of an opposing party, including the government, to obtain evidence through discovery or subpoena is an important procedural right. The exercise of that right can be frustrated if relevant material is altered, concealed or destroyed. Applicable law in many jurisdictions makes it an offense to destroy material for purpose of impairing its availability in a pending proceeding or one whose commencement can be foreseen. Falsifying evidence is also generally a criminal offense. Paragraph (a) applies to evidentiary material generally, including computerized information. Applicable law may permit a lawyer to take temporary possession of physical evidence of client crimes for the purpose of conducting a limited examination that will not alter or destroy material characteristics of the evidence. In such a case, applicable law may require the lawyer to turn the evidence over to the police or other prosecuting authority, depending on the circumstances.

[3] With regard to paragraph (b), it is not improper to pay a witness's expenses or to compensate an expert witness on terms permitted by law. The common law rule in most jurisdictions is that it is improper to pay an occurrence witness any fee for testifying and that it is improper to pay an expert witness a contingent fee.

[4] Paragraph (f) permits a lawyer to advise employees of a client to refrain from giving information to another party, for the employees may identify their interests with those of the client. See also Rule 4.2.

Rule 3.5 Impartiality and Decorum of the Tribunal

A lawyer shall not:

(a) seek to influence a judge, juror, prospective juror or other official by means prohibited by law;

(b) communicate ex parte with such a person during the proceeding unless authorized to do so by law or court order;

(c) communicate with a juror or prospective juror after discharge of the jury if:

(1) the communication is prohibited by law or court order;

(2) the juror has made known to the lawyer a desire not to communicate; or

(3) the communication involves misrepresentation, coercion, duress or harassment; or

(d) engage in conduct intended to disrupt a tribunal.

COMMENT

[1] Many forms of improper influence upon a tribunal are proscribed by criminal law. Others are specified in the ABA Model Code of Judicial Conduct, with which an advocate should be familiar. A lawyer is required to avoid contributing to a violation of such provisions.

[2] During a proceeding a lawyer may not communicate ex parte with persons serving in an official capacity in the proceeding, such as judges, masters or jurors, unless authorized to do so by law or court order.

[3] A lawyer may on occasion want to communicate with a juror or prospective juror after the jury has been discharged. The lawyer may do so unless the communication is prohibited by law or a court order but must respect the desire of the juror not to talk with the lawyer. The lawyer may not engage in improper conduct during the communication.

[4] The advocate's function is to present evidence and argument so that the cause may be decided according to law. Refraining from abusive or obstreperous conduct is a corollary of the advocate's right to speak on behalf of litigants. A lawyer may stand firm against abuse by a judge but should avoid reciprocation; the judge's default is no justification for similar dereliction by an advocate. An advocate can present the cause, protect the record for subsequent review and preserve professional integrity by patient firmness no less effectively than by belligerence or theatrics.

[5] The duty to refrain from disruptive conduct applies to any proceeding of a tribunal, including a deposition. See Rule 1.0(m).

Rule 3.6 Trial Publicity

(a) A lawyer who is participating or has participated in the investigation or litigation of a matter shall not make an extrajudicial statement that the lawyer knows or reasonably should know will be disseminated by means of public communication and will have a substantial likelihood of materially prejudicing an adjudicative proceeding in the matter.

(b) Notwithstanding paragraph (a), a lawyer may state:

(1) the claim, offense or defense involved and, except when prohibited by law, the identity of the persons involved;

(2) information contained in a public record;

(3) that an investigation of a matter is in progress;

(4) the scheduling or result of any step in litigation;

(5) a request for assistance in obtaining evidence and information necessary thereto;

(6) a warning of danger concerning the behavior of a person involved, when there is reason to believe that there exists the likelihood of substantial harm to an individual or to the public interest; and

(7) in a criminal case, in addition to subparagraphs (1) through (6):

(i) the identity, residence, occupation and family status of the accused;

(ii) if the accused has not been apprehended, information necessary to aid in apprehension of that person;

(iii) the fact, time and place of arrest; and

(iv) the identity of investigating and arresting officers or agencies and the length of the investigation.

(c) Notwithstanding paragraph (a), a lawyer may make a statement that a reasonable lawyer would believe is required to protect a client from the substantial undue prejudicial effect of recent publicity not initiated by the lawyer or the lawyer's client. A statement

made pursuant to this paragraph shall be limited to such information as is necessary to mitigate the recent adverse publicity.

(d) No lawyer associated in a firm or government agency with a lawyer subject to paragraph (a) shall make a statement prohibited by paragraph (a).

COMMENT

[1] It is difficult to strike a balance between protecting the right to a fair trial and safeguarding the right of free expression. Preserving the right to a fair trial necessarily entails some curtailment of the information that may be disseminated about a party prior to trial, particularly where trial by jury is involved. If there were no such limits, the result would be the practical nullification of the protective effect of the rules of forensic decorum and the exclusionary rules of evidence. On the other hand, there are vital social interests served by the free dissemination of information about events having legal consequences and about legal proceedings themselves. The public has a right to know about threats to its safety and measures aimed at assuring its security. It also has a legitimate interest in the conduct of judicial proceedings, particularly in matters of general public concern. Furthermore, the subject matter of legal proceedings is often of direct significance in debate and deliberation over questions of public policy.

[2] Special rules of confidentiality may validly govern proceedings in juvenile, domestic relations and mental disability proceedings, and perhaps other types of litigation. Rule 3.4(c) requires compliance with such rules.

[3] The Rule sets forth a basic general prohibition against a lawyer's making statements that the lawyer knows or should know will have a substantial likelihood of materially prejudicing an adjudicative proceeding. Recognizing that the public value of informed commentary is great and the likelihood of prejudice to a proceeding by the commentary of a lawyer who is not involved in the proceeding is small, the rule applies only to lawyers who are, or who have been involved in the investigation or litigation of a case, and their associates.

[4] Paragraph (b) identifies specific matters about which a lawyer's statements would not ordinarily be considered to present a substantial likelihood of material prejudice, and should not in any event be considered prohibited by the general prohibition of paragraph (a). Paragraph (b) is not intended to be an exhaustive listing of the subjects upon which a lawyer may make a statement, but statements on other matters may be subject to paragraph (a).

[5] There are, on the other hand, certain subjects that are more likely than not to have a material prejudicial effect on a proceeding, particularly when they refer to a civil matter triable to a jury, a criminal matter, or any other proceeding that could result in incarceration. These subjects relate to:

(1) the character, credibility, reputation or criminal record of a party, suspect in a criminal investigation or witness, or the identity of a witness, or the expected testimony of a party or witness;

(2) in a criminal case or proceeding that could result in incarceration, the possibility of a plea of guilty to the offense or the existence or contents of any confession, admission, or statement given by a defendant or suspect or that person's refusal or failure to make a statement;

(3) the performance or results of any examination or test or the refusal or failure of a person to submit to an examination or test, or the identity or nature of physical evidence expected to be presented;

(4) any opinion as to the guilt or innocence of a defendant or suspect in a criminal case or proceeding that could result in incarceration;

(5) information that the lawyer knows or reasonably should know is likely to be inadmissible as evidence in a trial and that would, if disclosed, create a substantial risk of prejudicing an impartial trial; or

(6) the fact that a defendant has been charged with a crime, unless there is included therein a statement explaining that the charge is merely an accusation and that the defendant is presumed innocent until and unless proven guilty.

[6] Another relevant factor in determining prejudice is the nature of the proceeding involved. Criminal jury trials will be most sensitive to extrajudicial speech. Civil trials may be less sensitive. Non-jury hearings and arbitration proceedings may be even less affected. The Rule will still place limitations on prejudicial comments in these cases, but the likelihood of prejudice may be different depending on the type of proceeding.

[7] Finally, extrajudicial statements that might otherwise raise a question under this Rule may be permissible when they are made in response to statements made publicly by another party, another party's lawyer, or third persons, where a reasonable lawyer would believe a public response is required in order to avoid prejudice to the lawyer's client. When prejudicial statements have been publicly made by others, responsive statements may have the salutary effect of lessening any resulting adverse impact on the adjudicative proceeding. Such responsive statements should be limited to contain only such information as is necessary to mitigate undue prejudice created by the statements made by others.

[8] See Rule 3.8(f) for additional duties of prosecutors in connection with extrajudicial statements about criminal proceedings.

Rule 3.7 Lawyer as Witness

(a) A lawyer shall not act as advocate at a trial in which the lawyer is likely to be a necessary witness unless:

(1) the testimony relates to an uncontested issue;

(2) the testimony relates to the nature and value of legal services rendered in the case; or

(3) disqualification of the lawyer would work substantial hardship on the client.

(b) A lawyer may act as advocate in a trial in which another lawyer in the lawyer's firm is likely to be called as a witness unless precluded from doing so by Rule 1.7 or Rule 1.9.

COMMENT

[1] Combining the roles of advocate and witness can prejudice the tribunal and the opposing party and can also involve a conflict of interest between the lawyer and client.

Advocate-Witness Rule

[2] The tribunal has proper objection when the trier of fact may be confused or misled by a lawyer serving as both advocate and witness. The opposing party has proper objection where the combination of roles may prejudice that party's rights in the litigation. A witness is required to testify on the basis of personal knowledge, while an advocate is expected to explain and comment on evidence given by others. It may not be clear whether a statement by an advocate-witness should be taken as proof or as an analysis of the proof.

[3] To protect the tribunal, paragraph (a) prohibits a lawyer from simultaneously serving as advocate and necessary witness except in those circumstances specified in paragraphs (a)(1) through (a)(3). Paragraph (a)(1) recognizes that if the testimony will be uncontested, the ambiguities in the dual role are purely theoretical. Paragraph (a)(2) recognizes that where the testimony concerns the extent and value of legal services rendered in the action in which the testimony is offered, permitting the lawyers to testify avoids the need for a second trial with new counsel to resolve that issue. Moreover, in such a situation the judge has firsthand knowledge of the matter in issue; hence, there is less dependence on the adversary process to test the credibility of the testimony.

[4] Apart from these two exceptions, paragraph (a)(3) recognizes that a balancing is required between the interests of the client and those of the tribunal and the opposing party. Whether the tribunal is likely to be misled or the opposing party is likely to suffer prejudice depends on the nature of the case, the importance and probable tenor of the lawyer's testimony, and the probability that the lawyer's testimony will conflict with that of other witnesses. Even if there is risk of such prejudice, in determining whether the lawyer should be disqualified, due regard must be given to the effect of disqualification on the lawyer's

client. It is relevant that one or both parties could reasonably foresee that the lawyer would probably be a witness. The conflict of interest principles stated in Rules 1.7, 1.9 and 1.10 have no application to this aspect of the problem.

[5] Because the tribunal is not likely to be misled when a lawyer acts as advocate in a trial in which another lawyer in the lawyer's firm will testify as a necessary witness, paragraph (b) permits the lawyer to do so except in situations involving a conflict of interest.

Conflict of Interest

[6] In determining if it is permissible to act as advocate in a trial in which the lawyer will be a necessary witness, the lawyer must also consider that the dual role may give rise to a conflict of interest that will require compliance with Rules 1.7 or 1.9. For example, if there is likely to be substantial conflict between the testimony of the client and that of the lawyer the representation involves a conflict of interest that requires compliance with Rule 1.7. This would be true even though the lawyer might not be prohibited by paragraph (a) from simultaneously serving as advocate and witness because the lawyer's disqualification would work a substantial hardship on the client. Similarly, a lawyer who might be permitted to simultaneously serve as an advocate and a witness by paragraph (a)(3) might be precluded from doing so by Rule 1.9. The problem can arise whether the lawyer is called as a witness on behalf of the client or is called by the opposing party. Determining whether or not such a conflict exists is primarily the responsibility of the lawyer involved. If there is a conflict of interest, the lawyer must secure the client's informed consent, confirmed in writing. In some cases, the lawyer will be precluded from seeking the client's consent. See Rule 1.7. See Rule 1.0(b) for the definition of "confirmed in writing" and Rule 1.0(e) for the definition of "informed consent."

[7] Paragraph (b) provides that a lawyer is not disqualified from serving as an advocate because a lawyer with whom the lawyer is associated in a firm is precluded from doing so by paragraph (a). If, however, the testifying lawyer would also be disqualified by Rule 1.7 or Rule 1.9 from representing the client in the matter, other lawyers in the firm will be precluded from representing the client by Rule 1.10 unless the client gives informed consent under the conditions stated in Rule 1.7.

Rule 3.8 Special Responsibilities of a Prosecutor*

The prosecutor in a criminal case shall:

(a) refrain from prosecuting a charge that the prosecutor knows is not supported by probable cause;

(b) make reasonable efforts to assure that the accused has been advised of the right to, and the procedure for obtaining, counsel and has been given reasonable opportunity to obtain counsel;

(c) not seek to obtain from an unrepresented accused a waiver of important pretrial rights, such as the right to a preliminary hearing;

(d) make timely disclosure to the defense of all evidence or information known to the prosecutor that tends to negate the guilt of the accused or mitigates the offense, and, in connection with sentencing, disclose to the defense and to the tribunal all unprivileged mitigating information known to the prosecutor, except when the prosecutor is relieved of this responsibility by a protective order of the tribunal;

(e) not subpoena a lawyer in a grand jury or other criminal proceeding to present evidence about a past or present client unless the prosecutor reasonably believes:

* In February 2008, the ABA House of Delegates amended Model Rule 3.8 to address concerns that our criminal justice system does not adequately minimize the occurrence of wrongful convictions. The amendment added new sections (g) and (h) and new comments 7, 8, and 9 and modified comment 1.

(1) the information sought is not protected from disclosure by any applicable privilege;

(2) the evidence sought is essential to the successful completion of an ongoing investigation or prosecution; and

(3) there is no other feasible alternative to obtain the information;

(f) except for statements that are necessary to inform the public of the nature and extent of the prosecutor's action and that serve a legitimate law enforcement purpose, refrain from making extrajudicial comments that have a substantial likelihood of heightening public condemnation of the accused and exercise reasonable care to prevent investigators, law enforcement personnel, employees or other persons assisting or associated with the prosecutor in a criminal case from making an extrajudicial statement that the prosecutor would be prohibited from making under Rule 3.6 or this Rule.

(g) When a prosecutor knows of new, credible and material evidence creating a reasonable likelihood that a convicted defendant did not commit an offense of which the defendant was convicted, the prosecutor shall:

(1) promptly disclose that evidence to an appropriate court or authority, and

(2) if the conviction was obtained in the prosecutor's jurisdiction,

(i) promptly disclose that evidence to the defendant unless a court authorizes delay, and

(ii) undertake further investigation, or make reasonable efforts to cause an investigation, to determine whether the defendant was convicted of an offense that the defendant did not commit.

(h) When a prosecutor knows of clear and convincing evidence establishing that a defendant in the prosecutor's jurisdiction was convicted of an offense that the defendant did not commit, the prosecutor shall seek to remedy the conviction.

COMMENT

[1] A prosecutor has the responsibility of a minister of justice and not simply that of an advocate. This responsibility carries with it specific obligations to see that the defendant is accorded procedural justice, that guilt is decided upon the basis of sufficient evidence, and that special precautions are taken to prevent and to rectify the conviction of innocent persons. The extent of mandated remedial action is a matter of debate and varies in different jurisdictions. Many jurisdictions have adopted the ABA Standards of Criminal Justice Relating to the Prosecution Function, which are the product of prolonged and careful deliberation by lawyers experienced in both criminal prosecution and defense. Competent representation of the sovereignty may require a prosecutor to undertake some procedural and remedial measures as a matter of obligation. Applicable law may require other measures by the prosecutor and knowing disregard of those obligations or a systematic abuse of prosecutorial discretion could constitute a violation of Rule 8.4.

[2] In some jurisdictions, a defendant may waive a preliminary hearing and thereby lose a valuable opportunity to challenge probable cause. Accordingly, prosecutors should not seek to obtain waivers of preliminary hearings or other important pretrial rights from unrepresented accused persons. Paragraph (c) does not apply, however, to an accused appearing pro se with the approval of the tribunal. Nor does it forbid the lawful questioning of an uncharged suspect who has knowingly waived the rights to counsel and silence.

[3] The exception in paragraph (d) recognizes that a prosecutor may seek an appropriate protective order from the tribunal if disclosure of information to the defense could result in substantial harm to an individual or to the public interest.

[4] Paragraph (e) is intended to limit the issuance of lawyer subpoenas in grand jury and other criminal proceedings to those situations in which there is a genuine need to intrude into the client-lawyer relationship.

[5] Paragraph (f) supplements Rule 3.6, which prohibits extrajudicial statements that have a substantial likelihood of prejudicing an adjudicatory proceeding. In the context of a criminal prosecution, a prosecutor's extrajudicial statement can create the additional problem of increasing public condemnation of the accused. Although the announcement of an indictment, for example, will necessarily have severe consequences for the accused, a prosecutor can, and should, avoid comments which have no legitimate law enforcement purpose and have a substantial likelihood of increasing public opprobrium of the accused. Nothing in this Comment is intended to restrict the statements which a prosecutor may make which comply with Rule 3.6(b) or 3.6(c).

[6] Like other lawyers, prosecutors are subject to Rules 5.1 and 5.3, which relate to responsibilities regarding lawyers and nonlawyers who work for or are associated with the lawyer's office. Paragraph (f) reminds the prosecutor of the importance of these obligations in connection with the unique dangers of improper extrajudicial statements in a criminal case. In addition, paragraph (f) requires a prosecutor to exercise reasonable care to prevent persons assisting or associated with the prosecutor from making improper extrajudicial statements, even when such persons are not under the direct supervision of the prosecutor. Ordinarily, the reasonable care standard will be satisfied if the prosecutor issues the appropriate cautions to law-enforcement personnel and other relevant individuals.

[7] When a prosecutor knows of new, credible and material evidence creating a reasonable likelihood that a person outside the prosecutor's jurisdiction was convicted of a crime that the person did not commit, paragraph (g) requires prompt disclosure to the court or other appropriate authority, such as the chief prosecutor of the jurisdiction where the conviction occurred. If the conviction was obtained in the prosecutor's jurisdiction, paragraph (g) requires the prosecutor to examine the evidence and undertake further investigation to determine whether the defendant is in fact innocent or make reasonable efforts to cause another appropriate authority to undertake the necessary investigation, and to promptly disclose the evidence to the court and, absent court-authorized delay, to the defendant. Consistent with the objectives of Rules 4.2 and 4.3, disclosure to a represented defendant must be made through the defendant's counsel, and, in the case of an unrepresented defendant, would ordinarily be accompanied by a request to a court for the appointment of counsel to assist the defendant in taking such legal measures as may be appropriate.

[8] Under paragraph (h), once the prosecutor knows of clear and convincing evidence that the defendant was convicted of an offense that the defendant did not commit, the prosecutor must seek to remedy the conviction. Necessary steps may include disclosure of the evidence to the defendant, requesting that the court appoint counsel for an unrepresented indigent defendant and, where appropriate, notifying the court that the prosecutor has knowledge that the defendant did not commit the offense of which the defendant was convicted.

[9] A prosecutor's independent judgment, made in good faith, that the new evidence is not of such nature as to trigger the obligations of sections (g) and (h), though subsequently determined to have been erroneous, does not constitute a violation of this Rule.

Rule 3.9 Advocate in Nonadjudicative Proceedings

A lawyer representing a client before a legislative body or administrative agency in a nonadjudicative proceeding shall disclose that the appearance is in a representative capacity and shall conform to the provisions of Rules 3.3(a) through (c), 3.4(a) through (c), and 3.5.

COMMENT

[1] In representation before bodies such as legislatures, municipal councils, and executive and administrative agencies acting in a rule-making or policy-making capacity, lawyers present facts, formulate issues and advance argument in the matters under consideration. The decision-making body, like a court, should be able to rely on the integrity of the submissions made to it. A lawyer appearing before such a body must deal with it honestly and in conformity with applicable rules of procedure. See Rules 3.3(a) through (c), 3.4(a) through (c) and 3.5.

[2] Lawyers have no exclusive right to appear before nonadjudicative bodies, as they do before a court. The requirements of this Rule therefore may subject lawyers to regulations inapplicable to advocates

who are not lawyers. However, legislatures and administrative agencies have a right to expect lawyers to deal with them as they deal with courts.

[3] This Rule only applies when a lawyer represents a client in connection with an official hearing or meeting of a governmental agency or a legislative body to which the lawyer or the lawyer's client is presenting evidence or argument. It does not apply to representation of a client in a negotiation or other bilateral transaction with a governmental agency or in connection with an application for a license or other privilege or the client's compliance with generally applicable reporting requirements, such as the filing of income-tax returns. Nor does it apply to the representation of a client in connection with an investigation or examination of the client's affairs conducted by government investigators or examiners. Representation in such matters is governed by Rules 4.1 through 4.4.

TRANSACTIONS WITH PERSONS OTHER THAN CLIENTS

Rule 4.1 Truthfulness in Statements to Others

In the course of representing a client a lawyer shall not knowingly:

(a) make a false statement of material fact or law to a third person; or

(b) fail to disclose a material fact when disclosure is necessary to avoid assisting a criminal or fraudulent act by a client, unless disclosure is prohibited by Rule 1.6.

COMMENT

Misrepresentation

[1] A lawyer is required to be truthful when dealing with others on a client's behalf, but generally has no affirmative duty to inform an opposing party of relevant facts. A misrepresentation can occur if the lawyer incorporates or affirms a statement of another person that the lawyer knows is false. Misrepresentations can also occur by partially true but misleading statements or omissions that are the equivalent of affirmative false statements. For dishonest conduct that does not amount to a false statement or for misrepresentations by a lawyer other than in the course of representing a client, see Rule 8.4.

Statements of Fact

[2] This Rule refers to statements of fact. Whether a particular statement should be regarded as one of fact can depend on the circumstances. Under generally accepted conventions in negotiation, certain types of statements ordinarily are not taken as statements of material fact. Estimates of price or value placed on the subject of a transaction and a party's intentions as to an acceptable settlement of a claim are ordinarily in this category, and so is the existence of an undisclosed principal except where nondisclosure of the principal would constitute fraud. Lawyers should be mindful of their obligations under applicable law to avoid criminal and tortious misrepresentation.

Crime or Fraud by Client

[3] Under Rule 1.2(d), a lawyer is prohibited from counseling or assisting a client in conduct that the lawyer knows is criminal or fraudulent. Paragraph (b) states a specific application of the principle set forth in Rule 1.2(d) and addresses the situation where a client's crime or fraud takes the form of a lie or misrepresentation. Ordinarily, a lawyer can avoid assisting a client's crime or fraud by withdrawing from the representation. Sometimes it may be necessary for the lawyer to give notice of the fact of withdrawal and to disaffirm an opinion, document, affirmation or the like. In extreme cases, substantive law may require a lawyer to disclose information relating to the representation to avoid being deemed to have assisted the client's crime or fraud. If the lawyer can avoid assisting a client's crime or fraud only by disclosing this information, then under paragraph (b) the lawyer is required to do so, unless the disclosure is prohibited by Rule 1.6.

Rule 4.2 Communication With Person Represented by Counsel

In representing a client, a lawyer shall not communicate about the subject of the representation with a person the lawyer knows to be represented by another lawyer in the

matter, unless the lawyer has the consent of the other lawyer or is authorized to do so by law or a court order.

COMMENT

[1] This Rule contributes to the proper functioning of the legal system by protecting a person who has chosen to be represented by a lawyer in a matter against possible overreaching by other lawyers who are participating in the matter, interference by those lawyers with the client-lawyer relationship and the uncounselled disclosure of information relating to the representation.

[2] This Rule applies to communications with any person who is represented by counsel concerning the matter to which the communication relates.

[3] The Rule applies even though the represented person initiates or consents to the communication. A lawyer must immediately terminate communication with a person if, after commencing communication, the lawyer learns that the person is one with whom communication is not permitted by this Rule.

[4] This Rule does not prohibit communication with a represented person, or an employee or agent of such a person, concerning matters outside the representation. For example, the existence of a controversy between a government agency and a private party, or between two organizations, does not prohibit a lawyer for either from communicating with nonlawyer representatives of the other regarding a separate matter. Nor does this Rule preclude communication with a represented person who is seeking advice from a lawyer who is not otherwise representing a client in the matter. A lawyer may not make a communication prohibited by this Rule through the acts of another. See Rule 8.4(a). Parties to a matter may communicate directly with each other, and a lawyer is not prohibited from advising a client concerning a communication that the client is legally entitled to make. Also, a lawyer having independent justification or legal authorization for communicating with a represented person is permitted to do so.

[5] Communications authorized by law may include communications by a lawyer on behalf of a client who is exercising a constitutional or other legal right to communicate with the government. Communications authorized by law may also include investigative activities of lawyers representing governmental entities, directly or through investigative agents, prior to the commencement of criminal or civil enforcement proceedings. When communicating with the accused in a criminal matter, a government lawyer must comply with this Rule in addition to honoring the constitutional rights of the accused. The fact that a communication does not violate a state or federal constitutional right is insufficient to establish that the communication is permissible under this Rule.

[6] A lawyer who is uncertain whether a communication with a represented person is permissible may seek a court order. A lawyer may also seek a court order in exceptional circumstances to authorize a communication that would otherwise be prohibited by this Rule, for example, where communication with a person represented by counsel is necessary to avoid reasonably certain injury.

[7] In the case of a represented organization, this Rule prohibits communications with a constituent of the organization who supervises, directs or regularly consults with the organization's lawyer concerning the matter or has authority to obligate the organization with respect to the matter or whose act or omission in connection with the matter may be imputed to the organization for purposes of civil or criminal liability. Consent of the organization's lawyer is not required for communication with a former constituent. If a constituent of the organization is represented in the matter by his or her own counsel, the consent by that counsel to a communication will be sufficient for purposes of this Rule. Compare Rule 3.4(f). In communicating with a current or former constituent of an organization, a lawyer must not use methods of obtaining evidence that violate the legal rights of the organization. See Rule 4.4.

[8] The prohibition on communications with a represented person only applies in circumstances where the lawyer knows that the person is in fact represented in the matter to be discussed. This means that the lawyer has actual knowledge of the fact of the representation; but such actual knowledge may be inferred from the circumstances. See Rule 1.0(f). Thus, the lawyer cannot evade the requirement of obtaining the consent of counsel by closing eyes to the obvious.

[9] In the event the person with whom the lawyer communicates is not known to be represented by counsel in the matter, the lawyer's communications are subject to Rule 4.3.

Rule 4.3 Dealing With Unrepresented Person

In dealing on behalf of a client with a person who is not represented by counsel, a lawyer shall not state or imply that the lawyer is disinterested. When the lawyer knows or reasonably should know that the unrepresented person misunderstands the lawyer's role in the matter, the lawyer shall make reasonable efforts to correct the misunderstanding. The lawyer shall not give legal advice to an unrepresented person, other than the advice to secure counsel, if the lawyer knows or reasonably should know that the interests of such a person are or have a reasonable possibility of being in conflict with the interests of the client.

COMMENT

[1] An unrepresented person, particularly one not experienced in dealing with legal matters, might assume that a lawyer is disinterested in loyalties or is a disinterested authority on the law even when the lawyer represents a client. In order to avoid a misunderstanding, a lawyer will typically need to identify the lawyer's client and, where necessary, explain that the client has interests opposed to those of the unrepresented person. For misunderstandings that sometimes arise when a lawyer for an organization deals with an unrepresented constituent, see Rule 1.13(d).

[2] The Rule distinguishes between situations involving unrepresented persons whose interests may be adverse to those of the lawyer's client and those in which the person's interests are not in conflict with the client's. In the former situation, the possibility that the lawyer will compromise the unrepresented person's interests is so great that the Rule prohibits the giving of any advice, apart from the advice to obtain counsel. Whether a lawyer is giving impermissible advice may depend on the experience and sophistication of the unrepresented person, as well as the setting in which the behavior and comments occur. This Rule does not prohibit a lawyer from negotiating the terms of a transaction or settling a dispute with an unrepresented person. So long as the lawyer has explained that the lawyer represents an adverse party and is not representing the person, the lawyer may inform the person of the terms on which the lawyer's client will enter into an agreement or settle a matter, prepare documents that require the person's signature and explain the lawyer's own view of the meaning of the document or the lawyer's view of the underlying legal obligations.

Rule 4.4 Respect for Rights of Third Persons*

(a) In representing a client, a lawyer shall not use means that have no substantial purpose other than to embarrass, delay, or burden a third person, or use methods of obtaining evidence that violate the legal rights of such a person.

(b) A lawyer who receives a document or electronically stored information relating to the representation of the lawyer's client and knows or reasonably should know that the document or electronically stored information was inadvertently sent shall promptly notify the sender.

COMMENT**

[1] Responsibility to a client requires a lawyer to subordinate the interests of others to those of the client, but that responsibility does not imply that a lawyer may disregard the rights of third persons. It is impractical to catalogue all such rights, but they include legal restrictions on methods of obtaining evidence from third persons and unwarranted intrusions into privileged relationships, such as the client-lawyer relationship.

[2] Paragraph (b) recognizes that lawyers sometimes receive a documents or electronically stored information that was mistakenly sent or produced by opposing parties or their lawyers. A document or electronically stored information is inadvertently sent when it is accidentally transmitted, such as when an

* In August 2012, the ABA House of Delegates amended Rule 4.4(b) to add the phrase "electronically stored information" to the text.

** In August 2012, the ABA House of Delegates substantially expanded Comment 2 and slightly amended Comment 3 to reflect the addition of "electronically stored information" to the rule.

email or letter is misaddressed or a document or electronically stored information is accidentally included with information that was intentionally transmitted. If a lawyer knows or reasonably should know that such a document or electronically stored information was sent inadvertently, then this Rule requires the lawyer to promptly notify the sender in order to permit that person to take protective measures. Whether the lawyer is required to take additional steps, such as returning or deleting the document or electronically stored information, is a matter of law beyond the scope of these Rules, as is the question of whether the privileged status of a document or electronically stored information has been waived. Similarly, this Rule does not address the legal duties of a lawyer who receives a document or electronically stored information that the lawyer knows or reasonably should know may have been inappropriately obtained by the sending person. For purposes of this Rule, "document or electronically stored information" includes, in addition to paper documents, email and other forms of electronically stored information, including embedded data (commonly referred to as "metadata"), that is subject to being read or put into readable form. Metadata in electronic documents creates an obligation under this Rule only if the receiving lawyer knows or reasonably should know that the metadata was inadvertently sent to the receiving lawyer.

[3] Some lawyers may choose to return a document or delete electronically stored information unread, for example, when the lawyer learns before receiving it that it was inadvertently sent. Where a lawyer is not required by applicable law to do so, the decision to voluntarily return such a document or delete electronically stored information is a matter of professional judgment ordinarily reserved to the lawyer. See Rules 1.2 and 1.4.

LAW FIRMS AND ASSOCIATIONS

Rule 5.1 Responsibilities of Partners, Managers, and Supervisory Lawyers

(a) A partner in a law firm, and a lawyer who individually or together with other lawyers possesses comparable managerial authority in a law firm, shall make reasonable efforts to ensure that the firm has in effect measures giving reasonable assurance that all lawyers in the firm conform to the Rules of Professional Conduct.

(b) A lawyer having direct supervisory authority over another lawyer shall make reasonable efforts to ensure that the other lawyer conforms to the Rules of Professional Conduct.

(c) A lawyer shall be responsible for another lawyer's violation of the Rules of Professional Conduct if:

(1) the lawyer orders or, with knowledge of the specific conduct, ratifies the conduct involved; or

(2) the lawyer is a partner or has comparable managerial authority in the law firm in which the other lawyer practices, or has direct supervisory authority over the other lawyer, and knows of the conduct at a time when its consequences can be avoided or mitigated but fails to take reasonable remedial action.

COMMENT

[1] Paragraph (a) applies to lawyers who have managerial authority over the professional work of a firm. See Rule 1.0(c). This includes members of a partnership, the shareholders in a law firm organized as a professional corporation, and members of other associations authorized to practice law; lawyers having comparable managerial authority in a legal services organization or a law department of an enterprise or government agency; and lawyers who have intermediate managerial responsibilities in a firm. Paragraph (b) applies to lawyers who have supervisory authority over the work of other lawyers in a firm.

[2] Paragraph (a) requires lawyers with managerial authority within a firm to make reasonable efforts to establish internal policies and procedures designed to provide reasonable assurance that all lawyers in the firm will conform to the Rules of Professional Conduct. Such policies and procedures include those designed to detect and resolve conflicts of interest, identify dates by which actions must be taken in

pending matters, account for client funds and property and ensure that inexperienced lawyers are properly supervised.

[3] Other measures that may be required to fulfill the responsibility prescribed in paragraph (a) can depend on the firm's structure and the nature of its practice. In a small firm of experienced lawyers, informal supervision and periodic review of compliance with the required systems ordinarily will suffice. In a large firm, or in practice situations in which difficult ethical problems frequently arise, more elaborate measures may be necessary. Some firms, for example, have a procedure whereby junior lawyers can make confidential referral of ethical problems directly to a designated senior partner or special committee. See Rule 5.2. Firms, whether large or small, may also rely on continuing legal education in professional ethics. In any event, the ethical atmosphere of a firm can influence the conduct of all its members and the partners may not assume that all lawyers associated with the firm will inevitably conform to the Rules.

[4] Paragraph (c) expresses a general principle of personal responsibility for acts of another. See also Rule 8.4(a).

[5] Paragraph (c)(2) defines the duty of a partner or other lawyer having comparable managerial authority in a law firm, as well as a lawyer who has direct supervisory authority over performance of specific legal work by another lawyer. Whether a lawyer has supervisory authority in particular circumstances is a question of fact. Partners and lawyers with comparable authority have at least indirect responsibility for all work being done by the firm, while a partner or manager in charge of a particular matter ordinarily also has supervisory responsibility for the work of other firm lawyers engaged in the matter. Appropriate remedial action by a partner or managing lawyer would depend on the immediacy of that lawyer's involvement and the seriousness of the misconduct. A supervisor is required to intervene to prevent avoidable consequences of misconduct if the supervisor knows that the misconduct occurred. Thus, if a supervising lawyer knows that a subordinate misrepresented a matter to an opposing party in negotiation, the supervisor as well as the subordinate has a duty to correct the resulting misapprehension.

[6] Professional misconduct by a lawyer under supervision could reveal a violation of paragraph (b) on the part of the supervisory lawyer even though it does not entail a violation of paragraph (c) because there was no direction, ratification or knowledge of the violation.

[7] Apart from this Rule and Rule 8.4(a), a lawyer does not have disciplinary liability for the conduct of a partner, associate or subordinate. Whether a lawyer may be liable civilly or criminally for another lawyer's conduct is a question of law beyond the scope of these Rules.

[8] The duties imposed by this Rule on managing and supervising lawyers do not alter the personal duty of each lawyer in a firm to abide by the Rules of Professional Conduct. See Rule 5.2(a).

Rule 5.2 Responsibilities of a Subordinate Lawyer

(a) A lawyer is bound by the Rules of Professional Conduct notwithstanding that the lawyer acted at the direction of another person.

(b) A subordinate lawyer does not violate the Rules of Professional Conduct if that lawyer acts in accordance with a supervisory lawyer's reasonable resolution of an arguable question of professional duty.

COMMENT

[1] Although a lawyer is not relieved of responsibility for a violation by the fact that the lawyer acted at the direction of a supervisor, that fact may be relevant in determining whether a lawyer had the knowledge required to render conduct a violation of the Rules. For example, if a subordinate filed a frivolous pleading at the direction of a supervisor, the subordinate would not be guilty of a professional violation unless the subordinate knew of the document's frivolous character.

[2] When lawyers in a supervisor-subordinate relationship encounter a matter involving professional judgment as to ethical duty, the supervisor may assume responsibility for making the judgment. Otherwise a consistent course of action or position could not be taken. If the question can reasonably be answered only one way, the duty of both lawyers is clear and they are equally responsible for fulfilling it. However, if the question is reasonably arguable, someone has to decide upon the course of action. That authority ordinarily

reposes in the supervisor, and a subordinate may be guided accordingly. For example, if a question arises whether the interests of two clients conflict under Rule 1.7, the supervisor's reasonable resolution of the question should protect the subordinate professionally if the resolution is subsequently challenged.

Rule 5.3 Responsibilities Regarding Nonlawyer Assistance*

With respect to a nonlawyer employed or retained by or associated with a lawyer:

(a) a partner, and a lawyer who individually or together with other lawyers possesses comparable managerial authority in a law firm shall make reasonable efforts to ensure that the firm has in effect measures giving reasonable assurance that the person's conduct is compatible with the professional obligations of the lawyer;

(b) a lawyer having direct supervisory authority over the nonlawyer shall make reasonable efforts to ensure that the person's conduct is compatible with the professional obligations of the lawyer; and

(c) a lawyer shall be responsible for conduct of such a person that would be a violation of the Rules of Professional Conduct if engaged in by a lawyer if:

(1) the lawyer orders or, with the knowledge of the specific conduct, ratifies the conduct involved; or

(2) the lawyer is a partner or has comparable managerial authority in the law firm in which the person is employed, or has direct supervisory authority over the person, and knows of the conduct at a time when its consequences can be avoided or mitigated but fails to take reasonable remedial action.

COMMENT*

[1] Paragraph (a) requires lawyers with managerial authority within a law firm to make reasonable efforts to ensure that the firm has in effect measures giving reasonable assurance that nonlawyers in the firm and nonlawyers outside the firm who work on firm matters act in a way compatible with the professional obligations of the lawyer. See Comment [6] to Rule 1.1 (retaining lawyers outside the firm) and Comment [1] to Rule 5.1. (responsibilities with respect to lawyers within a firm). Paragraph (b) applies to lawyers who have supervisory authority over such nonlawyers within or outside the firm. Paragraph (c) specifies the circumstances in which a lawyer is responsible for the conduct of such nonlawyers within or outside the firm that would be a violation of the Rules of Professional Conduct if engaged in by a lawyer.

Nonlawyers Within the Firm

[2] Lawyers generally employ assistants in their practice, including secretaries, investigators, law student interns, and paraprofessionals. Such assistants, whether employees or independent contractors, act for the lawyer in rendition of the lawyer's professional services. A lawyer must give such assistants appropriate instruction and supervision concerning the ethical aspects of their employment, particularly regarding the obligation not to disclose information relating to representation of the client, and should be responsible for their work product. The measures employed in supervising nonlawyers should take account of the fact that they do not have legal training and are not subject to professional discipline.

Nonlawyers Outside the Firm

[3] A lawyer may use nonlawyers outside the firm to assist the lawyer in rendering legal services to the client. Examples include the retention of an investigative or paraprofessional service, hiring a document management company to create and maintain a database for complex litigation, sending client documents to a third party for printing or scanning, and using an Internet-based service to store client information. When using such services outside the firm, a lawyer must make reasonable efforts to ensure that the services

---

* In August 2012, the ABA House of Delegates changed the word "Assistants" to "Assistance" in the title of the rule.

* In August 2012, the ABA House of Delegates reversed the order of the comments and substantially expanded new Comment 1. The ABA also added new Comments 3 and 4.

are provided in a manner that is compatible with the lawyer's professional obligations. The extent of this obligation will depend upon the circumstances, including the education, experience and reputation of the nonlawyer; the nature of the services involved; the terms of any arrangements concerning the protection of client information; and the legal and ethical environments of the jurisdictions in which the services will be performed, particularly with regard to confidentiality. See also Rules 1.1 (competence), 1.2 (allocation of authority), 1.4 (communication with client), 1.6 (confidentiality), 5.4(a) (professional independence of the lawyer), and 5.5(a) (unauthorized practice of law). When retaining or directing a nonlawyer outside the firm, a lawyer should communicate directions appropriate under the circumstances to give reasonable assurance that the nonlawyer's conduct is compatible with the professional obligations of the lawyer.

[4] Where the client directs the selection of a particular nonlawyer service provider outside the firm, the lawyer ordinarily should agree with the client concerning the allocation of responsibility for monitoring as between the client and the lawyer. See Rule 1.2. When making such an allocation in a matter pending before a tribunal, lawyers and parties may have additional obligations that are a matter of law beyond the scope of these Rules.

Rule 5.4 Professional Independence of a Lawyer

(a) A lawyer or law firm shall not share legal fees with a nonlawyer, except that:

(1) an agreement by a lawyer with the lawyer's firm, partner, or associate may provide for the payment of money, over a reasonable period of time after the lawyer's death, to the lawyer's estate or to one or more specified persons;

(2) a lawyer who purchases the practice of a deceased, disabled, or disappeared lawyer may, pursuant to the provisions of Rule 1.17, pay to the estate or other representative of that lawyer the agreed-upon purchase price;

(3) a lawyer or law firm may include nonlawyer employees in a compensation or retirement plan, even though the plan is based in whole or in part on a profit-sharing arrangement; and

(4) a lawyer may share court-awarded legal fees with a nonprofit organization that employed, retained or recommended employment of the lawyer in the matter.

(b) A lawyer shall not form a partnership with a nonlawyer if any of the activities of the partnership consist of the practice of law.

(c) A lawyer shall not permit a person who recommends, employs, or pays the lawyer to render legal services for another to direct or regulate the lawyer's professional judgment in rendering such legal services.

(d) A lawyer shall not practice with or in the form of a professional corporation or association authorized to practice law for a profit, if:

(1) a nonlawyer owns any interest therein, except that a fiduciary representative of the estate of a lawyer may hold the stock or interest of the lawyer for a reasonable time during administration;

(2) a nonlawyer is a corporate director or officer thereof or occupies the position of similar responsibility in any form of association other than a corporation; or

(3) a nonlawyer has the right to direct or control the professional judgment of a lawyer.

COMMENT

[1] The provisions of this Rule express traditional limitations on sharing fees. These limitations are to protect the lawyer's professional independence of judgment. Where someone other than the client pays the lawyer's fee or salary, or recommends employment of the lawyer, that arrangement does not modify the lawyer's obligation to the client. As stated in paragraph (c), such arrangements should not interfere with the lawyer's professional judgment.

[2] This Rule also expresses traditional limitations on permitting a third party to direct or regulate the lawyer's professional judgment in rendering legal services to another. See also Rule 1.8(f) (lawyer may accept compensation from a third party as long as there is no interference with the lawyer's independent professional judgment and the client gives informed consent).

Rule 5.5 Unauthorized Practice of Law; Multijurisdictional Practice of Law*

(a) A lawyer shall not practice law in a jurisdiction in violation of the regulation of the legal profession in that jurisdiction, or assist another in doing so.

(b) A lawyer who is not admitted to practice in this jurisdiction shall not:

(1) except as authorized by these Rules or other law, establish an office or other systematic and continuous presence in this jurisdiction for the practice of law; or

(2) hold out to the public or otherwise represent that the lawyer is admitted to practice law in this jurisdiction.

(c) A lawyer admitted in another United States jurisdiction, and not disbarred or suspended from practice in any jurisdiction, may provide legal services on a temporary basis in this jurisdiction that:

(1) are undertaken in association with a lawyer who is admitted to practice in this jurisdiction and who actively participates in the matter;

(2) are in or reasonably related to a pending or potential proceeding before a tribunal in this or another jurisdiction, if the lawyer, or a person the lawyer is assisting, is authorized by law or order to appear in such proceeding or reasonably expects to be so authorized;

(3) are in or reasonably related to a pending or potential arbitration, mediation, or other alternative dispute resolution proceeding in this or another jurisdiction, if the services arise out of or are reasonably related to the lawyer's practice in a jurisdiction in which the lawyer is admitted to practice and are not services for which the forum requires pro hac vice admission; or

(4) are not within paragraphs (c)(2) or (c)(3) and arise out of or are reasonably related to the lawyer's practice in a jurisdiction in which the lawyer is admitted to practice.

(d) A lawyer admitted in another United States jurisdiction or in a foreign jurisdiction, and not disbarred or suspended from practice in any jurisdiction or the equivalent thereof, or a person otherwise lawfully practicing as an in-house counsel under the laws of a foreign jurisdiction, may provide legal services through an office or other systematic and continuous presence in this jurisdiction that:

(1) are provided to the lawyer's employer or its organizational affiliates, are not services for which the forum requires pro hac vice admission; and when performed by

---

* In August 2002, the ABA adopted the recommendations of the Multijurisdictional Practice of Law Commission and enacted new Model Rule 5.5. The old rule text read as follows:

A lawyer shall not:

(a) practice law in a jurisdiction where doing so violates the regulation of the legal profession in that jurisdiction; or

(b) assist a person who is not a member of the bar in the performance of activity that constitutes the unauthorized practice of law.

In August 2012, the ABA House of Delegates made minor changes to Rule 5.5(d) and Comments 1 and 4. In February 2013, the ABA further amended Rule 5.5(d) to permit foreign lawyers to represent clients on foreign law issues. In February 2016, the ABA amended Rule 5.5(d) and (e) in order to permit foreign licensed attorneys from serving as in-house counsel of an employer client.

a foreign lawyer and requires advice on the law of this or another U.S. jurisdiction or of the United States, such advice shall be based upon the advice of a lawyer who is duly licensed and authorized by the jurisdiction to provide such advice; or

(2) are services that the lawyer is authorized by federal or other law or rule to provide in this jurisdiction.

(e) For purposes of paragraph (d),

(1) the foreign lawyer must be a member in good standing of a recognized legal profession in a foreign jurisdiction, the members of which are admitted to practice as lawyers or counselors at law or the equivalent, and subject to effective regulation and discipline by a duly constituted professional body or a public authority, or,

(2) the person otherwise lawfully practicing as an in-house counsel under the laws of a foreign jurisdiction must be authorized to practice under this rule by, in the exercise of its discretion, [the highest court of this jurisdiction].

COMMENT*

[1] A lawyer may practice law only in a jurisdiction in which the lawyer is authorized to practice. A lawyer may be admitted to practice law in a jurisdiction on a regular basis or may be authorized by court rule or order or by law to practice for a limited purpose or on a restricted basis. Paragraph (a) applies to unauthorized practice of law by a lawyer, whether through the lawyer's direct action or by the lawyer assisting another person. For example, a lawyer may not assist a person in practicing law in violation of the rules governing professional conduct in that person's jurisdiction.

[2] The definition of the practice of law is established by law and varies from one jurisdiction to another. Whatever the definition, limiting the practice of law to members of the bar protects the public against rendition of legal services by unqualified persons. This Rule does not prohibit a lawyer from employing the services of paraprofessionals and delegating functions to them, so long as the lawyer supervises the delegated work and retains responsibility for their work. See Rule 5.3.

[3] A lawyer may provide professional advice and instruction to nonlawyers whose employment requires knowledge of the law; for example, claims adjusters, employees of financial or commercial institutions, social workers, accountants and persons employed in government agencies. Lawyers also may assist independent nonlawyers, such as paraprofessionals, who are authorized by the law of a jurisdiction to provide particular law-related services. In addition, a lawyer may counsel nonlawyers who wish to proceed pro se.

[4] Other than as authorized by law or this Rule, a lawyer who is not admitted to practice generally in this jurisdiction violates paragraph (b)(1) if the lawyer establishes an office or other systematic and continuous presence in this jurisdiction for the practice of law. Presence may be systematic and continuous even if the lawyer is not physically present here. Such a lawyer must not hold out to the public or otherwise represent that the lawyer is admitted to practice law in this jurisdiction. See also Rules 7.1(a) and 7.5(b).

[5] There are occasions in which a lawyer admitted to practice in another United States jurisdiction, and not disbarred or suspended from practice in any jurisdiction, may provide legal services on a temporary basis in this jurisdiction under circumstances that do not create an unreasonable risk to the interests of their clients, the public or the courts. Paragraph (c) identifies four such circumstances. The fact that conduct is not so identified does not imply that the conduct is or is not authorized. With the exception of paragraphs (d)(1) and (d)(2), this Rule does not authorize a U.S. or foreign lawyer to establish an office or other systematic and continuous presence in this jurisdiction without being admitted to practice generally here.

[6] There is no single test to determine whether a lawyer's services are provided on a "temporary basis" in this jurisdiction, and may therefore be permissible under paragraph (c). Services may be "temporary" even though the lawyer provides services in this jurisdiction on a recurring basis, or for an

* In February 2007, the ABA House of Delegates added the last line to Comment 14 of Model Rule 5.5 to address unauthorized practice of law issues created by major disasters. This sentence refers to a standalone Model Rule on Provision of Legal Services Following Determination of a Major Disaster. This rule is reprinted in Part VII of the full edition of this book.

extended period of time, as when the lawyer is representing a client in a single lengthy negotiation or litigation.

[7] Paragraphs (c) and (d) apply to lawyers who are admitted to practice law in any United States jurisdiction, which includes the District of Columbia and any state, territory or commonwealth of the United States. Paragraph (d) also applies to lawyers admitted in a foreign jurisdiction. The word "admitted" in paragraphs (c), (d) and (e) contemplates that the lawyer is authorized to practice in the jurisdiction in which the lawyer is admitted and excludes a lawyer who while technically admitted is not authorized to practice, because, for example, the lawyer is on inactive status.

[8] Paragraph (c)(1) recognizes that the interests of clients and the public are protected if a lawyer admitted only in another jurisdiction associates with a lawyer licensed to practice in this jurisdiction. For this paragraph to apply, however, the lawyer admitted to practice in this jurisdiction must actively participate in and share responsibility for the representation of the client.

[9] Lawyers not admitted to practice generally in a jurisdiction may be authorized by law or order of a tribunal or an administrative agency to appear before the tribunal or agency. This authority may be granted pursuant to formal rules governing admission pro hac vice or pursuant to informal practice of the tribunal or agency. Under paragraph (c)(2), a lawyer does not violate this Rule when the lawyer appears before a tribunal or agency pursuant to such authority. To the extent that a court rule or other law of this jurisdiction requires a lawyer who is not admitted to practice in this jurisdiction to obtain admission pro hac vice before appearing before a tribunal or administrative agency, this Rule requires the lawyer to obtain that authority.

[10] Paragraph (c)(2) also provides that a lawyer rendering services in this jurisdiction on a temporary basis does not violate this Rule when the lawyer engages in conduct in anticipation of a proceeding or hearing in a jurisdiction in which the lawyer is authorized to practice law or in which the lawyer reasonably expects to be admitted pro hac vice. Examples of such conduct include meetings with the client, interviews of potential witnesses, and the review of documents. Similarly, a lawyer admitted only in another jurisdiction may engage in conduct temporarily in this jurisdiction in connection with pending litigation in another jurisdiction in which the lawyer is or reasonably expects to be authorized to appear, including taking depositions in this jurisdiction.

[11] When a lawyer has been or reasonably expects to be admitted to appear before a court or administrative agency, paragraph (c)(2) also permits conduct by lawyers who are associated with that lawyer in the matter, but who do not expect to appear before the court or administrative agency. For example, subordinate lawyers may conduct research, review documents, and attend meetings with witnesses in support of the lawyer responsible for the litigation.

[12] Paragraph (c)(3) permits a lawyer admitted to practice law in another jurisdiction to perform services on a temporary basis in this jurisdiction if those services are in or reasonably related to a pending or potential arbitration, mediation, or other alternative dispute resolution proceeding in this or another jurisdiction, if the services arise out of or are reasonably related to the lawyer's practice in a jurisdiction in which the lawyer is admitted to practice. The lawyer, however, must obtain admission pro hac vice in the case of a court-annexed arbitration or mediation or otherwise if court rules or law so require.

[13] Paragraph (c)(4) permits a lawyer admitted in another jurisdiction to provide certain legal services on a temporary basis in this jurisdiction that arise out of or are reasonably related to the lawyer's practice in a jurisdiction in which the lawyer is admitted but are not within paragraphs (c)(2) or (c)(3). These services include both legal services and services that nonlawyers may perform but that are considered the practice of law when performed by lawyers.

[14] Paragraphs (c)(3) and (c)(4) require that the services arise out of or be reasonably related to the lawyer's practice in a jurisdiction in which the lawyer is admitted. A variety of factors evidence such a relationship. The lawyer's client may have been previously represented by the lawyer, or may be resident in or have substantial contacts with the jurisdiction in which the lawyer is admitted. The matter, although involving other jurisdictions, may have a significant connection with that jurisdiction. In other cases, significant aspects of the lawyer's work might be conducted in that jurisdiction or a significant aspect of the matter may involve the law of that jurisdiction. The necessary relationship might arise when the client's

activities or the legal issues involve multiple jurisdictions, such as when the officers of a multinational corporation survey potential business sites and seek the services of their lawyer in assessing the relative merits of each. In addition, the services may draw on the lawyer's recognized expertise developed through the regular practice of law on behalf of clients in matters involving a particular body of federal, nationally uniform, foreign, or international law. Lawyers desiring to provide *pro bono* legal services on a temporary basis in a jurisdiction that has been affected by a major disaster, but in which they are not otherwise authorized to practice law, as well as lawyers from the affected jurisdiction who seek to practice law temporarily in another jurisdiction, but in which they are not otherwise authorized to practice law, should consult the [*Model Court Rule on Provision of Legal Services Following Determination of Major Disaster*].

[15] Paragraph (d) identifies two circumstances in which a lawyer who is admitted to practice in another United States or foreign jurisdiction, and is not disbarred or suspended from practice in any jurisdiction, or the equivalent thereof, may establish an office or other systematic and continuous presence in this jurisdiction for the practice of law. Pursuant to paragraph (c) of this Rule, a lawyer admitted in any U.S. jurisdiction may also provide legal services in this jurisdiction on a temporary basis. See also Model Rule on Temporary Practice by Foreign Lawyers. Except as provided in paragraphs (d)(1) and (d)(2), a lawyer who is admitted to practice law in another United States or foreign jurisdiction and who establishes an office or other systematic or continuous presence in this jurisdiction must become admitted to practice law generally in this jurisdiction.

[16] Paragraph (d)(1) applies to a U.S. or foreign lawyer who is employed by a client to provide legal services to the client or its organizational affiliates, i.e., entities that control, are controlled by, or are under common control with the employer. This paragraph does not authorize the provision of personal legal services to the employer's officers or employees. The paragraph applies to in-house corporate lawyers, government lawyers and others who are employed to render legal services to the employer. The lawyer's ability to represent the employer outside the jurisdiction in which the lawyer is licensed generally serves the interests of the employer and does not create an unreasonable risk to the client and others because the employer is well situated to assess the lawyer's qualifications and the quality of the lawyer's work. To further decrease any risk to the client, when advising on the domestic law of a United States jurisdiction or on the law of the United States, the foreign lawyer authorized to practice under paragraph (d)(1) of this Rule needs to base that advice on the advice of a lawyer licensed and authorized by the jurisdiction to provide it.

[17] If an employed lawyer establishes an office or other systematic presence in this jurisdiction for the purpose of rendering legal services to the employer, the lawyer may be subject to registration or other requirements, including assessments for client protection funds and mandatory continuing legal education. See Model Rule for Registration of In-House Counsel.

[18] Paragraph (d)(2) recognizes that a U.S. or foreign lawyer may provide legal services in a jurisdiction in which the lawyer is not licensed when authorized to do so by federal or other law, which includes statute, court rule, executive regulation or judicial precedent. See, e.g., The ABA Model Rule on Practice Pending Admission.

[19] A lawyer who practices law in this jurisdiction pursuant to paragraphs (c) or (d) or otherwise is subject to the disciplinary authority of this jurisdiction. See Rule 8.5(a).

[20] In some circumstances, a lawyer who practices law in this jurisdiction pursuant to paragraphs (c) or (d) may have to inform the client that the lawyer is not licensed to practice law in this jurisdiction. For example, that may be required when the representation occurs primarily in this jurisdiction and requires knowledge of the law of this jurisdiction. See Rule 1.4(b).

[21] Paragraphs (c) and (d) do not authorize communications advertising legal services in this jurisdiction by lawyers who are admitted to practice in other jurisdictions. Whether and how lawyers may communicate the availability of their services in this jurisdiction is governed by Rules 7.1 to 7.5.

Rule 5.6 Restrictions on Right to Practice

A lawyer shall not participate in offering or making:

(a) a partnership, shareholders, operating, employment, or other similar type of agreement that restricts the right of a lawyer to practice after termination of the relationship, except an agreement concerning benefits upon retirement; or

(b) an agreement in which a restriction on the lawyer's right to practice is part of the settlement of a client controversy.

COMMENT

[1] An agreement restricting the right of lawyers to practice after leaving a firm not only limits their professional autonomy but also limits the freedom of clients to choose a lawyer. Paragraph (a) prohibits such agreements except for restrictions incident to provisions concerning retirement benefits for service with the firm.

[2] Paragraph (b) prohibits a lawyer from agreeing not to represent other persons in connection with settling a claim on behalf of a client.

[3] This Rule does not apply to prohibit restrictions that may be included in the terms of the sale of a law practice pursuant to Rule 1.17.

Rule 5.7 Responsibilities Regarding Law-Related Services

(a) A lawyer shall be subject to the Rules of Professional Conduct with respect to the provision of law-related services, as defined in paragraph (b), if the law-related services are provided:

(1) by the lawyer in circumstances that are not distinct from the lawyer's provision of legal services to clients; or

(2) in other circumstances by an entity controlled by the lawyer individually or with others if the lawyer fails to take reasonable measures to assure that a person obtaining the law-related services knows that the services are not legal services and that the protections of the client-lawyer relationship do not exist.

(b) The term "law-related services" denotes services that might reasonably be performed in conjunction with and in substance are related to the provision of legal services, and that are not prohibited as unauthorized practice of law when provided by a nonlawyer.

COMMENT

[1] When a lawyer performs law-related services or controls an organization that does so, there exists the potential for ethical problems. Principal among these is the possibility that the person for whom the law-related services are performed fails to understand that the services may not carry with them the protections normally afforded as part of the client-lawyer relationship. The recipient of the law-related services may expect, for example, that the protection of client confidences, prohibitions against representation of persons with conflicting interests, and obligations of a lawyer to maintain professional independence apply to the provision of law-related services when that may not be the case.

[2] Rule 5.7 applies to the provision of law-related services by a lawyer even when the lawyer does not provide any legal services to the person for whom the law-related services are performed and whether the law-related services are performed through a law firm or a separate entity. The Rule identifies the circumstances in which all of the Rules of Professional Conduct apply to the provision of law-related services. Even when those circumstances do not exist, however, the conduct of a lawyer involved in the provision of law-related services is subject to those Rules that apply generally to lawyer conduct, regardless of whether the conduct involves the provision of legal services. See, e.g., Rule 8.4.

[3] When law-related services are provided by a lawyer under circumstances that are not distinct from the lawyer's provision of legal services to clients, the lawyer in providing the law-related services must adhere to the requirements of the Rules of Professional Conduct as provided in paragraph (a)(1). Even when the law-related and legal services are provided in circumstances that are distinct from each other, for

example through separate entities or different support staff within the law firm, the Rules of Professional Conduct apply to the lawyer as provided in paragraph (a)(2) unless the lawyer takes reasonable measures to assure that the recipient of the law-related services knows that the services are not legal services and that the protections of the client-lawyer relationship do not apply.

[4] Law-related services also may be provided through an entity that is distinct from that through which the lawyer provides legal services. If the lawyer individually or with others has control of such an entity's operations, the Rule requires the lawyer to take reasonable measures to assure that each person using the services of the entity knows that the services provided by the entity are not legal services and that the Rules of Professional Conduct that relate to the client-lawyer relationship do not apply. A lawyer's control of an entity extends to the ability to direct its operation. Whether a lawyer has such control will depend upon the circumstances of the particular case.

[5] When a client-lawyer relationship exists with a person who is referred by a lawyer to a separate law-related service entity controlled by the lawyer, individually or with others, the lawyer must comply with Rule 1.8(a).

[6] In taking the reasonable measures referred to in paragraph (a)(2) to assure that a person using law-related services understands the practical effect or significance of the inapplicability of the Rules of Professional Conduct, the lawyer should communicate to the person receiving the law-related services, in a manner sufficient to assure that the person understands the significance of the fact, that the relationship of the person to the business entity will not be a client-lawyer relationship. The communication should be made before entering into an agreement for provision of or providing law-related services, and preferably should be in writing.

[7] The burden is upon the lawyer to show that the lawyer has taken reasonable measures under the circumstances to communicate the desired understanding. For instance, a sophisticated user of law-related services, such as a publicly held corporation, may require a lesser explanation than someone unaccustomed to making distinctions between legal services and law-related services, such as an individual seeking tax advice from a lawyer-accountant or investigative services in connection with a lawsuit.

[8] Regardless of the sophistication of potential recipients of law-related services, a lawyer should take special care to keep separate the provision of law-related and legal services in order to minimize the risk that the recipient will assume that the law-related services are legal services. The risk of such confusion is especially acute when the lawyer renders both types of services with respect to the same matter. Under some circumstances the legal and law-related services may be so closely entwined that they cannot be distinguished from each other, and the requirement of disclosure and consultation imposed by paragraph (a)(2) of the Rule cannot be met. In such a case a lawyer will be responsible for assuring that both the lawyer's conduct and, to the extent required by Rule 5.3, that of nonlawyer employees in the distinct entity that the lawyer controls complies in all respects with the Rules of Professional Conduct.

[9] A broad range of economic and other interests of clients may be served by lawyers' engaging in the delivery of law-related services. Examples of law-related services include providing title insurance, financial planning, accounting, trust services, real estate counseling, legislative lobbying, economic analysis, social work, psychological counseling, tax preparation, and patent, medical or environmental consulting.

[10] When a lawyer is obliged to accord the recipients of such services the protections of those Rules that apply to the client-lawyer relationship, the lawyer must take special care to heed the proscriptions of the Rules addressing conflict of interest (Rules 1.7 through 1.11, especially Rules 1.7(a)(2) and 1.8(a), (b) and (f)), and to scrupulously adhere to the requirements of Rule 1.6 relating to disclosure of confidential information. The promotion of the law-related services must also in all respects comply with Rules 7.1 through 7.3, dealing with advertising and solicitation. In that regard, lawyers should take special care to identify the obligations that may be imposed as a result of a jurisdiction's decisional law.

[11] When the full protections of all of the Rules of Professional Conduct do not apply to the provision of law-related services, principles of law external to the Rules, for example, the law of principal and agent, govern the legal duties owed to those receiving the services. Those other legal principles may establish a different degree of protection for the recipient with respect to confidentiality of information, conflicts of interest and permissible business relationships with clients. See also Rule 8.4 (Misconduct).

PUBLIC SERVICE

Rule 6.1 Voluntary Pro Bono Publico Service

Every lawyer has a professional responsibility to provide legal services to those unable to pay. A lawyer should aspire to render at least (50) hours of pro bono publico legal services per year. In fulfilling this responsibility, the lawyer should:

(a) provide a substantial majority of the (50) hours of legal services without fee or expectation of fee to:

(1) persons of limited means or

(2) charitable, religious, civic, community, governmental and educational organizations in matters that are designed primarily to address the needs of persons of limited means; and

(b) provide any additional services through:

(1) delivery of legal services at no fee or substantially reduced fee to individuals, groups or organizations seeking to secure or protect civil rights, civil liberties or public rights, or charitable, religious, civic, community, governmental and educational organizations in matters in furtherance of their organizational purposes, where the payment of standard legal fees would significantly deplete the organization's economic resources or would be otherwise inappropriate;

(2) delivery of legal services at a substantially reduced fee to persons of limited means; or

(3) participation in activities for improving the law, the legal system or the legal profession. In addition, a lawyer should voluntarily contribute financial support to organizations that provide legal services to persons of limited means.

COMMENT

[1] Every lawyer, regardless of professional prominence or professional work load, has a responsibility to provide legal services to those unable to pay, and personal involvement in the problems of the disadvantaged can be one of the most rewarding experiences in the life of a lawyer. The American Bar Association urges all lawyers to provide a minimum of 50 hours of pro bono services annually. States, however, may decide to choose a higher or lower number of hours of annual service (which may be expressed as a percentage of a lawyer's professional time) depending upon local needs and local conditions. It is recognized that in some years a lawyer may render greater or fewer hours than the annual standard specified, but during the course of his or her legal career, each lawyer should render on average per year, the number of hours set forth in this Rule. Services can be performed in civil matters or in criminal or quasi-criminal matters for which there is no government obligation to provide funds for legal representation, such as post-conviction death penalty appeal cases.

[2] Paragraphs (a)(1) and (2) recognize the critical need for legal services that exists among persons of limited means by providing that a substantial majority of the legal services rendered annually to the disadvantaged be furnished without fee or expectation of fee. Legal services under these paragraphs consist of a full range of activities, including individual and class representation, the provision of legal advice, legislative lobbying, administrative rule making and the provision of free training or mentoring to those who represent persons of limited means. The variety of these activities should facilitate participation by government lawyers, even when restrictions exist on their engaging in the outside practice of law.

[3] Persons eligible for legal services under paragraphs (a)(1) and (2) are those who qualify for participation in programs funded by the Legal Services Corporation and those whose incomes and financial resources are slightly above the guidelines utilized by such programs but nevertheless, cannot afford counsel. Legal services can be rendered to individuals or to organizations such as homeless shelters, battered women's centers and food pantries that serve those of limited means. The term "governmental

organizations" includes, but is not limited to, public protection programs and sections of governmental or public sector agencies.

[4] Because service must be provided without fee or expectation of fee, the intent of the lawyer to render free legal services is essential for the work performed to fall within the meaning of paragraphs (a)(1) and (2). Accordingly, services rendered cannot be considered pro bono if an anticipated fee is uncollected, but the award of statutory attorneys' fees in a case originally accepted as pro bono would not disqualify such services from inclusion under this section. Lawyers who do receive fees in such cases are encouraged to contribute an appropriate portion of such fees to organizations or projects that benefit persons of limited means.

[5] While it is possible for a lawyer to fulfill the annual responsibility to perform pro bono services exclusively through activities described in paragraphs (a)(1) and (2), to the extent that any hours of service remained unfulfilled, the remaining commitment can be met in a variety of ways as set forth in paragraph (b). Constitutional, statutory or regulatory restrictions may prohibit or impede government and public sector lawyers and judges from performing the pro bono services outlined in paragraphs (a)(1) and (2). Accordingly, where those restrictions apply, government and public sector lawyers and judges may fulfill their pro bono responsibility by performing services outlined in paragraph (b).

[6] Paragraph (b)(1) includes the provision of certain types of legal services to those whose incomes and financial resources place them above limited means. It also permits the pro bono lawyer to accept a substantially reduced fee for services. Examples of the types of issues that may be addressed under this paragraph include First Amendment claims, Title VII claims and environmental protection claims. Additionally, a wide range of organizations may be represented, including social service, medical research, cultural and religious groups.

[7] Paragraph (b)(2) covers instances in which lawyers agree to and receive a modest fee for furnishing legal services to persons of limited means. Participation in judicare programs and acceptance of court appointments in which the fee is substantially below a lawyer's usual rate are encouraged under this section.

[8] Paragraph (b)(3) recognizes the value of lawyers engaging in activities that improve the law, the legal system or the legal profession. Serving on bar association committees, serving on boards of pro bono or legal services programs, taking part in Law Day activities, acting as a continuing legal education instructor, a mediator or an arbitrator and engaging in legislative lobbying to improve the law, the legal system or the profession are a few examples of the many activities that fall within this paragraph.

[9] Because the provision of pro bono services is a professional responsibility, it is the individual ethical commitment of each lawyer. Nevertheless, there may be times when it is not feasible for a lawyer to engage in pro bono services. At such times a lawyer may discharge the pro bono responsibility by providing financial support to organizations providing free legal services to persons of limited means. Such financial support should be reasonably equivalent to the value of the hours of service that would have otherwise been provided. In addition, at times it may be more feasible to satisfy the pro bono responsibility collectively, as by a firm's aggregate pro bono activities.

[10] Because the efforts of individual lawyers are not enough to meet the need for free legal services that exists among persons of limited means, the government and the profession have instituted additional programs to provide those services. Every lawyer should financially support such programs, in addition to either providing direct pro bono services or making financial contributions when pro bono service is not feasible.

[11] Law firms should act reasonably to enable and encourage all lawyers in the firm to provide the pro bono legal services called for by this Rule.

[12] The responsibility set forth in this Rule is not intended to be enforced through disciplinary process.

Rule 6.2 Accepting Appointments

A lawyer shall not seek to avoid appointment by a tribunal to represent a person except for good cause, such as:

(a) representing the client is likely to result in violation of the Rules of Professional Conduct or other law;

(b) representing the client is likely to result in an unreasonable financial burden on the lawyer; or

(c) the client or the cause is so repugnant to the lawyer as to be likely to impair the client-lawyer relationship or the lawyer's ability to represent the client.

COMMENT

[1] A lawyer ordinarily is not obliged to accept a client whose character or cause the lawyer regards as repugnant. The lawyer's freedom to select clients is, however, qualified. All lawyers have a responsibility to assist in providing pro bono publico service. See Rule 6.1. An individual lawyer fulfills this responsibility by accepting a fair share of unpopular matters or indigent or unpopular clients. A lawyer may also be subject to appointment by a court to serve unpopular clients or persons unable to afford legal services.

Appointed Counsel

[2] For good cause a lawyer may seek to decline an appointment to represent a person who cannot afford to retain counsel or whose cause is unpopular. Good cause exists if the lawyer could not handle the matter competently, see Rule 1.1, or if undertaking the representation would result in an improper conflict of interest, for example, when the client or the cause is so repugnant to the lawyer as to be likely to impair the client-lawyer relationship or the lawyer's ability to represent the client. A lawyer may also seek to decline an appointment if acceptance would be unreasonably burdensome, for example, when it would impose a financial sacrifice so great as to be unjust.

[3] An appointed lawyer has the same obligations to the client as retained counsel, including the obligations of loyalty and confidentiality, and is subject to the same limitations on the client-lawyer relationship, such as the obligation to refrain from assisting the client in violation of the Rules.

Rule 6.3 Membership in Legal Services Organizations

A lawyer may serve as a director, officer or member of a legal services organization, apart from the law firm in which the lawyer practices, notwithstanding that the organization serves persons having interests adverse to a client of the lawyer. The lawyer shall not knowingly participate in a decision or action of the organization:

(a) if participating in the decision or action would be incompatible with the lawyer's obligations to a client under Rule 1.7; or

(b) where the decision or action could have a material adverse effect on the representation of a client of the organization whose interests are adverse to a client of the lawyer.

COMMENT

[1] Lawyers should be encouraged to support and participate in legal service organizations. A lawyer who is an officer or a member of such an organization does not thereby have a client-lawyer relationship with persons served by the organization. However, there is potential conflict between the interests of such persons and the interests of the lawyer's clients. If the possibility of such conflict disqualified a lawyer from serving on the board of a legal services organization, the profession's involvement in such organizations would be severely curtailed.

[2] It may be necessary in appropriate cases to reassure a client of the organization that the representation will not be affected by conflicting loyalties of a member of the board. Established, written policies in this respect can enhance the credibility of such assurances.

Rule 6.4 Law Reform Activities Affecting Client Interests

A lawyer may serve as a director, officer or member of an organization involved in reform of the law or its administration notwithstanding that the reform may affect the interests of a client of the lawyer. When the lawyer knows that the interests of a client may be materially benefitted by a decision in which the lawyer participates, the lawyer shall disclose that fact but need not identify the client.

COMMENT

[1] Lawyers involved in organizations seeking law reform generally do not have a client-lawyer relationship with the organization. Otherwise, it might follow that a lawyer could not be involved in a bar association law reform program that might indirectly affect a client. See also Rule 1.2(b). For example, a lawyer specializing in antitrust litigation might be regarded as disqualified from participating in drafting revisions of rules governing that subject. In determining the nature and scope of participation in such activities, a lawyer should be mindful of obligations to clients under other Rules, particularly Rule 1.7. A lawyer is professionally obligated to protect the integrity of the program by making an appropriate disclosure within the organization when the lawyer knows a private client might be materially benefitted.

Rule 6.5 Non-profit and Court-Annexed Limited Legal-Services Programs

(a) A lawyer who, under the auspices of a program sponsored by a nonprofit organization or court, provides short-term limited legal services to a client without expectation by either the lawyer or the client that the lawyer will provide continuing representation in the matter:

(1) is subject to Rules 1.7 and 1.9(a) only if the lawyer knows that the representation of the client involves a conflict of interest; and

(2) is subject to Rule 1.10 only if the lawyer knows that another lawyer associated with the lawyer in a law firm is disqualified by Rule 1.7 or 1.9(a) with respect to the matter.

(b) Except as provided in paragraph (a)(2), Rule 1.10 is inapplicable to a representation governed by this Rule.

COMMENT

[1] Legal services organizations, courts and various nonprofit organizations have established programs through which lawyers provide short-term limited legal services—such as advice or the completion of legal forms—that will assist persons to address their legal problems without further representation by a lawyer. In these programs, such as legal-advice hotlines, advice-only clinics or pro se counseling programs, a client-lawyer relationship is established, but there is no expectation that the lawyer's representation of the client will continue beyond the limited consultation. Such programs are normally operated under circumstances in which ii is not feasible for a lawyer to systematically screen for conflicts of interest as is generally required before undertaking a representation. See, e.g., Rules 1.7, 1.9 and 1.10.

[2] A lawyer who provides short-term limited legal services pursuant to this Rule must secure the clients informed consent to the limited scope of the representation. See Rule 1.2(c). If a short-term limited representation would not be reasonable under the circumstances, the lawyer may offer advice to the client but must also advise the client of the need for further assistance of counsel. Except as provided in this Rule, the Rules of Professional Conduct, including Rules 1.6 and 1.9(c), are applicable to the limited representation.

[3] Because a lawyer who is representing a client in the circumstances addressed by this Rule ordinarily is not able to check systematically for conflicts of interest, paragraph (a) requires compliance with Rules 1.7 or 1.9(a) only if the lawyer knows that the representation presents a conflict of interest for the lawyer, and with Rule 1.10 only if the lawyer knows that another lawyer in the lawyer's firm is disqualified by Rules 1.7 or 1.9(a) in the matter.

[4] Because the limited nature of the services significantly reduces the risk of conflicts of interest with other matters being handled by the lawyer's firm, paragraph (b) provides that Rule 1.10 is inapplicable to a representation governed by this Rule except as provided by paragraph (a)(2). Paragraph (a)(2) requires the participating lawyer to comply with Rule 1.10 when the lawyer knows that the lawyer's firm is disqualified by Rules 1.7 or 1.9(a). By virtue of paragraph (b), however, a lawyer's participation in a short-term limited legal services program will not preclude the lawyer's firm from undertaking or continuing the representation of a client with interests adverse to a client being represented under the program's auspices. Nor will the personal disqualification of a lawyer participating in the program be imputed to other lawyers participating in the program.

[5] If, after commencing a short-term limited representation in accordance with this Rule, a lawyer undertakes to represent the client in the matter on an ongoing basis, Rules 1.7, 1.9(a) and 1.10 become applicable.

INFORMATION ABOUT LEGAL SERVICES

Rule 7.1 Communications Concerning a Lawyer's Services

A lawyer shall not make a false or misleading communication about the lawyer or the lawyer's services. A communication is false or misleading if it contains a material misrepresentation of fact or law, or omits a fact necessary to make the statement considered as a whole not materially misleading.

COMMENT*

[1] This Rule governs all communications about a lawyer's services, including advertising permitted by Rule 7.2. Whatever means are used to make known a lawyer's services, statements about them must be truthful.

[2] Truthful statements that are misleading are also prohibited by this Rule. A truthful statement is misleading if it omits a fact necessary to make the lawyer's communication considered as a whole not materially misleading. A truthful statement is also misleading if there is a substantial likelihood that it will lead a reasonable person to formulate a specific conclusion about the lawyer or the lawyer's services for which there is no reasonable factual foundation.

[3] An advertisement that truthfully reports a lawyer's achievements on behalf of clients or former clients may be misleading if presented so as to lead a reasonable person to form an unjustified expectation that the same results could be obtained for other clients in similar matters without reference to the specific factual and legal circumstances of each client's case. Similarly, an unsubstantiated comparison of the lawyer's services or fees with the services or fees of other lawyers may be misleading if presented with such specificity as would lead a reasonable person to conclude that the comparison can be substantiated. The inclusion of an appropriate disclaimer or qualifying language may preclude a finding that a statement is likely to create unjustified expectations or otherwise mislead the public.

[4] See also Rule 8.4(e) for the prohibition against stating or implying an ability to influence improperly a government agency or official or to achieve results by means that violate the Rules of Professional Conduct or other law.

Rule 7.2 Advertising**

(a) Subject to the requirements of Rules 7.1 and 7.3, a lawyer may advertise services through written, recorded or electronic communication, including public media.

---

* In August 2012, the ABA House of Delegates amended Comment 3 to change the words, "a prospective client" to "the public."

** In November 2002, the ABA added subsection (b)(4) and Comment 8 to permit reciprocal referral agreements between lawyers and others.

(b) A lawyer shall not give anything of value to a person for recommending the lawyer's services except that a lawyer may

(1) pay the reasonable costs of advertisements or communications permitted by this Rule;

(2) pay the usual charges of a legal service plan or a not-for-profit or qualified lawyer referral service. A qualified lawyer referral service is a lawyer referral service that has been approved by an appropriate regulatory authority;

(3) pay for a law practice in accordance with Rule 1.17; and

(4) refer clients to another lawyer or a nonlawyer professional pursuant to an agreement not otherwise prohibited under these Rules that provides for the other person to refer clients or customers to the lawyer, if

(i) the reciprocal referral agreement is not exclusive, and

(ii) the client is informed of the existence and nature of the agreement.

(c) Any communication made pursuant to this rule shall include the name and office address of at least one lawyer or law firm responsible for its content.

COMMENT

[1] To assist the public in learning about and obtaining legal services, lawyers should be allowed to make known their services not only through reputation but also through organized information campaigns in the form of advertising. Advertising involves an active quest for clients, contrary to the tradition that a lawyer should not seek clientele. However, the public's need to know about legal services can be fulfilled in part through advertising. This need is particularly acute in the case of persons of moderate means who have not made extensive use of legal services. The interest in expanding public information about legal services ought to prevail over considerations of tradition. Nevertheless, advertising by lawyers entails the risk of practices that are misleading or overreaching.

[2] This Rule permits public dissemination of information concerning a lawyer's name or firm name, address email address, website, and telephone number; the kinds of services the lawyer will undertake; the basis on which the lawyer's fees are determined, including prices for specific services and payment and credit arrangements; a lawyer's foreign language ability; names of references and, with their consent, names of clients regularly represented; and other information that might invite the attention of those seeking legal assistance.

[3] Questions of effectiveness and taste in advertising are matters of speculation and subjective judgment. Some jurisdictions have had extensive prohibitions against television and other forms of advertising, against advertising going beyond specified facts about a lawyer, or against "undignified" advertising. Television, the Internet, and other forms of electronic communication are now among the most powerful media for getting information to the public, particularly persons of low and moderate income; prohibiting television, Internet, and other forms of electronic advertising, therefore, would impede the flow of information about legal services to many sectors of the public. Limiting the information that may be advertised has a similar effect and assumes that the bar can accurately forecast the kind of information that the public would regard as relevant. But see Rule 7.3(a) for the prohibition against a solicitation through a real-time electronic exchange initiated by the lawyer.

[4] Neither this Rule nor Rule 7.3 prohibits communications authorized by law, such as notice to members of a class in class action litigation.

Paying Others to Recommend a Lawyer

[5] Except as permitted under paragraphs (b)(1)–(b)(4), lawyers are not permitted to pay others for recommending the lawyer's services or for channeling professional work in a manner that violates Rule 7.3. A communication contains a recommendation if it endorses or vouches for a lawyer's credentials, abilities,

---

In August 2012, the ABA House of Delegates amended Comments 1, 2, 3, 5, 6, and 7 to reflect modern advertising practices.

competence, character, or other professional qualities. Paragraph (b)(1), however, allows a lawyer to pay for advertising and communications permitted by this Rule, including the costs of print directory listings, on-line directory listings, newspaper ads, television and radio airtime, domain-name registrations, sponsorship fees, Internet-based advertisements, and group advertising. A lawyer may compensate employees, agents and vendors who are engaged to provide marketing or client development services, such as publicists, public-relations personnel, business-development staff and website designers. Moreover, a lawyer may pay others for generating client leads, such as Internet-based client leads, as long as the lead generator does not recommend the lawyer, any payment to the lead generator is consistent with Rules 1.5(e) (division of fees) and 5.4 (professional independence of the lawyer), and the lead generator's communications are consistent with Rule 7.1 (communications concerning a lawyer's services). To comply with Rule 7.1, a lawyer must not pay a lead generator that states, implies, or creates a reasonable impression that it is recommending the lawyer, is making the referral without payment from the lawyer, or has analyzed a person's legal problems when determining which lawyer should receive the referral. See also Rule 5.3 (duties of lawyers and law firms with respect to the conduct of nonlawyers); Rule 8.4(a) (duty to avoid violating the Rules through the acts of another).

[6] A lawyer may pay the usual charges of a legal service plan or a not-for-profit or qualified lawyer referral service. A legal service plan is a prepaid or group legal service plan or a similar delivery system that assists people who seek to secure legal representation. A lawyer referral service, on the other hand, is any organization that holds itself out to the public as a lawyer referral service. Such referral services are understood by the public to be consumer-oriented organizations that provide unbiased referrals to lawyers with appropriate experience in the subject matter of the representation and afford other client protections, such as complaint procedures or malpractice insurance requirements. Consequently, this Rule only permits a lawyer to pay the usual charges of a not-for-profit or qualified lawyer referral service. A qualified lawyer referral service is one that is approved by an appropriate regulatory authority as affording adequate protections for the public. See, e.g., the American Bar Association's Model Supreme Court Rules Governing Lawyer Referral Services and Model Lawyer Referral and Information Service Quality Assurance Act (requiring that organizations that are identified as lawyer referral services (i) permit the participation of all lawyers who are licensed and eligible to practice in the jurisdiction and who meet reasonable objective eligibility requirements as may be established by the referral service for the protection of the public; (ii) require each participating lawyer to carry reasonably adequate malpractice insurance; (iii) act reasonably to assess client satisfaction and address client complaints; and (iv) do not make referrals to lawyers who own, operate or are employed by the referral service.)

[7] A lawyer who accepts assignments or referrals from a legal service plan or referrals from a lawyer referral service must act reasonably to assure that the activities of the plan or service are compatible with the lawyer's professional obligations. See Rule 5.3. Legal service plans and lawyer referral services may communicate with the public, but such communication must be in conformity with these Rules. Thus, advertising must not be false or misleading, as would be the case if the communications of a group advertising program or a group legal services plan would mislead the public to think that it was a lawyer referral service sponsored by a state agency or bar association. Nor could the lawyer allow in-person, telephonic, or real-time contacts that would violate Rule 7.3.

[8] A lawyer also may agree to refer clients to another lawyer or a nonlawyer professional, in return for the undertaking of that person to refer clients or customers to the lawyer. Such reciprocal referral arrangements must not interfere with the lawyer's professional judgment as to making referrals or as to providing substantive legal services. See Rules 2.1 and 5.4(c). Except as provided in Rule 1.5(e), a lawyer who receives referrals from a lawyer or nonlawyer professional must not pay anything solely for the referral, but the lawyer does not violate paragraph (b) of this Rule by agreeing to refer clients to the other lawyer or nonlawyer professional, so long as the reciprocal referral agreement is not exclusive and the client is informed of the referral agreement. Conflicts of interest created by such arrangements are governed by Rule 1.7. Reciprocal referral agreements should not be of indefinite duration and should be reviewed periodically to determine whether they comply with these Rules. This Rule does not restrict referrals or divisions of revenues or net income among lawyers within firms comprised of multiple entities.

Rule 7.3 Solicitation of Clients*

(a) A lawyer shall not by in-person, live telephone or real-time electronic contact solicit professional employment when a significant motive for the lawyer's doing so is the lawyer's pecuniary gain, unless the person contacted:

(1) is a lawyer; or

(2) has a family, close personal, or prior professional relationship with the lawyer.

(b) A lawyer shall not solicit professional employment from a prospective client by written, recorded or electronic communication or by in-person, telephone or real-time electronic contact even when not otherwise prohibited by paragraph (a), if:

(1) the target of the solicitation has made known to the lawyer a desire not to be solicited by the lawyer; or

(2) the solicitation involves coercion, duress or harassment.

(c) Every written, recorded or electronic communication from a lawyer soliciting professional employment from anyone known to be in need of legal services in a particular matter shall include the words "Advertising Material" on the outside envelope, if any, and at the beginning and ending of any recorded or electronic communication, unless the recipient of the communication is a person specified in paragraphs (a)(1) or (a)(2).

(d) Notwithstanding the prohibitions in paragraph (a), a lawyer may participate with a prepaid or group legal service plan operated by an organization not owned or directed by the lawyer that uses in-person or telephone contact to solicit memberships or subscriptions for the plan from persons who are not known to need legal services in a particular matter covered by the plan.

COMMENT*

[1] A solicitation is a targeted communication initiated by the lawyer that is directed to a specific person and that offers to provide, or can reasonably be understood as offering to provide, legal services. In contrast, a lawyer's communication typically does not constitute a solicitation if it is directed to the general public, such as through a billboard, an Internet banner advertisement, a website or a television commercial, or if it is in response to a request for information or is automatically generated in response to Internet searches.

[2] There is a potential for abuse when a solicitation involves direct in-person, live telephone or real-time electronic contact by a lawyer with someone known to need legal services. These forms of contact subject a person to the private importuning of the trained advocate in a direct interpersonal encounter. The person, who may already feel overwhelmed by the circumstances giving rise to the need for legal services, may find it difficult fully to evaluate all available alternatives with reasoned judgment and appropriate self-interest in the face of the lawyer's presence and insistence upon being retained immediately. The situation is fraught with the possibility of undue influence, intimidation, and over-reaching.

[3] This potential for abuse inherent in direct in-person, live telephone or real-time electronic solicitation justifies its prohibition, particularly since lawyers have alternative means of conveying necessary information to those who may be in need of legal services. In particular, communications can be mailed or transmitted by email or other electronic means that do not involve real-time contact and do not violate other laws governing solicitation. These forms of communication and solicitations make it possible for a prospective client to be informed about the need for legal services, and about the qualifications of available lawyers and law firms, without subjecting the public to direct in-person, telephone or real-time electronic persuasion that may overwhelm a person's judgment.

---

* In August 2012, the ABA House of Delegates amended Rule 7.3 to remove the words "prospective client."

* In August 2012, the ABA House of Delegates added a new Comment 1, renumbered and slightly modified the rest of the comments.

[4] The use of general advertising and written, recorded or electronic communications to transmit information from lawyer to the public, rather than direct in-person, live telephone or real-time electronic contact, will help to assure that the information flows cleanly as well as freely. The contents of advertisements and communications permitted under Rule 7.2 can be permanently recorded so that they cannot be disputed and may be shared with others who know the lawyer. This potential for informal review is itself likely to help guard against statements and claims that might constitute false and misleading communications, in violation of Rule 7.1. The contents of direct in-person, live telephone or real-time electronic contact conversations between a lawyer and a prospective client can be disputed and may not be subject to third-party scrutiny. Consequently, they are much more likely to approach (and occasionally cross) the dividing line between accurate representations and those that are false and misleading.

[5] There is far less likelihood that a lawyer would engage in abusive practices against a former client, or a person with whom the lawyer has close personal or family relationship, or in situations in which the lawyer is motivated by considerations other than the lawyer's pecuniary gain. Nor is there a serious potential for abuse when the person contacted is a lawyer. Consequently, the general prohibition in Rule 7.3(a) and the requirements of Rule 7.3(c) are not applicable in those situations. Also, paragraph (a) is not intended to prohibit a lawyer from participating in constitutionally protected activities of public or charitable legal-service organizations or bona fide political, social, civic, fraternal, employee or trade organizations whose purposes include providing or recommending legal services to their members or beneficiaries.

[6] But even permitted forms of solicitation can be abused. Thus, any solicitation which contains information which is false or misleading within the meaning of Rule 7.1, which involves coercion, duress or harassment within the meaning of Rule 7.3(b)(2), or which involves contact with someone who has made known to the lawyer a desire not to be solicited by the lawyer within the meaning of Rule 7.3(b)(1) is prohibited. Moreover, if after sending a letter or other communication as permitted by Rule 7.2 the lawyer receives no response, any further effort to communicate with the recipient of the communication may violate the provisions of Rule 7.3(b).

[7] This Rule is not intended to prohibit a lawyer from contacting representatives of organizations or groups that may be interested in establishing a group or prepaid legal plan for their members, insureds, beneficiaries or other third parties for the purpose of informing such entities of the availability of and details concerning the plan or arrangement which the lawyer or lawyer's firm is willing to offer. This form of communication is not directed to people who are seeking legal services for themselves. Rather, it is usually addressed to an individual acting in a fiduciary capacity seeking a supplier of legal services for others who may, if they choose, become prospective clients of the lawyer. Under these circumstances, the activity which the lawyer undertakes in communicating with such representatives and the type of information transmitted to the individual are functionally similar to and serve the same purpose as advertising permitted under Rule 7.2.

[8] The requirement in Rule 7.3(c) that certain communications be marked "Advertising Material" does not apply to communications sent in response to requests of potential clients or their spokespersons or sponsors. General announcements by lawyers, including changes in personnel or office location, do not constitute communications soliciting professional employment from a client known to be in need of legal services within the meaning of this Rule.

[9] Paragraph (d) of this Rule permits a lawyer to participate with an organization which uses personal contact to solicit members for its group or prepaid legal service plan, provided that the personal contact is not undertaken by any lawyer who would be a provider of legal services through the plan. The organization must not be owned by or directed (whether as manager or otherwise) by any lawyer or law firm that participates in the plan. For example, paragraph (d) would not permit a lawyer to create an organization controlled directly or indirectly by the lawyer and use the organization for the in-person or telephone solicitation of legal employment of the lawyer through memberships in the plan or otherwise. The communication permitted by these organizations also must not be directed to a person known to need legal services in a particular matter, but is to be designed to inform potential plan members generally of another means of affordable legal services. Lawyers who participate in a legal service plan must reasonably assure that the plan sponsors are in compliance with Rules 7.1, 7.2 and 7.3(b). See 8.4(a).

Rule 7.4 Communication of Fields of Practice and Specialization

(a) A lawyer may communicate the fact that the lawyer does or does not practice in particular fields of law.

(b) A lawyer admitted to engage in patent practice before the United States Patent and Trademark Office may use the designation "Patent Attorney" or a substantially similar designation.

(c) A lawyer engaged in Admiralty practice may use the designation "Admiralty," "Proctor in Admiralty" or a substantially similar designation.

(d) A lawyer shall not state or imply that a lawyer is certified as a specialist in a particular field of law, unless:

(1) the lawyer has been certified as a specialist by an organization that has been approved by an appropriate state authority or that has been accredited by the American Bar Association; and

(2) the name of the certifying organization is clearly identified in the communication.

COMMENT

[1] Paragraph (a) of this Rule permits a lawyer to indicate areas of practice in communications about the lawyer's services. If a lawyer practices only in certain fields, or will not accept matters except in a specified field or fields, the lawyer is permitted to so indicate. A lawyer is generally permitted to state that the lawyer is a "specialist," practices a "specialty," or "specializes in" particular fields, but such communications are subject to the "false and misleading" standard applied in Rule 7.1 to communications concerning a lawyer's services.

[2] Paragraph (b) recognizes the long-established policy of the Patent and Trademark Office for the designation of lawyers practicing before the Office. Paragraph (c) recognizes that designation of Admiralty practice has a long historical tradition associated with maritime commerce and the federal courts.

[3] Paragraph (d) permits a lawyer to state that the lawyer is certified as a specialist in a field of law if such certification is granted by an organization approved by an appropriate state authority or accredited by the American Bar Association or another organization, such as a state bar association, that has been approved by the state authority to accredit organizations that certify lawyers as specialists. Certification signifies that an objective entity has recognized an advanced degree of knowledge and experience in the specialty area greater than is suggested by general licensure to practice law. Certifying organizations may be expected to apply standards of experience, knowledge and proficiency to insure that a lawyer's recognition as a specialist is meaningful and reliable. In order to insure that consumers can obtain access to useful information about an organization granting certification, the name of the certifying organization must be included in any communication regarding the certification.

Rule 7.5 Firm Names and Letterheads

(a) A lawyer shall not use a firm name, letterhead or other professional designation that violates Rule 7.1. A trade name may be used by a lawyer in private practice if it does not imply a connection with a government agency or with a public or charitable legal services organization and is not otherwise in violation of Rule 7.1.

(b) A law firm with offices in more than one jurisdiction may use the same name or other professional designation in each jurisdiction, but identification of the lawyers in an office of the firm shall indicate the jurisdictional limitations on those not licensed to practice in the jurisdiction where the office is located.

(c) The name of a lawyer holding a public office shall not be used in the name of a law firm, or in communications on its behalf, during any substantial period in which the lawyer is not actively and regularly practicing with the firm.

(d) Lawyers may state or imply that they practice in a partnership or other organization only when that is the fact.

COMMENT

[1] A firm may be designated by the names of all or some of its members, by the names of deceased members where there has been a continuing succession in the firm's identity or by a trade name such as the "ABC Legal Clinic." A lawyer or law firm may also be designated by a distinctive website address or comparable professional designation. Although the United States Supreme Court has held that legislation may prohibit the use of trade names in professional practice, use of such names in law practice is acceptable so long as it is not misleading. If a private firm uses a trade name that includes a geographical name such as "Springfield Legal Clinic," an express disclaimer that it is a public legal aid agency may be required to avoid a misleading implication. It may be observed that any firm name including the name of a deceased partner is, strictly speaking, a trade name. The use of such names to designate law firms has proven a useful means of identification. However, it is misleading to use the name of a lawyer not associated with the firm or a predecessor of the firm, or the name of a nonlawyer.

[2] With regard to paragraph (d), lawyers sharing office facilities, but who are not in fact associated with each other in a law firm, may not denominate themselves as, for example, "Smith and Jones," for that title suggests that they are practicing law together in a firm.

Rule 7.6 Political Contributions to Obtain Government Legal Engagements or Appointments by Judges

A lawyer or law firm shall not accept a government legal engagement or an appointment by a judge if the lawyer or law firm makes a political contribution or solicits political contributions for the purpose of obtaining or being considered for that type of legal engagement or appointment.

COMMENT

[1] Lawyers have a right to participate fully in the political process, which includes making and soliciting political contributions to candidates for judicial and other public office. Nevertheless, when lawyers make or solicit political contributions in order to obtain an engagement for legal work awarded by a government agency, or to obtain appointment by a judge, the public may legitimately question whether the lawyers engaged to perform the work are selected on the basis of competence and merit. In such a circumstance, the integrity of the profession is undermined.

[2] The term "political contribution" denotes any gift, subscription, loan, advance or deposit of anything of value made directly or indirectly to a candidate, incumbent, political party or campaign committee to influence or provide financial support for election to or retention in judicial or other government office. Political contributions in initiative and referendum elections are not included. For purposes of this Rule, the term "political contribution" does not include uncompensated services.

[3] Subject to the exceptions below, (i) the term "government legal engagement" denotes any engagement to provide legal services that a public official has the direct or indirect power to award; and (ii) the term "appointment by a judge" denotes an appointment to a position such as referee, commissioner, special master, receiver, guardian or other similar position that is made by a judge. Those terms do not, however, include (a) substantially uncompensated services; (b) engagements or appointments made on the basis of experience, expertise, professional qualifications and cost following a request for proposal or other process that is free from influence based upon political contributions; and (c) engagements or appointments made on a rotational basis from a list compiled without regard to political contributions.

[4] The term "lawyer or law firm" includes a political action committee or other entity owned or controlled by a lawyer or law firm.

[5] Political contributions are for the purpose of obtaining or being considered for a government legal engagement or appointment by a judge if, but for the desire to be considered for the legal engagement or appointment, the lawyer or law firm would not have made or solicited the contributions. The purpose may be determined by an examination of the circumstances in which the contributions occur. For example, one

or more contributions that in the aggregate are substantial in relation to other contributions by lawyers or law firms, made for the benefit of an official in a position to influence award of a government legal engagement, and followed by an award of the legal engagement to the contributing or soliciting lawyer or the lawyer's firm would support an inference that the purpose of the contributions was to obtain the engagement, absent other factors that weigh against existence of the proscribed purpose. Those factors may include among others that the contribution or solicitation was made to further a political, social, or economic interest or because of an existing personal, family, or professional relationship with a candidate.

[6] If a lawyer makes or solicits a political contribution under circumstances that constitute bribery or another crime, Rule 8.4(b) is implicated.

MAINTAINING THE INTEGRITY OF THE PROFESSION

Rule 8.1 Bar Admission and Disciplinary Matters

An applicant for admission to the bar, or a lawyer in connection with a bar admission application or in connection with a disciplinary matter, shall not:

(a) knowingly make a false statement of material fact; or

(b) fail to disclose a fact necessary to correct a misapprehension known by the person to have arisen in the matter, or knowingly fail to respond to a lawful demand for information from an admissions or disciplinary authority, except that this rule does not require disclosure of information otherwise protected by Rule 1.6.

COMMENT

[1] The duty imposed by this Rule extends to persons seeking admission to the bar as well as to lawyers. Hence, if a person makes a material false statement in connection with an application for admission, it may be the basis for subsequent disciplinary action if the person is admitted, and in any event may be relevant in a subsequent admission application. The duty imposed by this Rule applies to a lawyer's own admission or discipline as well as that of others. Thus, it is a separate professional offense for a lawyer to knowingly make a misrepresentation or omission in connection with a disciplinary investigation of the lawyer's own conduct. Paragraph (b) of this Rule also requires correction of any prior misstatement in the matter that the applicant or lawyer may have made and affirmative clarification of any misunderstanding on the part of the admissions or disciplinary authority of which the person involved becomes aware.

[2] This Rule is subject to the provisions of the fifth amendment of the United States Constitution and corresponding provisions of state constitutions. A person relying on such a provision in response to a question, however, should do so openly and not use the right of nondisclosure as a justification for failure to comply with this Rule.

[3] A lawyer representing an applicant for admission to the bar, or representing a lawyer who is the subject of a disciplinary inquiry or proceeding, is governed by the rules applicable to the client-lawyer relationship, including Rule 1.6 and, in some cases, Rule 3.3.

Rule 8.2 Judicial and Legal Officials

(a) A lawyer shall not make a statement that the lawyer knows to be false or with reckless disregard as to its truth or falsity concerning the qualifications or integrity of a judge, adjudicatory officer or public legal officer, or of a candidate for election or appointment to judicial or legal office.

(b) A lawyer who is a candidate for judicial office shall comply with the applicable provisions of the Code of Judicial Conduct.

COMMENT

[1] Assessments by lawyers are relied on in evaluating the professional or personal fitness of persons being considered for election or appointment to judicial office and to public legal offices, such as attorney general, prosecuting attorney and public defender. Expressing honest and candid opinions on such matters

contributes to improving the administration of justice. Conversely, false statements by a lawyer can unfairly undermine public confidence in the administration of justice.

[2] When a lawyer seeks judicial office, the lawyer should be bound by applicable limitations on political activity.

[3] To maintain the fair and independent administration of justice, lawyers are encouraged to continue traditional efforts to defend judges and courts unjustly criticized.

Rule 8.3 Reporting Professional Misconduct

(a) A lawyer who knows that another lawyer has committed a violation of the Rules of Professional Conduct that raises a substantial question as to that lawyer's honesty, trustworthiness or fitness as a lawyer in other respects, shall inform the appropriate professional authority.

(b) A lawyer who knows that a judge has committed a violation of applicable rules of judicial conduct that raises a substantial question as to the judge's fitness for office shall inform the appropriate authority.

(c) This Rule does not require disclosure of information otherwise protected by Rule 1.6 or information gained by a lawyer or judge while participating in an approved lawyers assistance program.

COMMENT

[1] Self-regulation of the legal profession requires that members of the profession initiate disciplinary investigation when they know of a violation of the Rules of Professional Conduct. Lawyers have a similar obligation with respect to judicial misconduct. An apparently isolated violation may indicate a pattern of misconduct that only a disciplinary investigation can uncover. Reporting a violation is especially important where the victim is unlikely to discover the offense.

[2] A report about misconduct is not required where it would involve violation of Rule 1.6. However, a lawyer should encourage a client to consent to disclosure where prosecution would not substantially prejudice the client's interests.

[3] If a lawyer were obliged to report every violation of the Rules, the failure to report any violation would itself be a professional offense. Such a requirement existed in many jurisdictions but proved to be unenforceable. This Rule limits the reporting obligation to those offenses that a self-regulating profession must vigorously endeavor to prevent. A measure of judgment is, therefore, required in complying with the provisions of this Rule. The term "substantial" refers to the seriousness of the possible offense and not the quantum of evidence of which the lawyer is aware. A report should be made to the bar disciplinary agency unless some other agency, such as a peer review agency, is more appropriate in the circumstances. Similar considerations apply to the reporting of judicial misconduct.

[4] The duty to report professional misconduct does not apply to a lawyer retained to represent a lawyer whose professional conduct is in question. Such a situation is governed by the Rules applicable to the client-lawyer relationship.

[5] Information about a lawyer's or judge's misconduct or fitness may be received by a lawyer in the course of that lawyer's participation in an approved lawyers or judges assistance program. In that circumstance, providing for an exception to the reporting requirements of paragraphs (a) and (b) of this Rule encourages lawyers and judges to seek treatment through such a program. Conversely, without such an exception, lawyers and judges may hesitate to seek assistance from these programs, which may then result in additional harm to their professional careers and additional injury to the welfare of clients and the public. These Rules do not otherwise address the confidentiality of information received by a lawyer or judge participating in an approved lawyers assistance program; such an obligation, however, may be imposed by the rules of the program or other law.

Rule 8.4 Misconduct

It is professional misconduct for a lawyer to:

(a) violate or attempt to violate the Rules of Professional Conduct, knowingly assist or induce another to do so, or do so through the acts of another;

(b) commit a criminal act that reflects adversely on the lawyer's honesty, trustworthiness or fitness as a lawyer in other respects;

(c) engage in conduct involving dishonesty, fraud, deceit or misrepresentation;

(d) engage in conduct that is prejudicial to the administration of justice;

(e) state or imply an ability to influence improperly a government agency or official or to achieve results by means that violate the Rules of Professional Conduct or other law; or

(f) knowingly assist a judge or judicial officer in conduct that is a violation of applicable rules of judicial conduct or other law.

COMMENT

[1] Lawyers are subject to discipline when they violate or attempt to violate the Rules of Professional Conduct, knowingly assist or induce another to do so or do so through the acts of another, as when they request or instruct an agent to do so on the lawyer's behalf. Paragraph (a), however, does not prohibit a lawyer from advising a client concerning action the client is legally entitled to take.

[2] Many kinds of illegal conduct reflect adversely on fitness to practice law, such as offenses involving fraud and the offense of willful failure to file an income tax return. However, some kinds of offenses carry no such implication. Traditionally, the distinction was drawn in terms of offenses involving "moral turpitude." That concept can be construed to include offenses concerning some matters of personal morality, such as adultery and comparable offenses, that have no specific connection to fitness for the practice of law. Although a lawyer is personally answerable to the entire criminal law, a lawyer should be professionally answerable only for offenses that indicate lack of those characteristics relevant to law practice. Offenses involving violence, dishonesty, breach of trust, or serious interference with the administration of justice are in that category. A pattern of repeated offenses, even ones of minor significance when considered separately, can indicate indifference to legal obligation.

[3] A lawyer who, in the course of representing a client, knowingly manifests by words or conduct, bias or prejudice based upon race, sex, religion, national origin, disability, age, sexual orientation or socioeconomic status, violates paragraph (d) when such actions are prejudicial to the administration of justice. Legitimate advocacy respecting the foregoing factors does not violate paragraph (d). A trial judge's finding that peremptory challenges were exercised on a discriminatory basis does not alone establish a violation of this rule.

[4] A lawyer may refuse to comply with an obligation imposed by law upon a good faith belief that no valid obligation exists. The provisions of Rule 1.2(d) concerning a good faith challenge to the validity, scope, meaning or application of the law apply to challenges of legal regulation of the practice of law.

[5] Lawyers holding public office assume legal responsibilities going beyond those of other citizens. A lawyer's abuse of public office can suggest an inability to fulfill the professional role of lawyers. The same is true of abuse of positions of private trust such as trustee, executor, administrator, guardian, agent and officer, director or manager of a corporation or other organization.

Rule 8.5 Disciplinary Authority: Choice of Law*

(a) Disciplinary Authority. A lawyer admitted to practice in this jurisdiction is subject to the disciplinary authority of this jurisdiction, regardless of where the lawyer's

* In November 2002, the ABA amended this rule to reflect the recommendations of the multijurisdictional practice of law commission.

conduct occurs. A lawyer not admitted in this jurisdiction is also subject to the disciplinary authority of this jurisdiction if the lawyer provides or offers to provide any legal services in this jurisdiction. A lawyer may be subject to the disciplinary authority of both this jurisdiction and another jurisdiction for the same conduct.

(b) Choice of Law. In any exercise of the disciplinary authority of this jurisdiction, the rules of professional conduct to be applied shall be as follows:

(1) for conduct in connection with a matter pending before a tribunal, the rules of the jurisdiction in which the tribunal sits, unless the rules of the tribunal provide otherwise; and

(2) for any other conduct, the rules of the jurisdiction in which the lawyer's conduct occurred, or, if the predominant effect of the conduct is in a different jurisdiction, the rules of that jurisdiction shall be applied to the conduct. A lawyer shall not be subject to discipline if the lawyer's conduct conforms to the rules of a jurisdiction in which the lawyer reasonably believes the predominant effect of the lawyer's conduct will occur.

COMMENT

Disciplinary Authority

[1] It is longstanding law that the conduct of a lawyer admitted to practice in this jurisdiction is subject to the disciplinary authority of this jurisdiction. Extension of the disciplinary authority of this jurisdiction to other lawyers who provide or offer to provide legal services in this jurisdiction is for the protection of the citizens of this jurisdiction. Reciprocal enforcement of a jurisdiction's disciplinary findings and sanctions will further advance the purposes of this Rule. See, Rules 6 and 22, ABA Model Rules for Lawyer Disciplinary Enforcement. A lawyer who is subject to the disciplinary authority of this jurisdiction under Rule 8.5(a) appoints an official to be designated by this Court to receive service of process in this jurisdiction. The fact that the lawyer is subject to the disciplinary authority of this jurisdiction may be a factor in determining whether personal jurisdiction may be asserted over the lawyer for civil matters.

Choice of Law*

[2] A lawyer may be potentially subject to more than one set of rules of professional conduct which impose different obligations. The lawyer may be licensed to practice in more than one jurisdiction with differing rules, or may be admitted to practice before a particular court with rules that differ from those of the jurisdiction or jurisdictions in which the lawyer is licensed to practice. Additionally, the lawyer's conduct may involve significant contacts with more than one jurisdiction.

[3] Paragraph (b) seeks to resolve such potential conflicts. Its premise is that minimizing conflicts between rules, as well as uncertainty about which rules are applicable, is in the best interest of both clients and the profession (as well as the bodies having authority to regulate the profession). Accordingly, it takes the approach of (i) providing that any particular conduct of a lawyer shall be subject to only one set of rules of professional conduct, (ii) making the determination of which set of rules applies to particular conduct as straightforward as possible, consistent with recognition of appropriate regulatory interests of relevant jurisdictions, and (iii) providing protection from discipline for lawyers who act reasonably in the face of uncertainty.

[4] Paragraph (b)(1) provides that as to a lawyer's conduct relating to a proceeding pending before a tribunal, the lawyer shall be subject only to the rules of the jurisdiction in which the tribunal sits unless the rules of the tribunal, including its choice of law rule, provide otherwise. As to all other conduct, including conduct in anticipation of a proceeding not yet pending before a tribunal, paragraph (b)(2) provides that a lawyer shall be subject to the rules of the jurisdiction in which the lawyer's conduct occurred, or, if the predominant effect of the conduct is in another jurisdiction, the rules of that jurisdiction shall be applied to the conduct. In the case of conduct in anticipation of a proceeding that is likely to be before a tribunal, the

---

* In February 2013, the ABA House of Delegates added the last line to Comment 5 to allow lawyers and clients to contractually choose a forum's rules of professional responsibility.

predominant effect of such conduct could be where the conduct occurred, where the tribunal sits or in another jurisdiction.

[5] When a lawyer's conduct involves significant contacts with more than one jurisdiction, it may not be clear whether the predominant effect of the lawyer's conduct will occur in a jurisdiction other than the one in which the conduct occurred. So long as the lawyer's conduct conforms to the rules of a jurisdiction in which the lawyer reasonably believes the predominant effect will occur, the lawyer shall not be subject to discipline under this Rule. With respect to conflicts of interest, in determining a lawyer's reasonable belief under paragraph (b)(2), a written agreement between the lawyer and client that reasonably specifies a particular jurisdiction as within the scope of that paragraph may be considered if the agreement was obtained with the client's informed consent confirmed in the agreement.

[6] If two admitting jurisdictions were to proceed against a lawyer for the same conduct, they should, applying this rule, identify the same governing ethics rules. They should take all appropriate steps to see that they do apply the same rule to the same conduct, and in all events should avoid proceeding against a lawyer on the basis of two inconsistent rules.

[7] The choice of law provision applies to lawyers engaged in transnational practice, unless international law, treaties or other agreements between competent regulatory authorities in the affected jurisdictions provide otherwise.

INDEX TO ABA MODEL RULES

D

INDEX

INDEX

J

K

L

M

N

A CHART COMPARING THE LANGUAGE OF THE STATE CONFIDENTIALITY RULES

I have created this confidentiality chart to allow students to quickly compare any jurisdiction's confidentiality rules with the ABA Model Rules and to locate the rule number for additional research. It does not take into account case law or ethics opinions which may modify these rules and it does not take into account federal and state statutes which may lead to a different result in a specific substantive area. To do so would complicate the usability of the chart and would in fact be misleading. Thus, this chart does not address noisy withdrawal unless such a concept is included in the rule itself, see Arkansas. I also have not included a category based upon Model Rule 4.1—Truthfulness in Statements to Others—because virtually all states' 4.1 rules permit disclosure only to the extent that their confidentiality rules (1.6 and 3.3) allow disclosure. In my opinion, the 4.1 concept is resolved in this chart. I have also chosen to exclude footnotes to increase ease of use. This chart was created by looking up the state ethics rules on the State Ethics Rules subcategory of the Ethics and Professional Responsibility topical database on Westlaw. I checked my research with the excellent chart prepared by the Attorneys' Liability Assurance Society, Inc. An excellent source of state implementation of the ABA Model Rules can be found at http://www.americanbar.org/groups/professional_responsibility/policy.html.

DISCLOSURE

Jurisdiction	To Prevent Serious Bodily Crime	To Prevent Non-Bodily Crime	To Prevent Non-Criminal Fraud	To Rectify Past Crime/Fraud When Lawyers Services Used	Fraud on Court
ABA 2001 Model Rules	May Reveal 1.6(b)(1)	Must Not 1.6	Must Not 1.6	Must Not 1.6	Must Reveal 3.3(a)(2)
ABA 2015 Model Rules	May Reveal if crime involves reasonably certain death or substantial bodily harm 1.6(b)(1)	May Reveal to prevent client from committing a crime reasonably certain to result in substantial injury to financial interests or property of another and when lawyer's services were used.	May Reveal to prevent client from committing a fraud reasonably certain to result in substantial injury financial interest or property of another and when legal services were used.	May Reveal to prevent, mitigate or rectify substantial injury to the financial interests or property of another that has or is reasonably certain to result from client's commission of a crime or fraud in furtherance of which the client has used the lawyer's services.	Must Take Reasonable Remedial Measures including, if necessary, disclosure to court 3.3(b)

CONFIDENTIALITY CHART

Jurisdiction	To Prevent Serious Bodily Crime	To Prevent Non-Bodily Crime	To Prevent Non-Criminal Fraud	To Rectify Past Crime/Fraud When Lawyers Services Used	Fraud on Court
Alabama	May Reveal 1.6(b)(1)	Must Not 1.6	Must Not 1.6	Must Not 1.6	Must Disclose 3.3(a)(2)
Alaska	May Reveal 1.6(b)(1)	May Reveal 1.6(b)(1)	Must Not 1.6	Shall Not 1.6	Must Disclose 3.3(a)(2)
Arizona	Shall Reveal 1.6(b)	ABA 2005 language 1.6(d)(1)	ABA 2005 language 1.6(d)(1)	ABA 2005 language 1.6(d)(2)	Must Disclose 3.3(a)(2)
Arkansas	May Reveal 1.6(b)(1)	May Reveal 1.6(b)(1)	May Reveal 1.6(b)(2)	May Reveal, but allows lawyer to disclose fact of withdrawal and to disavow opinions and documents 1.6(b)(3), 1.6(c)	Must Disclose 3.3
California Statute	May Reveal Bus. Prof. Code § 6068(e)	Must Not Bus. Prof. Code § 6068(e)	Must Not Bus. Prof. Code § 6068(e)	Must Not Bus. Prof. Code § 6068(e)	"shall not seek to mislead judge" Rule 5–200(B)
California Ethics Code	May Reveal 3–100(B)	Must Not 3–100	Must Not 3–100	Must Not 3–100	above
Colorado	May Reveal 1.6(b)	May Reveal 1.6(b)	May Reveal 1.6	Must Not 1.6	Must Disclose 3.3(a)(2)
Connecticut	Must Reveal 1.6(b)	Shall Reveal 1.6(c)(2)	Must Not 1.6	May Reveal 1.6(c)(2)	Must Disclose 3.3(a)(2)
Delaware	May Reveal 1.6(b)(1)	ABA 2005 language 1.6(b)(2)	ABA 2005 language 1.6(b)(2)	ABA 2005 language 1.6(b)(3)	Must Disclose 3.3(a)(2)

CONFIDENTIALITY CHART

Jurisdiction	To Prevent Serious Bodily Crime	To Prevent Non-Bodily Crime	To Prevent Non-Criminal Fraud	To Rectify Past Crime/Fraud When Lawyers Services Used	Fraud on Court
District of Columbia	May Reveal 1.6(c)(1)	Shall Not 1.6	Must Not 1.6	Must Not 1.6	When fraud on court is present or future, lawyer may not participate directly and may use a narrative of client perjury is involved. 3.3(b). When fraud on the court is past, may not reveal if protected by Rule 1.6. 3.3(d)
Florida	Must Reveal 4–1.6(b)(2)	Must Reveal 4–1.6(b)(1)	Must Not 4–1.6	Must Not 4–1.6	Must Disclose 4–3.3(a)(2)
Georgia	May Reveal 1.6(b)(1)(ii)	May Reveal 1.6(b)(1)	Must Not 1.6	Must Not 1.6	Must Disclose 3.3(a)(2)
Hawaii	May Reveal 1.6(c)(1)	May Reveal 1.6(c)(1)	May Reveal 1.6(c)(1)	Shall Reveal information which clearly establishes criminal or fraudulent act by client. 1.6(b). May Reveal information which lawyer reasonably believes to have been criminal or fraudulent. 1.6(c)(2)	Must Disclose 3.3(a)(2)

CONFIDENTIALITY CHART

Jurisdiction	To Prevent Serious Bodily Crime	To Prevent Non-Bodily Crime	To Prevent Non-Criminal Fraud	To Rectify Past Crime/Fraud When Lawyers Services Used	Fraud on Court
Idaho	May Reveal 1.6(b)(1)	May Reveal 1.6(b)(2)	Must Not 1.6	May Reveal 1.6	Must Disclose 3.3(a)(2)
Illinois	Shall Reveal 1.6(b)	May Reveal 1.6(c)(2)	Must Not 1.6	Must Not 1.6	Must Disclose 3.3(a)(2)
Indiana	May Reveal 1.6(b)(1)	ABA 2005 language 1.6(b)(2)	ABA 2005 language 1.6(b)(2)	ABA 2005 language 1.6(b)(3)	Must Disclose 3.3(a)(2)
Iowa	May Reveal 32:1.6(b)(1)	ABA 2005 language 32:1.6(b)(2)	ABA 2005 language 32:1.6(b)(2)	ABA 2005 language 32:1.6(b)(3)	Must Disclose 32:3.3(a)(2)
Kansas	May Reveal 1.6(b)(1)	May Reveal 1.6(b)(1)	Must Not 1.6	Must Not 1.6	Must Disclose 3.3(a)(2)
Kentucky	May Reveal 3.130 (1.6(b)(1))	Must Not 3.130(1.6)	Must Not 3.130 (1.6)	Must Not 3.310 (1.6)	Must Disclose 3.130 (3.3(a)(2))
Louisiana	May Reveal 1.6(b)(1)	ABA 2005 language 1.6(b)(2)	ABA 2005 language 1.6(b)(2)	ABA 2005 language 1.6(b)(3)	Must Reveal 3.3(b)

CONFIDENTIALITY CHART

Jurisdiction	To Prevent Serious Bodily Crime	To Prevent Non-Bodily Crime	To Prevent Non-Criminal Fraud	To Rectify Past Crime/Fraud When Lawyers Services Used	Fraud on Court
Maine	May Disclose 3.6(h)(4)	May Disclose 3.6(h)(4)	Must Not 3.6(h)	Must Not 3.6(h)	When fraud on court is perpetuated by a client, lawyer must urge client to rectify situation. When fraud continues, lawyer shall reveal fraud to court unless it involved privileged information. 3.6(b). When fraud is perpetuated by non-client, lawyer shall disclose fraud on the court. 3.6(b)
Maryland	May Reveal 1.6(b)(1)	May Reveal if crime is likely to result in "substantial injury to financial interests or property of another" 1.6(b)(1)	May Reveal if fraud is likely to result in "substantial injury to financial interests or property of another" 1.6(b)(1)	May Reveal 1.6(b)(2)	Must Disclose 3.3(a)(2)

CONFIDENTIALITY CHART

Jurisdiction	To Prevent Serious Bodily Crime	To Prevent Non-Bodily Crime	To Prevent Non-Criminal Fraud	To Rectify Past Crime/Fraud When Lawyers Services Used	Fraud on Court
Massachusetts	May Reveal to prevent death or substantial bodily harm or "wrongful execution or incarceration of another" 1.6(b)(1)	May Reveal if fraud is likely to result in "substantial injury to financial interests or property of another" 1.6(b)(1)	May Reveal if fraud is likely to result in "substantial injury to financial interests or property of another" 1.6(b)(1)	May Reveal 1.6(b)(3)	Must Disclose 3.3(a)(2)
Michigan	May Reveal 1.6(c)(4)	May Reveal 1.6(c)(4)	Must Not 1.6	May Reveal 1.6(c)(3)	Must Disclose 3.3(a)(2)
Minnesota	May Reveal 1.6(b)(6)	May Reveal 1.6(b)(3)	May Reveal 1.6(b)(4)	May Reveal 1.6(b)(5)	Must Disclose 3.3(b)
Mississippi	May Reveal 1.6(b)(1)	May Reveal 1.6(b)(1)	Must Not 1.6	Must Not 1.6	Must Disclose 3.3(a)(2)
Missouri	May Reveal 4–1.6(b)(1)	Must Not 4–1.6	Must Not 4–1.6	Must Not 4–1.6	Must Disclose 4–3.3(a)(2)
Montana	May Reveal 1.6(b)(1)	Must Not 1.6	Must Not 1.6	Must Not 1.6	Must Disclose 3.3(b)
Nebraska	May Reveal 1.6(b)(1)	Must Not 1.6	Must Not 1.6	Must Not 1.6	Must Reveal 3.3(b)
Nevada	Must Reveal 1.6(b)(1)	May Reveal, but shall where practicable first ask client to take suitable action 1.6(b)(2)	May Reveal but shall when practicable first ask client to take suitable action 1.6(b)(2)	May Reveal, but lawyer first shall attempt to persuade client to take corrective action. 1.6(b)(3)	Must Disclose 3.3(b)(2)

CONFIDENTIALITY CHART

Jurisdiction	To Prevent Serious Bodily Crime	To Prevent Non-Bodily Crime	To Prevent Non-Criminal Fraud	To Rectify Past Crime/Fraud When Lawyers Services Used	Fraud on Court
New Hampshire	May Reveal 1.6(b)(1)	May Reveal if it is likely to result in substantial injury to the financial interest or property of another 1.6(b)(1)	Must Not 1.6	Must Not 1.6	Must take reasonable remedial measures only if the fraud relates to evidence that the lawyer has offered in the past and the lawyer now realizes that it was false when offered. 3.3(a)(3)
New Jersey	Shall Reveal to prevent the client from committing a "criminal, illegal, or fraudulent act" likely to result in "death or substantial bodily harm". 1.6(b)(1)	Shall Reveal to prevent the client from committing a "criminal, illegal, or fraudulent act" likely to result in "substantial injury to the financial interest or property of another". 1.6(b)(1)	Shall Reveal to prevent the client from committing a "criminal, illegal, or fraudulent act" likely to result in "substantial injury to the financial interest or property of another". 1.6(b)(1)	May Reveal 1.6(d)(1)	Must Reveal 1.6(b)(2), 3.3(a)(2)
New Mexico	Should Reveal 16–106(B)	May Reveal 16–106(C)	Must Not 16–106	Must Not 16–106	Must Reveal 16–303(A)(2)

CONFIDENTIALITY CHART

Jurisdiction	To Prevent Serious Bodily Crime	To Prevent Non-Bodily Crime	To Prevent Non-Criminal Fraud	To Rectify Past Crime/Fraud When Lawyers Services Used	Fraud on Court
New York	May Reveal 4–101(C)(3)	May Reveal 4–101(C)(3)	Must Not 4–101	Must Not 4–101	When fraud on court is perpetuated by a client, lawyer shall promptly urge client to rectify situation. If fraud is not corrected, lawyer must reveal fraud to court unless it is a client confidence or secret. 7–102(B)(1)
North Carolina	May Reveal 1.6(b)(3)	May Reveal 1.6(b)(2)	Must Not 1.6	May Reveal 1.6(b)(4)	Must Disclose 3.3(a)(2)

CONFIDENTIALITY CHART

Jurisdiction	To Prevent Serious Bodily Crime	To Prevent Non-Bodily Crime	To Prevent Non-Criminal Fraud	To Rectify Past Crime/Fraud When Lawyers Services Used	Fraud on Court
North Dakota	Must Reveal 1.6(a)	May Reveal 1.6(d)	May Reveal 1.6(d)	May Reveal 1.6(f)	Must Reveal if fraud on court related to evidence that lawyer introduced other than the client's testimony. 3.3(c). Must Not reveal if fraud on the court comes from client's testimony. Lawyer shall urge a client to rectify the fraud and shall attempt to withdraw if client refuses. However, lawyer may not disclose the confidence. 3.3(d)
Ohio	May Reveal 4–101(C)(3)	May Reveal 4–101(C)(3)	Shall Not 4–101	Must Reveal 7–102(B)(1)	Must Reveal 7–102(B)(1)
Oklahoma	May Reveal 1.6(b)(1)	May Reveal 1.6(b)(1)	Shall Not 1.6	May Reveal 1.6(b)(2)	Must Disclose 3.3(a)(2)
Oregon	May Reveal 1.6(b)(2)	May Reveal 1.6(b)(1)	Shall Not 1.6	Must Not 1.6	Must Disclose 3.3(b)

CONFIDENTIALITY CHART

Jurisdiction	To Prevent Serious Bodily Crime	To Prevent Non-Bodily Crime	To Prevent Non-Criminal Fraud	To Rectify Past Crime/Fraud When Lawyers Services Used	Fraud on Court
Pennsylvania	May Reveal 1.6(c)(1)	May Reveal 1.6(c)(2)	Shall Not 1.6	May Reveal 1.6(c)(3)	Must Disclose 3.3(b)(2), 1.6(b)
Rhode Island	May Reveal 1.6(b)(1)	Shall Not 1.6	Must Not 1.6	Must Not 1.6	Must Disclose 3.3(a)(2)
South Carolina	May Reveal 1.6(b)(2)	May Reveal 1.6(b)(1)	May Reveal 1.6(b)(3)	May Reveal 1.6(b)(4)	Must Disclose 3.3(b)(2)
South Dakota	May Reveal 1.6(b)(1)	Shall Not 1.6	Shall Not 1.6	May Reveal 1.6(b)(4)	Must Disclose 3.3(b)(2)
Tennessee	Shall Reveal information to prevent reasonably certain death or substantial bodily harm 1.6(c)(1)	May Reveal 1.6(b)(1)	Must Not Reveal confidential information except to withdraw from the representa-tion and give notice of withdrawal and disavow opinions and other legal work when a third person will continue to rely on them. 4.1(b), 1.6	Must Not Disclose confidential information except to withdraw from the representation and give notice of withdrawal and disaffirm opinions and other legal work when a third person will continue to rely on them. 4.1(c)	Must Not Disclose, except when fraud involves juror misconduct. Tenn. Rule 3.3 has many nuances for dissuading client from committing fraud and allowing for with-drawal. But generally the rule is extremely protective of client confi-dences.
Texas	Must Reveal 1.05(e)	May Reveal 1.05(c)(7)	May Reveal 1.05(c)(7)	May Reveal 1.05(c)(8)	Shall Disclose 3.03(a)(2)

CONFIDENTIALITY CHART

Jurisdiction	To Prevent Serious Bodily Crime	To Prevent Non-Bodily Crime	To Prevent Non-Criminal Fraud	To Rectify Past Crime/Fraud When Lawyers Services Used	Fraud on Court
Utah	May Reveal 1.6(b)(1)	May Reveal crimes likely to result in substantial injury to the financial interests or property of another 1.6(b)(2)	May Reveal non-criminal fraud likely to result in substantial injury to the financial interests or property of another 1.6(b)(3)	May Reveal 1.6(b)(2)	Must Disclose 3.3(b)
Vermont	Must Reveal 1.6(b)(1)	Must Reveal if failure to disclose a material fact to a third person would assist a criminal or fraudulent act by a client 1.6(b)(2)	Must Disclose if failure to disclose a material fact to a third person would assist a criminal or fraudulent act by a client 1.6(b)(2)	Must Not 1.6	Must Disclose 3.3(a)(2)
Virginia	Shall Promptly Reveal 1.6(c)(1)	Shall Promptly Reveal 1.6(c)(1)	Must Not 1.6	May Reveal 1.6(b)(3)	Shall Promptly Reveal 1.6(c)(2), 3.3(a)(2)
Washington	May Reveal 1.6(b)(1)	May Reveal 1.6(b)(1)	Shall Not 1.6	Shall Not 1.6	Shall Not Disclose fraud on the court when such information is protected by 1.6 confidentiality. 3.3(a)(2), 3.3(c)
West Virginia	May Reveal 1.6(b)(1)	May Reveal 1.6(b)(1)	Shall Not 1.6	Shall Not 1.6	Must Disclose 3.3(a)(2)

CONFIDENTIALITY CHART

Jurisdiction	To Prevent Serious Bodily Crime	To Prevent Non-Bodily Crime	To Prevent Non-Criminal Fraud	To Rectify Past Crime/Fraud When Lawyers Services Used	Fraud on Court
Wisconsin	Shall Reveal 20:1.6(b)	Shall Reveal to prevent substantial injury to financial interests or property of another 20:1.6(b)	Shall Reveal to prevent substantial injury to financial interests or property of another 20:1.6(b)	May Reveal 20:1.6(c)(1)	Must Disclose 20:3.3(a)(2)
Wyoming	May Reveal 1.6(b)(1)	May Reveal 1.6(b)(1)	Must Not 1.6	Must Not 1.6	Must Disclose 3.3(a)(2)

SELECTED SIGNIFICANT STATE MODIFICATIONS TO THE ABA MODEL RULES

The ABA Model Rules are designed to serve as a model for the states to consider and adopt. The enactment of the Model Rules caused most of the states to at least reconsider their local codes of ethics. As of the date of this publication, forty-seven states have replaced codes based upon the Model Code and have enacted codes based upon the structure and content of the Model Rules. Every one of these states has in some way amended the Model Rules provisions. Three states (New York, Oregon, and Virginia) have amended their version of the Model Code to reflect certain Model Rules' provisions. One state, California, did not base its code on the Model Code originally and refused to base a 1989 revision on the Model Rules.

In light of the many state modifications to the Model Rules, it is useful to examine selected significant state amendments. Some of these amendments illustrate substantive disagreements with the position adopted by the ABA in the Model Rules. Other modifications reflect local practices that the states have chosen to memorialize in the local code. Still other changes illustrate the desire to be more elaborative with respect to the language in the text. The selected state variations presented in this section fall within each of these categories.

The selected significant state modifications to the ABA Model Rules are presented under the order of the rules and within this framework by alphabetical order of the states. In the advertising section, however, the Arizona and Texas rules are grouped under each state. This section is intended to be illustrative and not exhaustive of the many state modifications. The comments to the state rule are included only if they are relevant to the rule that is illustrated.

TABLE OF CONTENTS

CLIENT-LAWYER RELATIONSHIP

Texas Rule 1.01 *(Modification of Model Rules 1.1 and 1.3)*

[Texas has combined Model Rule 1.1 (competence) and 1.3 (diligence) into one rule.]

RULE 1.01 Competent and Diligent Representation

(a) A lawyer shall not accept or continue employment in a legal matter which the lawyer knows or should know is beyond the lawyer's competence, unless:

(1) another lawyer who is competent to handle the matter is, with the prior informed consent of the client, associated in the matter; or

(2) the advice or assistance of the lawyer is reasonably required in an emergency and the lawyer limits the advice and assistance to that which is reasonably necessary in the circumstances.

(b) In representing a client, a lawyer shall not:

(1) neglect a legal matter entrusted to the lawyer; or

(2) frequently fail to carry out completely the obligations that the lawyer owes to a client or clients.

(c) As used in this Rule, "neglect" signifies inattentiveness involving a conscious disregard for the responsibilities owed to a client or clients.

COMMENT:

Accepting Employment

[1] A lawyer generally should not accept or continue employment in any area of the law in which the lawyer is not and will not be prepared to render competent legal services. "Competence" is defined in Terminology as possession of the legal knowledge, skill, and training reasonably necessary for the representation. Competent representation contemplates appropriate application by the lawyer of that legal knowledge, skill and training, reasonable thoroughness in the study and analysis of the law and facts, and reasonable attentiveness to the responsibilities owed to the client.

[2] In determining whether a matter is beyond a lawyer's competence, relevant factors include the relative complexity and specialized nature of the matter, the lawyer's general experience in the field in question, the preparation and study the lawyer will be able to give the matter, and whether it is feasible either to refer the matter to or associate a lawyer of established competence in the field in question. The required attention and preparation are determined in part by what is at stake; major litigation and complex transactions ordinarily require more elaborate treatment than matters of lesser consequences.

[3] A lawyer may not need to have special training or prior experience to accept employment to handle legal problems of a type with which the lawyer is unfamiliar. Although expertise in a particular field of law may be useful in some circumstances, the appropriate proficiency in many instances is that of a general practitioner. A newly admitted lawyer can be as competent in some matters as a practitioner with long experience. Some important legal skills, such as the analysis of precedent, the evaluation of evidence and legal drafting, are required in all legal problems. Perhaps the most fundamental legal skill consists of determining what kind of legal problems a situation may involve, a skill that necessarily transcends any particular specialized knowledge.

[4] A lawyer possessing the normal skill and training reasonably necessary for the representation of a client in an area of law is not subject to discipline for accepting employment in a matter in which, in order to represent the client properly, the lawyer must become more competent in regard to relevant legal knowledge by additional study and investigation. If the additional study and preparation will result in unusual delay or expense to the client, the lawyer should not accept employment except with the informed consent of the client.

[5] A lawyer offered employment or employed in a matter beyond the lawyer's competence generally must decline or withdraw from the employment or, with the prior informed consent of the client, associate a lawyer who is competent in the matter. Paragraph (a)(2) permits a lawyer, however, to give advice or assistance in an emergency in a matter even though the lawyer does not have the skill ordinarily required if referral to or consultation with another lawyer would be impractical and if the assistance is limited to that which is reasonably necessary in the circumstances.

Competent and Diligent Representation

[6] Having accepted employment, a lawyer should act with competence, commitment and dedication to the interest of the client and with zeal in advocacy upon the client's behalf. A lawyer should feel a moral or professional obligation to pursue a matter on behalf of a client with reasonable diligence and promptness despite opposition, obstruction or personal inconvenience to the lawyer. A lawyer's workload should be controlled so that each matter can be handled with diligence and competence. As provided in paragraph (a), an incompetent lawyer is subject to discipline.

Neglect

[7] Perhaps no professional shortcoming is more widely resented than procrastination. A client's interests often can be adversely affected by the passage of time or the change of conditions; in extreme instances, as when a lawyer overlooks a statute of limitations, the client's legal position may be destroyed. Under paragraph (b), a lawyer is subject to professional discipline for neglecting a particular legal matter as well as for frequent failures to carry out fully the obligations owed to one or more clients. A lawyer who acts in good faith is not subject to discipline, under those provisions for an isolated inadvertent or unskilled act or omission, tactical error, or error of judgment. Because delay can cause a client needless anxiety and

undermine confidence in the lawyer's trustworthiness, there is a duty to communicate reasonably with clients; see Rule 1.03.

Maintaining Competence

[8] Because of the vital role of lawyers in the legal process, each lawyer should strive to become and remain proficient and competent in the practice of law. To maintain the requisite knowledge and skill of a competent practitioner, a lawyer should engage in continuing study and education. If a system of peer review has been established, the lawyer should consider making use of it in appropriate circumstances. Isolated instances of faulty conduct or decision should be identified for purposes of additional study or instruction.

Michigan Rule 1.2

[Michigan has amended Model Rule 1.2(a) to read as follows:]

RULE 1.2 Scope of Representation

(a) A lawyer shall seek the lawful objectives of a client through reasonably available means permitted by law and these rules. A lawyer does not violate this rule by acceding to reasonable requests of opposing counsel that do not prejudice the rights of the client, by being punctual in fulfilling all professional commitments, by avoiding offensive tactics. A lawyer shall abide by a client's decision whether to accept an offer of settlement or mediation evaluation of a matter. In a criminal case, the lawyer shall abide by the client's decision, after consultation with the lawyer, as to a plea to be entered, whether to waive jury trial, and whether the client will testify. In representing a client, a lawyer may, where permissible, exercise professional judgment to waive or fail to assert a right or position of the client.

* * *

Florida Rule 4–1.5 *(Modification of Model Rule 1.5)*

[Florida has amended Model Rule 1.5 to read as follows:]

RULE 4–1.5 Fees and Costs for Legal Services

(a) Illegal, Prohibited, or Clearly Excessive Fees and Costs. An attorney shall not enter into an agreement for, charge, or collect an illegal, prohibited, or clearly excessive fee or cost or a fee generated by employment that was obtained through advertising or solicitation not in compliance with the Rules Regulating The Florida Bar. A fee or cost is clearly excessive when:

(1) after a review of the facts, a lawyer of ordinary prudence would be left with a definite and firm conviction that the fee or the cost exceeds a reasonable fee or cost for services provided to such a degree as to constitute clear overreaching or an unconscionable demand by the attorney; or

(2) the fee or cost is sought or secured by the attorney by means of intentional misrepresentation or fraud upon the client, a nonclient party, or any court, as to either entitlement to, or amount of, the fee.

(b) Factors to Be Considered in Determining Reasonable Fee and Costs.

(1) Factors to be considered as guides in determining a reasonable fee include:

(A) the time and labor required, the novelty, complexity, and difficulty of the questions involved, and the skill requisite to perform the legal service properly;

(B) the likelihood that the acceptance of the particular employment will preclude other employment by the lawyer;

(C) the fee, or rate of fee, customarily charged in the locality for legal services of a comparable or similar nature;

(D) the significance of, or amount involved in, the subject matter of the representation, the responsibility involved in the representation, and the results obtained;

(E) the time limitations imposed by the client or by the circumstances and, as between attorney and client, any additional or special time demands or requests of the attorney by the client;

(F) the nature and length of the professional relationship with the client;

(G) the experience, reputation, diligence, and ability of the lawyer or lawyers performing the service and the skill, expertise, or efficiency of effort reflected in the actual providing of such services; and

(H) whether the fee is fixed or contingent, and, if fixed as to amount or rate, then whether the client's ability to pay rested to any significant degree on the outcome of the representation.

(2) Factors to be considered as guides in determining reasonable costs include:

(A) the nature and extent of the disclosure made to the client about the costs;

(B) whether a specific agreement exists between the lawyer and client as to the costs a client is expected to pay and how a cost is calculated that is charged to a client;

(C) the actual amount charged by third party provider of services to the attorney;

(D) whether specific costs can be identified and allocated to an individual client or a reasonable basis exists to estimate the costs charged;

(E) in-house service to a client if the cost is an in-house charge for services; and

(F) the relationship and past course of conduct between the lawyer and the client.

All costs are subject to the test of reasonableness set forth in subdivision (a) above. When the parties have a written contract in which the method is established for charging costs, the costs charged thereunder shall be presumed reasonable.

(c) Consideration of All Factors. In determining a reasonable fee, the time devoted to the representation and customary rate of fee need not be the sole or controlling factors. All factors set forth in this rule should be considered, and may be applied, in justification of a fee higher or lower than that which would result from application of only the time and rate factors.

(d) Enforceability of Fee Contracts. Contracts or agreements for attorney's fees between attorney and client will ordinarily be enforceable according to the terms of such contracts or agreements, unless found to be illegal, obtained through advertising or solicitation not in compliance with the Rules Regulating The Florida Bar, prohibited by this rule, or clearly excessive as defined by this rule.

(e) Duty to Communicate Basis or Rate of Fee or Costs to Client and Definitions.

(1) Duty to Communicate. When the lawyer has not regularly represented the client, the basis or rate of the fee and costs shall be communicated to the client, preferably in writing, before or within a reasonable time after commencing the representation. A fee for legal services that is nonrefundable in any part shall be confirmed in writing and shall explain the intent of the parties as to the nature and amount of the nonrefundable fee. The test of reasonableness found in subdivision (b), above, applies to all fees for legal services without regard to their characterization by the parties.

The fact that a contract may not be in accord with these rules is an issue between the attorney and client and a matter of professional ethics, but is not the proper basis for an action or defense by an opposing party when fee-shifting litigation is involved.

(2) Definitions.

(A) Retainer. A retainer is a sum of money paid to a lawyer to guarantee the lawyer's future availability. A retainer is not payment for past legal services and is not payment for future services.

(B) Flat Fee. A flat fee is a sum of money paid to a lawyer for all legal services to be provided in the representation. A flat fee may be termed "non-refundable."

(C) Advance Fee. An advanced fee is a sum of money paid to the lawyer against which the lawyer will bill the client as legal services are provided.

(f) Contingent Fees. As to contingent fees:

(1) A fee may be contingent on the outcome of the matter for which the service is rendered, except in a matter in which a contingent fee is prohibited by paragraph (f)(3) or by law. A contingent fee agreement shall be in writing and shall state the method by which the fee is to be determined, including the percentage or percentages that shall accrue to the lawyer in the event of settlement, trial, or appeal, litigation and other expenses to be deducted from the recovery, and whether such expenses are to be deducted before or after the contingent fee is calculated. Upon conclusion of a contingent fee matter, the lawyer shall provide the client with a written statement stating the outcome of the matter and, if there is a recovery, showing the remittance to the client and the method of its determination.

(2) Every lawyer who accepts a retainer or enters into an agreement, express or implied, for compensation for services rendered or to be rendered in any action, claim, or proceeding whereby the lawyer's compensation is to be dependent or contingent in whole or in part upon the successful prosecution or settlement thereof shall do so only where such fee arrangement is reduced to a written contract, signed by the client, and by a lawyer for the lawyer or for the law firm representing the client. No lawyer or firm may participate in the fee without the consent of the client in writing. Each participating lawyer or law firm shall sign the contract with the client and shall agree to assume joint legal responsibility to the client for the performance of the services in question as if each were partners of the other lawyer or law firm involved. The client shall be furnished with a copy of the signed contract and any subsequent notices or consents. All provisions of this rule shall apply to such fee contracts.

(3) A lawyer shall not enter into an arrangement for, charge, or collect:

(A) any fee in a domestic relations matter, the payment or amount of which is contingent upon the securing of a divorce or upon the amount of alimony or support, or property settlement in lieu thereof; or

(B) a contingent fee for representing a defendant in a criminal case.

(4) A lawyer who enters into an arrangement for, charges, or collects any fee in an action or claim for personal injury or for property damages or for death or loss of services resulting from personal injuries based upon tortious conduct of another, including products liability claims, whereby the compensation is to be dependent or contingent in whole or in part upon the successful prosecution or settlement thereof shall do so only under the following requirements:

(A) The contract shall contain the following provisions:

(i) "The undersigned client has, before signing this contract, received and read the statement of client's rights and understands each of the rights set forth

therein. The undersigned client has signed the statement and received a signed copy to refer to while being represented by the undersigned attorney(s)."

(ii) "This contract may be cancelled by written notification to the attorney at any time within 3 business days of the date the contract was signed, as shown below, and if cancelled the client shall not be obligated to pay any fees to the attorney for the work performed during that time. If the attorney has advanced funds to others in representation of the client, the attorney is entitled to be reimbursed for such amounts as the attorney has reasonably advanced on behalf of the client."

(B) The contract for representation of a client in a matter set forth in subdivision (f)(4) may provide for a contingent fee arrangement as agreed upon by the client and the lawyer, except as limited by the following provisions:

(i) Without prior court approval as specified below, any contingent fee that exceeds the following standards shall be presumed, unless rebutted, to be clearly excessive:

a. Before the filing of an answer or the demand for appointment of arbitrators or, if no answer is filed or no demand for appointment of arbitrators is made, the expiration of the time period provided for such action:

1. 33–1/3% of any recovery up to $1 million; plus

2. 30% of any portion of the recovery between $1 million and $2 million; plus

3. 20% of any portion of the recovery exceeding $2 million.

b. After the filing of an answer or the demand for appointment of arbitrators or, if no answer is filed or no demand for appointment of arbitrators is made, the expiration of the time period provided for such action, through the entry of judgment.

1. 40% of any recovery up to $1 million; plus

2. 30% of any portion of the recovery between $1 million and $2 million; plus

3. 20% of any portion of the recovery exceeding $2 million.

c. If all defendants admit liability at the time of filing their answers and request a trial only on damages:

1. 33⅓% of any recovery up to $1 million; plus

2. 20% of any portion of the recovery between $1 million and $2 million; plus

3. 15% of any portion of the recovery for any amount exceeding $2 million.

d. An additional 5% of any recovery after notice of appeal is filed or post-judgment relief or action is required for recovery on the judgment.

(ii) If any client is unable to obtain an attorney of the client's choice because of the limitations set forth in (f)(4)(B)(i), the client may petition the court in which the matter would be filed, if litigation is necessary, or if such court will not accept jurisdiction for the fee division, the circuit court wherein the cause of action arose, for approval of any fee contract between the client and an attorney of the client's choosing. Such authorization shall be given if the court determines the client has a complete understanding of the client's rights and the terms of the proposed contract. The application for authorization of such a contract can be filed as a separate proceeding before suit or simultaneously with the filing of a complaint. Proceedings thereon may occur before service on the defendant and

this aspect of the file may be sealed. A petition under this subdivision shall contain a certificate showing service on the client and, if the petition is denied, a copy of the petition and order denying the petition shall be served on The Florida Bar in Tallahassee by the member of the bar who has filed the petition. Authorization of such a contract shall not bar subsequent inquiry as to whether the fee actually claimed or charged is clearly excessive under subdivisions (a) and (b).

(iii) Subject to the provisions of 4–1.5(f)(4)(B)(i) and (ii) a lawyer who enters into an arrangement for, charges, or collects any fee in an action or claim for medical liability whereby the compensation is dependent or contingent in whole or in part upon the successful prosecution or settlement thereof shall provide the language of article I, section 26 of the Florida Constitution to the client in writing and shall orally inform the client that:

a. Unless waived, in any medical liability claim involving a contingency fee, the claimant is entitled to receive no less than 70% of the first $250,000.00 of all damages received by the claimant, exclusive of reasonable and customary costs, whether received by judgment, settlement, or otherwise, and regardless of the number of defendants. The claimant is entitled to 90% of all damages in excess of $250,000.00, exclusive of reasonable and customary costs and regardless of the number of defendants.

b. If a lawyer chooses not to accept the representation of a client under the terms of article I, section 26 of the Florida Constitution, the lawyer shall advise the client, both orally and in writing of alternative terms, if any, under which the lawyer would accept the representation of the client, as well as the client's right to seek representation by another lawyer willing to accept the representation under the terms of article I, section 26 of the Florida Constitution, or a lawyer willing to accept the representation on a fee basis that is not contingent.

c. If any client desires to waive any rights under article I, section 26 of the Florida Constitution in order to obtain a lawyer of the client's choice, a client may do so by waiving such rights in writing, under oath, and in the form provided in this rule. The lawyer shall provide each client a copy of the written waiver and shall afford each client a full and complete opportunity to understand the rights being waived as set forth in the waiver. A copy of the waiver, signed by each client and lawyer, shall be given to each client to retain, and the lawyer shall keep a copy in the lawyer's file pertaining to the client. The waiver shall be retained by the lawyer with the written fee contract and closing statement under the same conditions and requirements provided in 4–1.5(f)(5).

WAIVER OF THE CONSTITUTIONAL RIGHT PROVIDED IN ARTICLE I, SECTION 26 OF THE FLORIDA CONSTITUTION

On November 2, 2004, voters in the State of Florida approved The Medical Liability Claimant's Compensation Amendment that was identified as Amendment 3 on the ballot. The amendment is set forth below:

The Florida Constitution

Article I, Section 26 is created to read "Claimant's right to fair compensation." In any medical liability claim involving a contingency fee, the claimant is entitled to receive no less than 70% of the first $250,000 in all damages received by the claimant, exclusive of reasonable and customary costs, whether received by judgment, settlement or otherwise, and regardless of the number of defendants. The claimant is entitled to 90% of all damages in excess of $250,000, exclusive of reasonable and customary costs and regardless of the number of defendants. This provision is self-executing and does not require implementing legislation.

The undersigned client understands and acknowledges that (initial each provision):

______ I have been advised that signing this waiver releases an important constitutional right; and

______ I have been advised that I may consult with separate counsel before signing this waiver; and that I may request a hearing before a judge to further explain this waiver; and

______ By signing this waiver I agree to an increase in the attorney fee that might otherwise be owed if the constitutional provision listed above is not waived. Without prior court approval, the increased fee that I agree to may be up to the maximum contingency fee percentages set forth in Rule Regulating The Florida Bar 4–1.5(f)(4)(B)(i). Depending on the circumstances of my case, the maximum agreed upon fee may range from 33 1/3% to 40% of any recovery up to $1 million; plus 20% to 30% of any portion of the recovery between $1 million and $2 million; plus 15% to 20% of any recovery exceeding $2 million; and

______ I have three (3) business days following execution of this waiver in which to cancel this waiver; and

______ I wish to engage the legal services of the lawyers or law firms listed below in an action or claim for medical liability the fee for which is contingent in whole or in part upon the successful prosecution or settlement thereof, but I am unable to do so because of the provisions of the constitutional limitation set forth above. In consideration of the lawyers' or law firms' agreements to represent me and my desire to employ the lawyers or law firms listed below, I hereby knowingly, willingly, and voluntarily waive any and all rights and privileges that I may have under the constitutional provision set forth above, as apply to the contingency fee agreement only. Specifically, I waive the percentage restrictions that are the subject of the constitutional provision and confirm the fee percentages set forth in the contingency fee agreement; and

______ I have selected the lawyers or law firms listed below as my counsel of choice in this matter and would not be able to engage their services without this waiver; and I expressly state that this waiver is made freely and voluntarily, with full knowledge of its terms, and that all questions have been answered to my satisfaction.

ACKNOWLEDGMENT BY CLIENT FOR PRESENTATION TO THE COURT

The undersigned client hereby acknowledges, under oath, the following:

I have read and understand this entire waiver of my rights under the constitutional provision set forth above.

I am not under the influence of any substance, drug, or condition (physical, mental, or emotional) that interferes with my understanding of this entire waiver in which I am entering and all the consequences thereof.

I have entered into and signed this waiver freely and voluntarily.

I authorize my lawyers or law firms listed below to present this waiver to the appropriate court, if required for purposes of approval of the contingency fee agreement. Unless the court requires my attendance at a hearing for that purpose, my lawyers or law firms are authorized to provide this waiver to the court for its consideration without my presence.

DATED this ___ day of ______, ___.

By: ______

CLIENT

Sworn to and subscribed before me this ___ day of ______, ___ by ______, who is personally known to me, or has produced the following identification: ______.

______

______

Notary Public

My Commission Expires:

Dated this ___ day of ______, ___.

By: ______

ATTORNEY

(C) Before a lawyer enters into a contingent fee contract for representation of a client in a matter set forth in this rule, the lawyer shall provide the client with a copy of the statement of client's rights and shall afford the client a full and complete opportunity to understand each of the rights as set forth therein. A copy of the statement, signed by both the client and the lawyer, shall be given to the client to retain and the lawyer shall keep a copy in the client's file. The statement shall be retained by the lawyer with the written fee contract and closing statement under the same conditions and requirements as subdivision (f)(5).

(D) As to lawyers not in the same firm, a division of any fee within subdivision (f)(4) shall be on the following basis:

(i) To the lawyer assuming primary responsibility for the legal services on behalf of the client, a minimum of 75% of the total fee.

(ii) To the lawyer assuming secondary responsibility for the legal services on behalf of the client, a maximum of 25% of the total fee. Any fee in excess of 25% shall be presumed to be clearly excessive.

(iii) The 25% limitation shall not apply to those cases in which 2 or more lawyers or firms accept substantially equal active participation in the providing of legal services. In such circumstances counsel shall apply to the court in which the matter would be filed, if litigation is necessary, or if such court will not accept jurisdiction for the fee division, the circuit court wherein the cause of action arose, for authorization of the fee division in excess of 25%, based upon a sworn petition signed by all counsel that shall disclose in detail those services to be performed. The application for authorization of such a contract may be filed as a separate proceeding before suit or simultaneously with the filing of a complaint, or within 10 days of execution of a contract for division of fees when new counsel is engaged. Proceedings thereon may occur before service of process on any party and this aspect of the file may be sealed. Authorization of such contract shall not bar subsequent inquiry as to whether the fee actually claimed or charged is clearly excessive. An application under this subdivision shall contain a certificate showing service on the client and, if the application is denied, a copy of the petition and order denying the petition shall be served on The Florida Bar in Tallahassee by the member of the bar who filed the petition. Counsel may proceed with representation of the client pending court approval.

(iv) The percentages required by this subdivision shall be applicable after deduction of any fee payable to separate counsel retained especially for appellate purposes.

(5) In the event there is a recovery, upon the conclusion of the representation, the lawyer shall prepare a closing statement reflecting an itemization of all costs and expenses, together with the amount of fee received by each participating lawyer or law firm. A copy of the closing statement shall be executed by all participating lawyers, as well as the client, and each shall receive a copy. Each participating lawyer shall retain a copy of the written fee contract and closing statement for 6 years after execution of the closing statement. Any contingent fee contract and closing statement shall be available for inspection at reasonable times by the client, by any other person upon judicial order, or by the appropriate disciplinary agency.

(6) In cases in which the client is to receive a recovery that will be paid to the client on a future structured or periodic basis, the contingent fee percentage shall be calculated only on the cost of the structured verdict or settlement or, if the cost is unknown, on the present money value of the structured verdict or settlement, whichever is less. If the damages and the fee are to be paid out over the long term future schedule, this limitation does not apply. No attorney may negotiate separately with the defendant for that attorney's fee in a structured verdict or settlement when such separate negotiations would place the attorney in a position of conflict.

(g) Division of Fees Between Lawyers in Different Firms. Subject to the provisions of subdivision (f)(4)(D), a division of fee between lawyers who are not in the same firm may be made only if the total fee is reasonable and:

(1) the division is in proportion to the services performed by each lawyer; or

(2) by written agreement with the client:

(A) each lawyer assumes joint legal responsibility for the representation and agrees to be available for consultation with the client; and

(B) the agreement fully discloses that a division of fees will be made and the basis upon which the division of fees will be made.

(h) Credit Plans. A lawyer or law firm may accept payment under a credit plan. No higher fee shall be charged and no additional charge shall be imposed by reason of a lawyer's or law firm's participation in an approved credit plan.

(i) Arbitration Clauses. A lawyer shall not make an agreement with a potential client prospectively providing for mandatory arbitration of fee disputes without first advising that person in writing that the potential client should consider obtaining independent legal advice as to the advisability of entering into an agreement containing such mandatory arbitration provisions. A lawyer shall not make an agreement containing such mandatory arbitration provisions unless the agreement contains the following language in bold print:

NOTICE: This agreement contains provisions requiring arbitration of fee disputes. Before you sign this agreement you should consider consulting with another lawyer about the advisability of making an agreement with mandatory arbitration requirements. Arbitration proceedings are ways to resolve disputes without use of the court system. By entering into agreements that require arbitration as the way to resolve fee disputes, you give up (waive) your right to go to court to resolve those disputes by a judge or jury. These are important rights that should not be given up without careful consideration.

STATEMENT OF CLIENT'S RIGHTS FOR CONTINGENCY FEES

Before you, the prospective client, arrange a contingent fee agreement with a lawyer, you should understand this statement of your rights as a client. This statement is not a part of the actual contract between you and your lawyer, but, as a prospective client, you should be aware of these rights:

1. There is no legal requirement that a lawyer charge a client a set fee or a percentage of money recovered in a case. You, the client, have the right to talk with your lawyer about the proposed fee and to bargain about the rate or percentage as in any other contract. If you do not reach an agreement with one lawyer you may talk with other lawyers.

2. Any contingent fee contract must be in writing and you have 3 business days to reconsider the contract. You may cancel the contract without any reason if you notify your lawyer in writing within 3 business days of signing the contract. If you withdraw from the contract within the first 3 business days, you do not owe the lawyer a fee although you may be responsible for the lawyer's actual costs during that time. If your lawyer begins to represent you, your lawyer may not withdraw from the case without giving you notice, delivering necessary papers to you, and allowing you time to employ another lawyer. Often, your lawyer must obtain court approval before withdrawing from a case. If you discharge your lawyer without good cause after the 3-day period, you may have to pay a fee for work the lawyer has done.

3. Before hiring a lawyer, you, the client, have the right to know about the lawyer's education, training, and experience. If you ask, the lawyer should tell you specifically about the lawyer's actual experience dealing with cases similar to yours. If you ask, the lawyer should provide information about special training or knowledge and give you this information in writing if you request it.

4. Before signing a contingent fee contract with you, a lawyer must advise you whether the lawyer intends to handle your case alone or whether other lawyers will be helping with the case. If your lawyer intends to refer the case to other lawyers, the lawyer should tell you what kind of fee sharing arrangement will be made with the other lawyers. If lawyers from different law firms will represent you, at least 1 lawyer from each law firm must sign the contingent fee contract.

5. If your lawyer intends to refer your case to another lawyer or counsel with other lawyers, your lawyer should tell you about that at the beginning. If your lawyer takes the case and later decides to refer it to another lawyer or to associate with other lawyers, you should sign a new contract that includes the new lawyers. You, the client, also have the right to consult with each lawyer working on your case and each lawyer is legally responsible to represent your interests and is legally responsible for the acts of the other lawyers involved in the case.

6. You, the client, have the right to know in advance how you will need to pay the expenses and the legal fees at the end of the case. If you pay a deposit in advance for costs, you may ask reasonable questions about how the money will be or has been spent and how much of it remains unspent. Your lawyer should give a reasonable estimate about future necessary costs. If your lawyer agrees to lend or advance you money to prepare or research the case, you have the right to know periodically how much money your lawyer has spent on your behalf. You also have the right to decide, after consulting with your lawyer, how much money is to be spent to prepare a case. If you pay the expenses, you have the right to decide how much to spend. Your lawyer should also inform you whether the fee will be based on the gross amount recovered or on the amount recovered minus the costs.

7. You, the client, have the right to be told by your lawyer about possible adverse consequences if you lose the case. Those adverse consequences might include money that you might have to pay to your lawyer for costs and liability you might have for attorney's fees to the other side.

8. You, the client, have the right to receive and approve a closing statement at the end of the case before you pay any money. The statement must list all of the financial details of the entire case, including the amount recovered, all expenses, and a precise statement of your lawyer's fee. Until you approve the closing statement your lawyer cannot pay money to anyone, including you, without an appropriate order of the court. You also have the right to have every lawyer or law firm working on your case sign this closing statement.

9. You, the client, have the right to ask your lawyer at reasonable intervals how the case is progressing and to have these questions answered to the best of your lawyer's ability.

10. You, the client, have the right to make the final decision regarding settlement of a case. Your lawyer must notify you of all offers of settlement before and after the trial. Offers during the trial must be immediately communicated and you should consult with your lawyer regarding whether to accept a settlement. However, you must make the final decision to accept or reject a settlement.

11. If at any time you, the client, believe that your lawyer has charged an excessive or illegal fee, you have the right to report the matter to The Florida Bar, the agency that oversees the practice and behavior of all lawyers in Florida. For information on how to reach The Florida Bar, call 850–561–5600, or contact the local bar association. Any disagreement between you and your lawyer about a fee can be taken to court and you may wish to hire another lawyer to help you resolve this disagreement. Usually fee disputes must be handled in a separate lawsuit unless your fee contract provides for arbitration. You can request, but may not require, that a provision for arbitration (under chapter 682, Florida Statutes, or under the fee arbitration rule of the Rules Regulating The Florida Bar) be included in your fee contract.

______________________	______________________
Client Signature	Attorney Signature
______________________	______________________
Date	Date

COMMENT:

Bases or rate of fees and costs

When the lawyer has regularly represented a client, they ordinarily will have evolved an understanding concerning the basis or rate of the fee. The conduct of the lawyer and client in prior relationships is relevant when analyzing the requirements of this rule. In a new client-lawyer relationship, however, an understanding as to the fee should be promptly established. It is not necessary to recite all the factors that underlie the basis of the fee but only those that are directly involved in its computation. It is sufficient, for example, to state the basic rate is an hourly charge or a fixed amount or an estimated amount, or to identify the factors that may be taken into account in finally fixing the fee. Although hourly billing or a fixed fee may be the most common bases for computing fees in an area of practice, these may not be the only bases for computing fees. A lawyer should, where appropriate, discuss alternative billing methods with the client. When developments occur during the representation that render an earlier estimate substantially inaccurate, a revised estimate should be provided to the client. A written statement concerning the fee reduces the possibility of misunderstanding. Furnishing the client with a simple memorandum or a copy of the lawyer's customary fee schedule is sufficient if the basis or rate of the fee is set forth.

General overhead should be accounted for in a lawyer's fee, whether the lawyer charges hourly, flat, or contingent fees. Filing fees, transcription, and the like should be charged to the client at the actual amount paid by the lawyer. A lawyer may agree with the client to charge a reasonable amount for in-house costs or services. In-house costs include items such as copying, faxing, long distance telephone, and computerized research. In-house services include paralegal services, investigative services, accounting services, and courier services. The lawyer should sufficiently communicate with the client regarding the costs charged to the client so that the client understands the amount of costs being charged or the method for calculation of those costs. Costs appearing in sufficient detail on closing statements and approved by the parties to the transaction should meet the requirements of this rule.

Rule 4–1.8(e) should be consulted regarding a lawyer's providing financial assistance to a client in connection with litigation.

In order to avoid misunderstandings concerning the nature of legal fees, written documentation is required when any aspect of the fee is nonrefundable. A written contract provides a method to resolve misunderstandings and to protect the lawyer in the event of continued misunderstanding. Rule 4–1.5(e) does not require the client to sign a written document memorializing the terms of the fee. A letter from the lawyer to the client setting forth the basis or rate of the fee and the intent of the parties in regard to the nonrefundable nature of the fee is sufficient to meet the requirements of this rule.

All legal fees and contracts for legal fees are subject to the requirements of the Rules Regulating The Florida Bar. In particular, the test for reasonableness of legal fees found in rule 4–1.5(b) applies to all types of legal fees and contracts related to them.

Terms of payment

A lawyer may require advance payment of a fee but is obliged to return any unearned portion. See rule 4–1.16(d). A lawyer is not, however, required to return retainers that, pursuant to an agreement with a client, are not refundable. A nonrefundable retainer or nonrefundable flat fee is the property of the lawyer and should not be held in trust. If a client gives the lawyer a negotiable instrument that represents both an advance on costs plus either a nonrefundable retainer or a nonrefundable flat fee, the entire amount should be deposited into the lawyer's trust account, then the portion representing the earned nonrefundable retainer or nonrefundable flat fee should be withdrawn within a reasonable time. An advance fee must be held in trust until it is earned. Nonrefundable fees are, as all fees, subject to the prohibition against excessive fees.

A lawyer may accept property in payment for services, such as an ownership interest in an enterprise, providing this does not involve acquisition of a proprietary interest in the cause of action or subject matter of the litigation contrary to rule 4–1.8(i). However, a fee paid in property instead of money may be subject to special scrutiny because it involves questions concerning both the value of the services and the lawyer's special knowledge of the value of the property.

An agreement may not be made whose terms might induce the lawyer improperly to curtail services for the client or perform them in a way contrary to the client's interest. For example, a lawyer should not enter into an agreement whereby services are to be provided only up to a stated amount when it is foreseeable that more extensive services probably will be required, unless the situation is adequately explained to the client. Otherwise, the client might have to bargain for further assistance in the midst of a proceeding or transaction. However, it is proper to define the extent of services in light of the client's ability to pay. A lawyer should not exploit a fee arrangement based primarily on hourly charges by using wasteful procedures. When there is doubt whether a contingent fee is consistent with the client's best interest, the lawyer should offer the client alternative bases for the fee and explain their implications. Applicable law may impose limitations on contingent fees, such as a ceiling on the percentage.

Prohibited contingent fees

Subdivision (f)(3)(A) prohibits a lawyer from charging a contingent fee in a domestic relations matter when payment is contingent upon the securing of a divorce or upon the amount of alimony or support or property settlement to be obtained. This provision does not preclude a contract for a contingent fee for legal representation in connection with the recovery of post-judgment balances due under support, alimony, or other financial orders because such contracts do not implicate the same policy concerns.

Contingent fees are prohibited in criminal and certain domestic relations matters. In domestic relations cases, fees that include a bonus provision or additional fee to be determined at a later time and based on results obtained have been held to be impermissible contingency fees and therefore subject to restitution and disciplinary sanction as elsewhere stated in these Rules Regulating The Florida Bar.

Contingent fee regulation

Subdivision (e) is intended to clarify that whether the lawyer' s fee contract complies with these rules is a matter between the lawyer and client and an issue for professional disciplinary enforcement. The rules and subdivision (e) are not intended to be used as procedural weapons or defenses by others. Allowing opposing parties to assert noncompliance with these rules as a defense, including whether the fee is fixed or contingent, allows for potential inequity if the opposing party is allowed to escape responsibility for their actions solely through application of these rules.

Rule 4–1.5(f)(4) should not be construed to apply to actions or claims seeking property or other damages arising in the commercial litigation context.

Rule 4–1.5(f)(4)(B) is intended to apply only to contingent aspects of fee agreements. In the situation where a lawyer and client enter a contract for part noncontingent and part contingent attorney's fees, rule 4–1.5(f)(4)(B) should not be construed to apply to and prohibit or limit the noncontingent portion of the fee agreement. An attorney could properly charge and retain the noncontingent portion of the fee even if the matter was not successfully prosecuted or if the noncontingent portion of the fee exceeded the schedule set forth in rule 4–1.5(f)(4)(B). Rule 4–1.5(f)(4)(B) should, however, be construed to apply to any additional contingent portion of such a contract when considered together with earned noncontingent fees. Thus, under such a contract a lawyer may demand or collect only such additional contingent fees as would not cause the total fees to exceed the schedule set forth in rule 4–1.5(f)(4)(B).

The limitations in rule 4–1.5(f)(4)(B)(i)c are only to be applied in the case where all the defendants admit liability at the time they file their initial answer and the trial is only on the issue of the amount or extent of the loss or the extent of injury suffered by the client. If the trial involves not only the issue of damages but also such questions as proximate cause, affirmative defenses, seat belt defense, or other similar matters, the limitations are not to be applied because of the contingent nature of the case being left for resolution by the trier of fact.

Rule 4–1.5(f)(4)(B)(ii) provides the limitations set forth in subdivision (f)(4)(B)(i) may be waived by the client upon approval by the appropriate judge. This waiver provision may not be used to authorize a lawyer to charge a client a fee that would exceed rule 4–1.5(a) or (b). It is contemplated that this waiver provision will not be necessary except where the client wants to retain a particular lawyer to represent the client or the case involves complex, difficult, or novel questions of law or fact that would justify a contingent fee greater than the schedule but not a contingent fee that would exceed rule 4–1.5(b).

Upon a petition by a client, the trial court reviewing the waiver request must grant that request if the trial court finds the client: (a) understands the right to have the limitations in rule 4–1.5(f)(4)(B) applied in the specific matter; and (b) understands and approves the terms of the proposed contract. The consideration by the trial court of the waiver petition is not to be used as an opportunity for the court to inquire into the merits or details of the particular action or claim that is the subject of the contract.

The proceedings before the trial court and the trial court's decision on a waiver request are to be confidential and not subject to discovery by any of the parties to the action or by any other individual or entity except The Florida Bar. However, terms of the contract approved by the trial court may be subject to discovery if the contract (without court approval) was subject to discovery under applicable case law or rules of evidence.

Rule 4–1.5(f)(4)(B)(iii) is added to acknowledge the provisions of article 1, section 26 of the Florida Constitution, and to create an affirmative obligation on the part of an attorney contemplating a contingency fee contract to notify a potential client with a medical liability claim of the limitations provided in that constitutional provision. This addition to the rule is adopted prior to any judicial interpretation of the meaning or scope of the constitutional provision and this rule is not intended to make any substantive interpretation of the meaning or scope of that provision. The rule also provides that a client who wishes to waive the rights of the constitutional provision, as those rights may relate to attorney's fees, must do so in the form contained in the rule.

Rule 4–1.5(f)(6) prohibits a lawyer from charging the contingent fee percentage on the total, future value of a recovery being paid on a structured or periodic basis. This prohibition does not apply if the lawyer's fee is being paid over the same length of time as the schedule of payments to the client.

Fees that provide for a bonus or additional fees and that otherwise are not prohibited under the Rules Regulating the Florida Bar can be effective tools for structuring fees. For example, a fee contract calling for a flat fee and the payment of a bonus based on the amount of property retained or recovered in a general civil action is not prohibited by these rules. However, the bonus or additional fee must be stated clearly in amount or formula for calculation of the fee (basis or rate). Courts have held that unilateral bonus fees are unenforceable. The test of reasonableness and other requirements of this rule apply to permissible bonus fees.

Division of fee

A division of fee is a single billing to a client covering the fee of 2 or more lawyers who are not in the same firm. A division of fee facilitates association of more than 1 lawyer in a matter in which neither alone could serve the client as well, and most often is used when the fee is contingent and the division is between a referring lawyer and a trial specialist. Subject to the provisions of subdivision (f)(4)(D), subdivision (g) permits the lawyers to divide a fee on either the basis of the proportion of services they render or by agreement between the participating lawyers if all assume responsibility for the representation as a whole and the client is advised and does not object. It does require disclosure to the client of the share that each lawyer is to receive. Joint responsibility for the representation entails the obligations stated in rule 4–5.1 for purposes of the matter involved.

Disputes over fees

Since the fee arbitration rule (Chapter 14) has been established by the bar to provide a procedure for resolution of fee disputes, the lawyer should conscientiously consider submitting to it. Where law prescribes a procedure for determining a lawyer's fee, for example, in representation of an executor or administrator, a class, or a person entitled to a reasonable fee as part of the measure of damages, the lawyer entitled to such a fee and a lawyer representing another party concerned with the fee should comply with the prescribed procedure.

Referral fees and practices

A secondary lawyer shall not be entitled to a fee greater than the limitation set forth in rule 4–1.5(f)(4)(D)(ii) merely because the lawyer agrees to do some or all of the following: (a) consults with the client; (b) answers interrogatories; (c) attends depositions; (d) reviews pleadings; (e) attends the trial; or (f) assumes joint legal responsibility to the client. However, the provisions do not contemplate that a secondary lawyer who does more than the above is necessarily entitled to a larger percentage of the fee than that allowed by the limitation.

The provisions of rule 4–1.5(f)(4)(D)(iii) only apply where the participating lawyers have for purposes of the specific case established a co-counsel relationship. The need for court approval of a referral fee arrangement under rule 4–1.5(f)(4)(D)(iii) should only occur in a small percentage of cases arising under rule 4–1.5(f)(4) and usually occurs prior to the commencement of litigation or at the onset of the representation. However, in those cases in which litigation has been commenced or the representation has already begun, approval of the fee division should be sought within a reasonable period of time after the need for court approval of the fee division arises.

In determining if a co-counsel relationship exists, the court should look to see if the lawyers have established a special partnership agreement for the purpose of the specific case or matter. If such an agreement does exist, it must provide for a sharing of services or responsibility and the fee division is based upon a division of the services to be rendered or the responsibility assumed. It is contemplated that a co-counsel situation would exist where a division of responsibility is based upon, but not limited to, the following: (a) based upon geographic considerations, the lawyers agree to divide the legal work, responsibility, and representation in a convenient fashion. Such a situation would occur when different aspects of a case must be handled in different locations; (b) where the lawyers agree to divide the legal work and representation based upon their particular expertise in the substantive areas of law involved in the litigation; or (c) where the lawyers agree to divide the legal work and representation along established lines of division, such as liability and damages, causation and damages, or other similar factors.

The trial court's responsibility when reviewing an application for authorization of a fee division under rule 4–1.5(f)(4)(D)(iii) is to determine if a co-counsel relationship exists in that particular case. If the court determines a co-counsel relationship exists and authorizes the fee division requested, the court does not have any responsibility to review or approve the specific amount of the fee division agreed upon by the lawyers and the client.

Rule 4–1.5(f)(4)(D)(iv) applies to the situation where appellate counsel is retained during the trial of the case to assist with the appeal of the case. The percentages set forth in subdivision (f)(4)(D) are to be applicable after appellate counsel's fee is established. However, the effect should not be to impose an unreasonable fee on the client.

Credit plans

Credit plans include credit cards. If a lawyer accepts payment from a credit plan for an advance of fees and costs, the amount must be held in trust in accordance with chapter 5, Rules Regulating The Florida Bar, and the lawyer must add the lawyer's own money to the trust account in an amount equal to the amount charged by the credit plan for doing business with the credit plan.

Kansas Rule 1.5

[Kansas has substituted the following provisions for Model Rule 1.5(c) through (e):]

RULE 1.5

(c) A lawyer's fee shall be reasonable but a court determination that a fee is not reasonable shall not be presumptive evidence of a violation that requires discipline of the attorney.

(d) A fee may be contingent on the outcome of the matter for which the service is rendered, except in a matter in which a contingent fee is prohibited by paragraph (f) or other law. A contingent fee agreement shall be in writing and shall state the method by which the fee is to be determined, including the percentage or percentages that shall accrue to the lawyer in the event of settlement, trial or appeal, and the litigation and other expenses to be deducted from the recovery. All such expenses shall be deducted before the contingent fee is calculated. Upon conclusion of a contingent fee matter, the lawyer shall provide the client with a written statement stating the outcome of the matter and, if there is a recovery, showing the client's share and amount and the method of its determination. The statement shall advise the client of the right to have the fee reviewed as provided in subsection (e).

(e) Upon application by the client, all fee contracts shall be subject to review and approval by the appropriate court having jurisdiction of the matter and the court shall have the authority to determine whether the contract is reasonable. If the court finds the contract is not reasonable, it shall set and allow a reasonable fee.

Texas Rule 1.04

[Texas has modified several subsections of Model Rule 1.5 (fees) to read as follows:]

RULE 1.04 Fees

(f) A division or arrangement for division of a fee between lawyers who are not in the same firm may be made only if:

(1) the division is:

(i) in proportion to the professional services performed by each lawyer; or

(ii) made between lawyers who assume joint responsibility for the representation; and

(2) the client consents in writing to the terms of the arrangement prior to the time of the association or referral proposed, including:

(i) the identity of all lawyers or law firms who will participate in the fee-sharing agreement, and

(ii) whether fees will be divided based on the proportion of services performed or by lawyers agreeing to assume joint responsibility for the representation, and

(iii) the share of the fee that each lawyer or law firm will receive or, if the division is based on the proportion of services performed, the basis on which the division will be made; and

(3) the aggregate fee does not violate paragraph (a).

(g) Every agreement that allows a lawyer or law firm to associate other counsel in the representation of a person, or to refer the person to other counsel for such representation,

and that results in such an association with or referral to a different law firm or a lawyer in such a different firm, shall be confirmed by an arrangement conforming to paragraph (f). Consent by a client or a prospective client without knowledge of the information specified in subparagraph (f)(2) does not constitute a confirmation within the meaning of this rule. No attorney shall collect or seek to collect fees or expenses in connection with any such agreement that is not confirmed in that way, except for:

(1) the reasonable value of legal services provided to that person; and

(2) the reasonable and necessary expenses actually incurred on behalf of that person.

(h) Paragraph (f) of this rule does not apply to payment to a former partner or associate pursuant to a separation or retirement agreement, or to a lawyer referral program certified by the State Bar of Texas in accordance with the Texas Lawyer Referral Service Quality Act, Tex. Occ. Code 952.001 et seq., or any amendments or recodifications thereof.

COMMENT:

1. A lawyer in good conscience should not charge or collect more than a reasonable fee, although he may charge less or no fee at all. The determination of the reasonableness of a fee, or of the range of reasonableness, can be a difficult question, and a standard of "reasonableness" is too vague and uncertain to be an appropriate standard in a disciplinary action. For this reason, paragraph (a) adopts, for disciplinary purposes only, a clearer standard: the lawyer is subject to discipline for an illegal fee or an unconscionable fee. Paragraph (a) defines an unconscionable fee in terms of the reasonableness of the fee but in a way to eliminate factual disputes as to the fee's reasonableness. The Rule's "unconscionable" standard, however, does not preclude use of the "reasonableness" standard of paragraph (b) in other settings.

* * *

Division of Fees

10. A division of fees is a single billing to a client covering the fee of two or more lawyers who are not in the same firm. A division of fees facilitates association of more than one lawyer in a matter in which neither alone could serve the client as well, and most often is used when the fee is contingent and the division is between a referring or associating lawyer initially retained by the client and a trial specialist, but it applies in all cases in which two or more lawyers are representing a single client in the same matter, and without regard to whether litigation is involved. Paragraph (f) permits the lawyers to divide a fee either on the basis of the proportion of services they render or if each lawyer assumes joint responsibility for the representation.

11. Contingent fee agreements must be in a writing signed by the client and must otherwise comply with paragraph (d) of this Rule.

12. A division of a fee based on the proportion of services rendered by two or more lawyers contemplates that each lawyer is performing substantial legal services on behalf of the client with respect to the matter. In particular, it requires that each lawyer who participates in the fee have performed services beyond those involved in initially seeking to acquire and being engaged by the client. There must be a reasonable correlation between the amount or value of services rendered and responsibility assumed, and the share of the fee to be received. However, if each participating lawyer performs substantial legal services on behalf of the client, the agreed division should control even though the division is not directly proportional to actual work performed. If a division of fee is to be based on the proportion of services rendered, the arrangement may provide that the allocation not be made until the end of the representation. When the allocation is deferred until the end of the representation, the terms of the arrangement must include the basis by which the division will be made.

13. Joint responsibility for the representation entails ethical and perhaps financial responsibility for the representation. The ethical responsibility assumed requires that a referring or associating lawyer make reasonable efforts to assure adequacy of representation and to provide adequate client communication. Adequacy of representation requires that the referring or associating lawyer conduct a reasonable

investigation of the client's legal matter and refer the matter to a lawyer whom the referring or associating lawyer reasonably believes is competent to handle it. See Rule 1.01. Adequate attorney-client communication requires that a referring or associating lawyer monitor the matter throughout the representation and ensure that the client is informed of those matters that come to that lawyer's attention and that a reasonable lawyer would believe the client should be aware. See Rule 1.03. Attending all depositions and hearings or requiring that copies of all pleadings and correspondence be provided a referring or associating lawyer is not necessary in order to meet the monitoring requirement proposed by this rule. These types of activities may increase the transactional costs, which ultimately the client will bear and unless some benefit will be derived by the client, they should be avoided. The monitoring requirement is only that the referring lawyer be reasonably informed of the matter, respond to client questions, and assist the handling lawyer when necessary. Any referral or association of other counsel should be made based solely on the client's best interest.

14. In the aggregate, the minimum activities that must be undertaken by referring or associating lawyers pursuant to an arrangement for a division of fees are substantially greater than those assumed by a lawyer who forwarded a matter to other counsel, undertook no ongoing obligations with respect to it, and yet received a portion of the handling lawyer's fee once the matter was concluded, as was permitted under the prior version of this rule. Whether such activities, or any additional activities that a lawyer might agree to undertake, suffice to make one lawyer participating in such an arrangement responsible for the professional misconduct of another lawyer who is participating in it and, if so, to what extent, are intended to be resolved by Texas Civil Practice and Remedies Code, ch. 33, or other applicable law.

15. A client must consent in writing to the terms of the arrangement prior to the time of the association or referral proposed. For this consent to be effective, the client must have been advised of at least the key features of that arrangement. Those essential terms, which are specified in subparagraph (f)(2), are 1) the identity of all lawyers or law firms who will participate in the fee-sharing agreement, 2) whether fees will be divided based on the proportion of services performed or by lawyers agreeing to assume joint responsibility for the representation, and 3) the share of the fee that each lawyer or law firm will receive or the basis on which the division will he made if the division is based on proportion of service performed. Consent by a client or prospective client to the referral to or association of other counsel, made prior to any actual such referral or association, but without knowledge of the information specified in subparagraph (f)(2) does not constitute sufficient client confirmation within the meaning of this rule. The referring or associating lawyer or any other lawyer who employs another lawyer to assist in the representation has the primary duty to ensure full disclosure and compliance with this rule.

16. Paragraph (g) facilitates the enforcement of the requirements of paragraph (f). It does so by providing that agreements that authorize an attorney either to refer a person's case to another lawyer, or to associate other counsel in the handling of a client's case, and that actually result in such a referral or association with counsel in a different law firm from the one entering into the agreement, must be confirmed by an arrangement between the person and the lawyers involved that conforms to paragraph (f). As noted there, that arrangement must be presented to and agreed to by the person before the referral or association between the lawyers involved occurs. See subparagraph (f)(2). Because paragraph (g) refers to the party whose matter is involved as a "person" rather than as a "client," it is not possible to evade its requirements by having a referring lawyer not formally enter into an attorney-client relationship with the person involved before referring that person's matter to other counsel. Paragraph (g) does provide, however, for recovery in quantum meruit in instances where its requirements are not met. See subparagraphs (g)(1) and (g)(2).

17. What should be done with any otherwise agreed-to fee that is forfeited in whole or in part due to a lawyer's failure to comply with paragraph (g) is not resolved by these rules.

18. Subparagraph (f)(3) requires that the aggregate fee charged to clients in connection with a given matter by all of the lawyers involved meet the standards of paragraph (a)—that is, not be unconscionable.

Fee Disputes and Determinations

19. If a procedure has been established for resolution of fee disputes, such as an arbitration or mediation procedure established by a bar association, the lawyer should conscientiously consider submitting to it. Law may prescribe a procedure for determining a lawyer's fee, for example, in representation of an

executor or administrator, or when a class or a person is entitled to recover a reasonable attorney's fee as part of the measure of damages. All involved lawyers should comply with any prescribed procedures.

Michigan Rule 1.6

[Michigan has modified Model Rule 1.6 to read as follows:]

RULE 1.6 Confidentiality of Information

(a) "Confidence" refers to information protected by the client-lawyer privilege under applicable law, and "secret" refers to other information gained in the professional relationship that the client has requested be held inviolate or the disclosure of which would be embarrassing or would be likely to be detrimental to the client.

(b) Except when permitted under paragraph (c), a lawyer shall not knowingly:

(1) reveal a confidence or secret of a client;

(2) use a confidence or secret of a client to the disadvantage of the client; or

(3) use a confidence or secret of a client for the advantage of the lawyer or of a third person, unless the client consents after full disclosure.

(c) A lawyer may reveal:

(1) confidences or secrets with the consent of the client or clients affected, but only after full disclosure to them;

(2) confidences or secrets when permitted or required by these rules, or when required by law or by court order;

(3) confidences and secrets to the extent reasonably necessary to rectify the consequences of a client's illegal or fraudulent act in the furtherance of which the lawyer's services have been used;

(4) the intention of a client to commit a crime and the information necessary to prevent the crime; and

(5) confidences or secrets necessary to establish or collect a fee, or to defend the lawyer or the lawyer's employees or associates against an accusation of wrongful conduct.

(d) A lawyer shall exercise reasonable care to prevent employees, associates, and others whose services are utilized by the lawyer from disclosing or using confidences or secrets of a client, except that a lawyer may reveal the information allowed by paragraph (c) through an employee.

COMMENT:

The lawyer is part of a judicial system charged with upholding the law. One of the lawyer's functions is to advise clients so that they avoid any violation of the law in the proper exercise of their rights.

The observance of the ethical obligation of a lawyer to hold inviolate confidential information of the client not only facilitates the full development of facts essential to proper representation of the client, but also encourages people to seek early legal assistance.

Almost without exception, clients come to lawyers in order to determine what their rights are and what is, in the maze of laws and regulations, deemed to be legal and correct. The common law recognizes that the client's confidences must be protected from disclosure. Upon the basis of experience, lawyers know that almost all clients follow the advice given and that the law is upheld.

A fundamental principle in the client-lawyer relationship is that the lawyer maintain confidentiality of information relating to the representation. The client is thereby encouraged to communicate fully and frankly with the lawyer even as to embarrassing or legally damaging subject matter.

The principle of confidentiality is given effect in two related bodies of law, the client-lawyer privilege (which includes the work-product doctrine) in the law of evidence and the rule of confidentiality established in professional ethics. The client-lawyer privilege applies in judicial and other proceedings in which a lawyer may be called as a witness or otherwise required to produce evidence concerning a client. The rule of client-lawyer confidentiality applies in situations other than those where evidence is sought from the lawyer through compulsion of law. The confidentiality rule applies to confidences and secrets as defined in the rule. A lawyer may not disclose such information except as authorized or required by the Rules of Professional Conduct or other law. See also Scope, ante.

The requirement of maintaining confidentiality of information relating to representation applies to government lawyers who may disagree with the policy goals that their representation is designed to advance.

Authorized Disclosure. A lawyer is impliedly authorized to make disclosures about a client when appropriate in carrying out the representation, except to the extent that the client's instructions or special circumstances limit that authority. In litigation, for example, a lawyer may disclose information by admitting a fact that cannot properly be disputed, or, in negotiation, by making a disclosure that facilitates a satisfactory conclusion.

Lawyers in a firm may, in the course of the firm's practice, disclose to each other information relating to a client of the firm, unless the client has instructed that particular information be confined to specified lawyers, or unless the disclosure would breach a screen erected within the firm in accordance with Rules 1.10(b), 1.11(a), or 1.12(c).

Disclosure Adverse to Client. The confidentiality rule is subject to limited exceptions. In becoming privy to information about a client, a lawyer may foresee that the client intends to commit a crime. To the extent a lawyer is prohibited from making disclosure, the interests of the potential victim are sacrificed in favor of preserving the client's confidences even though the client's purpose is wrongful. To the extent a lawyer is required or permitted to disclose a client's purposes, the client may be inhibited from revealing facts which would enable the lawyer to counsel against a wrongful course of action. A rule governing disclosure of threatened harm thus involves balancing the interests of one group of potential victims against those of another. On the assumption that lawyers generally fulfill their duty to advise against the commission of deliberately wrongful acts, the public is better protected if full and open communication by the client is encouraged than if it is inhibited.

Generally speaking, information relating to the representation must be kept confidential as stated in paragraph (b). However, when the client is or will be engaged in criminal conduct or the integrity of the lawyer's own conduct is involved, the principle of confidentiality may appropriately yield, depending on the lawyer's knowledge about and relationship to the conduct in question, and the seriousness of that conduct. Several situations must be distinguished.

First, the lawyer may not counsel or assist a client in conduct that is illegal or fraudulent. See Rule 1.2(c). Similarly, a lawyer has a duty under Rule 3.3(a)(4) not to use false evidence. This duty is essentially a special instance of the duty prescribed in Rule 1.2(c) to avoid assisting a client in illegal or fraudulent conduct. The same is true of compliance with Rule 4.1 concerning truthfulness of a lawyer's own representations.

Second, the lawyer may have been innocently involved in past conduct by the client that was criminal or fraudulent. In such a situation the lawyer has not violated Rule 1.2(c), because to "counsel or assist" criminal or fraudulent conduct requires knowing that the conduct is of that character. Even if the involvement was innocent, however, the fact remains that the lawyer's professional services were made the instrument of the client's crime or fraud. The lawyer, therefore, has a legitimate interest in being able to rectify the consequences of such conduct, and has the professional right, although not a professional duty, to rectify the situation. Exercising that right may require revealing information relating to the representation. Paragraph (c)(3) gives the lawyer professional discretion to reveal such information to the extent necessary to accomplish rectification. However, the constitutional rights of defendants in criminal cases may limit the extent to which counsel for a defendant may correct a misrepresentation that is based on information provided by the client. See comment to Rule 3.3.

Third, the lawyer may learn that a client intends prospective conduct that is criminal. Inaction by the lawyer is not a violation of Rule 1.2(c), except in the limited circumstances where failure to act constitutes assisting the client. See comment to Rule 1.2(c). However, the lawyer's knowledge of the client's purpose may enable the lawyer to prevent commission of the prospective crime. If the prospective crime is likely to result in substantial injury, the lawyer may feel a moral obligation to take preventive action. When the threatened injury is grave, such as homicide or serious bodily injury, a lawyer may have an obligation under tort or criminal law to take reasonable preventive measures. Whether the lawyer's concern is based on moral or legal considerations, the interest in preventing the harm may be more compelling than the interest in preserving confidentiality of information relating to the client. As stated in paragraph (c)(4), the lawyer has professional discretion to reveal information in order to prevent a client's criminal act.

It is arguable that the lawyer should have a professional obligation to make a disclosure in order to prevent homicide or serious bodily injury which the lawyer knows is intended by the client. However, it is very difficult for a lawyer to "know" when such a heinous purpose will actually be carried out, for the client may have a change of mind. To require disclosure when the client intends such an act, at the risk of professional discipline if the assessment of the client's purpose turns out to be wrong, would be to impose a penal risk that might interfere with the lawyer's resolution of an inherently difficult moral dilemma.

The lawyer's exercise of discretion requires consideration of such factors as magnitude, proximity, and likelihood of the contemplated wrong; the nature of the lawyer's relationship with the client and with those who might be injured by the client; the lawyer's own involvement in the transaction; and factors that may extenuate the conduct in question. Where practical, the lawyer should seek to persuade the client to take suitable action. In any case, a disclosure adverse to the client's interest should be no greater than the lawyer reasonably believes necessary to the purpose. A lawyer's decision not to make a disclosure permitted by paragraph (c) does not violate this rule.

Where the client is an organization, the lawyer may be in doubt whether contemplated conduct will actually be carried out by the organization. Where necessary to guide conduct in connection with this rule, the lawyer should make an inquiry within the organization as indicated in Rule 1.13(b).

Paragraph (c)(3) does not apply where a lawyer is employed after a crime or fraud has been committed to represent the client in matters ensuing therefrom.

Withdrawal. If the lawyer's services will be used by the client in materially furthering a course of criminal or fraudulent conduct, the lawyer must withdraw, as stated in Rule 1.16(a)(1).

After withdrawal the lawyer is required to refrain from making disclosure of the client's confidences, except as otherwise provided in Rule 1.6. Neither this rule nor Rule 1.8(b) nor Rule 1.16(d) prevents the lawyer from giving notice of the fact of withdrawal, and the lawyer may also withdraw or disaffirm any opinion, document, affirmation, or the like.

Dispute Concerning Lawyer's Conduct. Where a legal claim or disciplinary charge alleges complicity of the lawyer in a client's conduct or other misconduct of the lawyer involving representation of the client, the lawyer may respond to the extent the lawyer reasonably believes necessary to establish a defense. The same is true with respect to a claim involving the conduct or representation of a former client. The lawyer's right to respond arises when an assertion of complicity or other misconduct has been made. Paragraph (c)(5) does not require the lawyer to await the commencement of an action or proceeding that charges complicity or other misconduct, so that the defense may be established by responding directly to a third party who has made such an assertion. The right to defend, of course, applies where a proceeding has been commenced. Where practicable and not prejudicial to the lawyer's ability to establish the defense, the lawyer should advise the client of the third party's assertion and request that the client respond appropriately. In any event, disclosure should be no greater than the lawyer reasonably believes is necessary to vindicate innocence, the disclosure should be made in a manner which limits access to the information to the tribunal or other persons having a need to know it, and appropriate protective orders or other arrangements should be sought by the lawyer to the fullest extent practicable.

If the lawyer is charged with wrongdoing in which the client's conduct is implicated, the rule of confidentiality should not prevent the lawyer from defending against the charge. Such a charge can arise in a civil, criminal, or professional disciplinary proceeding, and can be based on a wrong allegedly committed by the lawyer against the client, or on a wrong alleged by a third person, for example, a person claiming to have been defrauded by the lawyer and client acting together.

A lawyer entitled to a fee is permitted by paragraph (c)(5) to prove the services rendered in an action to collect it. This aspect of the rule expresses the principle that the beneficiary of a fiduciary relationship may not exploit it to the detriment of the fiduciary. As stated above, the lawyer must make every effort practicable to avoid unnecessary disclosure of information relating to a representation, to limit disclosure to those having the need to know it, and to obtain protective orders or make other arrangements minimizing the risk of disclosure.

Disclosures Otherwise Required or Authorized. The scope of the client-lawyer privilege is a question of law. If a lawyer is called as a witness to give testimony concerning a client, absent waiver by the client, paragraph (b)(1) requires the lawyer to invoke the privilege when it is applicable. The lawyer must comply with the final orders of a court or other tribunal of competent jurisdiction requiring the lawyer to give information about the client.

The Rules of Professional Conduct in various circumstances permit or require a lawyer to disclose information relating to the representation. See Rules 2.2, 2.3, 3.3 and 4.1. In addition to these provisions, a lawyer may be obligated or permitted by other provisions of law to give information about a client. Whether another provision of law supersedes Rule 1.6 is a matter of interpretation beyond the scope of these rules, but a presumption should exist against such a supersession.

Former Client. The duty of confidentiality continues after the client-lawyer relationship has terminated. See Rule 1.9.

***Texas Rule 1.05** (Modification of Model Rule 1.6)*

[Texas has modified Model Rule 1.6 (Confidentiality) to read as follows:]

RULE 1.05 Confidentiality of Information

(a) "Confidential information" includes both "privileged information" and "unprivileged client information." "Privileged information" refers to the information of a client protected by the lawyer-client privilege of Rule 503 of the Texas Rules of Evidence or of Rule 503 of the Texas Rules of Criminal Evidence or by the principles of attorney-client privilege governed by Rule 501 of the Federal Rules of Evidence for United States Courts and Magistrates. "Unprivileged client information" means all information relating to a client or furnished by the client, other than privileged information, acquired by the lawyer during the course of or by reason of the representation of the client.

(b) Except as permitted by paragraphs (c) and (d), or as required by paragraphs (e) and (f), a lawyer shall not knowingly:

(1) Reveal confidential information of a client or a former client to:

(i) a person that the client has instructed is not to receive the information; or

(ii) anyone else, other than the client, the client's representatives, or the members, associates, or employees of the lawyer's law firm.

(2) Use confidential information of a client to the disadvantage of the client unless the client consents after consultation.

(3) Use confidential information of a former client to the disadvantage of the former client after the representation is concluded unless the former client consents after consultation or the confidential information has become generally known.

(4) Use privileged information of a client for the advantage of the lawyer or of a third person, unless the client consents after consultation.

(c) A lawyer may reveal confidential information:

(1) When the lawyer has been expressly authorized to do so in order to carry out the representation.

(2) When the client consents after consultation.

(3) To the client, the client's representatives, or the members, associates, and employees of the lawyer's firm, except when otherwise instructed by the client.

(4) When the lawyer has reason to believe it is necessary to do so in order to comply with a court order, a Texas Disciplinary Rule of Professional Conduct, or other law.

(5) To the extent reasonably necessary to enforce a claim or establish a defense on behalf of the lawyer in a controversy between the lawyer and the client.

(6) To establish a defense to a criminal charge, civil claim or disciplinary complaint against the lawyer or the lawyer's associates based upon conduct involving the client or the representation of the client.

(7) When the lawyer has reason to believe it is necessary to do so in order to prevent the client from committing a criminal or fraudulent act.

(8) To the extent revelation reasonably appears necessary to rectify the consequences of a client's criminal or fraudulent act in the commission of which the lawyer's services had been used.

(d) A lawyer also may reveal unprivileged client information:

(1) When impliedly authorized to do so in order to carry out the representation.

(2) When the lawyer has reason to believe it is necessary to do so in order to:

(i) carry out the representation effectively;

(ii) defend the lawyer or the lawyer's employees or associates against a claim of wrongful conduct;

(iii) respond to allegations in any proceeding concerning the lawyer's representation of the client; or

(iv) prove the services rendered to a client, or the reasonable value thereof, or both, in an action against another person or organization responsible for the payment of the fee for services rendered to the client.

(e) When a lawyer has confidential information clearly establishing that a client is likely to commit a criminal or fraudulent act that is likely to result in death or substantial bodily harm to a person, the lawyer shall reveal confidential information to the extent revelation reasonably appears necessary to prevent the client from committing the criminal or fraudulent act.

(f) A lawyer shall reveal confidential information when required to do so by Rule 3.03(a)(2), 3.03(b), or by Rule 4.01(b).

COMMENT:

Confidentiality Generally

1. Both the fiduciary relationship existing between lawyer and client and the proper functioning of the legal system require the preservation by the lawyer of confidential information of one who has employed or sought to employ the lawyer. Free discussion should prevail between lawyer and client in order for the lawyer to be fully informed and for the client to obtain the full benefit of the legal system. The ethical obligation of the lawyer to protect the confidential information of the client not only facilitates the proper representation of the client but also encourages potential clients to seek early legal assistance.

2. Subject to the mandatory disclosure requirements of paragraphs (e) and (f) the lawyer generally should be required to maintain confidentiality of information acquired by the lawyer during the course of or by reason of the representation of the client. This principle involves an ethical obligation not to use the information to the detriment of the client or for the benefit of the lawyer or a third person. In regard to an evaluation of a matter affecting a client for use by a third person, see Rule 2.02.

3. The principle of confidentiality is given effect not only in the Texas Rules of Professional Conduct but also in the law of evidence regarding the attorney-client privilege and in the law of agency. The attorney-client privilege, developed through many decades, provides the client a right to prevent certain confidential communications from being revealed by compulsion of law. Several sound exceptions to confidentiality have been developed in the evidence law of privilege. Exceptions exist in evidence law where the services of the lawyer were sought or used by a client in planning or committing a crime or fraud as well as where issues have arisen as to breach of duty by the lawyer or by the client to the other.

4. Rule 1.05 reinforces the principles of evidence law relating to the attorney-client privilege. Rule 1.05 also furnishes considerable protection to other information falling outside the scope of the privilege. Rule 1.05 extends ethical protection generally to unprivileged information relating to the client or furnished by the client during the course of or by reason of the representation of the client. In this respect Rule 1.05 accords with general fiduciary principles of agency.

5. The requirement of confidentiality applies to government lawyers who may disagree with the policy goals that their representation is designed to advance.

Disclosure for Benefit of Client

6. A lawyer may be expressly authorized to make disclosures to carry out the representation and generally is recognized as having implied-in-fact authority to make disclosures about a client when appropriate in carrying out the representation to the extent that the client's instructions do not limit that authority. In litigation, for example, a lawyer may disclose information by admitting a fact that cannot properly be disputed, or in negotiation by making a disclosure that facilitates a satisfactory conclusion. The effect of Rule 1.05 is to require the lawyer to invoke, for the client, the attorney-client privilege when applicable; but if the court improperly denies the privilege, under paragraph (c)(4) the lawyer may testify as ordered by the court or may test the ruling as permitted by Rule 3.04(d).

7. In the course of a firm's practice, lawyers may disclose to each other and to appropriate employees information relating to a client, unless the client has instructed that particular information be confined to specified lawyers. Subparagraphs (b)(1) and (c)(3) continue these practices concerning disclosure of confidential information within the firm.

Use of Information

8. Following sound principles of agency law, subparagraphs (b)(2) and (4) subject a lawyer to discipline for using information relating to the representation in a manner disadvantageous to the client or beneficial to the lawyer or a third person, absent the informed consent of the client. The duty not to misuse client information continues after the client-lawyer relationship has terminated. Therefore, the lawyer is forbidden by subparagraph (b)(3) to use, in absence of the client's informed consent, confidential information of the former client to the client's disadvantage, unless the information is generally known.

Discretionary Disclosure Adverse to Client

9. In becoming privy to information about a client, a lawyer may foresee that the client intends serious and perhaps irreparable harm. To the extent a lawyer is prohibited from making disclosure, the interests of the potential victim are sacrificed in favor of preserving the client's information—usually unprivileged information—even though the client's purpose is wrongful. On the other hand, a client who knows or believes that a lawyer is required or permitted to disclose a client's wrongful purposes may be inhibited from revealing facts which would enable the lawyer to counsel effectively against wrongful action. Rule 1.05 thus involves balancing the interests of one group of potential victims against those of another. The criteria provided by the Rule are discussed below.

10. Rule 503(d)(1), Texas Rules of Civil Evidence (Tex.R.Civ.Evid.), and Rule 503(d)(1), Texas Rules of Criminal Evidence (Tex.R.Crim.Evid.), indicate the underlying public policy of furnishing no protection

to client information where the client seeks or uses the services of the lawyer to aid in the commission of a crime or fraud. That public policy governs the dictates of Rule 1.05. Where the client is planning or engaging in criminal or fraudulent conduct or where the culpability of the lawyer's conduct is involved, full protection of client information is not justified.

11. Several other situations must be distinguished. First, the lawyer may not counsel or assist a client in conduct that is criminal or fraudulent. See Rule 1.02(c). As noted in the Comment to that Rule, there can be situations where the lawyer may have to reveal information relating to the representation in order to avoid assisting a client's criminal or fraudulent conduct, and sub-paragraph (c)(4) permits doing so. A lawyer's duty under Rule 3.03(a) not to use false or fabricated evidence is a special instance of the duty prescribed in Rule 1.02(c) to avoid assisting a client in criminal or fraudulent conduct, and sub-paragraph (c)(4) permits revealing information necessary to comply with Rule 3.03(a) or (b). The same is true of compliance with Rule 4.01. See also paragraph (f).

12. Second, the lawyer may have been innocently involved in past conduct by the client that was criminal or fraudulent. In such a situation the lawyer has not violated Rule 1.02(c), because to "counsel or assist" criminal or fraudulent conduct requires knowing that the conduct is of that character. Since the lawyer's services were made an instrument of the client's crime or fraud, the lawyer has a legitimate interest both in rectifying the consequences of such conduct and in avoiding charges that the lawyer's participation was culpable. Sub-paragraph (c)(6) and (8) give the lawyer professional discretion to reveal both unprivileged and privileged information in order to serve those interests. See paragraph (g). In view of Tex.R.Civ.Evid. Rule 503(d)(1), and Tex.R.Crim.Evid. 503(d)(1), however, rarely will such information be privileged.

13. Third, the lawyer may learn that a client intends prospective conduct that is criminal or fraudulent. The lawyer's knowledge of the client's purpose may enable the lawyer to prevent commission of the prospective crime or fraud. When the threatened injury is grave, the lawyer's interest in preventing the harm may be more compelling than the interest in preserving confidentiality of information. As stated in subparagraph (c)(7), the lawyer has professional discretion, based on reasonable appearances, to reveal both privileged and unprivileged information in order to prevent the client's commission of any criminal or fraudulent act. In some situations of this sort, disclosure is mandatory. See paragraph (e) and Comments 18–20.

14. The lawyer's exercise of discretion under paragraphs (c) and (d) involves consideration of such factors as the magnitude, proximity, and likelihood of the contemplated wrong, the nature of the lawyer's relationship with the client and with those who might be injured by the client, the lawyer's own involvement in the transaction, and factors that may extenuate the client's conduct in question. In any case, a disclosure adverse to the client's interest should be no greater than the lawyer believes necessary to the purpose. Although preventive action is permitted by paragraphs (c) and (d), failure to take preventive action does not violate those paragraphs. But see paragraphs (e) and (f). *Because these rules do not define standards of civil liability of lawyers for professional conduct, paragraphs (c) and (d) do not create a duty on the lawyer to make any disclosure and no civil liability is intended to arise from the failure to make such disclosure.*

15. A lawyer entitled to a fee necessarily must be permitted to prove the services rendered in an action to collect it, and this necessity is recognized by sub-paragraphs (c)(5) and (d)(2)(iv). This aspect of the rule, in regard to privileged information, expresses the principle that the beneficiary of a fiduciary relationship may not exploit the relationship to the detriment of the fiduciary. Any disclosure by the lawyer, however, should be as protective of the client's interests as possible.

16. If the client is an organization, a lawyer also should refer to Rule 1.12 in order to determine the appropriate conduct in connection with this Rule.

Client Under a Disability

17. In some situations, Rule 1.02(g) requires a lawyer representing a client under a disability to seek the appointment of a legal representative for the client or to seek other orders for the protection of the client. The client may or may not, in a particular matter, effectively consent to the lawyer's revealing to the court confidential information and facts reasonably necessary to secure the desired appointment or order. Nevertheless, the lawyer is authorized by paragraph (c)(4) to reveal such information in order to comply with Rule 1.02(g). See also paragraph 5, Comment to Rule 1.03.

Mandatory Disclosure Adverse to Client

18. Rule 1.05(e) and (f) place upon a lawyer professional obligations in certain situations to make disclosure in order to prevent certain serious crimes by a client or to prevent involvement by the lawyer in a client's crimes or frauds. Except when death or serious bodily harm is likely to result, a lawyer's obligation is to dissuade the client from committing the crime or fraud or to persuade the client to take corrective action; see Rule 1.02(d) and (e).

19. Because it is very difficult for a lawyer to know when a client's criminal or fraudulent purpose actually will be carried out, the lawyer is required by paragraph (e) to act only if the lawyer has information "clearly establishing" the likelihood of such acts and consequences. If the information shows clearly that the client's contemplated crime or fraud is likely to result in death or serious injury, the lawyer must seek to avoid those lamentable results by revealing information necessary to prevent the criminal or fraudulent act. When the threatened crime or fraud is likely to have the less serious result of substantial injury to the financial interests or property of another, the lawyer is not required to reveal preventive information but may do so in conformity to paragraph (c)(7). See also paragraph (f); Rule 1.02(d) and (e); and Rule 3.03(b) and (c).

20. Although a violation of paragraph (e) will subject a lawyer to disciplinary action, the lawyer's decisions whether or how to act should not constitute grounds for discipline unless the lawyer's conduct in the light of those decisions was unreasonable under all existing circumstances as they reasonably appeared to the lawyer. This construction necessarily follows from the fact that paragraph (e) bases the lawyer's affirmative duty to act on how the situation "reasonably appears" to the lawyer, while that imposed by paragraph (f) arises only when a lawyer "knows" that the lawyer's services have been misused by the client. See also Rule 3.03(b).

Withdrawal

21. If the lawyer's services will be used by the client in materially furthering a course of criminal or fraudulent conduct, the lawyer must withdraw, as stated in Rule 1.15(a)(1). After withdrawal, a lawyer's conduct continues to be governed by Rule 1.05. However, the lawyer's duties of disclosure under paragraph (e) of the Rule, insofar as such duties are mandatory, do not survive the end of the relationship even though disclosure remains permissible under paragraphs (6), (7), and (8) if the further requirements of such paragraph are met. Neither this Rule nor Rule 1.15 prevents the lawyer from giving notice of the fact of withdrawal, and no rule forbids the lawyer to withdraw or disaffirm any opinion, document, affirmation, or the like.

Other Rules

22. Various other Texas Rules of Professional Conduct permit or require a lawyer to disclose information relating to the representation. See Rules 1.07, 1.12, 2.02, 3.03 and 4.01. In addition to these provisions, a lawyer may be obligated by other provisions of statutes or other law to give information about a client. Whether another provision of law supersedes Rule 1.05 is a matter of interpretation beyond the scope of these Rules, but sub-paragraph (c)(4) protects the lawyer from discipline who acts on reasonable belief as to the effect of such laws.

***Florida Rule 4–1.7** (Modification of Model Rule 1.7)*

[Florida has modified Model Rule 1.7 (Conflict of Interest) as follows:]

RULE 4–1.7 Conflict of Interest; General Rule

(a) Representing Adverse Interests. Except as provided in subdivision (b), a lawyer must not represent a client if:

(1) the representation of 1 client will be directly adverse to another client; or

(2) there is a substantial risk that the representation of 1 or more clients will be materially limited by the lawyer's responsibilities to another client, a former client or a third person or by a personal interest of the lawyer.

(b) Informed Consent. Notwithstanding the existence of a conflict of interest under subdivision (a), a lawyer may represent a client if:

(1) the lawyer reasonably believes that the lawyer will be able to provide competent and diligent representation to each affected client;

(2) the representation is not prohibited by law;

(3) the representation does not involve the assertion of a position adverse to another client when the lawyer represents both clients in the same proceeding before a tribunal; and

(4) each affected client gives informed consent, confirmed in writing or clearly stated on the record at a hearing.

(c) Explanation to Clients. When representation of multiple clients in a single matter is undertaken, the consultation must include an explanation of the implications of the common representation and the advantages and risks involved.

(d) Lawyers Related by Blood, Adoption, or Marriage. A lawyer related by blood, adoption, or marriage to another lawyer as parent, child, sibling, or spouse must not represent a client in a representation directly adverse to a person who the lawyer knows is represented by the other lawyer except with the client's informed consent, confirmed in writing or clearly stated on the record at a hearing.

(e) Representation of insureds. Upon undertaking the representation of an insured client at the expense of the insurer, a lawyer has a duty to ascertain whether the lawyer will be representing both the insurer and the insured as clients, or only the insured, and to inform both the insured and the insurer regarding the scope of the representation. All other Rules Regulating The Florida Bar related to conflicts of interest apply to the representation as they would in any other situation.

Texas Rule 1.06 *(Modification of Model Rule 1.7)*

[Texas has modified Model Rule 1.7 (Conflict of Interest) as follows:]

RULE 1.06 Conflict of Interest: General Rule

(a) A lawyer shall not represent opposing parties to the same litigation.

(b) In other situations and except to the extent permitted by paragraph (c), a lawyer shall not represent a person if the representation of that person:

(1) involves a substantially related matter in which that person's interests are materially and directly adverse to the interests of another client of the lawyer or the lawyer's firm; or

(2) reasonably appears to be or become adversely limited by the lawyer's or law firm's responsibilities to another client or to a third person or by the lawyer's or law firm's own interests.

(c) A lawyer may represent a client in the circumstances described in (b) if:

(1) the lawyer reasonably believes the representation of each client will not be materially affected; and

(2) each affected or potentially affected client consents to such representation after full disclosure of the existence, nature, implications, and possible adverse consequences of the common representation and the advantages involved, if any.

(d) A lawyer who has represented multiple parties in a matter shall not thereafter represent any of such parties in a dispute among the parties arising out of the matter, unless prior consent is obtained from all such parties to the dispute.

(e) If a lawyer has accepted representation in violation of this Rule, or if multiple representation properly accepted becomes improper under this Rule, the lawyer shall promptly withdraw from one or more representations to the extent necessary for any remaining representation not to be in violation of these Rules.

(f) If a lawyer would be prohibited by this Rule from engaging in particular conduct, no other lawyer while a member or associated with that lawyer's firm may engage in that conduct.

COMMENT:

Loyalty to a Client

1. Loyalty is an essential element in the lawyer's relationship to a client. An impermissible conflict of interest may exist before representation is undertaken, in which event the representation should be declined. If such a conflict arises after representation has been undertaken, the lawyer must take effective action to eliminate the conflict, including withdrawal if necessary to rectify the situation. See also Rule 1.16. When more than one client is involved and the lawyer withdraws because a conflict arises after representation, whether the lawyer may continue to represent any of the clients is determined by this Rule and Rules 1.05 and 1.09. See also Rule 1.07(c). Under this Rule, any conflict that prevents a particular lawyer from undertaking or continuing a representation of a client also prevents any other lawyer who is or becomes a member of or an associate with that lawyer's firm from doing so. See paragraph (f).

2. A fundamental principle recognized by paragraph (a) is that a lawyer may not represent opposing parties in litigation. The term "opposing parties" as used in this Rule contemplates a situation where a judgment favorable to one of the parties will directly impact unfavorably upon the other party. Moreover, as a general proposition loyalty to a client prohibits undertaking representation directly adverse to the representation of that client in a substantially related matter unless that client's fully informed consent is obtained and unless the lawyer reasonably believes that the lawyer's representation will be reasonably protective of that client's interests. Paragraphs (b) and (c) express that general concept.

Conflicts in Litigation

3. Paragraph (a) prohibits representation of opposing parties in litigation. Simultaneous representation of parties whose interests in litigation are not actually directly adverse but where the potential for conflict exists, such as co-plaintiffs or co-defendants, is governed by paragraph (b). An impermissible conflict may exist or develop by reason of substantial discrepancy in the parties' testimony, incompatibility in positions in relation to an opposing party or the fact that there are substantially different possibilities of settlement of the claims or liabilities in question. Such conflicts can arise in criminal cases as well as civil. The potential for conflict of interest in representing multiple defendants in a criminal case is so grave that ordinarily a lawyer should decline to represent more than one co-defendant. On the other hand, common representation of persons having similar interests is proper if the risk of adverse effect is minimal and the requirements of paragraph (b) are met. Compare Rule 1.07 involving intermediation between clients.

Conflict with Lawyer's Own Interests

4. Loyalty to a client is impaired not only by the representation of opposing parties in situations within paragraphs (a) and (b)(1) but also in any situation when a lawyer may not be able to consider, recommend or carry out an appropriate course of action for one client because of the lawyer's own interests or responsibilities to others. The conflict in effect forecloses alternatives that would otherwise be available to the client. Paragraph (b)(2) addresses such situations. A potential possible conflict does not itself necessarily preclude the representation. The critical questions are the likelihood that a conflict exists or will eventuate and, if it does, whether it will materially and adversely affect the lawyer's independent professional judgment in considering alternatives or foreclose courses of action that reasonably should be pursued on behalf of the client. It is for the client to decide whether the client wishes to accommodate the other interest involved. However, the client's consent to the representation by the lawyer of another whose interests are directly adverse is insufficient unless the lawyer also believes that there will be no materially adverse effect upon the interests of either client. See paragraph (c).

5. The lawyer's own interests should not be permitted to have adverse effect on representation of a client, even where paragraph (b)(2) is not violated. For example, a lawyer's need for income should not lead the lawyer to undertake matters that cannot be handled competently and at a reasonable fee. See Rules 1.01 and 1.04. If the probity of a lawyer's own conduct in a transaction is in question, it may be difficult for the lawyer to give a client detached advice. A lawyer should not allow related business interests to affect representation, for example, by referring clients to an enterprise in which the lawyer has an undisclosed interest.

Meaning of Directly Adverse

6. Within the meaning of Rule 1.06(b), the representation of one client is "directly adverse" to the representation of another client if the lawyer's independent judgment on behalf of a client or the lawyer's ability or willingness to consider, recommend or carry out a course of action will be or is reasonably likely to be adversely affected by the lawyer's representation of, or responsibilities to, the other client. The dual representation also is directly adverse if the lawyer reasonably appears to be called upon to espouse adverse positions in the same matter or a related matter. On the other hand, simultaneous representation in unrelated matters of clients whose interests are only generally adverse, such as competing economic enterprises, does not constitute the representation of directly adverse interests. Even when neither paragraph (a) nor (b) is applicable, a lawyer should realize that a business rivalry or personal differences between two clients or potential clients may be so important to one or both that one or the other would consider it contrary to its interests to have the same lawyer as its rival even in unrelated matters; and in those situations a wise lawyer would forego the dual representation.

Full Disclosure and Informed Consent

7. A client under some circumstances may consent to representation notwithstanding a conflict or potential conflict. However, as indicated in paragraph (c)(1), when a disinterested lawyer would conclude that the client should not agree to the representation under the circumstances, the lawyer involved should not ask for such agreement or provide representation on the basis of the client's consent. When more than one client is involved, the question of conflict must be resolved as to each client. Moreover, there may be circumstances where it is impossible to make the full disclosure necessary to obtain informed consent. For example, when the lawyer represents different clients in related matters and one of the clients refuses to consent to the disclosure necessary to permit the other client to make an informed decision, the lawyer cannot properly ask the latter to consent.

8. Disclosure and consent are not formalities. Disclosure sufficient for sophisticated clients may not be sufficient to permit less sophisticated clients to provide fully informed consent. While it is not required that the disclosure and consent be in writing, it would be prudent for the lawyer to provide potential dual clients with at least a written summary of the considerations disclosed.

9. In certain situations, such as in the preparation of loan papers or the preparation of a partnership agreement, a lawyer might have properly undertaken multiple representation and be confronted subsequently by a dispute among those clients in regard to that matter. Paragraph (d) forbids the representation of any of those parties in regard to that dispute unless informed consent is obtained from all of the parties to the dispute who had been represented by the lawyer in that matter.

10. A lawyer may represent parties having antagonistic positions on a legal question that has arisen in different cases, unless representation of either client would be adversely affected. Thus, it is ordinarily not improper to assert such positions in cases pending in different trial courts, but it may be improper to do so in cases pending at the same time in an appellate court.

11. Ordinarily, it is not advisable for a lawyer to act as advocate against a client the lawyer represents in some other matter, even if the other matter is wholly unrelated and even if paragraphs (a), (b), and (d) are not applicable. However, there are circumstances in which a lawyer may act as advocate against a client, for a lawyer is free to do so unless this Rule or another rule of the Texas Rules of Professional Conduct would be violated. For example, a lawyer representing an enterprise with diverse operations may accept employment as an advocate against the enterprise in a matter unrelated to any matter being handled for the enterprise if the representation of one client is not directly adverse to the representation of the other client. The propriety of concurrent representation can depend on the nature of the litigation. For example, a suit charging fraud entails conflict to a degree not involved in a suit for declaratory judgment concerning statutory interpretation.

Interest of Person Paying for a Lawyer's Service

12. A lawyer may be paid from a source other than the client, if the client is informed of that fact and consents and the arrangement does not compromise the lawyer's duty of loyalty to the client. See Rule 1.08(e). For example, when an insurer and its insured have conflicting interests in a matter arising from a liability insurance agreement, and the insurer is required to provide special counsel for the insured, the arrangement should assure the special counsel's professional independence. So also, when a corporation and its directors or employees are involved in a controversy in which they have conflicting interests, the corporation may provide funds for separate legal representation of the directors or employees, if the clients consent after consultation and the arrangement ensures the lawyer's professional independence.

Non-litigation Conflict Situations

13. Conflicts of interest in contexts other than litigation sometimes may be difficult to assess. Relevant factors in determining whether there is potential for adverse effect include the duration and intimacy of the lawyer's relationship with the client or clients involved, the functions being performed by the lawyer, the likelihood that actual conflict will arise and the likely prejudice to the client from the conflict if it does arise. The question is often one of proximity and degree.

14. For example, a lawyer may not represent multiple parties to a negotiation whose interests are fundamentally antagonistic to each other, but common representation may be permissible where the clients are generally aligned in interest even though there is some difference of interest among them.

15. Conflict questions may also arise in estate planning and estate administration. A lawyer may be called upon to prepare wills for several family members, such as husband and wife, and, depending upon the circumstances, a conflict of interest may arise. In estate administration it may be unclear whether the client is the fiduciary or is the estate or trust, including its beneficiaries. The lawyer should make clear the relationship to the parties involved.

16. A lawyer for a corporation or other organization who is also a member of its board of directors should determine whether the responsibilities of the two roles may conflict. The lawyer may be called on to advise the corporation in matters involving actions of the directors. Consideration should be given to the frequency with which such situations may arise, the potential intensity of the conflict, the effect of the lawyer's resignation from the board and the possibility of the corporation's obtaining legal advice from another lawyer in such situations. If there is material risk that the dual role will compromise the lawyer's independence of professional judgment, the lawyer should not serve as a director.

Conflict Charged by an Opposing Party

17. Raising questions of conflict of interest is primarily the responsibility of the lawyer undertaking the representation. In litigation, a court may raise the question when there is reason to infer that the lawyer has neglected the responsibility. In a criminal case, inquiry by the court is generally required when a lawyer represents multiple defendants. Where the conflict is such as clearly to call in question the fair or efficient administration of justice, opposing counsel may properly raise the question. Such an objection should be viewed with great caution, however, for it can be misused as a technique of harassment. See Preamble: Scope.

18. Except when the absolute prohibition of this rule applies or in litigation when a court passes upon issues of conflicting interests in determining a question of disqualification of counsel, resolving questions of conflict of interests may require decisions by all affected clients as well as by the lawyer.

District of Columbia Rule 1.8

[The District of Columbia has added subsection (i) to Model Rule 1.8]

RULE 1.8 Conflict of Interest: Prohibited Transactions

* * *

(i) A lawyer may acquire and enforce a lien granted by law to secure the lawyer's fees or expenses, but a lawyer shall not impose a lien upon any part of a client's files, except upon the lawyer's own work product, and then only to the extent that the work product has not been paid for. This work product exception shall not apply when the client has

become unable to pay, or when withholding the lawyer's work product would present a significant risk to the client of irreparable harm.

COMMENT:

Lawyer's Liens

[16] The substantive law of the District of Columbia has long permitted lawyers to assert and enforce liens against the property of clients. See, e.g., Redevelopment Land Agency v. Dowdey, 618 A.2d 153, 159–60 (D.C.1992), and cases cited therein. Whether a lawyer has a lien on money or property belonging to a client is generally a matter of substantive law as to which the ethics rules take no position. Exceptions to what the common law might otherwise permit are made with respect to contingent fees and retaining liens. See, respectively, Rule 1.5(c) and Rule 1.8(i).

[17] Rule 1.16(d) requires a lawyer to surrender papers and property to which the client is entitled when representation of the client terminates. Paragraph (i) of this Rule states a narrow exception to Rule 1.16(d): a lawyer may retain anything the law permits—including property—except for files. As to files, a lawyer may retain only the lawyer's own work product, and then only if the client has not paid for the work. However, if the client has paid for the work product, the client is entitled to receive it, even if the client has not previously seen or received a copy of the work product. Furthermore, the lawyer may not retain the work product for which the client has not paid, if the client has become unable to pay or if withholding the work product might irreparably harm the client's interest.

[18] Under Rule 1.16(d), for example, a lawyer would be required to return all papers received from a client, such as birth certificates, wills, tax returns, or "green cards." Rule 1.8(i) does not permit retention of such papers to secure payment of any fee due. Only the lawyer's own work product—results of factual investigations, legal research and analysis, and similar materials generated by the lawyer's own effort—could be retained. (The term "work product" as used in paragraph (i) is limited to materials falling within the "work product doctrine," but includes any material generated by the lawyer that would be protected under that doctrine whether or not created in connection with pending or anticipated litigation.) And a lawyer could not withhold all of the work product merely because a portion of the lawyer's fees had not been paid.

[19] There are situations in which withholding the work product would not be permissible because of irreparable harm to the client. The possibility of involuntary incarceration or criminal conviction constitutes one category of irreparable harm. The realistic possibility that a client might irretrievably lose a significant right or become subject to a significant liability because of the withholding of the work product constitutes another category of irreparable harm. On the other hand, the mere fact that the client might have to pay another lawyer to replicate the work product does not, standing alone, constitute irreparable harm. These examples are merely indicative of the meaning of the term "irreparable harm," and are not exhaustive.

Indiana Rule 1.8(l)

[Indiana has added the following provision to Model Rule 1.8.]

RULE 1.8 Conflict of Interest: Prohibited Transactions

* * *

(*l*) A part-time prosecutor or deputy prosecutor authorized by statute to otherwise engage in the practice of law shall refrain from representing a private client in any matter wherein exists an issue upon which said prosecutor has statutory prosecutorial authority or responsibilities. This restriction is not intended to prohibit representation in tort cases in which investigation and any prosecution of infractions has terminated, nor to prohibit representation in family law matters involving no issue subject to prosecutorial authority or responsibilities. Upon a prior, express written limitation of responsibility to exclude prosecutorial authority in matters related to family law, a part-time deputy prosecutor may fully represent private clients in cases involving family law.

Minnesota Rule 1.8(e)(3) & (j)

[Minnesota has added the following provision to Model Rule 1.8:]

RULE 1.8 Conflict of Interest: Prohibited Transactions

* * *

(e) A lawyer shall not provide financial assistance to a client in connection with pending or contemplated litigation, except that:

* * *

(3) a lawyer may guarantee a loan reasonably needed to enable the client to withstand delay in litigation that would otherwise put substantial pressure on the client to settle a case because of financial hardship rather than on the merits, provided the client remains ultimately liable for repayment of the loan without regard to the outcome of the litigation and, further provided, that no promise of such financial assistance was made to the client by the lawyer, or by another in the lawyer's behalf, prior to the employment of that lawyer by that client.

* * *

(j) A lawyer shall not have sexual relations with a current client unless a consensual sexual relationship existed between them when the lawyer-client relationship commenced. For purposes of this paragraph:

(1) "Sexual relations" means sexual intercourse or any other intentional touching of the intimate parts of a person or causing the person to touch the intimate parts of the lawyer.

(2) If the client is an organization, any individual who oversees the representation and gives instructions to the lawyer on behalf of the organization shall be deemed to be the client. In-house attorneys while representing governmental or corporate entities are governed by Rule 1.7(b) rather than by this rule with respect to sexual relations with other employees of the entity they represent.

(3) This paragraph does not prohibit a lawyer from engaging in sexual relations with a client of the lawyer's firm provided that the lawyer has no involvement in the performance of the legal work for the client.

(4) If a party other than the client alleges violation of this paragraph, and the complaint is not summarily dismissed, the Director, in determining whether to investigate the allegation and whether to charge any violation based on the allegations, shall consider the client's statement regarding whether the client would be unduly burdened by the investigation or charge.

Texas Rule 1.09 *(Modification of Model Rule 1.9)*

[Texas has modified Rule 1.9 (Former Client Conflicts) as follows:]

RULE 1.09 Conflict of Interest: Former Client

(a) Without prior consent, a lawyer who personally has formerly represented a client in a matter shall not thereafter represent another person in a matter adverse to the former client:

(1) in which such other person questions the validity of the lawyer's services or work product for the former client; or

(2) if the representation in reasonable probability will involve a violation of Rule 1.05.

(3) if it is the same or a substantially related matter;

(b) Except to the extent authorized by Rule 1.10, when lawyers are or have become members of or associated with a firm, none of them shall knowingly represent a client if any one of them practicing alone would be prohibited from doing so by paragraph (a).

(c) When the association of a lawyer with a firm has terminated, the lawyers who were then associated with that lawyer shall not knowingly represent a client if the lawyer whose association with that firm has terminated would be prohibited from doing so by paragraph (a)(1) or if the representation in reasonable probability will involve a violation of Rule 1.05.

COMMENT:

1. Rule 1.09 addresses the circumstances in which a lawyer in private practice, and other lawyers who were, are or become members of or associated with a firm in which that lawyer practiced or practices, may represent a client against a former client of that lawyer or the lawyer's former firm. Whether a lawyer, or that lawyer's present or former firm, is prohibited from representing a client in a matter by reason of the lawyer's successive government and private employment is governed by Rule 1.10 rather than by this Rule.

2. Paragraph (a) concerns the situation where a lawyer once personally represented a client and now wishes to represent a second client against that former client. Whether such a personal attorney-client relationship existed involves questions of both fact and law that are beyond the scope of these Rules. See Preamble: Scope. Among the relevant factors, however, would be how the former representation actually was conducted within the firm; the nature and scope of the former client's contacts with the firm (including any restrictions the client may have placed on the dissemination of confidential information within the firm); and the size of the firm.

3. Although paragraph (a) does not absolutely prohibit a lawyer from representing a client against a former client, it does provide that the latter representation is improper if any of three circumstances exists, except with prior consent. The first prohibition is against representation adverse to a former client if it is the same or a substantially related matter. The second circumstance is that the lawyer may not represent a client who questions the validity of the lawyer's services or work product for the former client. Thus, for example, a lawyer who drew a will leaving a substantial portion of the testator's property to a designated beneficiary would violate paragraph (a) by representing the testator's heirs at law in an action seeking to overturn the will.

4. Paragraph (a)'s third limitation on undertaking a representation against a former client is that it may not be done if there is a "reasonable probability" that the representation would cause the lawyer to violate the obligations owed the former client under Rule 1.05. Thus, for example, if there were a reasonable probability that the subsequent representation would involve either an unauthorized disclosure of confidential information under Rule 1.05(b)(1) or an improper use of such information to the disadvantage of the former client under Rule 1.05(b)(3), that representation would be improper under paragraph (a). Whether such a reasonable probability exists in any given case will be a question of fact.

5. Paragraph (b) extends paragraph (a)'s limitations on an individual lawyer's freedom to undertake a representation against that lawyer's former client to all other lawyers who are or become members of or associated with the firm in which that lawyer is practicing. Thus, for example, if a client severs the attorney-client relationship with a lawyer who remains in a firm, the entitlement of that individual lawyer to undertake a representation against that former client is governed by paragraph (a); and all other lawyers who are or become members of or associated with that lawyer's firm are treated in the same manner by paragraph (b). Similarly, if a lawyer severs his or her association with a firm and that firm retains as a client a person whom the lawyer personally represented while with the firm, that lawyer's ability thereafter to undertake a representation against that client is governed by paragraph (a); and all other lawyers who are or become members of or associates with that lawyer's new firm are treated in the same manner by paragraph (b).

6. Paragraph (c) addresses the situation of former partners or associates of a lawyer who once had represented a client when the relationship between the former partners or associates and the lawyer has been terminated. In that situation, the former partners or associates are prohibited from questioning the validity of such lawyer's work product and from undertaking representation which in reasonable probability will involve a violation of Rule 1.05. Such a violation could occur, for example, when the former partners or associates retained materials in their files from the earlier representation of the client that, if disclosed or used in connection with the subsequent representation, would violate Rule 1.05(b)(1) or (b)(3).

7. Thus, the effect of paragraphs (b) and (c) is to extend any inability of a particular lawyer under paragraph (a) to undertake a representation against a former client to all other lawyers who are or become members of or associated with any firm in which that lawyer is practicing. Should those other lawyers cease to be members of the same firm as the lawyer affected by paragraph (a) without themselves coming within its restrictions, they thereafter may undertake the representation against the lawyer's former client unless prevented from doing so by some other of these Rules.

8. Although not required to do so by Rule 1.05 or this Rule, some courts, as a procedural decision, disqualify a lawyer for representing a present client against a former client when the subject matter of the present representation is so closely related to the subject matter of the prior representation that confidences obtained from the former client might be useful in the representation of the present client. See Comment 17 to Rule 1.06. This so-called "substantial relationship" test is defended by asserting that to require a showing that confidences of the first client were in fact used for the benefit of the subsequent client as a condition to procedural disqualification would cause disclosure of the confidences that the court seeks to protect. A lawyer is not subject to discipline under Rule 1.05(b)(1), (3), or (4), however, unless the protected information is actually used. Likewise, a lawyer is not subject to discipline under this Rule unless the new representation by the lawyer in reasonable probability would result in a violation of those provisions.

9. Whether the "substantial relationship" test will continue to be employed as a standard for procedural disqualification is a matter beyond the scope of these Rules. See Preamble: Scope. The possibility that such a disqualification might be sought by the former client or granted by a court, however, is a matter that could be of substantial importance to the present client in deciding whether or not to retain or continue to employ a particular lawyer or law firm as its counsel. Consequently, a lawyer should disclose those possibilities, as well as their potential consequences for the representation, to the present client as soon as the lawyer becomes aware of them; and the client then should be allowed to decide whether or not to obtain new counsel. See Rules 1.03(b) and 1.06(b).

10. This Rule is primarily for the protection of clients and its protections can be waived by them. A waiver is effective only if there is consent after disclosure of the relevant circumstances, including the lawyer's past or intended role on behalf of each client, as appropriate. See Comments 7 and 8 to Rule 1.06.

District of Columbia Rule 1.11

[The District of Columbia has added the following provisions to Model Rule 1.11]

RULE 1.11 Successive Government and Private Employment

* * *

(d) Except as provided in paragraph (e), when any of counsel, lawyer, partner, or associate of a lawyer personally disqualified under paragraph (a) accepts employment in connection with a matter giving rise to the personal disqualification, the following notifications shall be required:

(1) The personally disqualified lawyer shall submit to the public department or agency by which the lawyer was formerly employed and serve on each other party to any pertinent proceeding a signed document attesting that during the period of disqualification the personally disqualified lawyer will not participate in any manner in the matter or the representation, will not discuss the matter or the representation with any partner, associate, or of counsel lawyer, and will not share in any fees for the matter or the representation.

(2) At least one affiliated lawyer shall submit to the same department or agency and serve on the same parties a signed document attesting that all affiliated lawyers are aware of the requirement that the personally disqualified lawyer be screened from participating in or discussing the matter or the representation and describing the procedures being taken to screen the personally disqualified lawyer.

(e) If a client requests in writing that the fact and subject matter of a representation subject to paragraph (d) not be disclosed by submitting the signed statements referred to in paragraph (d), such statements shall be prepared concurrently with undertaking the representation and filed with bar counsel under seal. If at any time thereafter the fact and subject matter of the representation are disclosed to the public or become a part of the public record, the signed statements previously prepared shall be promptly submitted as required by paragraph (d).

(f) Signed documents filed pursuant to paragraph (d) shall be available to the public, except to the extent that a lawyer submitting a signed document demonstrates to the satisfaction of the public department or agency upon which such documents are served that public disclosure is inconsistent with Rule 1.6 or provisions of law.

(g) This Rule applies to any matter involving a specific party or parties.

(h) A lawyer who participates in a program of temporary service to the office of corporation counsel of the kind described in Rule 1.10(e) shall be treated as having served as a public officer or employee for purposes of paragraph (a), and the provisions of paragraphs (b)–(e) shall apply to the lawyer and to lawyers affiliated with the lawyer.

New Hampshire Rule 1.11A

[New Hampshire has added the following provision to address the conduct of lawyer officials:]

RULE 1.11A Conduct of Lawyer-Officials

(a) Definitions. As used in this rule:

lawyer-official means a lawyer actively engaged in the practice of law, who is a member of a governmental body;

governmental body means any state or local governmental agency, board, body, council or commission, including any advisory committee established by any of such entities;

related body means a governmental body whose members are appointed or elected by the lawyer-official or the governmental body of which the lawyer-official is a member;

interest means a direct, personal and pecuniary interest, individually or on a client's behalf, in a matter which is under consideration by either the governmental body of which the lawyer-official is a member, or by a related body; and

advisory committee means any committee, council, commission, or other like body whose primary purpose is to consider an issue or issues designated by the appointing authority so as to provide such authority with advice or recommendations concerning the formulation of any public policy or legislation that may be promoted, modified, or opposed by such authority.

(b) No lawyer-official shall:

(1) participate in any hearing, debate, discussion or vote, or in any manner otherwise attempt to influence the outcome of a matter in which the lawyer-official has an interest;

(2) utilize information obtained in such capacity for his or her own personal benefit or that of his or her clients or the clients of the firm with which the lawyer-official is associated;

(3) appear on behalf of a client before any governmental body of which the lawyer-official is a member or any related body;

(4) accept anything of value from any person or organization when the lawyer-official knows or reasonably should know that the offer is for the purpose of influencing the lawyer-official's actions or decisions as a lawyer-official;

(5) use his or her official position to influence or to attempt to influence either the governmental body of which the lawyer is a member or a related body to act in favor of the lawyer-official or the lawyer-official's clients or clients of the firm with which the lawyer-official is associated.

(c) Other lawyers in the firm with which the lawyer-official is associated may appear on behalf of clients before the governmental body of which the lawyer-official is a member, if the lawyer-official publicly disqualifies himself or herself and refrains from participation in the matter in accordance with paragraph (b)(1) of this Rule and otherwise conducts himself or herself with respect to the matter in question in accordance with paragraph (b) of this Rule. Other lawyers in the firm with which the lawyer-official is associated may appear on behalf of clients before a related body, if the lawyer-official conducts himself or herself with respect to the matter in question in accordance with paragraph (b) of this Rule.

Montana Rule 1.17

[Montana has added Rule 1.17 which has no counterpart in the Model Rules]

RULE 1.17 Government Employment

An attorney employed full time by the State of Montana or a political subdivision shall not accept other employment during the course of which it would be possible to use or otherwise rely on information obtained by reason of government employment that is injurious, confidential or privileged and not otherwise discoverable.

COUNSELOR

Oregon Rule 2.4.

RULE 2.4 Lawyer Serving as Mediator

(a) A lawyer serving as a mediator:

(1) shall not act as a lawyer for any party against another party in the matter in mediation or in any related proceeding, and

(2) must clearly inform the parties of and obtain the parties' consent to the lawyer's role as mediator.

(b) A lawyer serving as a mediator:

(1) may prepare documents that memorialize and implement the agreement reached in mediation,

(2) shall recommend that each party seek independent legal advice before executing the documents, and

(3) with the consent of all parties, may record or may file the documents in court.

(c) The requirements of Rule 2.4(a)(2) and (b)(2) shall not apply to mediation programs established by operation of law or court order.

ADVOCATE

Kansas Rule 3.5

[Kansas has modified Model Rule 3.5 to read as follows:]

RULE 3.5 Impartiality and Decorum of the Tribunal

A lawyer shall not:

(a) give or lend anything of value to a judge, official, or employee of a tribunal except as permitted by Section D(5) of Canon 4 of the Code of Judicial Conduct as it may, from time to time be adopted in Kansas, nor may a lawyer attempt to improperly influence a judge, official or employee of a tribunal, but a lawyer may make a contribution to the campaign fund of a candidate for judicial office in conformity with Section C(2) and (4) of Canon 5 of the Code of Judicial Conduct;

(b) communicate or cause another to communicate with a member of a jury or the venire from which the jury will be selected about the matters under consideration other than in the course of official proceedings until after the discharge of the jury from further consideration of the case;

(c) communicate or cause another to communicate as to the merits of a cause with a judge or official before whom an adversary proceeding is pending except:

(1) in the course of official proceedings in the cause;

(2) in writing, if the lawyer promptly delivers a copy of the writing to opposing counsel or to the adverse party if unrepresented;

(3) orally upon adequate notice to opposing counsel or the adverse party if unrepresented;

(4) as otherwise authorized by law or court rule;

(d) engage in undignified or discourteous conduct degrading to a tribunal.

TRANSACTIONS WITH PERSONS OTHER THAN CLIENTS

Texas Rule 4.04 *(Modification of Model Rule 4.4)*

[Texas has modified Model Rule 4.4 as follows:]

RULE 4.04 Respect for Rights of Third Persons

* * *

(b) A lawyer shall not present, participate in presenting, or threaten to present:

(1) criminal or disciplinary charges solely to gain an advantage in a civil matter; or

(2) civil, criminal or disciplinary charges against a complainant, a witness, or a potential witness in a bar disciplinary proceeding solely to prevent participation by the complainant, witness or potential witness therein.

LAW FIRMS AND ASSOCIATIONS

District of Columbia Rule 5.4

RULE 5.4 Professional Independence of a Lawyer

(a) A lawyer or law firm shall not share legal fees with a nonlawyer, except that:

(1) an agreement by a lawyer with the lawyer's firm, partner, or associate may provide for the payment of money, over a reasonable period of time after the lawyer's death, to the lawyer's estate or to one or more specified persons;

(2) a lawyer who undertakes to complete unfinished legal business of a deceased lawyer may pay to the estate of the deceased lawyer that proportion of the total compensation which fairly represents the services rendered by the deceased lawyer. A lawyer who purchases the practice of a deceased, disabled, or disappeared lawyer may, pursuant to the provisions of Rule 1.17, pay the estate or other representative of that lawyer the agreed-upon purchase price.

(3) a lawyer or law firm may include nonlawyer employees in a compensation or retirement plan, even though the plan is based in whole or in part on a profit-sharing arrangement; and

(4) sharing of fees is permitted in a partnership or other form of organization which meets the requirements of paragraph (b).

* * *

(b) A lawyer may practice law in a partnership or other form of organization in which a financial interest is held or managerial authority is exercised by an individual nonlawyer who performs professional services which assist the organization in providing legal services to clients, but only if:

(1) the partnership or organization has as its sole purpose providing legal services to clients;

(2) all persons having such managerial authority or holding a financial interest undertake to abide by these rules of professional conduct;

(3) the lawyers who have a financial interest or managerial authority in the partnership or organization undertake to be responsible for the nonlawyer participants to the same extent as if nonlawyer participants were lawyers under rule 5.1;

(4) the foregoing conditions are set forth in writing.

(c) A lawyer shall not permit a person who recommends, employs, or pays the lawyer to render legal services for another to direct or regulate the lawyer's professional judgment in rendering such legal services.

COMMENT:

[1] The provisions of this Rule express traditional limitations on sharing fees with nonlawyers. (On sharing fees among lawyers not in the same firm, see Rule 1.5(e).) These limitations are to protect the lawyer's professional independence of judgment. Where someone other than the client pays the lawyer's fee or salary, or recommends employment of the lawyer, that arrangement does not modify the lawyer's obligation to the client. As stated in paragraph (c), such arrangements should not interfere with the lawyer's professional judgment.

[2] Traditionally, the canons of legal ethics and disciplinary rules prohibited lawyers from practicing law in a partnership that includes nonlawyers or in any other organization where a nonlawyer is a

shareholder, director, or officer. Notwithstanding these strictures, the profession implicitly recognized exceptions for lawyers who work for corporate law departments, insurance companies, and legal service organizations.

[3] As the demand increased for a broad range of professional services from a single source, lawyers employed professionals from other disciplines to work for them. So long as the nonlawyers remained employees of the lawyers, these relationships did not violate the disciplinary rules. However, when lawyers and nonlawyers considered forming partnerships and professional corporations to provide a combination of legal and other services to the public, they faced serious obstacles under the former rules.

[4] This Rule rejects an absolute prohibition against lawyers and nonlawyers joining together to provide collaborative services, but continues to impose traditional ethical requirements with respect to the organization thus created. Thus, a lawyer may practice law in an organization where nonlawyers hold a financial interest or exercise managerial authority, but only if the conditions set forth in subparagraphs (b)(1), (b)(2), and (b)(3) are satisfied, and, pursuant to subparagraph (b)(4), satisfaction of these conditions is set forth in a written instrument. The requirement of a writing helps ensure that these important conditions are not overlooked in establishing the organizational structure of entities in which nonlawyers enjoy an ownership or managerial role equivalent to that of a partner in a traditional law firm.

[5] Nonlawyer participants under Rule 5.4 ought not be confused with nonlawyer assistants under Rule 5.3. Nonlawyer participants are persons having managerial authority or financial interests in organizations which provide legal services. Within such organizations, lawyers with financial interests or managerial authority are held responsible for ethical misconduct by nonlawyer participants about which the lawyers know or reasonably should know. This is the same standard of liability contemplated by Rule 5.1, regarding the responsibilities of lawyers with direct supervisory authority over other lawyers.

[6] Nonlawyer assistants under Rule 5.3 do not have managerial authority or financial interests in the organization. Lawyers having direct supervisory authority over nonlawyer assistants are held responsible only for ethical misconduct by assistants about which the lawyers actually know.

[7] As the introductory portion of Subparagraph (b) makes clear, the purpose of liberalizing the rules regarding the possession of a financial interest or the exercise of management authority by a nonlawyer is to permit nonlawyer professionals to work with lawyers in the delivery of legal services without being relegated to the role of an employee. For example, the Rule permits economists to work in a firm with antitrust or public utility practitioners, psychologists or psychiatric social workers to work with family law practitioners to assist in counseling clients, nonlawyer lobbyists to work with lawyers who perform legislative services, certified public accountants to work in conjunction with tax lawyers or others who use accountants' services in performing legal services, and professional managers to serve as office managers, executive directors, or in similar positions. In all of these situations, the professionals may be given financial interests or managerial responsibility, so long as all of the requirements of subparagraph (c) are met.

[8] Subparagraph (b) does not permit an individual or entity to acquire all or any part of the ownership of a law partnership or other form of law practice organization for investment or other purposes. It thus does not permit a corporation, an investment banking firm, an investor, or any other person or entity to entitle itself to all or any portion of the income or profits of a law firm or other similar organization. Since such an investor would not be an individual performing professional services within the law firm or other organization, the requirements of subparagraph (b) would not be met.

[9] The term "individual" in subparagraph (b) is not intended to preclude the participation in a law firm or other organization by an individual professional corporation in the same manner as lawyers who have incorporated as a professional corporation currently participate in partnerships which include professional corporations.

[10] Some sharing of fees is likely to occur in the kinds of organizations permitted by paragraph (b). Subparagraph (a)(4) makes it clear that such fee-sharing is not prohibited.

* * *

Pennsylvania Rule 5.7

[Pennsylvania has enacted its own Rule 5.7 to govern lawyer involvement in nonlegal services.]

Rule 5.7. Responsibilities Regarding Nonlegal Services

(a) A lawyer who provides nonlegal services to a recipient that are not distinct from legal services provided to that recipient is subject to the Rules of Professional Conduct with respect to the provision of both legal and nonlegal services.

(b) A lawyer who provides nonlegal services to a recipient that are distinct from any legal services provided to the recipient is subject to the Rules of Professional Conduct with respect to the nonlegal services if the lawyer knows or reasonably should know that the recipient might believe that the recipient is receiving the protection of a client-lawyer relationship.

(c) A lawyer who is an owner, controlling party, employee, agent, or is otherwise affiliated with an entity providing nonlegal services to a recipient is subject to the Rules of Professional Conduct with respect to the nonlegal services if the lawyer knows or reasonably should know that the recipient might believe that the recipient is receiving the protection of a client-lawyer relationship.

(d) Paragraph (b) or (c) does not apply if the lawyer makes reasonable efforts to avoid any misunderstanding by the recipient receiving nonlegal services. Those efforts must include advising the recipient that the services are not legal services and that the protection of a client-lawyer relationship does not exist with respect to the provision of nonlegal services to the recipient.

(e) The term "nonlegal services" denotes services that might reasonably be performed in conjunction with and in substance are related to the provision of legal services, and that are not prohibited as unauthorized practice of law when provided by a nonlawyer.

COMMENT:

[1] For many years, lawyers have provided to their clients nonlegal services that are ancillary to the practice of law. Nonlegal services are those that are not prohibited as unauthorized practice of law when provided by a nonlawyer. Examples of nonlegal services include providing title insurance, financial planning, accounting, trust services, real estate counseling, legislative lobbying, economic analysis, social work, psychological counseling, tax return preparation, and patent, medical or environmental consulting. A broad range of economic and other interests of clients may be served by lawyers participating in the delivery of these services.

The Potential for Misunderstanding

[2] Whenever a lawyer directly provides nonlegal services, there exists the potential for ethical problems. Principal among these is the possibility that the person for whom the nonlegal services are performed may fail to understand that the services may not carry with them the protection normally afforded by the client-lawyer relationship. The recipient of the nonlegal services may expect, for example, that the protection of client confidences, prohibitions against representation of persons with conflicting interests, and obligations of a lawyer to maintain professional independence apply to the provision of nonlegal services when that may not be the case. The risk of such confusion is especially acute when the lawyer renders both types of services with respect to the same matter.

Providing Nonlegal Services That Are Not Distinct From Legal Services

[3] Under some circumstances, the legal and nonlegal services may be so closely entwined that they cannot be distinguished from each other. In this situation, confusion by the recipient as to when the protection of the client-lawyer relationship applies are likely to be unavoidable. Therefore, Rule 5.7(a) requires that the lawyer providing the nonlegal services adhere to all of the requirements of the Rules of Professional Conduct.

[4] In such a case, a lawyer will be responsible for assuring that both the lawyer's conduct and, to the extent required by Rule 5.3, that of nonlawyer employees comply in all respects with the Rules of Professional Conduct. When a lawyer is obliged to accord the recipients of such nonlegal services the protection of those Rules that apply to the client-lawyer relationship, the lawyer must take special care to heed the proscriptions of the Rules addressing conflict of interest (Rules 1.7 through 1.11, especially Rules 1.7(b) and 1.8(a), (b) and (f)), and to scrupulously adhere to the requirements of Rule 1.6 relating to disclosure of confidential information. The promotion of the nonlegal services must also in all respects comply with Rules 7.1 through 7.3, dealing with advertising and solicitation.

[5] Rule 5.7(a) applies to the provision of nonlegal services by a lawyer even when the lawyer does not personally provide any legal services to the person for whom the nonlegal services are performed if the person is also receiving legal services from another lawyer that are not distinct from the nonlegal services.

Avoiding Misunderstanding When A Lawyer Directly Provides Nonlegal Services That Are Distinct From Legal Services

[6] Even when the lawyer believes that his or her provision of nonlegal services is distinct from any legal services provided to the recipient, there is still a risk that the recipient of the nonlegal services will misunderstand the implications of receiving nonlegal services from a lawyer; the recipient might believe that the recipient is receiving the protection of a client-lawyer relationship. Where there is such a risk of misunderstanding, Rule 5.7(b) requires that the lawyer providing the nonlegal services adhere to all the Rules of Professional Conduct, unless exempted by Rule 5.7(d).

Avoiding Misunderstanding When a Lawyer is Indirectly Involved in the Provision of Nonlegal Services

[7] Nonlegal services also may be provided through an entity with which a lawyer is somehow affiliated, for example, as owner, employee, controlling party or agent. In this situation, there is still a risk that the recipient of the nonlegal services might believe that the recipient is receiving the protection of a client-lawyer relationship. Where there is such a risk of misunderstanding, Rule 5.7(c) requires that the lawyer involved with the entity providing nonlegal services adhere to all the Rules of Professional Conduct, unless exempted by Rule 5.7(d).

Avoiding the Application of Paragraphs (b) and (c)

[8] Paragraphs (b) and (c) specify that the Rules of Professional Conduct apply to a lawyer who directly provides or is otherwise involved in the provision of nonlegal services if there is a risk that the recipient might believe that the recipient is receiving the protection of a client-lawyer relationship. Neither the Rules of Professional Conduct nor paragraphs (b) or (c) will apply, however, if pursuant to paragraph (d), the lawyer takes reasonable efforts to avoid any misunderstanding by the recipient. In this respect, Rule 5.7 is analogous to Rule 4.3(c).

[9] In taking the reasonable measures referred to in paragraph (d), the lawyer must communicate to the person receiving the nonlegal services that the relationship will not be a client-lawyer relationship. The communication should be made before entering into an agreement for the provision of nonlegal services, in a manner sufficient to assure that the person understands the significance of the communication, and preferably should be in writing.

[10] The burden is upon the lawyer to show that the lawyer has taken reasonable measures under the circumstances to communicate the desired understanding. For instance, a sophisticated user of nonlegal services, such as a publicly-held corporation, may require a lesser explanation than someone unaccustomed to making distinctions between legal services and nonlegal services, such as an individual seeking tax advice from a lawyer-accountant or investigative services in connection with a lawsuit.

The Relationship Between Rule 5.7 and Other Rules of Professional Conduct

[11] Even before Rule 5.7 was adopted, a lawyer involved in the provision of nonlegal services was subject to those Rules of Professional Conduct that apply generally. For example, Rule 8.4(c) makes a lawyer responsible for fraud committed with respect to the provision of nonlegal services. Such a lawyer must also comply with Rule 1.8(a). Nothing in this rule is intended to suspend the effect of any otherwise applicable Rule of Professional Conduct such as Rule 1.7(b), Rule 1.8(a) and Rule 8.4(c).

[12] In addition to the Rules of Professional Conduct, principles of law external to the Rules, for example, the law of principal and agent, may govern the legal duties owed by a lawyer to those receiving the nonlegal services.

PUBLIC SERVICE

South Dakota Rule 6.1

[South Dakota has modified Model Rule 6.1 to read as follows:]

RULE 6.1 Voluntary Pro Bono Publico Service

A lawyer should render public interest legal service.

A lawyer may discharge this responsibility by:

(a) providing professional services at no fee or a reduced fee to persons of limited means or to public service or charitable groups or organizations; or

(b) by service without compensation in public interest activities that improve the law, the legal system or the legal profession; or

(c) by financial support for organizations that provide legal services to persons of limited means.

COMMENT:

[1] Every lawyer, regardless of professional prominence or professional work load, has a responsibility to provide legal services to those unable to pay, and personal involvement in the problems of the disadvantaged can be one of the most rewarding experiences in the life of a lawyer. The American Bar Association urges all lawyers to provide a minimum of 50 hours of pro bono services annually. States, however, may decide to choose a higher or lower number of hours of annual service (which may be expressed as a percentage of a lawyer's professional time) depending upon local needs and local conditions. It is recognized that in some years a lawyer may render greater or fewer hours than the annual standard specified, but during the course of his or her legal career, each lawyer should render on average per year, the number of hours set forth in this Rule. Services can be performed in civil matters or in criminal or quasi-criminal matters for which there is no government obligation to provide funds for legal representation, such as post-conviction death penalty appeal cases.

[2] Paragraphs (a)(1) and (2) recognize the critical need for legal services that exists among persons of limited means by providing that a substantial majority of the legal services rendered annually to the disadvantaged be furnished without fee or expectation of fee. Legal services under these paragraphs consist of a full range of activities, including individual and class representation, the provision of legal advice, legislative lobbying, administrative rule making and the provision of free training or mentoring to those who represent persons of limited means. The variety of these activities should facilitate participation by government lawyers, even when restrictions exist on their engaging in the outside practice of law.

[3] Persons eligible for legal services under paragraphs (a)(1) and (2) are those who qualify for participation in programs funded by the Legal Services Corporation and those whose incomes and financial resources are slightly above the guidelines utilized by such programs but nevertheless, cannot afford counsel. Legal services can be rendered to individuals or to organizations such as homeless shelters, battered women's centers and food pantries that serve those of limited means. The term "governmental organizations" includes, but is not limited to, public protection programs and sections of governmental or public sector agencies.

[4] Because service must be provided without fee or expectation of fee, the intent of the lawyer to render free legal services is essential for the work performed to fall within the meaning of paragraphs (a)(1) and (2). Accordingly, services rendered cannot be considered pro bono if an anticipated fee is uncollected, but the award of statutory attorneys' fees in a case originally accepted as pro bono would not disqualify such services from inclusion under this section. Lawyers who do receive fees in such cases are encouraged to

contribute an appropriate portion of such fees to organizations or projects that benefit persons of limited means.

[5] While it is possible for a lawyer to fulfill the annual responsibility to perform pro bono services exclusively through activities described in paragraphs (a)(1) and (2), to the extent that any hours of service remained unfulfilled, the remaining commitment can be met in a variety of ways as set forth in paragraph (b). Constitutional, statutory or regulatory restrictions may prohibit or impede government and public sector lawyers and judges from performing the pro bono services outlined in paragraphs (a)(1) and (2). Accordingly, where those restrictions apply, government and public sector lawyers and judges may fulfill their pro bono responsibility by performing services outlined in paragraph (b).

[6] Paragraph (b)(1) includes the provision of certain types of legal services to those whose incomes and financial resources place them above limited means. It also permits the pro bono lawyer to accept a substantially reduced fee for services. Examples of the types of issues that may be addressed under this paragraph include First Amendment claims, Title VII claims and environmental protection claims. Additionally, a wide range of organizations may be represented, including social service, medical research, cultural and religious groups.

[7] Paragraph (b)(2) covers instances in which lawyers agree to and receive a modest fee for furnishing legal services to persons of limited means. Participation in judicare programs and acceptance of court appointments in which the fee is substantially below a lawyer's usual rate are encouraged under this section.

[8] Paragraph (b)(3) recognizes the value of lawyers engaging in activities that improve the law, the legal system or the legal profession. Serving on bar association committees, serving on boards of pro bono or legal services programs, taking part in Law Day activities, acting as a continuing legal education instructor, a mediator or an arbitrator and engaging in legislative lobbying to improve the law, the legal system or the profession are a few examples of the many activities that fall within this paragraph.

[9] Because the provision of pro bono services is a professional responsibility, it is the individual ethical commitment of each lawyer. Nevertheless, there may be times when it is not feasible for a lawyer to engage in pro bono services. At such times a lawyer may discharge the pro bono responsibility by providing financial support to organizations providing free legal services to persons of limited means. Such financial support should be reasonably equivalent to the value of the hours of service that would have otherwise been provided. In addition, at times it may be more feasible to satisfy the pro bono responsibility collectively, as by a firm's aggregate pro bono activities.

[10] Because the efforts of individual lawyers are not enough to meet the need for free legal services that exists among persons of limited means, the government and the profession have instituted additional programs to provide those services. Every lawyer should financially support such programs, in addition to either providing direct pro bono services or making financial contributions when pro bono service is not feasible.

[11] Law firms should act reasonably to enable and encourage all lawyers in the firm to provide the pro bono legal services called for by this Rule.

[12] The responsibility set forth in this Rule is not intended to be enforced through disciplinary process.

INFORMATION ABOUT LEGAL SERVICES

Texas Disciplinary Rules 7.01–7.07

Texas Disciplinary Rule 7.01

RULE 7.01 Firm Names and Letterhead

(a) A lawyer in private practice shall not practice under a trade name, a name that is misleading as to the identity of the lawyer or lawyers practicing under such name, or a firm name containing names other than those of one or more of the lawyers in the firm, except that the names of a professional corporation, professional association, limited

liability partnership, or professional limited liability company may contain "P.C.," "L.L.P.," "P.L.L.C.," or similar symbols indicating the nature of the organization, and if otherwise lawful a firm may use as, or continue to include in, its name the name or names of one or more deceased or retired members of the firm or of a predecessor firm in a continuing line of succession. Nothing herein shall prohibit a married woman from practicing under her maiden name.

(b) A firm with offices in more than one jurisdiction may use the same name in each jurisdiction, but identification of the lawyers in an office of the firm shall indicate the jurisdictional limitations on those not licensed to practice in the jurisdiction where the office is located.

(c) The name of a lawyer occupying a judicial, legislative, or public executive or administrative position shall not be used in the name of a firm, or in communications on its behalf, during any substantial period in which the lawyer is not actively and regularly practicing with the firm.

(d) A lawyer shall not hold himself or herself out as being a partner, shareholder, or associate with one or more other lawyers unless they are in fact partners, shareholders, or associates.

(e) A lawyer shall not advertise in the public media or seek professional employment by any communication under a trade or fictitious name, except that a lawyer who practices under a firm name as authorized by paragraph (a) of this Rule may use that name in such advertisement or communication but only if that name is the firm name that appears on the lawyer's letterhead, business cards, office sign, fee contracts, and with the lawyer's signature on pleadings and other legal documents.

(f) A lawyer shall not use a firm name, letterhead, or other professional designation that violates Rule 7.02(a).

COMMENT:

1. A lawyer or law firm may not practice law using a name that is misleading as to the identity of the lawyers practicing under such name, but the continued use of the name of a deceased or retired member of the firm or of a predecessor firm is not considered to be misleading. Trade names are generally considered inherently misleading. Other types of firm names can be misleading as well, such as a firm name that creates the appearance that lawyers are partners or employees of a single law firm when in fact they are merely associated for the purpose of sharing expenses. In such cases, the lawyers involved may not denominate themselves in any manner suggesting such an ongoing professional relationship as, for example, "Smith and Jones" or "Smith and Jones Associates" or "Smith and Associates." Such titles create the false impression that the lawyers named have assumed a joint professional responsibility for clients' legal affairs. See paragraph (d).

2. The practice of law firms having offices in more than one state is commonplace. Although it is not necessary that the name of an interstate firm include Texas lawyers, a letterhead including the name of any lawyer not licensed in Texas must indicate the lawyer is not licensed in Texas.

3. Paragraph (c) is designed to prevent the exploitation of a lawyer's public position for the benefit of the lawyer's firm. Likewise, because it may be misleading under paragraph (a), a lawyer who occupies a judicial, legislative, or public executive or administrative position should not indicate that fact on a letterhead which identifies that person as an attorney in the private practice of law. However, a firm name may include the name of a public official who is actively and regularly practicing law with the firm. But see Rule 7.02(a)(4).

4. With certain limited exceptions, paragraph (a) forbids a lawyer from using a trade name or fictitious name. Paragraph (e) sets out this same prohibition with respect to advertising in public media or written communications seeking professional employment and contains additional restrictions on the use of trade names or fictitious names in those contexts. In a largely overlapping measure, paragraph (f) forbids

the use of any such name or designation if it would amount to a "false or misleading communication" under Rule 7.02(a).

(Comment amended by State Bar Board of Directors Jan. 20, 1995.)

Texas Disciplinary Rule 7.02

RULE 7.02 Communications Concerning a Lawyer's Services

(a) A lawyer shall not make or sponsor a false or misleading communication about the qualifications or the services of any lawyer or firm. A communication is false or misleading if it:

(1) contains a material misrepresentation of fact or law, or omits a fact necessary to make the statement considered as a whole not materially misleading;

(2) contains any reference in a public media advertisement to past successes or results obtained unless

(i) the communicating lawyer or member of the law firm served as lead counsel in the matter giving rise to the recovery, or was primarily responsible for the settlement or verdict;

(ii) the amount involved was actually received by the client;

(iii) the reference is accompanied by adequate information regarding the nature of the case or matter and the damages or injuries sustained by the client, and

(iv) if the gross amount received is stated, the attorney's fees and litigation expenses withheld from the amount are stated as well;

(3) is likely to create an unjustified expectation about results the lawyer can achieve, or states or implies that the lawyer can achieve results by means that violate these rules or other law;

(4) compares the lawyer's services with other lawyers' services, unless the comparison can be substantiated by reference to verifiable, objective data;

(5) states or implies that the lawyer is able to influence improperly or upon irrelevant grounds any tribunal, legislative body, or public official; or

(6) designates one or more specific areas of practice in an advertisement in the public media or in a solicitation communication unless the advertising or soliciting lawyer is competent to handle legal matters in each such area of practice; or

(7) uses an actor or model to portray a client of the lawyer or law firm.

(b) Rule 7.02(a)(5) does not require that a lawyer be certified by the Texas Board of Legal Specialization at the time of advertising in a specific area of practice, but such certification shall conclusively establish that such lawyer satisfies the requirements of Rule 7.02(a)(5) with respect to the area(s) of practice in which such lawyer is certified.

(c) A lawyer shall not advertise in the public media or state in a solicitation communication that the lawyer is a specialist, except as permitted under Rule 7.04.

(d) Any statement or disclaimer required by these rules shall be made in each language used in the advertisement or solicitation communication with respect to which such required statement or disclaimer relates; provided however, the mere statement that a particular language is spoken or understood shall not alone result in the need for a statement or disclaimer in that language.

(Former Rule 7.01 adopted eff. Jan. 1, 1990; redesignated and amended to be eff. April 1, 1995; on March 31, 1995, the Texas Supreme Court extended the effective date 120 days after the date of judgment of the U.S. District Court in Texans Against Censorship, Inc. v. State Bar of Texas, 888 F.Supp. 1328 (E.D.Tex. 1995).)

COMMENT:

1. The Rules within Part VII are intended to regulate communications made for the purpose of obtaining professional employment. They are not intended to affect other forms of speech by lawyers, such as political advertisements or political commentary, except insofar as a lawyer's effort to obtain employment is linked to a matter of current public debate.

2. This Rule governs all communications about a lawyer's services, including advertisements regulated by Rule 7.04 and solicitation communications regulated by Rules 7.03 and 7.05. Whatever means are used to make known a lawyer's services, statements about them must be truthful and nondeceptive.

3. Sub-paragraph (a)(1) recognizes that statements can be misleading both by what they contain and what they leave out. Statements that are false or misleading for either reason are prohibited. A truthful statement is misleading if it omits a fact necessary to make the lawyer's communication considered as a whole not materially misleading. A truthful statement is also misleading if there is a substantial likelihood that it will lead a reasonable person to formulate a specific conclusion about the lawyer or the lawyer's services for which there is no reasonable factual foundation.

4. Sub-paragraphs (a)(2) and (3) recognize that statements may create "unjustified expectations". For example, an advertisement that truthfully reports that a lawyer obtained a jury verdict of a certain amount on behalf of a client would nonetheless be misleading if it were to turn out that the verdict was overturned on appeal or later compromised for a substantially reduced amount, and the advertisement did not disclose such facts as well. Even an advertisement that fully and accurately reports a lawyer's achievements on behalf of clients or former clients may be misleading if presented so as to lead a reasonable person to form an unjustified expectation that the same results could be obtained for other clients in similar matters without reference to the specific factual and legal circumstances of each client's case. Those unique circumstances would ordinarily preclude advertisements in the public media and written solicitation communications that discuss the results obtained on behalf of a client, such as the amount of a damage award, the lawyer's record in obtaining favorable settlements or verdicts, as well as those that contain client endorsements.

5. Sub-paragraph (a)(4) recognizes that comparisons of lawyers' services may also be misleading unless those comparisons "can be substantiated by reference to verifiable objective data." Similarly, an unsubstantiated comparison of a lawyer's services or fees with the services or fees of other lawyers may be misleading if presented with such specificity as would lead a reasonable person to conclude that the comparison can be substantiated. Statements comparing a lawyer's services with those of another where the comparisons are not susceptible of precise measurement or verification, such as "we are the toughest lawyers in town", "we will get money for you when other lawyers can't", or "we are the best law firm in Texas if you want a large recovery" can deceive or mislead prospective clients.

6. The inclusion of a disclaimer or qualifying language may preclude a finding that a statement is likely to create unjustified expectations or otherwise mislead a prospective client, but it will not necessarily do so. Unless any such qualifications and disclaimers are both sufficient and displayed with equal prominence to the information to which they pertain, that information can still readily mislead prospective clients into believing that similar results can be obtained for them without reference to their specific factual and legal circumstances. Consequently, in order not to be false, misleading, or deceptive, other of these Rules require that appropriate disclaimers or qualifying language must be presented in the same manner as the communication and with equal prominence. See Rules 7.04(q) and 7.05(a)(2).

7. On the other hand, a simple statement of a lawyer's own qualifications devoid of comparisons to other lawyers does not pose the same risk of being misleading and so does not violate sub-paragraph (a)(4). Similarly, a lawyer making a referral to another lawyer may express a good faith subjective opinion regarding that other lawyer.

8. Thus, this Rule does not prohibit communication of information concerning a lawyer's name or firm name, address and telephone numbers; the basis on which the lawyer's fees are determined, including

prices for specific services and payment and credit arrangements; names of references and, with their consent, names of clients regularly represented; and other truthful information that might invite the attention of those seeking legal assistance. When a communication permitted by Rule 7.02 is made in the public media, the lawyer should consult Rule 7.04 for further guidance and restrictions. When a communication permitted by Rule 7.02 is made by a lawyer through a written solicitation, the lawyer should consult Rules 7.03 and 7.05 for further guidance and restrictions.

Communication of Fields of Practice

9. Sub-paragraph (a)(5) prohibits a lawyer from stating or implying that the lawyer has an ability to influence a tribunal, legislative body, or other public official through improper conduct or upon irrelevant grounds. Such conduct brings the profession into disrepute, even though the improper or irrelevant activities referred to are never carried out, and so are prohibited without regard to the lawyer's actual intent to engage in such activities.

10. Paragraphs (a)(6), (b) and (c) of Rule 7.02 regulate communications concerning a lawyer's fields of practice and should be construed together with Rule 7.04 or 7.05, as applicable. If a lawyer in a public media advertisement or in a written solicitation designates one or more specific areas of practice, that designation is at least an implicit representation that the lawyer is qualified in the areas designated. Accordingly, Rule 7.02(a)(5) prohibits the designation of a field of practice unless the communicating lawyer is in fact competent in the area.

11. Typically, one would expect competency to be measured by special education, training, or experience in the particular area of law designated. Because certification by the Texas Board of Legal Specialization involves special education, training, and experience, certification by the Texas Board of Legal Specialization conclusively establishes that a lawyer meets the requirements of Rule 7.02(a)(6) in any area in which the Board has certified the lawyer. However, competency may be established by means other than certification by the Texas Board of Legal Specialization. See Rule 7.04(b).

12. Lawyers who wish to advertise in the public media that they specialize should refer to Rule 7.04(a), (b) and (c). Lawyers who wish to assert a specialty in a written solicitation should refer to Rule 7.05(a)(4) and (b)(1).

Actor Portrayal of Clients

13. Sub-paragraph (a)(7) further protects prospective clients from false, misleading, or deceptive advertisements and solicitations by prohibiting the use of actors to portray clients of a lawyer or law firm. Other rules prohibit the use of actors to portray lawyers in the advertising or soliciting lawyer's firm. See Rules 7.04(g), 7.05(a). The truthfulness of such portrayals is extremely difficult to monitor, and almost inevitably they involve actors whose apparent physical and mental attributes differ in a number of material respects from those of the actual clients portrayed.

Communication in a Second Language

14. The ability of lawyers to communicate in a second language can facilitate the delivery and receipt of legal services. Accordingly, it is in the best interest of the public that potential clients be made aware of a lawyer's language ability. A lawyer may state an ability to communicate in a second language without any further elaboration. However, if a lawyer chooses to communicate with potential clients in a second language, all statements or disclaimers required by the Texas Disciplinary Rules of Professional Conduct must also be made in that language. See paragraph (d). Communicating some information in one language while communicating the rest in another is potentially misleading if the recipient understands only one of the languages.

(Comment amended by State Bar Board of Directors Jan. 20, 1995.)

Texas Disciplinary Rule 7.03

RULE 7.03 Prohibited Solicitations and Payments

(a) A lawyer shall not by in-person contact, or by regulated telephone or other electronic contact as defined in paragraph (f) seek professional employment concerning a matter arising out of a particular occurrence or event, or series of occurrences or events,

from a prospective client or nonclient who has not sought the lawyer's advice regarding employment or with whom the lawyer has no family or past or present attorney-client relationship when a significant motive for the lawyer's doing so is the lawyer's pecuniary gain. Notwithstanding the provisions of this paragraph, a lawyer for a qualified nonprofit organization may communicate with the organization's members for the purpose of educating the members to understand the law, to recognize legal problems, to make intelligent selection of counsel, or to use legal services. In those situations where in-person or telephone or other electronic contact is permitted by this paragraph, a lawyer shall not have such a contact with a prospective client if:

(1) the communication involves coercion, duress, fraud, overreaching, intimidation, undue influence, or harassment;

(2) the communication contains information prohibited by Rule 7.02(a); or

(3) the communication contains a false, fraudulent, misleading, deceptive, or unfair statement or claim.

(b) A lawyer shall not pay, give, or offer to pay or give anything of value to a person not licensed to practice law for soliciting prospective clients for, or referring clients or prospective clients to, any lawyer or firm, except that a lawyer may pay reasonable fees for advertising and public relations services rendered in accordance with this Rule and may pay the usual charges of a lawyer referral service that meets the requirements of Occupational Code Title 5, Subtitle B, Chapter 952.

(c) A lawyer, in order to solicit professional employment, shall not pay, give, advance, or offer to pay, give, or advance anything of value, other than actual litigation expenses and other financial assistance as permitted by Rule 1.08(d), to a prospective client or any other person; provided however, this provision does not prohibit the payment of legitimate referral fees as permitted by paragraph (b) of this Rule.

(d) A lawyer shall not enter into an agreement for, charge for, or collect a fee for professional employment obtained in violation of Rule 7.03(a), (b), or (c).

(e) A lawyer shall not participate with or accept referrals from a lawyer referral service unless the lawyer knows or reasonably believes that the lawyer referral service meets the requirements of Occupational Code Title 5, Subtitle B, Chapter 952.

(f) As used in paragraph (a), "regulated telephone or other electronic contact" means any electronic communication initiated by a lawyer or by any person acting on behalf of a lawyer or law firm that will result in the person contacted communicating in a live, interactive manner with any other person by telephone or other electronic means. For purposes of this Rule a website for a lawyer or law firm is not considered a communication initiated by or on behalf of that lawyer or firm.

COMMENT:

1. In many situations, in-person or telephone solicitations by lawyers involve well-known opportunities for abuse of prospective clients. Nonetheless, paragraph (a) unconditionally prohibits those activities only when profit for the lawyer is a significant motive and the solicitation concerns matters arising out of a particular occurrence, event, or series of occurrences or events. The reason for this limited outright ban is that there are circumstances where the dangers of such contacts can be reduced. As long as the conditions of subparagraphs (a)(1) through (a)(3) are not violated by a given contact, a lawyer may engage in telephone or in-person solicitations when the solicitation is unrelated to a specific occurrence, event, or series of occurrences or events. Similarly, subject to the same restrictions, in-person or telephone solicitations are permitted where the prospective client either has a family or past or present attorney-client relationship with the lawyer or where the potential client had previously contacted the lawyer about possible employment in the matter.

2. In addition, Rule 7.03(a) does not prohibit a lawyer for a qualified non-profit organization from in-person or telephone solicitation of prospective clients for purposes related to that organization. Historically and by law, nonprofit legal aid agencies, unions, and other qualified nonprofit organizations and their lawyers have been permitted to solicit clients in-person or by telephone, and Rule 7.03(a) is not in derogation of their constitutional rights to do so. Attorneys for such nonprofit organizations, however, remain subject to this Rule's general prohibitions against undue influence, intimidation, overreaching, and the like.

Paying for Solicitation

3. Rule 7.03(b) does not prohibit a lawyer from paying standard commercial fees for advertising or public relations services rendered in accordance with these Rules. In addition, a lawyer may pay the fees required by a lawyer referral service that meets the requirements of Article 320(d), Revised Statutes. However, paying, giving, or offering to pay or give anything of value to persons not licensed to practice law who solicit prospective clients for lawyers has always been considered to be against the best interest of both the public and the legal profession. Such actions circumvent these Rules by having a nonlawyer do what a lawyer is ethically proscribed from doing. Accordingly, the practice is forbidden by Rule 7.03(b). As to payments or gifts of value to licensed lawyers for soliciting prospective clients, see Rule 1.04(f).

4. Rule 7.03(c) prohibits a lawyer from paying or giving value directly to a prospective client or any other person as consideration for employment by that client except as permitted by Rule 1.08(d).

5. Paragraph (d) prohibits a lawyer from agreeing to or charging for professional employment obtained in violation of Rule 7.03. Paragraph (e) further requires a lawyer to decline business generated by a lawyer referral service unless the lawyer knows or reasonably believes that service is operated in conformity with statutory requirements.

6. References to "a lawyer" in this and other Rules include lawyers who practice in law firms. A lawyer associated with a firm cannot circumvent these Rules by soliciting or advertising in the name of that firm in a way that violates these Rules. See Rule 7.04(e).

(Comment amended by State Bar Board of Directors Jan. 20, 1995.)

Texas Disciplinary Rule 7.04

RULE 7.04 Advertisements in the Public Media

(a) A lawyer shall not advertise in the public media by stating that the lawyer is a specialist, except as permitted under Rule 7.04(b) or as follows:

(1) A lawyer admitted to practice before the United States Patent Office may use the designation "Patents," "Patent Attorney," or "Patent Lawyer," or any combination of those terms. A lawyer engaged in the trademark practice may use the designation "Trademark," "Trademark Attorney," or "Trademark Lawyer," or any combination of those terms. A lawyer engaged in patent and trademark practice may hold himself or herself out as specializing in "Intellectual Property Law," "Patent, Trademark, Copyright Law and Unfair Competition," or any of those terms.

(2) A lawyer may permit his or her name to be listed in lawyer referral service offices that meet the requirements of Occupational Code Title 5, Subtitle B, Chapter 952, according to the areas of law in which the lawyer will accept referrals.

(3) A lawyer available to practice in a particular area of law or legal service may distribute to other lawyers and publish in legal directories and legal newspapers (whether written or electronic) a listing or an announcement of such availability. The listing shall not contain a false or misleading representation of special competence or experience, but may contain the kind of information that traditionally has been included in such publications.

(b) A lawyer who advertises in the public media:

(1) shall publish or broadcast the name of at least one lawyer who is responsible for the content of such advertisement; and

(2) shall not include a statement that the lawyer has been certified or designated by an organization as possessing special competence or a statement that the lawyer is a member of an organization the name of which implies that its members possess special competence, except that:

(i) a lawyer who has been awarded a Certificate of Special Competence by the Texas Board of Legal Specialization in the area so advertised, may state with respect to each such area, "Board Certified, [area of specialization]—Texas Board of Legal Specialization;" and

(ii) a lawyer who is a member of an organization the name of which implies that its members possess special competence, or who has been certified or designated by an organization as possessing special competence, may include a factually accurate statement of such membership or may include a factually accurate statement, "Certified [area of specialization] [name of certifying organization]," but such statements may be made only if that organization has been accredited by the Texas Board of Legal Specialization as a bona fide organization that admits to membership or grants certification only on the basis of objective, exacting, publicly available standards (including high standards of individual character, conduct, and reputation) that are reasonably relevant to the special training or special competence that is implied and that are in excess of the level of training and competence generally required for admission to the Bar.

(3) shall, in the case of infomercial or comparable presentation, state that the presentation is an advertisement:

(i) both verbally and in writing at its outset, after any commercial interruption, and at its conclusion; and

(ii) in writing during any portion of the presentation that explains how to contact a lawyer or law firm.

(c) Separate and apart from any other statements, the statements referred to in paragraph (b) shall be displayed conspicuously and in language easily understood by an ordinary consumer.

(d) Subject to the requirements of Rules 7.02 and 7.03 and of paragraphs (a), (b), and (c) of this Rule, a lawyer may, either directly or through a public relations or advertising representative, advertise services in the public media, such as (but not limited to) a telephone directory, legal directory, newspaper or other periodical, outdoor display, radio, television, the internet, or electronic or digital media.

(e) All advertisements in the public media for a lawyer or firm must be reviewed and approved in writing by the lawyer or a lawyer in the firm.

(f) A copy or recording of each advertisement in the public media and relevant approval referred to in paragraph (e), and a record of when and where the advertisement was used, shall be kept by the lawyer or firm for four years after its last dissemination.

(g) In advertisements in the public media, any person who portrays a lawyer whose services or whose firm's services are being advertised, or who narrates an advertisement as if he or she were such a lawyer, shall be one or more of the lawyers whose services are being advertised.

(h) If an advertisement in the public media by a lawyer or firm discloses the willingness or potential willingness of the lawyer or firm to render services on a contingent fee basis, the advertisement must state whether the client will be obligated to pay all or any portion of the court costs and, if a client may be liable for other expenses, this fact must be disclosed. If specific percentage fees or fee ranges of contingent fee work are disclosed in such advertisement, it must also disclose whether the percentage is computed before or after expenses are deducted from the recovery.

(i) A lawyer who advertises in the public media a specific fee or range of fees for a particular service shall conform to the advertised fee or range of fees for the period during which the advertisement is reasonably expected to be in circulation or otherwise expected to be effective in attracting clients, unless the advertisement specifies a shorter period; but in no instance is the lawyer bound to conform to the advertised fee or range of fees for a period of more than one year after the date of publication.

*(j) A lawyer or firm who advertises in the public media must disclose the geographic location, by city or town, of the lawyer's or firm's principal office. A lawyer or firm shall not advertise the existence of any office other than the principal office unless:

(1) that other office is staffed by a lawyer at least three days a week; or

(2) the advertisement discloses the days and times during which a lawyer will be present at that office.

(k) A lawyer may not, directly or indirectly, pay all or a part of the cost of an advertisement in the public media for a lawyer not in the same firm unless such advertisement discloses the name and address of the financing lawyer, the relationship between the advertising lawyer and the financing lawyer, and whether the advertising lawyer is likely to refer cases received through the advertisement to the financing lawyer.

(*l*) If an advertising lawyer knows or should know at the time of an advertisement in the public media that a case or matter will likely be referred to another lawyer or firm, a statement of such fact shall be conspicuously included in such advertisement.

(m) No motto, slogan, or jingle that is false or misleading may be used in any advertisement in the public media.

(n) A lawyer shall not include in any advertisement in the public media the lawyer's association with a lawyer referral service unless the lawyer knows or reasonably believes that the lawyer referral service meets the requirements of Occupational Code Title 5, Subtitle B, Chapter 952.

(*o*) A lawyer may not advertise in the public media as part of an advertising cooperative or venture of two or more lawyers not in the same firm unless each such advertisement:

(1) states that the advertisement is paid for by the cooperating lawyers;

(2) names each of the cooperating lawyers;

(3) sets forth conspicuously the special competency requirements required by Rule 7.04(b) of lawyers who advertise in the public media;

(4) does not state or imply that the lawyers participating in the advertising cooperative or venture possess professional superiority, are able to perform services in a superior manner, or possess special competence in any area of law advertised,

---

* **Publisher's Note:** In Texans Against Censorship, Inc. v. State Bar of Texas, 888 F.Supp. 1328 (E.D.Tex. 1995), the U.S. District Court for the Eastern District of Texas held Rule 7.04(j) unconstitutional as applied to one of the plaintiffs. Affirmed, Texans v. State Bar of Texas, 100 F.3d 953 (5th Cir. 1996).

except that the advertisement may contain the information permitted by Rule 7.04(b)(2); and

(5) does not otherwise violate the Texas Disciplinary Rules of Professional Conduct.

(p) Each lawyer who advertises in the public media as part of an advertising cooperative or venture shall be individually responsible for:

(1) ensuring that each advertisement does not violate this Rule; and

(2) complying with the filing requirements of Rule 7.07.

(q) If these rules require that specific qualifications, disclaimers, or disclosures of information accompany communications concerning a lawyer's services, the required qualifications, disclaimers, or disclosures must be presented in the same manner as the communication and with equal prominence.

(r) A lawyer who advertises on the internet must display the statements and disclosures required by Rule 7.04.

(Adopted to be eff. April 1, 1995; on March 31, 1995, the Texas Supreme Court extended the effective date 120 days after the date of judgment of the U.S. District Court in Texans Against Censorship, Inc. v. State Bar of Texas, 888 F.Supp. 1328 (E.D.Tex. 1995).)

COMMENT:

1. Neither Rule 7.04 nor Rule 7.05 prohibits communications authorized by law, such as notice to members of a class in class action litigation.

Advertising Areas of Practice and Special Competence

2. Paragraphs (a) and (b) permit a lawyer, under the restrictions set forth, to indicate areas of practice in advertisements about the lawyer's services. See also paragraph (d). The restrictions are designed primarily to require that accurate information be conveyed. These restrictions recognize that a lawyer has a right protected by the United States Constitution to advertise publicly, but that the right may be regulated by reasonable restrictions designed to protect the public from false or misleading information. The restrictions contained in Rule 7.04 are based on the experience of the legal profession in the State of Texas and are designed to curtail what experience has shown to be misleading and deceptive advertising. To ensure accountability, sub-paragraph (b)(1) requires identification of at least one lawyer responsible for the content of the advertisement.

3. Because of long-standing tradition a lawyer admitted to practice before the United States Patent Office may use the designation "patents," "patent attorney" or "patent lawyer" or any combination of those terms. As recognized by paragraph (a)(1), a lawyer engaged in patent and trademark practice may hold himself or herself out as concentrating in "intellectual property law," "patents, or trademarks and related matters," or "patent, trademark, copyright law and unfair competition" or any of those terms.

4. Paragraph (a)(2) recognizes the propriety of listing a lawyer's name in legal directories according to the areas of law in which the lawyer will accept new matters. The same right is given with respect to lawyer referral service offices, but only if those services comply with statutory guidelines. The restriction in paragraph (a)(2) does not prevent a legal aid agency or prepaid legal services plan from advertising legal services provided under its auspices.

5. Paragraph (a)(3) permits advertisements by lawyers to other lawyers in legal directories and legal newspapers, subject to the same requirements of truthfulness that apply to all other forms of lawyer advertising. Such advertisements traditionally contain information about the name, location, telephone numbers, and general availability of a lawyer to work on particular legal matters. Other information may be included so long as it is not false or misleading. Because advertisements in these publications are not available to the general public, lawyers who list various areas of practice are not required to comply with paragraph (b).

6. Some advertisements, sometimes known as tombstone advertisements, mention only such matters as the name of the lawyer or law firm, a listing of lawyers associated with the firm, office addresses and telephone numbers, office and telephone service hours, dates of admission to bars, the acceptance of credit cards, and fees. The content of such advertisements is not the kind of information intended to be regulated by Rule 7.04(b). However, if the advertisement in the public media mentions any area of the law in which the lawyer practices, then, because of the likelihood of misleading material, the lawyer must comply with paragraph (b).

7. Sometimes lawyers choose to advertise in the public media the fact that they have been certified or designated by a particular organization or that they are members of a particular organization. Such statements naturally lead the public to believe that the lawyer possesses special competence in the area of law mentioned. Consequently, in order to ensure that the public will not be misled by such statements, sub-paragraph (b)(2) and paragraph (c) place limited but necessary restrictions upon a lawyer's basic right to advertise those affiliations.

8. Rule 7.04(b)(2) gives lawyers who possess certificates of specialization from the Texas Board of Legal Specialization or other meritorious credentials from organizations approved by the Board the option of stating that fact. If a lawyer mentions in an advertisement in the public media an area of the law in which the lawyer practices and that lawyer has not been awarded a Certificate in the area advertised, then the lawyer must disclaim or, where applicable, state that no certification is available. See sub-paragraph (b)(3). Sub-paragraphs (b)(2) and (b)(3) require that the restrictions set forth be complied with as to each area of law advertised.

9. Paragraph (c) is intended to ensure against misleading or material variations from the statements required by paragraph (b).

10. Paragraphs (e) and (f) provide the advertising lawyer, the Bar, and the public with requisite records should questions arise regarding the propriety of a public media advertisement. Paragraph (e), like paragraph (b)(1), ensures that a particular attorney accepts responsibility for the advertisement. It is in the public interest and in the interest of the legal profession that the records of those advertisements and approvals be maintained.

Examples of Prohibited Advertising

11. Paragraphs (g) through (*o*) regulate conduct that has been found to mislead or be likely to mislead the public. Each paragraph is designed to protect the public and to guard the legal profession against these documented misleading practices while at the same time respecting the constitutional rights of any lawyer to advertise.

12. Paragraph (g) is a limited regulation of video and audio forms of advertising. It prohibits lawyers from misleading the public into believing a nonlawyer portrayor or narrator in the advertisement is one of the lawyers prepared to perform services for the public. It does not prohibit the narration of an advertisement in the third person by an actor, as long as it is clear to those hearing or seeing the advertisement that the actor is not a lawyer prepared to perform services for the public.

13. Contingent fee contracts present unusual opportunities for deception by lawyers or for misunderstanding by the public. By requiring certain disclosures, paragraph (h) safeguards the public from misleading or potentially misleading advertisements that involve representation on a contingent fee basis. The affirmative requirements of paragraph (h) are not triggered solely by the expression of "contingent fee" or "percentage fee" in the advertisement. To the contrary, they encompass advertisements in the public media where the lawyer or firm expresses a mere willingness or potential willingness to render services for a contingent fee. Therefore, statements in an advertisement such as "no fee if no recovery" or "fees in the event of recovery only" are clearly included as a form of advertisement subject to the disclosure requirements of paragraph (h).

14. Paragraphs (i), (j), (k) and (*l*) jointly address the problem of advertising that experience has shown misleads the public concerning the fees that will be charged, the location where services will be provided, or the attorney who will be performing these services. Together they prohibit the same sort of "bait and switch" advertising tactics by lawyers that are universally condemned.

15. Paragraph (i) requires a lawyer who advertises a specific fee or range of fees in the public media to honor those commitments for the period during which the advertisement is reasonably expected to be in circulation or otherwise expected to be effective in attracting clients, unless the advertisement itself specifies a shorter period. In no event, however, is a lawyer required to honor an advertised fee or range of fees for more than one year after publication.

16. Paragraph (j) prohibits advertising the availability of a satellite office that is not staffed by a lawyer at least on a part-time basis. Paragraph (j) does not require, however, that a lawyer or firm identify the particular office as its principal one. Experience has shown that, in the absence of such regulation, members of the public have been misled into employing a lawyer in a distant city who advertises that there is a nearby satellite office, only to learn later that the lawyer is rarely available to the client because the nearby office is seldom open or is staffed only by lay personnel. Paragraph (k) is not intended to restrict the ability of legal services programs to advertise satellite offices in remote parts of the program's service area even if those satellite offices are staffed irregularly by attorneys. Otherwise low-income individuals in and near such communities might be denied access to the only legal services truly available to them.

17. When a lawyer or firm advertises, the public has a right to expect that lawyer or firm will perform the legal services. Experience has shown that attorneys not in the same firm may create a relationship wherein one will finance advertising for the other in return for referrals. Nondisclosure of such a referral relationship is misleading to the public. Accordingly, paragraph (k) prohibits such a relationship between an advertising lawyer and a lawyer who finances the advertising unless the advertisement discloses the nature of the financial relationship between the two lawyers. Paragraph (*l*) addresses the same problem from a different perspective, requiring a lawyer who advertises the availability of legal services and who knows or should know at the time that the advertisement is placed in the media that business will likely be referred to another lawyer or firm, to include a conspicuous statement of that fact in any such advertising. This requirement applies whether or not the lawyer to whom the business is referred is financing the advertisements of the referring lawyer. It does not, however, require disclosure of all possible scenarios under which a referral could occur, such as an unforeseen need to associate with a specialist in accordance with Rule 1.01(a) or the possibility of a referral if a prospective client turns out to have a conflict of interest precluding representation by the advertising lawyer.

18. Paragraph (m) protects the public by forbidding mottos, slogans, and jingles that are false or misleading. There are, however, mottos, slogans, and jingles that are informative rather than false or misleading. Accordingly, paragraph (m) recognizes an advertising lawyer's constitutional right to include appropriate mottos, slogans, and jingles in advertising.

19. Some lawyers choose to band together in a cooperative or joint venture to advertise. Although those arrangements are lawful, the fact that several independent lawyers have joined together in a single advertisement increases the risk of misrepresentation or other forms of inappropriate expression. Special care must be taken to ensure that cooperative advertisements identify each cooperating lawyer, state that each cooperating lawyer is paying for the advertisement, and accurately describe the professional qualifications of each cooperating lawyer. See paragraph (*o*). Furthermore, each cooperating lawyer must comply with the filing requirements of Rule 7.07. See paragraph (p).

(Comment adopted by State Bar Board of Directors Jan. 20, 1995.)

Texas Disciplinary Rule 7.05

RULE 7.05 Prohibited Written, Electronic or Digital Solicitations

(a) A lawyer shall not send, deliver, or transmit, or knowingly permit or knowingly cause another person to send, deliver, or transmit, a written, audio, audiovisual, digital media, recorded telephone message, or other electronic communication to a prospective client for the purpose of obtaining professional employment on behalf of any lawyer or law firm if:

(1) the communication involves coercion, duress, fraud, overreaching, intimidation, undue influence, or harassment;

(2) the communication contains information prohibited by Rule 7.02 or fails to satisfy each of the requirements of Rule 7.04(a) through (c), and (g) through (q) that would be applicable to the communication if it were an advertisement in the public media; or

(3) the communication contains a false, fraudulent, misleading, deceptive, or unfair statement or claim.

(b) Except as provided in paragraph (f) of this Rule, a written, electronic, or digital solicitation communication to prospective clients for the purpose of obtaining professional employment:

(1) shall, in the case of a non-electronically transmitted written communication, be plainly marked "ADVERTISEMENT" on its first page and on the face of the envelope or other packaging used to transmit the communication. If the written communication is in the form of a self-mailing brochure or pamphlet, the word "ADVERTISEMENT" shall be:

(i) in a color that contrasts sharply with the background color; and

(ii) in a size of at least 3/8″ vertically or three times the vertical height of the letters used in the body of such communication, whichever is larger;

(2) shall, in the ease of an electronic mail message, be plainly marked "ADVERTISEMENT" in the subject portion of the electronic mail and at the beginning of the message's text;

(3) shall not be made to resemble legal pleadings or other legal documents;

(4) shall not reveal on the envelope or other packaging or electronic mail subject line used to transmit the communication, or on the outside of a self-mailing brochure or pamphlet, the nature of the legal problem of the prospective client or non-client; and

(5) shall disclose how the lawyer obtained the information prompting the communication to solicit professional employment if such contact was prompted by a specific occurrence involving the recipient of the communication or a family member of such person(s).

(c) Except as provided in paragraph (f) of this Rule, an audio, audio-visual, digital media, recorded telephone message, or other electronic communication sent to prospective clients for the purpose of obtaining professional employment:

(1) shall, in the case of any such communication delivered to the recipient by non-electronic means, plainly and conspicuously state in writing on the outside of any envelope or other packaging used to transmit the communication, that it is an "ADVERTISEMENT";

(2) shall not reveal on any such envelope or other packaging the nature of the legal problem of the prospective client or non-client;

(3) shall disclose, either in the communication itself or in accompanying transmittal message, how the lawyer obtained the information prompting such audio, audiovisual, digital media, recorded telephone message, or other electronic communication to solicit professional employment, if such contact was promoted by a specific occurrence involving the recipient of the communication or a family member of such person(s);

(4) shall, in the case of a recorded audio presentation or a recorded telephone message, plainly state that it is an advertisement prior to any other words being spoken and again at the presentation's or message's conclusion; and

(5) shall, in the case of an audio-visual or digital media presentation, plainly state that the presentation is an advertisement:

(i) both verbally and in writing at the outset of the presentation and again at its conclusion; and

(ii) in writing during any portion of the presentation that explains how to contact a lawyer or law firm.

(d) All written, audio, audio-visual, digital media, recorded telephone message, or other electronic communications made to a prospective client for the purpose of obtaining professional employment of a lawyer or law firm must be reviewed and either signed by or approved in writing by the lawyer or a lawyer in the firm.

(e) A copy of each written, audio, audio-visual, digital media, recorded telephone message, or other electronic solicitation communication, the relevant approval thereof, and a record of the date of each such communication; the name, address, telephone number, or electronic address to which each such communication was sent; and the means by which each such communication was sent shall be kept by the lawyer or firm for four years after its dissemination.

(f) The provisions of paragraphs (b) and (c) of this Rule do not apply to a written audio audiovisual, digital media, recorded telephone message, or other form of electronic solicitation communication:

(1) directed to a family member or a person with whom the lawyer had or has an attorney client relationship;

(2) that is not motivated by or concerned with a particular past occurrence or event or a particular series of past occurrences or events, and also is not motivated by or concerned with the prospective client's specific existing legal problem of which the lawyer is aware;

(3) if the lawyer's use of the communication to secure professional employment was not significantly motivated by a desire for, or by the possibility of obtaining, pecuniary gain; or

(4) that is requested by the prospective client.

COMMENT:

1. Rule 7.03 deals with in-person or telephone contact between a lawyer and a prospective client wherein the lawyer seeks professional employment. Rule 7.04 deals with advertisements in the public media by a lawyer seeking professional employment. This Rule deals with written solicitations between a lawyer and a prospective client. Typical examples are letters or other forms of correspondence addressed to a prospective client.

2. Written solicitations raise more concerns than do comparable written advertisements. Being private, they are more difficult to monitor, and for that reason paragraph (d) requires retention for four years of certain information regarding written solicitations. See also Rule 7.07(a). Paragraph (a) addresses such concerns as well as problems stemming from exceptionally outrageous communications such as written solicitations involving fraud, intimidation, or deceptive and misleading claims. Because receipt of multiple solicitations appears to be most pronounced and vexatious in situations involving accident victims, paragraph (b)(7) requires disclosure of the source of information if the solicitation was prompted by a specific occurrence.

3. Because experience has shown that many written solicitations have been intrusive or misleading by reason of being personalized or being disguised as some form of official communication special prohibitions against such practices are necessary. The requirements of paragraph (b) greatly lessen those dangers of deception and harassment.

4. Newsletters or other works published by a lawyer that are not circulated for the purpose of obtaining professional employment are not within the ambit of paragraph (b).

5. In addition to addressing these special problems posed by written solicitations, Rule 7.05 regulates the content of those communications. It does so by incorporating the standards of Rule 7.02 and those of Rule 7.04 that would apply to the written solicitation were it instead a written advertisement in the public media. See paragraphs (a)(2), (3), and (b)(1). In brief, this approach means that, a lawyer may not include or omit anything from a written solicitation unless the lawyer could do so were the communication a written advertisement in the public media, except for those statements or disclaimers required by Rule 7.04(a)–(c). See sub-paragraph (b)(1).

6. Paragraph (e) provides that none of the restrictions in paragraph (b) apply in certain situations because the dangers of deception, harassment, vexation and overreaching are quite low. For example, a written solicitation may be directed to a family member or a present or a former client, or in response to a request by a prospective client. Similarly, a written solicitation may be used in seeking general employment in commercial matters from a bank or other corporation, when there is neither concern with specific existing legal problems nor concern with a particular past event or series of events. All such communications, however, remain subject to Rule 7.02 and paragraphs (h) through (*o*) of Rule 7.04. See sub-paragraph (a)(2).

7. In addition, paragraph (e) allows such communications in situations not involving the lawyer's pecuniary gain. For purposes of these rules, it is presumed that communications made on behalf of a nonprofit legal aid agency, union, or other qualified nonprofit organization are not motivated by a desire for, or by the possibility of obtaining, pecuniary gain, but that presumption may be rebutted.

(Comment adopted by State Bar Board of Directors Jan. 20, 1995.)

Texas Disciplinary Rule 7.06

RULE 7.06 Prohibited Employment

(a) A lawyer shall not accept or continue employment in a matter when that employment was procured by conduct prohibited by any of Rules 7.01 through 7.05, 8.04(a)(2), or 8.04(a)(9), engaged in by that lawyer personally or by any other person whom the lawyer ordered, encouraged, or knowingly permitted to engage in such conduct.

(b) A lawyer shall not accept or continue employment in a matter when the lawyer knows or reasonably should know that employment was procured by conduct prohibited by any of Rules 7.01 through 7.05, 8.04(a)(2), or 8.04(a)(9), engaged in by any other person or entity that is a shareholder, partner, or member of, an associate in, or of counsel to that lawyer's firm; or by any other person whom any of the foregoing persons or entities ordered, encouraged, or knowingly permitted to engage in such conduct.

(c) A lawyer who has not violated paragraph (a) or (b) in accepting employment in a matter shall not continue employment in that matter once the lawyer knows or reasonably should know that the person procuring the lawyer's employment in the matter engaged in, or ordered, encouraged, or knowingly permitted another to engage in, conduct prohibited by any of Rules 7.01 through 7.05, 8.04(a)(2), or 8.04(a)(9) in connection with the matter unless nothing of value is given thereafter in return for that employment.

A lawyer shall not accept or continue employment when the lawyer knows or reasonably should know that that the person who seeks the lawyer's services does so as a result of conduct prohibited by these rules.

(Former Rule 7.03 adopted eff. Jan. 1, 1990; redesignated and amended to be eff. April 1, 1995; on March 31, 1995, the Texas Supreme Court extended the effective date 120 days after the date of judgment of the U.S. District Court in Texans Against Censorship, Inc. v. State Bar of Texas, 888 F.Supp. 1328 (E.D.Tex. 1995).)

COMMENT:

Selection of a lawyer by a client often is a result of the advice and recommendation of third parties—relatives, friends, acquaintances, business associates and other lawyers. Although that method of referral is perfectly legitimate, the client is best served if the recommendation is disinterested and informed. All lawyers must guard against creating situations where referral from others is the consequence of some form of prohibited compensation or from some form of false or misleading communication, or by virtue of some other violation of these rules. This prohibition on accepting or continuing employment applies even if the lawyer whose services are involved had no direct or indirect involvement with the underlying violation of these Rules, provided that lawyer knows of the violation. See also Rule 7.03(d), forbidding a lawyer to charge or collect a fee where the misconduct involves violations of Rule 7.03(a), (b), or (c).

(Comment amended by State Bar Board of Directors Jan. 20, 1995.)

Texas Disciplinary Rule 7.07

RULE 7.07 Filing Requirements for Public Advertisements and Written, Recorded, Electronic, or Other Digital Solicitations

(a) Except as provided in paragraphs (c) and (e) of this Rule, a lawyer shall file with the Advertising Review Committee of the State Bar of Texas, no later than the mailing or sending by any means, including electronic, of a written, audio, audio-visual, digital or other electronic solicitation communication:

(1) a copy of the written, audio, audio-visual, digital, or other electronic solicitation communication being sent or to be sent to one or more prospective clients for the purpose of obtaining professional employment, together with a representative sample of the envelopes or other packaging in which the communications are enclosed;

(2) a completed lawyer advertising and solicitation communication application form; and

(3) a check or money order payable to the State Bar of Texas for the fee set by the Board of Directors. Such fee shall be for the sole purpose of defraying the expense of enforcing the rules related to such solicitations.

(b) Except as provided in paragraph (e) of this Rule, a lawyer shall file with the Advertising Review Committee of the State Bar of Texas, no later than the first dissemination of an advertisement in the public media, a copy of each of the lawyer's advertisements in the public media. The filing shall include:

(1) a copy of the advertisement in the form in which it appears or will be disseminated appear upon dissemination, such as a videotape, audiotape, DVD, CD, a print copy, or a photograph of outdoor advertising;

(2) a production script of the advertisement setting forth all words used and describing in detail the actions, events, scenes, and background sounds used in such advertisement together with a listing of the names and addresses of persons portrayed or heard to speak, if the advertisement is in or will be in a form in which the advertised message is not fully revealed by a print copy or photograph;

(3) a statement of when and where the advertisement has been, is, or will be used;

(4) a completed lawyer advertising and solicitation communication application form; and

(5) a check or money order payable to the State Bar of Texas for the fee set by the Board of Directors. Such fee shall be for the sole purpose of defraying the expense of enforcing the rules related to such advertisements.

(c) Except as provided in paragraph (e) of this Rule, a lawyer shall file with the Advertising Review Committee of the State Bar of Texas no later than its first posting on the internet or other comparable network of computers information concerning the lawyer's or lawyer's firm's website. As used in this Rule, a "website" means a single or

multiple page file, posted on a computer server, which describes a lawyer or law firm's practice or qualifications, to which public access is provided through publication of a uniform resource locator (URL). The filing shall include:

(1) the intended initial access page of a website;

(2) a completed lawyer advertising and solicitation communication application form; and

(3) a check or money order payable to the State Bar of Texas for the fee set by the Board of Directors. Such fee shall be set for the sole purpose of defraying the expense of enforcing the rules related to such websites.

(d) A lawyer who desires to secure an advance advisory opinion, referred to as a request for pre-approval, concerning compliance of a contemplated written-solicitation communication or advertisement may submit to the Advertising Review Committee, not less than thirty (30) days prior to the date of first dissemination, the material specified in paragraph (a) or (b) or the intended initial access page submitted pursuant to paragraph (c), including the application form and required fee; provided however, it shall not be necessary to submit a videotape or DVD if the videotape or DVD has not then been prepared and the production script submitted reflects in detail and accurately the actions, events, scenes, and background sounds that will be depicted or contained on such videotapes or DVDs, when prepared, as well as the narrative transcript of the verbal and printed portions of such advertisement. If a lawyer submits an advertisement or solicitation communication for pre-approval, a finding of noncompliance by the Advertising Review Committee is not binding in a disciplinary proceeding or disciplinary action, but a finding of compliance is binding in favor of the submitting lawyer as to all materials actually submitted for pre-approval if the representations, statements, materials, facts, and written assurances received in connection therewith are true and are not misleading. The finding of compliance constitutes admissible evidence if offered by a party.

(e) The filing requirements of paragraphs (a), (b), and (c) do not extend to any of the following materials, provided those materials comply with Rule 7.02(a) through (c) and, where applicable, Rule 7.04(a) through (c):

(1) an advertisement in the public media that contains only part or all of the following information:

(i) the name of the lawyer or firm and lawyers associated with the firm, with office addresses, electronic addresses, telephone numbers, office and telephone service hours, telecopier numbers, and a designation of the profession such as "attorney," "lawyer," "law office," or "firm";

(ii) the particular areas of law in which the lawyer or firm specializes or possesses special competence;

(iii) the particular areas of law in which the lawyer or firm practices or concentrates or to which it limits its practice;

(iv) the date of admission of the lawyer or lawyers to the State Bar of Texas, to particular federal courts, and to the bars of other jurisdictions;

(v) technical and professional licenses granted by this state and other recognized licensing authorities;

(vi) foreign language ability;

(vii) fields of law in which one or more lawyers are certified or designated, provided the statement of this information is in compliance with Rule 7.02(a) through (c);

(viii) identification of prepaid or group legal service plans in which the lawyer participates;

(ix) the acceptance or nonacceptance of credit cards;

(x) any fee for initial consultation and fee schedule;

(xi) other publicly available information concerning legal issues, not prepared or paid for by the firm or any of its lawyers, such as news articles, legal articles, editorial opinions, or other legal developments or events, such as proposed or enacted rules, regulations, or legislation;

(xii) in the case of a website, links to other websites;

(xiii) that the lawyer or firm is a sponsor of a charitable, civic, or community program or event, or is a sponsor of a public service announcement;

(xiv) any disclosure or statement required by these rules; and

(xv) any other information specified from time to time in orders promulgated by the Supreme Court of Texas;

(2) an advertisement in the public media that:

(i) identifies one or more lawyers or a firm as a contributor to a specified charity or as a sponsor of a specified charitable, community, or public interest program, activity, or event; and

(ii) contains no information about the lawyers or firm other than names of the lawyers or firm or both, location of the law offices, and the fact of the sponsorship or contribution;

(3) a listing or entry in a regularly published law list;

(4) an announcement card stating new or changed associations, new offices, or similar changes relating to a lawyer or firm, or a tombstone professional card;

(5) in the case of communications sent, delivered, or transmitted to, rather than accessed by, intended recipients, a newsletter, whether written, digital, or electronic, provided that it is sent, delivered, or transmitted mailed only to:

(i) existing or former clients;

(ii) other lawyers or professionals; or

(iii) members of a nonprofit organization that meets the following conditions: the primary purposes of the organization do not include the rendition of legal services; the recommending, furnishing, paying for, or educating persons regarding legal services is incidental and reasonably related to the primary purposes of the organization; the organization does not derive a financial benefit from the rendition of legal services by a lawyer; and the person for whom the legal services are rendered, and not the organization, is recognized as the client of the lawyer who is recommended, furnished, or paid by the organization;

(6) a solicitation communication that is not motivated by or concerned with a particular past occurrence or event or a particular series of past occurrences or events, and also is not motivated by or concerned with the prospective client's specific existing legal problem of which the lawyer is aware;

(7) a solicitation communication if the lawyer's use of the communication to secure professional employment was not significantly motivated by a desire for, or by the possibility of obtaining, pecuniary gain; or

(8) a solicitation communication that is requested by the prospective client.

(f) If requested by the Advertising Review Committee, a lawyer shall promptly submit information to substantiate statements or representations made or implied in any advertisement in the public media or solicitation communication by which the lawyer seeks paid professional employment.

(Adopted to be eff. April 1, 1995; on March 31, 1995, the Texas Supreme Court extended the effective date 120 days after the date of judgment of the U.S. District Court in Texans Against Censorship, Inc. v. State Bar of Texas, 888 F.Supp. 1328 (E.D.Tex. 1995).)

COMMENT:

1. Rule 7.07 covers the filing requirements for public media advertisements (see Rule 7.04) and written solicitations (see Rule 7.05). Rule 7.07(a) deals with those written solicitations sent by a lawyer to one or more specified prospective clients. Rule 7.07(b) deals with advertisements in the public media. Each provision allows the Bar to charge a fee for reviewing submitted materials, but requires that fee be set solely to defray the expenses of enforcing those provisions.

2. Copies of non-exempt written solicitations or advertisements in the public media must be provided to the Advertising Review Committee of the State Bar of Texas either in advance or concurrently with dissemination, together with the fee required by the State Bar of Texas Board of Directors. Presumably, the Advertising Review Committee will report to the appropriate grievance committee any lawyer whom it finds from the reviewed products has disseminated an advertisement in the public media or written solicitation that violates Rules 7.02, 7.03, 7.04, or 7.05, or, at a minimum, any lawyer whose violation raises a substantial question as to that lawyer's honesty, trustworthiness, or fitness as a lawyer in other respects. See Rule 8.03(a).

3. Paragraphs (a) and (b) do not require that a lawyer submit a copy of each and every written solicitation letter a lawyer sends. If the same form letter is sent to several people, only a representative sample of each form letter, along with a representative sample of the envelopes used to mail the letters, need be filed.

4. A lawyer wishing to do so may secure an advisory opinion from the Advertising Review Committee concerning any proposed advertisement in the public media or any written solicitation in advance of its first use or mailing by complying with Rule 7.07(c). This procedure is intended as a service to those lawyers who want to resolve any possible doubts about their proposed advertisements' or written solicitations' compliance with these Rules before utilizing them. Its use is purely optional. No lawyer is required to obtain advance clearance of any advertisement or written solicitation communication from the State Bar. Although a finding of noncompliance by the Advertising Review Committee is not binding in a disciplinary proceeding, a finding of compliance is binding in favor of the submitting lawyer, as long as the lawyer's presentation to the Advertising Review Committee in connection with that advisory opinion is true and not misleading.

5. Under its Internal Rules and Operating Procedures, the Advertising Review Committee is to complete its evaluations no later than 25 days after the date of receipt of a filing. The only way that the Committee can extend that review period is to: (1) determine that there is reasonable doubt whether the advertisement or written solicitation communication complies with these Rules; (2) conclude that further examination is warranted but cannot be completed within the 25-day period; and (3) advise the lawyer of those determinations in writing within that 25-day period. The Committee's Internal Rules and Operating Procedures also provide that a failure to send such a communication to the lawyer within the 25-day period constitutes approval of the advertisement or written solicitation communication. Consequently, if an attorney submits an advertisement in the public media or written solicitation communication to the Committee for advance approval not less than 30 days prior to the date of first dissemination as required by these Rules, the attorney will receive an assessment of that advertisement or communication before the date of its first intended use.

6. Consistent with the effort to protect the first amendment rights of lawyers while ensuring the right of the public to be free from misleading advertising and the right of the Texas legal profession to maintain its integrity, paragraph (d) exempts certain types of advertisements and written solicitations prepared for the purpose of seeking paid professional employment from the filing requirements of

paragraphs (a) and (b). Those types of communications need not be filed at all if they were not prepared to secure paid professional employment.

7. For the most part, the types of exempted advertising listed in subparagraphs (d)(1)–(5) are objective and less likely to result in false, misleading or fraudulent content. Similarly the types of exempted written solicitations listed in subparagraphs (d)(6)–(8) are those found least likely to result in harm to the public. See Rule 7.05(e), and comment 5 to Rule 7.05. The fact that a particular advertisement or written solicitation made by a lawyer is exempted from the filing requirements of this Rule does not exempt a lawyer from the other applicable obligations of these Rules. See generally Rules 7.01 through 7.06.

8. Paragraph (e) does not empower the Advertising Review Committee to seek information from a lawyer to substantiate statements or representations made or implied in advertisements or written communications that do not seek to obtain paid professional employment for that lawyer.

(Comment adopted by State Bar Board of Directors Jan. 20, 1995.)

MAINTAINING THE INTEGRITY OF THE PROFESSION

Florida Rule 8.4(d)

[Florida has modified Model Rule 8.4 to read as follows:]

RULE 4–8.4 Misconduct

A lawyer shall not:

* * *

(d) engage in conduct in connection with the practice of law that is prejudicial to the administration of justice, including to knowingly, or through callous indifference, disparage, humiliate, or discriminate against litigants, jurors, witnesses, court personnel, or other lawyers on any basis, including, but not limited to, on account of race, ethnicity, gender, religion, national origin, disability, marital status, sexual orientation, age, socioeconomic status, employment, or physical characteristic;

* * *

(h) willfully refuse, as determined by a court of competent jurisdiction, to timely pay a child support obligation; or

(i) engage in sexual conduct with a client or a representative of a client that exploits or adversely affects the interests of the client or the lawyer-client relationship.

If the sexual conduct commenced after the lawyer-client relationship was formed it shall be presumed that the sexual conduct exploits or adversely affects the interests of the client or the lawyer-client relationship. A lawyer may rebut this presumption by proving by a preponderance of the evidence that the sexual conduct did not exploit or adversely affect the interests of the client or the lawyer-client relationship.

The prohibition and presumption stated in this rule do not apply to a lawyer in the same firm as another lawyer representing the client if the lawyer involved in the sexual conduct does not personally provide legal services to the client and is screened from access to the file concerning the legal representation.

Minnesota Rule 8.4

[Minnesota, one of the first states to include a prohibition against discriminatory conduct by lawyers, has amended Model Rule 8.4 to add the following:]

RULE 8.4 Misconduct

It is professional misconduct for a lawyer to:

* * *

(g) harass a person on the basis of sex, race, age, creed, religion, color, national origin, disability, sexual orientation or marital status in connection with a lawyer's professional activities;

(h) commit a discriminatory act, prohibited by federal, state or local statute or ordinance, that reflects adversely on the lawyer's fitness as a lawyer. Whether a discriminatory act reflects adversely on a lawyer's fitness as a lawyer shall be determined after consideration of all the circumstances, including: (1) the seriousness of the act, (2) whether the lawyer knew that it was prohibited by statute or ordinance, (3) whether it was part of a pattern of prohibited conduct, and (4) whether it was committed in connection with the lawyer's professional activities.

(i) refuse to honor a final and binding fee arbitration award after agreeing to arbitrate a fee dispute.

COMMENT—2005:

* * *

[4] Paragraph (g) specifies a particularly egregious type of discriminatory act—harassment on the basis of sex, race, age, creed, religion, color, national origin, disability, sexual preference, or marital status. What constitutes harassment in this context may be determined with reference to antidiscrimination legislation and case law thereunder. This harassment ordinarily involves the active burdening of another, rather than mere passive failure to act properly.

[5] Harassment on the basis of sex, race, age, creed, religion, color, national origin, disability, sexual preference, or marital status may violate either paragraph (g) or paragraph (h). The harassment violates paragraph (g) if the lawyer committed it in connection with the lawyer's professional activities. Harassment, even if not committed in connection with the lawyer's professional activities, violates paragraph (h) if the harassment (1) is prohibited by antidiscrimination legislation and (2) reflects adversely on the lawyer's fitness as a lawyer, determined as specified in paragraph (h).

[6] Paragraph (h) reflects the premise that the concept of human equality lies at the very heart of our legal system. A lawyer whose behavior demonstrates hostility toward or indifference to the policy of equal justice under the law may thereby manifest a lack of character required of members of the legal profession. Therefore, a lawyer's discriminatory act prohibited by statute or ordinance may reflect adversely on his or her fitness as a lawyer even if the unlawful discriminatory act was not committed in connection with the lawyer's professional activities.

[7] Whether an unlawful discriminatory act reflects adversely on fitness as a lawyer is determined after consideration of all relevant circumstances, including the four factors listed in paragraph (h). It is not required that the listed factors be considered equally, nor is the list intended to be exclusive. For example, it would also be relevant that the lawyer reasonably believed that his or her conduct was protected under the state or federal constitution or that the lawyer was acting in a capacity for which the law provides an exemption from civil liability. See, e.g., Minn.Stat. Section 317A.257 (unpaid director or officer of nonprofit organization acting in good faith and not willfully or recklessly).

[8] A lawyer may refuse to comply with an obligation imposed by law upon a good faith belief that no valid obligation exists. The provisions of Rule 1.2(c)(d) concerning a good faith challenge to the validity, scope, meaning or application of the law apply to challenges of legal regulation of the practice of law.

New Jersey Rule 8.4(g)

[New Jersey has modified Model Rule 8.4 to read as follows:]

RULE 8.4 Misconduct

It is professional misconduct for a lawyer to:

* * *

(g) engage, in a professional capacity, in conduct involving discrimination (except employment discrimination unless resulting in a final agency or judicial determination) because of race, color, religion, age, sex, sexual orientation, national origin, language, marital status, socioeconomic status, or handicap where the conduct is intended or likely to cause harm.

Comment by Supreme Court:

This rule amendment (the addition of paragraph g) is intended to make discriminatory conduct unethical when engaged in by lawyers in their professional capacity. It would, for example, cover activities in the court house, such as a lawyer's treatment of court support staff, as well as conduct more directly related to litigation; activities related to practice outside of the court house, whether or not related to litigation, such as treatment of other attorneys and their staff; bar association and similar activities; and activities in the lawyer's office and firm. Except to the extent that they are closely related to the foregoing, purely private activities are not intended to be covered by this rule amendment, although they may possibly constitute a violation of some other ethical rule. Nor is employment discrimination in hiring, firing, promotion, or partnership status intended to be covered unless it has resulted in either an agency or judicial determination of discriminatory conduct. The Supreme Court believes that existing agencies and courts are better able to deal with such matters, that the disciplinary resources required to investigate and prosecute discrimination in the employment area would be disproportionate to the benefits to the system given remedies available elsewhere, and that limiting ethics proceedings in this area to cases where there has been an adjudication represents a practical resolution of conflicting needs.

"Discrimination" is intended to be construed broadly. It includes sexual harassment, derogatory or demeaning language, and, generally, any conduct towards the named groups that is both harmful and discriminatory.

Case law has already suggested both the area covered by this amendment and the possible direction of future cases. *In re Vincenti*, 114 *N.J.* 275 (554 *A.2d* 470) (1989). The Court believes the administration of justice would be better served, however, by the adoption of this general rule than by a case by case development of the scope of the professional obligation.

While the origin of this rule was a recommendation of the Supreme Court's Task Force on Women in the Courts, the Court concluded that the protection, limited to women and minorities in that recommendation, should be expanded. The groups covered in the initial proposed amendment to the rule are the same as those named in Canon 3A(4) of the Code of Judicial Conduct.

Following the initial publication of this proposed subsection (g) and receipt of various comments and suggestions, the Court revised the proposed amendment by making explicit its intent to limit the rule to conduct by attorneys in a professional capacity, to exclude employment discrimination unless adjudicated, to restrict the scope to conduct intended or likely to cause harm, and to include discrimination because of sexual orientation or socioeconomic status, these categories having been proposed by the ABA's Standing Committee on Ethics and Professional Responsibility as additions to the groups now covered in Canon 3A(4) of the New Jersey Code of Judicial Conduct. That Committee has also proposed that judges require attorneys, in proceedings before a judge, refrain from manifesting by words or conduct any bias or prejudice based on any of these categories. See proposed Canon 3A(6). This revision to the RPC further reflects the Court's intent to cover all discrimination where the attorney intends to cause harm such as inflicting emotional distress or obtaining a tactical advantage and not to cover instances when no harm is intended unless its occurrence is likely regardless of intent, e.g., where discriminatory comments or behavior is repetitive. While obviously the language of the rule cannot explicitly cover every instance of possible discriminatory conduct, the Court believes that, along with existing case law, it sufficiently narrows the breadth of the rule to avoid any suggestion that it is overly broad. See, e.g., *In re Vincenti*, 114 *N.J.* 275 (554 *A.2d* 470) (1989).

District of Columbia Rule 9.1

[The District of Columbia has added the following provision which has no counterpart in the Model Rules]

NONDISCRIMINATION BY MEMBERS OF THE BAR

RULE 9.1 Nondiscrimination

A lawyer shall not discriminate against any individual in conditions of employment because of the individual's race, color, religion, national origin, sex, age, marital status, sexual orientation, family responsibility, or physical handicap.

COMMENT:

[1] This provision is modeled after the D.C. Human Rights Act, D.C. Code § 2–1402.11 (2001), though in some respects more limited in scope. There are also provisions of federal law that contain certain prohibitions on discrimination in employment. The rule is not intended to create ethical obligations that exceed those imposed on a lawyer by applicable law.

[3] The investigation and adjudication of discrimination claims may involve particular expertise of the kind found within the D.C. Office of Human Rights and the federal Equal Employment Opportunity Commission. Such experience may involve, among other things, methods of analysis of statistical data regarding discrimination claims. These agencies also have, in appropriate circumstances, the power to award remedies to the victims of discrimination, such as reinstatement or back pay, which extend beyond the remedies that are available through the disciplinary process. Remedies available through the disciplinary process include such sanctions as disbarment, suspension, censure, and admonition, but do not extend to monetary awards or other remedies that could alter the employment status to take into account the impact of prior acts of discrimination.

[4] If proceedings are pending before other organizations, such as the D.C. Office of Human Rights or the Equal Employment Opportunity Commission, the processing of complaints by Bar Counsel may be deferred or abated where there is substantial similarity between the complaint filed with Bar Counsel and material allegations involved in such other proceedings. See § 19(d) of Rule XI of the Rules Governing the Bar of the District of Columbia.

Appendix:

States That Have Adopted a Version of the Model Rules*

Alabama—revised for Ethics 2000.

Alaska—revised for Ethics 2000.

Arizona—revised for Ethics 20/20.

Arkansas—revised for Ethics 20/20.

California—revised for Ethics 2000.

Colorado—revised for Ethics 2000.

Connecticut—revised for Ethics 20/20.

Delaware—revised for Ethics 20/20.

District of Columbia—revised for Ethics 2000.

Florida—revised for Ethics 2000.

Georgia

Hawaii

Idaho—revised for Ethics 20/20.

Illinois—revised for Ethics 2000.

Indiana—revised for Ethics 2000.

Iowa—revised for Ethics 2000.

Kansas—revised for Ethics 20/20.

Kentucky—revised for Ethics 2000.

Louisiana—revised for Ethics 20/20.

Maryland—revised for Ethics 2000.

Massachusetts—revised for Ethics 20/20.

Michigan—revised for Ethics 2000.

Minnesota—revised for Ethics 20/20.

Mississippi—revised for Ethics 2000.

Missouri—revised for Ethics 2000.

Montana—revised for Ethics 2000.

Nebraska—revised for Ethics 2000.

Nevada—revised for Ethics 20/20.

New Hampshire—revised for Ethics 2000.

New Jersey—revised for Ethics 2000.

New Mexico—revised for Ethics 20/20.

New York (Amended version of code to include many Model Rules provisions)

---

* Source: ABA/BNA Manual on Professional Conduct 01:3 (2015) (State Ethics Rules) and ABA Center for Professional Responsibility website. http://www.americanbar.org/content/dam/aba/administrative/professional_responsibility/state_implementation_selected_e20_20_rules.authcheckdam.pdf.

North Carolina—revised for Ethics 2000.

North Dakota—revised for Ethics 2000.

Ohio—revised for Ethics 20/20.

Oklahoma—revised for Ethics 2000.

Oregon—revised for Ethics 20/20.

Pennsylvania—revised for Ethics 2000.

Rhode Island—revised for Ethics 2000.

South Carolina—revised for Ethics 2000.

South Dakota—revised for Ethics 2000.

Tennessee—revised for Ethics 2000.

Texas

Utah—revised for Ethics 2000.

Vermont—revised for Ethics 2000.

Virginia—revised for Ethics 2000.

Washington—revised for Ethics 2000.

West Virginia—revised for Ethics 20/20.

Wisconsin—revised for Ethics 2000.

Wyoming—revised for Ethics 20/20.

OTHER SELECTED STATE STANDARDS, RULES, AND STATUTES

TABLE OF CONTENTS

Introduction

This section presents a more in depth perspective on how two states have chosen to regulate lawyers. The California Rules of Professional Conduct for governing lawyers' conduct differ substantially from the ABA codes of ethics. The California approach to regulating lawyer must also consider the legislature's control over lawyers. This form of regulation is contained in the California Business and Professions Code. Selected sections are reproduced below. We include the Disciplinary Rules of the New York Code of Professional Responsibility as an example of a state that continues to retain significant language its old code based rule when it adopted the Model Rules format in 2009.

CALIFORNIA RULES OF PROFESSIONAL CONDUCT

Approved by Supreme Court August 13, 1992, and current as of January 1, 2015

CHAPTER 1. PROFESSIONAL INTEGRITY IN GENERAL

CHAPTER 2. RELATIONSHIP AMONG MEMBERS

CHAPTER 3. PROFESSIONAL RELATIONSHIP WITH CLIENTS

CHAPTER 4. FINANCIAL RELATIONSHIP WITH CLIENTS

CHAPTER 5. ADVOCACY AND REPRESENTATION

CHAPTER 1. PROFESSIONAL INTEGRITY IN GENERAL

Rule 1-100. Rules of Professional Conduct, in General

(A) Purpose and Function.

The following rules are intended to regulate professional conduct of members of the State Bar through discipline. They have been adopted by the Board of Governors of the State Bar of California and approved by the Supreme Court of California pursuant to Business and Professions Code sections 6076 and 6077 to protect the public and to promote respect and confidence in the legal profession. These rules together with any standards adopted by the Board of Governors pursuant to these rules shall be binding upon all members of the State Bar.

For a willful breach of any of these rules, the Board of Governors has the power to discipline members as provided by law.

The prohibition of certain conduct in these rules is not exclusive. Members are also bound by applicable law including the State Bar Act (Bus. & Prof. Code, § 6000 et seq.) and opinions of California courts. Although not binding, opinions of ethics committees in California should be consulted by members for guidance on proper professional conduct. Ethics opinions and rules and standards promulgated by other jurisdictions and bar associations may also be considered.

These rules are not intended to create new civil causes of action. Nothing in these rules shall be deemed to create, augment, diminish, or eliminate any substantive legal duty of lawyers or the non-disciplinary consequences of violating such a duty.

(B) Definitions.

(1) "Law Firm" means:

(a) two or more lawyers whose activities constitute the practice of law, and who share its profits, expenses, and liabilities; or

(b) a law corporation which employs more than one lawyer; or

(c) a division, department, office, or group within a business entity, which includes more than one lawyer who performs legal services for the business entity; or

(d) a publicly funded entity which employs more than one lawyer to perform legal services.

(2) "Member" means a member of the State Bar of California.

(3) "Lawyer" means a member of the State Bar of California or a person who is admitted in good standing of and eligible to practice before the bar of any United States court or the highest court of the District of Columbia or any state, territory, or insular possession of the United States or is licensed to practice law is, or is admitted in good standing and is eligible to

practice before the bar of the highest court of a foreign country or any political subdivision thereof.

(4) "Associate" means an employee or fellow employee who is employed as a lawyer.

(5) "Shareholder" means a shareholder in a professional corporation pursuant to Business and Professions Code section 6160 et seq.

(C) Purpose of Discussions.

Because it is a practical impossibility to convey in black letter form all of the nuances of these disciplinary rules, the comments contained in the Discussions of the rules, while they do not add independent basis for imposing discipline, are intended to provide guidance for interpreting the rules and practicing in compliance with them.

(D) Geographic Scope of Rules.

(1) As to members:

These rules shall govern the activities of members in and outside this state, except as members lawfully practicing outside this state may be specifically required by a jurisdiction in which they are practicing to follow rules of professional conduct different from these rules.

(2) As to lawyers from other jurisdictions who are not members:

These rules shall also govern the activities of lawyers while engaged in the performance of lawyer functions in this state; but nothing contained in these rules shall be deemed to authorize the performance of such functions by such persons in this state except as otherwise permitted by law.

(E) These rules may be cited and referred to as "Rules of Professional Conduct of the State Bar of California."

Discussion:

The Rules of Professional Conduct are intended to establish the standards for members for purposes of discipline. (See *Ames v. State Bar* (1973) 8 Cal.3d 910 [106 Cal.Rptr. 489].) The fact that a member has engaged in conduct that may be contrary to these rules does not automatically give rise to a civil cause of action. (See *Noble v. Sears, Roebuck & Co.* (1973) 33 Cal.App.3d 654 [109 Cal.Rptr. 269]; *Wilhelm v. Pray, Price, Williams & Russell* (1986) 186 Cal.App.3d 1324 [231 Cal.Rptr. 355].) These rules are not intended to supercede existing law relating to members in non-disciplinary contexts. (See, e.g., *Klemm v. Superior Court* (1977) 75 Cal.App.3d 893 [142 Cal.Rptr. 509] (motion for disqualification of counsel due to a conflict of interest); *Academy of California Optometrists, Inc. v. Superior Court* (1975) 51 Cal.App.3d 999 [124 Cal.Rptr. 668] (duty to return client files); *Chronometrics, Inc. v. Sysgen, Inc.* (1980) 110 Cal.App.3d 597 [168 Cal.Rptr. 196] (disqualification of member appropriate remedy for improper communication with adverse party)).

Law firm, as defined by subparagraph (B)(1), is not intended to include an association of lawyers who do not share profits, expenses, and liabilities. The subparagraph is not intended to imply that a law firm may include a person who is not a member in violation of the law governing the unauthorized practice of law.

Rule 1-110. Disciplinary Authority of the State Bar

A member shall comply with conditions attached to public or private reprovals or other discipline administered by the State Bar pursuant to Business and Professions Code sections 6077 and 6078 and rule 19, California Rules of Court.

Rule 1–120. Assisting, Soliciting, or Inducing Violations

A member shall not knowingly assist in, solicit, or induce any violation of these rules or the State Bar Act.

Rule 1–200. False Statement Regarding Admission to the State Bar

(A) A member shall not knowingly make a false statement regarding a material fact or knowingly fail to disclose a material fact in connection with an application for admission to the State Bar.

(B) A member shall not further an application for admission to the State Bar of a person whom the member knows to be unqualified in respect to character, education, or other relevant attributes.

(C) This rule shall not prevent a member from serving as counsel of record for an applicant for admission to practice in proceedings related to such admission.

Discussion:

For purposes of rule 1–200 "admission" includes readmission.

Rule 1–300. Unauthorized Practice of Law

(A) A member shall not aid any person or entity in the unauthorized practice of law.

(B) A member shall not practice law in a jurisdiction where to do so would be in violation of regulations of the profession in that jurisdiction.

Rule 1–310. Forming a Partnership With a Non-lawyer

A member shall not form a partnership with a person who is not a lawyer if any of the activities of that partnership consist of the practice of law.

Discussion:

Rule 1–310 is not intended to govern members' activities which cannot be considered to constitute the practice of law. It is intended solely to preclude a member from being involved in the practice of law with a person who is not lawyer.

Rule 1–311. Employment of Disbarred, Suspended, Resigned, or Involuntarily Inactive Member

(A) For purposes of this rule:

(1) "Employ" means to engage the services of another, including employees, agents, independent contractors and consultants, regardless of whether any compensation is paid;

(2) "Involuntarily inactive member" means a member who is ineligible to practice law as a result of action taken pursuant to Business and Professions Code sections 6007, 6203(c), or California Rule of Court 31; and

(3) "Resigned member" means a member who has resigned from the State Bar while disciplinary charges are pending.

(B) A member shall not employ, associate professionally with, or aid a person the member knows or reasonably should know is a disbarred, suspended, resigned, or involuntarily inactive member to perform the following on behalf of the member's client:

(1) Render legal consultation or advice to the client;

(2) Appear on behalf of a client in any hearing or proceeding or before any judicial officer, arbitrator, mediator, court, public agency, referee, magistrate, commissioner, or hearing officer;

(3) Appear as a representative of the client at a deposition or other discovery matter;

(4) Negotiate or transact any matter for or on behalf of the client with third parties;

(5) Receive, disburse or otherwise handle the client's funds; or

(6) Engage in activities which constitute the practice of law.

(C) A member may employ, associate professionally with, or aid a disbarred, suspended, resigned, or involuntarily inactive member to perform research, drafting or clerical activities, including but not limited to:

(1) Legal work of a preparatory nature, such as legal research, the assemblage of data and other necessary information, drafting of pleadings, briefs, and other similar documents;

(2) Direct communication with the client or third parties regarding matters such as scheduling, billing, updates, confirmation of receipt or sending of correspondence and messages; or

(3) Accompanying an active member in attending a deposition or other discovery matter for the limited purpose of providing clerical assistance to the active member who will appear as the representative of the client.

(D) Prior to or at the time of employing a person the member knows or reasonably should know is a disbarred, suspended, resigned, or involuntarily inactive member, the member shall serve upon the State Bar written notice of the employment, including a full description of such person's current bar status. The written notice shall also list the activities prohibited in paragraph (B) and state that the disbarred, suspended, resigned, or involuntarily inactive member will not perform such activities. The member shall serve similar written notice upon each client on whose specific matter such person will work, prior to or at the time of employing such person to work on the client's specific matter. The member shall obtain proof of service of the client's written notice and shall retain such proof and a true and correct copy of the client's written notice for two years following termination of the member's employment with the client.

(E) A member may, without client or State Bar notification, employ a disbarred, suspended, resigned or involuntarily inactive member whose sole function is to perform office physical plant or equipment maintenance, courier or delivery services, catering, reception, typing or transcription, or other similar support activities.

(F) Upon termination of the disbarred, suspended, resigned, or involuntarily inactive member, the member shall promptly serve upon the State Bar written notice of the termination.

Discussion

For discussion of the activities that constitute the practice of law, see *Farnham v. State Bar* (1976) 17 Cal.3d 605 [131 Cal.Rptr. 611]; *Bluestein v. State Bar* (1974) 13 Cal.3d 162 [118 Cal.Rptr. 175]; *Baron v. City of Los Angeles* (1970) 2 Cal.3d 535 [86 Cal.Rptr. 673]; *Crawford v. State Bar* (1960) 54 Cal.2d 659 [7 Cal.Rptr. 746]; *People v. Merchants Protective Corporation* (1922) 189 Cal. 531, 535 [209 P. 363]; *People v. Landlords Professional Services* (1989) 215 Cal.App.3d 1599 [264 Cal.Rptr. 548]; and *People v. Sipper* (1943) 61 Cal.App.2d Supp. 844 [142 P.2d 960].

Paragraph (D) is not intended to prevent or discourage a member from fully discussing with the client the activities that will be performed by the disbarred, suspended, resigned, or involuntarily inactive member on the client's matter. If a member's client is an organization, then the written notice required by paragraph (D) shall be served upon the highest authorized officer, employee, or constituent overseeing the particular engagement. (See rule 3–600.)

Nothing in rule 1–311 shall be deemed to limit or preclude any activity engaged in pursuant to rules 983, 983.1, 983.2, and 988 of the California Rules of Court, or any local rule of a federal district court concerning admission pro hac vice.

Rule 1–320. Financial Arrangements With Non-lawyers

(A) Neither a member nor a law firm shall directly or indirectly share legal fees with a person who is not a lawyer, except that:

(1) An agreement between a member and a law firm, partner, or associate may provide for the payment of money after the member's death to the member's estate or to one or more specified persons over a reasonable period of time; or

(2) A member or law firm undertaking to complete unfinished legal business of a deceased member may pay to the estate of the deceased member or other person legally entitled thereto that proportion of the total compensation which fairly represents the services rendered by the deceased member;

(3) A member or law firm may include non-member employees in a compensation, profit-sharing, or retirement plan even though the plan is based in whole or in part on a profit-sharing arrangement, if such plan does not circumvent these rules or Business and Professions Code section 6000 et seq.; or

(4) A member may pay a prescribed registration, referral, or participation fee to a lawyer referral service established, sponsored, and operated in accordance with the State Bar of California's Minimum Standards for a Lawyer Referral Service in California.

(B) A member shall not compensate, give, or promise anything of value to any person or entity for the purpose of recommending or securing employment of the member or the member's law firm by a client, or as a reward for having made a recommendation resulting in employment of the member or the member's law firm by a client. A member's offering of or giving a gift or gratuity to any person or entity having made a recommendation resulting in the employment of the member or the member's law firm shall not of itself violate this rule, provided that the gift or gratuity was not offered or given in consideration of any promise, agreement, or understanding that such a gift or gratuity would be forthcoming or that referrals would be made or encouraged in the future.

(C) A member shall not compensate, give, or promise anything of value to any representative of the press, radio, television, or other communication medium in anticipation of or in return for publicity of the member, the law firm, or any other member as such in a news item, but the incidental provision of food or beverage shall not of itself violate this rule.

Discussion:

Rule 1–320(C) is not intended to preclude compensation to the communications media in exchange for advertising the member's or law firm's availability for professional employment.

Rule 1–400. Advertising and Solicitation

(A) For purposes of this rule, "communication" means any message or offer made by or on behalf of a member concerning the availability for professional employment of a member or a law firm directed to any former, present, or prospective client, including but not limited to the following:

(1) Any use of firm name, trade name, fictitious name, or other professional designation of such member or law firm; or

(2) Any stationery, letterhead, business card, sign, brochure, or other comparable written material describing such member, law firm, or lawyers; or

(3) Any advertisement (regardless of medium) of such member or law firm directed to the general public or any substantial portion thereof; or

(4) Any unsolicited correspondence from a member or law firm directed to any person or entity.

(B) For purposes of this rule, a "solicitation" means any communication:

(1) Concerning the availability for professional employment of a member or a law firm in which a significant motive is pecuniary gain; and

(2) Which is;

(a) delivered in person or by telephone, or

(b) directed by any means to a person known to the sender to be represented by counsel in a matter which is a subject of the communication.

(C) A solicitation shall not be made by or on behalf of a member or law firm to a prospective client with whom the member or law firm has no family or prior professional relationship, unless the solicitation is protected from abridgment by the Constitution of the United States or by the Constitution of the State of California. A solicitation to a former or present client in the discharge of a member's or law firm's professional duties is not prohibited.

(D) A communication or a solicitation (as defined herein) shall not:

(1) Contain any untrue statement; or

(2) Contain any matter, or present or arrange any matter in a manner or format which is false, deceptive, or which tends to confuse, deceive, or mislead the public; or

(3) Omit to state any fact necessary to make the statements made, in the light of circumstances under which they are made, not misleading to the public; or

(4) Fail to indicate clearly, expressly, or by context, that it is a communication or solicitation, as the case may be; or

(5) Be transmitted in any manner which involves intrusion, coercion, duress, compulsion, intimidation, threats, or vexatious or harassing conduct.

(6) State that a member is a "certified specialist" unless the member holds a current certificate as a specialist issued by the Board of Legal Specialization, or any other entity accredited by the State Bar to designate specialists pursuant to standards adopted by the Board of Governors, and states the complete name of the entity which granted certification.

(E) The Board of Governors of the State Bar shall formulate and adopt standards as to communications which will be presumed to violate this rule 1–400. The standards shall only be used as presumptions affecting the burden of proof in disciplinary proceedings involving alleged violations of these rules. "Presumption affecting the burden of proof" means that presumption defined in Evidence Code sections 605 and 606. Such standards formulated and adopted by the Board, as from time to time amended, shall be effective and binding on all members.

(F) A member shall retain for two years a true and correct copy or recording of any communication made by written or electronic media. Upon written request, the member shall make any such copy or recording available to the State Bar, and, if requested, shall provide to the State Bar evidence to support any factual or objective claim contained in the communication.

Standards:

Pursuant to Rule 1–400(E) the Board of Governors of the State Bar has adopted the following standards effective May 27, 1989 as forms of "communication" defined in rule 1–400(A) which are presumed to be in violation of Rule 1–400:

(1) A "communication" which contains guarantees, warranties, or predictions regarding the result of the representation.

(2) A "communication" which contains testimonials about or endorsements of a member unless such communication also contains an express disclaimer such as "this testimonial or endorsement does not constitute a guarantee, warranty, or prediction regarding the outcome of your legal matter."

(3) A "communication" which is delivered to a potential client whom the member knows or should reasonably know is in such a physical, emotional, or mental state that he or she would not be expected to exercise reasonable judgment as to the retention of counsel.

(4) A "communication" which is transmitted at the scene of an accident or at or en route to a hospital, emergency care center, or other health care facility.

(5) A "communication," except professional announcements, seeking professional employment for pecuniary gain, which is transmitted by mail or equivalent means which does not bear the word "Advertisement," "Newsletter" or words of similar import in 12 point print on the first page. If such communication, including firm brochures, newsletters, recent legal development advisories, and similar materials, is transmitted in an envelope, the envelope shall bear the word "Advertisement," "Newsletter" or words of similar import on the outside thereof.

(6) A "communication" in the form of a firm name, trade name, fictitious name, or other professional designation which states or implies a relationship between any member in private practice and a government agency or instrumentality or a public or non-profit legal services organization.

(7) A "communication" in the form of a firm name, trade name, fictitious name, or other professional designation which states or implies that a member has a relationship to any other lawyer or a law firm as a partner or associate, or officer or shareholder pursuant to Business and Professions Code sections 6160–6172 unless such relationship in fact exists.

(8) A "communication" which states or implies that a member or law firm is "of counsel" to another lawyer or a law firm unless the former has a relationship with the latter (other than as a partner or associate, or officer or shareholder pursuant to Business and Professions Code sections 6160–6172) which is close, personal, continuous, and regular.

(9) A "communication" in the form of a firm name, trade name, fictitious name, or other professional designation used by a member or law firm in private practice which differs materially from any other such designation used by such member or law firm at the same time in the same community.

(10) A "communication" which implies that the member or law firm is participating in a lawyer referral service which has been certified by the State Bar of California or as having satisfied the Minimum Standards for Lawyer Referral Services in California, when that is not the case.

(11) [Repealed eff. June 1, 1997.] A "communication" which states or implies that a member is a "certified specialist" unless such communication also states the complete name of the entity which granted the certification as a specialist.

(12) A "communication," except professional announcements, in the form of an advertisement primarily directed to seeking professional employment primarily for pecuniary gain transmitted to the general public or any substantial portion thereof by mail or equivalent means or by means of television, radio, newspaper, magazine or other form of commercial mass media which does not state the name of the member responsible for the communication. When the communication is made on behalf of a law firm, the communication shall state the name of at least one member responsible for it.

(13) A "communication" which contains a dramatization unless such communication contains a disclaimer which states "this is a dramatization" or words of similar import.

(14) A "communication" which states or implies "no fee without recovery" unless such communication also expressly discloses whether or not the client will be liable for costs.

(15) A "communication" which states or implies that a member is able to provide legal services in a language other than English unless the member can actually provide legal services in

such language or the communication also states in the language of the communication (a) the employment title of the person who speaks such language and (b) that the person is not a member of the State Bar of California, if that is the case.

(16) An unsolicited "communication" transmitted to the general public or any substantial portion thereof primarily directed to seeking professional employment primarily for pecuniary gain which sets forth a specific fee or range of fees for a particular service where, in fact, the member charges a greater fee than advertised in such communication within a period of 90 days following dissemination of such communication, unless such communication expressly specifies a shorter period of time regarding the advertised fee. Where the communication is published in the classified or "yellow pages" section of telephone, business or legal directories or in other media not published more frequently than once a year, the member shall conform to the advertised fee for a period of one year from initial publication, unless such communication expressly specifies a shorter period of time regarding the advertised fee.

Rule 1–500. Agreements Restricting a Member's Practice

(A) A member shall not be a party to or participate in offering or making an agreement, whether in connection with the settlement of a lawsuit or otherwise, if the agreement restricts the right of a member to practice law, except that this rule shall not prohibit such an agreement which:

(1) Is a part of an employment, shareholders' or partnership agreement among members provided the restrictive agreement does not survive the termination of the employment, shareholder, or partnership relationship; or

(2) Requires payments to a member upon the member's retirement from the practice of law.

(3) Is authorized by Business and Professions Code Sections 6092.5, subdivision (i) on 6093.

(B) A member shall not be a party to or participate in offering or making an agreement which precludes the reporting of a violation of these rules.

Discussion:

Paragraph (A) makes it clear that the practice, in connection with settlement agreements, of proposing that a member refrain from representing other clients in similar litigation, is prohibited. Neither counsel may demand or suggest such provisions nor may opposing counsel accede or agree to such provisions.

Paragraph (A) permits a restrictive covenant in a law corporation, partnership, or employment agreement. The law corporation shareholder, partner, or associate may agree not to have a separate practice during the existence of the relationship; however, upon termination of the relationship (whether voluntary or involuntary), the member is free to practice law without any contractual restriction except in the case of retirement from the active practice of law.

Rule 1–600. Legal Service Programs

(A) A member shall not participate in a nongovernmental program activity, or organization furnishing, recommending, or paying for legal services, which allows any third person or organization to interfere with the member's independence of professional judgment, or with the client-lawyer relationship, or allows unlicensed persons to practice law, or allows any third person or organization to receive directly or indirectly any part of the consideration paid to the member except as permitted by these rules, or otherwise violates the State Bar Act or these rules.

(B) The Board of Governors of the State Bar shall formulate and adopt Minimum Standards for Lawyer Referral Services, which, as from time to time amended, shall be binding on members.

Discussion:

The participation of a member in a lawyer referral service established, sponsored, supervised, and operated in conformity with the Minimum Standards for a Lawyer Referral Service in California is encouraged and is not, of itself, a violation of these rules.

Rule 1–600 is not intended to override any contractual agreement or relationship between insurers and insureds regarding the provision of legal services.

Rule 1–600 is not intended to apply to the activities of a public agency responsible for providing legal services to a government or to the public.

For purposes of paragraph (A), "a nongovernmental program, activity, or organization" includes, but is not limited to group, prepaid, and voluntary legal service programs, activities, or organizations.

Rule 1–650. Limited Legal Services Programs

(A) A member who, under the auspices of a program sponsored by a court, government agency, bar association, law school, or nonprofit organization, provides short-term limited legal services to a client without expectation by either the member or the client that the member will provide continuing representation in the matter:

(1) is subject to rule 3–310 only if the member knows that the representation of the client involves a conflict of interest; and

(2) has an imputed conflict of interest only if the member knows that another lawyer associated with the member in a law firm would have a conflict of interest under rule 3–310 with respect to the matter.

(B) Except as provided in paragraph (A)(2), a conflict of interest that arises from a member's participation in a program under paragraph (A) will not be imputed to the member's law firm.

(C) The personal disqualification of a lawyer participating in the program will not be imputed to other lawyers participating in the program.

Discussion:

[1] Courts, government agencies, bar associations, law schools and various nonprofit organizations have established programs through which lawyers provide short-term limited legal services—such as advice or the completion of legal forms—that will assist persons in addressing their legal problems without further representation by a lawyer. In these programs, such as legal-advice hotlines, advice-only clinics or pro se counseling programs, whenever a lawyer-client relationship is established, there is no expectation that the lawyer's representation of the client will continue beyond that limited consultation. Such programs are normally operated under circumstances in which it is not feasible for a lawyer to systematically screen for conflicts of interest as is generally required before undertaking a representation.

[2] A member who provides short-term limited legal services pursuant to rule 1–650 must secure the client's informed consent to the limited scope of the representation. If a short-term limited representation would not be reasonable under the circumstances, the member may offer advice to the client but must also advise the client of the need for further assistance of counsel. See rule 3–110. Except as provided in this rule 1–650, the Rules of Professional Conduct and the State Bar Act, including the member's duty of confidentiality under Business and Professions Code § 6068(e)(1), are applicable to the limited representation.

[3] A member who is representing a client in the circumstances addressed by rule 1–650 ordinarily is not able to check systematically for conflicts of interest. Therefore, paragraph (A)(1) requires compliance with rule 3–310 only if the member knows that the representation presents a conflict of interest for the member. In addition, paragraph (A)(2) imputes conflicts of interest to the member only if the member knows that another lawyer in the member's law firm would be disqualified under rule 3–310.

[4] Because the limited nature of the services significantly reduces the risk of conflicts of interest with other matters being handled by the member's law firm, paragraph (B) provides that imputed conflicts of interest are inapplicable to a representation governed by this rule except as provided by paragraph (A)(2).

Paragraph (A)(2) imputes conflicts of interest to the participating member when the member knows that any lawyer in the member's firm would be disqualified under rule 3–310. By virtue of paragraph (B), moreover, a member's participation in a short-term limited legal services program will not be imputed to the member's law firm or preclude the member's law firm from undertaking or continuing the representation of a client with interests adverse to a client being represented under the program's auspices. Nor will the personal disqualification of a lawyer participating in the program be imputed to other lawyers participating in the program.

[5] If, after commencing a short-term limited representation in accordance with rule 1–650, a member undertakes to represent the client in the matter on an ongoing basis, rule 3–310 and all other rules become applicable.

Rule 1–700. Member as Candidate for Judicial Office

(A) A member who is a candidate for judicial office in California shall comply with Canon 5 of the Code of Judicial Ethics.

(B) For purposes of this rule, "candidate for judicial office" means a member seeking judicial office by election. The determination of when a member is a candidate for judicial office is defined in the terminology section of the California Code of Judicial Ethics. A member's duty to comply with paragraph (A) shall end when the member announces withdrawal of the member's candidacy or when the results of the election are final, whichever occurs first.

Discussion:

Nothing in rule 1–700 shall be deemed to limit the applicability of any rule or law.

Rule 1–710. Member as Temporary Judge, Referee, or Court-Appointed Arbitrator

A member who is serving as a temporary judge, referee, or court-appointed arbitrator, and is subject under the Code of Judicial Ethics to Canon 6D, shall comply with the terms of that canon.

Discussion:

This rule is intended to permit the State Bar to discipline members who violate applicable portions of the Code of Judicial Ethics while acting in a judicial capacity pursuant to an order or appointment by a court.

Nothing in rule 1–710 shall be deemed to limit the applicability of any other rule or law.

CHAPTER 2. RELATIONSHIP AMONG MEMBERS

Rule 2–100. Communication With a Represented Party

(A) While representing a client, a member shall not communicate directly or indirectly about the subject of the representation with a party the member knows to be represented by another lawyer in the matter, unless the member has the consent of the other lawyer.

(B) For purposes of this rule, a "party" includes:

(1) An officer, director, or managing agent of a corporation or association, and a partner or managing agent of a partnership; or

(2) An association member or an employee of an association, corporation, or partnership, if the subject of the communication is any act or omission of such person in connection with the matter which may be binding upon or imputed to the organization for purposes of civil or criminal liability or whose statement may constitute an admission on the part of the organization.

(C) This rule shall not prohibit:

(1) Communications with a public officer, board, committee, or body;

(2) Communications initiated by a party seeking advice or representation from an independent lawyer of the party's choice; or

(3) Communications otherwise authorized by law.

Discussion:

Rule 2–100 is intended to control communications between a member and persons the member knows to be represented by counsel unless a statutory scheme or case law will override the rule. There are a number of express statutory schemes which authorize communications between a member and person who would otherwise be subject to this rule. These statutes protect a variety of other rights such as the right of employees to organize and to engage in collective bargaining, employee health and safety, or equal employment opportunity. Other applicable law also includes the authority of government prosecutors and investigators to conduct criminal investigations, as limited by the relevant decisional law.

Rule 2–100 is not intended to prevent the parties themselves from communicating with respect to the subject matter of the representation, and nothing in the rule prevents a member from advising the client that such communication can be made. Moreover, the rule does not prohibit a member who is also a party to a legal matter from directly or indirectly communicating on his or her own behalf with a represented party. Such a member has independent rights as a party which should not be abrogated because of his or her professional status. To prevent any possible abuse in such situations, the counsel for the opposing party may advise that party (1) about the risks and benefits of communications with a lawyer-party, and (2) not to accept or engage in communications with the lawyer-party.

Rule 2–100 also addresses the situation in which member A is contacted by an opposing party who is represented and, because of dissatisfaction with that party's counsel, seeks A's independent advice. Since A is employed by the opposition, the member cannot give independent advice.

As used in paragraph (A), "the subject of the representation," "matter," and "party" are not limited to a litigation context.

Paragraph (B) is intended to apply only to persons employed at the time of the communication. See *Triple A Machine Shop, Inc. v. State of California* (1989) 213 Cal.App.3d 131 [261 Cal.Rptr. 493].

Subparagraph (C)(2) is intended to permit a member to communicate with a party seeking to hire new counsel or to obtain a second opinion. A member contacted by such a party continues to be bound by other Rules of Professional Conduct. (See, e.g., rules 1–400 and 3–310.)

Rule 2–200. Financial Arrangements Among Lawyers

(A) A member shall not divide a fee for legal services with a lawyer who is not a partner of, associate of, or shareholder with the member unless:

(1) The client has consented in writing thereto after a full disclosure has been made in writing that a division of fees will be made and the terms of such division; and

(2) The total fee charged by all lawyers is not increased solely by reason of the provision for division of fees and is not unconscionable as that term is defined in rule 4–200.

(B) Except as permitted in paragraph (A) of this rule or rule 2–300, a member shall not compensate, give, or promise anything of value to any lawyer for the purpose of recommending or securing employment of the member or the member's law firm by a client, or as a reward for having made a recommendation resulting in employment of the member or the member's law firm by a client. A member's offering of or giving a gift or gratuity to any lawyer who has made a recommendation resulting in the employment of the member or the member's law firm shall not of itself violate this rule, provided that the gift or gratuity was not offered in consideration of any promise, agreement, or understanding that such a gift or gratuity would be forthcoming or that referrals would be made or encouraged in the future.

Rule 2–300. Sale or Purchase of a Law Practice of a Member, Living or Deceased

All or substantially all of the law practice of a member, living or deceased, including goodwill, may be sold to another member or law firm subject to all the following conditions:

(A) Fees charged to clients shall not be increased solely by reason of such sale.

(B) If the sale contemplates the transfer of responsibility for work not yet completed or responsibility for client files or information protected by Business and Professions Code section 6068, subdivision (e), then:

(1) if the seller is deceased, has a conservator or other person acting in a representative capacity, and no member has been appointed to act for the seller pursuant to Business and Professions Code section 6180.5, then prior to the transfer:

(a) the purchaser shall cause a written notice to be given to the client stating that the interest in the law practice is being transferred to the purchaser; that the client has the right to retain other counsel; that the client may take possession of any client papers and property, as required by rule 3–700(D); and that if no response is received to the notification within 90 days of the sending of such notice, or in the event the client's rights would be prejudiced by a failure to act during that time, the purchaser may act on behalf of the client until otherwise notified by the client. Such notice shall comply with the requirements as set forth in rule 1–400(D) and any provisions relating to attorney-client fee arrangements, and

(b) the purchaser shall obtain the written consent of the client provided that such consent shall be presumed until otherwise notified by the client if no response is received to the notification specified in subparagraph (a) within 90 days of the date of the sending of such notification to the client's last address as shown on the records of the seller, or the client's rights would be prejudiced by a failure to act during such 90-day period.

(2) in all other circumstances, not less than 90 days prior to the transfer:

(a) the seller, or the member appointed to act for the seller pursuant to Business and Professions Code section 6180.5 shall cause a written notice to be given to the client stating that the interest in the law practice is being transferred to the purchaser; that the client has the right to retain other counsel; that the client may take possession of any client papers and property, as required by rule 3–700(D); and that if no response is received to the notification within 90 days of the sending of such notice, the purchaser may act on behalf of the client until otherwise notified by the client. Such notice shall comply with the requirements as set forth in rule 1–400(D) and any provisions relating to attorney-client fee arrangements, and

(b) the seller, or the member appointed to act for the seller pursuant to Business and Professions Code section 6180.5 shall obtain the written consent of the client prior to the transfer provided that such consent shall be presumed until otherwise notified by the client if no response is received to the notification specified in subparagraph (a) within 90 days of the date of the sending of such notification to the client's last address as shown on the records of the seller.

(C) If substitution is required by the rules of a tribunal in which a matter is pending, all steps necessary to substitute a member shall be taken.

(D) All activity of a purchaser or potential purchaser under this rule shall be subject to compliance with rules 3–300 and 3–310 where applicable.

(E) Confidential information shall not be disclosed to a nonmember in connection with a sale under this rule.

(F) Admission to or retirement from a law partnership or law corporation, retirement plans and similar arrangements, or sale of tangible assets of a law practice shall not be deemed a sale or purchase under this rule.

Discussion:

Paragraph (A) is intended to prohibit the purchaser from charging the former clients of the seller a higher fee than the purchaser is charging his or her existing clients.

"All or substantially all of the law practice of a member" means, for purposes of rule 2–300, that, for example, a member may retain one or two clients who have such a longstanding personal and professional relationship with the member that transfer of those clients' files is not feasible. Conversely, rule 2–300 is not intended to authorize the sale of a law practice in a piecemeal fashion except as may be required by subparagraph (B)(1)(a) or paragraph (D).

Transfer of individual client matters, where permitted, is governed by rule 2–200. Payment of a fee to a non-lawyer broker for arranging the sale or purchase of a law practice is governed by rule 1–320.

Rule 2–400. Prohibited Discriminatory Conduct in a Law Practice

(A) For purposes of this rule:

(1) "law practice" includes sole practices, law partnerships, law corporations, corporate and governmental legal departments, and other entities which employ members to practice law;

(2) "knowingly permit" means a failure to advocate corrective action where the member knows of a discriminatory policy or practice which results in the unlawful discrimination prohibited in paragraph (B); and

(3) "unlawfully" and "unlawful" shall be determined by reference to applicable state or federal statutes or decisions making unlawful discrimination in employment and in offering goods and services to the public.

(B) In the management or operation of a law practice, a member shall not unlawfully discriminate or knowingly permit unlawful discrimination on the basis of race, national origin, sex, sexual orientation, religion, age or disability in:

(1) hiring, promoting, discharging or otherwise determining the conditions of employment of any person; or

(2) accepting or terminating representation of any client.

(C) No disciplinary investigation or proceeding may be initiated by the State Bar against a member under this rule unless and until a tribunal of competent jurisdiction, other than a disciplinary tribunal, shall have first adjudicated a complaint of alleged discrimination and found that unlawful conduct occurred. Upon such adjudication, the tribunal finding or verdict shall then be admissible evidence of the occurrence or non-occurrence of the alleged discrimination in any disciplinary proceeding initiated under this rule. In order for discipline to be imposed under this rule, however, the finding of unlawfulness must be upheld and final after appeal, the time for filing an appeal must have expired, or the appeal must have been dismissed.

Discussion:

In order for discriminatory conduct to be actionable under this rule, it must first be found to be unlawful by an appropriate civil administrative or judicial tribunal under applicable state or federal law. Until there is a finding of civil unlawfulness, there is no basis for disciplinary action under this rule.

A complaint of misconduct based on this rule may be filed with the State Bar following a finding of unlawfulness in the first instance even though that finding is thereafter appealed.

A disciplinary investigation or proceeding for conduct coming within this rule may be initiated and maintained, however, if such conduct warrants discipline under California Business and Professions Code sections 6106 and 6068, the California Supreme Court's inherent authority to impose discipline, or other disciplinary standard.

Adopted, eff. March 1, 1994.

CHAPTER 3. PROFESSIONAL RELATIONSHIP WITH CLIENTS

Rule 3–100. Confidential Information of a Client

(A) A member shall not reveal information protected from disclosure by Business and Professions Code section 6068, subdivision (e)(1) without the informed consent of the client, or as provided in paragraph (B) of this rule.

(B) A member may, but is not required to, reveal confidential information relating to the representation of a client to the extent that the member reasonably believes the disclosure is necessary to prevent a criminal act that the member reasonably believes is likely to result in death of, or substantial bodily harm to, an individual.

(C) Before revealing confidential information to prevent a criminal act as provided in paragraph (B), a member shall, if reasonable under the circumstances:

(1) make a good faith effort to persuade the client: (i) not to commit or to continue the criminal act or (ii) to pursue a course of conduct that will prevent the threatened death or substantial bodily harm; or do both (i) and (ii); and

(2) inform the client, at an appropriate time, of the member's ability or decision to reveal information as provided in paragraph (B).

(D) In revealing confidential information as provided in paragraph (B), the member's disclosure must be no more than is necessary to prevent the criminal act, given the information known to the member at the time of the disclosure.

(E) A member who does not reveal information permitted by paragraph (B) does not violate this rule.

Discussion:

[1] Duty of confidentiality. Paragraph (A) relates to a member's obligations under Business and Professions Code section 6068, subdivision (e)(*l*), which provides it is a duty of a member: "To maintain inviolate the confidence, and at every peril to himself or herself to preserve the secrets, of his or her client." A member's duty to preserve the confidentiality of client information involves public policies of paramount importance. (In Re Jordan (1974) 12 Cal.3d 575, 580 [116 Cal.Rptr. 371].) Preserving the confidentiality of client information contributes to the trust that is the hallmark of the client-lawyer relationship. The client is thereby encouraged to seek legal assistance and to communicate fully and frankly with the lawyer even as to embarrassing or legally damaging subject matter. The lawyer needs this information to represent the client effectively and, if necessary, to advise the client to refrain from wrongful conduct. Almost without exception, clients come to lawyers in order to determine their rights and what is, in the complex of laws and regulations, deemed to be legal and correct. Based upon experience, lawyers know that almost all clients follow the advice given, and the law is upheld. Paragraph (A) thus recognizes a fundamental principle in the client lawyer relationship, that, in the absence of the client's informed consent, a member must not reveal information relating to the representation. (See, e.g., *Commercial Standard Title Co. v. Superior Court* (1979) 92 Cal.App.3d 934, 945 [155 Cal.Rptr. 393].)

[2] Client-lawyer confidentiality encompasses the attorney-client privilege, the work-product doctrine and ethical standards of confidentiality. The principle of client-lawyer confidentiality applies to information relating to the representation, whatever its source, and encompasses matters communicated in confidence by the client, and therefore protected by the attorney-client privilege, matters protected by the work product doctrine, and matters protected under ethical standards of confidentiality, all as established in law, rule and policy. (See *In the Matter of Johnson* (Rev. Dept. 2000) 4 Cal. State Bar Ct. Rptr. 179; *Goldstein v. Lees* (1975) 46 Cal.3d 614, 621 [120 Cal. Rptr. 253].) The attorney-client privilege and work-product doctrine apply in judicial and other proceedings in which a member may be called as a witness or be otherwise compelled to produce evidence concerning a client. A member's ethical duty of confidentiality is not so limited in its scope of protection for the client-lawyer relationship of trust and prevents a member from revealing the client's confidential information even when not confronted with such compulsion. Thus, a member may not reveal such information except with the consent of the client or as authorized or required by the State Bar Act, these rules, or other law.

[3] Narrow exception to duty of confidentiality under this Rule. Notwithstanding the important public policies promoted by lawyers adhering to the core duty of confidentiality, the overriding value of life permits disclosures otherwise prohibited under Business & Professions Code section 6068(e), subdivision (1). Paragraph (B), which restates Business and Professions Code section 6068, subdivision (e)(2), identifies a narrow confidentiality exception, absent the client's informed consent, when a member reasonably believes that disclosure is necessary to prevent a criminal act that the member reasonably believes is likely to result in the death of, or substantial bodily harm to an individual. Evidence Code section 956.5, which relates to the evidentiary attorney client privilege, sets forth a similar express exception. Although a member is not permitted to reveal confidential information concerning a client's past, completed criminal acts, the policy favoring the preservation of human life that underlies this exception to the duty of confidentiality and the evidentiary privilege permits disclosure to prevent a future or ongoing criminal act.

[4] Member not subject to discipline for revealing confidential information as permitted under this Rule. Rule 3–100, which restates Business and Professions Code section 6068, subdivision (e)(2), reflects a balancing between the interests of preserving client confidentiality and of preventing a criminal act that a member reasonably believes is likely to result in death or substantial bodily harm to an individual. A member who reveals information as permitted under this rule is not subject to discipline.

[5] No duty to reveal confidential information. Neither Business and Professions Code section 6068, subdivision (e)(2) nor this rule imposes an affirmative obligation on a member to reveal information in order to prevent harm. (See rule 1–100(A).) A member may decide not to reveal confidential information. Whether a member chooses to reveal confidential information as permitted under this rule is a matter for the individual member to decide, based on all the facts and circumstances, such as those discussed in paragraph [6] of this discussion.

[6] Deciding to reveal confidential information as permitted under paragraph (B). Disclosure permitted under paragraph (B) is ordinarily a last resort, when no other available action is reasonably likely to prevent the criminal act. Prior to revealing information as permitted under paragraph (B), the member must, if reasonable under the circumstances, make a good faith effort to persuade the client to take steps to avoid the criminal act or threatened harm. Among the factors to be considered in determining whether to disclose confidential information are the following:

(1) the amount of time that the member has to make a decision about disclosure;

(2) whether the client or a third party has made similar threats before and whether they have ever acted or attempted to act upon them;

(3) whether the member believes the member's efforts to persuade the client or a third person not to engage in the criminal conduct have or have not been successful;

(4) the extent of adverse effect to the client's rights under the Fifth, Sixth and Fourteenth Amendments of the United States Constitution and analogous rights and privacy rights under Article I of the Constitution of the State of California that may result from disclosure contemplated by the member;

(5) the extent of other adverse effects to the client that may result from disclosure contemplated by the member; and

(6) the nature and extent of information that must be disclosed to prevent the criminal act or threatened harm.

A member may also consider whether the prospective harm to the victim or victims is imminent in deciding whether to disclose the confidential information. However, the imminence of the harm is not a prerequisite to disclosure and a member may disclose the information without waiting until immediately before the harm is likely to occur.

[7] Counseling client or third person not to commit a criminal act reasonably likely to result in death of substantial bodily harm. Subparagraph (C)(1) provides that before a member may reveal confidential information, the member must, if reasonable under the circumstances, make a good faith effort to persuade the client not to commit or to continue the criminal act, or to persuade the client to otherwise pursue a course of conduct that will prevent the threatened death or substantial bodily harm, or if necessary, do both. The interests protected by such counseling is the client's interest in limiting disclosure of confidential information and in taking responsible action to deal with situations attributable to the client. If a client, whether in response to the member's counseling or otherwise, takes corrective action—such as by ceasing the criminal act before harm is caused—the option for permissive disclosure by the member would cease as the threat posed by the criminal act would no longer be present. When the actor is a nonclient or when the act is deliberate or malicious, the member who contemplates making adverse disclosure of confidential information may reasonably conclude that the compelling interests of the member or others in their own personal safety preclude personal contact with the actor. Before counseling an actor who is a nonclient, the member should, if reasonable under the circumstances, first advise the client of the member's intended course of action. If a client or another person has already acted but the intended harm has not yet occurred, the member should consider, if reasonable under the circumstances, efforts to persuade the client or third person to warn the victim or consider other appropriate action to prevent the harm. Even when the member has concluded that paragraph (B) does not permit the member to reveal confidential information, the member nevertheless is permitted to counsel the client as to why it may be in the client's best interest to consent to the attorney's disclosure of that information.

[8] Disclosure of confidential information must be no more than is reasonably necessary to prevent the criminal act. Under paragraph (D), disclosure of confidential information, when made, must be no more extensive than the member reasonably believes necessary to prevent the criminal act. Disclosure should allow access to the confidential information to only those persons who the member reasonably believes can act to prevent the harm. Under some circumstances, a member may determine that the best course to pursue is to make an anonymous disclosure to the potential victim or relevant law-enforcement authorities. What particular measures are reasonable depends on the circumstances known to the member. Relevant circumstances include the time available, whether the victim might be unaware of the threat, the member's prior course of dealings with the client, and the extent of the adverse effect on the client that may result from the disclosure contemplated by the member.

[9] Informing client of member's ability or decision to reveal confidential information under subparagraph (C)(2). A member is required to keep a client reasonably informed about significant developments regarding the employment or representation. Rule 3–500; Business and Professions Code, section 6068, subdivision (m). Paragraph (C)(2), however, recognizes that under certain circumstances, informing a client of the member's ability or decision to reveal confidential information under paragraph (B) would likely increase the risk of death or substantial bodily harm, not only to the originally intended victims of the criminal act, but also to the client or members of the client's family, or to the member or the member's family or associates. Therefore, paragraph (C)(2) requires a member to inform the client of the member's ability or decision to reveal confidential information as provided in paragraph (B) only if it is reasonable to do so under the circumstances. Paragraph (C)(2) further recognizes that the appropriate time for the member to inform the client may vary depending upon the circumstances. (See paragraph [10] of this discussion.) Among the factors to be considered in determining an appropriate time, if any, to inform a client are:

(1) whether the client is an experienced user of legal services;

(2) the frequency of the member's contact with the client;

(3) the nature and length of the professional relationship with the client;

(4) whether the member and client have discussed the member's duty of confidentiality or any exceptions to that duty;

(5) the likelihood that the client's matter will involve information within paragraph (B);

(6) the member's belief, if applicable, that so informing the client is likely to increase the likelihood that a criminal act likely to result in the death of, or substantial bodily harm to, an individual; and

(7) the member's belief, if applicable, that good faith efforts to persuade a client not to act on a threat have failed.

[10] Avoiding a chilling effect on the lawyer-client relationship. The foregoing flexible approach to the member's informing a client of his or her ability or decision to reveal confidential information recognizes the concern that informing a client about limits on confidentiality may have a chilling effect on client communication. (See Discussion paragraph [1].) To avoid that chilling effect, one member may choose to inform the client of the member's ability to reveal information as early as the outset of the representation, while another member may choose to inform a client only at a point when that client has imparted information that may fall under paragraph (B), or even choose not to inform a client until such time as the member attempts to counsel the client as contemplated in Discussion paragraph [7]. In each situation, the member will have discharged properly the requirement under subparagraph (C)(2), and will not be subject to discipline.

[11] Informing client that disclosure has been made; termination of the lawyer-client relationship. When a member has revealed confidential information under paragraph (B), in all but extraordinary cases the relationship between member and client will have deteriorated so as to make the member's representation of the client impossible. Therefore, the member is required to seek to withdraw from the representation (see rule 3–700(B)), unless the member is able to obtain the client's informed consent to the member's continued representation. The member must inform the client of the fact of the member's disclosure unless the member has a compelling interest in not informing the client, such as to protect the member, the member's family or a third person from the risk of death or substantial bodily harm.

[12] Other consequences of the member's disclosure. Depending upon the circumstances of a member's disclosure of confidential information, there may be other important issues that a member must address. For example, if a member will he called as a witness in the client's matter, then rule 5–210 should be considered. Similarly, the member should consider his or her duties of loyalty and competency (rule 3 110).

[13] Other exceptions to confidentiality under California law. Rule 3–100 is not intended to augment, diminish, or preclude reliance upon, any other exceptions to the duty to preserve the confidentiality of client information recognized under California law.

Rule 3–110. Failing to Act Competently

(A) A member shall not intentionally, recklessly, or repeatedly fail to perform legal services with competence.

(B) For purposes of this rule, "competence" in any legal service shall mean to apply the 1) diligence, 2) learning and skill, and 3) mental, emotional, and physical ability reasonably necessary for the performance of such service.

(C) If a member does not have sufficient learning and skill when the legal service is undertaken, the member may nonetheless perform such services competently by 1) associating with or, where appropriate, professionally consulting another lawyer reasonably believed to be competent, or 2) by acquiring sufficient learning and skill before performance is required.

Discussion:

The duties set forth in rule 3–110 include the duty to supervise the work of subordinate attorney and non-attorney employees or agents. (See, e.g., *Waysman v. State Bar* (1986) 41 Cal.3d 452; *Trousil v. State Bar* (1985) 38 Cal.3d 337, 342 [211 Cal.Rptr. 525]; *Palomo v. State Bar* (1984) 36 Cal.3d 785 [205 Cal.Rptr. 834]; *Crane v. State Bar* (1981) 30 Cal.3d 117, 122; *Black v. State Bar* (1972) 7 Cal.3d 676, 692 [103 Cal.Rptr. 288; 499 P.2d 968]; *Vaughn v. State Bar* (1972) 6 Cal.3d 847, 857–858 [100 Cal.Rptr. 713; 494 P.2d 1257]; *Moore v. State Bar* (1964) 62 Cal.2d 74, 81 [41 Cal.Rptr. 161; 396 P.2d 577].)

In an emergency a lawyer may give advice or assistance in a matter in which the lawyer does not have the skill ordinarily required where referral to or consultation with another lawyer would be impractical. Even in an emergency, however, assistance should be limited to that reasonably necessary in the circumstances.

Rule 3–120. Sexual Relations With Client

(A) For purposes of this rule, "sexual relations" means sexual intercourse or the touching of an intimate part of another person for the purpose of sexual arousal, gratification, or abuse.

(B) A member shall not:

(1) Require or demand sexual relations with a client incident to or as a condition of any professional representation; or

(2) Employ coercion, intimidation, or undue influence in entering into sexual relations with a client; or

(3) Continue representation of a client with whom the member has sexual relations if such sexual relations cause the member to perform legal services incompetently in violation of rule 3–110.

(C) Paragraph (B) shall not apply to sexual relations between members and their spouses or to ongoing consensual sexual relationships which predate the initiation of the lawyer-client relationship.

(D) Where a lawyer in a firm has sexual relations with a client but does not participate in the representation of that client, the lawyers in the firm shall not be subject to discipline under this rule solely because of the occurrence of such sexual relations.

Discussion:

Rule 3–120 is intended to prohibit sexual exploitation by a lawyer in the course of a professional representation. Often, based upon the nature of the underlying representation, a client exhibits great emotional vulnerability and dependence upon the advice and guidance of counsel. Attorneys owe the utmost duty of good faith and fidelity to clients. (See, e.g., Greenbaum v. State Bar (1976) 15 Cal.3d 893, 903 [126 Cal.Rptr. 785]; Alkow v. State Bar (1971) 3 Cal.3d 924, 935 [92 Cal.Rptr. 279]; Cutler v. State Bar (1969) 71 Cal.2d 241, 251 [78 Cal.Rptr. 172]; Clancy v. State Bar (1969) 71 Cal.2d 140, 146 [77 Cal.Rptr. 657].) The relationship between an attorney and client is a fiduciary relationship of the very highest character and all dealings between an attorney and client that are beneficial to the attorney will be closely scrutinized with the utmost strictness for unfairness. (See, e.g., Giovanazzi v. State Bar (1980) 28 Cal.3d 465, 472 [169 Cal.Rptr. 581]; Benson v. State Bar (1975) 13 Cal.3d 581, 586 [119 Cal.Rptr. 297]; Lee v. State Bar (1970) 2 Cal.3d 927, 939 [88 Cal.Rptr. 361]; Clancy v. State Bar (1969) 71 Cal.2d 140, 146 [77 Cal.Rptr. 657].) Where attorneys exercise undue influence over clients or take unfair advantage of clients, discipline is appropriate. (See, e.g., Magee v. State Bar (1962) 58 Cal.2d 423 [24 Cal.Rptr. 839]; Lantz v. State Bar (1931) 212 Cal. 213 [298 P. 497].) In all client matters, a member is advised to keep clients' interests paramount in the course of the member's representation.

For purposes of this rule, if the client is an organization, any individual overseeing the representation shall be deemed to be the client. (See rule 3–600.)

Although paragraph (C) excludes representation of certain clients from the scope of rule 3–120, such exclusion is not intended to preclude the applicability of other Rules of Professional Conduct, including rule 3–110.

Rule 3–200. Prohibited Objectives of Employment

A member shall not seek, accept, or continue employment if the member knows or should know that the objective of such employment is:

(A) To bring an action, conduct a defense, assert a position in litigation, or take an appeal, without probable cause and for the purpose of harassing or maliciously injuring any person; or

(B) To present a claim or defense in litigation that is not warranted under existing law, unless it can be supported by a good faith argument for an extension, modification, or reversal of such existing law.

Rule 3–210. Advising the Violation of Law

A member shall not advise the violation of any law, rule, or ruling of a tribunal unless the member believes in good faith that such law, rule, or ruling is invalid. A member may take appropriate steps in good faith to test the validity of any law, rule, or ruling of a tribunal.

Discussion:

Rule 3–210 is intended to apply not only to the prospective conduct of a client but also to the interaction between the member and client and to the specific legal service sought by the client from the member. An example of the former is the handling of physical evidence of a crime in the possession of the client and offered to the member. (See *People v. Meredith* (1981) 29 Cal.3d 682 [175 Cal.Rptr. 612].) An example of the latter is a request that the member negotiate the return of stolen property in exchange for the owner's agreement not to report the theft to the police or prosecutorial authorities. (See *People v. Pic'l* (1982) 31 Cal.3d 731 [183 Cal.Rptr. 685].)

Rule 3–300. Avoiding Interests Adverse to a Client

A member shall not enter into a business transaction with a client; or knowingly acquire an ownership, possessory, security, or other pecuniary interest adverse to a client, unless each of the following requirements has been satisfied:

(A) The transaction or acquisition and its terms are fair and reasonable to the client and are fully disclosed and transmitted in writing to the client in a manner which should reasonably have been understood by the client; and

(B) The client is advised in writing that the client may seek the advice of an independent lawyer of the client's choice and is given a reasonable opportunity to seek that advice; and

(C) The client thereafter consents in writing to the terms of the transaction or the terms of the acquisition.

Discussion:

Rule 3–300 is not intended to apply to the agreement by which the member is retained by the client, unless the agreement confers on the member an ownership, possessory, security, or other pecuniary interest adverse to the client. Such an agreement is governed, in part, by rule 4–200.

Rule 3–300 is not intended to apply where the member and client each make an investment on terms offered to the general public or a significant portion thereof. For example, rule 3–300 is not intended to apply where A, a member, invests in a limited partnership syndicated by a third party. B, A's client, makes the same investment. Although A and B are each investing in the same business, A did not enter into the transaction "with" B for the purposes of the rule.

Rule 3–300 is intended to apply where the member wishes to obtain an interest in client's property in order to secure the amount of the member's past due or future fees.

Rule 3–310. Avoiding the Representation of Adverse Interests

(A) For purposes of this rule:

(1) "Disclosure" means informing the client or former client of the relevant circumstances and of the actual and reasonably foreseeable adverse consequences to the client or former client;

(2) "Informed written consent" means the client's or former client's written agreement to the representation following written disclosure;

(3) "Written" means any writing as defined in Evidence Code section 250.

(B) A member shall not accept or continue representation of a client without providing written disclosure to the client where:

(1) The member has a legal, business, financial, professional, or personal relationship with a party or witness in the same matter; or

(2) The member knows or reasonably should know that:

(a) the member previously had a legal, business, financial, professional, or personal relationship with a party or witness in the same matter; and

(b) the previous relationship would substantially affect the member's representation; or

(3) The member has or had a legal, business, financial, professional, or personal relationship with another person or entity the member knows or reasonably should know would be affected substantially by resolution of the matter; or

(4) The member has or had a legal, business, financial, or professional interest in the subject matter of the representation.

(C) A member shall not, without the informed written consent of each client:

(1) Accept representation of more than one client in a matter in which the interests of the clients potentially conflict; or

(2) Accept or continue, representation of more than one client in a matter in which the interests of the clients actually conflict; or

(3) Represent a client in a matter and at the same time in a separate matter accept as a client a person or entity whose interest in the first matter is adverse to the client in the first matter.

(D) A member who represents two or more clients shall not enter into an aggregate settlement of the claims of or against the clients without the informed written consent of each client.

(E) A member shall not, without the informed written consent of the client or former client, accept employment adverse to the client or former client where, by reason of the representation of the client or former client, the member has obtained confidential information material to the employment.

(F) A member shall not accept compensation for representing a client from one other than the client unless:

(1) There is no interference with the member's independence of professional judgment or with the client-lawyer relationship; and

(2) Information relating to representation of the client is protected as required by Business and Professions Code section 6068, subdivision (e); and

(3) The member obtains the client's informed written consent, provided that no disclosure or consent is required if:

(a) such nondisclosure is otherwise authorized by law; or

(b) the member is rendering legal services on behalf of any public agency which provides legal services to other public agencies or the public.

Discussion:

Rule 3–310 is not intended to prohibit a member from representing parties having antagonistic positions on the same legal question that has arisen in different cases, unless representation of either client would be adversely affected.

Other rules and laws may preclude making adequate disclosure under this rule. If such disclosure is precluded, informed written consent is likewise precluded. (See, e.g., Business and Professions Code section 6068, subsection (e).)

Paragraph (B) is not intended to apply to the relationship of a member to another party's lawyer. Such relationships are governed by rule 3–320.

Paragraph (B) is not intended to require either the disclosure of the new engagement to a former client or the consent of the former client to the new engagement. However, such disclosure or consent is required if paragraph (E) applies.

While paragraph (B) deals with the issues of adequate disclosure to the present client or clients of the member's present or past relationships to other parties or witnesses or present interest in the subject matter of the representation, paragraph (E) is intended to protect the confidences of another present or former client. These two paragraphs are to apply as complementary provisions.

Paragraph (B) is intended to apply only to a member's own relationships or interests, unless the member knows that a partner or associate in the same firm as the member has or had a relationship with another party or witness or has or had an interest in the subject matter of the representation.

Subparagraphs (C)(1) and (C)(2) are intended to apply to all types of legal employment, including the concurrent representation of multiple parties in litigation or in a single transaction or in some other common enterprise or legal relationship. Examples of the latter include the formation of a partnership for several partners or a corporation for several shareholders, the preparation of an ante-nuptial agreement, or joint or reciprocal wills for a husband and wife, or the resolution of an "uncontested" marital dissolution. In such situations, for the sake of convenience or economy, the parties may well prefer to employ a single counsel, but a member must disclose the potential adverse aspects of such multiple representation (e.g., Evid.Code, § 962) and must obtain the informed written consent of the clients thereto pursuant to subparagraph (C)(1). Moreover, if the potential adversity should become actual, the member must obtain the further informed written consent of the clients pursuant to subparagraph (C)(2).

Subparagraph (C)(3) is intended to apply to representations of clients in both litigation and transactional matters.

In *State Farm Mutual Automobile Insurance Company v. Federal Insurance Company* (1999) 72 Cal.App.4th 1422 [86 Cal.Rptr.2d 20], the court held that subparagraph (C)(3) was violated when a member, retained by an insurer to defend one suit, and while that suit was still pending, filed a direct action against the same insurer in an unrelated action without securing the insurer's consent. Notwithstanding *State Farm*, subparagraph (C)(3) is not intended to apply with respect to the relationship between an insurer and a member when, in each matter, the insurer's interest is only as an indemnity provider and not as a direct party to the action.

There are some matters in which the conflicts are such that written consent may not suffice for non-disciplinary purposes. (See Woods v. Superior Court (1983) 149 Cal.App.3d 931 [197 Cal.Rptr. 185]; Klemm v. Superior Court (1977) 75 Cal.App.3d 893 [142 Cal.Rptr. 509]; Ishmael v. Millington (1966) 241 Cal.App.2d 520 [50 Cal.Rptr. 592].)

Paragraph (D) is not intended to apply to class action settlements subject to court approval.

Paragraph (F) is not intended to abrogate existing relationships between insurers and insureds whereby the insurer has the contractual right to unilaterally select counsel for the insured, where there is no conflict of interest. (See San Diego Navy Federal Credit Union v. Cumis Insurance Society (1984) 162 Cal.App.3d 358 [208 Cal.Rptr. 494].)

Rule 3–320. Relationship With Other Party's Lawyer

A member shall not represent a client in a matter in which another party's lawyer is a spouse, parent, child, or sibling of the member, lives with the member, is a client of the member, or has an intimate personal relationship with the member, unless the member informs the client in writing of the relationship.

Discussion:

Rule 3–320 is not intended to apply to circumstances in which a member fails to advise the client of a relationship with another lawyer who is merely a partner or associate in the same law firm as the adverse party's counsel, and who has no direct involvement in the matter.

Rule 3–400. Limiting Liability to Client

A member shall not:

(A) Contract with a client prospectively limiting the member's liability to the client for the member's professional malpractice; or

(B) Settle a claim or potential claim for the member's liability to the client for the member's professional malpractice unless the client is informed in writing that the client may seek the advice of an independent lawyer of the client's choice regarding the settlement and is given a reasonable opportunity to seek that advice.

Discussion:

Rule 3–400 is not intended to apply to customary qualifications and limitations in legal opinions and memoranda, nor is it intended to prevent a member from reasonably limiting the scope of the member's employment or representation.

Rule 3–410. Disclosure of Professional Liability Insurance

(A) A member who knows or should know that he or she does not have professional liability insurance shall inform a client in writing, at the time of the client's engagement of the member, that the member does not have professional liability insurance whenever it is reasonably foreseeable that the total amount of the member's legal representation of the client in the matter will exceed four hours.

(B) If a member does not provide the notice required under paragraph (A) at the time of a client's engagement of the member, and the member subsequently knows or should know that he or she no longer has professional liability insurance during the representation of the client, the member shall inform the client in writing within thirty days of the date that the member knows or should know that he or she no longer has professional liability insurance.

(C) This rule does not apply to a member who is employed as a government lawyer or in-house counsel when that member is representing or providing legal advice to a client in that capacity.

(D) This rule does not apply to legal services rendered in an emergency to avoid foreseeable prejudice to the rights or interests of the client.

(E) This rule does not apply where the member has previously advised the client under Paragraph (A) or (B) that the member does not have professional liability insurance.

Discussion:

[1] The disclosure obligation imposed by Paragraph (A) of this rule applies with respect to new clients and new engagements with returning clients.

[2] A member may use the following language in making the disclosure required by Rule 3–410(A), and may include that language in a written fee agreement with the client or in a separate writing:

"Pursuant to California Rule of Professional Conduct 3–410, I am informing you in writing that I do not have professional liability insurance."

[3] A member may use the following language in making the disclosure required by Rule 3–410(B):

"Pursuant to California Rule of Professional Conduct 3–410, I am informing you in writing that I no longer have professional liability insurance."

[4] Rule 3–410(C) provides an exemption for a "government lawyer or in-house counsel when that member is representing or providing legal advice to a client in that capacity." The basis of both exemptions is essentially the same. The purpose of this rule is to provide information directly to a client if a member is not covered by professional liability insurance. If a member is employed directly by and provides legal services directly for a private entity or a federal, state or local governmental entity, that entity presumably

knows whether the member is or is not covered by professional liability insurance. The exemptions under this rule are limited to situations involving direct employment and representation, and do not, for example, apply to outside counsel for a private or governmental entity, or to counsel retained by an insurer to represent an insured.

Rule 3–500. Communication

A member shall keep a client reasonably informed about significant developments relating to the employment or representation, including promptly complying with reasonable requests for information and copies of significant documents when necessary to keep the client so informed.

Discussion:

Rule 3–500 is not intended to change a member's duties to his or her clients. It is intended to make clear that, while a client must be informed of significant developments in the matter, a member will not be disciplined for failing to communicate insignificant or irrelevant information. (See Bus. & Prof.Code, § 6068, subd. (m).)

A member may contract with the client in their employment agreement that the client assumes responsibility for the cost of copying significant documents. This rule is not intended to prohibit a claim for the recovery of the member's expense in any subsequent legal proceeding.

Rule 3–500 is not intended to create. augment, diminish, or eliminate any application of the work product rule. The obligation of the member to provide work product to the client shall be governed by relevant statutory and decisional law. Additionally, this rule is not intended to apply any document or correspondence that is subject to a protective order or non-disclosure agreement, or to override applicable statutory or decisional law requiring that certain information not be provided to criminal defendants who are clients of the member.

Rule 3–510. Communication of Settlement Offer

(A) A member shall promptly communicate to the member's client:

(1) All terms and conditions of any offer made to the client in a criminal matter; and

(2) All amounts, terms, and conditions of any written offer of settlement made to the client in all other matters.

(B) As used in this rule, "client" includes a person who possesses the authority to accept an offer of settlement or plea, or, in a class action, all the named representatives of the class.

Discussion:

Rule 3–510 is intended to require that counsel in a criminal matter convey all offers, whether written or oral, to the client, as give and take negotiations are less common in criminal matters, and, even were they to occur, such negotiations should require the participation of the accused.

Any oral offers of settlement made to the client in a civil matter should also be communicated if they are "significant" for the purposes of rule 3–500.

Rule 3–600. Organization as Client

(A) In representing an organization, a member shall conform his or her representation to the concept that the client is the organization itself, acting through its highest authorized officer, employee, body, or constituent overseeing the particular engagement.

(B) If a member acting on behalf of an organization knows that an actual or apparent agent of the organization acts or intends or refuses to act in a manner that is or may be a violation of law reasonably imputable to the organization, or in a manner which is likely to result in substantial injury to the organization, the member shall not violate his or her duty of protecting all confidential information as provided in Business and Professions Code section 6068, subdivision (e). Subject to Business and Professions Code section 6068, subdivision (e), the member may take such actions as appear to the member to be in the best lawful interest of the organization. Such actions may include among others:

(1) Urging reconsideration of the matter while explaining its likely consequences to the organization; or

(2) Referring the matter to the next higher authority in the organization, including, if warranted by the seriousness of the matter, referral to the highest internal authority that can act on behalf of the organization.

(C) If, despite the member's actions in accordance with paragraph (B), the highest authority that can act on behalf of the organization insists upon action or a refusal to act that is a violation of law and is likely to result in substantial injury to the organization, the member's response is limited to the member's right, and, where appropriate, duty to resign in accordance with rule 3–700.

(D) In dealing with an organization's directors, officers, employees, members, shareholders, or other constituents, a member shall explain the identity of the client for whom the member acts, whenever it is or becomes apparent that the organization's interests are or may become adverse to those of the constituent(s) with whom the member is dealing. The member shall not mislead such a constituent into believing that the constituent may communicate confidential information to the member in a way that will not be used in the organization's interest if that is or becomes adverse to the constituent.

(E) A member representing an organization may also represent any of its directors, officers, employees, members, shareholders, or other constituents, subject to the provisions of rule 3–310. If the organization's consent to the dual representation is required by rule 3–310, the consent shall be given by an appropriate constituent of the organization other than the individual or constituent who is to be represented, or by the shareholder(s) or organization members.

Discussion:

Rule 3–600 is not intended to enmesh members in the intricacies of the entity and aggregate theories of partnership.

Rule 3–600 is not intended to prohibit members from representing both an organization and other parties connected with it, as for instance (as simply one example) in establishing employee benefit packages for closely held corporations or professional partnerships.

Rule 3–600 is not intended to create or to validate artificial distinctions between entities and their officers, employees, or members, nor is it the purpose of the rule to deny the existence or importance of such formal distinctions. In dealing with a close corporation or small association, members commonly perform professional engagements for both the organization and its major constituents. When a change in control occurs or is threatened, members are faced with complex decisions involving personal and institutional relationships and loyalties and have frequently had difficulty in perceiving their correct duty. (See *People ex rel. Deukmejian v. Brown* (1981) 29 Cal.3d 150 [172 Cal.Rptr. 478]; *Goldstein v. Lees* (1975) 46 Cal.App.3d 614 [120 Cal.Rptr. 253]; *Woods v. Superior Court* (1983) 149 Cal.App.3d 931 [197 Cal.Rptr. 185]; *In re Banks* (1978) 283 Ore. 459 [584 P.2d 284]; 1 A.L.R.4th 1105.) In resolving such multiple relationships, members must rely on case law.

Rule 3–700. Termination of Employment

(A) In General.

(1) If permission for termination of employment is required by the rules of a tribunal, a member shall not withdraw from employment in a proceeding before that tribunal without its permission.

(2) A member shall not withdraw from employment until the member has taken reasonable steps to avoid reasonably foreseeable prejudice to the rights of the client, including giving

due notice to the client, allowing time for employment of other counsel, complying with rule 3–700(D), and complying with applicable laws and rules.

(B) Mandatory Withdrawal.

A member representing a client before a tribunal shall withdraw from employment with the permission of the tribunal, if required by its rules, and a member representing a client in other matters shall withdraw from employment, if:

(1) The member knows or should know that the client is bringing an action, conducting a defense, asserting a position in litigation, or taking an appeal, without probable cause and for the purpose of harassing or maliciously injuring any person; or

(2) The member knows or should know that continued employment will result in violation of these rules or of the State Bar Act; or

(3) The member's mental or physical condition renders it unreasonably difficult to carry out the employment effectively.

(C) Permissive Withdrawal.

If rule 3–700(B) is not applicable, a member may not request permission to withdraw in matters pending before a tribunal, and may not withdraw in other matters, unless such request or such withdrawal is because:

(1) The client

(a) insists upon presenting a claim or defense that is not warranted under existing law and cannot be supported by good faith argument for an extension, modification, or reversal of existing law, or

(b) seeks to pursue an illegal course of conduct, or

(c) insists that the member pursue a course of conduct that is illegal or that is prohibited under these rules or the State Bar Act, or

(d) by other conduct renders it unreasonably difficult for the member to carry out the employment effectively, or

(e) insists, in a matter not pending before a tribunal, that the member engage in conduct that is contrary to the judgment and advice of the member but not prohibited under these rules or the State Bar Act, or

(f) breaches an agreement or obligation to the member as to expenses or fees.

(2) The continued employment is likely to result in a violation of these rules or of the State Bar Act; or

(3) The inability to work with co-counsel indicates that the best interests of the client likely will be served by withdrawal; or

(4) The member's mental or physical condition renders it difficult for the member to carry out the employment effectively; or

(5) The client knowingly and freely assents to termination of the employment; or

(6) The member believes in good faith, in a proceeding pending before a tribunal, that the tribunal will find the existence of other good cause for withdrawal.

(D) Papers, Property and Fees.

A member whose employment has terminated shall:

(1) Subject to any protective order or non-disclosure agreement, promptly release to the client, at the request of the client, all the client papers and property. "Client papers and property"

includes correspondence, pleadings, deposition transcripts, exhibits, physical evidence, expert's reports, and other items reasonably necessary to the client's representation, whether the client has paid for them or not; and

(2) Promptly refund any part of a fee paid in advance that has not been earned. This provision is not applicable to a true retainer fee which is paid solely for the purpose of ensuring the availability of the member for the matter.

Discussion:

Subparagraph (A)(2) provides that "a member shall not withdraw from employment until the member has taken reasonable steps to avoid reasonably foreseeable prejudice to the rights of the clients." What such steps would include, of course, will vary according to the circumstances. Absent special circumstances, "reasonable steps" do not include providing additional services to the client once the successor counsel has been employed and rule 3–700(D) has been satisfied.

Paragraph (D) makes clear the member's duties in the recurring situation in which new counsel seeks to obtain client files from a member discharged by the client. It codifies existing case law. (See *Academy of California Optometrists v. Superior Court* (1975) 51 Cal.App.3d 999 [124 Cal.Rptr. 668]; *Weiss v. Marcus* (1975) 51 Cal.App.3d 590 [124 Cal.Rptr. 297].) Paragraph (D) also requires that the member "promptly" return unearned fees paid in advance. If a client disputes the amount to be returned, the member shall comply with rule 4–100(A)(2).

Paragraph (D) is not intended to prohibit a member from making, at the member's own expense, and retaining copies of papers released to the client, nor to prohibit a claim for the recovery of the member's expense in any subsequent legal proceeding.

CHAPTER 4. FINANCIAL RELATIONSHIP WITH CLIENTS

Rule 4–100. Preserving Identity of Funds and Property of a Client

(A) All funds received or held for the benefit of clients by a member or law firm, including advances for costs and expenses, shall be deposited in one or more identifiable bank accounts labelled "Trust Account," "Client's Funds Account" or words of similar import, maintained in the State of California, or, with written consent of the client, in any other jurisdiction where there is a substantial relationship between the client or the client's business and the other jurisdiction. No funds belonging to the member or the law firm shall be deposited therein or otherwise commingled therewith except as follows:

(1) Funds reasonably sufficient to pay bank charges.

(2) In the case of funds belonging in part to a client and in part presently or potentially to the member or the law firm, the portion belonging to the member or law firm must be withdrawn at the earliest reasonable time after the member's interest in that portion becomes fixed. However, when the right of the member or law firm to receive a portion of trust funds is disputed by the client, the disputed portion shall not be withdrawn until the dispute is finally resolved.

(B) A member shall:

(1) Promptly notify a client of the receipt of the client's funds, securities, or other properties.

(2) Identify and label securities and properties of a client promptly upon receipt and place them in a safe deposit box or other place of safekeeping as soon as practicable.

(3) Maintain complete records of all funds, securities, and other properties of a client coming into the possession of the member or law firm and render appropriate accounts to the client regarding them; preserve such records for a period of no less than five years after final appropriate distribution of such funds or properties; and comply with any order for an audit of such records issued pursuant to the Rules of Procedure of the State Bar.

(4) Promptly pay or deliver, as requested by the client, any funds, securities, or other properties in the possession of the member which the client is entitled to receive.

(C) The Board of Governors of the State Bar shall have the authority to formulate and adopt standards as to what "records" shall be maintained by members and law firms in accordance with subparagraph (B)(3). The standards formulated and adopted by the Board, as from time to time amended, shall be effective and binding on all members.

Standards:

Pursuant to rule 4–100(C) the Board of Governors of the State Bar adopted the following standards as to what "records" shall be maintained by members and law firms in accordance with subparagraph (B)(3).

(1) A member shall, from the date of receipt of client funds through the period ending five years from the date of appropriate disbursement of such funds, maintain:

(a) a written ledger for each client on whose behalf funds are held that sets forth:

(i) the name of such client,

(ii) the date, amount and source of all funds received on behalf of such client,

(iii) the date, amount, payee and purpose of each disbursement made on behalf of such client, and

(iv) the current balance for such client;

(b) a written journal for each bank account that sets forth:

(i) the name of such account,

(ii) the date, amount and client affected by each debit and credit, and

(iii) the current balance in such account;

(c) all bank statements and cancelled checks for each bank account; and

(d) each monthly reconciliation (balancing) of (a), (b), and (c).

(2) A member shall, from the date of receipt of all securities and other properties held for the benefit of client through the period ending five years from the date of appropriate disbursement of such securities and other properties, maintain a written journal that specifies:

(a) each item of security and property held;

(b) the person on whose behalf the security or property is held;

(c) the date of receipt of the security or property;

(d) the date of distribution of the security or property; and

(e) person to whom the security or property was distributed.

(Trust Account Record Keeping Standards as Adopted by the Board of Governors on July 11, 1992 Effective on January 1, 1993)

Rule 4–200. Fees for Legal Services

(A) A member shall not enter into an agreement for, charge, or collect an illegal or unconscionable fee.

(B) Unconscionability of a fee shall be determined on the basis of all the facts and circumstances existing at the time the agreement is entered into except where the parties contemplate that the fee will be affected by later events. Among the factors to be considered, where appropriate, in determining the conscionability of a fee are the following:

(1) The amount of the fee in proportion to the value of the services performed.

(2) The relative sophistication of the member and the client.

(3) The novelty and difficulty of the questions involved and the skill requisite to perform the legal service properly.

(4) The likelihood, if apparent to the client, that the acceptance of the particular employment will preclude other employment by the member.

(5) The amount involved and the results obtained.

(6) The time limitations imposed by the client or by the circumstances.

(7) The nature and length of the professional relationship with the client.

(8) The experience, reputation, and ability of the member or members performing the services.

(9) Whether the fee is fixed or contingent.

(10) The time and labor required.

(11) The informed consent of the client to the fee.

Rule 4–210. Payment of Personal or Business Expenses Incurred by or for a Client

(A) A member shall not directly or indirectly pay or agree to pay, guarantee, represent, or sanction a representation that the member or member's law firm will pay the personal or business expenses of a prospective or existing client, except that this rule shall not prohibit a member:

(1) With the consent of the client, from paying or agreeing to pay such expenses to third persons from funds collected or to be collected for the client as a result of the representation; or

(2) After employment, from lending money to the client upon the client's promise in writing to repay such loan; or

(3) From advancing the costs of prosecuting or defending a claim or action or otherwise protecting or promoting the client's interests, the repayment of which may be contingent on the outcome of the matter. Such costs within the meaning of this subparagraph (3) shall be limited to all reasonable expenses of litigation or reasonable expenses in preparation for litigation or in providing any legal services to the client.

(B) Nothing in rule 4–210 shall be deemed to limit rules 3–300, 3–310, and 4–300.

Rule 4–300. Purchasing Property at a Foreclosure or a Sale Subject to Judicial Review

(A) A member shall not directly or indirectly purchase property at a probate, foreclosure, receiver's, trustee's or judicial sale in an action or proceeding in which such member or any lawyer affiliated by reason of personal, business, or professional relationship with that member or with that member's law firm is acting as a lawyer for a party or as executor, receiver, trustee, administrator, guardian, or conservator.

(B) A member shall not represent the seller at a probate, foreclosure, receiver, trustee, or judicial sale in an action or proceeding in which the purchaser is a spouse or relative of the member or of another lawyer in the member's law firm or is an employee of the member or the member's law firm.

Rule 4–400. Gifts From Client

A member shall not induce a client to make a substantial gift, including a testamentary gift, to the member or to the member's parent, child, sibling, or spouse, except where the client is related to the member.

Discussion:

A member may accept a gift from a member's client, subject to general standards of fairness and absence of undue influence. The member who participates in the preparation of an instrument memorializing a gift which is otherwise permissible ought not to be subject to professional discipline. On the other hand, where impermissible influence occurred, discipline is appropriate. (See *Magee v. State Bar* (1962) 58 Cal.2d 423 [24 Cal.Rptr. 839].)

CHAPTER 5. ADVOCACY AND REPRESENTATION

Rule 5–100. Threatening Criminal, Administrative, or Disciplinary Charges

(A) A member shall not threaten to present criminal, administrative, or disciplinary charges to obtain an advantage in a civil dispute.

(B) As used in paragraph (A) of this rule, the term "administrative charges" means the filing or lodging of a complaint with a federal, state, or local governmental entity which may order or recommend the loss or suspension of a license, or may impose or recommend the imposition of a fine, pecuniary sanction, or other sanction of a quasi-criminal nature but does not include filing charges with an administrative entity required by law as a condition precedent to maintaining a civil action.

(C) As used in paragraph (A) of this rule, the term "civil dispute" means a controversy or potential controversy over the rights and duties of two or more parties under civil law, whether or not an action has been commenced, and includes an administrative proceeding of a quasi-civil nature pending before a federal, state, or local governmental entity.

Discussion:

Rule 5–100 is not intended to apply to a member's threatening to initiate contempt proceedings against a party for a failure to comply with a court order.

Paragraph (B) is intended to exempt the threat of filing an administrative charge which is a prerequisite to filing a civil complaint on the same transaction or occurrence.

For purposes of paragraph (C), the definition of "civil dispute" makes clear that the rule is applicable prior to the formal filing of a civil action.

Rule 5–110. Performing the Duty of Member in Government Service

A member in government service shall not institute or cause to be instituted criminal charges when the member knows or should know that the charges are not supported by probable cause. If, after the institution of criminal charges, the member in government service having responsibility for prosecuting the charges becomes aware that those charges are not supported by probable cause, the member shall promptly so advise the court in which the criminal matter is pending.

Rule 5–120. Trial Publicity

(A) A member who is participating or has participated in the investigation or litigation of a matter shall not make an extrajudicial statement that a reasonable person would expect to be disseminated by means of public communication if the member knows or reasonably should know that it will have a substantial likelihood of materially prejudicing an adjudicative proceeding in the matter.

(B) Notwithstanding paragraph (A), a member may state:

(1) the claim, offense or defense involved and, except when prohibited by law, the identity of the persons involved;

(2) the information contained in a public record;

(3) that an investigation of the matter is in progress;

(4) the scheduling or result of any step in litigation;

(5) a request for assistance in obtaining evidence and information necessary thereto;

(6) a warning of danger concerning the behavior of a person involved, when there is reason to believe that there exists the likelihood of substantial harm to an individual or the public interest; and

(7) in a criminal case, in addition to subparagraphs (1) through (6):

(a) the identity, residence, occupation, and family status of the accused;

(b) if the accused has not been apprehended, information necessary to aid in apprehension of that person;

(c) the fact, time, and place of arrest; and

(d) the identity of investigating and arresting officers or agencies and the length of the investigation.

(C) Notwithstanding paragraph (A), a member may make a statement that a reasonable member would believe is required to protect a client from the substantial undue prejudicial effect of recent publicity not initiated by the member or the member's client. A statement made pursuant to this paragraph shall be limited to such information as is necessary to mitigate the recent adverse publicity.

Discussion

Rule 5–120 is intended to apply equally to prosecutors and criminal defense counsel. Whether an extrajudicial statement violates rule 5–120 depends on many factors, including:

(1) whether the extrajudicial statement presents information clearly inadmissible as evidence in the matter for the purpose of proving or disproving a material fact in issue;

(2) whether the extrajudicial statement presents information the member knows is false, deceptive, or the use of which would violate Business and Professions Code section 6068(d);

(3) whether the extrajudicial statement violates a lawful "gag" order, or protective order, statute, rule of court, or special rule of confidentiality (for example, in juvenile, domestic, mental disability, and certain criminal proceedings); and

(4) the timing of the statement.

Paragraph (A) is intended to apply to statements made by or on behalf of the member. Subparagraph (B)(6) is not intended to create, augment, diminish, or eliminate any application of the lawyer-client privilege or of Business and Professions Code section 6068(e) regarding the member's duty to maintain client confidence and secrets.

Rule 5–200. Trial Conduct

In presenting a matter to a tribunal, a member:

(A) Shall employ, for the purpose of maintaining the causes confided to the member such means only as are consistent with truth;

(B) Shall not seek to mislead the judge, judicial officer, or jury by an artifice or false statement of fact or law;

(C) Shall not intentionally misquote to a tribunal the language of a book, statute, or decision;

(D) Shall not, knowing its invalidity, cite as authority a decision that has been overruled or a statute that has been repealed or declared unconstitutional; and

(E) Shall not assert personal knowledge of the facts at issue, except when testifying as a witness.

Rule 5–210. Member as Witness

A member shall not act as an advocate before a jury which will hear testimony from the member unless:

(A) The testimony relates to an uncontested matter; or

(B) The testimony relates to the nature and value of legal services rendered in the case; or

(C) The member has the informed, written consent of the client. If the member represents the People or a governmental entity, the consent shall be obtained from the head of the office or a designee of the head of the office by which the member is employed and shall be consistent with principles of recusal.

Discussion:

Rule 5–210 is intended to apply to situations in which the member knows or should know that he or she ought to be called as a witness in litigation in which there is a jury. This rule is not intended to encompass situations in which the member is representing the client in an adversarial proceeding and is testifying before a judge. In non-adversarial proceedings, as where the lawyer testifies on behalf of the client, in a hearing before a legislative body, rule 5–210 is not applicable.

Rule 5–210 is not intended to apply to circumstances in which a lawyer in an advocate's firm will be a witness.

Rule 5–220. Suppression of Evidence

A member shall not suppress any evidence that the member or the member's client has a legal obligation to reveal or to produce.

Rule 5–300. Contact With Officials

(A) A member shall not directly or indirectly give or lend anything of value to a judge, official, or employee of a tribunal unless the personal or family relationship between the member and the judge, official, or employee is such that gifts are customarily given and exchanged. Nothing contained in this rule shall prohibit a member from contributing to the campaign fund of a judge running for election or confirmation pursuant to applicable law pertaining to such contributions.

(B) A member shall not directly or indirectly communicate with or argue to a judge or judicial officer upon the merits of a contested matter pending before such judge or judicial officer, except:

(1) In open court; or

(2) With the consent of all other counsel in such matter; or

(3) In the presence of all other counsel in such matter; or

(4) In writing with a copy thereof furnished to such other counsel; or

(5) In ex parte matters.

(C) As used in this rule, "judge" and "judicial officer" shall include law clerks, research attorneys, or other court personnel who participate in the decision-making process.

Rule 5–310. Prohibited Contact With Witnesses

A member shall not:

(A) Advise or directly or indirectly cause a person to secrete himself or herself or to leave the jurisdiction of a tribunal for the purpose of making that person unavailable as a witness therein.

(B) Directly or indirectly pay, offer to pay, or acquiesce in the payment of compensation to a witness contingent upon the content of the witness's testimony or the outcome of the case. Except where prohibited by law, a member may advance, guarantee, or acquiesce in the payment of:

(1) Expenses reasonably incurred by a witness in attending or testifying.

(2) Reasonable compensation to a witness for loss of time in attending or testifying.

(3) A reasonable fee for the professional services of an expert witness.

Rule 5–320. Contact With Jurors

(A) A member connected with a case shall not communicate directly or indirectly with anyone the member knows to be a member of the venire from which the jury will be selected for trial of that case.

(B) During trial a member connected with the case shall not communicate directly or indirectly with any juror.

(C) During trial a member who is not connected with the case shall not communicate directly or indirectly concerning the case with anyone the member knows is a juror in the case.

(D) After discharge of the jury from further consideration of a case a member shall not ask questions of or make comments to a member of that jury that are intended to harass or embarrass the juror or to influence the juror's actions in future jury service.

(E) A member shall not directly or indirectly conduct an out of court investigation of a person who is either a member of the venire or a juror in a manner likely to influence the state of mind of such person in connection with present or future jury service.

(F) All restrictions imposed by this rule also apply to communications with or investigations of members of the family of a person who is either a member of the venire or a juror.

(G) A member shall reveal promptly to the court improper conduct by a person who is either a member of a venire or a juror, or by another toward a person who is either a member of a venire or a juror or a member of his or her family, of which the member has knowledge.

(H) This Rule does not prohibit a member from communicating with persons who are members of a venire or jurors as a part of the official proceedings.

(I) For purposes of this Rule, "juror" means any empaneled, discharged, or excused juror.

CALIFORNIA RULES ON MULTIJURISDICTIONAL PRACTICE

[On April 8, 2004, the California Supreme Court approved several rules on out-of-state lawyers who are practicing in California. In 2007, these rules were renumbered and restructured as follows.]

Rule 9.45. Registered legal services attorneys

(a) Definitions

The following definitions apply in this rule:

(1) "Qualifying legal services provider" means either of the following, provided that the qualifying legal services provider follows quality-control procedures approved by the State Bar of California:

(A) A nonprofit entity incorporated and operated exclusively in California that as its primary purpose and function provides legal services without charge in civil matters to indigent persons, especially underserved client groups, such as the elderly, persons with disabilities, juveniles, and non-English-speaking persons; or

(B) A program operated exclusively in California by a nonprofit law school approved by the American Bar Association or accredited by the State Bar of California that has operated for at least two years at a cost of at least $20,000 per year as an identifiable law school unit with a primary purpose and function of providing legal services without charge to indigent persons.

(2) "Active member in good standing of the bar of a United States state, jurisdiction, possession, territory, or dependency" means an attorney who:

(A) Is a member in good standing of the entity governing the practice of law in each jurisdiction in which the member is licensed to practice law;

(B) Remains an active member in good standing of the entity governing the practice of law in at least one United States state, jurisdiction, possession, territory, or dependency other than California while practicing law as a registered legal services attorney in California; and

(C) Has not been disbarred, has not resigned with charges pending, or is not suspended from practicing law in any other jurisdiction.

(b) Scope of practice

Subject to all applicable rules, regulations, and statutes, an attorney practicing law under this rule may practice law in California only while working, with or without pay, at a qualifying legal services provider, as defined in this rule, and, at that institution and only on behalf of its clients, may engage, under supervision, in all forms of legal practice that are permissible for a member of the State Bar of California.

(c) Requirements

For an attorney to practice law under this rule, the attorney must:

(1) Be an active member in good standing of the bar of a United States state, jurisdiction, possession, territory, or dependency;

(2) Register with the State Bar of California and file an Application for Determination of Moral Character;

(3) Meet all of the requirements for admission to the State Bar of California, except that the attorney:

(A) Need not take the California bar examination or the Multistate Professional Responsibility Examination; and

(B) May practice law while awaiting the result of his or her Application for Determination of Moral Character;

(4) Comply with the rules adopted by the Board of Governors relating to the State Bar Registered Legal Services Attorney Program;

(5) Practice law exclusively for a single qualifying legal services provider, except that, if so qualified, an attorney may, while practicing under this rule, simultaneously practice law as registered in-house counsel;

(6) Practice law under the supervision of an attorney who is employed by the qualifying legal services provider and who is a member in good standing of the State Bar of California;

(7) Abide by all of the laws and rules that govern members of the State Bar of California, including the Minimum Continuing Legal Education (MCLE) requirements;

(8) Satisfy in his or her first year of practice under this rule all of the MCLE requirements, including ethics education, that members of the State Bar of California must complete every three years; and

(9) Not have taken and failed the California bar examination within five years immediately preceding application to register under this rule.

(d) Application

To qualify to practice law as a registered legal services attorney, the attorney must:

(1) Register as an attorney applicant and file an Application for Determination of Moral Character with the Committee of Bar Examiners;

(2) Submit to the State Bar of California a declaration signed by the attorney agreeing that he or she will be subject to the disciplinary authority of the Supreme Court of California and the State Bar of California and attesting that he or she will not practice law in California other than under supervision at a qualifying legal services provider during the time he or she practices law as a registered legal services attorney in California, except that, if so qualified, the attorney may, while practicing under this rule, simultaneously practice law as registered in-house counsel; and

(3) Submit to the State Bar of California a declaration signed by a qualifying supervisor on behalf of the qualifying legal services provider in California attesting that the applicant will work, with or without pay, as an attorney for the organization; that the applicant will be supervised as specified in this rule; and that the qualifying legal services provider and the supervising attorney assume professional responsibility for any work performed by the applicant under this rule.

(e) Duration of practice

An attorney may practice for no more than a total of three years under this rule.

(f) Application and registration fees

The State Bar of California may set appropriate application fees and initial and annual registration fees to be paid by registered legal services attorneys.

(g) State Bar Registered Legal Services Attorney Program

The State Bar may establish and administer a program for registering California legal services attorneys under rules adopted by the Board of Governors of the State Bar.

(h) Supervision

To meet the requirements of this rule, an attorney supervising a registered legal services attorney:

(1) Must be an active member in good standing of the State Bar of California;

(2) Must have actively practiced law in California and been a member in good standing of the State Bar of California for at least the two years immediately preceding the time of supervision;

(3) Must have practiced law as a full-time occupation for at least four years;

(4) Must not supervise more than two registered legal services attorneys concurrently;

(5) Must assume professional responsibility for any work that the registered legal services attorney performs under the supervising attorney's supervision;

(6) Must assist, counsel, and provide direct supervision of the registered legal services attorney in the activities authorized by this rule and review such activities with the supervised attorney, to the extent required for the protection of the client;

(7) Must read, approve, and personally sign any pleadings, briefs, or other similar documents prepared by the registered legal services attorney before their filing, and must read and approve any documents prepared by the registered legal services attorney for execution by any person who is not a member of the State Bar of California before their submission for execution; and

(8) May, in his or her absence, designate another attorney meeting the requirements of (1) through (7) to provide the supervision required under this rule.

(i) Inherent power of Supreme Court

Nothing in this rule may be construed as affecting the power of the Supreme Court of California to exercise its inherent jurisdiction over the practice of law in California.

(j) Effect of rule on multijurisdictional practice

Nothing in this rule limits the scope of activities permissible under existing law by attorneys who are not members of the State Bar of California.

Rule 9.46. Registered in-house counsel

(a) Definitions

The following definitions apply to terms used in this rule:

(1) "Qualifying institution" means a corporation, a partnership, an association, or other legal entity, including its subsidiaries and organizational affiliates. Neither a

governmental entity nor an entity that provides legal services to others can be a qualifying institution for purposes of this rule. A qualifying institution must:

(A) Employ at least 10 employees full time in California; or

(B) Employ in California an attorney who is an active member in good standing of the State Bar of California.

(2) "Active member in good standing of the bar of a United States state, jurisdiction, possession, territory, or dependency" means an attorney who meets all of the following criteria:

(A) Is a member in good standing of the entity governing the practice of law in each jurisdiction in which the member is licensed to practice law;

(B) Remains an active member in good standing of the entity governing the practice of law in at least one United States state, jurisdiction, possession, territory, or dependency, other than California, while practicing law as registered in-house counsel in California; and

(C) Has not been disbarred, has not resigned with charges pending, or is not suspended from practicing law in any other jurisdiction.

(b) Scope of practice

Subject to all applicable rules, regulations, and statutes, an attorney practicing law under this rule is:

(1) Permitted to provide legal services in California only to the qualifying institution that employs him or her;

(2) Not permitted to make court appearances in California state courts or to engage in any other activities for which *pro hac vice* admission is required if they are performed in California by an attorney who is not a member of the State Bar of California; and

(3) Not permitted to provide personal or individual representation to any customers, shareholders, owners, partners, officers, employees, servants, or agents of the qualifying institution.

(c) Requirements

For an attorney to practice law under this rule, the attorney must:

(1) Be an active member in good standing of the bar of a United States state, jurisdiction, possession, territory, or dependency;

(2) Register with the State Bar of California and file an Application for Determination of Moral Character;

(3) Meet all of the requirements for admission to the State Bar of California, except that the attorney:

(A) Need not take the California bar examination or the Multistate Professional Responsibility Examination; and

(B) May practice law while awaiting the result of his or her Application for Determination of Moral Character;

(4) Comply with the rules adopted by the Board of Governors relating to the State Bar Registered In-House Counsel Program;

(5) Practice law exclusively for a single qualifying institution, except that, while practicing under this rule, the attorney may, if so qualified, simultaneously practice law as a registered legal services attorney;

(6) Abide by all of the laws and rules that govern members of the State Bar of California, including the Minimum Continuing Legal Education (MCLE) requirements;

(7) Satisfy in his or her first year of practice under this rule all of the MCLE requirements, including ethics education, that members of the State Bar of California must complete every three years and, thereafter, satisfy the MCLE requirements applicable to all members of the State Bar; and

(8) Reside in California.

(d) Application

To qualify to practice law as registered in-house counsel, an attorney must:

(1) Register as an attorney applicant and file an Application for Determination of Moral Character with the Committee of Bar Examiners;

(2) Submit to the State Bar of California a declaration signed by the attorney agreeing that he or she will be subject to the disciplinary authority of the Supreme Court of California and the State Bar of California and attesting that he or she will not practice law in California other than on behalf of the qualifying institution during the time he or she is registered in-house counsel in California, except that if so qualified, the attorney may, while practicing under this rule, simultaneously practice law as a registered legal services attorney; and

(3) Submit to the State Bar of California a declaration signed by an officer, a director, or a general counsel of the applicant's employer, on behalf of the applicant's employer, attesting that the applicant is employed as an attorney for the employer, that the nature of the employment conforms to the requirements of this rule, that the employer will notify the State Bar of California within 30 days of the cessation of the applicant's employment in California, and that the person signing the declaration believes, to the best of his or her knowledge after reasonable inquiry, that the applicant qualifies for registration under this rule and is an individual of good moral character.

(e) Duration of practice

A registered in-house counsel must renew his or her registration annually. There is no limitation on the number of years in-house counsel may register under this rule. Registered in-house counsel may practice law under this rule only for as long as he or she remains employed by the same qualifying institution that provided the declaration in support of his or her application. If an attorney practicing law as registered in-house counsel leaves the employment of his or her employer or changes employers, he or she must notify the State Bar of California within 30 days. If an attorney wishes to practice law under this rule for a new employer, he or she must first register as in-house counsel for that employer.

(f) Eligibility

An application to register under this rule may not be denied because:

(1) The attorney applicant has practiced law in California as in-house counsel before the effective date of this rule.

(2) The attorney applicant is practicing law as in-house counsel at or after the effective date of this rule, provided that the attorney applies under this rule within six months of its effective date.

(g) Application and registration fees

The State Bar of California may set appropriate application fees and initial and annual registration fees to be paid by registered in-house counsel.

(h) State Bar Registered In-House Counsel Program

The State Bar must establish and administer a program for registering California in-house counsel under rules adopted by the Board of Governors.

(i) Inherent power of Supreme Court

Nothing in this rule may be construed as affecting the power of the Supreme Court of California to exercise its inherent jurisdiction over the practice of law in California.

(j) Effect of rule on multijurisdictional practice

Nothing in this rule limits the scope of activities permissible under existing law by attorneys who are not members of the State Bar of California.

Rule 9.47. Attorneys practicing law temporarily in California as part of litigation

(a) Definitions

The following definitions apply to the terms used in this rule:

(1) "A formal legal proceeding" means litigation, arbitration, mediation, or a legal action before an administrative decision-maker.

(2) "Authorized to appear" means the attorney is permitted to appear in the proceeding by the rules of the jurisdiction in which the formal legal proceeding is taking place or will be taking place.

(3) "Active member in good standing of the bar of a United States state, jurisdiction, possession, territory, or dependency" means an attorney who meets all of the following criteria:

(A) Is a member in good standing of the entity governing the practice of law in each jurisdiction in which the member is licensed to practice law;

(B) Remains an active member in good standing of the entity governing the practice of law in at least one United States state, jurisdiction, possession, territory, or dependency while practicing law under this rule; and

(C) Has not been disbarred, has not resigned with charges pending, or is not suspended from practicing law in any other jurisdiction.

(b) Requirements

For an attorney to practice law under this rule, the attorney must:

(1) Maintain an office in a United States jurisdiction other than California and in which the attorney is licensed to practice law;

(2) Already be retained by a client in the matter for which the attorney is providing legal services in California, except that the attorney may provide legal advice to a potential client, at the potential client's request, to assist the client in deciding whether to retain the attorney;

(3) Indicate on any Web site or other advertisement that is accessible in California either that the attorney is not a member of the State Bar of California or that the attorney is admitted to practice law only in the states listed; and

(4) Be an active member in good standing of the bar of a United States state, jurisdiction, possession, territory, or dependency.

(c) Permissible activities

An attorney meeting the requirements of this rule, who complies with all applicable rules, regulations, and statutes, is not engaging in the unauthorized practice of law in California if the attorney's services are part of:

(1) A formal legal proceeding that is pending in another jurisdiction and in which the attorney is authorized to appear;

(2) A formal legal proceeding that is anticipated but is not yet pending in California and in which the attorney reasonably expects to be authorized to appear;

(3) A formal legal proceeding that is anticipated but is not yet pending in another jurisdiction and in which the attorney reasonably expects to be authorized to appear; or

(4) A formal legal proceeding that is anticipated or pending and in which the attorney's supervisor is authorized to appear or reasonably expects to be authorized to appear.

The attorney whose anticipated authorization to appear in a formal legal proceeding serves as the basis for practice under this rule must seek that authorization promptly after it becomes possible to do so. Failure to seek that authorization promptly, or denial of that authorization, ends eligibility to practice under this rule.

(d) Restrictions

To qualify to practice law in California under this rule, an attorney must not:

(1) Hold out to the public or otherwise represent that he or she is admitted to practice law in California;

(2) Establish or maintain a resident office or other systematic or continuous presence in California for the practice of law;

(3) Be a resident of California;

(4) Be regularly employed in California;

(5) Regularly engage in substantial business or professional activities in California; or

(6) Have been disbarred, have resigned with charges pending, or be suspended from practicing law in any other jurisdiction.

(e) Conditions

By practicing law in California under this rule, an attorney agrees that he or she is providing legal services in California subject to:

(1) The jurisdiction of the State Bar of California;

(2) The jurisdiction of the courts of this state to the same extent as is a member of the State Bar of California; and

(3) The laws of the State of California relating to the practice of law, the State Bar Rules of Professional Conduct, the rules and regulations of the State Bar of California, and these rules.

(f) Inherent power of Supreme Court

Nothing in this rule may be construed as affecting the power of the Supreme Court of California to exercise its inherent jurisdiction over the practice of law in California.

(g) Effect of rule on multijurisdictional practice

Nothing in this rule limits the scope of activities permissible under existing law by attorneys who are not members of the State Bar of California.

Rule 9.48. Nonlitigating attorneys temporarily in California to provide legal services

(a) Definitions

The following definitions apply to terms used in this rule:

(1) "A transaction or other nonlitigation matter" includes any legal matter other than litigation, arbitration, mediation, or a legal action before an administrative decision-maker.

(2) "Active member in good standing of the bar of a United States state, jurisdiction, possession, territory, or dependency" means an attorney who meets all of the following criteria:

(A) Is a member in good standing of the entity governing the practice of law in each jurisdiction in which the member is licensed to practice law;

(B) Remains an active member in good standing of the entity governing the practice of law in at least one United States state, jurisdiction, possession, territory, or dependency other than California while practicing law under this rule; and

(C) Has not been disbarred, has not resigned with charges pending, or is not suspended from practicing law in any other jurisdiction.

(b) Requirements

For an attorney to practice law under this rule, the attorney must:

(1) Maintain an office in a United States jurisdiction other than California and in which the attorney is licensed to practice law;

(2) Already be retained by a client in the matter for which the attorney is providing legal services in California, except that the attorney may provide legal advice to a potential client, at the potential client's request, to assist the client in deciding whether to retain the attorney;

(3) Indicate on any Web site or other advertisement that is accessible in California either that the attorney is not a member of the State Bar of California or that the attorney is admitted to practice law only in the states listed; and

(4) Be an active member in good standing of the bar of a United States state, jurisdiction, possession, territory, or dependency.

(c) Permissible activities

An attorney who meets the requirements of this rule and who complies with all applicable rules, regulations, and statutes is not engaging in the unauthorized practice of law in California if the attorney:

(1) Provides legal assistance or legal advice in California to a client concerning a transaction or other nonlitigation matter, a material aspect of which is taking place

in a jurisdiction other than California and in which the attorney is licensed to provide legal services;

(2) Provides legal assistance or legal advice in California on an issue of federal law or of the law of a jurisdiction other than California to attorneys licensed to practice law in California; or

(3) Is an employee of a client and provides legal assistance or legal advice in California to the client or to the client's subsidiaries or organizational affiliates.

(d) Restrictions

To qualify to practice law in California under this rule, an attorney must not:

(1) Hold out to the public or otherwise represent that he or she is admitted to practice law in California;

(2) Establish or maintain a resident office or other systematic or continuous presence in California for the practice of law;

(3) Be a resident of California;

(4) Be regularly employed in California;

(5) Regularly engage in substantial business or professional activities in California; or

(6) Have been disbarred, have resigned with charges pending, or be suspended from practicing law in any other jurisdiction.

(e) Conditions

By practicing law in California under this rule, an attorney agrees that he or she is providing legal services in California subject to:

(1) The jurisdiction of the State Bar of California;

(2) The jurisdiction of the courts of this state to the same extent as is a member of the State Bar of California; and

(3) The laws of the State of California relating to the practice of law, the State Bar Rules of Professional Conduct, the rules and regulations of the State Bar of California, and these rules.

(f) Scope of practice

An attorney is permitted by this rule to provide legal assistance or legal services concerning only a transaction or other nonlitigation matter.

(g) Inherent power of Supreme Court

Nothing in this rule may be construed as affecting the power of the Supreme Court of California to exercise its inherent jurisdiction over the practice of law in California.

(h) Effect of rule on multijurisdictional practice

Nothing in this rule limits the scope of activities permissible under existing law by attorneys who are not members of the State Bar of California.

CALIFORNIA BUSINESS & PROFESSIONS CODE

(Selected Sections)

CHAPTER 4. ATTORNEYS

TABLE OF CONTENTS

ARTICLE 4. ADMISSION TO THE PRACTICE OF LAW

ARTICLE 14. FUNDS FOR THE PROVISION OF LEGAL SERVICES TO INDIGENT PERSONS

ARTICLE 4. ADMISSION TO THE PRACTICE OF LAW

§ 6067. Oath

Every person on his admission shall take an oath to support the Constitution of the United States and the Constitution of the State of California, and faithfully to discharge the duties of any attorney at law to the best of his knowledge and ability. A certificate of the oath shall be indorsed upon his license.

§ 6068. Duties of attorney

It is the duty of an attorney:

(a) To support the Constitution and laws of the United States and of this State.

(b) To maintain the respect due to the courts of justice and judicial officers.

(c) To counsel or maintain such actions, proceedings or defenses only as appear to him legal or just, except the defense of a person charged with a public offense.

(d) To employ, for the purpose of maintaining the causes confided to him or her such means only as are consistent with truth, and never to seek to mislead the judge or any judicial officer by an artifice or false statement of fact or law.

(e)(1) To maintain inviolate the confidence, and at every peril to himself or herself to preserve the secrets, of his or her client.

(2) Notwithstanding paragraph (1), an attorney may, but is not required to, reveal confidential information relating to the representation of a client to the extent that the attorney reasonably believes the disclosure is necessary to prevent a criminal act that the attorney reasonably believes is likely to result in death of, or substantial bodily harm to, an individual.

(f) To advance no fact prejudicial to the honor or reputation of a party or witness, unless required by the justice of the cause with which he or she is charged.

(g) Not to encourage either the commencement or the continuance of an action or proceeding from any corrupt motive of passion or interest.

(h) Never to reject, for any consideration personal to himself or herself, the cause of the defenseless or the oppressed.

(i) To cooperate and participate in any disciplinary investigation or other regulatory or disciplinary proceeding pending against himself or herself. However, this subdivision shall not be construed to deprive an attorney of any privilege guaranteed by the Fifth Amendment to the Constitution of the United States or any other constitutional or statutory privileges. This subdivision shall not be construed to require an attorney to cooperate with a request that requires him or her to waive any constitutional or statutory privilege or to comply with a request for information or other matters within an unreasonable period of time in light of the time constraints of the attorney's practice. Any exercise by an attorney of any constitutional or statutory privilege shall not be used against the attorney in a regulatory or disciplinary proceeding against him or her.

(j) To comply with the requirements of Section 6002.1.

(k) To comply with all conditions attached to any disciplinary probation, including a probation imposed with the concurrence of the attorney.

(*l*) To keep all agreements made in lieu of disciplinary prosecution with the agency charged with attorney discipline.

(m) To respond promptly to reasonable status inquiries of clients and to keep clients reasonably informed of significant developments in matters with regard to which the attorney has agreed to provide legal services.

(n) To provide copies to the client of certain documents under time limits and as prescribed in a rule of professional conduct which the board shall adopt.

(*o*) To report to the agency charged with attorney discipline, in writing, within 30 days of the time the attorney has knowledge of any of the following:

(1) The filing of three or more lawsuits in a 12-month period against the attorney for malpractice or other wrongful conduct committed in a professional capacity.

(2) The entry of judgment against the attorney in a civil action for fraud, misrepresentation, breach of fiduciary duty, or gross negligence committed in a professional capacity.

(3) The imposition of any judicial sanctions against the attorney, except for sanctions for failure to make discovery or monetary sanctions of less than one thousand dollars ($1,000).

(4) The bringing of an indictment or information charging a felony against the attorney.

(5) The conviction of the attorney, including any verdict of guilty, or plea of guilty or no contest, of a felony, or a misdemeanor committed in the course of the practice of law, or in a manner in which a client of the attorney was the victim, or a necessary element of which, as determined by the statutory or common law definition of the misdemeanor, involves improper conduct of an attorney, including dishonesty or other moral turpitude, or an attempt or a conspiracy or solicitation of another to commit a felony or a misdemeanor of that type.

(6) The imposition of discipline against the attorney by a professional or occupational disciplinary agency or licensing board, whether in California or elsewhere.

(7) Reversal of judgment in a proceeding based in whole or in part upon misconduct, grossly incompetent representation, or wilful misrepresentation by an attorney.

(8) As used in this subdivision, "against the attorney" includes claims and proceedings against any firm of attorneys for the practice of law in which the attorney was a partner at the time of the conduct complained of and any law corporation in which the attorney was a shareholder at the time of the conduct complained of unless the matter has to the attorney's knowledge already been reported by the law firm or corporation.

(9) The State Bar may develop a prescribed form for the making of reports required by this section, usage of which it may require by rule or regulation.

(10) This subdivision is only intended to provide that the failure to report as required herein may serve as a basis of discipline.

§ 6090.5 Settlements; prohibited agreements

(a) It is cause for suspension, disbarment, or other discipline for any member, whether as a party or as an attorney for a party, to agree or seek agreement, that:

(1) The professional misconduct or the terms of a settlement of a claim for professional misconduct shall not be reported to the disciplinary agency.

(2) The plaintiff shall withdraw a disciplinary complaint or shall not cooperate with the investigation or prosecution conducted by the disciplinary agency.

(3) The record of any civil action for professional misconduct shall be sealed from review by the disciplinary agency.

(b) The section applies to all settlements, whether made before or after the commencement of a civil action.

ARTICLE 6. DISCIPLINARY AUTHORITY OF THE COURTS

§ 6100. Disbarment or suspension

For any of the causes provided in this article, arising after an attorney's admission to practice, he or she may be disbarred or suspended by the Supreme Court. Nothing in this article limits the inherent power of the Supreme Court to discipline, including to summarily disbar, any attorney.

§ 6101. Conviction of crime; notice of pendency of action; record of conviction; proceedings

(a) Conviction of a felony or misdemeanor, involving moral turpitude, constitutes a cause for disbarment or suspension.

In any proceeding, whether under this article or otherwise, to disbar or suspend an attorney on account of that conviction, the record of conviction shall be conclusive evidence of guilt of the crime of which he or she has been convicted.

(b) The district attorney, city attorney, or other prosecuting agency shall notify the Office of the State Bar of California of the pendency of an action against an attorney charging a felony or misdemeanor immediately upon obtaining information that the defendant is an attorney. The notice shall identify the attorney and describe the crimes charged and the alleged facts. The prosecuting agency shall also notify the clerk of the court in which the action is pending that the defendant is an attorney, and the clerk shall record prominently in the file that the defendant is an attorney.

(c) The clerk of the court in which an attorney is convicted of a crime shall, within 48 hours after the conviction, transmit a certified copy of the record of conviction to the Office of the State Bar. Within five days of receipt, the Office of the State Bar shall transmit the record of any conviction which involves or may involve moral turpitude to the Supreme Court with such other records and information as may be appropriate to establish the Supreme Court's jurisdiction. The State Bar of California may procure and transmit the record of conviction to the Supreme Court when the clerk has not done so or when the conviction was had in a court other than a court of this state.

(d) The proceedings to disbar or suspend an attorney on account of such a conviction shall be undertaken by the Supreme Court pursuant to the procedure provided in this section and Section 6102, upon the receipt of the certified copy of the record of conviction.

(e) A plea or verdict of guilty, an acceptance of a nolo contendere plea, or a conviction after a plea of nolo contendere is deemed to be a conviction within the meaning of those sections.

§ 6102. Immediate suspension and subsequent disbarment upon conviction of crime; crimes involving moral turpitude or felonies; procedure

(a) Upon the receipt of the certified copy of the record of conviction, if it appears therefrom that the crime of which the attorney was convicted involved or that there is probable cause to believe that it involved moral turpitude or is a felony under the laws of California, the United States, or any state or territory thereof, the Supreme Court shall suspend the attorney until the time for appeal has elapsed, if no appeal has been taken, or until the judgment of conviction has been affirmed on appeal, or has otherwise become final, and until the further order of the court. Upon its own motion or upon good cause shown the court may decline to impose, or may set aside, the suspension when it appears to be in the interest of justice to do so, with due regard being given to maintaining the integrity of and confidence in the profession.

(b) For the purposes of this section, a crime is a felony under the law of California if it is declared to be so specifically or by subdivision (a) of Section 17 of the Penal Code, unless it is charged as a misdemeanor pursuant to paragraph (4) or (5) of subdivision (b) of Section 17 of the Penal Code, irrespective of whether in a particular case the crime may be considered a misdemeanor as a result of postconviction proceedings, including proceedings resulting in punishment or probation set forth in paragraph (1) or (3) of subdivision (b) of Section 17 of the Penal Code.

(c) After the judgment of conviction of an offense specified in subdivision (a) has become final or, irrespective of any subsequent order under Section 1203.4 of the Penal Code or similar statutory provision, an order granting probation has been made suspending the imposition of sentence, the Supreme Court shall summarily disbar the attorney if the offense is a felony under the laws of California, the United States, or any state or territory thereof, and an element of the offense is the specific intent to deceive, defraud, steal, or make or suborn a false statement or involved moral turpitude.

(d) For purposes of this section, a conviction under the laws of another state or territory of the United States shall be deemed a felony if:

(1) The judgment or conviction was entered as a felony irrespective of any subsequent order suspending sentence or granting probation and irrespective of whether the crime may be considered a misdemeanor as a result of postconviction proceedings.

(2) The elements of the offense for which the member was convicted would constitute a felony under the laws of the State of California at the time the offense was committed.

(e) Except as provided in subdivision (c), if after adequate notice and opportunity to be heard (which hearing shall not be had until the judgment of conviction has become final or, irrespective of any subsequent order under Section 1203.4 of the Penal Code, an order granting probation has been made suspending the imposition of sentence), the court finds that the crime of which the attorney was convicted, or the circumstances of its commission, involved moral turpitude, it shall enter an order disbarring the attorney or suspending him or her from practice for a limited time, according to the gravity of the crime and the circumstances of the case; otherwise it shall dismiss the proceedings. In determining the extent of the discipline to be imposed in a proceeding pursuant to this article any prior discipline imposed upon the attorney may be considered.

(f) The court may refer the proceedings or any part thereof or issue therein, including the nature or extent of discipline, to the State Bar for hearing, report, and recommendation.

(g) The record of the proceedings resulting in the conviction, including a transcript of the testimony therein, may be received in evidence.

(h) The Supreme Court shall prescribe rules for the practice and procedure in proceedings conducted pursuant to this section and Section 6101.

(i) The other provisions of this article providing a procedure for the disbarment or suspension of an attorney do not apply to proceedings pursuant to this section and Section 6101, unless expressly made applicable.

§ 6103. Disobedience of court order; violation of oath or attorney's duties

A wilful disobedience or violation of an order of the court requiring him to do or forbear an act connected with or in the course of his profession, which he ought in good faith to do or forbear, and any violation of the oath taken by him, or of his duties as such attorney, constitute causes for disbarment or suspension.

§ 6103.5 Written offers of settlement; required communication to client; discovery

(a) A member of the State Bar shall promptly communicate to the member's client all amounts, terms, and conditions of any written offer of settlement made by or on behalf of an opposing party. As used in this section, "client" includes any person employing the member of the State Bar who possesses the authority to accept an offer of settlement, or in a class action, who is a representative of the class.

(b) Any written offer of settlement or any required communication of a settlement offer, as described in subdivision (a), shall be discoverable by either party in any action in which the existence or communication of the offer of settlement is an issue before the trier of fact.

§ 6103.7 Reporting or threatening to report suspected immigration status

It is cause for suspension, disbarment, or other discipline for any member of the State Bar to report suspected immigration status or threaten to report suspected immigration status of a witness or party to a civil or administrative action or his or her family member to a federal, state, or local agency because the witness or party exercises or has exercised a right related to his or her employment, broadly interpreted. As used in this section, "family member" means a spouse, parent, sibling, child, uncle, aunt, niece, nephew, cousin, grandparent, or grandchild related by blood, adoption, marriage, or domestic partnership.

§ 6104. Unauthorized appearance

Corruptly or wilfully and without authority appearing as attorney for a party to an action or proceeding constitutes a cause for disbarment or suspension.

§ 6105. Permitting misuse of name

Lending his name to be used as attorney by another person who is not an attorney constitutes a cause for disbarment or suspension.

§ 6106. Moral turpitude, dishonesty or corruption irrespective of criminal conviction

The commission of any act involving moral turpitude, dishonesty or corruption, whether the act is committed in the course of his relations as an attorney or otherwise, and whether the act is a felony or misdemeanor or not, constitutes a cause for disbarment or suspension.

If the act constitutes a felony or misdemeanor, conviction thereof in a criminal proceeding is not a condition precedent to disbarment or suspension from practice therefor.

§ 6106.1 Advocacy of overthrow of government

Advocating the overthrow of the Government of the United States or of this State by force, violence, or other unconstitutional means, constitutes a cause for disbarment or suspension.

§ 6106.5 Insurance claims; fraud

It shall constitute cause for disbarment or suspension for an attorney to engage in any conduct prohibited under Section 1871.4 of the Insurance Code or Section 550 of the Penal Code.

§ 6106.7 Miller-Ayala Athlete Agents Act; violation of requirements

It shall constitute cause for the imposition of discipline of an attorney within the meaning of this chapter for an attorney to violate any provision of the Miller-Ayala Athlete Agents Act (Chapter 2.5 (commencing with Section 18895) of Division 8), or to violate any provision of Chapter 1 (commencing with Section 1500) of Part 6 of Division 2 of the Labor Code, prior to January 1, 1997, or to violate any provision of the law of any other state regulating athlete agents.

§ 6106.8 Sexual involvement between lawyers and clients; rule of professional conduct

(a) The Legislature hereby finds and declares that there is no rule that governs propriety of sexual relationships between lawyers and clients. The Legislature further finds and declares that it is difficult to separate sound judgment from emotion or bias which may result from sexual involvement between a lawyer and his or her client during the period that an attorney-client relationship exists, and that emotional detachment is essential to the lawyer's ability to render competent legal services. Therefore, in order to ensure that a lawyer acts in the best interest of his or her client, a rule of professional conduct governing sexual relations between attorneys and their clients shall be adopted.

(b) With the approval of the Supreme Court, the State Bar shall adopt a rule of professional conduct governing sexual relations between attorneys and their clients in cases involving, but not limited to, probate matters and domestic relations, including dissolution proceedings, child custody cases, and settlement proceedings.

(c) The State Bar shall submit the proposed rule to the Supreme Court for approval no later than January 1, 1991.

(d) Intentional violation of this rule shall constitute a cause for suspension or disbarment.

§ 6106.9 Sexual relations between attorney and client; cause for discipline; complaints to state bar

(a) It shall constitute cause for the imposition of discipline of an attorney within the meaning of this chapter for an attorney to do any of the following:

(1) Expressly or impliedly condition the performance of legal services for a current or prospective client upon the client's willingness to engage in sexual relations with the attorney.

(2) Employ coercion, intimidation, or undue influence in entering into sexual relations with a client.

(3) Continue representation of a client with whom the attorney has sexual relations if the sexual relations cause the attorney to perform legal services incompetently in violation of Rule 3–110 of the Rules of Professional Conduct of the State Bar of California, or if the sexual relations would, or would be likely to, damage or prejudice the client's case.

(b) Subdivision (a) shall not apply to sexual relations between attorneys and their spouses or persons in an equivalent domestic relationship or to ongoing consensual sexual relationships that predate the initiation of the attorney-client relationship.

(c) Where an attorney in a firm has sexual relations with a client but does not participate in the representation of that client, the attorneys in the firm shall not be subject to discipline under this section solely because of the occurrence of those sexual relations.

(d) For the purposes of this section, "sexual relations" means sexual intercourse or the touching of an intimate part of another person for the purpose of sexual arousal, gratification, or abuse.

(e) Any complaint made to the State Bar alleging a violation of subdivision (a) shall be verified under oath by the person making the complaint.

§ 6107. Proceedings upon court's own knowledge or upon information

The proceedings to disbar or suspend an attorney, on grounds other than the conviction of a felony or misdemeanor, involving moral turpitude, may be taken by the court for the matters within its knowledge, or may be taken upon the information of another.

§ 6108. Accusation

If the proceedings are upon the information of another, the accusation shall be in writing and shall state the matters charged, and be verified by the oath of some person, to the effect that the charges therein contained are true.

The verification may be made upon information and belief when the accusation is presented by an organized bar association.

§ 6109. Order to appear and answer; service

Upon receiving the accusation, the court shall make an order requiring the accused to appear and answer it at a specified time, and shall cause a copy of the order and of the accusation to be served upon the accused at least five days before the day appointed in the order.

§ 6110. Citation

The court or judge may direct the service of a citation to the accused, requiring him to appear and answer the accusation, to be made by publication for thirty days in a newspaper of general circulation published in the county in which the proceeding is pending, if it appears by affidavit to the satisfaction of the court or judge that the accused either:

(a) Resides out of the State.

(b) Has departed from the State.

(c) Can not, after due diligence, be found within the State.

(d) Conceals himself to avoid the service of the order to show cause.

The citation shall be:

(a) Directed to the accused.

(b) Recite the date of the filing of the accusation, the name of the accuser, and the general nature of the charges against him.

(c) Require him to appear and answer the accusation at a specified time.

On proof of the publication of the citation as herein required, the court has jurisdiction to proceed to hear the accusation and render judgment with like effect as if an order to show cause and a copy of the accusation had been personally served on the accused.

§ 6111. Appearance; determination upon default

The accused shall appear at the time appointed in the order, and answer the accusation, unless, for sufficient cause, the court assigns another day for that purpose. If he does not appear, the court may proceed and determine the accusation in his absence.

§ 6112. Answer

The accused may answer to the accusation either by objecting to its sufficiency or by denying it.

If he objects to the sufficiency of the accusation, the objection shall be in writing, but need not be in any specific form. It is sufficient if it presents intelligibly the grounds of the objection.

If he denies the accusation, the denial may be oral and without oath, and shall be entered upon the minutes.

§ 6113. Time for answer after objection

If an objection to the sufficiency of the accusation is not sustained, the accused shall answer within the time designated by the court.

§ 6114. Judgment upon plea of guilty or failure to answer; trial upon denial of charges

If the accused pleads guilty, or refuses to answer the accusation, the court shall proceed to judgment of disbarment or suspension.

If he denies the matters charged, the court shall, at such time as it may appoint, proceed to try the accusation.

§ 6115. Reference to take depositions

The court may, in its discretion, order a reference to a committee to take depositions in the matter.

§ 6116. Judgment

When an attorney has been found guilty of the charges made in proceedings not based upon a record of conviction, judgment shall be rendered disbarring the attorney or suspending him from practice for a limited time, according to the gravity of the offense charged.

§ 6117. Effect of disbarment or suspension

During such disbarment or suspension, the attorney shall be precluded from practicing law. When disbarred, his name shall be stricken from the roll of attorneys.

ARTICLE 7. UNLAWFUL PRACTICE OF LAW

§ 6125. Necessity of active membership in state bar

No person shall practice law in California unless the person is an active member of the State Bar.

§ 6126. Unauthorized practice, advertising or holding out; penalties

(a) Any person advertising or holding himself or herself out as practicing or entitled to practice law or otherwise practicing law who is not an active member of the State Bar, or otherwise authorized pursuant to statute or court rule to practice law in this state at the time of doing so, is guilty of a misdemeanor punishable by up to one year in a county jail or by a fine of up to one thousand dollars ($1,000), or by both that fine and imprisonment. Upon a second or subsequent conviction, the person shall be confined in a county jail for not less than 90 days, except in an unusual case where the interests of justice would be served by imposition of a lesser sentence or a fine. If the court imposes only a fine or a sentence of less than 90 days for a second or subsequent conviction under this subdivision, the court shall state the reasons for its sentencing choice on the record.

(b) Any person who has been involuntarily enrolled as an inactive member of the State Bar, or has been suspended from membership from the State Bar, or has been disbarred, or has resigned from the State Bar with charges pending, and thereafter practices or attempts to practice law, advertises or holds himself or herself out as practicing or otherwise entitled to practice law, is guilty of a crime punishable by imprisonment pursuant to subdivision (h) of Section 1170 of the Penal Code or in a county jail for a period not to exceed six months. However, any person who has been involuntarily enrolled as an inactive member of the State Bar pursuant to paragraph (1) of subdivision (e) of Section 6007 and who knowingly thereafter practices or attempts to practice law, or advertises or holds himself or herself out as practicing or otherwise entitled to practice law, is guilty of a crime punishable by imprisonment pursuant to subdivision (h) of Section 1170 of the Penal Code or in a county jail for a period not to exceed six months.

(c) The willful failure of a member of the State Bar, or one who has resigned or been disbarred, to comply with an order of the Supreme Court to comply with Rule 9.20 of the California Rules of Court, constitutes a crime punishable by imprisonment in the state prison or county jail.

(d) The penalties provided in this section are cumulative to each other and to any other remedies or penalties provided by law.

§ 6126.3 Jurisdiction of court over unauthorized person's files, records and practice; intervention by the superior court or State Bar; order to show cause; appointment of counsel; notice of cessation of law practice

(a) In addition to any criminal penalties pursuant to Section 6126 or to any contempt proceedings pursuant to Section 6127, the courts of the state shall have the jurisdiction provided in this section when a person advertises or holds himself or herself out as practicing or entitled to practice law, or otherwise practices law, without being an active member of the State Bar or otherwise authorized pursuant to statute or court rule to practice law in this state at the time of doing so.

(b) The State Bar, or the superior court on its own motion, may make application to the superior court for the county where the person described in subdivision (a) maintains or more recently has maintained his or her principal office for the practice of law or where he or she resides, for assumption by the court of jurisdiction over the practice to the extent provided in this section. In any proceeding under this section, the State Bar shall be permitted to intervene and to assume primary responsibility for conducting the action.

(c) An application made pursuant to subdivision (b) shall be verified, and shall state facts showing all of the following:

(1) Probable cause to believe that the facts set forth in subdivision (a) of Section 6126 have occurred.

(2) The interest of the applicant.

(3) Probable cause to believe that the interests of a client or of an interested person or entity will be prejudiced if the proceeding is not maintained.

(d) The application shall be set for hearing, and an order to show cause shall be issued directing the person to show cause why the court should not assume jurisdiction over the practice as provided in this section. A copy of the application and order to show cause shall be served upon the person by personal delivery or, as an alternate method of service, by certified or registered mail, return receipt requested, addressed to the person either at the address at which he or she maintains, or more recently has maintained, his or her principal office or at the address where he or she resides. Service is complete at the time of mailing, but any prescribed period of notice and any right or duty to do any act or make any response within that prescribed period or on a date certain after notice is served by mail shall be extended five days if the place of address is within the State of California, 10 days if the place of address is outside the State of California but within the United States, and 20 days if the place of address is outside the United States. If the State Bar is not the applicant, copies shall also be served upon the Office of the Chief Trial Counsel of the State Bar in similar manner at the time of service on the person who is the subject of the application. The court may prescribe additional or alternative methods of service of the application and order to show cause, and may prescribe methods of notifying and serving notices and process upon other persons and entities in cases not specifically provided herein.

(e) If the court finds that the facts set forth in subdivision (a) of Section 6126 have occurred and that the interests of a client or an interested person or entity will be prejudiced if the proceeding provided herein is not maintained, the court may make an order assuming jurisdiction over the person's practice pursuant to this section. If the person to whom the order to show cause is directed does not appear, the court may make its order upon the verified application or upon such proof as it may require. Thereupon, the court shall appoint one or more active members of the State Bar to act under its direction to mail a notice of cessation of practice, pursuant to subdivision (g), and may order those appointed attorneys to do one or more of the following:

(1) Examine the files and records of the practice and obtain information as to any pending matters that may require attention.

(2) Notify persons and entities who appear to be clients of the person of the occurrence of the event or events stated in subdivision (a) of Section 6126, and inform them that it may be in their best interest to obtain other legal counsel.

(3) Apply for an extension of time pending employment of legal counsel by the client.

(4) With the consent of the client, file notices, motions, and pleadings on behalf of the client where jurisdictional time limits are involved and other legal counsel has not yet been obtained.

(5) Give notice to the depositor and appropriate persons and entities who may be affected, other than clients, of the occurrence of the event or events.

(6) Arrange for the surrender or delivery of clients' papers or property.

(7) Arrange for the appointment of a receiver, where applicable, to take possession and control of any and all bank accounts relating to the affected person's practice.

(8) Do any other acts that the court may direct to carry out the purposes of this section.

The court shall have jurisdiction over the files and records and over the practice of the affected person for the limited purposes of this section, and may make all orders necessary or appropriate to exercise this jurisdiction. The court shall provide a copy of any order issued pursuant to this section to the Office of the Chief Trial Counsel of the State Bar.

(f) Anyone examining the files and records of the practice of the person described in subdivision (a) shall observe any lawyer-client privilege under Sections 950 and 952 of the Evidence Code and shall make disclosure only to the extent necessary to carry out the purposes of this section. That disclosure shall be a disclosure that is reasonably necessary for the accomplishment of the purpose for which the person described in subdivision (a) was consulted. The appointment of a member of the State Bar pursuant to this section shall not affect the lawyer-client privilege, which privilege shall apply to communications by or to the appointed members to the same extent as it would have applied to communications by or to the person described in subdivision (a).

(g) The notice of cessation of law practice shall contain any information that may be required by the court, including, but not limited to, the finding by the court that the facts set forth in subdivision (a) of Section 6126 have occurred and that the court has assumed jurisdiction of the practice. The notice shall be mailed to all clients, to opposing counsel, to courts and agencies in which the person has pending matters with an identification of the matter, to the Office of the Chief Trial Counsel of the State Bar, and to any other person or entity having reason to be informed of the court's assumption of the practice.

(h) Nothing in this section shall authorize the court or an attorney appointed by it pursuant to this section to approve or disapprove of the employment of legal counsel, to fix terms of legal employment, or to supervise or in any way undertake the conduct of the practice, except to the limited extent provided by paragraphs (3) and (4) of subdivision (e).

(i) Unless court approval is first obtained, neither the attorney appointed pursuant to this section, nor his or her corporation, nor any partner or associate of the attorney shall accept employment as an attorney by any client of the affected person on any matter pending at the time of the appointment. Action taken pursuant to paragraphs (3) and (4) of subdivision (e) shall not be deemed employment for purposes of this subdivision.

(j) Upon a finding by the court that it is more likely than not that the application will be granted and that delay in making the orders described in subdivision (e) will result in substantial injury to clients or to others, the court, without notice or upon notice as it shall prescribe, may make interim orders containing any provisions that the court deems appropriate under the circumstances. Such an interim order shall be served in the manner provided in subdivision (d) and, if the application and order to show cause have not yet been served, the application and order to show cause shall be served at the time of serving the interim order.

(k) No person or entity shall incur any liability by reason of the institution or maintenance of a proceeding brought under this section. No person or entity shall incur any liability for an act done or omitted to be done pursuant to order of the court under this section. No person or entity shall be liable for failure to apply for court jurisdiction under this section. Nothing in this section shall affect any obligation otherwise existing between the affected person and any other person or entity.

(*l*) An order pursuant to this section is not appealable and shall not be stayed by petition for a writ, except as ordered by the superior court or by the appellate court.

(m) A member of the State Bar appointed pursuant to this section shall serve without compensation. However, the member may be paid reasonable compensation by the State Bar in cases where the State Bar has determined that the member has devoted extraordinary time and services that were necessary to the performance of the member's duties under this article. All payments of compensation for time and services shall be at the discretion of the State Bar. Any member shall be entitled to reimbursement from the State Bar for necessary expenses incurred in the performance of the member's duties under this article. Upon court approval of expenses or compensation for time and services, the State Bar shall be entitled to reimbursement therefor from the person described in subdivision (a) or his or her estate.

§ 6126.5 Additional remedies and penalties

(a) In addition to any remedies and penalties available in any enforcement action brought in the name of the people of the State of California by the Attorney General, a district attorney, or a city attorney, acting as a public prosecutor, the court shall award relief in the enforcement action for any person who obtained services offered or provided in violation of Section 6125 or 6126 or who purchased any goods, services, or real or personal property in connection with services offered or provided in violation of Section 6125 or 6126 against the person who violated Section 6125 or 6126, or who sold goods, services, or property in connection with that violation. The court shall consider the following relief:

(1) Actual damages.

(2) Restitution of all amounts paid.

(3) The amount of penalties and tax liabilities incurred in connection with the sale or transfer of assets to pay for any goods, services, or property.

(4) Reasonable attorney's fees and costs expended to rectify errors made in the unlawful practice of law.

(5) Prejudgment interest at the legal rate from the date of loss to the date of judgment.

(6) Appropriate equitable relief, including the rescission of sales made in connection with a violation of law.

(b) The relief awarded under paragraphs (1) to (6), inclusive, of subdivision (a) shall be distributed to, or on behalf of, the person for whom it was awarded or, if it is impracticable to do so, shall be distributed as may be directed by the court pursuant to its equitable powers.

(c) The court shall also award the Attorney General, district attorney, or city attorney reasonable attorney's fees and costs and, in the court's discretion, exemplary damages as provided in Section 3294 of the Civil Code.

(d) This section shall not be construed to create, abrogate, or otherwise affect claims, rights, or remedies, if any, that may be held by a person or entity other than those law enforcement agencies described in subdivision (a). The remedies provided in this section are cumulative to each other and to the remedies and penalties provided under other laws.

§ 6127. Contempt of court

The following acts or omissions in respect to the practice of law are contempts of the authority of the courts:

(a) Assuming to be an officer or attorney of a court and acting as such, without authority.

(b) Advertising or holding oneself out as practicing or as entitled to practice law or otherwise practicing law in any court, without being an active member of the State Bar.

Proceedings to adjudge a person in contempt of court under this section are to be taken in accordance with the provisions of Title V of Part III of the Code of Civil Procedure.

§ 6127.5 Law corporation under professional corporation act

Nothing in Sections 6125, 6126 and 6127 shall be deemed to apply to the acts and practices of a law corporation duly certificated pursuant to the Professional Corporation Act, as contained in Part 4 (commencing with Section 13400) of Division 3 of Title 1 of the Corporations Code, and pursuant to Article 10 (commencing with Section 6160) of Chapter 4 of Division 3 of this code, when the law corporation is in compliance with the requirements of (a) the Professional Corporation Act; (b) Article 10 (commencing with Section 6160) of Chapter 4 of Division 3 of this code; and (c) all other statutes and all rules and regulations now or hereafter enacted or adopted pertaining to such corporation and the conduct of its affairs.

§ 6128. Deceit, collusion, delay of suit and improper receipt of money as misdemeanors

Every attorney is guilty of a misdemeanor who either:

(a) Is guilty of any deceit or collusion, or consents to any deceit or collusion, with intent to deceive the court or any party.

(b) Wilfully delays his client's suit with a view to his own gain.

(c) Wilfully receives any money or allowance for or on account of any money which he has not laid out or become answerable for.

Any violation of the provisions of this section is punishable by imprisonment in the county jail not exceeding six months, or by a fine not exceeding two thousand five hundred dollars ($2,500), or by both.

§ 6129. Buying claim as misdemeanor

Every attorney who, either directly or indirectly, buys or is interested in buying any evidence of debt or thing in action, with intent to bring suit thereon, is guilty of a misdemeanor.

Any violation of the provisions of this section is punished by imprisonment in the county jail not exceeding six months, or by a fine not exceeding two thousand five hundred dollars ($2,500), or by both.

§ 6130. Disbarred or suspended attorney suing as assignee

No person, who has been an attorney, shall while a judgment of disbarment or suspension is in force appear on his own behalf as plaintiff in the prosecution of any action where the subject of the action has been assigned to him subsequent to the entry of the judgment of disbarment or suspension and solely for purpose of collection.

§ 6131. Aiding defense where partner or self has acted as public prosecutor; misdemeanor and disbarment

Every attorney is guilty of a misdemeanor and, in addition to the punishment prescribed therefor, shall be disbarred:

(a) Who directly or indirectly advises in relation to, or aids, or promotes the defense of any action or proceeding in any court the prosecution of which is carried on, aided or promoted by any person as district attorney or other public prosecutor with whom such person is directly or indirectly connected as a partner.

(b) Who, having himself prosecuted or in any manner aided or promoted any action or proceeding in any court as district attorney or other public prosecutor, afterwards, directly or indirectly, advises in relation to or takes any part in the defense thereof, as attorney or otherwise, or who takes or receives any valuable consideration from or on behalf of any defendant in any such action upon any understanding or agreement whatever having relation to the defense thereof.

This section does not prohibit an attorney from defending himself in person, as attorney or counsel, when prosecuted, either civilly or criminally.

§ 6132. Firm names; removal of names of attorneys under discipline

Any law firm, partnership, corporation, or association which contains the name of an attorney who is disbarred, or who resigned with charges pending, in its business name shall remove the name of that attorney from its business name, and from all signs, advertisements, letterhead, and other materials containing that name, within 60 days of the disbarment or resignation.

§ 6133. Resigned, suspended or disbarred attorneys; supervision of activities by firms

Any attorney or any law firm, partnership, corporation, or association employing an attorney who has resigned, or who is under actual suspension from the practice of law, or is disbarred, shall not permit that attorney to practice law or so advertise or hold himself or herself out as practicing law and shall supervise him or her in any other assigned duties. A willful violation of this section constitutes a cause for discipline.

ARTICLE 8.5 FEE AGREEMENTS

§ 6146. Limitations; periodic payments

(a) An attorney shall not contract for or collect a contingency fee for representing any person seeking damages in connection with an action for injury or damage against a health care provider based upon such person's alleged professional negligence in excess of the following limits:

(1) Forty percent of the first fifty thousand dollars ($50,000) recovered.

(2) Thirty-three and one-third percent of the next fifty thousand dollars ($50,000) recovered.

(3) Twenty-five percent of the next five hundred thousand dollars ($500,000) recovered.

(4) Fifteen percent of any amount on which the recovery exceeds six hundred thousand dollars ($600,000).

The limitations shall apply regardless of whether the recovery is by settlement, arbitration, or judgment, or whether the person for whom the recovery is made is a responsible adult, an infant, or a person of unsound mind.

(b) If periodic payments are awarded to the plaintiff pursuant to Section 667.7 of the Code of Civil Procedure, the court shall place a total value on these payments based upon the projected life expectancy of the plaintiff and include this amount in computing the total award from which attorney's fees are calculated under this section.

(c) For purposes of this section:

(1) "Recovered" means the net sum recovered after deducting any disbursements or costs incurred in connection with prosecution or settlement of the claim. Costs of medical care incurred by the plaintiff and the attorney's office-overhead costs or charges are not deductible disbursements or costs for such purpose.

(2) "Health care provider" means any person licensed or certified pursuant to Division 2 (commencing with Section 500), or licensed pursuant to the Osteopathic Initiative Act, or the Chiropractic Initiative Act, or licensed pursuant to Chapter 2.5 (commencing with Section 1440)

of Division 2 of the Health and Safety Code; and any clinic, health dispensary, or health facility, licensed pursuant to Division 2 (commencing with Section 1200) of the Health and Safety Code. "Health care provider" includes the legal representatives of a health care provider.

(3) "Professional negligence" is a negligent act or omission to act by a health care provider in the rendering of professional services, which act or omission is the proximate cause of a personal injury or wrongful death, provided that the services are within the scope of services for which the provider is licensed and which are not within any restriction imposed by the licensing agency or licensed hospital.

§ 6147. Contingency fee contracts; duplicate copy; contents; effect of noncompliance; recovery of workers' compensation benefits

(a) An attorney who contracts to represent a client on a contingency fee basis shall, at the time the contract is entered into, provide a duplicate copy of the contract, signed by both the attorney and the client, or the client's guardian or representative, to the client, or to the client's guardian or representative. The contract shall be in writing and shall include, but is not limited to, all of the following:

(1) A statement of the contingency fee rate that the client and attorney have agreed upon.

(2) A statement as to how disbursements and costs incurred in connection with the prosecution or settlement of the claim will affect the contingency fee and the client's recovery.

(3) A statement as to what extent, if any, the client could be required to pay any compensation to the attorney for related matters that arise out of their relationship not covered by their contingency fee contract. This may include any amounts collected for the plaintiff by the attorney.

(4) Unless the claim is subject to the provisions of Section 6146, a statement that the fee is not set by law but is negotiable between attorney and client.

(5) If the claim is subject to the provisions of Section 6146, a statement that the rates set forth in that section are the maximum limits for the contingency fee agreement, and that the attorney and client may negotiate a lower rate.

(b) Failure to comply with any provision of this section renders the agreement voidable at the option of the plaintiff, and the attorney shall thereupon be entitled to collect a reasonable fee.

(c) This section shall not apply to contingency fee contracts for the recovery of workers' compensation benefits.

(d) This section shall become operative on January 1, 2000.

§ 6147.5 Contingency fee contracts; recovery of claims between merchants

(a) Sections 6147 and 6148 shall not apply to contingency fee contracts for the recovery of claims between merchants as defined in Section 2104 of the Commercial Code, arising from the sale or lease of goods or services rendered, or money loaned for use, in the conduct of a business or profession if the merchant contracting for legal services employs 10 or more individuals.

(b)(1) In the instances in which no written contract for legal services exists as permitted by subdivision (a), an attorney shall not contract for or collect a contingency fee in excess of the following limits:

(A) Twenty percent of the first three hundred dollars ($300) collected.

(B) Eighteen percent of the next one thousand seven hundred dollars ($1,700) collected.

(C) Thirteen percent of sums collected in excess of two thousand dollars ($2,000).

(2) However, the following minimum charges may be charged and collected:

(A) Twenty-five dollars ($25) in collections of seventy-five dollars ($75) to one hundred twenty-five dollars ($125).

(B) Thirty-three and one-third percent of collections less than seventy-five dollars ($75).

§ 6148. Contracts for services in cases not coming within § 6147; bills rendered by attorney; contents; failure to comply

(a) In any case not coming within Section 6147 in which it is reasonably foreseeable that total expense to a client, including attorney fees will exceed one thousand dollars ($1,000), the contract for services in the case shall be in writing. At the time the contract is entered into, the attorney shall provide a duplicate copy of the contract signed by both the attorney and the client, or the client's guardian or representative, to the client or the client's guardian or representative. The written contract shall contain all of the following:

(1) Any basis of compensation including, but not limited to, hourly rates, statutory fees or flat fees, and other standard rates, fees, and charges applicable to the case.

(2) The general nature of the legal services to be provided to the client.

(3) The respective responsibilities of the attorney and the client as to the performance of the contract.

(b) All bills rendered by an attorney to a client shall clearly state the basis thereof. Bills for the fee portion of the bill shall include the amount, rate, basis for calculation, or other method of determination of the attorney's fees and costs. Bills for the cost and expense portion of the bill shall clearly identify the costs and expenses incurred and the amount of the costs and expenses. Upon request by the client, the attorney shall provide a bill to the client no later than 10 days following the request unless the attorney has provided a bill to the client within 31 days prior to the request, in which case the attorney may provide a bill to the client no later than 31 days following the date the most recent bill was provided. The client is entitled to make similar requests at intervals of no less than 30 days following the initial request. In providing responses to client requests for billing information, the attorney may use billing data that is currently effective on the date of the request, or, if any fees or costs to that date cannot be accurately determined, they shall be described and estimated.

(c) Failure to comply with any provision of this section renders the agreement voidable at the option of the client, and the attorney shall, upon the agreement being voided, be entitled to collect a reasonable fee.

(d) This section shall not apply to any of the following:

(1) Services rendered in an emergency to avoid foreseeable prejudice to the rights or interests of the client or where a writing is otherwise impractical.

(2) An arrangement as to the fee implied by the fact that the attorney's services are of the same general kind as previously rendered to and paid for by the client.

(3) If the client knowingly states in writing, after full disclosure of this section, that a writing concerning fees is not required.

(4) If the client is a corporation.

(e) This section applies prospectively only to fee agreements following its operative date.

(f) This section shall become operative on January 1, 2000.

§ 6149. Written fee contract as confidential communication

A written fee contract shall be deemed to be a confidential communication within the meaning of subdivision (e) of Section 6068 and of Section 952 of the Evidence Code.

§ 6149.5 Third-party liability claim; settlement by insurer; notice to claimant; effect on action or defense

(a) Upon the payment of one hundred dollars ($100) or more in settlement of any third-party liability claim the insurer shall provide written notice to the claimant if both of the following apply:

(1) The claimant is a natural person.

(2) The payment is delivered to the claimant's lawyer or other representative by draft, check, or otherwise.

(b) For purposes of this section, "written notice" includes providing to the claimant a copy of the cover letter sent to the claimant's attorney or other representative that accompanied the settlement payment.

(c) This section shall not create any cause of action for any person against the insurer based upon the insurer's failure to provide the notice to a claimant required by this section. This section shall not create a defense for any party to any cause of action based upon the insurer's failure to provide this notice.

ARTICLE 9. UNLAWFUL SOLICITATION

§ 6150. Relation of article to chapter

This article is a part of Chapter 4 of this division of the Business and Professions Code, but the phrase "this chapter" as used in Chapter 4 does not apply to the provisions of this article unless expressly made applicable.

§ 6151. Definitions

As used in this article:

(a) A runner or capper is any person, firm, association or corporation acting for consideration in any manner or in any capacity as an agent for an attorney at law or law firm, whether the attorney or any member of the law firm is admitted in California or any other jurisdiction, in the solicitation or procurement of business for the attorney at law or law firm as provided in this article.

(b) An agent is one who represents another in dealings with one or more third persons.

§ 6152. Prohibition of solicitation

(a) It is unlawful for:

(1) Any person, in an individual capacity or in a capacity as a public or private employee, or for any firm, corporation, partnership or association to act as a runner or capper for any attorneys or to solicit any business for any attorneys in and about the state prisons, county jails, city jails, city prisons, or other places of detention of persons, city receiving hospitals, city and county receiving hospitals, county hospitals, superior courts, or in any public institution or in any public place or upon any public street or highway or in and about private hospitals, sanitariums or in and about any private institution or upon private property of any character whatsoever.

(2) Any person to solicit another person to commit or join in the commission of a violation of subdivision (a).

(b) A general release from a liability claim obtained from any person during the period of the first physical confinement, whether as an inpatient or outpatient, in a clinic or health facility, as defined in Sections 1203 and 1250 of the Health and Safety Code, as a result of the injury alleged to have given rise to the claim and primarily of treatment of the injury, is presumed fraudulent if the release is executed within 15 days after the commencement of confinement or prior to release from confinement, which ever occurs first.

(c) Nothing in this section shall be construed to prevent the recommendation of professional employment where that recommendation is not prohibited by the Rules of Professional Conduct of the State Bar of California.

(d) Nothing in this section shall be construed to mean that a public defender or assigned counsel may not make known his or her services as a criminal defense attorney to persons unable to afford legal counsel whether those persons are in custody or otherwise.

§ 6153. Violation; penalty

Any person, firm, partnership, association, or corporation violating subdivision (a) of Section 6152 is punishable, upon a first conviction by imprisonment in a county jail for not more than one year or by a fine not exceeding fifteen thousand dollars ($15,000), or by both that imprisonment and fine. Upon a second or subsequent conviction, a person, firm, partnership, association, or corporation is punishable by imprisonment in a county jail for not more than one year, or by imprisonment pursuant to subdivision (h) of Section 1170 of the Penal Code for 2, 3 or 4 years, or by a fine not exceeding fifteen thousand dollars ($15,000), or by both that imprisonment and fine.

Any person employed either as an officer, director, trustee, clerk, servant or agent of this State or of any county or other municipal corporation or subdivision thereof, who is found guilty of violating any of the provisions of this article, shall forfeit the right to his office and employment in addition to any other penalty provided in this article.

§ 6154. Runner or capper used to procure business's void contract; divesting of fees and other compensation; fees recovered from workers' compensation actions

(a) Any contract for professional services secured by any attorney at law or law firm in this state through the services of a runner or capper is void. In any action against any attorney or law firm under the Unfair Practices Act, Chapter 4 (commencing with Section 17000) of Division 7, or Chapter 5 (commencing with Section 17200) of Division 7, any judgment shall include an order divesting the attorney or law firm of any fees and other compensation received pursuant to any such void contract. Those fees and compensation shall be recoverable as additional civil penalties under Chapter 4 (commencing with Section 17000) or Chapter 5 (commencing with Section 17200) of Division 7.

(b) Notwithstanding Section 17206 or any other provision of law, any fees recovered pursuant to subdivision (a) in an action involving professional services related to the provision of workers' compensation shall be allocated as follows: if the action is brought by the Attorney General, one-half of the penalty collected shall be paid to the State General Fund, and one-half of the penalty collected shall be paid to the Workers' Compensation Fraud Account in the Insurance Fund; if the action is brought by a district attorney, one-half of the penalty collected shall be paid to the treasurer of the county in which the judgment was entered, and one-half of the penalty collected shall be paid to the Workers' Compensation Fraud Account in the Insurance Fund; if the action is brought by a city attorney or city prosecutor, one-half of the penalty collected shall be paid to the Workers' Compensation Fraud Account in the Insurance Fund. Moneys deposited into the Workers' Compensation Fraud Account pursuant to this subdivision shall be used in the investigation and prosecution of workers' compensation fraud, as appropriated by the Legislature.

§ 6155. Referral services; conflicts of interest; enforcement; rules and regulations; duration of section

(a) An individual, partnership, corporation, association, or any other entity shall not operate for the direct or indirect purpose, in whole or in part, of referring potential clients to attorneys, and no attorney shall accept a referral of such potential clients, unless all of the following requirements are met:

(1) The service is registered with the State Bar of California and (a) on July 1, 1988, is operated in conformity with minimum standards for a lawyer referral service established by the State Bar, or (b) upon approval by the Supreme Court of minimum standards for a lawyer referral service, is operated in conformity with those standards.

(2) The combined charges to the potential client by the referral service and the attorney to whom the potential client is referred do not exceed the total cost that the client would normally pay if no referral service were involved.

(b) A referral service shall not be owned or operated, in whole or in part, directly or indirectly, by those lawyers to whom, individually or collectively, more than 20 percent of referrals are made. For purposes of this subdivision, a referral service that is owned or operated by a bar association, as defined in the minimum standards, shall be deemed to be owned or operated by its governing committee so long as the governing committee is constituted and functions in the manner prescribed by the minimum standards.

(c) None of the following is a lawyer referral service:

(1) A plan of legal insurance as defined in Section 119.6 of the Insurance Code.

(2) A group or prepaid legal plan, whether operated by a union, trust, mutual benefit or aid association, public or private corporation, or other entity or person, which meets both of the following conditions:

(A) It recommends, furnishes, or pays for legal services to its members or beneficiaries.

(B) It provides telephone advice or personal consultation.

(3) A program having as its purpose the referral of clients to attorneys for representation on a pro bono basis.

(d) The following are in the public interest and do not constitute an unlawful restraint of trade or commerce:

(1) An agreement between a referral service and a participating attorney to eliminate or restrict the attorney's fee for an initial office consultation for each potential client or to provide free or reduced fee services.

(2) Requirements by a referral service that attorneys meet reasonable participation requirements, including experience, education, and training requirements.

(3) Provisions of the minimum standards as approved by the Supreme Court.

(4) Requirements that the application and renewal fees for certification as a lawyer referral service be determined, in whole or in part, by a consideration of any combination of the following factors: a referral service's gross annual revenues, number of panels, number of panel members, amount of fees charged to panel members, or for-profit or nonprofit status; provided that the application and renewal fees do not exceed ten thousand dollars ($10,000) or 1 percent of the gross annual revenues, whichever is less.

(5) Requirements that, to increase access to the justice system for all Californians, lawyer referral services establish separate ongoing activities or arrangements that serve persons of limited means.

(e) A violation or threatened violation of this section may be enjoined by any person.

(f) With the approval of the Supreme Court, the State Bar shall formulate and enforce rules and regulations for carrying out this section, including rules and regulations which do the following:

(1) Establish minimum standards for lawyer referral services. The minimum standards shall include provisions ensuring that panel membership shall be open to all attorneys practicing in the geographical area served who are qualified by virtue of suitable experience, and limiting attorney registration and membership fees to reasonable sums which do not discourage widespread attorney membership.

(2) Require that an entity seeking to qualify as a lawyer referral service register with the State Bar and obtain from the State Bar a certificate of compliance with the minimum standards for lawyer referral services.

(3) Require that the certificate may be obtained, maintained, suspended, or revoked pursuant to procedures set forth in the rules and regulations.

(4) Require the lawyer referral service to pay an application and renewal fee for the certificate in such reasonable amounts as may be determined by the State Bar. The State Bar shall adopt rules authorizing the waiver or reduction of the fees upon a demonstration of financial necessity. The State Bar may require that the application and renewal fees for certification as a lawyer referral service be determined, in whole or in part, by a consideration of any combination of the following factors: a referral service's gross annual revenues, number of panels, number of panel members, amount of fees charged to panel members, or for-profit or nonprofit status; provided that the application and renewal fees do not exceed ten thousand dollars ($10,000) or 1 percent of the gross annual revenues, whichever is less.

(5) Require that, to increase access to the justice system for all Californians, lawyer referral services establish separate ongoing activities or arrangements that serve persons of limited means.

(6) Require each lawyer who is a member of a certified lawyer referral service to comply with all applicable professional standards, rules, and regulations, and to possess a policy of errors and omissions insurance in an amount not less than one hundred thousand dollars ($100,000) for each occurrence and three hundred thousand dollars ($300,000) aggregate, per year. By rule, the State Bar may provide for alternative proof of financial responsibility to meet this requirement.

(g) Provide that cause for denial of certification or recertification or revocation of certification of a lawyer referral service shall include, but not be limited to:

(1) Noncompliance with the statutes or minimum standards governing lawyer referral services as adopted and from time to time amended.

(2) Sharing common or cross ownership, interests, or operations with any entity which engages in referrals to licensed or unlicensed health care providers.

(3) Direct or indirect consideration regarding referrals between an owner, operator, or member of a lawyer referral service and any licensed or unlicensed health care provider.

(4) Advertising on behalf of attorneys in violation of the Rules of Professional Conduct or the Business and Professions Code.

(h) This section shall not be construed to prohibit attorneys from jointly advertising their services.

(1) Permissible joint advertising, among other things, identifies by name the advertising attorneys or law firms whom the consumer of legal services may select and initiate contact with.

(2) Certifiable referral activity involves, among other things, some person or entity other than the consumer and advertising attorney or law firms which, in person, electronically, or otherwise, refers the consumer to an attorney or law firm not identified in the advertising.

(i) A lawyer referral service certified under this section and operating in full compliance with this section, and in full compliance with the minimum standards and the rules and regulations of the State Bar governing lawyer referral services, shall not be deemed to be in violation of Section 3215 of the Labor Code or Section 750 of the Insurance Code.

(j) The payment by an attorney or law firm member of a certified referral service of the normal fees of that service shall not be deemed to be in violation of Section 3215 of the Labor Code or Section 750 of the Insurance Code, provided that the attorney or law firm member is in full compliance with the minimum standards and the rules and regulations of the State Bar governing lawyer referral services.

(k) Certifications of lawyer referral services issued by the State Bar shall not be transferable.

[Ed. Note: The California Bar has prepared two documents relating to referral services: (1) Minimum Standards for a Lawyer Referral Service in California, and (2) Certification and Renewal Fees for Lawyer Referral Services. These documents are omitted from this publication.]

ARTICLE 9.5 LEGAL ADVERTISING

§ 6157. Definitions

As used in this article, the following definitions apply:

(a) "Member" means a member in good standing of the State Bar and includes the terms "lawyer" and "attorney" and includes any agent of the member and any law firm or law corporation doing business in the State of California.

(b) "Lawyer" means a member of the State Bar or a person who is admitted in good standing and eligible to practice before the bar of any United States court or the highest court of the District of Columbia or any state, territory, or insular possession of the United States, or is licensed to practice law in, or is admitted in good standing and eligible to practice before the bar of the highest court of, a foreign country or any political subdivision thereof, and includes any agent of the lawyer, law firm, or law corporation doing business in the state.

(c) "Advertise" or "advertisement" means any communication, disseminated by television or radio, by any print medium, including, but not limited to, newspapers and billboards, or by means of a mailing directed generally to members of the public and not to a specific person, that solicits employment of legal services provided by a member, and is directed to the general public and is paid for by, or on the behalf of, an attorney.

(d) "Electronic medium" means television, radio, or computer networks.

§ 6157.1 False, misleading or deceptive statements; prohibition

No advertisement shall contain any false, misleading, or deceptive statement or omit to state any fact necessary to make the statements made, in light of circumstances under which they are made, not false, misleading, or deceptive.

§ 6157.2 Prohibited statements regarding outcome; dramatizations; contingent fee basis representations

No advertisement shall contain or refer to any of the following:

(a) Any guarantee or warranty regarding the outcome of a legal matter as a result of representation by the member.

(b) Statements or symbols stating that the member featured in the advertisement can generally obtain immediate cash or quick settlements.

(c)(1) An impersonation of the name, voice, photograph, or electronic image of any person other than the lawyer, directly or implicitly purporting to be that of a lawyer.

(2) An impersonation of the name, voice, photograph, or electronic image of any person directly or implicitly purporting to be a client of the member featured in the advertisement, or a dramatization of events, unless disclosure of the impersonation or dramatization is made in the advertisement.

(3) A spokesperson, including a celebrity spokesperson, unless there is a disclosure of the spokesperson's title.

(d) A statement that a member offers representation on a contingent basis unless the statement also advises whether a client will be held responsible for any costs advanced by the member when no recovery is obtained on behalf of the client. If the client will not be held responsible for costs, no disclosure is required.

§ 6157.3 Advertisements made on behalf of member; required representations

Any advertisement made on behalf of a member, which is not paid for by the member, shall disclose any business relationship, past or present, between the member and the person paying for the advertisement.

§ 6157.4 Lawyer referral service advertising

Any advertisement that is created or disseminated by a lawyer referral service shall disclose whether the attorneys on the organization's referral list, panel, or system, paid any consideration, other than a proportional share of actual cost, to be included on that list, panel, or system.

§ 6157.5 Immigration and naturalization services advertising; member seeking professional employment; application of section

(a) All advertisements published, distributed, or broadcasted by or on behalf of a member seeking professional employment for the member in providing services relating to immigration or naturalization shall include a statement that he or she is an active member of the State Bar, licensed to practice law in this state. If the advertisement seeks employment for a law firm or law corporation employing more than one attorney, the advertisement shall include a statement that all the services relating to immigration and naturalization provided by the firm or corporation shall be provided by an active member of the State Bar or by a person under the supervision of an active member of the State Bar. This subdivision shall not apply to classified or "yellow pages" listings in a telephone or business directory of three lines or less that state only the name, address, and telephone number of the listed entity.

(b) If the advertisement is in a language other than English, the statement required by subdivision (a) shall be in the same language as the advertisement.

(c) This section shall not apply to members employed by public agencies or by nonprofit entities registered with the Secretary of State.

(d) A violation of this section by a member shall be cause for discipline by the State Bar.

§ 6158. Electronic media advertising; false, misleading or deceptive message; factual substantiation

In advertising by electronic media, to comply with Sections 6157.1 and 6157.2, the message as a whole may not be false, misleading, or deceptive, and the message as a whole must be factually substantiated. The message means the effect in combination of the spoken word, sound, background, action, symbols, visual image, or any other technique employed to create the message. Factually substantiated means capable of verification by a credible source.

§ 6158.1 False, misleading or deceptive messages; rebuttable presumption

There shall be a rebuttable presumption affecting the burden of producing evidence that the following messages are false, misleading, or deceptive within the meaning of Section 6158:

(a) A message as to the ultimate result of a specific case or cases presented out of context without adequately providing information as to the facts or law giving rise to the result.

(b) The depiction of an event through methods such as the use of displays of injuries, accident scenes, or portrayals of other injurious events which may or may not be accompanied by sound effects and which may give rise to a claim for compensation.

(c) A message referring to or implying money received by or for a client in a particular case or cases, or to potential monetary recovery for a prospective client. A reference to money or monetary recovery includes, but is not limited to, a specific dollar amount, characterization of a sum of money, monetary symbols, or the implication of wealth.

§ 6158.2 Information presumed to be in compliance with article

The following information shall be presumed to be in compliance with this article for purposes of advertising by electronic media, provided the message as a whole is not false, misleading, or deceptive:

(a) Name, including name of law firm, names of professional associates, addresses, telephone numbers, and the designation "lawyer," "attorney," "law firm," or the like.

(b) Fields of practice, limitation of practice, or specialization.

(c) Fees for routine legal services, subject to the requirements of subdivision (d) of Section 6157.2 and the Rules of Professional Conduct.

(d) Date and place of birth.

(e) Date and place of admission to the bar of state and federal courts.

(f) Schools attended, with dates of graduation, degrees, and other scholastic distinctions.

(g) Public or quasi-public offices.

(h) Military service.

(i) Legal authorship.

(j) Legal teaching positions.

(k) Memberships, offices, and committee assignments in bar associations.

(*l*) Memberships and offices in legal fraternities and legal societies.

(m) Technical and professional licenses.

(n) Memberships in scientific, technical, and professional associations and societies.

(*o*) Foreign language ability of the advertising lawyer or a member of lawyer's firm.

§ 6158.3 Electronic media advertising; required disclosures

In addition to any disclosure required by Section 6157.2, Section 6157.3, and the Rules of Professional Conduct, the following disclosure shall appear in advertising by electronic media. Use of the following disclosure alone may not rebut any presumption created in Section 6158.1. If an advertisement in the electronic media conveys a message portraying a result in a particular case or cases, the advertisement must state, in either an oral or printed communication, either of the following disclosures: The advertisement must adequately disclose the factual and legal circumstances that justify the result portrayed in the message, including the basis for liability and the nature of injury or damage sustained, or the advertisement must state that the result portrayed in the advertisement was dependent on the facts of that case, and that the results will differ if based on different facts.

§ 6158.4 Violation; complaint; contents; procedure

(a) Any person claiming a violation of Section 6158, 6158.1, or 6158.3 may file a complaint with the State Bar that states the name of the advertiser, a description of the advertisement claimed to violate these sections, and that specifically identifies the alleged violation. A copy of the complaint shall be served simultaneously upon the advertiser. The advertiser shall have nine days from the date of service of the complaint to voluntarily withdraw from broadcast the advertisement that is the subject of the complaint. If the advertiser elects to withdraw the advertisement, the advertiser shall notify the State Bar of that fact, and no further action may be taken by the complainant. The advertiser shall provide a copy of the complained of advertisement to the State Bar for review within seven days of service of the complaint. Within 21 days of the delivery of the complained of advertisement, the State Bar shall determine whether substantial evidence of a violation of these sections exists. The review shall be conducted by a State Bar attorney who has expertise in the area of lawyer advertising.

(b)(1) Upon a State Bar determination that substantial evidence of a violation exists, if the member or certified lawyer referral service withdraws that advertisement from broadcast within 72 hours, no further action may be taken by the complainant.

(2) Upon a State Bar determination that substantial evidence of a violation exists, if the member or certified lawyer referral service fails to withdraw the advertisement within 72 hours, a civil enforcement action brought pursuant to subdivision (e) may be commenced within one year of the State Bar decision. If the member or certified lawyer referral service withdraws an advertisement upon a State Bar determination that substantial evidence of a violation exists and subsequently rebroadcasts the same advertisement without a finding by the trier of fact in an action brought pursuant to subdivision (c) or (e) that the advertisement does not violate Section 6158, 6158.1, or 6158.3, a civil enforcement action may be commenced within one year of the rebroadcast.

(3) Upon a determination that substantial evidence of a violation does not exist, the complainant is barred from bringing a civil enforcement action pursuant to subdivision (e), but may bring an action for declaratory relief pursuant to subdivision (c).

(c) Any member or certified lawyer referral service who was the subject of a complaint and any complainant affected by the decision of the State Bar may bring an action for declaratory relief in the superior court to obtain a judicial declaration of whether Section 6158, 6158.1, or 6158.3 has been violated, and, if applicable, may also request injunctive relief. Any defense otherwise available at law may be raised for the first time in the declaratory relief action, including any constitutional challenge. Any civil enforcement action filed pursuant to subdivision (e) shall be stayed pending the resolution of the declaratory relief action. The action shall be defended by the real party in interest. The State Bar shall not be considered a party to the action unless it elects to intervene in the action.

(1) Upon a State Bar determination that substantial evidence of a violation exists, if the complainant or the member or certified lawyer referral service brings an action for declaratory relief to obtain a judicial declaration of whether the advertisement violates Section 6158, 6158.1, or 6158.3, and the court declares that the advertisement violates one or more of the sections, a civil enforcement action pursuant to subdivision (e) may be filed or maintained if the member or certified lawyer referral service failed to withdraw the advertisement within 72 hours of the State Bar determination. The decision of the court that an advertisement violates Section 6158, 6158.1, or 6158.3 shall be binding on the issue of whether the advertisement is unlawful in any pending

or prospective civil enforcement action brought pursuant to subdivision (e) if that binding effect is supported by the doctrine of collateral estoppel or res judicata.

If, in that declaratory relief action, the court declares that the advertisement does not violate Section 6158, 6158.1, or 6158.3, the member or lawyer referral service may broadcast the advertisement. The decision of the court that an advertisement does not violate Section 6158, 6158.1, or 6158.3 shall bar any pending or prospective civil enforcement action brought pursuant to subdivision (e) if that prohibitive effect is supported by the doctrine of collateral estoppel or res judicata.

(2) If, following a State Bar determination that does not find substantial evidence that an advertisement violates Section 6158, 6158.1, or 6158.3, the complainant or the member or certified lawyer referral service brings an action for declaratory relief to obtain a judicial declaration of whether the advertisement violates Section 6158, 6158.1, or 6158.3, and the court declares that the advertisement violates one or more of the sections, a civil enforcement action pursuant to subdivision (e) may be filed or maintained if the member or certified lawyer referral service broadcasts the same advertisement following the decision in the declaratory relief action. The decision of the court that an advertisement violates Section 6158, 6158.1, or 6158.3 shall be binding on the issue of whether the advertisement is unlawful in any pending or prospective civil enforcement action brought pursuant to subdivision (e) if that binding effect is supported by the doctrine of collateral estoppel or res judicata.

If, in that declaratory relief action, the court declares that the advertisement does not violate Section 6158, 6158.1, or 6158.3, the member or lawyer referral service may continue broadcast of the advertisement. The decision of the court that an advertisement does not violate Section 6158, 6158.1, or 6158.3 shall bar any pending or prospective civil enforcement action brought pursuant to subdivision (e) if that prohibitive effect is supported by the doctrine of collateral estoppel or res judicata.

(d) The State Bar review procedure shall apply only to members and certified referral services. A direct civil enforcement action for a violation of Section 6158, 6158.1, or 6158.3 may be maintained against any other advertiser after first giving 14 days' notice to the advertiser of the alleged violation. If the advertiser does not withdraw from broadcast the advertisement that is the subject of the notice within 14 days of service of the notice, a civil enforcement action pursuant to subdivision (e) may be commenced. The civil enforcement action shall be commenced within one year of the date of the last publication or broadcast of the advertisement that is the subject of the action.

(e) Subject to Section 6158.5, a violation of Section 6158, 6158.1, or 6158.3 shall be cause for a civil enforcement action brought by any person residing within the State of California for an amount up to five thousand dollars ($5,000) for each individual broadcast that violates Section 6158, 6158.1, or 6158.3. Venue shall be in a county where the advertisement was broadcast.

(f) In any civil action brought pursuant to this section, the matter shall be determined according to the law and procedure relating to the trial of civil actions, including trial by jury, if demanded.

(g) The decision of the State Bar pursuant to subdivision (a) shall be admissible in the civil enforcement action brought pursuant to subdivision (e). However, the State Bar shall not be a party or a witness in either a declaratory relief proceeding brought pursuant to subdivision (c) or the civil enforcement action brought pursuant to subdivision (e). Additionally, no direct action may be filed against the State Bar challenging the State Bar's decision pursuant to subdivision (a).

(h) Amounts recovered pursuant to this section shall be paid into the Client Security Fund maintained by the State Bar.

(i) In any civil action brought pursuant to this section, the court shall award attorney's fees pursuant to Section 1021.5 of the Code of Civil Procedure if the court finds that the action has resulted in the enforcement of an important public interest or that a significant benefit has been conferred on the public.

(j) The State Bar shall maintain records of all complainants and complaints filed pursuant to subdivision (a) for a period of seven years. If a complainant files five or more unfounded complaints within seven years, the complainant shall be considered a vexatious litigant for purposes of this section. The State Bar shall require any person deemed a vexatious litigant to post security in the minimum amount of twenty-five thousand dollars ($25,000) prior to considering any complaint filed by that person and shall refrain from taking any action until the security is posted. In any civil action arising from this section brought by a person deemed a vexatious litigant, the defendant may advise the court and trier of fact that the plaintiff is deemed to be a vexatious litigant under the provisions of this section and disclose the basis for this determination.

(k) Nothing in this section shall restrict any other right available under existing law or otherwise available to a citizen seeking redress for false, misleading, or deceptive advertisements.

§ 6158.5 Application of article

This article applies to all lawyers, members, law partnerships, law corporations, entities subject to regulation under Section 6155, advertising collectives, cooperatives, or other individuals, including nonlawyers, or groups advertising the availability of legal services. Subdivisions (a) to (k), inclusive, of Section 6158.4 do not apply to qualified legal services projects as defined in Article 14 (commencing with Section 6210) and nonprofit lawyer referral services certified under Section 6155. Sections 6157 to 6158.5, inclusive, do not apply to the media in which the advertising is displayed or to an advertising agency that prepares the contents of an advertisement and is not directly involved in the formation or operation of lawyer advertising collectives or cooperatives, referral services, or other groups existing primarily for the purpose of advertising the availability of legal services or making referrals to attorneys.

§ 6158.7 Violation as cause for discipline by state bar

A violation of Section 6158, 6158.1, or 6158.3 by a member shall be cause for discipline by the State Bar. In addition to the existing grounds for initiating a disciplinary proceeding set forth in a statute or in the Rules of Professional Conduct, the State Bar may commence an investigation based upon a complaint filed by a person pursuant to Section 6158.4. The State Bar's decision pursuant to subdivision (a) of Section 6158.4 shall be admissible, but shall not be determinative, in any disciplinary proceeding brought as a result of that complaint.

§ 6159. Report by court of article violators

The court shall report the name, address, and professional license number of any person found in violation of this article to the appropriate professional licensing agency for review and possible disciplinary action.

§ 6159.1 Retention of advertising copy by payor

A true and correct copy of any advertisement made by a person or member shall be retained for one year by the person or member who pays for an advertisement soliciting employment of legal services.

§ 6159.2 Rights and duties under other laws

(a) Nothing in this article shall be deemed to limit or preclude enforcement of any other provision of law, or of any court rule, or of the State Bar Rules of Professional Conduct.

(b) Nothing in this article shall limit the right of advertising protected under the Constitution of the State of California or of the United States. If any provision of this article is found to violate either Constitution, that provision is severable and the remaining provisions shall be enforceable without the severed provision.

ARTICLE 13. ARBITRATION OF ATTORNEYS' FEES

§ 6200. Establishment of system and procedure; applicability of article; voluntary or mandatory nature; rules; immunity of arbitrator; powers of arbitrator; confidentiality of mediation

(a) The board of trustees shall, by rule, establish, maintain, and administer a system and procedure for the arbitration, and may establish, maintain, and administer a system and procedure for mediation of disputes concerning fees, costs, or both, charged for professional services by members of the State Bar or by members of the bar of other jurisdictions. The rules may include provision for a filing fee in the amount as the board may, from time to time, determine.

(b) This article shall not apply to any of the following:

(1) Disputes where a member of the State Bar of California is also admitted to practice in another jurisdiction or where an attorney is only admitted to practice in another jurisdiction, and he or she maintains no office in the State of California, and no material portion of the services were rendered in the State of California.

(2) Claims for affirmative relief against the attorney for damages or otherwise based upon alleged malpractice or professional misconduct, except as provided in subdivision (a) of Section 6203.

(3) Disputes where the fee or cost to be paid by the client or on his or her behalf has been determined pursuant to statute or court order.

(c) Unless the client has agreed in writing to arbitration under this article of all disputes concerning fees, costs, or both, arbitration under this article shall be voluntary for a client and shall be mandatory for an attorney if commenced by a client. Mediation under this article shall be voluntary for an attorney and a client.

(d) The board of trustees shall adopt rules to allow arbitration and mediation of attorney fee and cost disputes under this article to proceed under arbitration and mediation systems sponsored by local bar associations in this state. Rules of procedure promulgated by local bar associations are subject to review by the board or a committee designated by the board to ensure that they provide for a fair, impartial, and speedy hearing and award.

(e) In adopting or reviewing rules of arbitration under this section the board shall provide that the panel shall include one attorney member whose area of practice is either, at the option of the client, civil law, if the attorney's representation involved civil law, or criminal law, if the attorney's representation involved criminal law, as follows:

(1) If the panel is composed of three members the panel shall include one attorney member whose area of practice is either, at the option of the client, civil or criminal law, and shall include one lay member.

(2) If the panel is composed of one member, that member shall be an attorney whose area of practice is either, at the option of the client, civil or criminal law.

(f) In any arbitration or mediation conducted pursuant to this article by the State Bar or by a local bar association, pursuant to rules of procedure approved by the board of trustees, an arbitrator or mediator, as well as the arbitrating association and its directors, officers, and employees, shall have the same immunity which attaches in judicial proceedings.

(g) In the conduct of arbitrations under this article the arbitrator or arbitrators may do all of the following:

(1) Take and hear evidence pertaining to the proceeding.

(2) Administer oaths and affirmations.

(3) Issue subpoenas for the attendance of witnesses and the production of books, papers, and documents pertaining to the proceeding.

(h) Participation in mediation is a voluntary consensual process, based on direct negotiations between the attorney and his or her client, and is an extension of the negotiated settlement process. All discussions and offers of settlement are confidential and may not be disclosed in any subsequent arbitration or other proceedings.

§ 6201. Notice to client and state bar; stay of action; right to arbitration; waiver by client

(a) The rules adopted by the board of trustees shall provide that an attorney shall forward a written notice to the client prior to or at the time of service of summons or claim in an action against the client or prior to or at the commencement of any other proceeding against client under a contract between attorney and client which provides for an alternative to arbitration under this article, for recovery of fees, costs, or both. The written notice shall be in the form that the board of trustees prescribes, and shall include a statement of the client's right to arbitration under this article. Failure to give this notice shall be a ground for the dismissal of the action or other proceeding. The notice shall not be required, however, prior to initiating mediation of the dispute.

The rules adopted by the board of trustees shall provide that the client's failure to request arbitration within 30 days after receipt of notice from the attorney shall be deemed a waiver of the client's right to arbitration under the provisions of this article.

(b) If an attorney, or the attorney's assignee, commences an action in any court or any other proceeding and the client is entitled to maintain arbitration under this article, and the dispute is not one to which subdivision (b) of Section 6200 applies, the client may stay the action or other proceeding by serving and filing a request for arbitration in accordance with the rules established by the board of trustees pursuant to subdivision (a) of Section 6200. The request for arbitration shall be served and filed prior to the filing of an answer in the action or equivalent response in the other proceeding; failure to so request arbitration prior to the filing of an answer or equivalent response shall be deemed a waiver of the client's right to arbitration under the provisions of this article if notice of the client's right to arbitration was given pursuant to subdivision (a).

(c) Upon filing and service of the request for arbitration, the action or other proceeding shall be automatically stayed until the award of the arbitrators is issued or the arbitration is otherwise terminated. The stay may be vacated in whole or in part, after a hearing duly noticed by any party or the court, if and to the extent the court finds that the matter is not appropriate for arbitration under the provisions of this article. The action or other proceeding may thereafter proceed subject to the provisions of Section 6204.

(d) A client's right to request or maintain arbitration under the provisions of this article is waived by the client commencing an action or filing any pleading seeking either of the following: (1) Judicial resolution of a fee dispute to which this article applies. (2) Affirmative relief against the attorney for damages or otherwise based upon alleged malpractice or professional misconduct.

(e) If the client waives the right to arbitration under this article, the parties may stipulate to set aside the waiver and to proceed with arbitration.

§ 6203. Award; contents; damages and offset; fees and costs; finality of award; appellate fees and costs; attorney inactive status and penalties

(a) The award shall be in writing and signed by the arbitrators concurring therein. It shall include a determination of all the questions submitted to the arbitrators, the decision of which is necessary in order to determine the controversy. The award shall not include any award to either party for costs or attorney's fees incurred in preparation for or in the course of the fee arbitration proceeding, notwithstanding any contract between the parties providing for such an award or attorney's fees. However, the filing fee paid may be allocated between the parties by the arbitrators. This section shall not preclude an award of costs or attorney's fees to either party by a court pursuant to subdivision (c) of this section or of subdivision (d) of Section 6204. The State Bar, or the local bar association delegated by the State Bar to conduct the arbitration, shall deliver to each of the parties with the award, an original declaration of service of the award.

Evidence relating to claims of malpractice and professional misconduct, shall be admissible only to the extent that those claims bear upon the fees, costs, or both, to which the attorney is entitled. The arbitrators shall not award affirmative relief, in the form of damages or offset or otherwise, for injuries underlying the claim. Nothing in this section shall be construed to prevent the arbitrators from awarding a refund of unearned prepaid fees.

(b) Even if the parties to the arbitration have not agreed in writing to be bound, the arbitration award shall become binding upon the passage of 30 days after service of notice of the award, unless a party has, within the 30 days, sought a trial after arbitration pursuant to Section 6204. If an action has previously been filed in any court, any petition to confirm, correct, or vacate the award shall be to the court in which the action is pending, and may be served by mail on any party who has appeared, as provided in Chapter 4 (commencing with Section 1003) of Title 14 of Part 2 of the Code of Civil Procedure; otherwise it shall be in the same manner as provided in Chapter 4 (commencing with Section 1285) of Title 9 of Part 3 of the Code of Civil Procedure. If no action is pending in any court, the award may be confirmed, corrected, or vacated by petition to the court having jurisdiction over the amount of the arbitration award, but otherwise in the same manner as provided in Chapter 4 (commencing with Section 1285) of Title 9 of Part 3 of the Code of Civil Procedure.

(c) Neither party to the arbitration may recover costs or attorney's fees incurred in preparation for or in the course of the fee arbitration proceeding with the exception of the filing fee paid pursuant to subdivision (a) of this section. However, a court confirming, correcting, or vacating an award under this section may award to the prevailing party reasonable fees and costs including, if applicable, fees or costs on appeal, incurred in obtaining confirmation, correction, or vacation of the award. The party obtaining judgment confirming, correcting, or vacating the award shall be the prevailing party except that, without regard to consideration of who the prevailing party may be, if a party did not appear at the arbitration hearing in the manner provided by the rules adopted by the board of trustees, that party shall not be entitled to attorney's fees or costs upon confirmation, correction, or vacation of the award.

(d)(1) In any matter arbitrated under this article in which the award is binding or has become binding by operation of law or has become a judgment either after confirmation under subdivision (c) or after a trial after arbitration under Section 6204, or in any matter mediated under this article, if: (A) the award, judgment, or agreement reached after mediation includes a refund of fees or costs, or both, to the client and (B) the attorney has not complied with that award, judgment, or agreement the State Bar shall enforce the award, judgment, or agreement by placing the attorney on involuntary inactive status until the refund has been paid.

(2) The State Bar shall provide for an administrative procedure to determine whether an award, judgment, or agreement should be enforced pursuant to this subdivision. An award, judgment, or agreement shall be so enforced if either of the following applies:

(A) The State Bar shows that the attorney has failed to comply with a binding fee arbitration award, judgment, or agreement rendered pursuant to this article.

(B) The attorney has not proposed a payment plan acceptable to the client or the State Bar.

However, the award, judgment, or agreement shall not be so enforced if the attorney has demonstrated that he or she (i) is not personally responsible for making or ensuring payment of the refund, or (ii) is unable to pay the refund.

(3) An attorney who has failed to comply with a binding award, judgment, or agreement shall pay administrative penalties or reasonable costs, or both, as directed by the State Bar. Penalties imposed shall not exceed 20 percent of the amount to be refunded to the client or one thousand dollars ($1,000), whichever is greater. Any penalties or costs, or both, that are not paid shall be added to the membership fee of the attorney for the next calendar year.

(4) The board shall terminate the inactive enrollment upon proof that the attorney has complied with the award, judgment, or agreement and upon payment of any costs or penalties, or both, assessed as a result of the attorney's failure to comply.

(5) A request for enforcement under this subdivision shall be made within four years from the date (A) the arbitration award was mailed, (B) the judgment was entered, or (C) the date the agreement was signed. In an arbitrated matter, however, in no event shall a request be made prior to 100 days from the date of the service of a signed copy of the award. In cases where the award is appealed, a request shall not be made prior to 100 days from the date the award has become final as set forth in this section.

ARTICLE 14. FUNDS FOR THE PROVISION OF LEGAL SERVICES TO INDIGENT PERSONS

§ 6210. Legislative findings; purpose

The Legislature finds that, due to insufficient funding, existing programs providing free legal services in civil matters to indigent persons, especially underserved client groups, such as the elderly, the disabled, juveniles, and non-English-speaking persons, do not adequately meet the needs of these persons. It is the purpose of this article to expand the availability and improve the quality of existing free legal services in civil matters to indigent persons, and to initiate new programs that will provide services to them. The Legislature finds that the use of funds collected by the State Bar pursuant to this article for these purposes is in the public interest, is a proper use of the funds, and is consistent with essential public and governmental purposes in the judicial branch of government. The Legislature further finds that the expansion, improvement, and initiation of legal services to indigent persons will aid in the advancement of the science of jurisprudence and the improvement of the administration of justice.

§ 6211. Establishment by attorney by IOLTA account; interest and dividends earned to be paid to state bar; other accounts not prohibited; rules of professional conduct, authority of supreme court or state bar not affected

(a) An attorney or law firm, which in the course of the practice of law receives or disburses trust funds, shall establish and maintain an IOLTA account in which the attorney or law firm shall deposit or invest all client deposits or funds invested for a short period of time. All such client funds may be deposited in a single unsegregated account. The interest and dividends earned on all such accounts shall be paid to the State Bar of California to be used for the purposes set forth in this article.

(b) Nothing in this article shall be construed to prohibit an attorney or law firm from establishing one or more interest bearing bank accounts or other trust investments as may be permitted by the Supreme Court, with the interest or dividends earned on the accounts payable to clients for trust funds not deposited in accordance with subdivision (a).

(c) With the approval of the Supreme Court, the State Bar may formulate and enforce rules of professional conduct pertaining to the use by attorneys or law firms of interest bearing trust accounts for unsegregated client funds pursuant to this article.

(d) Nothing in this article shall be construed as affecting or impairing the disciplinary powers and authority of the Supreme Court or of the State Bar or as modifying the statutes and rules governing the conduct of members of the State Bar.

§ 6212. Establishment by attorney of IOLTA account; amount of interest; remittance to state bar; reporting of IOLTA account compliance and other information; statements and reports

An attorney who, or a law firm which, establishes an interest bearing demand trust account pursuant to subdivision (a) of Section 6211 shall comply with all of the following provisions:

(a) The IOLTA account shall be established and maintained with an eligible institution offering or making available an IOLTA account that meets the requirements of this article. The IOLTA account shall be established and maintained consistent with the attorney or law firm's duties of professional responsibility. An eligible financial institution shall have no responsibility for selecting the deposit or investment product chosen for the IOLTA account.

(b) Except as provided in subdivision (f), the rate of interest or dividends payable on any IOLTA account shall not be less than the interest rate or dividends generally paid by the eligible institution to nonattorney customers on accounts of the same type meeting the same minimum balance and other eligibility requirements as the IOLTA account. In determining the interest rate or dividend payable on any IOLTA account, an eligible institution may consider, in addition to the balance in the IOLTA account, risk or other factors customarily considered by the eligible institution when setting the interest rate or dividends for its non-IOLTA accounts, provided that the factors do not discriminate between IOLTA customers and non-IOLTA customers and that these factors do not include the fact that the account is an IOLTA account. The eligible institution shall calculate interest and dividends in accordance with its standard practice for non-IOLTA customers. Nothing in this article shall preclude an eligible institution from paying a higher interest rate or dividend on an IOLTA account or from electing to waive any fees and service charges on an IOLTA account.

(c) Reasonable fees may be deducted from the interest or dividends remitted on an IOLTA account only at the rates and in accordance with the customary practices of the eligible institution for non-IOLTA customers. No other fees or service charges may be deducted from the interest or dividends earned on an IOLTA account. Unless and until the State Bar enacts regulations exempting from compliance with subdivision (a) of Section 6211 those accounts for which maintenance fees exceed the interest or dividends paid, an eligible institution may deduct the fees and service charges in excess of the interest or dividends paid on an IOLTA account from the aggregate interest and dividends remitted to the State Bar. Fees and service charges other than reasonable fees shall be the sole responsibility of, and may only be charged to, the attorney or law firm maintaining the IOLTA account. Fees and charges shall not be assessed against or deducted from the principal of any IOLTA account. It is the intent of the Legislature that the State Bar develop policies so that eligible institutions not incur uncompensated administrative costs in adapting their systems to comply with the provisions of Chapter 422 of the Statutes of 2007 or in making investment products available to IOLTA members.

(d) The attorney or law firm shall report IOLTA account compliance and all other IOLTA account information required by the State Bar in the manner specified by the State Bar.

(e) The eligible institution shall be directed to do all of the following:

(1) To remit interest or dividends on the IOLTA account, less reasonable fees, to the State Bar, at least quarterly.

(2) To transmit to the State Bar with each remittance a statement showing the name of the attorney or law firm for which the remittance is sent, for each account the rate of interest applied or dividend paid, the amount and type of fees deducted, if any, and the average balance for each account for each month of the period for which the report is made.

(3) To transmit to the attorney or law firm customer at the same time a report showing the amount paid to the State Bar for that period, the rate of interest or dividend applied, the amount of fees and service charges deducted, if any, and the average daily account balance for each month of the period for which the report is made.

(f) An eligible institution has no affirmative duty to offer or make investment products available to IOLTA customers. However, if an eligible institution offers or makes investment products available to non-IOLTA customers, in order to remain an IOLTA-eligible institution, it shall make those products available to IOLTA customers or pay an interest rate on the IOLTA deposit account that is comparable to the rate of return or the dividends generally paid on that investment product for similar customers meeting the same minimum balance and other requirements applicable to the investment product. If the eligible institution elects to pay that higher interest rate, the eligible institution may subject the IOLTA deposit account to equivalent fees and charges assessable against the investment product.

§ 6213. Definitions

As used in this article:

(a) "Qualified legal services project" means either of the following:

(1) A nonprofit project incorporated and operated exclusively in California that provides as its primary purpose and function legal services without charge to indigent persons and that has quality control procedures approved by the State Bar of California.

(2) A program operated exclusively in California by a nonprofit law school accredited by the State Bar of California that meets the requirements of subparagraphs (A) and (B).

(A) The program shall have operated for at least two years at a cost of at least twenty thousand dollars ($20,000) per year as an identifiable law school unit with a primary purpose and function of providing legal services without charge to indigent persons.

(B) The program shall have quality control procedures approved by the State Bar of California.

(b) "Qualified support center" means an incorporated nonprofit legal services center that has as its primary purpose and function the provision of legal training, legal technical assistance, or advocacy support without charge and which actually provides through an office in California a significant level of legal training, legal technical assistance, or advocacy support without charge to qualified legal services projects on a statewide basis in California.

(c) "Recipient" means a qualified legal services project or support center receiving financial assistance under this article.

(d) "Indigent person" means a person whose income is (1) 125 percent or less of the current poverty threshold established by the United States Office of Management and Budget, or (2) who is eligible for Supplemental Security Income or free services under the Older Americans Act or Developmentally Disabled Assistance Act. With regard to a project that provides free services of attorneys in private practice without compensation, "indigent person" also means a person whose income is 75 percent or less of the maximum levels of income for lower income households as defined in Section 50079.5 of the Health and Safety Code. For the purpose of this subdivision, the income of a person who is disabled shall be determined after deducting the costs of medical and other disability-related special expenses.

(e) "Fee generating case" means any case or matter that, if undertaken on behalf of an indigent person by an attorney in private practice, reasonably may be expected to result in payment of a fee for legal services from an award to a client, from public funds, or from the opposing party. A case shall not be considered fee generating if adequate representation is unavailable and any of the following circumstances exist:

(1) The recipient has determined that free referral is not possible because of any of the following reasons:

(A) The case has been rejected by the local lawyer referral service, or if there is no such service, by two attorneys in private practice who have experience in the subject matter of the case.

(B) Neither the referral service nor any attorney will consider the case without payment of a consultation fee.

(C) The case if of the type that attorneys in private practice in the area ordinarily do not accept, or do not accept without prepayment of a fee.

(D) Emergency circumstances compel immediate action before referral can be made, but the client is advised that, if appropriate and consistent with professional responsibility, referral will be attempted at a later time.

(2) Recovery of damages is not the principal object of the case and a request for damages is merely ancillary to an action for equitable or other nonpecuniary relief, or inclusion of a counterclaim requesting damages is necessary for effective defense or because of applicable rules governing joinder of counterclaims.

(3) A court has appointed a recipient or an employee of a recipient pursuant to a statute or a court rule or practice of equal applicability to all attorneys in the jurisdiction.

(4) The case involves the rights of a claimant under a publicly supported benefit program for which entitlement to benefit is based on need.

(f) "Legal Services Corporation" means the Legal Services Corporation established under the Legal Services Corporation Act of 1974, (P.L. 93–355; 42 U.S.C. Sec. 2996 et seq.).

(g) "Older Americans Act" means the Older Americans Act of 1965, as amended (P.L. 89–73; 42 U.S.C. Sec. 3001 et seq.).

(h) "Developmentally Disabled Assistance Act" means the Developmentally Disabled Assistance and Bill of Rights Act of 1975, as amended (P.L. 94–103; 42 U.S.C. Sec. 6001 et seq.).

(i) "Supplemental security income recipient" means an individual receiving or eligible to receive payments under Title XVI of the federal Social Security Act, or payments under Chapter 3 (commencing with Section 12000) of Part 3 of Division 9 of the Welfare and Institutions Code.

(j) "IOLTA account" means an account or investment product established and maintained pursuant to subdivision (a) of Section 6211 that is any of the following:

(1) An interest-bearing checking account.

(2) An investment sweep product that is a daily (overnight) financial institution repurchase agreement or an open-end money-market fund.

(3) An investment product authorized by California Supreme Court rule or order.

A daily financial institution repurchase agreement shall be fully collateralized by United States Government Securities or other comparably conservative debt securities, and may be established only with any eligible institution that is "well-capitalized" or "adequately capitalized" as those terms are defined by applicable federal statutes and regulations. An open-end money-market fund shall be invested solely in United States Government Securities or repurchase agreements fully collateralized by United States Government Securities or other comparably conservative debt securities, shall hold itself out as a "money-market fund" as that term is defined by federal statutes and regulations under the Investment Company Act of 1940 (15 U.S.C. Sec. 80a–1 et seq.), and, at the time of the investment, shall have total assets of at least two hundred fifty million dollars ($250,000,000).

(k) "Eligible institution" means either of the following:

(1) A bank, savings and loan, or other financial institution regulated by a federal or state agency that pays interest or dividends in the IOLTA account and carries deposit insurance from an agency of the federal government.

(2) Any other type of financial institution authorized by the Supreme Court.

§ 6214. Qualified legal service projects

(a) Projects meeting the requirements of subdivision (a) of Section 6213 which are funded either in whole or part by the Legal Services Corporation or with Older American Act funds shall be presumed qualified legal services projects for the purpose of this article.

(b) Projects meeting the requirements of subdivision (a) of Section 6213 but not qualifying under the presumption specified in subdivision (a) shall qualify for funds under this article if they meet all of the following additional criteria:

(1) They receive cash funds from other sources in the amount of at least twenty thousand dollars ($20,000) per year to support free legal representation to indigent persons.

(2) They have demonstrated community support for the operation of a viable ongoing program.

(3) They provide one or both of the following special services:

(A) The coordination of the recruitment of substantial numbers of attorneys in private practice to provide free legal representation to indigent persons or to qualified legal services projects in California.

(B) The provision of legal representation, training, or technical assistance on matters concerning special client groups, including the elderly, the disabled, juveniles, and non-English-speaking groups, or on matters of specialized substantive law important to the special client groups.

§ 6214.5 Qualified legal services projects; eligibility for distributions of funds

A law school program that meets the definition of a "qualified legal services project" as defined in paragraph (2) of subdivision (a) of Section 6213, and that applied to the State Bar for funding under this article not later than February 17, 1984, shall be deemed eligible for all distributions of funds made under Section 6216.

§ 6215. Qualified support centers

(a) Support centers satisfying the qualifications specified in subdivision (b) of Section 6213 which were operating an office and providing services in California on December 31, 1980, shall be presumed to be qualified support centers for the purposes of this article.

(b) Support centers not qualifying under the presumption specified in subdivision (a) may qualify as a support center by meeting both of the following additional criteria:

(1) Meeting quality control standards established by the State Bar.

(2) Being deemed to be of special need by a majority of the qualified legal services projects.

§ 6216. Distribution of funds

The State Bar shall distribute all moneys received under the program established by this article for the provision of civil legal services to indigent persons. The funds first shall be distributed 18 months from the effective date of this article, or upon such a date, as shall be determined by the State Bar, that adequate funds are available to initiate the program. Thereafter, the funds shall be distributed on an annual basis. All distributions of funds shall be made in the following order and in the following manner:

(a) To pay the actual administrative costs of the program, including any costs incurred after the adoption of this article and a reasonable reserve therefor.

(b) Eighty-five percent of the funds remaining after payment of administrative costs allocated pursuant to this article shall be distributed to qualified legal services projects. Distribution shall be by a pro rata county-by-county formula based upon the number of persons whose income is 125 percent or less of the current poverty threshold per county. For the purposes of this section, the source of data identifying the number of persons per county shall be the latest available figures from the United States Department of Commerce, Bureau of the Census. Projects from more than one county may pool their funds to operate a joint, multicounty legal services project serving each of their respective counties.

(1)(A) In any county which is served by more than one qualified legal services project, the State Bar shall distribute funds for the county to those projects which apply on a pro rata basis, based upon the amount of their total budget expended in the prior year for legal services in that county as compared to the total expended in the prior year for legal services by all qualified legal services projects applying therefor in the county. In determining the amount of funds to be allocated to a qualified legal services project specified in paragraph (2) of subdivision (a) of Section 6213, the State Bar shall recognize only expenditures attributable to the representation of indigent persons as constituting the budget of the program.

(B) The State Bar shall reserve 10 percent of the funds allocated to the county for distribution to programs meeting the standards of subparagraph (A) of paragraph (3) and paragraphs (1) and (2) of subdivision (b) of Section 6214 and which perform the services described in subparagraph (A) of paragraph (3) of Section 6214 as their principal means of delivering legal services. The State Bar shall distribute the funds for that county to those programs which apply on a pro rata basis, based upon the amount of their total budget expended for free legal services in that county as compared to the total expended for free legal services by all programs meeting the standards of subparagraph (A) of paragraph (3) and paragraphs (1) and (2) of subdivision (b) of Section 6214 in that county. The State Bar shall distribute any funds for which no program has qualified pursuant hereto, in accordance with the provisions of subparagraph (A) of paragraph (1) of this subdivision.

(2) In any county in which there is no qualified legal services projects providing services, the State Bar shall reserve for the remainder of the fiscal year for distribution the pro rata share of funds as provided for by this article. Upon application of a qualified legal services project proposing to provide legal services to the indigent of the county, the State Bar shall distribute the funds to the project. Any funds not so distributed shall be added to the funds to be distributed the following year.

(c) Fifteen percent of the funds remaining after payment of administrative costs allocated for the purposes of this article shall be distributed equally by the State Bar to qualified support centers which apply for the funds. The funds provided to support centers shall be used only for the provision of legal services within California. Qualified support centers that receive funds to provide services to qualified legal services projects from sources other than this article, shall submit and shall have approved by the State Bar a plan assuring that the services funded under this article are in addition to those already funded for qualified legal services projects by other sources.

§ 6217. Maintenance of quality services, professional standards, attorney-client privilege; funds to be expended in accordance with article; interference with attorney prohibited

With respect to the provision of legal assistance under this article, each recipient shall ensure all of the following:

(a) The maintenance of quality service and professional standards.

(b) The expenditure of funds received in accordance with the provisions of this article.

(c) The preservation of the attorney-client privilege in any case, and the protection of the integrity of the adversary process from any impairment in furnishing legal assistance to indigent persons.

(d) That no one shall interfere with any attorney funded in whole or in part by this article in carrying out his or her professional responsibility to his or her client as established by the rules of professional responsibility and this chapter.

§ 6218. Eligibility for services; establishment of guidelines; funds to be expended in accordance with article

All legal services projects and support centers receiving funds pursuant to this article shall adopt financial eligibility guidelines for indigent persons.

(a) Qualified legal services programs shall ensure that funds appropriated pursuant to this article shall be used solely to defray the costs of providing legal services to indigent persons or for such other purposes as set forth in this article.

(b) Funds received pursuant to this article by support centers shall only be used to provide services to qualified legal services projects as defined in subdivision (a) of Section 6213 which are used pursuant to a plan as required by subdivision (c) of Section 6216, or as permitted by Section 6219.

§ 6219. Provision of work opportunities and scholarships for disadvantaged law students

Qualified legal services projects and support centers may use funds provided under this article to provide work opportunities with pay, and where feasible, scholarships for disadvantaged law students to help defray their law school expenses.

§ 6220. Private attorneys providing legal services without charge; support center services

Attorneys in private practice who are providing legal services without charge to indigent persons shall not be disqualified from receiving the services of the qualified support centers.

§ 6221. Services for indigent members of disadvantaged and underserved groups

Qualified legal services projects shall make significant efforts to utilize 20 percent of the funds allocated under this article for increasing the availability of services to the elderly, the disabled, juveniles, or other indigent persons who are members of disadvantaged and underserved groups within their service area.

§ 6222. Financial statements; submission to state bar; state bar report

A recipient of funds allocated pursuant to this article annually shall submit a financial statement to the State Bar, including an audit of the funds by a certified public accountant or a fiscal review approved by the State Bar, a report demonstrating the programs on which they were expended, a report on the recipient's compliance with the requirements of Section 6217, and progress in meeting the service expansion requirements of Section 6221.

The Board of Governors of the State Bar shall include a report of receipts of funds under this article, expenditures for administrative costs, and disbursements of the funds, on a county-by-county basis, in the annual report of State Bar receipts and expenditures required pursuant to Section 6145.

§ 6223. Expenditure of funds; prohibitions

No funds allocated by the State Bar pursuant to this article shall be used for any of the following purposes:

(a) The provision of legal assistance with respect to any fee generating case, except in accordance with guidelines which shall be promulgated by the State Bar.

(b) The provision of legal assistance with respect to any criminal proceeding.

(c) The provision of legal assistance, except to indigent persons or except to provide support services to qualified legal services projects as defined by this article.

§ 6224. State bar; powers; determination of qualifications to receive funds; denial of funds; termination; procedures

The State Bar shall have the power to determine that an applicant for funding is not qualified to receive funding, to deny future funding, or to terminate existing funding because the recipient is not operating in compliance with the requirements or restrictions of this article.

A denial of an application for funding or for future funding or an action by the State Bar to terminate an existing grant of funds under this article shall not become final until the applicant or recipient has been afforded reasonable notice and an opportunity for a timely and fair hearing. Pending final determination of any hearing held with reference to termination of funding, financial assistance shall be continued at its existing level on a month-to-month basis. Hearings for denial shall be conducted by an impartial hearing officer whose decision shall be final. The hearing officer shall render a decision no later than 30 days after the conclusion of the hearing. Specific procedures governing the conduct of the hearings of this section shall be determined by the State Bar pursuant to Section 6225.

§ 6225. Implementation of article; adoption of rules and regulations; procedures

The Board of Trustees of the State Bar shall adopt the regulations and procedures necessary to implement this article and to ensure that the funds allocated herein are utilized to provide civil legal services to indigent persons, especially underserved client groups such as but not limited to the elderly, the disabled, juveniles, and non-English-speaking persons.

In adopting the regulations the Board of Trustees shall comply with the following procedures:

(a) The board shall publish a preliminary draft of the regulations and procedures, which shall be distributed, together with notice of the hearings required by subdivision (b), to commercial banking institutions, to members of the State Bar, and to potential recipients of funds.

(b) The board shall hold at least two public hearings, one in southern California and one in northern California where affected and interested parties shall be afforded an opportunity to present oral and written testimony regarding the proposed regulations and procedures.

§ 6226. Implementation of article; resolution

The program authorized by this article shall become operative only upon the adoption of a resolution by the Board of Trustees of the State Bar stating that regulations have been adopted pursuant to Section 6225 which conform the program to all applicable tax and banking statutes, regulations, and rulings.

§ 6227. Credit of state not pledged

Nothing in this article shall create an obligation or pledge of the credit of the State of California or of the State Bar of California. Claims arising by reason of acts done pursuant to this article shall be limited to the moneys generated hereunder.

§ 6228. Severability

If any provision of this article or the application thereof to any group or circumstances is held invalid, such invalidity shall not affect the other provisions or applications of this article which can be given effect without the invalid provision or application, and to this end the provisions of this article are severable.

NEW YORK RULES OF PROFESSIONAL CONDUCT (2016)

(Effective 1/1/16)

[In 2008, New York adopted a set of rules based upon the Model Rules. It is effective on April 1, 2009. The Court amended these rules in 2013 and in 2015. Ed.]

Table of Contents

Rule 1.0: Terminology

(a) "Advertisement" means any public or private communication made by or on behalf of a lawyer or law firm about that lawyer or law firm's services, the primary purpose of which is for the retention of the lawyer or law firm. It does not include communications to existing clients or other lawyers.

(b) "Belief" or "believes" denotes that the person involved actually believes the fact in question to be true. A person's belief may be inferred from circumstances.

(c) "Computer-accessed communication" means any communication made by or on behalf of a lawyer or law firm that is disseminated through the use of a computer or related electronic device, including, but not limited to, web sites, weblogs, search engines, electronic mail, banner advertisements, pop-up and pop-under advertisements, chat rooms, list servers, instant messaging, or other internet presences, and any attachments or links related thereto.

(d) "Confidential information" is defined in Rule 1.6.

(e) "Confirmed in writing" denotes (i) a writing from the person to the lawyer confirming that the person has given consent, (ii) a writing that the lawyer promptly transmits to the person confirming the person's oral consent, or (iii) a statement by the person made on the record of any proceeding before a tribunal. If it is not feasible to obtain or transmit the writing at the time the person gives oral consent, then the lawyer must obtain or transmit it within a reasonable time thereafter.

(f) "Differing interests" include every interest that will adversely affect either the judgment or the loyalty of a lawyer to a client, whether it be a conflicting, inconsistent, diverse, or other interest.

(g) "Domestic relations matter" denotes representation of a client in a claim, action or proceeding, or preliminary to the filing of a claim, action or proceeding, in either Supreme Court or Family Court, or in any court of appellate jurisdiction, for divorce, separation, annulment, custody, visitation, maintenance, child support or alimony, or to enforce or modify a judgment or order in connection with any such claim, action or proceeding.

(h) "Firm" or "law firm" includes, but is not limited to, a lawyer or lawyers in a law partnership, professional corporation, sole proprietorship or other association authorized to practice law; or lawyers employed in a qualified legal assistance organization, a government law office, or the legal department of a corporation or other organization.

(i) "Fraud" or "fraudulent" denotes conduct that is fraudulent under the substantive or procedural law of the applicable jurisdiction or has a purpose to deceive, provided that it does not include conduct that, although characterized as fraudulent by statute or administrative rule, lacks an element of scienter, deceit, intent to mislead, or knowing failure to correct misrepresentations that can be reasonably expected to induce detrimental reliance by another.

(j) "Informed consent" denotes the agreement by a person to a proposed course of conduct after the lawyer has communicated information adequate for the person to make an informed decision, and after the lawyer has adequately explained to the person the material risks of the proposed course of conduct and reasonably available alternatives.

(k) "Knowingly," "known," "know," or "knows" denotes actual knowledge of the fact in question. A person's knowledge may be inferred from circumstances.

(*l*) "Matter" includes any litigation, judicial or administrative proceeding, case, claim, application, request for a ruling or other determination, contract, controversy, investigation, charge, accusation, arrest, negotiation, arbitration, mediation or any other representation involving a specific party or parties.

(m) "Partner" denotes a member of a partnership, a shareholder in a law firm organized as a professional legal corporation or a member of an association authorized to practice law.

(n) "Person" includes an individual, a corporation, an association, a trust, a partnership, and any other organization or entity.

(*o*) "Professional legal corporation" means a corporation, or an association treated as a corporation, authorized by law to practice law for profit.

(p) "Qualified legal assistance organization" means an office or organization of one of the four types listed in Rule 7.2(b)(1)-(4) that meets all of the requirements thereof.

(q) "Reasonable" or "reasonably," when used in relation to conduct by a lawyer, denotes the conduct of a reasonably prudent and competent lawyer. When used in the context of conflict of interest determinations, "reasonable lawyer" denotes a lawyer acting from the perspective of a reasonably prudent and competent lawyer who is personally disinterested in commencing or continuing the representation.

(r) "Reasonable belief" or "reasonably believes," when used in reference to a lawyer, denotes that the lawyer believes the matter in question and that the circumstances are such that the belief is reasonable.

(s) "Reasonably should know," when used in reference to a lawyer, denotes that a lawyer of reasonable prudence and competence would ascertain the matter in question.

(t) "Screened" or "screening" denotes the isolation of a lawyer from any participation in a matter through the timely imposition of procedures within a firm that are reasonably adequate under the circumstances to protect information that the isolated lawyer or the firm is obligated to protect under these Rules or other law.

(u) "Sexual relations" denotes sexual intercourse or the touching of an intimate part of the lawyer or another person for the purpose of sexual arousal, sexual gratification or sexual abuse.

(v) "State" includes the District of Columbia, Puerto Rico, and other federal territories and possessions.

(w) "Tribunal" denotes a court, an arbitrator in an arbitration proceeding or a legislative body, administrative agency or other body acting in an adjudicative capacity. A legislative body, administrative agency or other body acts in an adjudicative capacity when a neutral official, after the presentation of evidence or legal argument by a party or parties, will render a legal judgment directly affecting a party's interests in a particular matter.

(x) "Writing" or "written" denotes a tangible or electronic record of a communication or representation, including handwriting, typewriting, printing, photocopying, photography, audio or video recording and email. A "signed" writing includes an electronic sound, symbol or process attached to or logically associated with a writing and executed or adopted by a person with the intent to sign the writing.

Rule 1.1: Competence

(a) A lawyer should provide competent representation to a client. Competent representation requires the legal knowledge, skill, thoroughness and preparation reasonably necessary for the representation.

(b) A lawyer shall not handle a legal matter that the lawyer knows or should know that the lawyer is not competent to handle, without associating with a lawyer who is competent to handle it.

(c) A lawyer shall not intentionally:

(1) fail to seek the objectives of the client through reasonably available means permitted by law and these Rules; or

(2) prejudice or damage the client during the course of the representation except as permitted or required by these Rules.

Rule 1.2: Scope of Representation and Allocation of Authority Between Client and Lawyer

(a) Subject to the provisions herein, a lawyer shall abide by a client's decisions concerning the objectives of representation and, as required by Rule 1.4, shall consult with the client as to the means by which they are to be pursued. A lawyer shall abide by a client's decision whether to settle a matter. In a criminal case, the lawyer shall abide by the client's decision, after consultation with the lawyer, as to a plea to be entered, whether to waive jury trial and whether the client will testify.

(b) A lawyer's representation of a client, including representation by appointment, does not constitute an endorsement of the client's political, economic, social or moral views or activities.

(c) A lawyer may limit the scope of the representation if the limitation is reasonable under the circumstances, the client gives informed consent and where necessary notice is provided to the tribunal and/or opposing counsel.

(d) A lawyer shall not counsel a client to engage, or assist a client, in conduct that the lawyer knows is illegal or fraudulent, except that the lawyer may discuss the legal consequences of any proposed course of conduct with a client.

(e) A lawyer may exercise professional judgment to waive or fail to assert a right or position of the client, or accede to reasonable requests of opposing counsel, when doing so does not prejudice the rights of the client.

(f) A lawyer may refuse to aid or participate in conduct that the lawyer believes to be unlawful, even though there is some support for an argument that the conduct is legal.

(g) A lawyer does not violate this Rule by being punctual in fulfilling all professional commitments, by avoiding offensive tactics, and by treating with courtesy and consideration all persons involved in the legal process.

Rule 1.3: Diligence

(a) A lawyer shall act with reasonable diligence and promptness in representing a client.

(b) A lawyer shall not neglect a legal matter entrusted to the lawyer.

(c) A lawyer shall not intentionally fail to carry out a contract of employment entered into with a client for professional services, but the lawyer may withdraw as permitted under these Rules.

Rule 1.4: Communication

(a) A lawyer shall:

(1) promptly inform the client of:

(i) any decision or circumstance with respect to which the client's informed consent, as defined in Rule 1.0(j), is required by these Rules;

(ii) any information required by court rule or other law to be communicated to a client; and

(iii) material developments in the matter including settlement or plea offers.

(2) reasonably consult with the client about the means by which the client's objectives are to be accomplished;

(3) keep the client reasonably informed about the status of the matter;

(4) promptly comply with a client's reasonable requests for information; and

(5) consult with the client about any relevant limitation on the lawyer's conduct when the lawyer knows that the client expects assistance not permitted by these Rules or other law.

(b) A lawyer shall explain a matter to the extent reasonably necessary to permit the client to make informed decisions regarding the representation.

Rule 1.5: Fees and Division of Fees

(a) A lawyer shall not make an agreement for, charge, or collect an excessive or illegal fee or expense. A fee is excessive when, after a review of the facts, a reasonable lawyer would be left with a definite and firm conviction that the fee is excessive. The factors to be considered in determining whether a fee is excessive may include the following:

(1) the time and labor required, the novelty and difficulty of the questions involved, and the skill requisite to perform the legal service properly;

(2) the likelihood, if apparent or made known to the client, that the acceptance of the particular employment will preclude other employment by the lawyer;

(3) the fee customarily charged in the locality for similar legal services;

(4) the amount involved and the results obtained;

(5) the time limitations imposed by the client or by circumstances;

(6) the nature and length of the professional relationship with the client;

(7) the experience, reputation and ability of the lawyer or lawyers performing the services; and

(8) whether the fee is fixed or contingent.

(b) A lawyer shall communicate to a client the scope of the representation and the basis or rate of the fee and expenses for which the client will be responsible. This information shall be communicated to the client before or within a reasonable time after commencement of the representation and shall be in writing where required by statute or court rule. This provision shall not apply when the lawyer will charge a regularly represented client on the same basis or rate and perform services that are of the same general kind as previously rendered to and paid for by the client. Any changes in the scope of the representation or the basis or rate of the fee or expenses shall also be communicated to the client.

(c) A fee may be contingent on the outcome of the matter for which the service is rendered, except in a matter in which a contingent fee is prohibited by paragraph (d) or other law. Promptly after a lawyer has been employed in a contingent fee matter, the lawyer shall provide the client with a writing stating the method by which the fee is to be determined, including the percentage or percentages that shall accrue to the lawyer in the event of settlement, trial or appeal; litigation and other expenses to be deducted from the recovery; and whether such expenses are to be deducted before or, if not prohibited by statute or court rule, after the contingent fee is calculated. The writing must clearly notify the client of any expenses for which the client will be liable regardless of whether the client is the prevailing party. Upon conclusion of a contingent fee matter, the lawyer shall provide the client with a writing stating the outcome of the matter and, if there is a recovery, showing the remittance to the client and the method of its determination.

(d) A lawyer shall not enter into an arrangement for, charge or collect:

(1) a contingent fee for representing a defendant in a criminal matter;

(2) a fee prohibited by law or rule of court;

(3) a fee based on fraudulent billing;

(4) a nonrefundable retainer fee; provided that a lawyer may enter into a retainer agreement with a client containing a reasonable minimum fee clause if it defines in plain language and sets forth the circumstances under which such fee may be incurred and how it will be calculated; or

(5) any fee in a domestic relations matter if:

(i) the payment or amount of the fee is contingent upon the securing of a divorce or of obtaining child custody or visitation or is in any way determined by reference to the amount of maintenance, support, equitable distribution, or property settlement;

(ii) a written retainer agreement has not been signed by the lawyer and client setting forth in plain language the nature of the relationship and the details of the fee arrangement; or

(iii) the written retainer agreement includes a security interest, confession of judgment or other lien without prior notice being provided to the client in a signed retainer agreement and approval from a tribunal after notice to the adversary. A lawyer shall not foreclose on a mortgage placed on the marital residence while the spouse who consents to the mortgage remains the titleholder and the residence remains the spouse's primary residence.

(e) In domestic relations matters, a lawyer shall provide a prospective client with a statement of client's rights and responsibilities at the initial conference and prior to the signing of a written retainer agreement.

(f) Where applicable, a lawyer shall resolve fee disputes by arbitration at the election of the client pursuant to a fee arbitration program established by the Chief Administrator of the Courts and approved by the Administrative Board of the Courts.

(g) A lawyer shall not divide a fee for legal services with another lawyer who is not associated in the same law firm unless:

(1) the division is in proportion to the services performed by each lawyer or, by a writing given to the client, each lawyer assumes joint responsibility for the representation;

(2) the client agrees to employment of the other lawyer after a full disclosure that a division of fees will be made, including the share each lawyer will receive, and the client's agreement is confirmed in writing; and

(3) the total fee is not excessive.

(h) Rule 1.5(g) does not prohibit payment to a lawyer formerly associated in a law firm pursuant to a separation or retirement agreement.

Rule 1.6: Confidentiality of Information

(a) A lawyer shall not knowingly reveal confidential information, as defined in this Rule, or use such information to the disadvantage of a client or for the advantage of the lawyer or a third person, unless:

(1) the client gives informed consent, as defined in Rule 1.0(j);

(2) the disclosure is impliedly authorized to advance the best interests of the client and is either reasonable under the circumstances or customary in the professional community; or

(3) the disclosure is permitted by paragraph (b).

"Confidential information" consists of information gained during or relating to the representation of a client, whatever its source, that is (a) protected by the attorney-client privilege, (b) likely to be embarrassing or detrimental to the client if disclosed, or (c) information that the client has requested be kept confidential. "Confidential information" does not ordinarily include (i) a lawyer's legal knowledge or legal research or (ii) information that is generally known in the local community or in the trade, field or profession to which the information relates.

(b) A lawyer may reveal or use confidential information to the extent that the lawyer reasonably believes necessary:

(1) to prevent reasonably certain death or substantial bodily harm;

(2) to prevent the client from committing a crime;

(3) to withdraw a written or oral opinion or representation previously given by the lawyer and reasonably believed by the lawyer still to be relied upon by a third person, where the lawyer has discovered that the opinion or representation was based on materially inaccurate information or is being used to further a crime or fraud;

(4) to secure legal advice about compliance with these Rules or other law by the lawyer, another lawyer associated with the lawyer's firm or the law firm;

(5)(i) to defend the lawyer or the lawyer's employees and associates against an accusation of wrongful conduct; or

(ii) to establish or collect a fee; or

(6) when permitted or required under these Rules or to comply with other law or court order.

(c) A lawyer shall exercise reasonable care to prevent the lawyer's employees, associates, and others whose services are utilized by the lawyer from disclosing or using confidential information of a client, except that a lawyer may reveal the information permitted to be disclosed by paragraph (b) through an employee.

Rule 1.7: Conflict of Interest: Current Clients

(a) Except as provided in paragraph (b), a lawyer shall not represent a client if a reasonable lawyer would conclude that either:

(1) the representation will involve the lawyer in representing differing interests; or

(2) there is a significant risk that the lawyer's professional judgment on behalf of a client will be adversely affected by the lawyer's own financial, business, property or other personal interests.

(b) Notwithstanding the existence of a concurrent conflict of interest under paragraph (a), a lawyer may represent a client if:

(1) the lawyer reasonably believes that the lawyer will be able to provide competent and diligent representation to each affected client;

(2) the representation is not prohibited by law;

(3) the representation does not involve the assertion of a claim by one client against another client represented by the lawyer in the same litigation or other proceeding before a tribunal; and

(4) each affected client gives informed consent, confirmed in writing.

Rule 1.8: Current Clients: Specific Conflict of Interest Rules

(a) A lawyer shall not enter into a business transaction with a client if they have differing interests therein and if the client expects the lawyer to exercise professional judgment therein for the protection of the client, unless:

(1) the transaction is fair and reasonable to the client and the terms of the transaction are fully disclosed and transmitted in writing in a manner that can be reasonably understood by the client;

(2) the client is advised in writing of the desirability of seeking, and is given a reasonable opportunity to seek, the advice of independent legal counsel on the transaction; and

(3) the client gives informed consent, in a writing signed by the client, to the essential terms of the transaction and the lawyer's role in the transaction, including whether the lawyer is representing the client in the transaction.

(b) A lawyer shall not use information relating to representation of a client to the disadvantage of the client unless the client gives informed consent, except as permitted or required by these Rules.

(c) A lawyer shall not:

(1) solicit any gift from a client, including a testamentary gift, for the benefit of the lawyer or a person related to the lawyer; or

(2) prepare on behalf of a client an instrument giving the lawyer or a person related to the lawyer any gift, unless the lawyer or other recipient of the gift is related to the client and a reasonable lawyer would conclude that the transaction is fair and reasonable.

For purposes of this paragraph, related persons include a spouse, child, grandchild, parent, grandparent or other relative or individual with whom the lawyer or the client maintains a close, familial relationship.

(d) Prior to conclusion of all aspects of the matter giving rise to the representation or proposed representation of the client or prospective client, a lawyer shall not negotiate or enter into any arrangement or understanding with:

(1) a client or a prospective client by which the lawyer acquires an interest in literary or media rights with respect to the subject matter of the representation or proposed representation; or

(2) any person by which the lawyer transfers or assigns any interest in literary or media rights with respect to the subject matter of the representation of a client or prospective client.

(e) While representing a client in connection with contemplated or pending litigation, a lawyer shall not advance or guarantee financial assistance to the client, except that:

(1) a lawyer may advance court costs and expenses of litigation, the repayment of which may be contingent on the outcome of the matter;

(2) a lawyer representing an indigent or pro bono client may pay court costs and expenses of litigation on behalf of the client; and

(3) a lawyer, in an action in which an attorney's fee is payable in whole or in part as a percentage of the recovery in the action, may pay on the lawyer's own account court costs and expenses of litigation. In such case, the fee paid to the lawyer from the proceeds of the action may include an amount equal to such costs and expenses incurred.

(f) A lawyer shall not accept compensation for representing a client, or anything of value related to the lawyer's representation of the client, from one other than the client unless:

(1) the client gives informed consent;

(2) there is no interference with the lawyer's independent professional judgment or with the client-lawyer relationship; and

(3) the client's confidential information is protected as required by Rule 1.6.

(g) A lawyer who represents two or more clients shall not participate in making an aggregate settlement of the claims of or against the clients, absent court approval, unless each client gives informed consent in a writing signed by the client. The lawyer's disclosure shall include the existence and nature of all the claims involved and of the participation of each person in the settlement.

(h) A lawyer shall not:

(1) make an agreement prospectively limiting the lawyer's liability to a client for malpractice; or

(2) settle a claim or potential claim for such liability with an unrepresented client or former client unless that person is advised in writing of the desirability of seeking, and is given a reasonable opportunity to seek, the advice of independent legal counsel in connection therewith.

(i) A lawyer shall not acquire a proprietary interest in the cause of action or subject matter of litigation the lawyer is conducting for a client, except that the lawyer may:

(1) acquire a lien authorized by law to secure the lawyer's fee or expenses; and

(2) contract with a client for a reasonable contingent fee in a civil matter subject to Rule 1.5(d) or other law or court rule.

(j)(1) A lawyer shall not:

(i) as a condition of entering into or continuing any professional representation by the lawyer or the lawyer's firm, require or demand sexual relations with any person;

(ii) employ coercion, intimidation or undue influence in entering into sexual relations incident to any professional representation by the lawyer or the lawyer's firm; or

(iii) in domestic relations matters, enter into sexual relations with a client during the course of the lawyer's representation of the client.

(2) Rule 1.8(j)(1) shall not apply to sexual relations between lawyers and their spouses or to ongoing consensual sexual relationships that predate the initiation of the client-lawyer relationship.

(k) Where a lawyer in a firm has sexual relations with a client but does not participate in the representation of that client, the lawyers in the firm shall not be subject to discipline under this Rule solely because of the occurrence of such sexual relations.

Rule 1.9: Duties to Former Clients

(a) A lawyer who has formerly represented a client in a matter shall not thereafter represent another person in the same or a substantially related matter in which that person's interests are materially adverse to the interests of the former client unless the former client gives informed consent, confirmed in writing.

(b) Unless the former client gives informed consent, confirmed in writing, a lawyer shall not knowingly represent a person in the same or a substantially related matter in which a firm with which the lawyer formerly was associated had previously represented a client:

(1) whose interests are materially adverse to that person; and

(2) about whom the lawyer had acquired information protected by Rules 1. 6 or paragraph (c) of this Rule that is material to the matter.

(c) A lawyer who has formerly represented a client in a matter or whose present or former firm has formerly represented a client in a matter shall not thereafter:

(1) use confidential information of the former client protected by Rule 1.6 to the disadvantage of the former client, except as these Rules would permit or require with respect to a current client or when the information has become generally known; or

(2) reveal confidential information of the former client protected by Rule 1.6 except as these Rules would permit or require with respect to a current client.

Rule 1.10: Imputation of Conflicts of Interest

(a) While lawyers are associated in a firm, none of them shall knowingly represent a client when any one of them practicing alone would be prohibited from doing so by Rule 1.7, 1.8 or 1.9, except as otherwise provided therein.

(b) When a lawyer has terminated an association with a firm, the firm is prohibited from thereafter representing a person with interests that the firm knows or reasonably should know are materially adverse to those of a client represented by the formerly associated lawyer and not currently represented by the firm if the firm or any lawyer remaining in the firm has information protected by Rule 1.6 or Rule 1.9(c) that is material to the matter.

(c) When a lawyer becomes associated with a firm, the firm may not knowingly represent a client in a matter that is the same as or substantially related to a matter in which the newly associated lawyer, or a firm with which that lawyer was associated, formerly represented a client whose interests are materially adverse to the prospective or current client unless the newly associated lawyer did not acquire any information protected by Rule 1.6 or Rule 1.9(c) that is material to the current matter.

(d) A disqualification prescribed by this Rule may be waived by the affected client or former client under the conditions stated in Rule 1.7.

(e) A law firm shall make a written record of its engagements, at or near the time of each new engagement, and shall implement and maintain a system by which proposed engagements are checked against current and previous engagements when:

(1) the firm agrees to represent a new client;

(2) the firm agrees to represent an existing client in a new matter;

(3) the firm hires or associates with another lawyer; or

(4) an additional party is named or appears in a pending matter.

(f) Substantial failure to keep records or to implement or maintain a conflict-checking system that complies with paragraph (e) shall be a violation thereof regardless of whether there is another violation of these Rules.

(g) Where a violation of paragraph (e) by a law firm is a substantial factor in causing a violation of paragraph (a) by a lawyer, the law firm, as well as the individual lawyer, shall be responsible for the violation of paragraph (a).

(h) A lawyer related to another lawyer as parent, child, sibling or spouse shall not represent in any matter a client whose interests differ from those of another party to the matter who the lawyer knows is represented by the other lawyer unless the client consents to the representation after full disclosure and the lawyer concludes that the lawyer can adequately represent the interests of the client.

Rule 1.11: Special Conflicts of Interest for Former and Current Government Officers and Employees

(a) Except as law may otherwise expressly provide, a lawyer who has formerly served as a public officer or employee of the government:

(1) shall comply with Rule 1.9(c); and

(2) shall not represent a client in connection with a matter in which the lawyer participated personally and substantially as a public officer or employee, unless the appropriate government agency gives its informed consent, confirmed in writing, to the representation. This provision shall not apply to matters governed by Rule 1.12(a).

(b) When a lawyer is disqualified from representation under paragraph (a), no lawyer in a firm with which that lawyer is associated may knowingly undertake or continue representation in such a matter unless:

(1) the firm acts promptly and reasonably to:

(i) notify, as appropriate, lawyers and nonlawyer personnel within the firm that the personally disqualified lawyer is prohibited from participating in the representation of the current client;

(ii) implement effective screening procedures to prevent the flow of information about the matter between the personally disqualified lawyer and the others in the firm;

(iii) ensure that the disqualified lawyer is apportioned no part of the fee therefrom; and

(iv) give written notice to the appropriate government agency to enable it to ascertain compliance with the provisions of this Rule; and

(2) there are no other circumstances in the particular representation that create an appearance of impropriety.

(c) Except as law may otherwise expressly provide, a lawyer having information that the lawyer knows is confidential government information about a person, acquired when the lawyer was a public officer or employee, may not represent a private client whose interests are adverse to that person in a matter in which the information could be used to the material disadvantage of that person. As used in this Rule, the term "confidential government information" means information that has been obtained under governmental authority and that, at the time this Rule is applied, the government is prohibited by law from disclosing to the public or has a legal privilege not to disclose, and that is not otherwise available to the public. A firm with which that lawyer is associated may undertake or continue representation in the matter only if the disqualified lawyer is timely and effectively screened from any participation in the matter in accordance with the provisions of paragraph (b).

(d) Except as law may otherwise expressly provide, a lawyer currently serving as a public officer or employee shall not:

(1) participate in a matter in which the lawyer participated personally and substantially while in private practice or nongovernmental employment, unless under applicable law no one is, or by lawful delegation may be, authorized to act in the lawyer's stead in the matter; or

(2) negotiate for private employment with any person who is involved as a party or as lawyer for a party in a matter in which the lawyer is participating personally and substantially.

(e) As used in this Rule, the term "matter" as defined in Rule 1.0(*l*) does not include or apply to agency rulemaking functions.

(f) A lawyer who holds public office shall not:

(1) use the public position to obtain, or attempt to obtain, a special advantage in legislative matters for the lawyer or for a client under circumstances where the lawyer knows or it is obvious that such action is not in the public interest;

(2) use the public position to influence, or attempt to influence, a tribunal to act in favor of the lawyer or of a client; or

(3) accept anything of value from any person when the lawyer knows or it is obvious that the offer is for the purpose of influencing the lawyer's action as a public official.

Rule 1.12: Specific Conflicts of Interest for Former Judges, Arbitrators, Mediators or Other Third-Party Neutrals

(a) A lawyer shall not accept private employment in a matter upon the merits of which the lawyer has acted in a judicial capacity.

(b) Except as stated in paragraph (e), and unless all parties to the proceeding give informed consent, confirmed in writing, a lawyer shall not represent anyone in connection with a matter in which the lawyer participated personally and substantially as:

(1) an arbitrator, mediator or other third-party neutral; or

(2) a law clerk to a judge or other adjudicative officer or an arbitrator, mediator or other third-party neutral.

(c) A lawyer shall not negotiate for employment with any person who is involved as a party or as lawyer for a party in a matter in which the lawyer is participating personally and substantially as a judge or other adjudicative officer or as an arbitrator, mediator or other third-party neutral.

(d) When a lawyer is disqualified from representation under this Rule, no lawyer in a firm with which that lawyer is associated may knowingly undertake or continue representation in such a matter unless:

(1) the firm acts promptly and reasonably to:

(i) notify, as appropriate, lawyers and nonlawyer personnel within the firm that the personally disqualified lawyer is prohibited from participating in the representation of the current client;

(ii) implement effective screening procedures to prevent the flow of information about the matter between the personally disqualified lawyer and the others in the firm;

(iii) ensure that the disqualified lawyer is apportioned no part of the fee therefrom; and

(iv) give written notice to the parties and any appropriate tribunal to enable it to ascertain compliance with the provisions of this Rule; and

(2) there are no other circumstances in the particular representation that create an appearance of impropriety.

(e) An arbitrator selected as a partisan of a party in a multimember arbitration panel is not prohibited from subsequently representing that party.

Rule 1.13: Organization as Client

(a) When a lawyer employed or retained by an organization is dealing with the organization's directors, officers, employees, members, shareholders or other constituents, and it appears that the organization's interests may differ from those of the constituents with whom the lawyer is dealing, the lawyer shall explain that the lawyer is the lawyer for the organization and not for any of the constituents.

(b) If a lawyer for an organization knows that an officer, employee or other person associated with the organization is engaged in action or intends to act or refuses to act in a matter related to the representation that (i) is a violation of a legal obligation to the organization or a violation of law that reasonably might be imputed to the organization, and (ii) is likely to result in substantial injury to the organization, then the lawyer shall proceed as is reasonably necessary in the best interest of the organization. In determining how to proceed, the lawyer shall give due consideration to the seriousness of the violation and its consequences, the scope and nature of the lawyer's representation, the responsibility in the organization and the apparent motivation of the person involved, the policies of the organization concerning such matters and any other relevant considerations. Any measures taken shall be designed to minimize disruption of the organization and the risk of revealing information relating to the representation to persons outside the organization. Such measures may include, among others:

1. asking reconsideration of the matter;

2. advising that a separate legal opinion on the matter be sought for presentation to an appropriate authority in the organization; and

3. referring the matter to higher authority in the organization, including, if warranted by the seriousness of the matter, referral to the highest authority that can act in behalf of the organization as determined by applicable law.

(c) If, despite the lawyer's efforts in accordance with paragraph (b), the highest authority that can act on behalf of the organization insists upon action, or a refusal to act, that is clearly in violation of law and is likely to result in a substantial injury to the organization, the lawyer may reveal confidential information only if permitted by Rule 1.6, and may resign in accordance with Rule 1.16.

(d) A lawyer representing an organization may also represent any of its directors, officers, employees, members, shareholders or other constituents, subject to the provisions of Rule 1.7. If the organization's consent to the concurrent representation is required by Rule 1.7, the consent shall be given by an appropriate official of the organization other than the individual who is to be represented, or by the shareholders.

Rule 1.14: Client With Diminished Capacity

(a) When a client's capacity to make adequately considered decisions in connection with a representation is diminished, whether because of minority, mental impairment or for some other reason, the lawyer shall, as far as reasonably possible, maintain a conventional relationship with the client.

(b) When the lawyer reasonably believes that the client has diminished capacity, is at risk of substantial physical, financial or other harm unless action is taken and cannot adequately act in the client's own interest, the lawyer may take reasonably necessary protective action, including consulting with individuals or entities that have the ability to take action to protect the client and, in appropriate cases, seeking the appointment of a guardian ad litem, conservator or guardian.

(c) Information relating to the representation of a client with diminished capacity is protected by Rule 1.6. When taking protective action pursuant to paragraph (b), the lawyer is impliedly authorized under Rule 1.6(a) to reveal information about the client, but only to the extent reasonably necessary to protect the client's interests.

Rule 1.15: Preserving Identity of Funds and Property of Others; Fiduciary Responsibility; Commingling and Misappropriation of Client Funds or Property; Maintenance of Bank Accounts; Record Keeping; Examination of Records

(a) Prohibition Against Commingling and Misappropriation of Client Funds or Property.

A lawyer in possession of any funds or other property belonging to another person, where such possession is incident to his or her practice of law, is a fiduciary, and must not misappropriate such funds or property or commingle such funds or property with his or her own.

(b) Separate Accounts.

(1) A lawyer who is in possession of funds belonging to another person incident to the lawyer's practice of law shall maintain such funds in a banking institution within New York State that agrees to provide dishonored check reports in accordance with the provisions of 22 N.Y.C.R.R. Part 1300. "Banking institution" means a state or national bank, trust company, savings bank, savings and loan association or credit union. Such funds shall be maintained, in the lawyer's own name, or in the name of a firm of lawyers of which the lawyer is a member, or in the name of the lawyer or firm of lawyers by whom the lawyer is employed, in a special account or accounts, separate from any business or personal accounts of the lawyer or lawyer's firm, and separate from any accounts that the lawyer may maintain as executor, guardian, trustee or receiver, or in any other fiduciary capacity; into such special account or accounts all funds held in escrow or otherwise entrusted to the lawyer or firm shall be deposited; provided, however, that such funds may be maintained in a banking institution located outside New York State if such banking institution complies with 22 N.Y.C.R.R. Part 1300 and the lawyer has obtained the prior written approval of the person to whom such funds belong specifying the name and address of the office or branch of the banking institution where such funds are to be maintained.

(2) A lawyer or the lawyer's firm shall identify the special bank account or accounts required by Rule 1.15(b)(1) as an "Attorney Special Account," "Attorney Trust Account," or "Attorney Escrow Account," and shall obtain checks and deposit slips that bear such title. Such title may be accompanied by such other descriptive language as the lawyer may deem appropriate, provided that such additional language distinguishes such special account or accounts from other bank accounts that are maintained by the lawyer or the lawyer's firm.

(3) Funds reasonably sufficient to maintain the account or to pay account charges may be deposited therein.

(4) Funds belonging in part to a client or third person and in part currently or potentially to the lawyer or law firm shall be kept in such special account or accounts, but the portion belonging to the lawyer or law firm may be withdrawn when due unless the right of the lawyer or law firm to receive it is disputed by the client or third person, in which event the disputed portion shall not be withdrawn until the dispute is finally resolved.

(c) Notification of Receipt of Property; Safekeeping; Rendering Accounts; Payment or Delivery of Property.

A lawyer shall:

(1) promptly notify a client or third person of the receipt of funds, securities, or other properties in which the client or third person has an interest;

(2) identify and label securities and properties of a client or third person promptly upon receipt and place them in a safe deposit box or other place of safekeeping as soon as practicable;

(3) maintain complete records of all funds, securities, and other properties of a client or third person coming into the possession of the lawyer and render appropriate accounts to the client or third person regarding them; and

(4) promptly pay or deliver to the client or third person as requested by the client or third person the funds, securities, or other properties in the possession of the lawyer that the client or third person is entitled to receive.

(d) Required Bookkeeping Records.

(1) A lawyer shall maintain for seven years after the events that they record:

(i) the records of all deposits in and withdrawals from the accounts specified in Rule 1.15(b) and of any other bank account that concerns or affects the lawyer's practice of law; these records shall specifically identify the date, source and description of each item deposited, as well as the date, payee and purpose of each withdrawal or disbursement;

(ii) a record for special accounts, showing the source of all funds deposited in such accounts, the names of all persons for whom the funds are or were held, the amount of such funds, the description and amounts, and the names of all persons to whom such funds were disbursed;

(iii) copies of all retainer and compensation agreements with clients;

(iv) copies of all statements to clients or other persons showing the disbursement of funds to them or on their behalf;

(v) copies of all bills rendered to clients;

(vi) copies of all records showing payments to lawyers, investigators or other persons, not in the lawyer's regular employ, for services rendered or performed;

(vii) copies of all retainer and closing statements filed with the Office of Court Administration; and

(viii) all checkbooks and check stubs, bank statements, prenumbered canceled checks and duplicate deposit slips.

(2) Lawyers shall make accurate entries of all financial transactions in their records of receipts and disbursements, in their special accounts, in their ledger books or similar records, and in any other books of account kept by them in the regular course of their practice, which entries shall be made at or near the time of the act, condition or event recorded.

(3) For purposes of Rule 1.15(d), a lawyer may satisfy the requirements of maintaining "copies" by maintaining any of the following items: original records, photocopies, microfilm, optical imaging, and any other medium that preserves an image of the document that cannot be altered without detection.

(e) Authorized Signatories.

All special account withdrawals shall be made only to a named payee and not to cash. Such withdrawals shall be made by check or, with the prior written approval of the party entitled to the proceeds, by bank transfer. Only a lawyer admitted to practice law in New York State shall be an authorized signatory of a special account.

(f) Missing Clients.

Whenever any sum of money is payable to a client and the lawyer is unable to locate the client, the lawyer shall apply to the court in which the action was brought if in the unified court system, or, if no action was commenced in the unified court system, to the Supreme Court in the county in which the lawyer maintains an office for the practice of law, for an order directing payment to the lawyer of any fees and disbursements that are owed by the client and the balance, if any, to the Lawyers' Fund for Client Protection for safeguarding and disbursement to persons who are entitled thereto.

(g) Designation of Successor Signatories.

(1) Upon the death of a lawyer who was the sole signatory on an attorney trust, escrow or special account, an application may be made to the Supreme Court for an order designating a successor signatory for such trust, escrow or special account, who shall be a member of the bar in good standing and admitted to the practice of law in New York State.

(2) An application to designate a successor signatory shall be made to the Supreme Court in the judicial district in which the deceased lawyer maintained an office for the practice of law. The application may be made by the legal representative of the deceased lawyer's estate; a lawyer who was affiliated with the deceased lawyer in the practice of law; any person who has a beneficial interest in such trust, escrow or special account; an officer of a city or county bar association; or counsel for an attorney disciplinary committee. No lawyer may charge a legal fee for assisting with an application to designate a successor signatory pursuant to this Rule.

(3) The Supreme Court may designate a successor signatory and may direct the safeguarding of funds from such trust, escrow or special account, and the disbursement of such funds to persons who are entitled thereto, and may order that funds in such account be deposited with the Lawyers' Fund for Client Protection for safeguarding and disbursement to persons who are entitled thereto.

(h) Dissolution of a Firm.

Upon the dissolution of any firm of lawyers, the former partners or members shall make appropriate arrangements for the maintenance, by one of them or by a successor firm, of the records specified in Rule 1.15(d).

(i) Availability of Bookkeeping Records: Records Subject to Production in Disciplinary Investigations and Proceedings.

The financial records required by this Rule shall be located, or made available, at the principal New York State office of the lawyers subject hereto, and any such records shall be produced in response to a notice or subpoena duces tecum issued in connection with a complaint before or any investigation by the appropriate grievance or departmental disciplinary committee, or shall be produced at the direction of the appropriate Appellate Division before any person designated by it. All books and records produced pursuant to this Rule shall be kept confidential, except for the purpose of the particular proceeding, and their contents shall not be disclosed by anyone in violation of the attorney-client privilege.

(j) Disciplinary Action.

A lawyer who does not maintain and keep the accounts and records as specified and required by this Rule, or who does not produce any such records pursuant to this Rule, shall be deemed in violation of these Rules and shall be subject to disciplinary proceedings.

Rule 1.16: Declining or Terminating Representation

(a) A lawyer shall not accept employment on behalf of a person if the lawyer knows or reasonably should know that such person wishes to:

(1) bring a legal action, conduct a defense, or assert a position in a matter, or otherwise have steps taken for such person, merely for the purpose of harassing or maliciously injuring any person; or

(2) present a claim or defense in a matter that is not warranted under existing law, unless it can be supported by a good faith argument for an extension, modification, or reversal of existing law.

(b) Except as stated in paragraph (d), a lawyer shall withdraw from the representation of a client when:

(1) the lawyer knows or reasonably should know that the representation will result in a violation of these Rules or of law;

(2) the lawyer's physical or mental condition materially impairs the lawyer's ability to represent the client;

(3) the lawyer is discharged; or

(4) the lawyer knows or reasonably should know that the client is bringing the legal action, conducting the defense, or asserting a position in the matter, or is otherwise having steps taken, merely for the purpose of harassing or maliciously injuring any person.

(c) Except as stated in paragraph (d), a lawyer may withdraw from representing a client when:

(1) withdrawal can be accomplished without material adverse effect on the interests of the client;

(2) the client persists in a course of action involving the lawyer's services that the lawyer reasonably believes is criminal or fraudulent;

(3) the client has used the lawyer's services to perpetrate a crime or fraud;

(4) the client insists upon taking action with which the lawyer has a fundamental disagreement;

(5) the client deliberately disregards an agreement or obligation to the lawyer as to expenses or fees;

(6) the client insists upon presenting a claim or defense that is not warranted under existing law and cannot be supported by good faith argument for an extension, modification, or reversal of existing law;

(7) the client fails to cooperate in the representation or otherwise renders the representation unreasonably difficult for the lawyer to carry out employment effectively;

(8) the lawyer's inability to work with co-counsel indicates that the best interest of the client likely will be served by withdrawal;

(9) the lawyer's mental or physical condition renders it difficult for the lawyer to carry out the representation effectively;

(10) the client knowingly and freely assents to termination of the employment;

(11) withdrawal is permitted under Rule 1.13(c) or other law;

(12) the lawyer believes in good faith, in a matter pending before a tribunal, that the tribunal will find the existence of other good cause for withdrawal; or

(13) the client insists that the lawyer pursue a course of conduct which is illegal or prohibited under these Rules.

(d) If permission for withdrawal from employment is required by the rules of a tribunal, a lawyer shall not withdraw from employment in a matter before that tribunal without its permission. When ordered to do so by a tribunal, a lawyer shall continue representation notwithstanding good cause for terminating the representation.

(e) Even when withdrawal is otherwise permitted or required, upon termination of representation, a lawyer shall take steps, to the extent reasonably practicable, to avoid foreseeable prejudice to the rights of the client, including giving reasonable notice to the client, allowing time for employment of other counsel, delivering to the client all papers and property to which the client is entitled, promptly refunding any part of a fee paid in advance that has not been earned and complying with applicable laws and rules.

Rule 1.17: Sale of Law Practice

(a) A lawyer retiring from a private practice of law; a law firm, one or more members of which are retiring from the private practice of law with the firm; or the personal representative of a deceased, disabled or missing lawyer, may sell a law practice, including goodwill, to one or more lawyers or law firms, who may purchase the practice. The seller and the buyer may agree on reasonable restrictions on the seller's private practice of law, notwithstanding any other provision of these Rules. Retirement shall include the cessation of the private practice of law in the geographic area, that is, the county and city and any county or city contiguous thereto, in which the practice to be sold has been conducted.

(b) Confidential information.

(1) With respect to each matter subject to the contemplated sale, the seller may provide prospective buyers with any information not protected as confidential information under Rule 1.6.

(2) Notwithstanding Rule 1.6, the seller may provide the prospective buyer with information as to individual clients:

(i) concerning the identity of the client, except as provided in paragraph (b)(6);

(ii) concerning the status and general nature of the matter;

(iii) available in public court files; and

(iv) concerning the financial terms of the client-lawyer relationship and the payment status of the client's account.

(3) Prior to making any disclosure of confidential information that may be permitted under paragraph (b)(2), the seller shall provide the prospective buyer with information regarding the matters involved in the proposed sale sufficient to enable the prospective buyer to determine whether any conflicts of interest exist. Where sufficient information cannot be disclosed without revealing client confidential information, the seller may make the disclosures necessary for the prospective buyer to determine whether any conflict of interest exists, subject to paragraph (b)(6). If the prospective buyer determines that conflicts of interest exist prior to reviewing the information, or determines during the course of review that a conflict of interest exists, the prospective buyer shall not review or continue to review the information unless the seller shall have obtained the consent of the client in accordance with Rule 1.6(a)(1).

(4) Prospective buyers shall maintain the confidentiality of and shall not use any client information received in connection with the proposed sale in the same manner and to the same extent as if the prospective buyers represented the client.

(5) Absent the consent of the client after full disclosure, a seller shall not provide a prospective buyer with information if doing so would cause a violation of the attorney-client privilege.

(6) If the seller has reason to believe that the identity of the client or the fact of the representation itself constitutes confidential information in the circumstances, the seller may not provide such information to a prospective buyer without first advising the client of the identity of the prospective buyer and obtaining the client's consent to the proposed disclosure.

(c) Written notice of the sale shall be given jointly by the seller and the buyer to each of the seller's clients and shall include information regarding:

(1) the client's right to retain other counsel or to take possession of the file;

(2) the fact that the client's consent to the transfer of the client's file or matter to the buyer will be presumed if the client does not take any action or otherwise object within 90 days of the sending of the notice, subject to any court rule or statute requiring express approval by the client or a court;

(3) the fact that agreements between the seller and the seller's clients as to fees will be honored by the buyer;

(4) proposed fee increases, if any, permitted under paragraph (e); and

(5) the identity and background of the buyer or buyers, including principal office address, bar admissions, number of years in practice in New York State, whether the buyer has ever been disciplined for professional misconduct or convicted of a crime, and whether the buyer currently intends to resell the practice.

(d) When the buyer's representation of a client of the seller would give rise to a waivable conflict of interest, the buyer shall not undertake such representation unless the necessary waiver or waivers have been obtained in writing.

(e) The fee charged a client by the buyer shall not be increased by reason of the sale, unless permitted by a retainer agreement with the client or otherwise specifically agreed to by the client.

Rule 1.18: Duties to Prospective Clients

(a) A person who discusses with a lawyer the possibility of forming a client-lawyer relationship with respect to a matter is a "prospective client."

(b) Even when no client-lawyer relationship ensues, a lawyer who has had discussions with a prospective client shall not use or reveal information learned in the consultation, except as Rule 1.9 would permit with respect to information of a former client.

(c) A lawyer subject to paragraph (b) shall not represent a client with interests materially adverse to those of a prospective client in the same or a substantially related matter if the lawyer received information from the prospective client that could be significantly harmful to that person in the matter, except as provided in paragraph (d). If a lawyer is disqualified from representation under this paragraph, no lawyer in a firm with which that lawyer is associated may knowingly undertake or continue representation in such a matter, except as provided in paragraph (d).

(d) When the lawyer has received disqualifying information as defined in paragraph (c), representation is permissible if:

(1) both the affected client and the prospective client have given informed consent, confirmed in writing; or

(2) the lawyer who received the information took reasonable measures to avoid exposure to more disqualifying information than was reasonably necessary to determine whether to represent the prospective client; and

(i) the firm acts promptly and reasonably to notify, as appropriate, lawyers and nonlawyer personnel within the firm that the personally disqualified lawyer is prohibited from participating in the representation of the current client;

(ii) the firm implements effective screening procedures to prevent the flow of information about the matter between the disqualified lawyer and the others in the firm;

(iii) the disqualified lawyer is apportioned no part of the fee therefrom; and

(iv) written notice is promptly given to the prospective client; and

(3) a reasonable lawyer would conclude that the law firm will be able to provide competent and diligent representation in the matter.

(e) A person who:

(1) communicates information unilaterally to a lawyer, without any reasonable expectation that the lawyer is willing to discuss the possibility of forming a client-lawyer relationship; or

(2) communicates with a lawyer for the purpose of disqualifying the lawyer from handling a materially adverse representation on the same or a substantially related matter,

is not a prospective client with the meaning of paragraph (a).

Rule 2.1: Advisor

In representing a client, a lawyer shall exercise independent professional judgment and render candid advice. In rendering advice, a lawyer may refer not only to law but to other considerations such as moral, economic, social, psychological, and political factors that may be relevant to the client's situation.

[Rule 2.2: Reserved]

Rule 2.3: Evaluation for Use by Third Persons

(a) A lawyer may provide an evaluation of a matter affecting a client for the use of someone other than the client if the lawyer reasonably believes that making the evaluation is compatible with other aspects of the lawyer's relationship with the client.

(b) When the lawyer knows or reasonably should know that the evaluation is likely to affect the client's interests materially and adversely, the lawyer shall not provide the evaluation unless the client gives informed consent.

(c) Unless disclosure is authorized in connection with a report of an evaluation, information relating to the evaluation is protected by Rule 1.6.

Rule 2.4: Lawyer Serving as Third-Party Neutral

(a) A lawyer serves as a "third-party neutral" when the lawyer assists two or more persons who are not clients of the lawyer to reach a resolution of a dispute or other matter that has arisen between them. Service as a third-party neutral may include service as an arbitrator, a mediator or in such other capacity as will enable the lawyer to assist the parties to resolve the matter.

(b) A lawyer serving as a third-party neutral shall inform unrepresented parties that the lawyer is not representing them. When the lawyer knows or reasonably should know that a party does not understand the lawyer's role in the matter, the lawyer shall explain the difference between the lawyer's role as a third-party neutral and a lawyer's role as one who represents a client.

Rule 3.1: Non-Meritorious Claims and Contentions

(a) A lawyer shall not bring or defend a proceeding, or assert or controvert an issue therein, unless there is a basis in law and fact for doing so that is not frivolous. A lawyer for the defendant in a criminal proceeding or for the respondent in a proceeding that could result in incarceration may nevertheless so defend the proceeding as to require that every element of the case be established.

(b) A lawyer's conduct is "frivolous" for purposes of this Rule if:

(1) the lawyer knowingly advances a claim or defense that is unwarranted under existing law, except that the lawyer may advance such claim or defense if it can be supported by good faith argument for an extension, modification, or reversal of existing law;

(2) the conduct has no reasonable purpose other than to delay or prolong the resolution of litigation, in violation of Rule 3.2, or serves merely to harass or maliciously injure another; or

(3) the lawyer knowingly asserts material factual statements that are false.

Rule 3.2: Delay of Litigation

In representing a client, a lawyer shall not use means that have no substantial purpose other than to delay or prolong the proceeding or to cause needless expense.

Rule 3.3: Conduct Before a Tribunal

(a) A lawyer shall not knowingly:

(1) make a false statement of fact or law to a tribunal or fail to correct a false statement of material fact or law previously made to the tribunal by the lawyer;

(2) fail to disclose to the tribunal controlling legal authority known to the lawyer to be directly adverse to the position of the client and not disclosed by opposing counsel; or

(3) offer or use evidence that the lawyer knows to be false. If a lawyer, the lawyer's client, or a witness called by the lawyer has offered material evidence and the lawyer comes to know of its falsity, the lawyer shall take reasonable remedial measures, including, if necessary, disclosure to the tribunal. A lawyer may refuse to offer evidence, other than the testimony of a defendant in a criminal matter, that the lawyer reasonably believes is false.

(b) A lawyer who represents a client before a tribunal and who knows that a person intends to engage, is engaging or has engaged in criminal or fraudulent conduct related to the proceeding shall take reasonable remedial measures, including, if necessary, disclosure to the tribunal.

(c) The duties stated in paragraphs (a) and (b) apply even if compliance requires disclosure of information otherwise protected by Rule 1.6.

(d) In an ex parte proceeding, a lawyer shall inform the tribunal of all material facts known to the lawyer that will enable the tribunal to make an informed decision, whether or not the facts are adverse.

(e) In presenting a matter to a tribunal, a lawyer shall disclose, unless privileged or irrelevant, the identities of the clients the lawyer represents and of the persons who employed the lawyer.

(f) In appearing as a lawyer before a tribunal, a lawyer shall not:

(1) fail to comply with known local customs of courtesy or practice of the bar or a particular tribunal without giving to opposing counsel timely notice of the intent not to comply;

(2) engage in undignified or discourteous conduct;

(3) intentionally or habitually violate any established rule of procedure or of evidence; or

(4) engage in conduct intended to disrupt the tribunal.

Rule 3.4: Fairness to Opposing Party and Counsel

A lawyer shall not:

(a)(1) suppress any evidence that the lawyer or the client has a legal obligation to reveal or produce;

(2) advise or cause a person to hide or leave the jurisdiction of a tribunal for the purpose of making the person unavailable as a witness therein;

(3) conceal or knowingly fail to disclose that which the lawyer is required by law to reveal;

(4) knowingly use perjured testimony or false evidence;

(5) participate in the creation or preservation of evidence when the lawyer knows or it is obvious that the evidence is false; or

(6) knowingly engage in other illegal conduct or conduct contrary to these Rules;

(b) offer an inducement to a witness that is prohibited by law or pay, offer to pay or acquiesce in the payment of compensation to a witness contingent upon the content of the witness's testimony or the outcome of the matter. A lawyer may advance, guarantee or acquiesce in the payment of:

(1) reasonable compensation to a witness for the loss of time in attending, testifying, preparing to testify or otherwise assisting counsel, and reasonable related expenses; or

(2) a reasonable fee for the professional services of an expert witness and reasonable related expenses;

(c) disregard or advise the client to disregard a standing rule of a tribunal or a ruling of a tribunal made in the course of a proceeding, but the lawyer may take appropriate steps in good faith to test the validity of such rule or ruling;

(d) in appearing before a tribunal on behalf of a client:

(1) state or allude to any matter that the lawyer does not reasonably believe is relevant or that will not be supported by admissible evidence;

(2) assert personal knowledge of facts in issue except when testifying as a witness;

(3) assert a personal opinion as to the justness of a cause, the credibility of a witness, the culpability of a civil litigant or the guilt or innocence of an accused but the lawyer may argue, upon analysis of the evidence, for any position or conclusion with respect to the matters stated herein; or

(4) ask any question that the lawyer has no reasonable basis to believe is relevant to the case and that is intended to degrade a witness or other person; or

(e) present, participate in presenting, or threaten to present criminal charges solely to obtain an advantage in a civil matter.

Rule 3.5: Maintaining and Preserving the Impartiality of Tribunals and Jurors

(a) A lawyer shall not:

(1) seek to or cause another person to influence a judge, official or employee of a tribunal by means prohibited by law or give or lend anything of value to such judge, official, or employee of a tribunal when the recipient is prohibited from accepting the gift or loan but a lawyer may

make a contribution to the campaign fund of a candidate for judicial office in conformity with Part 100 of the Rules of the Chief Administrator of the Courts;

(2) in an adversarial proceeding communicate or cause another person to do so on the lawyer's behalf, as to the merits of the matter with a judge or official of a tribunal or an employee thereof before whom the matter is pending, except:

(i) in the course of official proceedings in the matter;

(ii) in writing, if the lawyer promptly delivers a copy of the writing to counsel for other parties and to a party who is not represented by a lawyer;

(iii) orally, upon adequate notice to counsel for the other parties and to any party who is not represented by a lawyer; or

(iv) as otherwise authorized by law, or by Part 100 of the Rules of the Chief Administrator of the Courts;

(3) seek to or cause another person to influence a juror or prospective juror by means prohibited by law;

(4) communicate or cause another to communicate with a member of the jury venire from which the jury will be selected for the trial of a case or, during the trial of a case, with any member of the jury unless authorized to do so by law or court order;

(5) communicate with a juror or prospective juror after discharge of the jury if:

(i) the communication is prohibited by law or court order;

(ii) the juror has made known to the lawyer a desire not to communicate;

(iii) the communication involves misrepresentation, coercion, duress or harassment; or

(iv) the communication is an attempt to influence the juror's actions in future jury service; or

(6) conduct a vexatious or harassing investigation of either a member of the venire or a juror or, by financial support or otherwise, cause another to do so.

(b) During the trial of a case a lawyer who is not connected therewith shall not communicate with or cause another to communicate with a juror concerning the case.

(c) All restrictions imposed by this Rule also apply to communications with or investigations of members of a family of a member of the venire or a juror.

(d) A lawyer shall reveal promptly to the court improper conduct by a member of the venire or a juror, or by another toward a member of the venire or a juror or a member of his or her family of which the lawyer has knowledge.

Rule 3.6: Trial Publicity

(a) A lawyer who is participating in or has participated in a criminal or civil matter shall not make an extrajudicial statement that the lawyer knows or reasonably should know will be disseminated by means of public communication and will have a substantial likelihood of materially prejudicing an adjudicative proceeding in the matter.

(b) A statement ordinarily is likely to prejudice materially an adjudicative proceeding when it refers to a civil matter triable to a jury, a criminal matter or any other proceeding that could result in incarceration, and the statement relates to:

(1) the character, credibility, reputation or criminal record of a party, suspect in a criminal investigation or witness, or the identity of a witness or the expected testimony of a party or witness;

(2) in a criminal matter that could result in incarceration, the possibility of a plea of guilty to the offense or the existence or contents of any confession, admission or statement given by a defendant or suspect, or that person's refusal or failure to make a statement;

(3) the performance or results of any examination or test, or the refusal or failure of a person to submit to an examination or test, or the identity or nature of physical evidence expected to be presented;

(4) any opinion as to the guilt or innocence of a defendant or suspect in a criminal matter that could result in incarceration;

(5) information the lawyer knows or reasonably should know is likely to be inadmissible as evidence in a trial and would, if disclosed, create a substantial risk of prejudicing an impartial trial; or

(6) the fact that a defendant has been charged with a crime, unless there is included therein a statement explaining that the charge is merely an accusation and that the defendant is presumed innocent until and unless proven guilty.

(c) Provided that the statement complies with paragraph (a), a lawyer may state the following without elaboration:

(1) the claim, offense or defense and, except when prohibited by law, the identity of the persons involved;

(2) information contained in a public record;

(3) that an investigation of a matter is in progress;

(4) the scheduling or result of any step in litigation;

(5) a request for assistance in obtaining evidence and information necessary thereto;

(6) a warning of danger concerning the behavior of a person involved, when there is reason to believe that there exists the likelihood of substantial harm to an individual or to the public interest; and

(7) in a criminal matter:

(i) the identity, age, residence, occupation and family status of the accused;

(ii) if the accused has not been apprehended, information necessary to aid in apprehension of that person;

(iii) the identity of investigating and arresting officers or agencies and the length of the investigation; and

(iv) the fact, time and place of arrest, resistance, pursuit and use of weapons, and a description of physical evidence seized, other than as contained only in a confession, admission or statement.

(d) Notwithstanding paragraph (a), a lawyer may make a statement that a reasonable lawyer would believe is required to protect a client from the substantial prejudicial effect of recent publicity not initiated by the lawyer or the lawyer's client. A statement made pursuant to this paragraph shall be limited to such information as is necessary to mitigate the recent adverse publicity.

(e) No lawyer associated in a firm or government agency with a lawyer subject to paragraph (a) shall make a statement prohibited by paragraph (a).

Rule 3.7: Lawyer as Witness

(a) A lawyer shall not act as advocate before a tribunal in a matter in which the lawyer is likely to be a witness on a significant issue of fact unless:

(1) the testimony relates solely to an uncontested issue;

(2) the testimony relates solely to the nature and value of legal services rendered in the matter;

(3) disqualification of the lawyer would work substantial hardship on the client;

(4) the testimony will relate solely to a matter of formality, and there is no reason to believe that substantial evidence will be offered in opposition to the testimony; or

(5) the testimony is authorized by the tribunal.

(b) A lawyer may not act as advocate before a tribunal in a matter if:

(1) another lawyer in the lawyer's firm is likely to be called as a witness on a significant issue other than on behalf of the client, and it is apparent that the testimony may be prejudicial to the client; or

(2) the lawyer is precluded from doing so by Rule 1.7 or Rule 1.9.

Rule 3.8: Special Responsibilities of Prosecutors and Other Government Lawyers

(a) A prosecutor or other government lawyer shall not institute, cause to be instituted or maintain a criminal charge when the prosecutor or other government lawyer knows or it is obvious that the charge is not supported by probable cause.

(b) A prosecutor or other government lawyer in criminal litigation shall make timely disclosure to counsel for the defendant or to a defendant who has no counsel of the existence of evidence or information known to the prosecutor or other government lawyer that tends to negate the guilt of the accused, mitigate the degree of the offense, or reduce the sentence, except when relieved of this responsibility by a protective order of a tribunal.

(c) When a prosecutor knows of new, credible and material evidence creating a reasonable likelihood that a convicted defendant did not commit an offense of which the defendant was convicted, the prosecutor shall within a reasonable time: (1) disclose that evidence to an appropriate court or prosecutor's office; or (2) if the conviction was obtained by that prosecutor's office, (A) notify the appropriate court and the defendant that the prosecutor's office possesses such evidence unless a court authorizes delay for good cause shown; (B) disclose that evidence to the defendant unless the disclosure would interfere with an ongoing investigation or endanger the safety of a witness or other person, and a court authorizes delay for good cause shown; and (C) undertake or make reasonable efforts to cause to be undertaken such further inquiry or investigation as may be necessary to provide a reasonable belief that the conviction should or should not be set aside. (d) When a prosecutor knows of clear and convincing evidence establishing that a defendant was convicted, in a prosecution by the prosecutor's office, of an offense that the defendant did not commit, the prosecutor shall seek a remedy consistent with justice, applicable law, and the circumstances of the case. (e) A prosecutor's independent judgment, made in good faith, that the new evidence is not of such nature as to trigger the obligations of sections (c) and (d), though subsequently determined to have been erroneous, does not constitute a violation of this rule.

Rule 3.9: Advocate in Non-Adjudicative Matters

A lawyer communicating in a representative capacity with a legislative body or administrative agency in connection with a pending non-adjudicative matter or proceeding shall disclose that the appearance is in a representative capacity, except when the lawyer seeks information from an agency that is available to the public.

Rule 4.1: Truthfulness in Statements to Others

In the course of representing a client, a lawyer shall not knowingly make a false statement of fact or law to a third person.

Rule 4.2: Communication With Person Represented by Counsel

(a) In representing a client, a lawyer shall not communicate or cause another to communicate about the subject of the representation with a party the lawyer knows to be represented by another lawyer in the matter, unless the lawyer has the prior consent of the other lawyer or is authorized to do so by law.

(b) Notwithstanding the prohibitions of paragraph (a), and unless otherwise prohibited by law, a lawyer may cause a client to communicate with a represented person unless the represented person is not legally competent, and may counsel the client with respect to those communications, provided the lawyer gives reasonable advance notice to the represented person's counsel that such communications will be taking place.

(c) A lawyer who is acting pro se or is represented by counsel in a matter is subject to paragraph (a), but may communicate with a represented person, unless otherwise prohibited by law and unless the represented person is not legally competent, provided the lawyer or the lawyer's counsel gives reasonable advance notice to the represented person's counsel that such communications will be taking place.

Rule 4.3: Communicating With Unrepresented Persons

In communicating on behalf of a client with a person who is not represented by counsel, a lawyer shall not state or imply that the lawyer is disinterested. When the lawyer knows or reasonably should know that the unrepresented person misunderstands the lawyer's role in the matter, the lawyer shall make reasonable efforts to correct the misunderstanding. The lawyer shall not give legal advice to an unrepresented person other than the advice to secure counsel if the lawyer knows or reasonably should know that the interests of such person are or have a reasonable possibility of being in conflict with the interests of the client.

Rule 4.4: Respect for Rights of Third Persons

(a) In representing a client, a lawyer shall not use means that have no substantial purpose other than to embarrass or harm a third person or use methods of obtaining evidence that violate the legal rights of such a person.

(b) A lawyer who receives a document relating to the representation of the lawyer's client and knows or reasonably should know that the document was inadvertently sent shall promptly notify the sender.

Rule 4.5: Communication After Incidents Involving Personal Injury or Wrongful Death

(a) In the event of a specific incident involving potential claims for personal injury or wrongful death, no unsolicited communication shall be made to an individual injured in the incident or to a family member or legal representative of such an individual, by a lawyer or law firm, or by any associate, agent, employee or other representative of a lawyer or law firm representing actual or potential defendants or entities that may defend and/or indemnify said defendants, before the 30th day after the date of the incident, unless a filing must be made within 30 days of the incident as a legal prerequisite to the particular claim, in which case no unsolicited communication shall be made before the 15th day after the date of the incident.

(b) An unsolicited communication by a lawyer or law firm, seeking to represent an injured individual or the legal representative thereof under the circumstance described in paragraph (a) shall comply with Rule 7.3(e).

Rule 5.1: Responsibilities of Law Firms, Partners, Managers and Supervisory Lawyers

(a) A law firm shall make reasonable efforts to ensure that all lawyers in the firm conform to these Rules.

(b)(1) A lawyer with management responsibility in a law firm shall make reasonable efforts to ensure that other lawyers in the law firm conform to these Rules.

(2) A lawyer with direct supervisory authority over another lawyer shall make reasonable efforts to ensure that the supervised lawyer conforms to these Rules.

(c) A law firm shall ensure that the work of partners and associates is adequately supervised, as appropriate. A lawyer with direct supervisory authority over another lawyer shall adequately supervise the work of the other lawyer, as appropriate. In either case, the degree of supervision required is that which is reasonable under the circumstances, taking into account factors such as the experience of the person whose work is being supervised, the amount of work involved in a particular matter, and the likelihood that ethical problems might arise in the course of working on the matter.

(d) A lawyer shall be responsible for a violation of these Rules by another lawyer if:

(1) the lawyer orders or directs the specific conduct or, with knowledge of the specific conduct, ratifies it; or

(2) the lawyer is a partner in a law firm or is a lawyer who individually or together with other lawyers possesses comparable managerial responsibility in a law firm in which the other lawyer practices or is a lawyer who has supervisory authority over the other lawyer; and

(i) knows of such conduct at a time when it could be prevented or its consequences avoided or mitigated but fails to take reasonable remedial action; or

(ii) in the exercise of reasonable management or supervisory authority should have known of the conduct so that reasonable remedial action could have been taken at a time when the consequences of the conduct could have been avoided or mitigated.

Rule 5.2: Responsibilities of a Subordinate Lawyer

(a) A lawyer is bound by these Rules notwithstanding that the lawyer acted at the direction of another person.

(b) A subordinate lawyer does not violate these Rules if that lawyer acts in accordance with a supervisory lawyer's reasonable resolution of an arguable question of professional duty.

Rule 5.3: Lawyer's Responsibility for Conduct of Nonlawyers

(a) A law firm shall ensure that the work of nonlawyers who work for the firm is adequately supervised, as appropriate. A lawyer with direct supervisory authority over a nonlawyer shall adequately supervise the work of the nonlawyer, as appropriate. In either case, the degree of supervision required is that which is reasonable under the circumstances, taking into account factors such as the experience of the person whose work is being supervised, the amount of work involved in a particular matter and the likelihood that ethical problems might arise in the course of working on the matter.

(b) A lawyer shall be responsible for conduct of a nonlawyer employed or retained by or associated with the lawyer that would be a violation of these Rules if engaged in by a lawyer, if:

(1) the lawyer orders or directs the specific conduct or, with knowledge of the specific conduct, ratifies it; or

(2) the lawyer is a partner in a law firm or is a lawyer who individually or together with other lawyers possesses comparable managerial responsibility in a law firm in which the nonlawyer is employed or is a lawyer who has supervisory authority over the nonlawyer; and

(i) knows of such conduct at a time when it could be prevented or its consequences avoided or mitigated but fails to take reasonable remedial action; or

(ii) in the exercise of reasonable management or supervisory authority should have known of the conduct so that reasonable remedial action could have been taken at a time when the consequences of the conduct could have been avoided or mitigated.

Rule 5.4: Professional Independence of a Lawyer

(a) A lawyer or law firm shall not share legal fees with a nonlawyer, except that:

(1) an agreement by a lawyer with the lawyer's firm or another lawyer associated in the firm may provide for the payment of money, over a reasonable period of time after the lawyer's death, to the lawyer's estate or to one or more specified persons;

(2) a lawyer who undertakes to complete unfinished legal business of a deceased lawyer may pay to the estate of the deceased lawyer that portion of the total compensation that fairly represents the services rendered by the deceased lawyer; and

(3) a lawyer or law firm may compensate a nonlawyer employee or include a nonlawyer employee in a retirement plan based in whole or in part on a profit-sharing arrangement.

(b) A lawyer shall not form a partnership with a nonlawyer if any of the activities of the partnership consist of the practice of law.

(c) Unless authorized by law, a lawyer shall not permit a person who recommends, employs or pays the lawyer to render legal service for another to direct or regulate the lawyer's professional judgment in rendering such legal services or to cause the lawyer to compromise the lawyer's duty to maintain the confidential information of the client under Rule 1.6.

(d) A lawyer shall not practice with or in the form of an entity authorized to practice law for profit, if:

(1) a nonlawyer owns any interest therein, except that a fiduciary representative of the estate of a lawyer may hold the stock or interest of the lawyer for a reasonable time during administration;

(2) a nonlawyer is a member, corporate director or officer thereof or occupies a position of similar responsibility in any form of association other than a corporation; or

(3) a nonlawyer has the right to direct or control the professional judgment of a lawyer.

Rule 5.5: Unauthorized Practice of Law

(a) A lawyer shall not practice law in a jurisdiction in violation of the regulation of the legal profession in that jurisdiction.

(b) A lawyer shall not aid a nonlawyer in the unauthorized practice of law.

Rule 5.6: Restrictions on Right to Practice

(a) A lawyer shall not participate in offering or making:

(1) a partnership, shareholder, operating, employment, or other similar type of agreement that restricts the right of a lawyer to practice after termination of the relationship, except an agreement concerning benefits upon retirement; or

(2) an agreement in which a restriction on a lawyer's right to practice is part of the settlement of a client controversy.

(b) This Rule does not prohibit restrictions that may be included in the terms of the sale of a law practice pursuant to Rule 1.17.

Rule 5.7: Responsibilities Regarding Nonlegal Services

(a) With respect to lawyers or law firms providing nonlegal services to clients or other persons:

(1) A lawyer or law firm that provides nonlegal services to a person that are not distinct from legal services being provided to that person by the lawyer or law firm is subject to these Rules with respect to the provision of both legal and nonlegal services.

(2) A lawyer or law firm that provides nonlegal services to a person that are distinct from legal services being provided to that person by the lawyer or law firm is subject to these Rules with respect to the nonlegal services if the person receiving the services could reasonably believe that the nonlegal services are the subject of a client-lawyer relationship.

(3) A lawyer or law firm that is an owner, controlling party or agent of, or that is otherwise affiliated with, an entity that the lawyer or law firm knows to be providing nonlegal services to a person is subject to these Rules with respect to the nonlegal services if the person receiving the services could reasonably believe that the nonlegal services are the subject of a client-lawyer relationship.

(4) For purposes of paragraphs (a)(2) and (a)(3), it will be presumed that the person receiving nonlegal services believes the services to be the subject of a client-lawyer relationship unless the lawyer or law firm has advised the person receiving the services in writing that the services are not legal services and that the protection of a client-lawyer relationship does not exist with respect to the nonlegal services, or if the interest of the lawyer or law firm in the entity providing nonlegal services is *de minimis*.

(b) Notwithstanding the provisions of paragraph (a), a lawyer or law firm that is an owner, controlling party, agent, or is otherwise affiliated with an entity that the lawyer or law firm knows is providing nonlegal services to a person shall not permit any nonlawyer providing such services or affiliated with that entity to direct or regulate the professional judgment of the lawyer or law firm in rendering legal services to any person, or to cause the lawyer or law firm to compromise its duty under Rule 1.6(a) and (c) with respect to the confidential information of a client receiving legal services.

(c) For purposes of this Rule, "nonlegal services" shall mean those services that lawyers may lawfully provide and that are not prohibited as an unauthorized practice of law when provided by a nonlawyer.

Rule 5.8: Contractual Relationship Between Lawyers and Nonlegal Professionals

(a) The practice of law has an essential tradition of complete independence and uncompromised loyalty to those it serves. Recognizing this tradition, clients of lawyers practicing in New York State are guaranteed "independent professional judgment and undivided loyalty uncompromised by conflicts of interest." Indeed, these guarantees represent the very foundation of the profession and allow and foster its continued role as a protector of the system of law. Therefore, a lawyer must remain completely responsible for his or her own independent professional judgment, maintain the confidences and secrets of clients, preserve funds of clients and third parties in his or her control, and otherwise comply with the legal and ethical principles governing lawyers in New York State.

Multi-disciplinary practice between lawyers and nonlawyers is incompatible with the core values of the legal profession and therefore, a strict division between services provided by lawyers and those provided by nonlawyers is essential to protect those values. However, a lawyer or law firm may enter into and maintain a contractual relationship with a nonlegal professional or nonlegal professional service firm for the purpose of offering to the public, on a systematic and continuing basis, legal services performed by the lawyer or law firm as well as other nonlegal professional services, notwithstanding the provisions of Rule 1.7(a), provided that:

(1) the profession of the nonlegal professional or nonlegal professional service firm is included in a list jointly established and maintained by the Appellate Divisions pursuant to Section 1205.3 of the Joint Appellate Division Rules;

(2) the lawyer or law firm neither grants to the nonlegal professional or nonlegal professional service firm, nor permits such person or firm to obtain, hold or exercise, directly or indirectly, any ownership or investment interest in, or managerial or supervisory right, power or position in connection with the practice of law by the lawyer or law firm, nor, as provided in Rule 7.2(a)(1), shares legal fees with a nonlawyer or receives or gives any monetary or other tangible benefit for giving or receiving a referral; and

(3) the fact that the contractual relationship exists is disclosed by the lawyer or law firm to any client of the lawyer or law firm before the client is referred to the nonlegal professional service firm, or to any client of the nonlegal professional service firm before that client receives legal services from the lawyer or law firm; and the client has given informed written consent and has been provided with a copy of the "Statement of Client's Rights In Cooperative Business Arrangements" pursuant to section 1205.4 of the Joint Appellate Divisions Rules.

(b) For purposes of paragraph (a):

(1) each profession on the list maintained pursuant to a Joint Rule of the Appellate Divisions shall have been designated sua sponte, or approved by the Appellate Divisions upon application of a member of a nonlegal profession or nonlegal professional service firm, upon a determination that the profession is composed of individuals who, with respect to their profession:

(a) have been awarded a bachelor's degree or its equivalent from an accredited college or university, or have attained an equivalent combination of educational credit from such a college or university and work experience;

(b) are licensed to practice the profession by an agency of the State of New York or the United States Government; and

(c) are required under penalty of suspension or revocation of license to adhere to a code of ethical conduct that is reasonably comparable to that of the legal profession;

(2) the term "ownership or investment interest" shall mean any such interest in any form of debt or equity, and shall include any interest commonly considered to be an interest accruing to or enjoyed by an owner or investor.

(c) This Rule shall not apply to relationships consisting solely of non-exclusive reciprocal referral agreements or understandings between a lawyer or law firm and a nonlegal professional or nonlegal professional service firm.

Rule 6.1: Voluntary Pro Bono Service

Lawyers are strongly encouraged to provide pro bono legal services to benefit poor persons.

(a) Every lawyer should aspire to:

(1) provide at least 50 hours of pro bono legal services each year to poor persons; and

(2) contribute financially to organizations that provide legal services to poor persons. Lawyers in private practice or employed by a for-profit entity should aspire to contribute annually in an amount at least equivalent to (i) the amount typically billed by the lawyer (or the firm with which the lawyer is associated) for one hour of time; or (ii) if the lawyer's work is performed on a contingency basis, the amount typically billed by lawyers in the community for one hour of time; or (iii) the amount typically paid by the organization employing the lawyer for one hour of the lawyer's time; or (iv) if the lawyer is underemployed, an amount not to exceed one-tenth of one percent of the lawyer's income.

(b) Pro bono legal services that meet this goal are:

(1) professional services rendered in civil matters, and in those criminal matters for which the government is not obliged to provide funds for legal representation, to persons who are financially unable to compensate counsel;

(2) activities related to improving the administration of justice by simplifying the legal process for, or increasing the availability and quality of legal services to, poor persons; and

(3) professional services to charitable, religious, civic and educational organizations in matters designed predominantly to address the needs of poor persons.

(c) Appropriate organizations for financial contributions are:

(1) organizations primarily engaged in the provision of legal services to the poor; and

(2) organizations substantially engaged in the provision of legal services to the poor, provided that the donated funds are to be used for the provision of such legal services.

(d) This Rule is not intended to be enforced through the disciplinary process, and the failure to fulfill the aspirational goals contained herein should be without legal consequence.

[Rule 6.2: Reserved]

Rule 6.3: Membership in a Legal Services Organization

A lawyer may serve as a director, officer or member of a not-for-profit legal services organization, apart from the law firm in which the lawyer practices, notwithstanding that the organization serves persons having interests that differ from those of a client of the lawyer or the lawyer's firm. The lawyer shall not knowingly participate in a decision or action of the organization:

(a) if participating in the decision or action would be incompatible with the lawyer's obligations to a client under Rules 1.7 through 1.13; or

(b) where the decision or action could have a material adverse effect on the representation of a client of the organization whose interests differ from those of a client of the lawyer or the lawyer's firm.

Rule 6.4: Law Reform Activities Affecting Client Interests (Amended 4/22/2010)

A lawyer may serve as a director, officer or member of an organization involved in reform of the law or its administration, notwithstanding that the reform may affect the interests of a client of the lawyer. When the lawyer knows that the interests of a client may be materially benefitted by a decision in which the lawyer actively participates, the lawyer shall disclose that fact to the organization, but need not identify the client. In determining the nature and scope of participation in such activities, a lawyer should be mindful of obligations to clients under other Rules, particularly Rule 1.7.

Rule 6.5: Participation in Limited Pro Bono Legal Service Programs

(a) A lawyer who, under the auspices of a program sponsored by a court, government agency, bar association or not-for-profit legal services organization, provides short-term limited legal services to a client without expectation by either the lawyer or the client that the lawyer will provide continuing representation in the matter:

(1) shall comply with Rules 1.7, 1.8 and 1.9, concerning restrictions on representations where there are or may be conflicts of interest as that term is defined in these Rules, only if the lawyer has actual knowledge at the time of commencement of representation that the representation of the client involves a conflict of interest; and

(2) shall comply with Rule 1.10 only if the lawyer has actual knowledge at the time of commencement of representation that another lawyer associated with the lawyer in a law firm is affected by Rules 1.7, 1.8 and 1.9.

(b) Except as provided in paragraph (a)(2), Rule 1.7 and Rule 1.9 are inapplicable to a representation governed by this Rule.

(c) Short-term limited legal services are services providing legal advice or representation free of charge as part of a program described in paragraph (a) with no expectation that the assistance will continue beyond what is necessary to complete an initial consultation, representation or court appearance.

(d) The lawyer providing short-term limited legal services must secure the client's informed consent to the limited scope of the representation, and such representation shall be subject to the provisions of Rule 1.6.

(e) This Rule shall not apply where the court before which the matter is pending determines that a conflict of interest exists or, if during the course of the representation, the lawyer providing the services becomes aware of the existence of a conflict of interest precluding continued representation.

Rule 7.1: Advertising

(a) A lawyer or law firm shall not use or disseminate or participate in the use or dissemination of any advertisement that:

(1) contains statements or claims that are false, deceptive or misleading; or

(2) violates a Rule.

(b) Subject to the provisions of paragraph (a), an advertisement may include information as to:

(1) legal and nonlegal education, degrees and other scholastic distinctions, dates of admission to any bar; areas of the law in which the lawyer or law firm practices, as authorized by these Rules; public offices and teaching positions held; publications of law related matters authored by the lawyer; memberships in bar associations or other professional societies or organizations, including offices and committee assignments therein; foreign language fluency; and bona fide professional ratings;

(2) names of clients regularly represented, provided that the client has given prior written consent;

(3) bank references; credit arrangements accepted; prepaid or group legal services programs in which the lawyer or law firm participates; nonlegal services provided by the lawyer or law firm or by an entity owned and controlled by the lawyer or law firm; the existence of contractual relationships between the lawyer or law firm and a nonlegal professional or nonlegal

professional service firm, to the extent permitted by Rule 5.8, and the nature and extent of services available through those contractual relationships; and

(4) legal fees for initial consultation; contingent fee rates in civil matters when accompanied by a statement disclosing the information required by paragraph (p); range of fees for legal and nonlegal services, provided that there be available to the public free of charge a written statement clearly describing the scope of each advertised service; hourly rates; and fixed fees for specified legal and nonlegal services.

(c) An advertisement shall not:

(1) include an endorsement of, or testimonial about, a lawyer or law firm from a client with respect to a matter still pending;

(2) include a paid endorsement of, or testimonial about, a lawyer or law firm without disclosing that the person is being compensated therefor;

(3) include the portrayal of a judge, the portrayal of a fictitious law firm, the use of a fictitious name to refer to lawyers not associated together in a law firm, or otherwise imply that lawyers are associated in a law firm if that is not the case;

(4) use actors to portray the lawyer, members of the law firm, or clients, or utilize depictions of fictionalized events or scenes, without disclosure of same;

(5) rely on techniques to obtain attention that demonstrate a clear and intentional lack of relevance to the selection of counsel, including the portrayal of lawyers exhibiting characteristics clearly unrelated to legal competence;

(6) be made to resemble legal documents; or

(7) utilize a nickname, moniker, motto or trade name that implies an ability to obtain results in a matter.

(d) An advertisement that complies with paragraph (e) may contain the following:

(1) statements that are reasonably likely to create an expectation about results the lawyer can achieve;

(2) statements that compare the lawyer's services with the services of other lawyers;

(3) testimonials or endorsements of clients, where not prohibited by paragraph (c)(1), and of former clients; or

(4) statements describing or characterizing the quality of the lawyer's or law firm's services.

(e) It is permissible to provide the information set forth in paragraph (d) provided:

(1) its dissemination does not violate paragraph (a);

(2) it can be factually supported by the lawyer or law firm as of the date on which the advertisement is published or disseminated; and

(3) it is accompanied by the following disclaimer: "Prior results do not guarantee a similar outcome."

(f) Every advertisement other than those appearing in a radio, television or billboard advertisement, in a directory, newspaper, magazine or other periodical (and any web sites related thereto), or made in person pursuant to Rule 7.3(a)(1), shall be labeled "Attorney Advertising" on the first page, or on the home page in the case of a web site. If the communication is in the form of a self-mailing brochure or postcard, the words "Attorney Advertising" shall appear therein. In the case of electronic mail, the subject line shall contain the notation "ATTORNEY ADVERTISING."

(g) A lawyer or law firm shall not utilize:

(1) a pop-up or pop-under advertisement in connection with computer-accessed communications, other than on the lawyer or law firm's own web site or other internet presence; or

(2) meta tags or other hidden computer codes that, if displayed, would violate these Rules.

(h) All advertisements shall include the name, principal law office address and telephone number of the lawyer or law firm whose services are being offered.

(i) Any words or statements required by this Rule to appear in an advertisement must be clearly legible and capable of being read by the average person, if written, and intelligible if spoken aloud. In the case of a web site, the required words or statements shall appear on the home page.

(j) A lawyer or law firm advertising any fixed fee for specified legal services shall, at the time of fee publication, have available to the public a written statement clearly describing the scope of each advertised service, which statement shall be available to the client at the time of retainer for any such service. Such legal services shall include all those services that are recognized as reasonable and necessary under local custom in the area of practice in the community where the services are performed.

(k) All advertisements shall be pre-approved by the lawyer or law firm, and a copy shall be retained for a period of not less than three years following its initial dissemination. Any advertisement contained in a computer-accessed communication shall be retained for a period of not less than one year. A copy of the contents of any web site covered by this Rule shall be preserved upon the initial publication of the web site, any major web site redesign, or a meaningful and extensive content change, but in no event less frequently than once every 90 days.

(*l*) If a lawyer or law firm advertises a range of fees or an hourly rate for services, the lawyer or law firm shall not charge more than the fee advertised for such services. If a lawyer or law firm advertises a fixed fee for specified legal services, or performs services described in a fee schedule, the lawyer or law firm shall not charge more than the fixed fee for such stated legal service as set forth in the advertisement or fee schedule, unless the client agrees in writing that the services performed or to be performed were not legal services referred to or implied in the advertisement or in the fee schedule and, further, that a different fee arrangement shall apply to the transaction.

(m) Unless otherwise specified in the advertisement, if a lawyer publishes any fee information authorized under this Rule in a publication that is published more frequently than once per month, the lawyer shall be bound by any representation made therein for a period of not less than 30 days after such publication. If a lawyer publishes any fee information authorized under this Rule in a publication that is published once per month or less frequently, the lawyer shall be bound by any representation made therein until the publication of the succeeding issue. If a lawyer publishes any fee information authorized under this Rule in a publication that has no fixed date for publication of a succeeding issue, the lawyer shall be bound by any representation made therein for a reasonable period of time after publication, but in no event less than 90 days.

(n) Unless otherwise specified, if a lawyer broadcasts any fee information authorized under this Rule, the lawyer shall be bound by any representation made therein for a period of not less than 30 days after such broadcast.

(*o*) A lawyer shall not compensate or give anything of value to representatives of the press, radio, television or other communication medium in anticipation of or in return for professional publicity in a news item.

(p) All advertisements that contain information about the fees charged by the lawyer or law firm, including those indicating that in the absence of a recovery no fee will be charged, shall comply with the provisions of Judiciary Law § 488(3).

(q) A lawyer may accept employment that results from participation in activities designed to educate the public to recognize legal problems, to make intelligent selection of counsel or to utilize available legal services.

(r) Without affecting the right to accept employment, a lawyer may speak publicly or write for publication on legal topics so long as the lawyer does not undertake to give individual advice.

Rule 7.2: Payment for Referrals

(a) A lawyer shall not compensate or give anything of value to a person or organization to recommend or obtain employment by a client, or as a reward for having made a recommendation resulting in employment by a client, except that:

(1) a lawyer or law firm may refer clients to a nonlegal professional or nonlegal professional service firm pursuant to a contractual relationship with such nonlegal professional or nonlegal professional service firm to provide legal and other professional services on a systematic and continuing basis as permitted by Rule 5.8, provided however that such referral shall not otherwise include any monetary or other tangible consideration or reward for such, or the sharing of legal fees; and

(2) a lawyer may pay the usual and reasonable fees or dues charged by a qualified legal assistance organization or referral fees to another lawyer as permitted by Rule 1.5(g).

(b) A lawyer or the lawyer's partner or associate or any other affiliated lawyer may be recommended, employed or paid by, or may cooperate with one of the following offices or organizations that promote the use of the lawyer's services or those of a partner or associate or any other affiliated lawyer, or request one of the following offices or organizations to recommend or promote the use of the lawyer's services or those of the lawyer's partner or associate, or any other affiliated lawyer as a private practitioner, if there is no interference with the exercise of independent professional judgment on behalf of the client:

(1) a legal aid office or public defender office:

(i) operated or sponsored by a duly accredited law school;

(ii) operated or sponsored by a bona fide, non-profit community organization;

(iii) operated or sponsored by a governmental agency; or

(iv) operated, sponsored, or approved by a bar association;

(2) a military legal assistance office;

(3) a lawyer referral service operated, sponsored or approved by a bar association or authorized by law or court rule; or

(4) any bona fide organization that recommends, furnishes or pays for legal services to its members or beneficiaries provided the following conditions are satisfied:

(i) Neither the lawyer, nor the lawyer's partner, nor associate, nor any other affiliated lawyer nor any nonlawyer, shall have initiated or promoted such organization for the primary purpose of providing financial or other benefit to such lawyer, partner, associate or affiliated lawyer;

(ii) Such organization is not operated for the purpose of procuring legal work or financial benefit for any lawyer as a private practitioner outside of the legal services program of the organization;

(iii) The member or beneficiary to whom the legal services are furnished, and not such organization, is recognized as the client of the lawyer in the matter;

(iv) The legal service plan of such organization provides appropriate relief for any member or beneficiary who asserts a claim that representation by counsel furnished, selected or approved by the organization for the particular matter involved would be unethical, improper or inadequate under the circumstances of the matter involved; and the plan provides an appropriate procedure for seeking such relief;

(v) The lawyer does not know or have cause to know that such organization is in violation of applicable laws, rules of court or other legal requirements that govern its legal service operations; and

(vi) Such organization has filed with the appropriate disciplinary authority, to the extent required by such authority, at least annually a report with respect to its legal service plan, if any, showing its terms, its schedule of benefits, its subscription charges, agreements with counsel and financial results of its legal service activities or, if it has failed to do so, the lawyer does not know or have cause to know of such failure.

Rule 7.3: Solicitation and Recommendation of Professional Employment

(a) A lawyer shall not engage in solicitation:

(1) by in-person or telephone contact, or by real-time or interactive computer-accessed communication unless the recipient is a close friend, relative, former client or existing client; or

(2) by any form of communication if:

(i) the communication or contact violates Rule 4.5, Rule 7.1(a), or paragraph (e) of this Rule;

(ii) the recipient has made known to the lawyer a desire not to be solicited by the lawyer;

(iii) the solicitation involves coercion, duress or harassment;

(iv) the lawyer knows or reasonably should know that the age or the physical, emotional or mental state of the recipient makes it unlikely that the recipient will be able to exercise reasonable judgment in retaining a lawyer; or

(v) the lawyer intends or expects, but does not disclose, that the legal services necessary to handle the matter competently will be performed primarily by another lawyer who is not affiliated with the soliciting lawyer as a partner, associate or of counsel.

(b) For purposes of this Rule, "solicitation" means any advertisement initiated by or on behalf of a lawyer or law firm that is directed to, or targeted at, a specific recipient or group of recipients, or their family members or legal representatives, the primary purpose of which is the retention of the lawyer or law firm, and a significant motive for which is pecuniary gain. It does not include a proposal or other writing prepared and delivered in response to a specific request of a prospective client.

(c) A solicitation directed to a recipient in this State shall be subject to the following provisions:

(1) A copy of the solicitation shall at the time of its dissemination be filed with the attorney disciplinary committee of the judicial district or judicial department wherein the lawyer or law firm maintains its principal office. Where no such office is maintained, the filing shall be made in the judicial department where the solicitation is targeted. A filing shall consist of:

(i) a copy of the solicitation;

(ii) a transcript of the audio portion of any radio or television solicitation; and

(iii) if the solicitation is in a language other than English, an accurate English-language translation.

(2) Such solicitation shall contain no reference to the fact of filing.

(3) If a solicitation is directed to a predetermined recipient, a list containing the names and addresses of all recipients shall be retained by the lawyer or law firm for a period of not less than three years following the last date of its dissemination.

(4) Solicitations filed pursuant to this subdivision shall be open to public inspection.

(5) The provisions of this paragraph shall not apply to:

(i) a solicitation directed or disseminated to a close friend, relative, or former or existing client;

(ii) a web site maintained by the lawyer or law firm, unless the web site is designed for and directed to or targeted at a prospective client affected by an identifiable actual event or occurrence or by an identifiable prospective defendant; or

(iii) professional cards or other announcements the distribution of which is authorized by Rule 7.5(a).

(d) A written solicitation shall not be sent by a method that requires the recipient to travel to a location other than that at which the recipient ordinarily receives business or personal mail or that requires a signature on the part of the recipient.

(e) No solicitation relating to a specific incident involving potential claims for personal injury or wrongful death shall be disseminated before the 30th day after the date of the incident, unless a filing must be made within 30 days of the incident as a legal prerequisite to the particular claim, in which case no unsolicited communication shall be made before the 15th day after the date of the incident.

(f) Any solicitation made in writing or by computer-accessed communication and directed to a pre-determined recipient, if prompted by a specific occurrence involving or affecting a recipient, shall disclose how the lawyer obtained the identity of the recipient and learned of the recipient's potential legal need.

(g) If a retainer agreement is provided with any solicitation, the top of each page shall be marked "SAMPLE" in red ink in a type size equal to the largest type size used in the agreement and the words "DO NOT SIGN" shall appear on the client signature line.

(h) Any solicitation covered by this section shall include the name, principal law office address and telephone number of the lawyer or law firm whose services are being offered.

(i) The provisions of this Rule shall apply to a lawyer or members of a law firm not admitted to practice in this State who shall solicit retention by residents of this State.

Rule 7.4: Identification of Practice and Specialty

(a) A lawyer or law firm may publicly identify one or more areas of law in which the lawyer or the law firm practices, or may state that the practice of the lawyer or law firm is limited to one or more areas of law, provided that the lawyer or law firm shall not state that the lawyer or law firm is a specialist or specializes in a particular field of law, except as provided in Rule 7.4(c).

(b) A lawyer admitted to engage in patent practice before the United States Patent and Trademark Office may use the designation "Patent Attorney" or a substantially similar designation.

(c) A lawyer may state that the lawyer has been recognized or certified as a specialist only as follows:

(1) A lawyer who is certified as a specialist in a particular area of law or law practice by a private organization approved for that purpose by the American Bar Association may state the fact of certification if, in conjunction therewith, the certifying organization is identified and the

following statement is prominently made: "This certification is not granted by any governmental authority;"

(2) A lawyer who is certified as a specialist in a particular area of law or law practice by the authority having jurisdiction over specialization under the laws of another state or territory may state the fact of certification if, in conjunction therewith, the certifying state or territory is identified and the following statement is prominently made: "This certification is not granted by any governmental authority within the State of New York."

(3) A statement is prominently made if:

(i) when written, it is clearly legible and capable of being read by the average person, and is at least two font sizes larger than the largest text used to state the fact of certification; and

(ii) when spoken, it is intelligible to the average person, and is at a cadence no faster, and a level of audibility no lower, than the cadence and level of audibility used to state the fact of certification.

Rule 7.5: Professional Notices, Letterheads, and Signs

(a) A lawyer or law firm may use internet web sites, professional cards, professional announcement cards, office signs, letterheads or similar professional notices or devices, provided the same do not violate any statute or court rule and are in accordance with Rule 7.1, including the following:

(1) a professional card of a lawyer identifying the lawyer by name and as a lawyer, and giving addresses, telephone numbers, the name of the law firm, and any information permitted under Rule 7.1(b) or Rule 7.4. A professional card of a law firm may also give the names of members and associates;

(2) a professional announcement card stating new or changed associations or addresses, change of firm name, or similar matters pertaining to the professional offices of a lawyer or law firm or any nonlegal business conducted by the lawyer or law firm pursuant to Rule 5.7. It may state biographical data, the names of members of the firm and associates, and the names and dates of predecessor firms in a continuing line of succession. It may state the nature of the legal practice if permitted under Rule 7.4;

(3) a sign in or near the office and in the building directory identifying the law office and any nonlegal business conducted by the lawyer or law firm pursuant to Rule 5.7. The sign may state the nature of the legal practice if permitted under Rule 7.4; or

(4) a letterhead identifying the lawyer by name and as a lawyer, and giving addresses, telephone numbers, the name of the law firm, associates and any information permitted under Rule 7.1(b) or Rule 7.4. A letterhead of a law firm may also give the names of members and associates, and names and dates relating to deceased and retired members. A lawyer or law firm may be designated "Of Counsel" on a letterhead if there is a continuing relationship with a lawyer or law firm, other than as a partner or associate. A lawyer or law firm may be designated as "General Counsel" or by similar professional reference on stationery of a client if the lawyer or the firm devotes a substantial amount of professional time in the representation of that client. The letterhead of a law firm may give the names and dates of predecessor firms in a continuing line of succession.

(b) A lawyer in private practice shall not practice under a trade name, a name that is misleading as to the identity of the lawyer or lawyers practicing under such name, or a firm name containing names other than those of one or more of the lawyers in the firm, except that the name of a professional corporation shall contain "PC" or such symbols permitted by law, the name of a limited liability company or partnership shall contain "LLC," "LLP" or such symbols permitted by law and, if otherwise lawful, a firm may use as, or continue to include in its name the name or names of one or more deceased or retired members of the firm or of a predecessor firm in a continuing line of succession. Such terms as "legal clinic," "legal aid," "legal service office," "legal assistance office," "defender office" and the like may be used only by qualified legal assistance organizations, except that the term "legal clinic" may be used by any lawyer or law firm provided the name of a participating lawyer or firm is incorporated therein. A lawyer or law firm may not include the name of a nonlawyer in its firm name, nor may a lawyer or law firm that has a contractual relationship with a nonlegal professional or nonlegal professional service firm pursuant to Rule 5.8 to provide legal and other professional services on a systematic and continuing basis include in its firm name the name of the nonlegal professional service firm or any individual nonlegal professional affiliated therewith. A lawyer who assumes a judicial, legislative or public executive or administrative post or office shall not permit the lawyer's name to remain in the name of a law firm or to be used in professional notices of the firm during any significant period in which the lawyer is not actively and regularly practicing law as a member of the firm and, during such period, other members of the firm shall not use the lawyer's name in the firm name or in professional notices of the firm.

(c) Lawyers shall not hold themselves out as having a partnership with one or more other lawyers unless they are in fact partners.

(d) A partnership shall not be formed or continued between or among lawyers licensed in different jurisdictions unless all enumerations of the members and associates of the firm on its letterhead and in other permissible listings make clear the jurisdictional limitations on those members and associates of the firm not licensed to practice in all listed jurisdictions; however, the same firm name may be used in each jurisdiction.

(e) A lawyer or law firm may utilize a domain name for an internet web site that does not include the name of the lawyer or law firm provided:

(1) all pages of the web site clearly and conspicuously include the actual name of the lawyer or law firm;

(2) the lawyer or law firm in no way attempts to engage in the practice of law using the domain name;

(3) the domain name does not imply an ability to obtain results in a matter; and

(4) the domain name does not otherwise violate these Rules.

(f) A lawyer or law firm may utilize a telephone number which contains a domain name, nickname, moniker or motto that does not otherwise violate these Rules.

Rule 8.1: Candor in the Bar Admission Process

(a) A lawyer shall be subject to discipline if, in connection with the lawyer's own application for admission to the bar previously filed in this state or in any other jurisdiction, or in connection with the application of another person for admission to the bar, the lawyer knowingly:

(1) has made or failed to correct a false statement of material fact; or

(2) has failed to disclose a material fact requested in connection with a lawful demand for information from an admissions authority.

Rule 8.2: Judicial Officers and Candidates

(a) A lawyer shall not knowingly make a false statement of fact concerning the qualifications, conduct or integrity of a judge or other adjudicatory officer or of a candidate for election or appointment to judicial office.

(b) A lawyer who is a candidate for judicial office shall comply with the applicable provisions of Part 100 of the Rules of the Chief Administrator of the Courts.

Rule 8.3: Reporting Professional Misconduct

(a) A lawyer who knows that another lawyer has committed a violation of the Rules of Professional Conduct that raises a substantial question as to that lawyer's honesty, trustworthiness or fitness as a lawyer shall report such knowledge to a tribunal or other authority empowered to investigate or act upon such violation.

(b) A lawyer who possesses knowledge or evidence concerning another lawyer or a judge shall not fail to respond to a lawful demand for information from a tribunal or other authority empowered to investigate or act upon such conduct.

(c) This Rule does not require disclosure of:

(1) information otherwise protected by Rule 1.6; or

(2) information gained by a lawyer or judge while participating in a bona fide lawyer assistance program.

Rule 8.4: Misconduct

A lawyer or law firm shall not:

(a) violate or attempt to violate the Rules of Professional Conduct, knowingly assist or induce another to do so, or do so through the acts of another;

(b) engage in illegal conduct that adversely reflects on the lawyer's honesty, trustworthiness or fitness as a lawyer;

(c) engage in conduct involving dishonesty, fraud, deceit or misrepresentation;

(d) engage in conduct that is prejudicial to the administration of justice;

(e) state or imply an ability:

(1) to influence improperly or upon irrelevant grounds any tribunal, legislative body or public official; or

(2) to achieve results using means that violate these Rules or other law;

(f) knowingly assist a judge or judicial officer in conduct that is a violation of applicable rules of judicial conduct or other law;

(g) unlawfully discriminate in the practice of law, including in hiring, promoting or otherwise determining conditions of employment on the basis of age, race, creed, color, national origin, sex, disability, marital status or sexual orientation. Where there is a tribunal with jurisdiction to hear a complaint, if timely brought, other than a Departmental Disciplinary Committee, a complaint based on unlawful discrimination shall be brought before such tribunal in the first instance. A certified copy of a determination by such a tribunal, which has become final and enforceable and as to which the right to judicial or appellate review has been exhausted, finding that the lawyer has engaged in an unlawful discriminatory practice shall constitute prima facie evidence of professional misconduct in a disciplinary proceeding; or

(h) engage in any other conduct that adversely reflects on the lawyer's fitness as a lawyer.

Rule 8.5: Disciplinary Authority and Choice of Law

(a) A lawyer admitted to practice in this state is subject to the disciplinary authority of this state, regardless of where the lawyer's conduct occurs. A lawyer may be subject to the disciplinary authority of both this state and another jurisdiction where the lawyer is admitted for the same conduct.

(b) In any exercise of the disciplinary authority of this state, the rules of professional conduct to be applied shall be as follows:

(1) For conduct in connection with a proceeding in a court before which a lawyer has been admitted to practice (either generally or for purposes of that proceeding), the rules to be applied shall be the rules of the jurisdiction in which the court sits, unless the rules of the court provide otherwise; and

(2) For any other conduct:

(i) If the lawyer is licensed to practice only in this state, the rules to be applied shall be the rules of this state, and

(ii) If the lawyer is licensed to practice in this state and another jurisdiction, the rules to be applied shall be the rules of the admitting jurisdiction in which the lawyer principally practices; provided, however, that if particular conduct clearly has its predominant effect in another jurisdiction in which the lawyer is licensed to practice, the rules of that jurisdiction shall be applied to that conduct.

AMERICAN BAR ASSOCIATION MODEL CODE OF PROFESSIONAL RESPONSIBILITY

As Amended and in Effect as of 1983.

[The Model Code of Professional Responsibility was the product of the Wright Committee's efforts to replace the Canons of Professional Ethics, which had grown from 32 canons in 1908 to 47 canons in 1964. The Model Code was enacted by the ABA in 1969, and subsequently, most states adopted codes of professional responsibility based upon the Model Code. The distinctive feature of the Model Code is its organization into canons, ethical considerations, and disciplinary rules. The canons provided the Model Code with a theoretical structure. Each canon was a general directive to lawyers about the law of professional responsibility. The ethical considerations were more detailed in that they discussed actual fact situations that arose under each canon. Each ethical consideration, however, was only aspirational in nature. Lawyers were supposed to strive to follow the ethical considerations, but they were not considered binding. The disciplinary rules were the provisions that lawyers needed to follow to avoid disciplinary liability. These rules established minimum standards that lawyers were required to follow and standards that were enforced by the disciplinary committees. The ABA replaced the Model Code with the Model Rules of Professional Conduct in 1983. Ed.]

TABLE OF CONTENTS *

---

* Prepared by Editor.

PREAMBLE AND PRELIMINARY STATEMENT

Preamble[1]

The continued existence of a free and democratic society depends upon recognition of the concept that justice is based upon the rule of law grounded in respect for the dignity of the individual and his capacity

---

[1] The footnotes are intended merely to enable the reader to relate the provisions of this Code to the ABA Canons of Professional Ethics adopted in 1908, as amended, the Opinions of the ABA Committee on Professional Ethics, and a limited number of other sources; they are not intended to be an annotation of the views taken by the ABA Special

through reason for enlightened self-government.[2] Law so grounded makes justice possible, for only through such law does the dignity of the individual attain respect and protection. Without it, individual rights become subject to unrestrained power, respect for law is destroyed, and rational self-government is impossible.

Lawyers as guardians of the law, play a vital role in the preservation of society. The fulfillment of this role requires an understanding by lawyers of their relationship with and function in our legal system.[3] A consequent obligation of lawyers is to maintain the highest standards of ethical conduct.

In fulfilling his professional responsibilities, a lawyer necessarily assumes various roles that require the performance of many difficult tasks. Not every situation which he may encounter can be foreseen,[4] but fundamental ethical principles are always present to guide him. Within the framework of these principles, a lawyer must with courage and foresight be able and ready to shape the body of the law to the ever-changing relationships of society.[5]

The Code of Professional Responsibility points the way to the aspiring and provides standards by which to judge the transgressor. Each lawyer must find within his own conscience the touchstone against which to test the extent to which his actions should rise above minimum standards. But in the last analysis it is the desire for the respect and confidence of the members of his profession and of the society which he serves that should provide to a lawyer the incentive for the highest possible degree of ethical conduct. The possible loss of that respect and confidence is the ultimate sanction. So long as its practitioners are guided by these principles, the law will continue to be a noble profession. This is its greatness and its strength, which permit of no compromise.

Preliminary Statement

In furtherance of the principles stated in the Preamble, the American Bar Association has promulgated this Code of Professional Responsibility, consisting of three separate but interrelated parts: Canons, Ethical Considerations, and Disciplinary Rules.[6] The Code is designed to be adopted by appropriate agencies both as an inspirational guide to the members of the profession and as a basis for disciplinary action when the conduct of a lawyer falls below the required minimum standards stated in the Disciplinary Rules.

Obviously the Canons, Ethical Considerations, and Disciplinary Rules cannot apply to non-lawyers; however, they do define the type of ethical conduct that the public has a right to expect not only of lawyers but also of their non-professional employees and associates in all matters pertaining to professional

---

Committee on Evaluation of Ethical Standards. Footnotes citing ABA Canons refer to the ABA Canons of Professional Ethics, adopted in 1908, as amended.

2 Cf. ABA Canons, Preamble.

3 "[T]he lawyer stands today in special need of a clear understanding of his obligations and of the vital connection between these obligations and the role his profession plays in society." *Professional Responsibility: Report of the Joint Conference,* 44 A.B.A.J. 1159, 1160 (1958).

4 "No general statement of the responsibilities of the legal profession can encompass all the situations in which the lawyer may be placed. Each position held by him makes its own peculiar demands. These demands the lawyer must clarify for himself in the light of the particular role in which he serves." *Professional Responsibility: Report of the Joint Conference,* 44 A.B.A.J. 1159, 1218 (1958).

5 "The law and its institutions change as social conditions change. They must change if they are to preserve, much less advance, the political and social values from which they derive their purposes and their life. This is true of the most important of legal institutions, the profession of law. The profession, too, must change when conditions change in order to preserve and advance the social values that are its reasons for being." Cheatham, *Availability of Legal Services: The Responsibility of the Individual Lawyer and the Organized Bar,* 12 U.C.L.A.L.Rev. 438, 440 (1965).

6 The Supreme Court of Wisconsin adopted a Code of Judicial Ethics in 1967. "The code is divided into standards and rules, the standards being statements of what the general desirable level of conduct should be, the rules being particular canons, the violation of which shall subject an individual judge to sanctions." In re Promulgation of a Code of Judicial Ethics, 36 Wis.2d 252, 255, 153 N.W.2d 873, 874 (1967).

The portion of the Wisconsin Code of Judicial Ethics entitled "Standards" states that "[t]he following standards set forth the significant qualities of the ideal judge. . . ." Id., 36 Wis.2d at 256, 153 N.W.2d at 875. The portion entitled "Rules" states that "[t]he court promulgates the following rules because the requirements of judicial conduct embodied therein are of sufficient gravity to warrant sanctions if they are not obeyed. . . ." Id., 36 Wis.2d at 259, 153 N.W.2d at 876.

employment. A lawyer should ultimately be responsible for the conduct of his employees and associates in the course of the professional representation of the client.

The Canons are statements of axiomatic norms, expressing in general terms the standards of professional conduct expected of lawyers in their relationships with the public, with the legal system, and with the legal profession. They embody the general concepts from which the Ethical Considerations and the Disciplinary Rules are derived.

The Ethical Considerations are aspirational in character and represent the objectives toward which every member of the profession should strive. They constitute a body of principles upon which the lawyer can rely for guidance in many specific situations.[7]

The Disciplinary Rules, unlike the Ethical Considerations, are mandatory in character. The Disciplinary Rules state the minimum level of conduct below which no lawyer can fall without being subject to disciplinary action. Within the framework of fair trial,[8] the Disciplinary Rules should be uniformly applied to all lawyers,[9] regardless of the nature of their professional activities.[10] The Code makes no attempt to prescribe either disciplinary procedures or penalties[11] for violation of a Disciplinary Rule,[12] nor does it undertake to define standards for civil liability of lawyers for professional conduct. The severity of judgment

---

[7] "Under the conditions of modern practice is it peculiarly necessary that the lawyer should understand, not merely the established standards of professional conduct, but the reasons underlying these standards. Today the lawyer plays a changing and increasingly varied role. In many developing fields the precise contribution of the legal profession is as yet undefined." *Professional Responsibility: Report of the Joint Conference,* 44 A.B.A.J. 1159 (1958).

"A true sense of professional responsibility must derive from an understanding of the reasons that lie back of specific restraints, such as those embodied in the Canons. The grounds for the lawyer's peculiar obligations are to be found in the nature of his calling. The lawyer who seeks a clear understanding of his duties will be led to reflect on the special services his profession renders to society and the services it might render if its full capacities were realized. When the lawyer fully understands the nature of his office, he will then discern what restraints are necessary to keep that office wholesome and effective." *Id.*

[8] "Disbarment, designed to protect the public, is a punishment or penalty imposed on the lawyer. * * * He is accordingly entitled to procedural due process, which includes fair notice of the charge." In re Ruffalo, 390 U.S. 544, 550, 20 L.Ed.2d 117, 122, 88 S.Ct. 1222, 1226 (1968), rehearing denied, 391 U.S. 961, 20 L.Ed.2d 874, 88 S.Ct. 1833 (1968).

"A State cannot exclude a person from the practice of law or from any other occupation in a manner or for reasons that contravene the Due Process or Equal Protection Clause of the Fourteenth Amendment. . . . A State can require high standards of qualification . . . but any qualification must have a rational connection with the applicant's fitness or capacity to practice law." Schware v. Bd. of Bar Examiners, 353 U.S. 232, 239, 1 L.Ed.2d 796, 801–02, 77 S.Ct. 752, 756 (1957).

"[A]n accused lawyer may expect that he will not be condemned out of a capricious self-righteousness or denied the essentials of a fair hearing." Kingsland v. Dorsey, 338 U.S. 318, 320, 94 L.Ed. 123, 126, 70 S.Ct. 123, 124–25 (1949).

"The attorney and counsellor being, by the solemn judicial act of the court, clothed with his office, does not hold it as a matter of grace and favor. The right which it confers upon him to appear for suitors, and to argue causes is something more than a mere indulgence, revocable at the pleasure of the court, or at the command of the legislature. It is a right of which he can only be deprived by the judgment of the court, for moral or professional delinquency." Ex parte Garland, 71 U.S. (4 Wall.) 333, 378–79, 18 L.Ed. 366, 370 (1866).

See generally Comment, *Procedural Due Process and Character Hearings for Bar Applicants,* 15 Stan.L.Rev. 500 (1963).

[9] "The canons of professional ethics must be enforced by the Courts and must be respected by members of the Bar if we are to maintain public confidence in the integrity and impartiality of the administration of justice." In re Meeker, 76 N.M. 354, 357, 414 P.2d 862, 864 (1966), appeal dismissed, 385 U.S. 449 (1967).

[10] See ABA Canon 45.

"The Canons of this Association govern all its members, irrespective of the nature of their practice, and the application of the Canons is not affected by statutes or regulations governing certain activities of lawyers which may prescribe less stringent standards." ABA Comm. on Professional Ethics, Opinions, No. 203 (1940) [hereinafter each Opinion is cited as "ABA Opinion"].

Cf. *ABA Opinion* 152 (1936).

[11] "There is generally no prescribed discipline for any particular type of improper conduct. The disciplinary measures taken are discretionary with the courts, which may disbar, suspend, or merely censure the attorney as the nature of the offense and past indicia of character may warrant." Note, 43 Cornell L.Q. 489, 495 (1958).

[12] The Code seeks only to specify conduct for which a lawyer should be disciplined. Recommendations as to the procedures to be used in disciplinary actions and the gravity of disciplinary measures appropriate for violations of the Code are within the jurisdiction of the American Bar Association Special Committee on Evaluation of Disciplinary Enforcement.

against one found guilty of violating a Disciplinary Rule should be determined by the character of the offense and the attendant circumstances.[13] An enforcing agency, in applying the Disciplinary Rules, may find interpretive guidance in the basic principles embodied in the Canons and in the objectives reflected in the Ethical Considerations.

CANON 1

A Lawyer Should Assist in Maintaining the Integrity and Competence of the Legal Profession

ETHICAL CONSIDERATIONS

EC 1–1 A basic tenet of the professional responsibility of lawyers is that every person in our society should have ready access to the independent professional services of a lawyer of integrity and competence. Maintaining the integrity and improving the competence of the bar to meet the highest standards is the ethical responsibility of every lawyer.

EC 1–2 The public should be protected from those who are not qualified to be lawyers by reason of a deficiency in education[1] or moral standards[2] or of other relevant factors[3] but who nevertheless seek to

---

13 "The severity of the judgment of this court should be in proportion to the gravity of the offenses, the moral turpitude involved, and the extent that the defendant's acts and conduct affect his professional qualifications to practice law." Louisiana State Bar Ass'n v. Steiner, 204 La. 1073, 1092–93, 16 So.2d 843, 850 (1944) (Higgins, J., concurring in decree).

"Certainly an erring lawyer who has been disciplined and who having paid the penalty has given satisfactory evidence of repentance and has been rehabilitated and restored to his place at the bar by the court which knows him best ought not to have what amounts to an order of permanent disbarment entered against him by a federal court solely on the basis of an earlier criminal record and without regard to his subsequent rehabilitation and present good character. . . . We think, therefore, that the district court should reconsider the appellant's application for admission and grant it unless the court finds it to be a fact that the appellant is not presently of good moral or professional character." In re Dreier, 258 F.2d 68, 69–70 (3d Cir.1958).

1 "[W]e cannot conclude that all educational restrictions [on bar admission] are unlawful. We assume that few would deny that a grammar school education requirement, before taking the bar examination, was reasonable. Or that an applicant had to be able to read or write. Once we conclude that *some* restriction is proper, then it becomes a matter of degree—the problem of drawing the line.

. . .

"We conclude the fundamental question here is whether Rule IV, Section 6 of the Rules Pertaining to Admission of Applicants to the State Bar of Arizona is 'arbitrary, capricious and unreasonable.' We conclude an educational requirement of graduation from an accredited law school is not." Hackin v. Lockwood, 361 F.2d 499, 503–04 (9th Cir.1966), cert. denied, 385 U.S. 960, 17 L.Ed.2d 305, 87 S.Ct. 396 (1966).

2 "Every state in the United States, as a prerequisite for admission to the practice of law, requires that applicants possess 'good moral character.' Although the requirement is of judicial origin, it is now embodied in legislation in most states." Comment, *Procedural Due Process and Character Hearings for Bar Applicants,* 15 Stan.L.Rev. 500 (1963).

"Good character in the members of the bar is essential to the preservation of the integrity of the courts. The duty and power of the court to guard its portals against intrusion by men and women who are mentally and morally dishonest, unfit because of bad character, evidenced by their course of conduct, to participate in the administrative law, would seem to be unquestioned in the matter of preservation of judicial dignity and integrity." In re Monaghan, 126 Vt. 53, 222 A.2d 665, 670 (1966).

"Fundamentally, the question involved in both situations [i.e. admission and disciplinary proceedings] is the same—is the applicant for admission or the attorney sought to be disciplined a fit and proper person to be permitted to practice law, and that usually turns upon whether he has committed or is likely to continue to commit acts of moral turpitude. At the time of oral argument the attorney for respondent frankly conceded that the test for admission and for discipline is and should be the same. We agree with this concession." Hallinan v. Comm. of Bar Examiners, 65 Cal.2d 447, 453, 421 P.2d 76, 81, 55 Cal.Rptr. 228, 233 (1966).

3 "Proceedings to gain admission to the bar are for the purpose of protecting the public and the courts from the ministrations of persons unfit to practice the profession. Attorneys are officers of the court appointed to assist the court in the administration of justice. Into their hands are committed the property, the liberty and sometimes the lives of their clients. This commitment demands a high degree of intelligence, knowledge of the law, respect for its function in society, sound and faithful judgment and, above all else, integrity of character in private and professional conduct." In re Monaghan, 126 Vt. 53, 222 A.2d 665, 676 (1966) (Holden, C.J., dissenting).

practice law. To assure the maintenance of high moral and educational standards of the legal profession, lawyers should affirmatively assist courts and other appropriate bodies in promulgating, enforcing, and improving requirements for admission to the bar.[4] In like manner, the bar has a positive obligation to aid in the continued improvement of all phases of pre-admission and post-admission legal education.

EC 1–3 Before recommending an applicant for admission, a lawyer should satisfy himself that the applicant is of good moral character. Although a lawyer should not become a self-appointed investigator or judge of applicants for admission, he should report to proper officials all unfavorable information he possesses relating to the character or other qualifications of an applicant.[5]

EC 1–4 The integrity of the profession can be maintained only if conduct of lawyers in violation of the Disciplinary Rules is brought to the attention of the proper officials. A lawyer should reveal voluntarily to those officials all unprivileged knowledge of conduct of lawyers which he believes clearly to be in violation of the Disciplinary Rules.[6] A lawyer should, upon request, serve on and assist committees and boards having responsibility for the administration of the Disciplinary Rules.[7]

EC 1–5 A lawyer should maintain high standards of professional conduct and should encourage fellow lawyers to do likewise. He should be temperate and dignified, and he should refrain from all illegal and morally reprehensible conduct.[8] Because of his position in society, even minor violations of law by a lawyer may tend to lessen public confidence in the legal profession. Obedience to law exemplifies respect for law. To lawyers especially, respect for the law should be more than a platitude.

EC 1–6 An applicant for admission to the bar or a lawyer may be unqualified, temporarily or permanently, for other than moral and educational reasons, such as mental or emotional instability. Lawyers should be diligent in taking steps to see that during a period of disqualification such person is not granted a license or, if licensed, is not permitted to practice.[9] In like manner, when the disqualification has terminated, members of the bar should assist such person in being licensed, or, if licensed, in being restored to his full right to practice.

---

4 "A bar composed of lawyers of good moral character is a worthy objective but it is unnecessary to sacrifice vital freedoms in order to obtain that goal. It is also important both to society and the bar itself that lawyers be unintimidated—free to think, speak, and act as members of an Independent Bar." Konigsberg v. State Bar, 353 U.S. 252, 273, 1 L.Ed.2d 810, 825, 77 S.Ct. 722, 733 (1957).

5 *See* ABA Canon 29.

6 ABA Canon 28 designates certain conduct as unprofessional and then states that: "A duty to the public and to the profession devolves upon every member of the Bar having knowledge of such practices upon the part of any practitioner immediately to inform thereof, to the end that the offender may be disbarred." ABA Canon 29 states a broader admonition: "Lawyers should expose without fear or favor before the proper tribunals corrupt or dishonest conduct in the profession."

7 "It is the obligation of the organized Bar and the individual lawyer to give unstinted cooperation and assistance to the highest court of the state in discharging its function and duty with respect to discipline and in purging the profession of the unworthy." *Report of the Special Committee on Disciplinary Procedures,* 80 A.B.A.Rep. 463, 470 (1955).

8 Cf. ABA Canon 32.

9 "We decline, on the present record, to disbar Mr. Sherman or to reprimand him—not because we condone his actions, but because, as heretofore indicated, we are concerned with whether he is mentally responsible for what he has done.

. . .

"The logic of the situation would seem to dictate the conclusion that, if he was mentally responsible for the conduct we have outlined, he should be disbarred; and, if he was not mentally responsible, he should not be permitted to practice law.

"However, the flaw in the logic is that he may have been mentally irresponsible [at the time of his offensive conduct] . . . , and, yet, have sufficiently improved in the almost two and one-half years intervening to be able to capably and competently represent his clients. . . .

. . .

"We would make clear that we are satisfied that a case has been made against Mr. Sherman, warranting a refusal to permit him to further practice law in this state unless he can establish his mental irresponsibility at the time of the offenses charged. The burden of proof is upon him.

"If he establishes such mental irresponsibility, the burden is then upon him to establish his present capability to practice law." In re Sherman, 58 Wash.2d 1, 6–7, 354 P.2d 888, 890 (1960), cert. denied, 371 U.S. 951, 9 L.Ed.2d 499, 83 S.Ct. 506 (1963).

DISCIPLINARY RULES

DR 1–101 Maintaining Integrity and Competence of the Legal Profession.

(A) A lawyer is subject to discipline if he has made a materially false statement in, or if he has deliberately failed to disclose a material fact requested in connection with, his application for admission to the bar.[10]

(B) A lawyer shall not further the application for admission to the bar of another person known by him to be unqualified in respect to character, education, or other relevant attribute.[11]

DR 1–102 Misconduct.

(A) A lawyer shall not:

(1) Violate a Disciplinary Rule.

(2) Circumvent a Disciplinary Rule through actions of another.[12]

(3) Engage in illegal conduct involving moral turpitude.[13]

---

10 "This Court has the inherent power to revoke a license to practice law in this State, where such license was issued by this Court, and its issuance was procured by the fraudulent concealment, or by the false and fraudulent representation by the applicant of a fact which was manifestly material to the issuance of the license." North Carolina ex rel. Attorney General v. Gorson, 209 N.C. 320, 326, 183 S.E. 392, 395 (1936), cert. denied, 298 U.S. 662, 80 L.Ed. 1387, 56 S.Ct. 752 (1936).

See also Application of Patterson, 318 P.2d 907, 913 (Or.1957), cert. denied, 356 U.S. 947, 2 L.Ed.2d 822, 78 S.Ct. 795 (1958).

11 See ABA Canon 29.

12 In *ABA Opinion* 95 (1933), which held that a municipal attorney could not permit police officers to interview persons with claims against the municipality when the attorney knew the claimants to be represented by counsel, the Committee on Professional Ethics said:

"The law officer is, of course, responsible for the acts of those in his department who are under his supervision and control." *Opinion 85.* In re Robinson, 136 N.Y.S. 548 (affirmed 209 N.Y. 354–1912) held that it was a matter of disbarment for an attorney to adopt a general course of approving the unethical conduct of employees of his client, even though he did not actively participate therein.

" '. . . The attorney should not advise or sanction acts by his client which he himself should not do.' *Opinion 75.*"

13 "The most obvious non-professional ground for disbarment is conviction for a felony. Most states make conviction for a felony grounds for automatic disbarment. Some of these states, including New York, make disbarment mandatory upon conviction for *any* felony, while others require disbarment only for those felonies which involve moral turpitude. There are strong arguments that some felonies, such as involuntary manslaughter, reflect neither on an attorney's fitness, trustworthiness, nor competence and, therefore, should not be grounds for disbarment, but most states tend to disregard these arguments and, following the common law rule, make disbarment mandatory on conviction for any felony." Note, 43 Cornell L.Q. 489, 490 (1958).

"Some states treat conviction for misdemeanors as grounds for automatic disbarment. . . . However, the vast majority, accepting the common law rule, require that the misdemeanor involve moral turpitude. While the definition of moral turpitude may prove difficult, it seems only proper that those minor offenses which do not affect the attorney's fitness to continue in the profession should not be grounds for disbarment. A good example is an assault and battery conviction which would not involve moral turpitude unless done with malice and deliberation." Id. at 491.

"The term 'moral turpitude' has been used in the law for centuries. It has been the subject of many decisions by the courts but has never been clearly defined because of the nature of the term. Perhaps the best general definition of the term 'moral turpitude' is that it imports an act of baseness, vileness or depravity in the duties which one person owes to another or to society in general, which is contrary to the usual, accepted and customary rule of right and duty which a person should follow. 58 C.J.S. at page 1201. Although offenses against revenue laws have been held to be crimes of moral turpitude, it has also been held that the attempt to evade the payment of taxes due to the government or any subdivision thereof, while wrong and unlawful, does not involve moral turpitude. 58 C.J.S. at page 1205." Comm. on Legal Ethics v. Scheer, 149 W.Va. 721, 726–27, 143 S.E.2d 141, 145 (1965).

"The right and power to discipline an attorney, as one of its officers, is inherent in the court. . . . This power is not limited to those instances of misconduct wherein he has been employed, or has acted, in a professional capacity; but, on

(4) Engage in conduct involving dishonesty, fraud, deceit, or misrepresentation.

(5) Engage in conduct that is prejudicial to the administration of justice.

(6) Engage in any other conduct that adversely reflects on his fitness to practice law.[14]

DR 1-103 Disclosure of Information to Authorities.

(A) A lawyer possessing unprivileged knowledge of a violation of DR 1-102 shall report such knowledge to a tribunal or other authority empowered to investigate or act upon such violation.[15]

(B) A lawyer possessing unprivileged knowledge or evidence concerning another lawyer or a judge shall reveal fully such knowledge or evidence upon proper request of a tribunal or other authority empowered to investigate or act upon the conduct of lawyers or judges.[16]

CANON 2

A Lawyer Should Assist the Legal Profession in Fulfilling Its Duty to Make Legal Counsel Available

ETHICAL CONSIDERATIONS

EC 2-1 The need of members of the public for legal services[1] is met only if they recognize their legal problems, appreciate the importance of seeking assistance,[2] and are able to obtain the services of acceptable legal counsel.[3] Hence, important functions of the legal profession are to educate laymen to recognize their

---

the contrary, this power may be exercised where his misconduct outside the scope of his professional relations shows him to be an unfit person to practice law." In re Wilson, 391 S.W.2d 914, 917–18 (Mo.1965).

[14] "It is a fair characterization of the lawyer's responsibility in our society that he stands 'as a shield,' to quote Devlin, J., in defense of right and to ward off wrong. From a profession charged with these responsibilities there must be exacted those qualities of truth-speaking, of a high sense of honor, of granite discretion, of the strictest observance of fiduciary responsibility, that have, throughout the centuries, been compendiously described as 'moral character.'" Schware v. Bd. of Bar Examiners, 353 U.S. 232, 247 L.Ed.2d 796, 806, 77 S.Ct. 752, 761 (1957) (Frankfurter, J., concurring).

"Particularly applicable here is Rule 4.47 providing that 'A lawyer should always maintain his integrity; and shall not willfully commit any act against the interest of the public; nor shall he violate his duty to the courts or his clients; *nor shall he, by any misconduct, commit any offense against the laws of Missouri or the United States of America, which amounts to a crime involving acts done by him contrary to justice, honesty, modesty or good morals;* nor shall he be guilty of any other misconduct whereby, for the protection of the public and those charged with the administration of justice, he should no longer be entrusted with the duties and responsibilities belonging to the office of an attorney.'" In re Wilson, 391 S.W.2d 914, 917 (Mo.1965).

[15] See ABA Canon 29; cf. ABA Canon 28.

[16] Cf. ABA Canons 28 and 29.

[1] "Men have need for more than a system of law; they have need for a system of law which functions, and that means they have need for lawyers." Cheatham, *The Lawyer's Role and Surroundings,* 25 Rocky Mt.L.Rev. 405 (1953).

[2] "Law is not self-applying; men must apply and utilize it in concrete cases. But the ordinary man is incapable. He cannot know the principles of law or the rules guiding the machinery of law administration; he does not know how to formulate his desires with precision and to put them into writing; he is ineffective in the presentation of his claims." Cheatham, *The Lawyer's Role and Surroundings,* 25 Rocky Mt.L.Rev. 405 (1953).

[3] "This need [to provide legal services] was recognized by . . . Mr. [Lewis F.] Powell [Jr., President, American Bar Association, 1963–64], who said: 'Looking at contemporary America realistically, we must admit that despite all our efforts to date (and these have not been insignificant), far too many persons are not able to obtain equal justice under law. This usually results because their poverty or their ignorance has prevented them from obtaining legal counsel.'" Address by E. Clinton Bamberger, Association of American Law Schools 1965 Annual Meeting, Dec. 28, 1965, in Proceedings, Part II, 1965, 61, 63–64 (1965).

"A wide gap separates the need for legal services and its satisfaction, as numerous studies reveal. Looked at from the side of the layman, one reason for the gap is poverty and the consequent inability to pay legal fees. Another set of reasons is ignorance of the need for and the value of legal services, and ignorance of where to find a dependable lawyer. There is fear of the mysterious processes and delays of the law, and there is fear of overreaching and overcharging by lawyers, a

problems, to facilitate the process of intelligent selection of lawyers, and to assist in making legal services fully available.[4]

Recognition of Legal Problems

EC 2–2 The legal profession should assist lay-persons to recognize legal problems because such problems may not be self-revealing and often are not timely noticed. Therefore, lawyers should encourage and participate in educational and public relations programs concerning our legal system with particular reference to legal problems that frequently arise. Preparation of advertisements and professional articles for lay publications[5] and participation in seminars, lectures, and civic programs should be motivated by a desire to educate the public to an awareness of legal needs and to provide information relevant to the selection of the most appropriate counsel rather than to obtain publicity for particular lawyers. The problems of advertising on television require special consideration, due to the style, cost, and transitory nature of such media. If the interests of laypersons in receiving relevant lawyer advertising are not adequately served by print media and radio advertising, and if adequate safeguards to protect the public can reasonably be formulated, television advertising may serve a public interest.

As amended in 1977.

EC 2–3 Whether a lawyer acts properly in volunteering in-person advice to a layperson to seek legal services depends upon the circumstances.[6] The giving of advice that one should take legal action could well be in fulfillment of the duty of the legal profession to assist laypersons in recognizing legal problems.[7] The advice is proper only if motivated by a desire to protect one who does not recognize that he may have legal problems or who is ignorant of his legal rights or obligations. It is improper if motivated by a desire to obtain personal benefit, secure personal publicity, or cause legal action to be taken merely to harass or injure another. A lawyer should not initiate an in-person contact with a non-client, personally or through a representative, for the purpose of being retained to represent him for compensation.

As amended in 1977.

---

fear stimulated by the occasional exposure of shysters." Cheatham, *Availability of Legal Services: The Responsibility of the Individual Lawyer and of the Organized Bar,* 12 U.C.L.A.L.Rev. 438 (1965).

4 "It is not only the right but the duty of the profession as a whole to utilize such methods as may be developed to bring the services of its members to those who need them, so long as this can be done ethically and with dignity." *ABA Opinion* 320 (1968).

"[T]here is a responsibility on the bar to make legal services available to those who need them. The maxim, 'privilege brings responsibilities,' can be expanded to read, exclusive privilege to render public service brings responsibility to assure that the service is available to those in need of it." Cheatham, *Availability of Legal Services: The Responsibility of the Individual Lawyer and of the Organized Bar,* 12 U.C.L.A.L.Rev. 438, 443 (1965).

"The obligation to provide legal services for those actually caught up in litigation carries with it the obligation to make preventive legal advice accessible to all. It is among those unaccustomed to business affairs and fearful of the ways of the law that such advice is often most needed. If it is not received in time, the most valiant and skillful representation in court may come too late." *Professional Responsibility: Report of the Joint Conference,* 44 A.B.A.J. 1159, 1216 (1958).

5 "A lawyer may with propriety write articles for publications in which he gives information upon the law. . . ." A.B.A. Canon 40.

6 See ABA Canon 28.

7 This question can assume constitutional dimensions: "We meet at the outset the contention that "solicitation" is wholly outside the area of freedoms protected by the First Amendment. To this contention there are two answers. The first is that a State cannot foreclose the exercise of constitutional rights by mere labels. The second is that abstract discussion is not the only species of communication which the Constitution protects; the First Amendment also protects vigorous advocacy, certainly of lawful ends, against governmental intrusion. . . .

. . .

"However valid may be Virginia's interest in regulating the traditionally illegal practice of barratry, maintenance and champerty, that interest does not justify the prohibition of the NAACP activities disclosed by this record. Malicious intent was of the essence of the common-law offenses of fomenting or stirring up litigation. And whatever may be or may have been true of suits against governments in other countries, the exercise in our own, as in this case of First Amendment rights to enforce Constitutional rights through litigation, as a matter of law, cannot be deemed malicious." NAACP v. Button, 371 U.S. 415, 429, 439–40, 9 L.Ed.2d 405, 415–16, 422, 83 S.Ct. 328, 336, 341 (1963).

EC 2–4 Since motivation is subjective and often difficult to judge, the motives of a lawyer who volunteers in-person advice likely to produce legal controversy may well be suspect if he receives professional employment or other benefits as a result.[8] A lawyer who volunteers in-person advice that one should obtain the services of a lawyer generally should not himself accept employment, compensation, or other benefit in connection with that matter. However, it is not improper for a lawyer to volunteer such advice and render resulting legal services to close friends, relatives, former clients (in regard to matters germane to former employment), and regular clients.[9]

As amended in 1977.

EC 2–5 A lawyer who writes or speaks for the purpose of educating members of the public to recognize their legal problems should carefully refrain from giving or appearing to give a general solution applicable to all apparently similar individual problems,[10] since slight changes in fact situations may require a material variance in the applicable advice; otherwise, the public may be mislead and misadvised. Talks and writings by lawyers for laypersons should caution them not to attempt to solve individual problems upon the basis of the information contained therein.[11]

As amended in 1977.

Selection of a Lawyer

EC 2–6 Formerly a potential client usually knew the reputations of local lawyers for competency and integrity and therefore could select a practitioner in whom he had confidence. This traditional selection process worked well because it was initiated by the client and the choice was an informed one.

EC 2–7 Changed conditions, however, have seriously restricted the effectiveness of the traditional selection process. Often the reputations of lawyers are not sufficiently known to enable laypersons to make intelligent choices.[12] The law has become increasingly complex and specialized. Few lawyers are willing and competent to deal with every kind of legal matter, and many laypersons have difficulty in determining the competence of lawyers to render different types of legal services. The selection of legal counsel is particularly difficult for transients, persons moving into new areas, persons of limited education or means, and others who have little or no contact with lawyers.[13] Lack of information about the availability of lawyers, the qualifications of particular lawyers, and the expense of legal representation leads laypersons to avoid seeking legal advice.

---

[8] "It is disreputable for an attorney to breed litigation by seeking out those who have claims for personal injuries or other grounds of action in order to secure them as clients, or to employ agents or runners, or to reward those who bring or influence the bringing of business to his office. . . . Moreover, it tends quite easily to the institution of baseless litigation and the manufacture of perjured testimony. From early times, this danger has been recognized in the law by the condemnation of the crime of common barratry, or the stirring up of suits or quarrels between individuals at law or otherwise." In re Ades, 6 F.Supp. 467, 474–75 (D.Mary.1934).

[9] "*Rule 2.*

"§ a. . . .

"[A] member of the State Bar shall not solicit professional employment by

"(1) Volunteering counsel or advice except where ties of blood relationship or trust make it appropriate." Cal.Business and Professions Code § 6076 (West 1962).

[10] "*Rule 18* . . . A member of the State Bar shall not advise inquirers or render opinions to them through or in connection with a newspaper, radio or other publicity medium of any kind in respect to their specific legal problems, whether or not such attorney shall be compensated for his services." Cal.Business and Professions Code § 6076 (West 1962).

[11] "In any case where a member might well apply the advice given in the opinion to his individual affairs, the lawyer rendering the opinion [concerning problems common to members of an association and distributed to the members through a periodic bulletin] should specifically state that this opinion should not be relied on by any member as a basis for handling his individual affairs, but that in every case he should consult his counsel. In the publication of the opinion the association should make a similar statement." *ABA Opinion* 273 (1946).

[12] "A group of recent interrelated changes bears directly on the availability of legal services. . . . [One] change is the constantly accelerating urbanization of the country and the decline of personal and neighborhood knowledge of whom to retain as a professional man." Cheatham, *Availability of Legal Services: The Responsibility of the Individual Lawyer and of the Organized Bar,* 12 U.C.L.A.L.Rev. 438, 440 (1965).

[13] Cf. Cheatham, *A Lawyer When Needed: Legal Services for the Middle Classes,* 63 Colum.L.Rev. 973, 974 (1963).

As amended in 1977.

EC 2–8 Selection of a lawyer by a layperson should be made on an informed basis. Advice and recommendation of third parties—relatives, friends, acquaintances, business associates, or other lawyers—and disclosure of relevant information about the lawyer and his practice may be helpful. A layperson is best served if the recommendation is disinterested and informed. In order that the recommendation be disinterested, a lawyer should not seek to influence another to recommend his employment. A lawyer should not compensate another person for recommending him, for influencing a prospective client to employ him, or to encourage future recommendations.[14] Advertisements and public communications, whether in law lists, telephone directories, newspapers, other forms of print media, television or radio, should be formulated to convey only information that is necessary to make an appropriate selection. Such information includes: (1) office information, such as, name, including name of law firm and names of professional associates; addresses; telephone numbers; credit card acceptability; fluency in foreign languages; and office hours; (2) relevant biographical information; (3) description of the practice, but only by using designations and definitions authorized by [the agency having jurisdiction of the subject under state law], for example, one or more fields of law in which the lawyer or law firm practices; a statement that practice is limited to one or more fields of law; and/or a statement that the lawyer or law firm specializes in a particular field of law practice, but only by using designations, definitions and standards authorized by [the agency having jurisdiction of the subject under state law]; and (4) permitted fee information. Self-laudation should be avoided.

As amended in 1978.

Selection of a Lawyer: Lawyer Advertising

EC 2–9 The lack of sophistication on the part of many members of the public concerning legal services, the importance of the interests affected by the choice of a lawyer and prior experience with unrestricted lawyer advertising, require that special care be taken by lawyers to avoid misleading the public and to assure that the information set forth in any advertising is relevant to the selection of a lawyer. The lawyer must be mindful that the benefits of lawyer advertising depend upon its reliability and accuracy. Examples of information in lawyer advertising that would be deceptive include misstatements of fact, suggestions that the ingenuity or prior record of a lawyer rather than the justice of the claim are the principal factors likely to determine the result, inclusion of information irrelevant to selecting a lawyer, and representations concerning the quality of service, which cannot be measured or verified. Since lawyer advertising is calculated and not spontaneous, reasonable regulation of lawyer advertising designed to foster compliance with appropriate standards serves the public interest without impeding the flow of useful, meaningful, and relevant information to the public.

As amended in 1977.

EC 2–10 A lawyer should ensure that the information contained in any advertising which the lawyer publishes, broadcasts or causes to be published or broadcast is relevant, is disseminated in an objective and understandable fashion, and would facilitate the prospective client's ability to compare the qualifications of the lawyers available to represent him. A lawyer should strive to communicate such information without undue emphasis upon style and advertising stratagems which serve to hinder rather than to facilitate intelligent selection of counsel. Because technological change is a recurrent feature of communications forms, and because perceptions of what is relevant in lawyer selection may change, lawyer advertising regulations should not be cast in rigid, unchangeable terms. Machinery is therefore available to advertisers and consumers for prompt consideration of proposals to change the rules governing lawyer advertising. The determination of any request for such change should depend upon whether the proposal is necessary in light of existing Code provisions, whether the proposal accords with standards of accuracy, reliability and truthfulness, and whether the proposal would facilitate informed selection of lawyers by potential consumers of legal services. Representatives of lawyers and consumers should be heard in addition to the applicant concerning any proposed change. Any change which is approved should be promulgated in the form of an amendment to the Code so that all lawyers practicing in the jurisdiction may avail themselves of its provisions.

---

[14] See ABA Canon 28.

As amended in 1977.

EC 2–11 The name under which a lawyer conducts his practice may be a factor in the selection process.[16] The use of a trade name or an assumed name could mislead laypersons concerning the identity, responsibility, and status of those practicing thereunder.[17] Accordingly, a lawyer in private practice should practice only under a designation containing his own name, the name of a lawyer employing him, the name of one or more of the lawyers practicing in a partnership, or, if permitted by law, the name of a professional legal corporation, which should be clearly designated as such. For many years some law firms have used a firm name retaining one or more names of deceased or retired partners and such practice is not improper if the firm is a bona fide successor of a firm in which the deceased or retired person was a member, if the use of the name is authorized by law or by contract, and if the public is not misled thereby.[18] However, the name of a partner who withdraws from a firm but continues to practice law should be omitted from the firm name in order to avoid misleading the public.

As amended in 1977.

EC 2–12 A lawyer occupying a judicial, legislative, or public executive or administrative position who has the right to practice law concurrently may allow his name to remain in the name of the firm if he actively continues to practice law as a member thereof. Otherwise, his name should be removed from the firm name,[19] and he should not be identified as a past or present member of the firm; and he should not hold himself out as being a practicing lawyer.

EC 2–13 In order to avoid the possibility of misleading persons with whom he deals, a lawyer should be scrupulous in the representation of his professional status.[20] He should not hold himself out as being a partner or associate of a law firm if he is not one in fact,[21] and thus should not hold himself out as partner or associate if he only shares offices with another lawyer.[22]

EC 2–14 In some instances a lawyer confines his practice to a particular field of law.[23] In the absence of state controls to insure the existence of special competence, a lawyer should not be permitted to hold himself

---

16 *Cf. ABA Opinion* 303 (1961).

17 *See* ABA Canon 33.

18 Id.

"The continued use of a firm name by one or more surviving partners after the death of a member of the firm whose name is in the firm title is expressly permitted by the Canons of Ethics. The reason for this is that all of the partners have by their joint and several efforts over a period of years contributed to the good will attached to the firm name. In the case of a firm having widespread connections, this good will is disturbed by a change in firm name every time a name partner dies, and that reflects a loss in some degree of the good will to the building up of which the surviving partners have contributed their time, skill and labor through a period of years. To avoid this loss the firm name is continued, and to meet the requirements of the Canon the individuals constituting the firm from time to time are listed." *ABA Opinion* 267 (1945).

"Accepted local custom in New York recognizes that the name of a law firm does not necessarily identify the individual members of the firm, and hence the continued use of a firm name after the death of one or more partners is not a deception and is permissible. . . . The continued use of a deceased partner's name in the firm title is not affected by the fact that another partner withdraws from the firm and his name is dropped, or the name of the new partner is added to the firm name." *Opinion* No. 45, Committee on Professional Ethics, New York State Bar Ass'n, 39 N.Y.St.B.J. 455 (1967).

19 Cf. ABA Canon 33 and *ABA Opinion* 315 (1965).

20 Cf. *ABA Opinions* 283 (1950) and 81 (1932).

21 See *ABA Opinion* 316 (1967).

22 "The word 'associates' has a variety of meanings. Principally through custom the word when used on the letterheads of law firms has come to be regarded as describing those who are employees of the firm. Because the word has acquired this special significance in connection with the practice of the law the use of the word to describe lawyer relationships other than employer-employee is likely to be misleading." In re Sussman and Tanner, 241 Ore. 246, 248, 405 P.2d 355, 356 (1965).

According to *ABA Opinion* 310 (1963), use of the term "associates" would be misleading in two situations: (1) where two lawyers are partners and they share both responsibility and liability for the partnership; and (2) where two lawyers practice separately, sharing no responsibility or liability, and only share a suite of offices and some costs.

23 "For a long time, many lawyers have, of necessity, limited their practice to certain branches of law. The increasing complexity of the law and the demand of the public for more expertness on the part of the lawyer has, in the past few

out as a specialist or as having official recognition as a specialist, other than in the fields of admiralty, trademark, and patent law where a holding out as a specialist historically has been permitted. A lawyer may, however, indicate in permitted advertising, if it is factual, a limitation of his practice or one or more particular areas or fields of law in which he practices using designations and definitions authorized for that purpose by [the state agency having jurisdiction]. A lawyer practicing in a jurisdiction which certifies specialists must also be careful not to confuse laypersons as to his status. If a lawyer discloses areas of law in which he practices or to which he limits his practice, but is not certified in [the jurisdiction], he, and the designation authorized in [the jurisdiction], should avoid any implication that he is in fact certified.

As amended in 1977.

EC 2–15 The legal profession has developed lawyer referral systems designed to aid individuals who are able to pay fees but need assistance in locating lawyers competent to handle their particular problems. Use of a lawyer referral system enables a layman to avoid an uninformed selection of a lawyer because such a system makes possible the employment of competent lawyers who have indicated an interest in the subject matter involved. Lawyers should support the principle of lawyer referral systems and should encourage the evolution of other ethical plans which aid in the selection of qualified counsel.

Financial Ability to Employ Counsel: Generally

EC 2–16 The legal profession cannot remain a viable force in fulfilling its role in our society unless its members receive adequate compensation for services rendered, and reasonable fees[24] should be charged in appropriate cases to clients able to pay them. Nevertheless, persons unable to pay all or a portion of a reasonable fee should be able to obtain necessary legal services,[25] and lawyers should support and participate in ethical activities designed to achieve that objective.[26]

Financial Ability to Employ Counsel: Persons Able to Pay Reasonable Fees

EC 2–17 The determination of a proper fee requires consideration of the interests of both client and lawyer.[27] A lawyer should not charge more than a reasonable fee,[28] for excessive cost of legal service would deter laymen from utilizing the legal system in protection of their rights. Furthermore, an excessive charge abuses the professional relationship between lawyer and client. On the other hand, adequate compensation is necessary in order to enable the lawyer to serve his client effectively and to preserve the integrity and independence of the profession.[29]

EC 2–18 The determination of the reasonableness of a fee requires consideration of all relevant circumstances,[30] including those stated in the Disciplinary Rules. The fees of a lawyer will vary according to many factors, including the time required, his experience, ability, and reputation, the nature of the employment, the responsibility involved, and the results obtained. It is a commendable and long-standing tradition of the bar that special consideration is given in the fixing of any fee for services rendered a brother lawyer or a member of his immediate family.

As amended in 1974.

---

years—particularly in the last ten years—brought about specialization on an increasing scale." *Report of the Special Committee on Specialization and Specialized Legal Services,* 79 A.B.A.Rep. 582, 584 (1954).

[24] See ABA Canon 12.

[25] Cf. ABA Canon 12.

[26] "If there is any fundamental proposition of government on which all would agree, it is that one of the highest goals of society must be to achieve and maintain equality before the law. Yet this ideal remains an empty form of words unless the legal profession is ready to provide adequate representation for those unable to pay the usual fees." *Professional Representation: Report of the Joint Conference,* 44 A.B.A.J. 1159, 1216 (1958).

[27] See ABA Canon 12.

[28] Cf. ABA Canon 12.

[29] "When members of the Bar are induced to render legal services for inadequate compensation as a consequence the quality of the service rendered may be lowered, the welfare of the profession injured and the administration of justice made less efficient." *ABA Opinion* 302 (1961).

[30] See ABA Canon 12.

EC 2–19 As soon as feasible after a lawyer has been employed, it is desirable that he reach a clear agreement with his client as to the basis of the fee charges to be made. Such a course will not only prevent later misunderstanding but will also work for good relations between the lawyer and the client. It is usually beneficial to reduce to writing the understanding of the parties regarding the fee, particularly when it is contingent. A lawyer should be mindful that many persons who desire to employ him may have had little or no experience with fee charges of lawyers, and for this reason he should explain fully to such persons the reasons for the particular fee arrangement he proposes.

EC 2–20 Contingent fee arrangements[31] in civil cases have long been commonly accepted in the United States in proceedings to enforce claims. The historical bases of their acceptance are that (1) they often, and in a variety of circumstances, provide the only practical means by which one having a claim against another can economically afford, finance, and obtain the services of a competent lawyer to prosecute his claim, and (2) a successful prosecution of the claim produces a *res* out of which the fee can be paid.[32] Although a lawyer generally should decline to accept employment on a contingent fee basis by one who is able to pay a reasonable fixed fee, it is not necessarily improper for a lawyer, where justified by the particular circumstances of a case, to enter into a contingent fee contract in a civil case with any client who, after being fully informed of all relevant factors, desires that arrangement. Because of the human relationships involved and the unique character of the proceedings, contingent fee arrangements in domestic relation cases are rarely justified. In administrative agency proceedings contingent fee contracts should be governed by the same consideration as in other civil cases. Public policy properly condemns contingent fee arrangements in criminal cases, largely on the ground that legal services in criminal cases do not produce a *res* with which to pay the fee.

EC 2–21 A lawyer should not accept compensation or any thing of value incident to his employment or services from one other than his client without the knowledge and consent of his client after full disclosure.[33]

EC 2–22 Without the consent of his client, a lawyer should not associate in a particular matter another lawyer outside his firm. A fee may properly be divided between lawyers[34] properly associated if the division is in proportion to the services performed and the responsibility assumed by each lawyer[35] and if the total fee is reasonable.

---

[31] See ABA Canon 13; see also MacKinnon, Contingent Fees for Legal Services (1964) (A report of the American Bar Foundation).

"A contract for a reasonable contingent fee where sanctioned by law is permitted by *Canon 13,* but the client must remain responsible to the lawyer for expenses advanced by the latter. 'There is to be no barter of the privilege of prosecuting a cause for gain in exchange for the promise of the attorney to prosecute at his own expense.' (Cardozo, C.J. In Matter of Gilman, 251 N.Y. 265, 270–271.)" *ABA Opinion* 246 (1942).

[32] See Comment, Providing Legal Services for the Middle Class in Civil Matters: The Problem, the Duty and a Solution, 26 U.Pitt.L.Rev. 811, 829 (1965).

[33] See ABA Canon 38.

"Of course, as . . . [Informal Opinion 679] points out, there must be full disclosure of the arrangement [that an entity other than the client pays the attorney's fee] by the attorney to the client. . . ." ABA Opinion 320 (1968).

[34] "Only lawyers may share in . . . a division of fees, but . . . it is not necessary that both lawyers be admitted to practice in the same state, so long as the division was based on the division of services or responsibility." ABA Opinion 316 (1967).

[35] See ABA Canon 34.

"We adhere to our previous rulings that where a lawyer merely brings about the employment of another lawyer but renders no service and assumes no responsibility in the matter, a division of the latter's fee is improper. (Opinions 18 and 153).

"It is assumed that the bar, generally, understands what acts or conduct of a lawyer may constitute 'services' to a client within the intendment of Canon 12. Such acts or conduct invariably, if not always involve 'responsibility' on the part of the lawyer, whether the word 'responsibility' be construed to denote the possible resultant legal or moral liability on the part of the lawyer to the client or to others, or the onus of deciding what should or should not be done in behalf of the client. The word 'services' in Canon 12 must be construed in this broad sense and may apply to the selection and retainer of associate counsel as well as to others acts or conduct in the client's behalf." ABA Opinion 204 (1940).

EC 2–23 A lawyer should be zealous in his efforts to avoid controversies over fees with clients[36] and should attempt to resolve amicably any differences on the subject.[37] He should not sue a client for a fee unless necessary to prevent fraud or gross imposition by the client.[38]

Financial Ability to Employ Counsel: Persons Unable to Pay Reasonable Fees

EC 2–24 A layman whose financial ability is not sufficient to permit payment of any fee cannot obtain legal services, other than in cases where a contingent fee is appropriate, unless the services are provided for him. Even a person of moderate means may be unable to pay a reasonable fee which is large because of the complexity, novelty, or difficulty of the problem or similar factors.[39]

EC 2–25 Historically, the need for legal services of those unable to pay reasonable fees has been met in part by lawyers who donated their services or accepted court appointments on behalf of such individuals. The basic responsibility for providing legal services for those unable to pay ultimately rests upon the individual lawyer, and personal involvement in the problems of the disadvantaged can be one of the most rewarding experiences in the life of a lawyer. Every lawyer, regardless of professional prominence or professional workload, should find time to participate in serving the disadvantaged. The rendition of free legal services to those unable to pay reasonable fees continues to be an obligation of each lawyer, but the efforts of individual lawyers are often not enough to meet the need.[40] Thus it has been necessary for the

---

[36] See ABA Canon 14.

[37] Cf. ABA Opinion 320 (1968).

[38] See ABA Canon 14.

"Ours is a learned profession, not a mere money-getting trade. . . . Suits to collect fees should be avoided. Only where the circumstances imperatively require, should resort be had to a suit to compel payment. And where a lawyer does resort to a suit to enforce payment of fees which involves a disclosure, he should carefully avoid any disclosure not clearly necessary to obtaining or defending his rights." ABA Opinion 250 (1943).

But cf. ABA Opinion 320 (1968).

[39] "As a society increases in size, sophistication and technology, the body of laws which is required to control that society also increases in size, scope and complexity. With this growth, the law directly affects more and more facets of individual behavior, creating an expanding need for legal services on the part of the individual members of the society. . . . As legal guidance in social and commercial behavior increasingly becomes necessary, there will come a concurrent demand from the layman that such guidance be made available to him. This demand will not come from those who are able to employ the best legal talent, nor from those who can obtain legal assistance at little or no cost. It will come from the large 'forgotten middle income class,' who can neither afford to pay proportionately large fees nor qualify for ultra-low-cost services. The legal profession must recognize this inevitable demand and consider methods whereby it can be satisfied. If the profession fails to provide such methods, the laity will." Comment, *Providing Legal Services for the Middle Class in Civil Matters: The Problem, the Duty and a Solution,* 26 U.Pitt.L.Rev. 811, 811–12 (1965).

"The issue is not whether we shall do something or do nothing. The demand for ordinary everyday legal justice is so great and the moral nature of the demand is so strong that the issue has become whether we devise, maintain, and support suitable agencies able to satisfy the demand, or by our own default, force the government to take over the job, supplant us, and ultimately dominate us." Smith, *Legal Service Offices for Persons of Moderate Means,* 1949 Wis.L.Rev. 416, 418 (1949).

[40] "Lawyers have peculiar responsibilities for the just administration of the law, and these responsibilities include providing advice and representation for needy persons. To a degree not always appreciated by the public at large, the bar has performed these obligations with zeal and devotion. The Committee is persuaded, however, that a system of justice that attempts, in mid-twentieth century America, to meet the needs of the financially incapacitated accused through primary or exclusive reliance on the uncompensated services of counsel will prove unsuccessful and inadequate. . . . A system of adequate representation, therefore, should be structured and financed in a manner reflecting its public importance. . . . We believe that fees for private appointed counsel should be set by the court within maximum limits established by the statute." Report of the Att'y Gen's Comm. on Poverty and the Administration of Criminal Justice 41–43 (1963).

profession to institute additional programs to provide legal services.[41] Accordingly, legal aid offices,[42] lawyer referral services, and other related programs have been developed, and others will be developed, by the profession.[43] Every lawyer should support all proper efforts to meet this need for legal services.[44]

Acceptance and Retention of Employment

EC 2–26 A lawyer is under no obligation to act as advisor or advocate for every person who may wish to become his client; but in furtherance of the objective of the bar to make legal services fully available, a lawyer should not lightly decline proffered employment. The fulfillment of this objective requires acceptance by a lawyer of his share of tendered employment which may be unattractive both to him and the bar generally.[45]

EC 2–27 History is replete with instances of distinguished and sacrificial services by lawyers who have represented unpopular clients and causes. Regardless of his personal feelings, a lawyer should not decline representation because a client or a cause is unpopular or community reaction is adverse.[46]

EC 2–28 The personal preference of a lawyer to avoid adversary alignment against judges, other lawyers,[47] public officials, or influential members of the community does not justify his rejection of tendered employment.

---

41 "At present this representation [of those unable to pay usual fees] is being supplied in some measure through the spontaneous generosity of individual lawyers, through legal aid societies, and—increasingly—through the organized efforts of the Bar. If those who stand in need of this service know of its availability and their need is in fact adequately met, the precise mechanism by which this service is provided becomes of secondary importance. It is of great importance, however, that both the impulse to render this service and the plan for making that impulse effective, should arise within the legal profession itself." *Professional Responsibility: Report of the Joint Conference,* 44 A.B.A.J. 1159, 1216 (1958).

42 "Free legal clinics carried on by the organized bar are not ethically objectionable. On the contrary, they serve a very worthwhile purpose and should be encouraged." *ABA Opinion* 191 (1939).

43 "Whereas the American Bar Association believes that it is a fundamental duty of the bar to see to it that all persons requiring legal advice be able to attain it, irrespective of their economic status. . . .

"Resolved, that the Association approves and sponsors the setting up by state and local bar associations of lawyer referral plans and low-cost legal service methods for the purpose of dealing with cases of persons who might not otherwise have the benefit of legal advice. . . ." *Proceedings of the House of Delegates of the American Bar Association,* Oct. 30, 1946, 71 A.B.A.Rep. 103, 109–10 (1946).

44 "The defense of indigent citizens, without compensation, is carried on throughout the country by lawyers representing legal aid societies, not only with the approval, but with the commendation of those acquainted with the work. Not infrequently services are rendered out of sympathy or for other philanthropic reasons, by individual lawyers who do not represent legal aid societies. There is nothing whatever in the Canons to prevent a lawyer from performing such an act, nor should there be." *ABA Opinion* 148 (1935).

45 But cf. ABA Canon 31.

46 "One of the highest services the lawyer can render to society is to appear in court on behalf of clients whose causes are in disfavor with the general public." *Professional Responsibility: Report of the Joint Conference,* 44 A.B.A.J. 1159, 1216 (1958).

One author proposes the following proposition to be included in "A Proper Oath for Advocates": "I recognize that it is sometimes difficult for clients with unpopular causes to obtain proper legal representation. I will do all that I can to assure that the client with the unpopular cause is properly represented, and that the lawyer representing such a client receives credit from and support of the bar for handling such a matter." Thode, *The Ethical Standard for the Advocate,* 39 Texas L.Rev. 575, 592 (1961).

"§ 6068. . . . It is the duty of an attorney.

. . .

"(h) Never to reject, for any consideration personal to himself, the cause of the defenseless or the oppressed." Cal.Business and Professions Code § 6068 (West 1962). Virtually the same language is found in the Oregon statutes at Ore.Rev.Stats. Ch. 9, § 9.460(8).

See Rostow, *The Lawyer and His Client,* 48 A.B.A.J. 25 and 146 (1962).

47 See ABA Canons 7 and 29.

"We are of the opinion that it is not professionally improper for a lawyer to accept employment to compel another lawyer to honor the just claim of a layman. On the contrary, it is highly proper that he do so. Unfortunately, there appears to be a widespread feeling among laymen that it is difficult, if not impossible, to obtain justice when they have claims against members of the Bar because other lawyers will not accept employment to proceed against them. The honor of the profession, whose members proudly style themselves officers of the court, must surely be sullied if its members bind themselves by custom to refrain from enforcing just claims of laymen against lawyers." *ABA Opinion* 144 (1935).

EC 2–29 When a lawyer is appointed by a court or requested by a bar association to undertake representation of a person unable to obtain counsel, whether for financial or other reasons, he should not seek to be excused from undertaking the representation except for compelling reasons.[48] Compelling reasons do not include such factors as the repugnance of the subject matter of the proceeding, the identity[49] or position of a person involved in the case, the belief of the lawyer that the defendant in a criminal proceeding is guilty,[50] or the belief of the lawyer regarding the merits of the civil case.[51]

EC 2–30 Employment should not be accepted by a lawyer when he is unable to render competent service[52] or when he knows or it is obvious that the person seeking to employ him desires to institute or maintain an action merely for the purpose of harassing or maliciously injuring another.[53] Likewise, a lawyer should decline employment if the intensity of his personal feeling, as distinguished from a community attitude, may impair his effective representation of a prospective client. If a lawyer knows a client has previously obtained counsel, he should not accept employment in the matter unless the other counsel approves[54] or withdraws, or the client terminates the prior employment.[55]

EC 2–31 Full availability of legal counsel requires both that persons be able to obtain counsel and that lawyers who undertake representation complete the work involved. Trial counsel for a convicted defendant should continue to represent his client by advising whether to take an appeal and, if the appeal is prosecuted, by representing him through the appeal unless new counsel is substituted or withdrawal is permitted by the appropriate court.

EC 2–32 A decision by a lawyer to withdraw should be made only on the basis of compelling circumstances,[56] and in a matter pending before a tribunal he must comply with the rules of the tribunal regarding withdrawal. A lawyer should not withdraw without considering carefully and endeavoring to minimize the possible adverse effect on the rights of his client and the possibility of prejudice to his client[57] as a result of his withdrawal. Even when he justifiably withdraws, a lawyer should protect the welfare of his client by giving due notice of his withdrawal,[58] suggesting employment of other counsel, delivering to the client all papers and property to which the client is entitled, cooperating with counsel subsequently

---

[48] ABA Canon 4 uses a slightly different test, saying, "A lawyer assigned as counsel for an indigent prisoner ought not to ask to be excused for any trivial reason. . . ."

[49] Cf. ABA Canon 7.

[50] See ABA Canon 5.

[51] Dr. Johnson's reply to Boswell upon being asked what he thought of "supporting a cause which you know to be bad" was: "Sir, you do not know it to be good or bad till the Judge determines it. I have said that you are to state facts fairly; so that your thinking, or what you call knowing, a cause to be bad, must be from reasoning, must be from supposing your arguments to be weak and inconclusive. But, Sir, that is not enough. An argument which does not convince yourself, may convince the Judge to whom you urge it; and if it does convince him, why, then, Sir, you are wrong, and he is right." 2 Boswell, The Life of Johnson 47–48 (Hill ed. 1887).

[52] "The lawyer deciding whether to undertake a case must be able to judge objectively whether he is capable of handling it and whether he can assume its burdens without prejudice to previous commitments. . . ." *Professional Responsibility: Report of the Joint Conference,* 44 A.B.A.J. 1158, 1218 (1958).

[53] "The lawyer must decline to conduct a civil cause or to make a defense when convinced that it is intended merely to harass or to injure the opposite party or to work oppression or wrong." ABA Canon 30.

[54] See ABA Canon 7.

[55] Id.

"From the facts stated we assume that the client has discharged the first attorney and given notice of the discharge. Such being the case, the second attorney may properly accept employment. *Canon 7; Opinions 10, 130, 149.*" *ABA Opinion* 209 (1941).

[56] See ABA Canon 44.

"I will carefully consider, before taking a case, whether it appears that I can fully represent the client within the framework of law. If the decision is in the affirmative, then it will take extreme circumstances to cause me to decide later that I cannot so represent him." Thode, *The Ethical Standard for the Advocate,* 39 Texas L.Rev. 575, 592 (1961) (from "A Proper Oath for Advocates").

[57] *ABA Opinion* 314 (1965) held that a lawyer should not disassociate himself from a cause when "it is obvious that the very act of disassociation would have the effect of violating *Canon 37.*"

[58] ABA Canon 44 enumerates instances in which ". . . the lawyer may be warranted in withdrawing on due notice to the client, allowing him time to employ another lawyer."

employed, and otherwise endeavoring to minimize the possibility of harm. Further, he should refund to the client any compensation not earned during the employment.[59]

EC 2–33 As a part of the legal profession's commitment to the principle that high quality legal services should be available to all, attorneys are encouraged to cooperate with qualified legal assistance organizations providing prepaid legal services. Such participation should at all times be in accordance with the basic tenets of the profession: independence, integrity, competence and devotion to the interests of individual clients. An attorney so participating should make certain that his relationship with a qualified legal assistance organization in no way interferes with his independent, professional representation of the interests of the individual client. An attorney should avoid situations in which officials of the organization who are not lawyers attempt to direct attorneys concerning the manner in which legal services are performed for individual members, and should also avoid situations in which considerations of economy are given undue weight in determining the attorneys employed by an organization or the legal services to be performed for the member or beneficiary rather than competence and quality of service. An attorney interested in maintaining the historic traditions of the profession and preserving the function of a lawyer as a trusted and independent advisor to individual members of society should carefully assess such factors when accepting employment by, or otherwise participating in, a particular qualified legal assistance organization, and while so participating should adhere to the highest professional standards of effort and competence.

Added in 1974; amended in 1975.

DISCIPLINARY RULES

DR 2–101 Publicity.

(A) A lawyer shall not, on behalf of himself, his partner, associate or any other lawyer affiliated with him or his firm, use or participate in the use of any form of public communication containing a false, fraudulent, misleading, deceptive, self-laudatory or unfair statement or claim.

(B) In order to facilitate the process of informed selection of a lawyer by potential consumers of legal services, a lawyer may publish or broadcast, subject to DR 2–103, the following information in print media distributed or over television or radio broadcast in the geographic area or areas in which the lawyer resides or maintains offices or in which a significant part of the lawyer's clientele resides, provided that the information disclosed by the lawyer in such publication or broadcast complies with DR 2–101(A), and is presented in a dignified manner:

(1) Name, including name of law firm and names of professional associates; addresses and telephone numbers;

(2) One or more fields of law in which the lawyer or law firm practices, a statement that practice is limited to one or more fields of law, or a statement that the lawyer or law firm specializes in a particular field of law practice, to the extent authorized under DR 2–105;

(3) Date and place of birth;

(4) Date and place of admission to the bar of state and federal courts;

(5) Schools attended, with dates of graduation, degrees and other scholastic distinctions;

(6) Public or quasi-public offices;

(7) Military service;

---

[59] *See* ABA Canon 44.

(8) Legal authorships;

(9) Legal teaching positions;

(10) Memberships, offices, and committee assignments, in bar associations;

(11) Membership and offices in legal fraternities and legal societies;

(12) Technical and professional licenses;

(13) Memberships in scientific, technical and professional associations and societies;

(14) Foreign language ability;

(15) Names and addresses of bank references;

(16) With their written consent, names of clients regularly represented;

(17) Prepaid or group legal services programs in which the lawyer participates;

(18) Whether credit cards or other credit arrangements are accepted;

(19) Office and telephone answering service hours;

(20) Fee for an initial consultation;

(21) Availability upon request of a written schedule of fees and/or an estimate of the fee to be charged for specific services;

(22) Contingent fee rates subject to DR 2–106(C), provided that the statement discloses whether percentages are computed before or after deduction of costs;

(23) Range of fees for services, provided that the statement discloses that the specific fee within the range which will be charged will vary depending upon the particular matter to be handled for each client and the client is entitled without obligation to an estimate of the fee within the range likely to be charged. In print size equivalent to the largest print used in setting forth the fee information;

(24) Hourly rate, provided that the statement discloses that the total fee charged will depend upon the number of hours which must be devoted to the particular matter to be handled for each client and the client is entitled to without obligation an estimate of the fee likely to be charged, in print size at least equivalent to the largest print used in setting forth the fee information;

(25) Fixed fees for specific legal services,* the description of which would not be misunderstood or be deceptive, provided that the statement discloses that the quoted fee will be available only to clients whose matters fall into the services described and that the client is entitled without obligation to a specific estimate of the fee likely to be charged in print size at least equivalent to the largest print used in setting forth the fee information.

(C) Any person desiring to expand the information authorized for disclosure in DR 2–101(B), or to provide for its dissemination through other forums may apply to [the agency having jurisdiction under state law]. Any such application shall be served upon [the agencies having jurisdiction under state law over the regulation of the legal profession and consumer matters] who shall be heard, together with the applicant, on the issue of whether the proposal is necessary in light of the existing provisions of the Code, accords with standards of accuracy, reliability and truthfulness, and would facilitate the process of informed selection of lawyers by potential consumers of legal

* The agency having jurisdiction under state law may desire to issue appropriate guidelines defining "specific legal services."

services. The relief granted in response to any such application shall be promulgated as an amendment to DR 2–101(B), universally applicable to all lawyers.*

(D) If the advertisement is communicated to the public over television or radio, it shall be prerecorded, approved for broadcast by the lawyer, and a recording of the actual transmission shall be retained by the lawyer.

(E) If a lawyer advertises a fee for a service, the lawyer must render that service for no more than the fee advertised.

(F) Unless otherwise specified in the advertisement if a lawyer publishes any fee information authorized under DR 2–101(B) in a publication that is published more frequently than one time per month, the lawyer shall be bound by any representation made therein for a period of not less than 30 days after such publication. If a lawyer publishes any fee information authorized under DR 2–101(B) in a publication that is published once a month or less frequently, he shall be bound by any representation made therein until the publication of the succeeding issue. If a lawyer publishes any fee information authorized under DR 2–101(B) in a publication which has no fixed date for publication of a succeeding issue, the lawyer shall be bound by any representation made therein for a reasonable period of time after publication but in no event less than one year.

(G) Unless otherwise specified, if a lawyer broadcasts any fee information authorized under DR 2–101(B), the lawyer shall be bound by any representation made therein for a period of not less than 30 days after such broadcast.

(H) This rule does not prohibit limited and dignified identification of a lawyer as a lawyer as well as by name:

(1) In political advertisements when his professional status is germane to the political campaign or to a political issue.

(2) In public notices when the name and profession of a lawyer are required or authorized by law or are reasonably pertinent for a purpose other than the attraction of potential clients.

(3) In routine reports and announcements of a bona fide business, civic, professional, or political organization in which he serves as a director or officer.

(4) In and on legal documents prepared by him.

(5) In and on legal textbooks, treatises, and other legal publications, and in dignified advertisements thereof.

(I) A lawyer shall not compensate or give any thing of value to representatives of the press, radio, television, or other communication medium in anticipation of or in return for professional publicity in a news item.

As amended in 1974, 1975, 1977 and 1978.

DR 2–102 Professional Notices, Letterheads and Offices.

(A) A lawyer or law firm shall not use or participate in the use of professional cards, professional announcement cards, office signs, letterheads, or similar professional notices or devices, except that the following may be used if they are in dignified form:

(1) A professional card of a lawyer identifying him by name and as a lawyer, and giving his addresses, telephone numbers, the name of his law firm, and any

* The agency having jurisdiction under state law should establish orderly and expeditious procedures for ruling on such applications.

information permitted under DR 2–105. A professional card of a law firm may also give the names of members and associates. Such cards may be used for identification.

(2) A brief professional announcement card stating new or changed associations or addresses, change of firm name, or similar matters pertaining to the professional offices of a lawyer or law firm, which may be mailed to lawyers, clients, former clients, personal friends, and relatives.[64] It shall not state biographical data except to the extent reasonably necessary to identify the lawyer or to explain the change in his association, but it may state the immediate past position of the lawyer.[65] It may give the names and dates of predecessor firms in a continuing line of succession. It shall not state the nature of the practice except as permitted under DR 2–105.[66]

(3) A sign on or near the door of the office and in the building directory identifying the law office. The sign shall not state the nature of the practice, except as permitted under DR 2–105.

(4) A letter head of a lawyer identifying him by name and as a lawyer, and giving his addresses, telephone numbers, the name of his law firm, associates and any information permitted under DR 2–105. A letterhead of a law firm may also give the names of members and associates,[67] and names and dates relating to deceased and retired members.[68] A lawyer may be designated "Of Counsel" on a letterhead if he has a continuing relationship with a lawyer or law firm, other than as a partner or associate. A lawyer or law firm may be designated as "General Counsel" or by similar professional reference on stationary of a client if he or the firm devotes a substantial amount of professional time in the representation of that client.[69] The letterhead of a law firm may give the names and dates of predecessor firms in a continuing line of succession.

(B) A lawyer in private practice shall not practice under a trade name, a name that is misleading as to the identity of the lawyer or lawyers practicing under such name, or a firm name containing names other than those of one or more of the lawyers in the firm, except that the name of a professional corporation or professional association may contain "P.C." or "P.A." or similar symbols indicating the nature of the organization, and if otherwise lawful a firm may use as, or continue to include in, its name the name or names of one or more deceased or retired members of the firm or of a predecessor firm in a continuing line of succession.[70] A lawyer who assumes a judicial, legislative, or public executive or administrative post or office shall not permit his name to remain in the name of a law firm or to be used in professional

---

64 See *ABA Opinion* 301 (1961).

65 "[I]t has become commonplace for many lawyers to participate in government service; to deny them the right, upon their return to private practice, to refer to their prior employment in a brief and dignified manner, would place an undue limitation upon a large element of our profession. It is entirely proper for a member of the profession to explain his absence from private practice, where such is the primary purpose of the announcement, by a brief and dignified reference to the prior employment.

". . . [A]ny such announcement should be limited to the immediate past connection of the lawyer with the government, made upon his leaving that position to enter private practice." *ABA Opinion* 301 (1961).

66 See *ABA Opinion* 251 (1943).

67 "Those lawyers who are working for an individual lawyer or a law firm may be designated on the letterhead and in other appropriate places as 'associates' " *ABA Opinion* 310 (1963).

68 See ABA Canon 33.

69 But see *ABA Opinion* 285 (1951).

70 See ABA Canon 33; cf. *ABA Opinions* 318 (1967), 267 (1945), 219 (1941), 208 (1940), 192 (1939), 97 (1933), and 6 (1925).

notices of the firm during any significant period in which he is not actively and regularly practicing law as a member of the firm,[71] and during such period other members of the firm shall not use his name in the firm name or in professional notices of the firm.[72]

(C) A lawyer shall not hold himself out as having a partnership with one or more other lawyers or professional corporations unless they are in fact partners.[74]

(D) A partnership shall not be formed or continued between or among lawyers licensed in different jurisdictions unless all enumerations of the members and associates of the firm on its letterhead and in other permissible listings make clear the jurisdictional limitations on those members and associates of the firm not licensed to practice in all listed jurisdictions;[75] however, the same firm name may be used in each jurisdiction.

(E) Nothing contained herein shall prohibit a lawyer from using or permitting the use of, in connection with his name, an earned degree or title derived therefrom indicating his training in the law.

As amended in 1976, 1977, 1979 and 1980.

DR 2–103 Recommendation of Professional Employment.[77]

(A) A lawyer shall not, except as authorized in DR 2–101(B), recommend employment as a private practitioner,[78] of himself, his partner, or associate to a layperson who has not sought his advice regarding employment of a lawyer.[79]

(B) A lawyer shall not compensate or give anything of value to a person or organization to recommend or secure his employment[80] by a client, or as a reward for having made a recommendation resulting in his employment[81] by a client, except that he may pay the usual and reasonable fees or dues charged by any of the organizations listed in DR 2–103(D).

---

[71] *ABA Opinion* 318 (1967) held, anything to the contrary in Formal Opinion 315 or in the other opinions cited notwithstanding that: Where a partner whose name appears in the name of a law firm is elected or appointed to high local, state or federal office, which office he intends to occupy only temporarily, at the end of which time he intends to return to his position with the firm, and provided that he is not precluded by holding such office from engaging in the practice of law and does not in fact sever his relationship with the firm but only takes a leave of absence, and provided that there is no local law, statute or custom to the contrary, his name may be retained in the firm name during his term or terms of office, but only if proper precautions are taken not to mislead the public as to his degree of participation in the firm's affairs.

Cf. *ABA Opinion* 143 (1935). New York County Opinion 67, and New York City Opinions 36 and 798; but cf. *ABA Opinion* 192 (1939) and Michigan Opinion 164.

[72] Cf. ABA Canon 33.

[74] See *ABA Opinion* 277 (1948); cf. ABA Canon 33 and *ABA Opinions* 318 (1967), 126 (1935), 115 (1934), and 106 (1934).

[75] See *ABA Opinions* 318 (1967) and 316 (1967); cf. ABA Canon 33.

[77] Cf. ABA Canon 28.

[78] "We think it clear that a lawyer's seeking employment in an ordinary law office, or appointment to a civil service position, is not prohibited by . . . [Canon 27]." *ABA Opinion* 197 (1939).

[79] "[A] lawyer may not seek from persons not his clients the opportunity to perform . . . a [legal] checkup." *ABA Opinion* 307 (1962).

[80] Cf. *ABA Opinion* 78 (1932).

[81] " 'No financial connection of any kind between the Brotherhood and any lawyer is permissible. No lawyer can properly pay any amount whatsoever to the Brotherhood or any of its departments, officers or members as compensation, reimbursement of expenses or gratuity in connection with the procurement of a case.' " In re Brotherhood of R.R. Trainmen, 13 Ill.2d 391, 398, 150 N.E.2d 163, 167 (1958), quoted in In re Ratner, 194 Kan. 362, 372, 399 P.2d 865, 873 (1956).

See *ABA Opinion* 147 (1935).

(C) A lawyer shall not request a person or organization to recommend or promote the use of his services or those of his partner or associate, or any other lawyer affiliated with him or his firm, as a private practitioner,[83] except as authorized in DR 2-101, and except that

(1) He may request referrals from a lawyer referral service operated, sponsored, or approved by a bar association and may pay its fees incident thereto.[84]

(2) He may cooperate with the legal service activities of any of the offices or organizations enumerated in DR 2-103(D)(1) through (4) and may perform legal services for those to whom he was recommended by it to do such work if:

(a) The person to whom the recommendation is made is a member or beneficiary of such office or organization; and

(b) The lawyer remains free to exercise his independent professional judgment on behalf of his client.

(D) A lawyer or his partner or associate or any other lawyer affiliated with him or his firm may be recommended, employed or paid by, or may cooperate with, one of the following offices or organizations that promote the use of his services or those of his partner or associate or any other lawyer affiliated with him or his firm if there is no interference with the exercise of independent professional judgment in behalf of his client:

(1) A legal aid office or public defender office:

(a) Operated or sponsored by a duly accredited law school.

(b) Operated or sponsored by a bona fide nonprofit community organization.

(c) Operated or sponsored by a governmental agency.

(d) Operated, sponsored, or approved by a bar association.[86]

(2) A military legal assistance office.

(3) A lawyer referral service operated, sponsored, or approved by a bar association.

(4) Any bona fide organization that recommends, furnishes or pays for legal services to its members or beneficiaries[87] provided the following conditions are satisfied:

(a) Such organization, including any affiliate, is so organized and operated that no profit is derived by it from the rendition of legal services by lawyers, and that, if the organization is organized for profit, the legal services are not rendered by lawyers employed, directed, supervised or selected by it except in connection with matters where such organization bears ultimate liability of its member or beneficiary.

---

[83] "This Court has condemned the practice of ambulance chasing through the media of runners and touters. In similar fashion we have with equal emphasis condemned the practice of direct solicitation by a lawyer. We have classified both offenses as serious breaches of the Canons of Ethics demanding severe treatment of the offending lawyer." State v. Dawson, 111 So.2d 427, 431 (Fla.1959).

[84] "Registrants [of a lawyer referral plan] may be required to contribute to the expense of operating it by a reasonable registration charge or by a reasonable percentage of fees collected by them." *ABA Opinion* 291 (1956).

Cf. *ABA Opinion* 227 (1941).

[86] Cf. *ABA Opinion* 148 (1935).

[87] United Mine Workers v. Ill. State Bar Ass'n., 389 U.S. 217, 19 L.Ed.2d 426, 88 S.Ct. 353 (1967); Brotherhood of R.R. Trainmen v. Virginia, 371 U.S. 1, 12 L.Ed.2d 89, 84 S.Ct. 1113 (1964); NAACP v. Button, 371 U.S. 415, 9 L.Ed.2d 405, 83 S.Ct. 328 (1963).

(b) Neither the lawyer, nor his partner, nor associate, nor any other lawyer affiliated with him or his firm, nor any non-lawyer, shall have initiated or promoted such organization for the primary purpose of providing financial or other benefit to such lawyer, partner, associate or affiliated lawyer.

(c) Such organization is not operated for the purpose of procuring legal work or financial benefit for any lawyer as a private practitioner outside of the legal services program of the organization.

(d) The member or beneficiary to whom the legal services are furnished, and not such organization, is recognized as the client of the lawyer in the matter.

(e) Any member or beneficiary who is entitled to have legal services furnished or paid for by the organization may, if such member or beneficiary so desires, select counsel other than that furnished, selected or approved by the organization for the particular matter involved; and the legal service plan of such organization provides appropriate relief for any member or beneficiary who asserts a claim that representation by counsel furnished, selected or approved would be unethical, improper or inadequate under the circumstances of the matter involved and the plan provides an appropriate procedure for seeking such relief.

(f) The lawyer does not know or have cause to know that such organization is in violation of applicable laws, rules of court and other legal requirements that govern its legal service operations.

(g) Such organization has filed with the appropriate disciplinary authority at least annually a report with respect to its legal service plan, if any, showing its terms, its schedule of benefits, its subscription charges, agreements with counsel, and financial results of its legal service activities or, if it has failed to do so, the lawyer does not know or have cause to know of such failure.

(E) A lawyer shall not accept employment when he knows or it is obvious that the person who seeks his services does so as a result of conduct prohibited under this Disciplinary Rule.

As amended in 1974, 1975 and 1977.

DR 2–104 Suggestion of Need of Legal Services.[89, 90]

(A) A lawyer who has given in-person unsolicited advice to a layperson that he should obtain counsel or take legal action shall not accept employment resulting from that advice,[91] except that:

(1) A lawyer may accept employment by a close friend, relative, former client (if the advice is germane to the former employment), or one whom the lawyer reasonably believes to be a client.[92]

---

[89] "If a bar association has embarked on a program of institutional advertising for an annual legal check-up and provides brochures and reprints, it is not improper to have these available in the lawyer's office for persons to read and take." *ABA Opinion* 307 (1962).

Cf. *ABA Opinion* 121 (1934).

[90] ABA Canon 28.

[91] Cf. *ABA Opinions* 229 (1941) and 173 (1937).

[92] "It certainly is not improper for a lawyer to advise his regular clients of new statutes, court decisions, and administrative rulings, which may affect the client's interests, provided the communication is strictly limited to such information. . . .

"When such communications go to concerns or individuals other than regular clients of the lawyer, they are thinly disguised advertisements for professional employment, and are obviously improper." *ABA Opinion* 213 (1941).

(2) A lawyer may accept employment that results from his participation in activities designed to educate laypersons to recognize legal problems, to make intelligent selection of counsel, or to utilize available legal services if such activities are conducted or sponsored by a qualified legal assistance organization.

(3) A lawyer who is recommended, furnished or paid by a qualified legal assistance organization enumerated in DR 2–103(D)(1) through (4) may represent a member or beneficiary thereof, to the extent and under the conditions prescribed therein.

(4) Without affecting his right to accept employment, a lawyer may speak publicly or write for publication on legal topics[95] so long as he does not emphasize his own professional experience or reputation and does not undertake to give individual advice.

(5) If success in asserting rights or defenses of his client in litigation in the nature of a class action is dependent upon the joinder of others, a lawyer may accept, but shall not seek, employment from those contacted for the purpose of obtaining their joinder.[96]

As amended in 1974, 1975 and 1977.

DR 2–105 Limitation of Practice.[97]

(A) A lawyer shall not hold himself out publicly as a specialist, as practicing in certain areas of law or as limiting his practice permitted under DR 2–101(B), except as follows:

(1) A lawyer admitted to practice before the United States Patent and Trademark Office may use the designation "Patents," "Patent Attorney," "Patent Lawyer," or "Registered Patent Attorney" or any combination of those terms, on his letterhead and office sign.

(2) A lawyer who publicly discloses fields of law in which the lawyer or the law firm practices or states that his practice is limited to one or more fields of law shall do so by using designations and definitions authorized and approved by [the agency having jurisdiction of the subject under state law].

(3) A lawyer who is certified as a specialist in a particular field of law or law practice by [the authority having jurisdiction under state law over the subject of specialization by lawyers] may hold himself out as such, but only in accordance with the rules prescribed by that authority.[98]

As amended in 1977.

"It is our opinion that where the lawyer has no reason to believe that he has been supplanted by another lawyer, it is not only his right, but it might even be his duty to advise his client of any change of fact or law which might defeat the client's testamentary purpose as expressed in the will.

"Periodic notices might be sent to the client for whom a lawyer has drawn a will, suggesting that it might be wise for the client to reexamine his will to determine whether or not there has been any change in his situation requiring a modification of his will." *ABA Opinion* 210 (1941).

Cf. ABA Canon 28.

[95] Cf. *ABA Opinion* 168 (1937).

[96] But cf. *ABA Opinion* 111 (1934).

[97] See ABA Canon 45; cf. ABA Canons 43, and 46.

[98] This provision is included to conform to action taken by the ABA House of Delegates at the Mid-Winter Meeting, January, 1969.

DR 2–106 Fees for Legal Services.[99]

(A) A lawyer shall not enter into an agreement for, charge, or collect an illegal or clearly excessive fee.[100]

(B) A fee is clearly excessive when, after a review of the facts, a lawyer of ordinary prudence would be left with a definite and firm conviction that the fee is in excess of a reasonable fee. Factors to be considered as guides in determining the reasonableness of a fee include the following:

(1) The time and labor required, the novelty and difficulty of the questions involved, and the skill requisite to perform the legal service properly.

(2) The likelihood, if apparent to the client, that the acceptance of the particular employment will preclude other employment by the lawyer.

(3) The fee customarily charged in the locality for similar legal services.

(4) The amount involved and the results obtained.

(5) The time limitations imposed by the client or by the circumstances.

(6) The nature and length of the professional relationship with the client.

(7) The experience, reputation, and ability of the lawyer or lawyers performing the services.

(8) Whether the fee is fixed or contingent.[101]

(C) A lawyer shall not enter into an arrangement for, charge, or collect a contingent fee for representing a defendant in a criminal case.[102]

DR 2–107 Division of Fees Among Lawyers.

(A) A lawyer shall not divide a fee for legal services with another lawyer who is not a partner in or associate of his law firm or law office, unless:

(1) The client consents to employment of the other lawyer after a full disclosure that a division of fees will be made.

---

[99] See ABA Canon 12.

[100] The charging of a "clearly excessive fee" is a ground for discipline. State ex rel. Nebraska State Bar Ass'n. v. Richards, 165 Neb. 80, 90, 84 N.W.2d 136, 143 (1957).

"An attorney has the right to contract for any fee he chooses so long as it is not excessive (see Opinion 190), and this Committee is not concerned with the amount of such fees unless so excessive as to constitute a misappropriation of the client's funds (see Opinion 27)." *ABA Opinion* 320 (1968).

Cf. *ABA Opinions* 209 (1940), 190 (1939), and 27 (1930) and State ex rel. Lee v. Buchanan, 191 So.2d 33 (Fla.1966).

[101] Cf. ABA Canon 13; see generally MacKinnon, Contingent Fees for Legal Services (1964) (A Report of the American Bar Foundation).

[102] "Contingent fees, whether in civil or criminal cases, are a special concern of the law. . . .

"In criminal cases, the rule is stricter because of the danger of corrupting justice. The second part of Section 542 of the Restatement [of Contracts] reads: 'A bargain to conduct a criminal case . . . in consideration of a promise of a fee contingent on success is illegal. . . .' " Peyton v. Margiotti, 398 Pa. 86, 156 A.2d 865, 967 (1959).

"The third area of practice in which the use of the contingent fee is generally considered to be prohibited is the prosecution and defense of criminal cases. However, there are so few cases, and these are predominantly old, that it is doubtful that there can be said to be any current law on the subject. . . . In the absence of cases on the validity of contingent fees for defense attorneys, it is necessary to rely on the consensus among commentators that such a fee is void as against public policy. The nature of criminal practice itself makes unlikely the use of contingent fee contracts." MacKinnon, Contingent Fees for Legal Services 52 (1964) (A Report of the American Bar Foundation).

(2) The division is made in proportion to the services performed and responsibility assumed by each.[103]

(3) The total fee of the lawyers does not clearly exceed reasonable compensation for all legal services they rendered the client.[104]

(B) This Disciplinary Rule does not prohibit payment to a former partner or associate pursuant to a separation or retirement agreement.

DR 2–108 Agreements Restricting the Practice of a Lawyer.

(A) A lawyer shall not be a party to or participate in a partnership or employment agreement with another lawyer that restricts the right of a lawyer to practice law after the termination of a relationship created by the agreement, except as a condition to payment of retirement benefits.[105]

(B) In connection with the settlement of a controversy or suit, a lawyer shall not enter into an agreement that restricts his right to practice law.

DR 2–109 Acceptance of Employment.

(A) A lawyer shall not accept employment on behalf of a person if he knows or it is obvious that such person wishes to:

(1) Bring a legal action, conduct a defense, or assert a position in litigation, or otherwise have steps taken for him, merely for the purpose of harassing or maliciously injuring any person.[106]

(2) Present a claim or defense in litigation that is not warranted under existing law, unless it can be supported by good faith argument for an extension, modification, or reversal of existing law.

DR 2–110 Withdrawal From Employment.[107]

(A) In general.

(1) If permission for withdrawal from employment is required by the rules of a tribunal, a lawyer shall not withdraw from employment in a proceeding before that tribunal without its permission.

(2) In any event, a lawyer shall not withdraw from employment until he has taken reasonable steps to avoid foreseeable prejudice to the rights of his client, including giving due notice to his client, allowing time for employment of other

---

[103] See ABA Canon 34 and *ABA Opinions* 316 (1967) and 294 (1958); see generally *ABA Opinions* 265 (1945), 204 (1940), 190 (1939), 171 (1937), 153 (1936), 97 (1933), 63 (1932), 28 (1930), 27 (1930), and 18 (1930).

[104] "*Canon 12* contemplates that a lawyer's fee should not exceed *the value of the services* rendered. . . .

"*Canon 12* applies, whether joint or separate fees are charged [by associate attorneys]. . . ." *ABA Opinion* 204 (1940).

[105] "[A] general covenant restricting an employed lawyer, after leaving the employment, from practicing in the community for a stated period, appears to this Committee to be an unwarranted restriction on the right of a lawyer to choose where he will practice and inconsistent with our professional status. Accordingly, the Committee is of the opinion it would be improper for the employing lawyer to require the covenant and likewise for the employed lawyer to agree to it." *ABA Opinion* 300 (1961).

[106] See ABA Canon 30.

"*Rule 13.* . . . A member of the State Bar shall not accept employment to prosecute or defend a case solely out of spite, or solely for the purpose of harassing or delaying another. . . ." Cal.Business and Professions Code § 6067 (West 1962).

[107] Cf. ABA Canon 44.

counsel, delivering to the client all papers and property to which the client is entitled, and complying with applicable laws and rules.

(3) A lawyer who withdraws from employment shall refund promptly any part of a fee paid in advance that has not been earned.

(B) Mandatory withdrawal.

A lawyer representing a client before a tribunal, with its permission if required by its rules, shall withdraw from employment, and a lawyer representing a client in other matters shall withdraw from employment, if:

(1) He knows or it is obvious that his client is bringing the legal action, conducting the defense, or asserting a position in the litigation, or is otherwise having steps taken for him, merely for the purpose of harassing or maliciously injuring any person.

(2) He knows or it is obvious that his continued employment will result in violation of a Disciplinary Rule.[108]

(3) His mental or physical condition renders it unreasonably difficult for him to carry out the employment effectively.

(4) He is discharged by his client.

(C) Permissive withdrawal.[109]

If DR 2-110(B) is not applicable, a lawyer may not request permission to withdraw in matters pending before a tribunal, and may not withdraw in other matters, unless such request or such withdrawal is because:

(1) His client:

(a) Insists upon presenting a claim or defense that is not warranted under existing law and cannot be supported by good faith argument for an extension, modification, or reversal of existing law.[110]

(b) Personally seeks to pursue an illegal course of conduct.

(c) Insists that the lawyer pursue a course of conduct that is illegal or that is prohibited under the Disciplinary Rules.

(d) By other conduct renders it unreasonably difficult for the lawyer to carry out his employment effectively.

(e) Insists, in a matter not pending before a tribunal, that the lawyer engage in conduct that is contrary to the judgment and advice of the lawyer but not prohibited under the Disciplinary Rules.

(f) Deliberately disregards an agreement or obligation to the lawyer as to expenses or fees.

(2) His continued employment is likely to result in a violation of a Disciplinary Rule.

(3) His inability to work with co-counsel indicates that the best interests of the client likely will be served by withdrawal.

(4) His mental or physical condition renders it difficult for him to carry out the employment effectively.

---

108 See also Code of Professional Responsibility, DR 5-102 and DR 5-105.

109 Cf. ABA Canon 4.

110 Cf. Anders v. California, 386 U.S. 738, 18 L.Ed.2d 493, 87 S.Ct. 1396 (1967), rehearing denied, 388 U.S. 924, 18 L.Ed.2d 1377, 87 S.Ct. 2094 (1967).

(5) His client knowingly and freely assents to termination of his employment.

(6) He believes in good faith, in a proceeding pending before a tribunal, that the tribunal will find the existence of other good cause for withdrawal.

CANON 3

A Lawyer Should Assist in Preventing the Unauthorized Practice of Law

ETHICAL CONSIDERATIONS

EC 3–1 The prohibition against the practice of law by a layman is grounded in the need of the public for integrity and competence of those who undertake to render legal services. Because of the fiduciary and personal character of the lawyer-client relationship and the inherently complex nature of our legal system, the public can better be assured of the requisite responsibility and competence if the practice of law is confined to those who are subject to the requirements and regulations imposed upon members of the legal profession.

EC 3–2 The sensitive variations in the considerations that bear on legal determinations often make it difficult even for a lawyer to exercise appropriate professional judgment, and it is therefore essential that the personal nature of the relationship of client and lawyer be preserved. Competent professional judgment is the product of a trained familiarity with law and legal processes, a disciplined, analytical approach to legal problems, and a firm ethical commitment.

EC 3–3 A non-lawyer who undertakes to handle legal matters is not governed as to integrity or legal competence by the same rules that govern the conduct of a lawyer. A lawyer is not only subject to that regulation but also is committed to high standards of ethical conduct. The public interest is best served in legal matters by a regulated profession committed to such standards.[1] The Disciplinary Rules protect the public in that they prohibit a lawyer from seeking employment by improper overtures, from acting in cases of divided loyalties, and from submitting to the control of others in the exercise of his judgment. Moreover, a person who entrusts legal matters to a lawyer is protected by the attorney-client privilege and by the duty of the lawyer to hold inviolate the confidences and secrets of his client.

EC 3–4 A layman who seeks legal services often is not in a position to judge whether he will receive proper professional attention. The entrustment of a legal matter may well involve the confidences, the reputation, the property, the freedom, or even the life of the client. Proper protection of members of the public demands that no person be permitted to act in the confidential and demanding capacity of a lawyer unless he is subject to the regulations of the legal profession.

EC 3–5 It is neither necessary nor desirable to attempt the formulation of a single, specific definition of what constitutes the practice of law.[2] Functionally, the practice of law relates to the rendition of services for others that call for the professional judgment of a lawyer. The essence of the professional judgment of the lawyer is his educated ability to relate the general body and philosophy of law to a specific legal problem of a client; and thus, the public interest will be better served if only lawyers are permitted to act in matters involving professional judgment. Where this professional judgment is not involved, non-lawyers, such as court clerks, police officers, abstracters, and many governmental employees, may engage in occupations that

---

[1] "The condemnation of the unauthorized practice of law is designed to protect the public from legal services by persons unskilled in the law. The prohibition of lay intermediaries is intended to insure the loyalty of the lawyer to the client unimpaired by intervening and possibly conflicting interests." Cheatham, *Availability of Legal Services: The Responsibility of the Individual Lawyer and of the Organized Bar,* 12 U.C.L.A.L.Rev. 438, 439 (1965).

[2] "What constitutes unauthorized practice of the law in a particular jurisdiction is a matter for determination by the courts of that jurisdiction." *ABA Opinion* 198 (1939).

"In the light of the historical development of the lawyer's functions, it is impossible to lay down an exhaustive definition of 'the practice of law' by attempting to enumerate every conceivable act performed by lawyers in the normal course of their work." State Bar of Arizona v. Arizona Land Title & Trust Co., 90 Ariz. 76, 87, 366 P.2d 1, 8–9 (1961), modified, 91 Ariz. 293, 371 P.2d 1020 (1962).

require a special knowledge of law in certain areas. But the services of a lawyer are essential in the public interest whenever the exercise of professional legal judgment is required.

EC 3–6 A lawyer often delegates tasks to clerks, secretaries, and other lay persons. Such delegation is proper if the lawyer maintains a direct relationship with his client, supervises the delegated work, and has complete professional responsibility for the work product.[3] This delegation enables a lawyer to render legal service more economically and efficiently.

EC 3–7 The prohibition against a non-lawyer practicing law does not prevent a layman from representing himself, for then he is ordinarily exposing only himself to possible injury. The purpose of the legal profession is to make educated legal representation available to the public; but anyone who does not wish to avail himself of such representation is not required to do so. Even so, the legal profession should help members of the public to recognize legal problems and to understand why it may be unwise for them to act for themselves in matters having legal consequences.

EC 3–8 Since a lawyer should not aid or encourage a layman to practice law, he should not practice law in association with a layman or otherwise share legal fees with a layman.[4] This does not mean, however, that the pecuniary value of the interest of a deceased lawyer in his firm or practice may not be paid to his estate or specified persons such as his widow or heirs.[5] In like manner, profit-sharing retirement plans of a lawyer or law firm which include non-lawyer office employees are not improper.[6] These limited exceptions to the rule against sharing legal fees with laymen are permissible since they do not aid or encourage laymen to practice law.

EC 3–9 Regulation of the practice of law is accomplished principally by the respective states.[7] Authority to engage in the practice of law conferred in any jurisdiction is not per se a grant of the right to practice

---

[3] "A lawyer can employ lay secretaries, lay investigators, lay detectives, lay researchers, accountants, lay scriveners, nonlawyer draftsmen or nonlawyer researchers. In fact he may employ nonlawyers to do any task for him except counsel clients about law matters, engage directly in the practice of law, appear in court or appear in formal proceedings a part of the judicial process, so long as it is he who takes the work and vouches for it to the client and becomes responsible to the client." *ABA Opinion* 316 (1967).

ABA Opinion 316 (1967) also stated that if a lawyer practices law as part of a law firm which includes lawyers from several states, he may delegate tasks to firm members in other states so long as he "is the person who, on behalf of the firm, vouched for the work of all of the others and, with the client and in the courts, did the legal acts defined by that state as the practice of law."

"A lawyer cannot delegate his professional responsibility to a law student employed in his office. He may avail himself of the assistance of the student in many of the fields of the lawyer's work, such as examination of case law, finding and interviewing witnesses, making collections of claims, examining court records, delivering papers, conveying important messages, and other similar matters. But the student is not permitted, until he is admitted to the Bar, to perform the professional functions of a lawyer, such as conducting court trials, giving professional advice to clients or drawing legal documents for them. The student in all his work must act as agent for the lawyer employing him, who must supervise his work and be responsible for his good conduct." *ABA Opinion* 85 (1932).

[4] "No division of fees for legal services is proper, except with another lawyer. . . ." ABA Canon 34. Otherwise, according to *ABA Opinion* 316 (1967), "[t]he Canons of Ethics do not examine into the method by which such persons are remunerated by the lawyer. . . . They may be paid a salary, a per diem charge, a flat fee, a contract price, etc."

See ABA Canons 33 and 47.

[5] "Many partnership agreements provide that the active partners, on the death of any one of them, are to make payments to the estate or to the nominee of a deceased partner on a pre-determined formula. It is only where the effect of such an arrangement is to make the estate or nominee a member of the partnership along with the surviving partners that it is prohibited by *Canon 34.* Where the payments are made in accordance with a pre-existing agreement entered into by the deceased partner during his lifetime and providing for a fixed method for determining their amount based upon the value of services rendered during the partner's lifetime and providing for a fixed period over which the payments are to be made, this is not the case. Under these circumstances, whether the payments are considered to be delayed payment of compensation earned but withheld during the partner's lifetime, or whether they are considered to be an approximation of his interest in matters pending at the time of his death, is immaterial. In either event, as Henry S. Drinker says in his book, Legal Ethics, at page 189: 'It would seem, however, that a reasonable agreement to pay the estate a proportion of the receipts for a reasonable period is a proper practical settlement for the lawyer's services to his retirement or death.' " *ABA Opinion* 308 (1963).

[6] Cf. ABA Opinion 311 (1964).

[7] "That the States have broad power to regulate the practice of law is, of course, beyond question." United Mine Workers v. Ill. State Bar Ass'n, 389 U.S. 217, 222 (1967).

elsewhere, and it is improper for a lawyer to engage in practice where he is not permitted by law or by court order to do so. However, the demands of business and the mobility of our society pose distinct problems in the regulation of the practice of law by the states.[8] In furtherance of the public interest, the legal profession should discourage regulation that unreasonably imposes territorial limitations upon the right of a lawyer to handle the legal affairs of his client or upon the opportunity of a client to obtain the services of a lawyer of his choice in all matters including the presentation of a contested matter in a tribunal before which the lawyer is not permanently admitted to practice.[9]

DISCIPLINARY RULES

DR 3–101 Aiding Unauthorized Practice of Law.[10]

(A) A lawyer shall not aid a non-lawyer in the unauthorized practice of law.[11]

(B) A lawyer shall not practice law in a jurisdiction where to do so would be in violation of regulations of the profession in that jurisdiction.[12]

DR 3–102 Dividing Legal Fees With a Non-lawyer.

(A) A lawyer or law firm shall not share legal fees with a non-lawyer,[13] except that:

(1) An agreement by a lawyer with his firm, partner, or associate may provide for the payment of money, over a reasonable period of time after his death, to his estate or to one or more specified persons.[14]

(2) A lawyer who undertakes to complete unfinished legal business of a deceased lawyer may pay to the estate of the deceased lawyer that proportion of the total compensation which fairly represents the services rendered by the deceased lawyer.

(3) A lawyer or law firm may include non-lawyer employees in a compensation or retirement plan, even though the plan is based in whole or in part on a profit-

---

"It is a matter of law, not of ethics, as to where an individual may practice law. Each state has its own rules." *ABA Opinion* 316 (1967).

8 "Much of clients' business crosses state lines. People are mobile, moving from state to state. Many metropolitan areas cross state lines. It is common today to have a single economic and social community involving more than one state. The business of a single client may involve legal problems in several states." *ABA Opinion* 316 (1967).

9 "[W]e reaffirmed the general principle that legal services to New Jersey residents with respect to New Jersey matters may ordinarily be furnished only by New Jersey counsel; but we pointed out that there may be multistate transactions where strict adherence to this thesis would not be in the public interest and that, under the circumstances, it would have been not only more costly to the client but also 'grossly impractical and inefficient' to have had the settlement negotiations conducted by separate lawyers from different states." In re Estate of Waring, 47 N.J. 367, 376, 221 A.2d 193, 197 (1966).

Cf. ABA Opinion 316 (1967).

10 Conduct permitted by the Disciplinary Rules of Canons 2 and 5 does not violate DR 3–101.

11 See ABA Canon 47.

12 It should be noted, however, that a lawyer may engage in conduct, otherwise prohibited by this Disciplinary Rule, where such conduct is authorized by preemptive federal legislation. See Sperry v. Florida, 373 U.S. 379, 10 L.Ed.2d 428, 83 S.Ct. 1322 (1963).

13 See ABA Canon 34 and *ABA Opinions* 316 (1967), 180 (1938), and 48 (1931).

"The receiving attorney shall not under any guise or form share his fee for legal services with a lay agency, personal or corporate, without prejudice, however, to the right of the lay forwarder to charge and collect from the creditor proper compensation for non-legal services rendered by the law [*sic*] forwarder which are separate and apart from the services performed by the receiving attorney." *ABA Opinion* 294 (1958).

14 See *ABA Opinion* 266 (1945).

sharing arrangement [15] providing such plan does not circumvent another disciplinary rule.[16]

As amended in 1980.

DR 3-103 Forming a Partnership With a Non-lawyer.

(A) A lawyer shall not form a partnership with a non-lawyer if any of the activities of the partnership consist of the practice of law.[17]

CANON 4

A Lawyer Should Preserve the Confidences and Secrets of a Client

Ethical Considerations

EC 4-1 Both the fiduciary relationship existing between lawyer and client and the proper functioning of the legal system require the preservation by the lawyer of confidences and secrets of one who has employed or sought to employ him.[1] A client must feel free to discuss whatever he wishes with his lawyer and a lawyer must be equally free to obtain information beyond that volunteered by his client.[2] A lawyer should be fully informed of all the facts of the matter he is handling in order for his client to obtain the full advantage of our legal system. It is for the lawyer in the exercise of his independent professional judgment to separate the relevant and important from the irrelevant and unimportant. The observance of the ethical obligation of a lawyer to hold inviolate the confidences and secrets of his client not only facilitates the full development of facts essential to proper representation of the client but also encourages laymen to seek early legal assistance.

---

15 Cf. *ABA Opinion* 311 (1964).

16 See ABA Informal Opinion 1440 (1979).

17 See ABA Canon 33; cf. *ABA Opinions* 239 (1942) and 201 (1940).

ABA Opinion 316 (1967) states that lawyers licensed in different jurisdictions may, under certain conditions, enter "into an arrangement for the practice of law" and that a lawyer licensed in State A is not, for such purpose a layman in State B.

1 See ABA Canons 6 and 37 and *ABA Opinions* 287 (1953). "The reason underlying the rule with respect to confidential communications between attorney and client is well stated in Mechem on Agency, 2d Ed., Vol. 2, § 2297, as follows: 'The purposes and necessities of the relation between a client and his attorney require, in many cases on the part of the client, the fullest and freest disclosures to the attorney of the client's objects, motives and acts. This disclosure is made in the strictest confidence, relying upon the attorney's honor and fidelity. To permit the attorney to reveal to others what is so disclosed, would be not only a gross violation of a sacred trust upon his part, but it would utterly destroy and prevent the usefulness and benefits to be derived from professional assistance. Based upon considerations of public policy, therefore, the law wisely declares that all confidential communications and disclosures, made by a client to his legal adviser for the purpose of obtaining his professional aid or advice, shall be strictly privileged:—that the attorney shall not be permitted, without the consent of his client,—and much less will he be compelled—to reveal or disclose communications made to him under such circumstances.' " *ABA Opinion* 250 (1943).

"While it is true that complete revelation of relevant facts should be encouraged for trial purposes, nevertheless an attorney's dealings with his client, if both are sincere, and if the dealings involve more than mere technical matters, should be immune to discovery proceedings. There must be freedom from fear of revealment of matters disclosed to an attorney because of the peculiarly intimate relationship existing." Ellis-Foster Co. v. Union Carbide & Carbon Corp., 159 F.Supp. 917, 919 (D.N.J.1958).

Cf. *ABA Opinions* 314 (1965), 274 (1946) and 268 (1945).

2 "While it is the great purpose of law to ascertain the truth, there is the countervailing necessity of insuring the right of every person to freely and fully confer and confide in one having knowledge of the law, and skilled in its practice, in order that the former may have adequate advice and a proper defense. This assistance can be made safely and readily available only when the client is free from the consequences of apprehension of disclosure by reason of the subsequent statements of the skilled lawyer." Baird v. Koerner, 279 F.2d 623, 629–30 (9th Cir.1960).

Cf. *ABA Opinion* 150 (1936).

EC 4–2 The obligation to protect confidences and secrets obviously does not preclude a lawyer from revealing information when his client consents after full disclosure,[3] when necessary to perform his professional employment, when permitted by a Disciplinary Rule, or when required by law. Unless the client otherwise directs, a lawyer may disclose the affairs of his client to partners or associates of his firm. It is a matter of common knowledge that the normal operation of a law office exposes confidential professional information to non-lawyer employees of the office, particularly secretaries and those having access to the files; and this obligates a lawyer to exercise care in selecting and training his employees so that the sanctity of all confidences and secrets of his clients may be preserved. If the obligation extends to two or more clients as to the same information, a lawyer should obtain the permission of all before revealing the information. A lawyer must always be sensitive to the rights and wishes of his client and act scrupulously in the making of decisions which may involve the disclosure of information obtained in his professional relationship.[4] Thus, in the absence of consent of his client after full disclosure, a lawyer should not associate another lawyer in the handling of a matter; nor should he, in the absence of consent, seek counsel from another lawyer if there is a reasonable possibility that the identity of the client or his confidences or secrets would be revealed to such lawyer. Both social amenities and professional duty should cause a lawyer to shun indiscreet conversations concerning his clients.

EC 4–3 Unless the client otherwise directs, it is not improper for a lawyer to give limited information from his files to an outside agency necessary for statistical, bookkeeping, accounting, data processing, banking, printing, or other legitimate purposes, provided he exercises due care in the selection of the agency and warns the agency that the information must be kept confidential.

EC 4–4 The attorney-client privilege is more limited than the ethical obligation of a lawyer to guard the confidence and secrets of his client. This ethical precept, unlike the evidentiary privilege, exists without regard to the nature or source of information or the fact that others share the knowledge. A lawyer should endeavor to act in a manner which preserves the evidentiary privilege; for example, he should avoid professional discussions in the presence of persons to whom the privilege does not extend. A lawyer owes an obligation to advise the client of the attorney-client privilege and timely to assert the privilege unless it is waived by the client.

EC 4–5 A lawyer should not use information acquired in the course of the representation of a client to the disadvantage of the client and a lawyer should not use, except with the consent of his client after full disclosure, such information for his own purposes.[5] Likewise, a lawyer should be diligent in his efforts to prevent the misuse of such information by his employees and associates.[6] Care should be exercised by a lawyer to prevent the disclosure of the confidences and secrets of one client to another,[7] and no employment should be accepted that might require such disclosure.

EC 4–6 The obligation of a lawyer to preserve the confidences and secrets of his client continues after the termination of his employment.[8] Thus a lawyer should not attempt to sell a law practice as a going business

---

3 "Where . . . [a client] knowingly and after full disclosure participates in a [legal fee] financing plan which requires the furnishing of certain information to the bank, clearly by his conduct he has waived any privilege as to that information." *ABA Opinion* 320 (1968).

4 "The lawyer must decide when he takes a case whether it is a suitable one for him to undertake and after this decision is made, he is not justified in turning against his client by exposing injurious evidence entrusted to him. . . . [D]oing something intrinsically regrettable, because the only alternative involves worse consequences, is a necessity in every profession." Williston, Life and Law 271 (1940).

Cf. *ABA Opinions* 177 (1938) and 83 (1932).

5 See ABA Canon 11.

6 See ABA Canon 37.

7 See ABA Canons 6 and 37.

"[A]n attorney must not accept professional employment against a client or a former client which will, or even *may* require him to use confidential information obtained by the attorney in the course of his professional relations with such client regarding the subject matter of the employment. . . ." *ABA Opinion* 165 (1936).

8 See ABA Canon 37.

"Confidential communications between an attorney and his client, made because of the relationship and concerning the subject-matter of the attorney's employment, are generally privileged from disclosure without the consent of the client, and this privilege outlasts the attorney's employment. *Canon 37.*" *ABA Opinion* 154 (1936).

because, among other reasons, to do so would involve the disclosure of confidences and secrets.[9] A lawyer should also provide for the protection of the confidences and secrets of his client following the termination of the practice of the lawyer, whether termination is due to death, disability, or retirement. For example, a lawyer might provide for the personal papers of the client to be returned to him and for the papers of the lawyer to be delivered to another lawyer or to be destroyed. In determining the method of disposition, the instructions and wishes of the client should be a dominant consideration.

DISCIPLINARY RULES

DR 4–101 Preservation of Confidences and Secrets of a Client.[10]

(A) "Confidence" refers to information protected by the attorney-client privilege under applicable law, and "secret" refers to other information gained in the professional relationship that the client has requested be held inviolate or the disclosure of which would be embarrassing or would be likely to be detrimental to the client.

(B) Except when permitted under DR 4–101(C), a lawyer shall not knowingly:

(1) Reveal a confidence or secret of his client.[11]

(2) Use a confidence or secret of his client to the disadvantage of the client.

(3) Use a confidence or secret of his client for the advantage of himself [12] or of a third person,[13] unless the client consents after full disclosure.

(C) A lawyer may reveal:

(1) Confidences or secrets with the consent of the client or clients affected, but only after a full disclosure to them.[14]

(2) Confidences or secrets when permitted under Disciplinary Rules or required by law or court order.[15]

---

9 Cf. *ABA Opinion* 266 (1945).

10 See ABA Canon 37; cf. ABA Canon 6.

11 "§ 6068 . . . It is the duty of an attorney: . . .

"(e) To maintain inviolate the confidence, and at every peril to himself to preserve the secrets, of his client." Cal. Business and Professions Code § 6068 (West 1962). Virtually the same provision is found in the Oregon statutes. Ore.Rev.Stat. ch. 9, § 9.460(5).

"Communications between lawyer and client are privileged (Wigmore on Evidence, 3d Ed., Vol. 8, §§ 2290–2329). The modern theory underlying the privilege is subjective and is to give the client freedom of apprehension in consulting his legal advisor (ibid., § 2290, p. 548). The privilege applies to communications made in seeking legal advice for any purpose (ibid., § 2294, p. 563). The mere circumstance that the advice is given without charge therefore does not nullify the privilege (ibid., § 2303)." *ABA Opinion* 216 (1941).

"It is the duty of an attorney to maintain the confidence and preserve inviolate the secrets of his client. . . ." *ABA Opinion* 155 (1936).

12 See ABA Canon 11.

"The provision respecting employment is in accord with the general rule announced in the adjudicated cases that a lawyer may not make use of knowledge or information acquired by him through his professional relations with his client, or in the conduct of his client's business, to his own advantage or profit (7 C.J.S., § 125, p. 958; Healy v. Gray, 184 Iowa 111, 168 N.W. 222; Baumgardner v. Hudson, D.C.App., 277 F. 552; Goodrum v. Clement, D.C.App., 277 F. 586)." *ABA Opinion* 250 (1943).

13 See *ABA Opinion* 177 (1938).

14 "[A lawyer] may not divulge confidential communications, information, and secrets imparted to him by the client or acquired during their professional relations, unless he is authorized to do so by the client (People v. Gerold, 265 Ill. 448, 107 N.E. 165, 178; Murphy v. Riggs, 238 Mich. 151, 213 N.W. 110, 112; Opinion of this Committee, No. 91)." *ABA Opinion* 202 (1940).

Cf. *ABA Opinion* 91 (1933).

15 "A defendant in a criminal case when admitted to bail is not only regarded as in the custody of his bail, but he is also in the custody of the law, and admission to bail does not deprive the court of its inherent power to deal with the person of the prisoner. Being in lawful custody, the defendant is guilty of an escape when he gains his liberty before he

(3) The intention of his client to commit a crime [16] and the information necessary to prevent the crime.[17]

(4) Confidences or secrets necessary to establish or collect his fee [18] or to defend himself or his employees or associates against an accusation of wrongful conduct.[19]

(D) A lawyer shall exercise reasonable care to prevent his employees, associates, and others whose services are utilized by him from disclosing or using confidences or secrets of a client, except that a lawyer may reveal the information allowed by DR 4–101(C) through an employee.

---

is delivered in due process of law, and is guilty of a separate offense for which he may be punished. In failing to disclose his client's whereabouts as a fugitive under these circumstances the attorney would not only be aiding his client to escape trial on the charge for which he was indicted, but would likewise be aiding him in evading prosecution for the additional offense of escape.

"It is the opinion of the committee that under such circumstances the attorney's knowledge of his client's whereabouts is not privileged, and that he may be disciplined for failing to disclose that information to the proper authorities. . . ." *ABA Opinion* 155 (1936).

"We held in *Opinion* 155 that a communication by a client to his attorney in respect to the future commission of an unlawful act or to a continuing wrong is not privileged from disclosure. Public policy forbids that the relation of attorney and client should be used to conceal wrongdoing on the part of the client.

. . .

"When an attorney representing a defendant in a criminal case applies on his behalf for probation or suspension of sentence, he represents to the court, by implication at least, that his client will abide by the terms and conditions of the court's order. When that attorney is later advised of a violation of that order, it is his duty to advise his client of the consequences of his act, and endeavor to prevent a continuance of the wrongdoing. If his client thereafter persists in violating the terms and conditions of his probation, it is the duty of the attorney as an officer of the court to advise the proper authorities concerning his client's conduct. Such information, even though coming to the attorney from the client in the course of his professional relations with respect to other matters in which he represents the defendant, is not privileged from disclosure. . . ." *ABA Opinion* 156 (1936).

See *ABA Opinion* 155 (1936).

[16] *ABA Opinion* 314 (1965) indicates that a lawyer must disclose even the confidences of his clients if "the facts in the attorney's possession indicate beyond reasonable doubt that a crime will be committed."

See *ABA Opinion* 155 (1936).

[17] See ABA Canon 37 and *ABA Opinion* 202 (1940).

[18] Cf. *ABA Opinion* 250 (1943).

[19] See ABA Canon 37 and *ABA Opinions* 202 (1940) and 19 (1930).

"[T]he adjudicated cases recognize an exception to the rule [that a lawyer shall not reveal the confidences of his client], where disclosure is necessary to protect the attorney's interests arising out of the relation of attorney and client in which disclosure was made.

"The exception is stated in Mechem on Agency, 2d Ed., Vol. 2, § 2313, as follows: 'But the attorney may disclose information received from the client when it becomes necessary for his own protection, as if the client should bring an action against the attorney for negligence or misconduct, and it became necessary for the attorney to show what his instructions were, or what was the nature of the duty which the client expected him to perform. So if it became necessary for the attorney to bring an action against the client, the client's privilege could not prevent the attorney from disclosing what was essential as a means of obtaining or defending his own rights.'

"Mr. Jones, in his Commentaries on Evidence, 2d Ed., Vol. 5, § 2165, states the exception thus: 'It has frequently been held that the rule as to privileged communications does not apply when litigation arises between attorney and client to the extent that their communications are relevant to the issue. In such cases, if the disclosure of privileged communications becomes necessary to protect the attorney's rights, he is released from those obligations of secrecy which the law places upon him. He should not, however, disclose more than is necessary for his own protection. It would be a manifest injustice to allow the client to take advantage of the rule of exclusion as to professional confidence to the prejudice of his attorney, or that it should be carried to the extent of depriving the attorney of the means of obtaining or defending his own rights. In such cases the attorney is exempted from the obligations of secrecy.' " *ABA Opinion* 250 (1943).

CANON 5

A Lawyer Should Exercise Independent Professional Judgment on Behalf of a Client

ETHICAL CONSIDERATIONS

EC 5–1 The professional judgment of a lawyer should be exercised, within the bounds of the law, solely for the benefit of his client and free of compromising influences and loyalties.[1] Neither his personal interests, the interests of other clients, nor the desires of third persons should be permitted to dilute his loyalty to his client.

Interests of a Lawyer That May Affect His Judgment

EC 5–2 A lawyer should not accept proffered employment if his personal interests or desires will, or there is a reasonable probability that they will, affect adversely the advice to be given or services to be rendered the prospective client.[2] After accepting employment, a lawyer carefully should refrain from acquiring a property right or assuming a position that would tend to make his judgment less protective of the interests of his client.

EC 5–3 The self-interest of a lawyer resulting from his ownership of property in which his client also has an interest or which may affect property of his client may interfere with the exercise of free judgment on behalf of his client. If such interference would occur with respect to a prospective client, a lawyer should decline employment proffered by him. After accepting employment, a lawyer should not acquire property rights that would adversely affect his professional judgment in the representation of his client. Even if the property interests of a lawyer do not presently interfere with the exercise of his independent judgment, but the likelihood of interference can reasonably be foreseen by him, a lawyer should explain the situation to his client and should decline employment or withdraw unless the client consents to the continuance of the relationship after full disclosure. A lawyer should not seek to persuade his client to permit him to invest in

---

1 Cf. ABA Canon 35.

"[A lawyer's] fiduciary duty is of the highest order and he must not represent interests adverse to those of the client. It is true that because of his professional responsibility and the confidence and trust which his client may legitimately repose in him, he must adhere to a high standard of honesty, integrity and good faith in dealing with his client. He is not permitted to take advantage of his position or superior knowledge to impose upon the client; nor to conceal facts or law, nor in any way deceive him without being held responsible therefor." Smoot v. Lund, 13 Utah 2d 168, 172, 369 P.2d 933, 936 (1962).

"When a client engages the services of a lawyer in a given piece of business he is entitled to feel that, until that business is finally disposed of in some manner, he has the undivided loyalty of the one upon whom he looks as his advocate and champion. If, as in this case, he is sued and his home attached by his own attorney, who is representing him in another matter, all feeling of loyalty is necessarily destroyed, and the profession is exposed to the charge that it is interested only in money." Grievance Comm. v. Rattner, 152 Conn. 59, 65, 203 A.2d 82, 84 (1964).

"One of the cardinal principles confronting every attorney in the representation of a client is the requirement of complete loyalty and service in good faith to the best of his ability. In a criminal case the client is entitled to a fair trial, but not a perfect one. These are fundamental requirements of due process under the Fourteenth Amendment. . . . The same principles are applicable in Sixth Amendment cases (not pertinent herein) and suggest that an attorney should have no conflict of interest and that he must devote his full and faithful efforts toward the defense of his client." Johns v. Smyth, 176 F.Supp. 949, 952 (E.D.Va.1959), modified, United States ex rel. Wilkins v. Banmiller, 205 F.Supp. 123, 128 n. 5 (E.D.Pa.1962), aff'd 325 F.2d 514 (3d Cir.1963), cert. denied, 379 U.S. 847, 13 L.Ed.2d 51, 85 S.Ct. 87 (1964).

2 "Attorneys must not allow their private interests to conflict with those of their clients. . . . They owe their entire devotion to the interests of their clients." United States v. Anonymous, 215 F.Supp. 111, 113 (E.D.Tenn.1963).

"[T]he court [below] concluded that a firm may not accept any action against a person whom they are presently representing even though there is no relationship between the two cases. In arriving at this conclusion, the court cites an opinion of the Committee on Professional Ethics of the New York County Lawyers' Association which stated in part: 'While under the circumstances . . . there may be no actual conflict of interest . . . "maintenance of public confidence in the Bar requires an attorney who has accepted representation of a client to decline, while representing such client, any employment from an adverse party in any matter even though wholly unrelated to the original retainer." See Question and Answer No. 350, N.Y. County L. Ass'n, Questions and Answer No. 450 (June 21, 1956).' " Grievance Comm. v. Rattner, 152 Conn. 59, 65, 203 A.2d 82, 84 (1964).

an undertaking of his client nor make improper use of his professional relationship to influence his client to invest in an enterprise in which the lawyer is interested.

EC 5–4 If, in the course of his representation of a client, a lawyer is permitted to receive from his client a beneficial ownership in publication rights relating to the subject matter of the employment, he may be tempted to subordinate the interests of his client to his own anticipated pecuniary gain. For example, a lawyer in a criminal case who obtains from his client television, radio, motion picture, newspaper, magazine, book, or other publication rights with respect to the case may be influenced, consciously or unconsciously, to a course of conduct that will enhance the value of his publication rights to the prejudice of his client. To prevent these potentially differing interests, such arrangements should be scrupulously avoided prior to the termination of all aspects of the matter giving rise to the employment, even though his employment has previously ended.

EC 5–5 A lawyer should not suggest to his client that a gift be made to himself or for his benefit. If a lawyer accepts a gift from his client, he is peculiarly susceptible to the charge that he unduly influenced or over-reached the client. If a client voluntarily offers to make a gift to his lawyer, the lawyer may accept the gift, but before doing so, he should urge that his client secure disinterested advice from an independent, competent person who is cognizant of all the circumstances.[3] Other than in exceptional circumstances, a lawyer should insist that an instrument in which his client desires to name him beneficially be prepared by another lawyer selected by the client.[4]

EC 5–6 A lawyer should not consciously influence a client to name him as executor, trustee, or lawyer in an instrument. In those cases where a client wishes to name his lawyer as such, care should be taken by the lawyer to avoid even the appearance of impropriety.[5]

EC 5–7 The possibility of an adverse effect upon the exercise of free judgment by a lawyer on behalf of his client during litigation generally makes it undesirable for the lawyer to acquire a proprietary interest in the cause of his client or otherwise to become financially interested in the outcome of the litigation.[6] However, it is not improper for a lawyer to protect his right to collect a fee for his services by the assertion of legally permissible liens, even though by doing so he may acquire an interest in the outcome of litigation. Although a contingent fee arrangement [7] gives a lawyer a financial interest in the outcome of litigation, a reasonable contingent fee is permissible in civil cases because it may be the only means by which a layman can obtain the services of a lawyer of his choice. But a lawyer, because he is in a better position to evaluate a cause of action, should enter into a continent fee arrangement only in those instances where the arrangement will be beneficial to the client.

EC 5–8 A financial interest in the outcome of litigation also results if monetary advances are made by the lawyer to his client.[8] Although this assistance generally is not encouraged, there are instances when it is not improper to make loans to a client. For example, the advancing or guaranteeing of payment of the costs

---

[3] "Courts of equity will scrutinize with jealous vigilance transactions between parties occupying fiduciary relations toward each other. . . . A deed will not be held invalid, however, if made by the grantor with full knowledge of its nature and effect, and because of the deliberate, voluntary and intelligent desire of the grantor. . . . Where a fiduciary relation exists, the burden of proof is on the grantee or beneficiary of an instrument executed during the existence of such relationship to show the fairness of the transaction, that it was equitable and just and that it did not proceed from undue influence. . . . The same rule has application where an attorney engages in a transaction with a client during the existence of the relation and is benefited thereby. . . . Conversely, an attorney is not prohibited from dealing with his client or buying his property, and such contracts, if open, fair and honest, when deliberately made, are as valid as contracts between other parties. . . . [I]mportant factors in determining whether a transaction is fair include a showing by the fiduciary (1) that he made a full and frank disclosure of all the relevant information that he had: (2) that the consideration was adequate; and (3) that the principal had independent advice before completing the transaction." McFail v. Braden, 19 Ill.2d 108, 117–18, 166 N.E.2d 46, 52 (1960).

[4] See State ex rel. Nebraska State Bar Ass'n v. Richards, 165 Neb. 80, 94–95, 84 N.W.2d 136, 146 (1957).

[5] See ABA Canon 9.

[6] See ABA Canon 10.

[7] See Code of Professional Responsibility, EC 2–20.

[8] See ABA Canon 42.

and expenses of litigation by a lawyer may be the only way a client can enforce his cause of action,[9] but the ultimate liability for such costs and expenses must be that of the client.

EC 5–9 Occasionally a lawyer is called upon to decide in a particular case whether he will be a witness or an advocate. If a lawyer is both counsel and witness, he becomes more easily impeachable for interest and thus may be a less effective witness. Conversely, the opposing counsel may be handicapped in challenging the credibility of the lawyer when the lawyer also appears as an advocate in the case. An advocate who becomes a witness is in the unseemly and ineffective position of arguing his own credibility. The roles of an advocate and of a witness are inconsistent; the function of an advocate is to advance or argue the cause of another, while that of a witness is to state facts objectively.

EC 5–10 Problems incident to the lawyer-witness relationship arise at different stages; they relate either to whether a lawyer should accept employment or should withdraw from employment.[10] Regardless of when the problem arises, his decision is to be governed by the same basic considerations. It is not objectionable for a lawyer who is a potential witness to be an advocate if it is unlikely that he will be called as a witness because his testimony would be merely cumulative or if his testimony will relate only to an uncontested issue.[11] In the exceptional situation where it will be manifestly unfair to the client for the lawyer to refuse employment or to withdraw when he will likely be a witness on a contested issue, he may serve as advocate even though he may be a witness.[12] In making such decision, he should determine the personal or financial sacrifice of the client that may result from his refusal of employment or withdrawal therefrom, the materiality of his testimony, and the effectiveness of his representation in view of his personal involvement. In weighing these factors, it should be clear that refusal or withdrawal will impose an unreasonable hardship upon the client before the lawyer accepts or continues the employment.[13] Where the question arises, doubts should be resolved in favor of the lawyer testifying and against his becoming or continuing as an advocate.[14]

---

[9] "*Rule 3a*. . . . A member of the State Bar shall not directly or indirectly pay or agree to pay, or represent or sanction the representation that he will pay, medical, hospital or nursing bills or other personal expenses incurred by or for a client, prospective or existing; provided this rule shall not prohibit a member:

"(1) with the consent of the client, from paying or agreeing to pay to third persons such expenses from funds collected or to be collected for the client; or

"(2) after he has been employed, from lending money to his client upon the client's promise in writing to repay such loan; or

"(3) from advancing the costs of prosecuting or defending a claim or action. Such costs within the meaning of this subparagraph (3) include all taxable costs or disbursements, costs or investigation and costs of obtaining and presenting evidence." Cal. Business and Professions Code § 6076 (West Supp.1967).

[10] "When a lawyer knows, prior to trial, that he will be a necessary witness, except as to merely formal matters such as identification or custody of a document or the like, neither he nor his firm or associates should conduct the trial. If, during the trial, he discovers that the ends of justice require his testimony, he should, from that point on, if feasible and not prejudicial to his client's case, leave further conduct of the trial to other counsel. If circumstances do not permit withdrawal from the conduct of the trial, the lawyer should not argue the credibility of his own testimony." *A Code of Trial Conduct: Promulgated by the American College of Trial Lawyers,* 43 A.B.A.J. 223, 224–25 (1957).

[11] Cf. Canon 19: "When a lawyer is a witness for his client, except as to merely formal matters, such as the attestation or custody of an instrument and the like, he should leave the trial of the case to other counsel."

[12] "It is the general rule that a lawyer may not testify in litigation in which he is an advocate unless circumstances arise which could not be anticipated and it is necessary to prevent a miscarriage of justice. In those rare cases where the testimony of an attorney is needed to protect his client's interests, it is not only proper but mandatory that it be forthcoming." Schwartz v. Wenger, 267 Minn. 40, 43–44, 124 N.W.2d 489, 492 (1963).

[13] "The great weight of authority in this country holds that the attorney who acts as counsel and witness, in behalf of his client, in the same cause on a material matter, not of a merely formal character, and not in an emergency, but having knowledge that he would be required to be a witness in ample time to have secured other counsel and given up his service in the case, violates a highly important provision of the Code of Ethics and a rule of professional conduct, but does not commit a legal error in so testifying, as a result of which a new trial will be granted." Erwin M. Jennings Co. v. DiGenova, 107 Conn. 491, 499, 141 A. 866, 869 (1928).

[14] "[C]ases may arise, and in practice often do arise, in which there would be a failure of justice should the attorney withhold his testimony. In such a case it would be a vicious professional sentiment which would deprive the client of the benefit of his attorney's testimony." Connolly v. Straw, 53 Wis. 645, 649, 11 N.W. 17, 19 (1881).

But see Canon 19. "Except when essential to the ends of justice, a lawyer should avoid testifying in court in behalf of his client."

EC 5–11 A lawyer should not permit his personal interests to influence his advice relative to a suggestion by his client that additional counsel be employed.[15] In like manner, his personal interests should not deter him from suggesting that additional counsel be employed; on the contrary, he should be alert to the desirability of recommending additional counsel when, in his judgment, the proper representation of his client requires it. However, a lawyer should advise his client not to employ additional counsel suggested by the client if the lawyer believes that such employment would be a disservice to the client, and he should disclose the reasons for his belief.

EC 5–12 Inability of co-counsel to agree on a matter vital to the representation of their client requires that their disagreement be submitted by them jointly to their client for his resolution, and the decision of the client shall control the action to be taken.[16]

EC 5–13 A lawyer should not maintain membership in or be influenced by any organization of employees that undertakes to prescribe, direct, or suggest when or how he should fulfill his professional obligations to a person or organization that employs him as a lawyer. Although it is not necessarily improper for a lawyer employed by a corporation or similar entity to be a member of an organization of employees, he should be vigilant to safeguard his fidelity as a lawyer to his employer, free from outside influences.

Interests of Multiple Clients

EC 5–14 Maintaining the independence of professional judgment required of a lawyer precludes his acceptance or continuation of employment that will adversely affect his judgment on behalf of or dilute his loyalty to a client.[17] This problem arises whenever a lawyer is asked to represent two or more clients who may have differing interests, whether such interests be conflicting, inconsistent, diverse, or otherwise discordant.[18]

EC 5–15 If a lawyer is requested to undertake or to continue representation of multiple clients having potentially differing interests, he must weigh carefully the possibility that his judgment may be impaired or his loyalty divided if he accepts or continues the employment. He should resolve all doubts against the propriety of the representation. A lawyer should never represent in litigation multiple clients with differing interests; [19] and there are few situations in which he would be justified in representing in litigation multiple clients with potentially differing interests. If a lawyer accepted such employment and the interests did become actually differing, he would have to withdraw from employment with likelihood of resulting hardship on the clients; and for this reason it is preferable that he refuse the employment initially. On the other hand, there are many instances in which a lawyer may properly serve multiple clients having potentially differing interests in matters not involving litigation. If the interests vary only slightly, it is generally likely that the lawyer will not be subjected to an adverse influence and that he can retain his independent judgment on behalf of each client; and if the interests become differing, withdrawal is less likely to have a disruptive effect upon the causes of his clients.

---

15 Cf. ABA Canon 7.

16 See ABA Canon 7.

17 See ABA Canon 6; cf. *ABA Opinions* 261 (1944), 242 (1942), 142 (1935), and 30 (1931).

18 The ABA Canons speak of "conflicting interests" rather than "differing interests" but make no attempt to define such other than the statement in Canon 6: "Within the meaning of this canon, a lawyer represents conflicting interests when, in behalf of one client, it is his duty to contend for that which duty to another client requires him to oppose."

19 "Canon 6 of the Canons of Professional Ethics, adopted by the American Bar Association on September 30, 1937, and by the Pennsylvania Bar Association on January 7, 1938, provides in part that 'It is unprofessional to represent conflicting interests, except by express consent of all concerned given after a full disclosure of the facts. Within the meaning of this Canon, a lawyer represents conflicting interests when, in behalf of one client, it is his duty to contend for that which duty to another client requires him to oppose.' The full disclosure required by this canon contemplates that the possibly adverse effect of the conflict be fully explained by the attorney to the client to be affected and by him thoroughly understood. . . .

"The foregoing canon applies to cases where the circumstances are such that possibly conflicting interests may permissibly be represented by the same attorney. But manifestly, there are instances where the conflicts of interest are so critically adverse as not to admit of one attorney's representing both sides. Such is the situation which this record presents. No one could conscionably contend that the same attorney may represent both the plaintiff and defendant in an adversary action. Yet, that is what is being done in this case." Jedwabny v. Philadelphia Transportation Co., 390 Pa. 231, 235, 135 A.2d 252, 254 (1957), cert. denied, 355 U.S. 966, 2 L.Ed.2d 541, 78 S.Ct. 557 (1958).

EC 5–16 In those instances in which a lawyer is justified in representing two or more clients having differing interests, it is nevertheless essential that each client be given the opportunity to evaluate his need for representation free of any potential conflict and to obtain other counsel if he so desires.[20] Thus before a lawyer may represent multiple clients, he should explain fully to each client the implications of the common representation and should accept or continue employment only if the clients consent.[21] If there are present other circumstances that might cause any of the multiple clients to question the undivided loyalty of the lawyer, he should also advise all of the clients of those circumstances.[22]

EC 5–17 Typically recurring situations involving potentially differing interests are those in which a lawyer is asked to represent co-defendants in a criminal case, co-plaintiffs in a personal injury case, an insured and his insurer,[23] and beneficiaries of the estate of a decedent. Whether a lawyer can fairly and adequately protect the interests of multiple clients in these and similar situations depends upon an analysis of each case. In certain circumstances, there may exist little chance of the judgment of the lawyer being adversely affected by the slight possibility that the interests will become actually differing; in other circumstances, the chance of adverse effect upon his judgment is not unlikely.

EC 5–18 A lawyer employed or retained by a corporation or similar entity owes his allegiance to the entity and not to a stockholder, director, officer, employee, representative, or other person connected with the entity. In advising the entity, a lawyer should keep paramount its interests and his professional judgment should not be influenced by the personal desires of any person or organization. Occasionally a lawyer for an entity is requested by a stockholder, director, officer, employee, representative, or other person connected with the entity to represent him in an individual capacity; in such case the lawyer may serve the individual only if the lawyer is convinced that differing interests are not present.

EC 5–19 A lawyer may represent several clients whose interests are not actually or potentially differing. Nevertheless, he should explain any circumstances that might cause a client to question his undivided loyalty.[24] Regardless of the belief of a lawyer that he may properly represent multiple clients, he must defer to a client who holds the contrary belief and withdraw from representation of that client.

EC 5–20 A lawyer is often asked to serve as an impartial arbitrator or mediator in matters which involve present or former clients. He may serve in either capacity if he first discloses such present or former

---

20 "Glasser wished the benefit of the undivided assistance of counsel of his own choice. We think that such a desire on the part of an accused should be respected. Irrespective of any conflict of interest, the additional burden of representing another party may conceivably impair counsel's effectiveness.

"To determine the precise degree of prejudice sustained by Glasser as a result of the court's appointment of Stewart as counsel for Kretske is at once difficult and unnecessary. The right to have the assistance of counsel is too fundamental and absolute to allow courts to indulge in nice calculations as to the amount of prejudice arising from its denial." Glasser v. United States, 315 U.S. 60, 75–76, 86 L.Ed. 680, 62 S.Ct. 457, 467 (1942).

21 See ABA Canon 6.

22 Id.

23 Cf. *ABA Opinion* 282 (1950).

"When counsel, although paid by the casualty company, undertakes to represent the policyholder and files his notice of appearance, he owes to his client, the assured, an undeviating and single allegiance. His fealty embraces the requirement to produce in court all witnesses, fact and expert, who are available and necessary for the proper protection of the rights of his client. . . .

" . . . The Canons of Professional Ethics make it pellucid that there are not two standards, one applying to counsel privately retained by a client, and the other to counsel paid by an insurance carrier." American Employers Ins. Co. v. Goble Aircraft Specialties, 205 Misc. 1066, 1075, 131 N.Y.S.2d 393, 401 (1954), motion to withdraw appeal granted, 1 App.Div.2d 1008, 154 N.Y.S.2d 835 (1956).

"[C]ounsel, selected by State Farm to defend Dorothy Walker's suit for $50,000 damages, was apprised by Walker that his earlier version of the accident was untrue and that actually the accident occurred because he lost control of his car in passing a Cadillac just ahead. At that point, Walker's counsel should have refused to participate further in view of the conflict of interest between Walker and State Farm. . . . Instead he participated in the ensuing deposition of the Walkers, even took an *ex parte* sworn statement from Mr. Walker in order to advise State Farm what action it should take, and later used the statement against Walker in the District Court. This action appears to contravene an Indiana attorney's duty 'at every peril to himself, to preserve the secrets of his client'. . . ." State Farm Mut. Auto Ins. Co. v. Walker, 382 F.2d 548, 552 (1967), cert. denied, 389 U.S. 1045, 19 L.Ed.2d 837, 88 S.Ct. 789 (1968).

24 See ABA Canon 6.

relationships. After a lawyer has undertaken to act as an impartial arbitrator or mediator, he should not thereafter represent in the dispute any of the parties involved.

Desires of Third Persons

EC 5–21 The obligation of a lawyer to exercise professional judgment solely on behalf of his client requires that he disregard the desires of others that might impair his free judgment.[25] The desires of a third person will seldom adversely affect a lawyer unless that person is in a position to exert strong economic, political, or social pressures upon the lawyer. These influences are often subtle, and a lawyer must be alert to their existence. A lawyer subjected to outside pressures should make full disclosure of them to his client; [26] and if he or his client believes that the effectiveness of his representation has been or will be impaired thereby, the lawyer should take proper steps to withdraw from representation of his client.

EC 5–22 Economic, political, or social pressures by third persons are less likely to impinge upon the independent judgment of a lawyer in a matter in which he is compensated directly by his client and his professional work is exclusively with his client. On the other hand, if a lawyer is compensated from a source other than his client, he may feel a sense of responsibility to someone other than his client.

EC 5–23 A person or organization that pays or furnishes lawyers to represent others possesses a potential power to exert strong pressures against the independent judgment of those lawyers. Some employers may be interested in furthering their own economic, political, or social goals without regard to the professional responsibility of the lawyer to his individual client. Others may be far more concerned with establishment or extension of legal principles than in the immediate protection of the rights of the lawyer's individual client. On some occasions, decisions on priority of work may be made by the employer rather than the lawyer with the result that prosecution of work already undertaken for clients is postponed to their detriment. Similarly, an employer may seek, consciously or unconsciously, to further its own economic interests through the action of the lawyers employed by it. Since a lawyer must always be free to exercise his professional judgment without regard to the interests or motives of a third person, the lawyer who is employed by one to represent another must constantly guard against erosion of his professional freedom.[27]

EC 5–24 To assist a lawyer in preserving his professional independence, a number of courses are available to him. For example, a lawyer should not practice with or in the form of a professional legal corporation, even though the corporate form is permitted by law,[28] if any director, officer, or stockholder of it is a non-lawyer. Although a lawyer may be employed by a business corporation with non-lawyers serving as directors or officers, and they necessarily have the right to make decisions of business policy, a lawyer must decline to accept direction of his professional judgment from any layman. Various types of legal aid offices are administered by boards of directors composed of lawyers and laymen. A lawyer should not accept

---

[25] See ABA Canon 35.

"Objection to the intervention of a lay intermediary, who may control litigation or otherwise interfere with the rendering of legal services in a confidential relationship, . . . derives from the element of pecuniary gain. Fearful of dangers thought to arise from that element, the courts of several States have sustained regulations aimed at these activities. We intimate no view one way or the other as to the merits of those decisions with respect to the particular arrangements against which they are directed. It is enough that the superficial resemblance in form between those arrangements and that at bar cannot obscure the vital fact that here the entire arrangement employs constitutionally privileged means of expression to secure constitutionally guaranteed civil rights." NAACP v. Button, 371 U.S. 415, 441–42, 9 L.Ed.2d 405, 423–24, 83 S.Ct. 328, 342–43 (1963).

[26] Cf. ABA Canon 38.

[27] "Certainly it is true that 'the professional relationship between an attorney and his client is highly personal, involving an intimate appreciation of each individual client's particular problem.' And this Committee does not condone practices which interfere with that relationship. However, the mere fact the lawyer is actually paid by some entity other than the client does not affect that relationship, so long as the lawyer is selected by and is directly responsible to the client. See Informal Opinions 469 and 679. Of course, as the latter decision points out, there must be full disclosure of the arrangement by the attorney to the client. . . ." *ABA Opinion* 320 (1968).

"[A] third party may pay the cost of legal services as long as control remains in the client and the responsibility of the lawyer is solely to the client. Informal Opinions 469 ad [*sic*] 679. See also *Opinion* 237." Id.

[28] *ABA Opinion* 303 (1961) recognized that "[s]tatutory provisions now exist in several states which are designed to make [the practice of law in a form that will be classified as a corporation for federal income tax purposes] legally possible, either as a result of lawyers incorporating or forming associations with various corporate characteristics."

employment from such an organization unless the board sets only broad policies and there is no interference in the relationship of the lawyer and the individual client he serves. Where a lawyer is employed by an organization, a written agreement that defines the relationship between him and the organization and provides for his independence is desirable since it may serve to prevent misunderstanding as to their respective roles. Although other innovations in the means of supplying legal counsel may develop, the responsibility of the lawyer to maintain his professional independence remains constant, and the legal profession must insure that changing circumstances do not result in loss of the professional independence of the lawyer.

DISCIPLINARY RULES

DR 5-101 Refusing Employment When the Interests of the Lawyer May Impair His Independent Professional Judgment.

(A) Except with the consent of his client after full disclosure, a lawyer shall not accept employment if the exercise of his professional judgment on behalf of his client will be or reasonably may be affected by his own financial, business, property, or personal interests.[29]

(B) A lawyer shall not accept employment in contemplated or pending litigation if he knows or it is obvious that he or a lawyer in his firm ought to be called as a witness, except that he may undertake the employment and he or a lawyer in his firm may testify:

(1) If the testimony will relate solely to an uncontested matter.

(2) If the testimony will relate solely to a matter of formality and there is no reason to believe that substantial evidence will be offered in opposition to the testimony.

(3) If the testimony will relate solely to the nature and value of legal services rendered in the case by the lawyer or his firm to the client.

(4) As to any matter, if refusal would work a substantial hardship on the client because of the distinctive value of the lawyer or his firm as counsel in the particular case.

DR 5-102 Withdrawal as Counsel When the Lawyer Becomes a Witness.[30]

(A) If, after undertaking employment in contemplated or pending litigation, a lawyer learns or it is obvious that he or a lawyer in his firm ought to be called as a witness on behalf of his client, he shall withdraw from the conduct of the trial and his firm, if any, shall not continue representation in the trial, except that he may continue the representation and he or a lawyer in his firm may testify in the circumstances enumerated in DR 5-101(B)(1) through (4).

---

[29] Cf. ABA Canon 6 and *ABA Opinions* 181 (1938), 104 (1934), 103 (1933), 72 (1932), 50 (1931), 49 (1931), and 33 (1931).

"New York County [Opinion] 203. . . . [A lawyer] should not advise a client to employ an investment company in which he is interested, without informing him of this." Drinker, *Legal Ethics* 956 (1953).

"In *Opinions* 72 and 49 this Committee held: The relations of partners in a law firm are such that neither the firm nor any member or associate thereof, may accept any professional employment which any member of the firm cannot properly accept.

"In *Opinion* 16 this Committee held that a member of a law firm could not represent a defendant in a criminal case which was being prosecuted by another member of the firm who was public prosecuting attorney. The Opinion stated that it was clearly unethical for one member of the firm to oppose the interest of the state while another member represented those interests. . . . Since the prosecutor himself could not represent both the public and the defendant, no member of his law firm could either." *ABA Opinion* 296 (1959).

[30] Cf. ABA Canon 19 and *ABA Opinions* 220 (1941), 185 (1938), 50 (1931), and 33 (1931); but cf. Erwin M. Jennings Co. v. DiGenova, 107 Conn. 491, 498–99, 141 A. 866, 868 (1928).

(B) If, after undertaking employment in contemplated or pending litigation, a lawyer learns or it is obvious that he or a lawyer in his firm may be called as a witness other than on behalf of his client, he may continue the representation until it is apparent that his testimony is or may be prejudicial to his client.[31]

DR 5-103 Avoiding Acquisition of Interest in Litigation.

(A) A lawyer shall not acquire a proprietary interest in the cause of action or subject matter of litigation he is conducting for a client,[32] except that he may:

(1) Acquire a lien granted by law to secure his fee or expenses.

(2) Contract with a client for a reasonable contingent fee in a civil case.[33]

(B) While representing a client in connection with contemplated or pending litigation, a lawyer shall not advance or guarantee financial assistance to his client,[34] except that a lawyer may advance or guarantee the expenses of litigation, including court costs, expenses of investigation, expenses of medical examination, and costs of obtaining and presenting evidence, provided the client remains ultimately liable for such expenses.

DR 5-104 Limiting Business Relations With a Client.

(A) A lawyer shall not enter into a business transaction with a client if they have differing interests therein and if the client expects the lawyer to exercise his professional judgment therein for the protection of the client, unless the client has consented after full disclosure.

(B) Prior to conclusion of all aspects of the matter giving rise to his employment, a lawyer shall not enter into any arrangement or understanding with a client or a prospective client by which he acquires an interest in publication rights with respect to the subject matter of his employment or proposed employment.

DR 5-105 Refusing to Accept or Continue Employment if the Interests of Another Client May Impair the Independent Professional Judgment of the Lawyer.

(A) A lawyer shall decline proffered employment if the exercise of his independent professional judgment in behalf of a client will be or is likely to be adversely affected by the acceptance of the proffered employment,[35] or if it would be likely to involve him in representing differing interests, except to the extent permitted under DR 5-105(C).[36]

(B) A lawyer shall not continue multiple employment if the exercise of his independent professional judgment in behalf of a client will be or is likely to be adversely affected

---

31 "This *Canon* [19] *of Ethics* needs no elaboration to be applied to the facts here. Apparently, the object of this precept is to avoid putting a lawyer in the obviously embarrassing predicament of testifying and then having to argue the credibility and effect of his own testimony. It was not designed to permit a lawyer to call opposing counsel as a witness and thereby disqualify him as counsel." Galarowicz v. Ward, 119 Utah 611, 620, 230 P.2d 576, 580 (1951).

32 ABA Canon 10 and *ABA Opinions* 279 (1949), 246 (1942) and 176 (1938).

33 See Code of Professional Responsibility, DR 2-106(C).

34 See ABA Canon 42; cf. *ABA Opinion* 288 (1954).

35 See ABA Canon 6; cf. *ABA Opinions* 167 (1937), 60 (1931), and 40 (1931).

36 *ABA Opinion* 247 (1942) held that an attorney could not investigate a night club shooting on behalf of one of the owner's liability insurers, obtaining the cooperation of the owner, and later represent the injured patron in an action against the owner and a different insurance company unless the attorney obtain the "express consent of all concerned given after a full disclosure of the facts," since to do so would be to represent conflicting interests.

See *ABA Opinions* 247 (1942), 224 (1941), 222 (1941), 218 (1941), 112 (1934), 83 (1932), and 86 (1932).

by his representation of another client, or if it would be likely to involve him in representing differing interests, except to the extent permitted under DR 5-105(C).[37]

(C) In the situations covered by DR 5-105(A) and (B), a lawyer may represent multiple clients if it is obvious that he can adequately represent the interest of each and if each consents to the representation after full disclosure of the possible effect of such representation on the exercise of his independent professional judgment on behalf of each.

(D) If a lawyer is required to decline employment or to withdraw from employment under a Disciplinary Rule, no partner or associate, or any other lawyer affiliated with him or his firm may accept or continue such employment.

As amended in 1974.

DR 5-106 Settling Similar Claims of Clients.[38]

(A) A lawyer who represents two or more clients shall not make or participate in the making of an aggregate settlement of the claims of or against his clients, unless each client has consented to the settlement after being advised of the existence and nature of all the claims involved in the proposed settlement, of the total amount of the settlement, and of the participation of each person in the settlement.

DR 5-107 Avoiding Influence by Others Than the Client.

(A) Except with the consent of his client after full disclosure, a lawyer shall not:

(1) Accept compensation for his legal services from one other than his client.

(2) Accept from one other than his client any thing of value related to his representation of or his employment by his client.[39]

(B) A lawyer shall not permit a person who recommends, employs, or pays him to render legal services for another to direct or regulate his professional judgment in rendering such legal services.[40]

(C) A lawyer shall not practice with or in the form of a professional corporation or association authorized to practice law for a profit, if:

(1) A non-lawyer owns any interest therein,[41] except that a fiduciary representative of the estate of a lawyer may hold the stock or interest of the lawyer for a reasonable time during administration;

(2) A non-lawyer is a corporate director or officer thereof; [42] or

---

[37] Cf. *ABA Opinions* 231 (1941) and 160 (1936).

[38] Cf. *ABA Opinions* 243 (1942) and 235 (1941).

[39] See ABA Canon 38.

"A lawyer who receives a commission (whether delayed or not) from a title insurance company or guaranty fund for recommending or selling the insurance to his client, or for work done for the client or the company, without either fully disclosing to the client his financial interest in the transaction, or crediting the client's bill with the amount thus received, is guilty of unethical conduct." *ABA Opinion* 304 (1962).

[40] See ABA Canon 35; cf. *ABA Opinion* 237 (1941).

"When the lay forwarder, as agent for the creditor, forwards a claim to an attorney, the direct relationship of attorney and client shall then exist between the attorney and the creditor, and the forwarder shall not interpose itself as an intermediary to control the activities of the attorney." *ABA Opinion* 294 (1958).

[41] "Permanent beneficial and voting rights in the organization set up to practice law, whatever its form, must be restricted to lawyers while the organization is engaged in the practice of law." *ABA Opinion* 303 (1961).

[42] "*Canon 33* . . . promulgates underlying principles that must be observed no matter in what form of organization lawyers practice law. Its requirement that no person shall be admitted or held out as a practitioner or member who is not

(3) A non-lawyer has the right to direct or control the professional judgment of a lawyer.[43]

CANON 6

A Lawyer Should Represent a Client Competently

ETHICAL CONSIDERATIONS

EC 6–1 Because of his vital role in the legal process, a lawyer should act with competence and proper care in representing clients. He should strive to become and remain proficient in his practice [1] and should accept employment only in matters which he is or intends to become competent to handle.

EC 6–2 A lawyer is aided in attaining and maintaining his competence by keeping abreast of current legal literature and developments, participating in continuing legal education programs,[2] concentrating in particular areas of the law, and by utilizing other available means. He has the additional ethical obligation to assist in improving the legal profession, and he may do so by participating in bar activities intended to advance the quality and standards of members of the profession. Of particular importance is the careful training of his younger associates and the giving of sound guidance to all lawyers who consult him. In short, a lawyer should strive at all levels to aid the legal profession in advancing the highest possible standards of integrity and competence and to meet those standards himself.

EC 6–3 While the licensing of a lawyer is evidence that he has met the standards then prevailing for admission to the bar, a lawyer generally should not accept employment in any area of the law in which he is not qualified.[3] However, he may accept such employment if in good faith he expects to become qualified through study and investigation, as long as such preparation would not result in unreasonable delay or expense to his client. Proper preparation and representation may require the association by the lawyer of professionals in other disciplines. A lawyer offered employment in a matter in which he is not and does not

---

a member of the legal profession duly authorized to practice, and amendable to professional discipline, makes it clear that any centralized management must be in lawyers to avoid a violation of this Canon." *ABA Opinion* 303 (1961).

[43] "There is no intervention of any lay agency between lawyer and client when centralized management provided only by lawyers may give guidance or direction to the services being rendered by a lawyer-member of the organization to a client. The language in *Canon 35* that a lawyer should avoid all relations which direct the performance of his duties by or in the interest of an intermediary refers to lay intermediaries and not lawyer intermediaries with whom he is associated in the practice of law." *ABA Opinion* 303 (1961).

[1] "[W]hen a citizen is faced with the need for a lawyer, he wants, and is entitled to, the best informed counsel he can obtain. Changing times produce changes in our laws and legal procedures. The natural complexities of law require continuing intensive study by a lawyer if he is to render his clients a maximum of efficient service. And, in so doing, he maintains the high standards of the legal profession; and he also increases respect and confidence by the general public." Rochelle & Payne, *The Struggle for Public Understanding,* 25 Texas B.J. 109, 160 (1962).

"We have undergone enormous changes in the last fifty years within the lives of most of the adults living today who may be seeking advice. Most of these changes have been accompanied by changes and developments in the law. . . . Every practicing lawyer encounters these problems and is often perplexed with his own inability to keep up, not only with changes in the law, but also with changes in the lives of his clients and their legal problems.

"To be sure, no client has a right to expect that his lawyer will have all of the answers at the end of his tongue or even in the back of his head at all times. But the client does have the right to expect that the lawyer will have devoted his time and energies to maintaining and improving his competence to know where to look for the answers, to know how to deal with the problems, and to know how to advise to the best of his legal talents and abilities." Levy & Sprague, *Accounting and Law: Is Dual Practice in the Public Interest?*, 52 A.B.A.J. 1110, 1112 (1966).

[2] "The whole purpose of continuing legal education, so enthusiastically supported by the ABA, is to make it possible for lawyers to make themselves better lawyers. But there are no nostrums for proficiency in the law; it must come through the hard work of the lawyer himself. To the extent that that work, whether it be in attending institutes or lecture courses, in studying after hours or in the actual day in and day out practice of his profession, can be concentrated within a limited field, the greater the proficiency and expertness that can be developed." *Report of the Special Committee on Specialization and Specialized Legal Education,* 79 A.B.A.Rep. 582, 588 (1954).

[3] "If the attorney is not competent to skillfully and properly perform the work, he should not undertake the service." Degen v. Steinbrink, 202 App.Div. 477, 481, 195 N.Y.S. 810, 814 (1922), aff'd mem., 236 N.Y. 669, 142 N.E. 328 (1923).

expect to become so qualified should either decline the employment or, with the consent of his client, accept the employment and associate a lawyer who is competent in the matter.

EC 6–4 Having undertaken representation, a lawyer should use proper care to safeguard the interests of his client. If a lawyer has accepted employment in a matter beyond his competence but in which he expected to become competent, he should diligently undertake the work and study necessary to qualify himself. In addition to being qualified to handle a particular matter, his obligation to his client requires him to prepare adequately for and give appropriate attention to his legal work.

EC 6–5 A lawyer should have pride in his professional endeavors. His obligation to act competently calls for higher motivation than that arising from fear of civil liability or disciplinary penalty.

EC 6–6 A lawyer should not seek, by contract or other means, to limit his individual liability to his client for his malpractice. A lawyer who handles the affairs of his client properly has no need to attempt to limit his liability for his professional activities and one who does not handle the affairs of his client properly should not be permitted to do so. A lawyer who is a stockholder in or is associated with a professional legal corporation may, however, limit his liability for malpractice of his associates in the corporation, but only to the extent permitted by law.[4]

DISCIPLINARY RULES

DR 6–101 Failing to Act Competently.

(A) A lawyer shall not:

(1) Handle a legal matter which he knows or should know that he is not competent to handle, without associating with him a lawyer who is competent to handle it.

(2) Handle a legal matter without preparation adequate in the circumstances.

(3) Neglect a legal matter entrusted to him.[5]

DR 6–102 Limiting Liability to Client.

(A) A lawyer shall not attempt to exonerate himself from or limit his liability to his client for his personal malpractice.

---

4 See *ABA Opinion* 303 (1961); cf. Code of Professional Responsibility EC 2–11.

5 The annual report for 1967–1968 of the Committee on Grievances of the Association of the Bar of the City of New York showed a receipt of 2,232 complaints; of the 828 offenses against clients, 76 involved conversion, 49 involved "overreaching," and 452, or more than half of all such offenses, involved neglect. *Annual Report of the Committee on Grievances of the Association of the Bar of the City of New York,* N.Y.L.J., Sept. 12, 1968, at 4, col. 5.

CANON 7

A Lawyer Should Represent a Client Zealously Within the Bounds of the Law

ETHICAL CONSIDERATIONS

EC 7–1 The duty of a lawyer, both to his client [1] and to the legal system, is to represent his client zealously [2] within the bounds of the law,[3] which includes Disciplinary Rules and enforceable professional regulations.[4]

---

1 "The right to be heard would be, in many cases, of little avail if it did not comprehend the right to be heard by counsel. Even the intelligent and educated layman has small and sometimes no skill in the science of law." Powell v. Alabama, 287 U.S. 45, 68–69, 77 L.Ed. 158, 170, 53 S.Ct. 55, 64 (1932).

2 Cf. ABA Canon 4.

"At times . . . [the tax lawyer] will be wise to discard some arguments and he should exercise discretion to emphasize the arguments which in his judgment are most likely to be persuasive. But this process involves legal judgment rather than moral attitudes. The tax lawyer should put aside private disagreements with Congressional and Treasury policies. His own notions of policy, and his personal view of what the law should be, are irrelevant. The job entrusted to him by his client is to use all his learning and ability to protect his client's rights, not to help in the process of promoting a better tax system. The tax lawyer need not accept his client's economic and social opinions, but the client is paying for technical attention and undivided concentration upon his affairs. He is equally entitled to performance unfettered by his attorney's economic and social predilections." Paul, *The Lawyer is a Tax Advisor,* 25 Rocky Mt.L.Rev. 412, 418 (1953).

3 See ABA Canons 15 and 32.

ABA Canon 5, although only speaking of one accused of crime, imposes a similar obligation on the lawyer: "[T]he lawyer is bound, by all fair and honorable means, to present every defense that the law of the land permits, to the end that no person may be deprived of life or liberty, but by due process of law."

"Any persuasion or pressure on the advocate which deters him from planning and carrying out the litigation on the basis of 'what, within the framework of the law, is best for my client's interest?' interferes with the obligation to represent the client fully within the law.

"This obligation, in its fullest sense, is the heart of the adversary process. Each attorney, as an advocate, acts for and seeks that which in his judgment is best for his client, within the bounds authoritatively established. The advocate does not *decide* what is just in this case—he would be usurping the function of the judge and jury—he acts for and seeks for his client that which he is entitled to under the law. He can do no less and properly represent the client." Thode, *The Ethical Standard for the Advocate,* 39 Texas L.Rev. 575, 584 (1961).

"The [Texas public opinion] survey indicates that distrust of the lawyer can be traced directly to certain factors. Foremost of these is a basic misunderstanding of the function of the lawyer as an advocate in an adversary system.

"Lawyers are accused of taking advantage of 'loopholes' and 'technicalities' to win. Persons who make this charge are unaware, or do not understand, that the lawyer is hired to win, and if he does not exercise every legitimate effort in his client's behalf, then he is betraying a sacred trust." Rochelle & Payne, *The Struggle for Public Understanding,* 25 Texas B.J. 109, 159 (1962).

"The importance of the attorney's undivided allegiance and faithful service to one accused of crime, irrespective of the attorney's personal opinion as to the guilt of his client, lies in Canon 5 of the American Bar Association Canon of Ethics.

"The difficulty lies, of course, in ascertaining whether the attorney has been guilty of an error of judgment, such as an election with respect to trial tactics, or has otherwise been actuated by his conscience or belief that his client should be convicted in any event. All too frequently courts are called upon to review actions of defense counsel which are, at the most, errors of judgment, not properly reviewable on habeas corpus unless the trial is a farce and a mockery of justice which requires the court to intervene. . . . But when defense counsel, in a truly adverse proceeding, admits that his conscience would not permit him to adopt certain customary trial procedures, this extends beyond the realm of judgment and strongly suggests an invasion of constitutional rights." Johns v. Smyth, 176 F.Supp. 949, 952 (E.D.Va.1959), modified, United States ex rel. Wilkins v. Banmiller, 205 F.Supp. 123, 128, n. 5 (E.D. Pa.1962), aff'd 325 F.2d 514 (3d Cir.1963), cert. denied, 379 U.S. 847, 13 L.Ed.2d 51, 85 S.Ct. 87 (1964).

"The adversary system in law administration bears a striking resemblance to the competitive economic system. In each we assume that the individual through partisanship or through self-interest will strive mightily for his side, and that kind of striving we must have. But neither system would be tolerable without restraints and modifications, and at times without outright departures from the system itself. Since the legal profession is entrusted with the system of law administration, a part of its task is to develop in its members appropriate restraints without impairing the values of partisan striving. An accompanying task is to aid in the modification of the adversary system or departure from it in areas to which the system is unsuited." Cheatham, *The Lawyer's Role and Surroundings,* 25 Rocky Mt.L.Rev. 405, 410 (1953).

The professional responsibility of a lawyer derives from his membership in a profession which has the duty of assisting members of the public to secure and protect available legal rights and benefits. In our government of laws and not of men, each member of our society is entitled to have his conduct judged and regulated in accordance with the law; [5] to seek any lawful objective [6] through legally permissible means; [7] and to present for adjudication any lawful claim, issue, or defense.

EC 7–2 The bounds of the law in a given case are often difficult to ascertain.[8] The language of legislative enactments and judicial opinions may be uncertain as applied to varying factual situations. The limits and specific meaning of apparently relevant law may be made doubtful by changing or developing constitutional interpretations, inadequately expressed statutes or judicial opinions, and changing public and judicial attitudes. Certainty of law ranges from well-settled rules through areas of conflicting authority to areas without precedent.

EC 7–3 Where the bounds of law are uncertain, the action of a lawyer may depend on whether he is serving as advocate or adviser. A lawyer may serve simultaneously as both advocate and adviser, but the two roles are essentially different.[9] In asserting a position on behalf of his client, an advocate for the most

---

4 "Rule 4.15 prohibits, in the pursuit of a client's cause, 'any manner of fraud or chicane'; Rule 4.22 requires 'candor and fairness' in the conduct of the lawyer, and forbids the making of knowing misquotations; Rule 4.47 provides that a lawyer 'should always maintain his integrity,' and generally forbids all misconduct injurious to the interests of the public, the courts, or his clients, and acts contrary to 'justice, honesty, modesty or good morals.' Our Commissioner has accurately paraphrased these rules as follows: 'An attorney does not have the duty to do all and whatever he can that may enable him to win his client's cause or to further his client's interest. His duty and efforts in these respects, although they should be prompted by his 'entire devotion' to the interest of his client, must be within and not without the bounds of the law.' " In re Wines, 370 S.W.2d 328, 333 (Mo.1963).

See Note, 38 Texas L.Rev. 107, 110 (1959).

5 "Under our system of government the process of adjudication is surrounded by safeguards evolved from centuries of experience. These safeguards are not designed merely to lend formality and decorum to the trial of causes. They are predicated on the assumption that to secure for any controversy a truly informed and dispassionate decision is a difficult thing, requiring for its achievement a special summoning and organization of human effort and the adoption of measures to exclude the biases and prejudgments that have free play outside the courtroom. All of this goes for naught if the man with an unpopular cause is unable to find a competent lawyer courageous enough to represent him. His chance to have his day in court loses much of its meaning if his case is handicapped from the outset by the very kind of prejudgment our rules of evidence and procedure are intended to prevent." *Professional Responsibility: Report of the Joint Conference,* 44 A.B.A.J. 1159, 1216 (1958).

6 "[I]t is . . . [the tax lawyer's] positive duty to show the client how to avail himself to the full of what the law permits. He is not the keeper of the Congressional conscience." Paul, *The Lawyer as a Tax Adviser,* 25 Rocky Mt.L.Rev. 412, 418 (1953).

7 See ABA Canons 15 and 30.

8 "The fact that it desired to evade the law, as it is called, is immaterial, because the very meaning of a line in the law is that you intentionally may go as close to it as you can if you do not pass it. . . . It is a matter of proximity and degree as to which minds will differ. . . ." Justice Holmes, in Superior Oil Co. v. Mississippi, 280 U.S. 390, 395–96, 74 L.Ed. 504, 508, 50 S.Ct. 169, 170 (1930).

9 "Today's lawyers perform two distinct types of functions, and our ethical standards should, but in the main do not, recognize these two functions. Judge Philbrick McCoy recently reported to the American Bar Association the need for a reappraisal of the Canons in light of the new and distinct function of counselor, as distinguished from advocate, which today predominates in the legal profession. . . .

". . . In the first place, any revision of the canons must take into account and speak to this new and now predominant function of the lawyer. . . . It is beyond the scope of this paper to discuss the ethical standards to be applied to the counselor except to state that in my opinion such standards should require a greater recognition and protection for the interest of the public generally than is presently expressed in the canons. Also, the counselor's obligation should extend to requiring him to inform and to impress upon the client a just solution of the problem, considering all interests involved." Thode, *The Ethical Standard for the Advocate,* 39 Texas L.Rev. 575, 578–79 (1961).

"The man who has been called into court to answer for his own actions is entitled to fair hearing. Partisan advocacy plays its essential part in such a hearing, and the lawyer pleading his client's case may properly present it in the most favorable light. A similar resolution of doubts in one direction becomes inappropriate when the lawyer acts as counselor. The reasons that justify and even require partisan advocacy in the trial of a cause do not grant any license to the lawyer to participate as legal advisor in a line of conduct that is immoral, unfair, or of doubtful legality. In saving himself from this unworthy involvement, the lawyer cannot be guided solely by an unreflective inner sense of good faith; he must be at pains to preserve a sufficient detachment from his client's interests so that he remains capable of a sound and objective appraisal of the propriety of what his client proposes to do." *Professional Responsibility: Report of the Joint Conference,* 44 A.B.J. 1159, 1161 (1958).

part deals with past conduct and must take the facts as he finds them. By contrast, a lawyer serving as adviser primarily assists his client in determining the course of future conduct and relationships. While serving as advocate, a lawyer should resolve in favor of his client doubts as to the bounds of the law.[10] In serving a client as adviser, a lawyer in appropriate circumstances should give his professional opinion as to what the ultimate decisions of the courts would likely be as to the applicable law.

Duty of the Lawyer to a Client

EC 7–4 The advocate may urge any permissible construction of the law favorable to his client, without regard to his professional opinion as to the likelihood that the construction will ultimately prevail.[11] His conduct is within the bounds of the law, and therefore permissible, if the position taken is supported by the law or is supportable by a good faith argument for an extension, modification, or reversal of the law. However, a lawyer is not justified in asserting a position in litigation that is frivolous.[12]

EC 7–5 A lawyer as adviser furthers the interest of his client by giving his professional opinion as to what he believes would likely be the ultimate decision of the courts on the matter at hand and by informing his client of the practical effect of such decision.[13] He may continue in the representation of his client even though his client has elected to pursue a course of conduct contrary to the advice of the lawyer so long as he does not thereby knowingly assist the client to engage in illegal conduct or to take a frivolous legal position. A lawyer should never encourage or aid his client to commit criminal acts or counsel his client on how to violate the law and avoid punishment therefor.[14]

---

[10] "[A] lawyer who is asked to advise his client . . . may freely urge the statement of positions most favorable to the client just as long as there is reasonable basis for those positions." *ABA Opinion* 314 (1965).

[11] "The lawyer . . . is not an umpire, but an advocate. He is under no duty to refrain from making every proper argument in support of any legal point because he is not convinced of its inherent soundness. . . . His personal belief in the soundness of his cause or of the authorities supporting it, is irrelevant." *ABA Opinion* 280 (1949).

"Counsel apparently misconceived his role. It was his duty to honorably present his client's contentions in the light most favorable to his client. Instead he presumed to advise the court as to the validity and sufficiency of prisoner's motion, by letter. We therefore conclude that the prisoner had no effective assistance of counsel and remand this case to the District Court with instructions to set aside the Judgment, appoint new counsel to represent the prisoner if he makes no objection thereto, and proceed anew." McCartney v. United States, 343 F.2d 471, 472 (9th Cir.1965).

[12] "Here the court-appointed counsel had the transcript but refused to proceed with the appeal because he found no merit in it. . . . We cannot say that there was a finding of frivolity by either of the California courts or that counsel acted in any greater capacity than merely as *amicus curiae* which was condemned in *Ellis,* supra. Hence California's procedure did not furnish petitioner with counsel acting in the role of an advocate nor did it provide that full consideration and resolution of the matter as is obtained when counsel is acting in that capacity. . . .

"The constitutional requirement of substantial equality and fair process can only be attained where counsel acts in the role of an active advocate in behalf of his client, as opposed to that of *amicus curiae.* The no-merit letter and the procedure it triggers do not reach that dignity. Counsel should, and can with honor and without conflict, be of more assistance to his client and to the court. His role as advocate requires that he support his client's appeal to the best of his ability. Of course, if counsel finds his case to be wholly frivolous, after a conscientious examination of it, he should so advise the court and request permission to withdraw. That request must, however, be accompanied by a brief referring to anything in the record that might arguably support the appeal. A copy of counsel's brief should be furnished the indigent and time allowed him to raise any points that he chooses; the court—not counsel—then proceeds, after a full examination of all the proceedings, to decide whether the case is wholly frivolous. If it so finds it may grant counsel's request to withdraw and dismiss the appeal insofar as federal requirements are concerned, or proceed to a decision on the merits, if state law so requires. On the other hand, if it finds any of the legal points arguable on their merits (and therefore not frivolous) it must, prior to decision afford the indigent the assistance of counsel to argue the appeal." *Anders v. California,* 386 U.S. 738, 744, 18 L.Ed.2d 493, 498, 87 S.Ct. 1396, 1399–1400 (1967), rehearing denied, 388 U.S. 924, 18 L.Ed.2d 1377, 87 S.Ct. 2094 (1967).

See Paul, *The Lawyer As a Tax Adviser,* 25 Rocky Mt.L.Rev. 412, 432 (1953).

[13] See ABA Canon 32.

[14] "For a lawyer to represent a syndicate notoriously engaged in the violation of the law for the purpose of advising the members how to break the law and at the same time escape it, is manifestly improper. While a lawyer may see to it that anyone accused of crime, no matter how serious and flagrant, has a fair trial, and present all available defenses, he may not co-operate in planning violations of the law. There is a sharp distinction, of course, between advising what can lawfully be done and advising how unlawful acts can be done in a way to avoid conviction. Where a lawyer accepts a retainer from an organization, known to be unlawful, and agrees in advance to defend its members when from time to time they are accused of crime arising out of its unlawful activities, this is equally improper."

EC 7–6 Whether the proposed action of a lawyer is within the bounds of the law may be a perplexing question when his client is contemplating a course of conduct having legal consequences that vary according to the client's intent, motive, or desires at the time of the action. Often a lawyer is asked to assist his client in developing evidence relevant to the state of mind of the client at a particular time. He may properly assist his client in the development and preservation of evidence of existing motive, intent, or desire; obviously, he may not do anything furthering the creation or preservation of false evidence. In many cases a lawyer may not be certain as to the state of mind of his client, and in those situations he should resolve reasonable doubts in favor of his client.

EC 7–7 In certain areas of legal representation not affecting the merits of the cause or substantially prejudicing the rights of a client, a lawyer is entitled to make decisions on his own. But otherwise the authority to make decisions is exclusively that of the client and, if made within the framework of the law, such decisions are binding on his lawyer. As typical examples in civil cases, it is for the client to decide whether he will accept a settlement offer or whether he will waive his right to plead an affirmative defense. A defense lawyer in a criminal case has the duty to advise his client fully on whether a particular plea to a charge appears to be desirable and as to the prospects of success on appeal, but it is for the client to decide what plea should be entered and whether an appeal should be taken.[15]

EC 7–8 A lawyer should exert his best efforts to insure that decisions of his client are made only after the client has been informed of relevant considerations. A lawyer ought to initiate this decision-making process if the client does not do so. Advice of a lawyer to his client need not be confined to purely legal considerations.[16] A lawyer should advise his client of the possible effect of each legal alternative.[17] A lawyer should bring to bear upon this decision-making process the fullness of his experience as well as his objective viewpoint.[18] In assisting his client to reach a proper decision, it is often desirable for a lawyer to point out those factors which may lead to a decision that is morally just as well as legally permissible.[19] He may emphasize the possibility of harsh consequences that might result from assertion of legally permissible positions. In the final analysis, however, the lawyer should always remember that the decision whether to forego legally available objectives or methods because of non-legal factors is ultimately for the client and not for himself. In the event that the client in a non-adjudicatory matter insists upon a course of conduct that is contrary to the judgment and advice of the lawyer but not prohibited by Disciplinary Rules, the lawyer may withdraw from the employment.[20]

"See also *Opinion* 155." *ABA Opinion* 281 (1952).

[15] See ABA Special Committee on Minimum Standards for the Administration of Criminal Justice, *Standards Relating to Pleas of Guilty,* pp. 69–70 (1968).

[16] "First of all, a truly great lawyer is a wise counselor to all manner of men in the varied crises of their lives when they most need disinterested advice. Effective counseling necessarily involves a thoroughgoing knowledge of the principles of the law not merely as they appear in the books but as they actually operate in action." Vanderbilt, *The Five Functions of the Lawyer: Service to Clients and the Public,* 40 A.B.A.J. 31 (1954).

[17] "A lawyer should endeavor to obtain full knowledge of his client's cause before advising thereon. . . ." ABA Canon 8.

[18] "[I]n devising charters of collaborative effort the lawyer often acts where all of the affected parties are present as participants. But the lawyer also performs a similar function in situations where this is not so, as, for example, in planning estates and drafting wills. Here the instrument defining the terms of collaboration may affect persons not present and often not born. Yet here, too, the good lawyer does not serve merely as a legal conduit for his client's desires, but as a wise counselor, experienced in the art of devising arrangements that will put in workable order the entangled affairs and interests of human beings." *Professional Responsibility: Report of the Joint Conference,* 44 A.B.A.J. 1159, 1162 (1958).

[19] See ABA Canon 8.

"Vital as is the lawyer's role in adjudication, it should not be thought that it is only as an advocate pleading in open court that he contributes to the administration of the law. The most effective realization of the law's aims often takes place in the attorney's office, where litigation is forestalled by anticipating its outcome, where the lawyer's quiet counsel takes the place of public force. Contrary to popular belief, the compliance with the law thus brought about is not generally lip-serving and narrow, for by reminding him of its long-run costs the lawyer often deters his client from a course of conduct technically permissible under existing law, though inconsistent with its underlying spirit and purpose." *Professional Responsibility: Report of the Joint Conference,* 44 A.B.A.J. 1159, 1161 (1958).

[20] "My summation of Judge Sharswood's view of the advocate's duty to the client is that he owes to the client the duty to use all legal means in support of the client's case. However, at the same time Judge Sharswood recognized that many advocates would find this obligation unbearable if applicable without exception. Therefore, the individual lawyer is given the choice of representing his client fully within the bounds set by the law *or of telling his client that he cannot*

EC 7–9 In the exercise of his professional judgment on those decisions which are for his determination in the handling of a legal matter,[21] a lawyer should always act in a manner consistent with the best interests of his client.[22] However, when an action in the best interest of his client seems to him to be unjust, he may ask his client for permission to forego such action.[23]

EC 7–10 The duty of a lawyer to represent his client with zeal does not militate against his concurrent obligation to treat with consideration all persons involved in the legal process and to avoid the infliction of needless harm.

EC 7–11 The responsibilities of a lawyer may vary according to the intelligence, experience, mental condition or age of a client, the obligation of a public officer, or the nature of a particular proceeding. Examples include the representation of an illiterate or an incompetent, service as a public prosecutor or other government lawyer, and appearances before administrative and legislative bodies.

EC 7–12 Any mental or physical condition of a client that renders him incapable of making a considered judgment on his own behalf casts additional responsibilities upon his lawyer. Where an incompetent is acting through a guardian or other legal representative, a lawyer must look to such representative for those decisions which are normally the prerogative of the client to make. If a client under disability has no legal representative, his lawyer may be compelled in court proceedings to make decisions on behalf of the client. If the client is capable of understanding the matter in question or of contributing to the advancement of his interests, regardless of whether he is legally disqualified from performing certain acts, the lawyer should obtain from him all possible aid. If the disability of a client and the lack of a legal representative compel the lawyer to make decisions for his client, the lawyer should consider all circumstances then prevailing and act with care to safeguard and advance the interests of his client. But obviously a lawyer cannot perform any act or make any decision which the law requires his client to perform or make, either acting for himself if competent, or by a duly constituted representative if legally incompetent.

EC 7–13 The responsibility of a public prosecutor differs from that of the usual advocate; his duty is to seek justice, not merely to convict.[24] This special duty exists because: (1) the prosecutor represents the sovereign and therefore should use restraint in the discretionary exercise of governmental powers, such as in the selection of cases to prosecute; (2) during trial the prosecutor is not only an advocate but he also may make decisions normally made by an individual client, and those affecting the public interest should be fair to all; and (3) in our system of criminal justice the accused is to be given the benefit of all reasonable doubts. With respect to evidence and witnesses, the prosecutor has responsibilities different from those of a lawyer in private practice: the prosecutor should make timely disclosure to the defense of available evidence, known to him, that tends to negate the guilt of the accused, mitigate the degree of the offense, or reduce the punishment. Further, a prosecutor should not intentionally avoid pursuit of evidence merely because he believes it will damage the prosecutor's case or aid the accused.

EC 7–14 A government lawyer who has discretionary power relative to litigation should refrain from instituting or continuing litigation that is obviously unfair. A government lawyer not having such

---

do so, so that the client may obtain another attorney if he wishes." Thode, *The Ethical Standard for the Advocate,* 39 Texas L.Rev. 575, 582 (1961).

Cf. Code of Professional Responsibility, DR 2–110(C).

[21] See ABA Canon 24.

[22] Thode, *The Ethical Standard for the Advocate,* 39 Texas L.Rev. 575, 592 (1961).

[23] Cf. *ABA Opinions* 253 (1946) and 178 (1938).

[24] See ABA Canon 5 and Berger v. United States, 295 U.S. 78, 79 L.Ed. 1314, 55 S.Ct. 629 (1935).

"The public prosecutor cannot take as a guide for the conduct of his office the standards of an attorney appearing on behalf of an individual client. The freedom elsewhere wisely granted to a partisan advocate must be severely curtailed if the prosecutor's duties are to be properly discharged. The public prosecutor must recall that he occupies a dual role, being obligated, on the one hand, to furnish that adversary element essential to the informed decision of any controversy, but being possessed, on the other, of important governmental powers that are pledged to the accomplishment of one objective only, that of impartial justice. Where the prosecutor is recreant to the trust implicit in his office, he undermines confidence, not only in his profession, but in government and the very ideal of justice itself." *Professional Responsibility: Report of the Joint Conference,* 44 A.B.A.J. 1159, 1218 (1958).

"The prosecuting attorney is the attorney for the state, and it is his primary duty not to convict but to see that justice is done." *ABA Opinion* 150 (1936).

discretionary power who believes there is lack of merit in a controversy submitted to him should so advise his superiors and recommend the avoidance of unfair litigation. A government lawyer in a civil action or administrative proceeding has the responsibility to seek justice and to develop a full and fair record, and he should not use his position or the economic power of the government to harass parties or to bring about unjust settlements or results.

EC 7–15 The nature and purpose of proceedings before administrative agencies vary widely. The proceedings may be legislative or quasi-judicial, or a combination of both. They may be *ex parte* in character, in which event they may originate either at the instance of the agency or upon motion of an interested party. The scope of an inquiry may be purely investigative or it may be truly adversary looking toward the adjudication of specific rights of a party or of classes of parties. The foregoing are but examples of some of the types of proceedings conducted by administrative agencies. A lawyer appearing before an administrative agency,[25] regardless of the nature of the proceeding it is conducting, has the continuing duty to advance the cause of his client within the bounds of the law.[26] Where the applicable rules of the agency impose specific obligations upon a lawyer, it is his duty to comply therewith, unless the lawyer has a legitimate basis for challenging the validity thereof. In all appearances before administrative agencies, a lawyer should identify himself, his client if identity of his client is not privileged,[27] and the representative nature of his appearance. It is not improper, however, for a lawyer to seek from an agency information available to the public without identifying his client.

EC 7–16 The primary business of a legislative body is to enact laws rather than to adjudicate controversies, although on occasion the activities of a legislative body may take on the characteristics of an adversary proceeding, particularly in investigative and impeachment matters. The role of a lawyer supporting or opposing proposed legislation normally is quite different from his role in representing a person under investigation or on trial by a legislative body. When a lawyer appears in connection with proposed legislation, he seeks to affect the lawmaking process, but when he appears on behalf of a client in investigatory or impeachment proceedings, he is concerned with the protection of the rights of his client. In either event, he should identify himself and his client, if identity of his client is not privileged, and should comply with applicable laws and legislative rules.[28]

EC 7–17 The obligation of loyalty to his client applies only to a lawyer in the discharge of his professional duties and implies no obligation to adopt a personal viewpoint favorable to the interests or desires of his client.[29] While a lawyer must act always with circumspection in order that his conduct will not adversely affect the rights of a client in a matter he is then handling, he may take positions on public issues and espouse legal reforms he favors without regard to the individual views of any client.

EC 7–18 The legal system in its broadest sense functions best when persons in need of legal advice or assistance are represented by their own counsel. For this reason a lawyer should not communicate on the subject matter of the representation of his client with a person he knows to be represented in the matter by

---

25 As to appearances before a department of government, Canon 26 provides: "A lawyer openly . . . may render professional services . . . in advocacy of claims before departments of government, upon the same principles of ethics which justify his appearance before the Courts. . . ."

26 "But as an advocate before a service which itself represents the adversary point of view, where his client's case is fairly arguable, a lawyer is under no duty to disclose its weaknesses, any more than he would be to make such a disclosure to a brother lawyer. The limitations within which he must operate are best expressed in Canon 22. . . ." *ABA Opinion* 314 (1965).

27 See Baird v. Koerner, 279 F.2d 623 (9th Cir.1960).

28 See ABA Canon 26.

29 "Law should be so practiced that the lawyer remains free to make up his own mind how he will vote, what causes he will support, what economic and political philosophy he will espouse. It is one of the glories of the profession that it admits of this freedom. Distinguished examples can be cited of lawyers whose views were at variance from those of their clients, lawyers whose skill and wisdom make them valued advisers to those who had little sympathy with their views as citizens." *Professional Responsibility: Report of the Joint Conference,* 44 A.B.A.J. 1159, 1217 (1958).

"No doubt some tax lawyers feel constrained to abstain from activities on behalf of a better tax system because they think that their clients may object. Clients have no right to object if the tax adviser handles their affairs competently and faithfully and independently of his private views as to tax policy. They buy his expert services, not his private opinions or his silence on issues that gravely affect the public interest." Paul, *The Lawyer as a Tax Adviser,* 25 Rocky Mt.L.Rev. 412, 434 (1953).

a lawyer, unless pursuant to law or rule of court or unless he has the consent of the lawyer for that person.[30] If one is not represented by counsel, a lawyer representing another may have to deal directly with the unrepresented person; in such an instance, a lawyer should not undertake to give advice to the person who is attempting to represent himself,[31] except that he may advise him to obtain a lawyer.

Duty of the Lawyer to the Adversary System of Justice

EC 7–19 Our legal system provides for the adjudication of disputes governed by the rules of substantive, evidentiary, and procedural law. An adversary presentation counters the natural human tendency to judge too swiftly in terms of the familiar that which is not yet fully known; [32] the advocate, by his zealous preparation and presentation of facts and law, enables the tribunal to come to the hearing with an open and neutral mind and to render impartial judgments.[33] The duty of a lawyer to his client and his duty to the legal system are the same: to represent his client zealously within the bounds of the law.[34]

EC 7–20 In order to function properly, our adjudicative process requires an informed, impartial tribunal capable of administering justice promptly and efficiently [35] according to procedures that command public confidence and respect.[36] Not only must there be competent, adverse presentation of evidence and issues, but a tribunal must be aided by rules appropriate to an effective and dignified process. The procedures under which tribunals operate in our adversary system have been prescribed largely by legislative enactments, court rules and decisions, and administrative rules. Through the years certain concepts of proper professional conduct have become rules of law applicable to the adversary adjudicative process. Many of these concepts are the bases for standards of professional conduct set forth in the Disciplinary Rules.

EC 7–21 The civil adjudicative process is primarily designed for the settlement of disputes between parties, while the criminal process is designed for the protection of society as a whole. Threatening to use, or using, the criminal process to coerce adjustment of private civil claims or controversies is a subversion of that process; [37] further, the person against whom the criminal process is so misused may be deterred from asserting his legal rights and thus the usefulness of the civil process in settling private disputes is impaired. As in all cases of abuse of judicial process, the improper use of criminal process tends to diminish public confidence in our legal system.

EC 7–22 Respect for judicial rulings is essential to the proper administration of justice; however, a litigant or his lawyer may, in good faith and within the framework of the law, take steps to test the correctness of a ruling of a tribunal.[38]

---

[30] See ABA Canon 9.

[31] Id.

[32] See *Professional Responsibility: Report of the Joint Conference,* 44 A.B.A.J. 1159, 1160 (1958).

[33] "Without the participation of someone who can act responsibly for each of the parties, this essential narrowing of the issues [by exchange of written pleadings or stipulations of counsel] becomes impossible. But here again the true significance of partisan advocacy lies deeper, touching once more the integrity of the adjudicative process itself. It is only through the advocate's participation that the hearing may remain in fact what it purports to be in theory: a public trial of the facts and issues. Each advocate comes to the hearing prepared to present his proofs and arguments, knowing at the same time that his arguments may fail to persuade and that his proof may be rejected as inadequate. . . . The deciding tribunal, on the other hand, comes to the hearing uncommitted. It has not represented to the public that any fact can be proved, that any argument is sound, or that any particular way of stating a litigant's case is the most effective expression of its merits." *Professional Responsibility: Report of the Joint Conference,* 44 A.B.A.J. 1159, 1160–61 (1958).

[34] Cf. ABA Canons 15 and 32.

[35] Cf. ABA Canon 21.

[36] See *Professional Responsibility: Report of the Joint Conference,* 44 A.B.A.J. 1159, 1216 (1958).

[37] "We are of the opinion that the letter in question was improper, and that in writing and sending it respondent was guilty of unprofessional conduct. This court has heretofore expressed its disapproval of using threats of criminal prosecution as a means of forcing settlement of civil claims. . . .

"Respondent has been guilty of a violation of a principle which condemns any confusion of threats of criminal prosecution with the enforcement of civil claims. For this misconduct he should be severely censured." Matter of Gelman, 230 App.Div. 524, 527, 245 N.Y.S. 416, 419 (1930).

[38] "An attorney has the duty to protect the interests of his client. He has a right to press legitimate argument and to protest an erroneous ruling." Gallagher v. Municipal Court, 31 Cal.2d 784, 796, 192 P.2d 905, 913 (1948).

EC 7–23 The complexity of law often makes it difficult for a tribunal to be fully informed unless the pertinent law is presented by the lawyers in the cause. A tribunal that is fully informed on the applicable law is better able to make a fair and accurate determination of the matter before it. The adversary system contemplates that each lawyer will present and argue the existing law in the light most favorable to his client.[39] Where a lawyer knows of legal authority in the controlling jurisdiction directly adverse to the position of his client, he should inform the tribunal of its existence unless his adversary has done so; but, having made such disclosure, he may challenge its soundness in whole or in part.[40]

EC 7–24 In order to bring about just and informed decisions, evidentiary and procedural rules have been established by tribunals to permit the inclusion of relevant evidence and argument and the exclusion of all other considerations. The expression by a lawyer of his personal opinion as to the justness of a cause, as to the credibility of a witness, as to the culpability of a civil litigant, or as to the guilt or innocence of an accused is not a proper subject for argument to the trier of fact.[41] It is improper as to factual matters because admissible evidence possessed by a lawyer should be presented only as sworn testimony. It is improper as to all other matters because, were the rule otherwise, the silence of a lawyer on a given occasion could be construed unfavorably to his client. However, a lawyer may argue, on his analysis of the evidence, for any position or conclusion with respect to any of the foregoing matters.

EC 7–25 Rules of evidence and procedure are designed to lead to just decisions and are part of the framework of the law. Thus while a lawyer may take steps in good faith and within the framework of the law to test the validity of rules, he is not justified in consciously violating such rules and he should be diligent in his efforts to guard against his unintentional violation of them.[42] As examples, a lawyer should subscribe to or verify only those pleadings that he believes are in compliance with applicable law and rules; a lawyer should not make any prefatory statement before a tribunal in regard to the purported facts of the case on trial unless he believes that his statement will be supported by admissible evidence; a lawyer should not ask a witness a question solely for the purpose of harassing or embarrassing him; and a lawyer should not by subterfuge put before a jury matters which it cannot properly consider.

EC 7–26 The law and Disciplinary Rules prohibit the use of fraudulent, false, or perjured testimony or evidence.[43] A lawyer who knowingly[44] participates in introduction of such testimony or evidence is subject to discipline. A lawyer should, however, present any admissible evidence his client desires to have presented unless he knows, or from facts within his knowledge should know, that such testimony or evidence is false, fraudulent, or perjured.[45]

"There must be protection, however, in the far more frequent case of the attorney who stands on his rights and combats the order in good faith and without disrespect believing with good cause that it is void, for it is here that the independence of the bar becomes valuable." Note, 39 Colum.L.Rev. 433, 438 (1939).

[39] "Too many do not understand that accomplishment of the layman's abstract ideas of justice is the function of the judge and jury, and that it is the lawyer's sworn duty to portray his client's case in its most favorable light." Rochelle and Payne, *The Struggle for Public Understanding,* 25 Texas B.J. 109, 159 (1962).

[40] "We are of the opinion that this Canon requires the lawyer to disclose such decisions [that are adverse to his client's contentions] to the court. He may, of course, after doing so, challenge the soundness of the decisions or present reasons which he believes would warrant the court in not following them in the pending case." *ABA Opinion* 146 (1935).

Cf. *ABA Opinion* 280 (1949) and Thode, *The Ethical Standard for the Advocate,* 39 Texas L.Rev. 575, 585–86 (1961).

[41] See ABA Canon 15.

"The traditional duty of an advocate is that he honorably uphold the contentions of his client. He should not voluntarily undermine them." Harders v. State of California, 373 F.2d 839, 842 (9th Cir.1967).

[42] See ABA Canon 22.

[43] Id. Cf. ABA Canon 41.

[44] See generally *ABA Opinion* 287 (1953) as to a lawyer's duty when he unknowingly participates in introducing perjured testimony.

[45] "Under any standard of proper ethical conduct an attorney should not sit by silently and permit his client to commit what may have been perjury, and which certainly would mislead the court and the opposing party on a matter vital to the issue under consideration. . . .

. . .

"Respondent next urges that it was his duty to observe the utmost good faith toward his client, and therefore he could not divulge any confidential information. This duty to the client of course does not extend to the point of authorizing collaboration with him in the commission of fraud." In re Carroll, 244 S.W.2d 474, 474–75 (Ky.1951).

EC 7–27 Because it interferes with the proper administration of justice, a lawyer should not suppress evidence that he or his client has a legal obligation to reveal or produce. In like manner, a lawyer should not advise or cause a person to secrete himself or to leave the jurisdiction of a tribunal for the purpose of making him unavailable as a witness therein.[46]

EC 7–28 Witnesses should always testify truthfully[47] and should be free from any financial inducements that might tempt them to do otherwise.[48] A lawyer should not pay or agree to pay a non-expert witness an amount in excess of reimbursement for expenses and financial loss incident to his being a witness; however, a lawyer may pay or agree to pay an expert witness a reasonable fee for his services as an expert. But in no event should a lawyer pay or agree to pay a contingent fee to any witness. A lawyer should exercise reasonable diligence to see that his client and lay associates conform to these standards.[49]

EC 7–29 To safeguard the impartiality that is essential to the judicial process, veniremen and jurors should be protected against extraneous influences.[50] When impartiality is present, public confidence in the judicial system is enhanced. There should be no extrajudicial communication with veniremen prior to trial or with jurors during trial by or on behalf of a lawyer connected with the case. Furthermore, a lawyer who is not connected with the case should not communicate with or cause another to communicate with a venireman or a juror about the case. After the trial, communication by a lawyer with jurors is permitted so long as he refrains from asking questions or making comments that tend to harass or embarrass the juror [51] or to influence actions of the juror in future cases. Were a lawyer to be prohibited from communicating after a trial with a juror, he could not ascertain if the verdict might be subject to legal challenge, in which event the invalidity of a verdict might go undetected.[52] When an extrajudicial communication by a lawyer with a juror is permitted by law, it should be made considerately and with deference to the personal feelings of the juror.

EC 7–30 Vexatious or harassing investigations of veniremen or jurors seriously impair the effectiveness of our jury system. For this reason, a lawyer or anyone on his behalf who conducts an investigation of veniremen or jurors should act with circumspection and restraint.

EC 7–31 Communications with or investigations of members of families of veniremen or jurors by a lawyer or by anyone on his behalf are subject to the restrictions imposed upon the lawyer with respect to his communications with or investigations of veniremen and jurors.

---

[46] See ABA Canon 5; cf. *ABA Opinion* 131 (1935).

[47] Cf. ABA Canon 39.

[48] "The prevalence of perjury is a serious menace to the administration of justice, to prevent which no means have as yet been satisfactorily devised. But there certainly can be no greater incentive to perjury than to allow a party to make payments to its opponents witnesses under any guise or on any excuse, and at least attorneys who are officers of the court to aid it in the administration of justice, must keep themselves clear of any connection which in the slightest degree tends to induce witnesses to testify in favor of their clients." In re Robinson, 151 App.Div. 589, 600, 136 N.Y.S. 548, 556–57 (1912), aff'd, 209 N.Y. 354, 103 N.E. 160 (1913).

[49] "It will not do for an attorney who seeks to justify himself against charges of this kind to show that he has escaped criminal responsibility under the Penal Law, nor can he blindly shut his eyes to a system which tends to suborn witnesses, to produce perjured testimony, and to suppress the truth. He has an active affirmative duty to protect the administration of justice from perjury and fraud, and that duty is not performed by allowing his subordinates and assistants to attempt to subvert justice and procure results for his clients based upon false testimony and perjured witnesses." Id., 151 App.Div. at 592, 136 N.Y.S. at 551.

[50] See ABA Canon 23.

[51] "[I]t is unfair to jurors to permit a disappointed litigant to pick over their private associations in search of something to discredit them and their verdict. And it would be unfair to the public too if jurors should understand that they cannot convict a man of means without risking an inquiry of that kind by paid investigators, with, to boot, the distortions an inquiry of that kind can produce." State v. LaFera, 42 N.J. 97, 107, 199 A.2d 630, 636 (1964).

[52] *ABA Opinion* 319 (1968) points out that "[m]any courts today, and the trend is in this direction, allow the testimony of jurors as to all irregularities in and out of the courtroom except those irregularities whose existence can be determined only by exploring the consciousness of a single particular juror, New Jersey v. Kociolek, 20 N.J. 92, 118 A.2d 812 (1955). Model Code of Evidence Rule 301. Certainly as to states in which the testimony and affidavits of jurors may be received in support of or against a motion for new trial, a lawyer, in his obligation to protect his client, must have the tools for ascertaining whether or not grounds for a new trial exist and it is not unethical for him to talk to and question jurors."

EC 7–32 Because of his duty to aid in preserving the integrity of the jury system, a lawyer who learns of improper conduct by or towards a venireman, a juror, or a member of the family of either should make a prompt report to the court regarding such conduct.

EC 7–33 A goal of our legal system is that each party shall have his case, criminal or civil, adjudicated by an impartial tribunal. The attainment of this goal may be defeated by dissemination of news or comments which tend to influence judge or jury.[53] Such news or comments may prevent prospective jurors from being impartial at the outset of the trial[54] and may also interfere with the obligation of jurors to base their verdict solely upon the evidence admitted in the trial.[55] The release by a lawyer of out-of-court statements regarding

---

[53] Generally see ABA Advisory Committee on Fair Trial and Free Press, Standards Relating to Fair Trial and Free Press (1966).

"[T]he trial court might well have proscribed extrajudicial statements by any lawyer, party, witness, or court official which divulged prejudicial matters. . . . See State v. Van Dwyne, 43 N.J. 369, 389, 204 A.2d 841, 852 (1964), in which the court interpreted Canon 20 of the American Bar Association's Canons of Professional Ethics to prohibit such statements. Being advised of the great public interest in the case, the mass coverage of the press, and the potential prejudicial impact of publicity, the court could also have requested the appropriate city and county officials to promulgate a regulation with respect to dissemination of information about the case by their employees. In addition, reporters who wrote or broadcast prejudicial stories, could have been warned as to the impropriety of publishing material not introduced in the proceedings. . . . In this manner, Sheppard's right to a trial free from outside interference would have been given added protection without corresponding curtailment of the news media. Had the judge, the other officers of the court, and the police placed the interest of justice first, the news media would have soon learned to be content with the task of reporting the case as it unfolded in the courtroom—not pieced together from extrajudicial statements." Sheppard v. Maxwell, 384 U.S. 333, 361–62, 16 L.Ed.2d 600, 619–20, 86 S.Ct. 1507, 1521–22 (1966).

"Court proceedings are held for the solemn purpose of endeavoring to ascertain the truth which is the *sine qua non* of a fair trial. Over the centuries Anglo-American courts have devised careful safeguards by rule and otherwise to protect and facilitate the performance of this high function. As a result, at this time those safeguards do not permit the televising and photographing of a criminal trial, save in two States and there only under restrictions. The federal courts prohibit it by specific rule. This is weighty evidence that our concepts of a fair trial do not tolerate such an indulgence. We have always held that the atmosphere essential to the preservation of a fair trial—the most fundamental of all freedoms—must be maintained at all costs." Estes v. State of Texas, 381 U.S. 532, 540, 14 L.Ed.2d 543, 549, 85 S.Ct. 1628, 1631–32 (1965), rehearing denied, 382 U.S. 875, 15 L.Ed.2d 118, 86 S.Ct. 18 (1965).

[54] "Pretrial can create a major problem for the defendant in a criminal case. Indeed, it may be more harmful than publicity during the trial for it may well set the community opinion as to guilt or innocence. . . . The trial witnesses present at the hearing, as well as the original jury panel, were undoubtedly made aware of the peculiar public importance of the case by the press and television coverage being provided, and by the fact that they themselves were televised live and their pictures rebroadcast on the evening show." Id., 381 U.S. at 536–37, 14 L.Ed.2d at 546–47, 85 S.Ct. at 1629–30.

[55] "The undeviating rule of this Court was expressed by Mr. Justice Holmes over half a century ago in Patterson v. Colorado, 205 U.S. 454, 462 (1907):

"The theory of our system is that the conclusions to be reached in a case will be induced only by evidence and argument in open court, and not by any outside influence, whether of private talk or public print."

Sheppard v. Maxwell, 384 U.S. 333, 351, 16 L.Ed.2d 600, 614, 86 S.Ct. 1507, 1516 (1966).

"The trial judge has a large discretion in ruling on the issue of prejudice resulting from the reading by jurors of news articles concerning the trial. . . . Generalizations beyond that statement are not profitable, because each case must turn on its special facts. We have here the exposure of jurors to information of a character which the trial judge ruled was so prejudicial it could not be directly offered as evidence. The prejudice to the defendant is almost certain to be as great when that evidence reaches the jury through news accounts as when it is a part of the prosecution's evidence. . . . It may indeed be greater for it is then not tempered by protective procedures." Marshall v. United States, 360 U.S. 310, 312–13, 3 L.Ed.2d 1250, 1252, 79 S.Ct. 1171, 1173 (1959).

"The experienced trial lawyer knows that an adverse public opinion is a tremendous disadvantage to the defense of his client. Although grand jurors conduct their deliberations in secret, they are selected from the body of the public. They are likely to know what the general public knows and to reflect the public attitude. Trials are open to the public, and aroused public opinion respecting the merits of a legal controversy creates a court room atmosphere which, without any vocal expression in the presence of the petit jury, makes itself felt and has its effect upon the action of the petit jury. Our fundamental concepts of justice and our American sense of fair play requires that the petit jury shall be composed of persons with fair and impartial minds and without preconceived views as to the merits of the controversy, and that it shall determine the issues presented to it solely upon the evidence adduced at the trial and according to the law given in the instructions of the trial judge.

"While we may doubt that the effect of public opinion would sway or bias the judgment of the trial judge in an equity proceeding, the defendant should not be called upon to run that risk and the trial court should not have his work made more difficult by any dissemination of statements to the public that would be calculated to create a public demand for a particular judgment in a prospective or pending case." *ABA Opinion* 199 (1940).

an anticipated or pending trial may improperly affect the impartiality of the tribunal.[56] For these reasons, standards for permissible and prohibited conduct of a lawyer with respect to trial publicity have been established.

EC 7–34 The impartiality of a public servant in our legal system may be impaired by the receipt of gifts or loans. A lawyer,[57] therefore, is never justified in making a gift or a loan to a judge, a hearing officer, or an official or employee of a tribunal, except as permitted by Section C(4) of Canon 5 of the Code of Judicial Conduct, but a lawyer may make a contribution to the campaign fund of a candidate for judicial office in conformity with Section B(2) under Canon 7 of the Code of Judicial Conduct.[58]

As amended in 1974.

EC 7–35 All litigants and lawyers should have access to tribunals on an equal basis. Generally, in adversary proceedings a lawyer should not communicate with a judge relative to a matter pending before, or which is to be brought before, a tribunal over which he presides in circumstances which might have the effect or give the appearance of granting undue advantage to one party.[59] For example, a lawyer should not communicate with a tribunal by a writing unless a copy thereof is promptly delivered to opposing counsel or to the adverse party if he is not represented by a lawyer. Ordinarily an oral communication by a lawyer with a judge or hearing officer should be made only upon adequate notice to opposing counsel, or, if there is none, to the opposing party. A lawyer should not condone or lend himself to private importunities by another with a judge or hearing officer on behalf of himself or his client.

EC 7–36 Judicial hearings ought to be conducted through dignified and orderly procedures designed to protect the rights of all parties. Although a lawyer has the duty to represent his client zealously, he should not engage in any conduct that offends the dignity and decorum of proceedings.[60] While maintaining his independence, a lawyer should be respectful, courteous, and above-board in his relations with a judge or hearing officer before whom he appears.[61] He should avoid undue solicitude for the comfort or convenience of judge or jury and should avoid any other conduct calculated to gain special consideration.

EC 7–37 In adversary proceedings, clients are litigants and though ill feeling may exist between clients, such ill feeling should not influence a lawyer in his conduct, attitude, and demeanor towards opposing lawyers.[62] A lawyer should not make unfair or derogatory personal reference to opposing counsel. Haranguing and offensive tactics by lawyers interfere with the orderly administration of justice and have no proper place in our legal system.

EC 7–38 A lawyer should be courteous to opposing counsel and should accede to reasonable requests regarding court proceedings, settings, continuances, waiver of procedural formalities, and similar matters which do not prejudice the rights of his client.[63] He should follow local customs of courtesy or practice, unless

---

Cf. Estes v. State of Texas, 381 U.S. 532, 544–45, 14 L.Ed.2d 543, 551, 85 S.Ct. 1628, 1634 (1965), rehearing denied, 381 U.S. 875, 15 L.Ed.2d 118, 86 S.Ct. 18 (1965).

[56] See ABA Canon 20.

[57] Canon 3 observes that a lawyer "deserves rebuke and denunciation for any device or attempt to gain from a Judge special personal consideration or favor."

See ABA Canon 32.

[58] "*Judicial Canon 32* provides:

" 'A judge should not accept any presents or favors from litigants, or from lawyers practicing before him or from others whose interests are likely to be submitted to him for judgment.'

"The language of this Canon is perhaps broad enough to prohibit campaign contributions by lawyers, practicing before the court upon which the candidate hopes to sit. However, we do not think it was intended to prohibit such contributions when the candidate is obligated, by force of circumstances over which he has no control, to conduct a campaign, the expense of which exceeds that which he should reasonably be expected to personally bear!" *ABA Opinion* 226 (1941).

[59] See ABA Canons 3 and 32.

[60] Cf. ABA Canon 18.

[61] See ABA Canons 1 and 3.

[62] See ABA Canon 17.

[63] See ABA Canon 24.

he gives timely notice to opposing counsel of his intention not to do so.[64] A lawyer should be punctual in fulfilling all professional commitments.[65]

EC 7-39 In the final analysis, proper functioning of the adversary system depends upon cooperation between lawyers and tribunals in utilizing procedures which will preserve the impartiality of tribunals and make their decisional processes prompt and just, without impinging upon the obligation of lawyers to represent their clients zealously within the framework of the law.

DISCIPLINARY RULES

DR 7-101 Representing a Client Zealously.

(A) A lawyer shall not intentionally: [66]

(1) Fail to seek the lawful objectives of his client through reasonably available means[67] permitted by law and the Disciplinary Rules, except as provided by DR 7-101(B). A lawyer does not violate this Disciplinary Rule, however, by acceding to reasonable requests of opposing counsel which do not prejudice the rights of his client, by being punctual in fulfilling all professional commitments, by avoiding offensive tactics, or by treating with courtesy and consideration all persons involved in the legal process.

(2) Fail to carry out a contract of employment entered into with a client for professional services, but he may withdraw as permitted under DR 2-110, DR 5-102, and DR 5-105.

(3) Prejudice or damage his client during the course of the professional relationship[68] except as required under DR 7-102(B).

(B) In his representation of a client, a lawyer may:

(1) Where permissible, exercise his professional judgment to waive or fail to assert a right or position of his client.

(2) Refuse to aid or participate in conduct that he believes to be unlawful, even though there is some support for an argument that the conduct is legal.

DR 7-102 Representing a Client Within the Bounds of the Law.

(A) In his representation of a client, a lawyer shall not:

(1) File a suit, assert a position, conduct a defense, delay a trial, or take other action on behalf of his client when he knows or when it is obvious that such action would serve merely to harass or maliciously injure another.[69]

(2) Knowingly advance a claim or defense that is unwarranted under existing law, except that he may advance such claim or defense it if can be supported by good faith argument for an extension, modification, or reversal of existing law.

(3) Conceal or knowingly fail to disclose that which he is required by law to reveal.

(4) Knowingly use perjured testimony or false evidence.[70]

---

64 See ABA Canon 25.

65 See ABA Canon 21.

66 See ABA Canon 15.

67 See ABA Canons 5 and 15; cf. ABA Canons 4 and 32.

68 Cf. ABA Canon 24.

69 See ABA Canon 30.

70 Cf. ABA Canons 22 and 29.

(5) Knowingly make a false statement of law or fact.

(6) Participate in the creation or preservation of evidence when he knows or it is obvious that the evidence is false.

(7) Counsel or assist his client in conduct that the lawyer knows to be illegal or fraudulent.

(8) Knowingly engage in other illegal conduct or conduct contrary to a Disciplinary Rule.

(B) A lawyer who receives information clearly establishing that:

(1) His client has, in the course of the representation, perpetrated a fraud upon a person or tribunal shall promptly call upon his client to rectify the same, and if his client refuses or is unable to do so, he shall reveal the fraud to the affected person or tribunal, except when the information is protected as a privileged communication.[71]

(2) A person other than his client has perpetrated a fraud upon a tribunal shall promptly reveal the fraud to the tribunal.[72]

As amended in 1974.

DR 7–103 Performing the Duty of Public Prosecutor or Other Government Lawyer.[73]

(A) A public prosecutor or other government lawyer shall not institute or cause to be instituted criminal charges when he knows or it is obvious that the charges are not supported by probable cause.

(B) A public prosecutor or other government lawyer in criminal litigation shall make timely disclosure to counsel for the defendant, or to the defendant if he has no counsel, of the existence of evidence, known to the prosecutor or other government lawyer, that tends to negate the guilt of the accused, mitigate the degree of the offense, or reduce the punishment.

DR 7–104 Communicating With One of Adverse Interest.[74]

(A) During the course of his representation of a client a lawyer shall not:

(1) Communicate or cause another to communicate on the subject of the representation with a party he knows to be represented by a lawyer in that matter unless he has the prior consent of the lawyer representing such other party [75] or is authorized by law to do so.

---

71 See ABA Canon 41; cf. Hinds v. State Bar, 19 Cal.2d 87, 92–93, 119 P.2d 134, 137 (1941); but see *ABA Opinion* 287 (1953) and Texas Canon 38. Also see Code of Professional Responsibility. DR 4–101(C)(2).

72 See Precision Inst. Mfg. Co. v. Automotive M.M. Co., 324 U.S. 806, 89 L.Ed. 1381, 65 S.Ct. 993 (1945).

73 Cf. ABA Canon 5.

74 "*Rule 12*. . . . A member of the State Bar shall not communicate with a party represented by counsel upon a subject of controversy, in the absence and without the consent of such counsel. This rule shall not apply to communications with a public officer, board, committee or body." Cal. Business and Professions Code § 6076 (West 1962).

75 See ABA Canon 9; cf. *ABA Opinions* 124 (1934), 108 (1934), 95 (1933), and 75 (1932); also see In re Schwabe, 242 Or. 169, 174–75, 408 P.2d 922, 924 (1965).

"It is clear from the earlier opinions of this committee that *Canon 9* is to be construed literally and does not allow a communication with an opposing party, without the consent of his counsel, though the purpose merely be to investigate the facts. *Opinions 117, 55, 66,*" *ABA Opinion* 187 (1938).

(2) Give advice to a person who is not represented by a lawyer, other than the advice to secure counsel,[76] if the interests of such person are or have a reasonable possibility of being in conflict with the interests of his client.[77]

DR 7–105 Threatening Criminal Prosecution.

(A) A lawyer shall not present, participate in presenting, or threaten to present criminal charges solely to obtain an advantage in a civil matter.

DR 7–106 Trial Conduct.

(A) A lawyer shall not disregard or advise his client to disregard a standing rule of a tribunal or a ruling of a tribunal made in the course of a proceeding, but he may take appropriate steps in good faith to test the validity of such rule or ruling.

(B) In presenting a matter to a tribunal, a lawyer shall disclose:[78]

(1) Legal authority in the controlling jurisdiction known to him to be directly adverse to the position of his client and which is not disclosed by opposing counsel.[79]

(2) Unless privileged or irrelevant, the identities of the clients he represents and of the persons who employed him.[80]

(C) In appearing in his professional capacity before a tribunal, a lawyer shall not:

(1) State or allude to any matter that he has no reasonable basis to believe is relevant to the case or that will not be supported by admissible evidence.[81]

---

76 Cf. *ABA Opinion* 102 (1933).

77 Cf. ABA Canon 9 and *ABA Opinion* 58 (1931).

78 Cf. Note, 38 Texas L.Rev. 107, 108–09 (1959).

79 "In the brief summary in the 1947 edition of the Committee's decisions (p. 17), *Opinion 146* was thus summarized: *Opinion 146*—A lawyer should disclose to the court a decision directly adverse to his client's case that is unknown to his adversary.

"We would not confine the Opinion to 'controlling authorities'—i.e., those decisive of the pending case—but, in accordance with the tests hereafter suggested, would apply it to a decision directly adverse to any proposition of law on which the lawyer expressly relies, which would reasonably be considered important by the judge sitting on the case.

* * *

". . . The test in every case should be: Is the decision which opposing counsel has overlooked one which the court should clearly consider in deciding the case? Would a reasonable judge properly feel that a lawyer who advanced, as the law, a proposition adverse to the undisclosed decision, was lacking in candor and fairness to him? Might the judge consider himself misled by an implied representation that the lawyer knew of no adverse authority?" *ABA Opinion* 280 (1949).

80 "The authorities are substantially uniform against any privilege as applied to the fact of retainer or identity of the client. The privilege is limited to confidential communications, and a retainer is not a confidential communication, although it cannot come into existence without some communication between the attorney and the—at that stage prospective—client." United States v. Pape, 144 F.2d 778, 782 (2d Cir. 1944), cert. denied, 323 U.S. 752 89 L.Ed.2d 602, 65 S.Ct. 86 (1944).

"To be sure, there may be circumstances under which the identification of a client may amount to the prejudicial disclosure of a confidential communication, as where the substance of a disclosure has already been revealed but not its source." Colton v. United States, 306 F.2d 633, 637 (2d Cir. 1962).

81 See ABA Canon 22; cf. ABA Canon 17.

"The rule allowing counsel when addressing the jury the widest latitude in discussing the evidence and presenting the client's theories falls far short of authorizing the statement by counsel of matter not in evidence, or indulging in argument founded on no proof, or demanding verdicts for purposes other than the just settlement of the matters at issue between the litigants, or appealing to prejudice or passion. The rule confining counsel to legitimate argument is not based on etiquette, but on justice. Its violation is not merely an overstepping of the bounds of propriety, but a violation of a party's rights. The jurors must determine the issues upon the evidence. Counsel's address should help them do this, not tend to lead them astray." Cherry Creek Nat. Bank v. Fidelity & Cas. Co., 207 App.Div. 787, 790–91, 202 N.Y.S. 611, 614 (1924).

(2) **Ask any question that he has no reasonable basis to believe is relevant to the case and that is intended to degrade a witness or other person.**[82]

(3) **Assert his personal knowledge of the facts in issue, except when testifying as a witness.**

(4) **Assert his personal opinion as to the justness of a cause, as to the credibility of a witness, as to the culpability of a civil litigant, or as to the guilt or innocence of an accused;** [83] **but he may argue, on his analysis of the evidence, for any position or conclusion with respect to the matters stated herein.**

(5) **Fail to comply with known local customs of courtesy or practice of the bar or a particular tribunal without giving to opposing counsel timely notice of his intent not to comply.**[84]

(6) **Engage in undignified or discourteous conduct which is degrading to a tribunal.**

(7) **Intentionally or habitually violate any established rule of procedure or of evidence.**

DR 7-107 Trial Publicity.[85]

(A) **A lawyer participating in or associated with the investigation of a criminal matter shall not make or participate in making an extrajudicial statement that a reasonable person would expect to be disseminated by means of public communication and that does more than state without elaboration:**

---

[82] Cf. ABA Canon 18.

§ 6068. . . . It is the duty of an attorney:

* * *

"(f) To abstain from all offensive personality, and to advance no fact prejudicial to the honor or reputation of a party or witness, unless required by the justice of the cause with which he is charged." Cal.Business and Professions Code § 6068 (West 1962).

[83] "The record in the case at bar was silent concerning the qualities and character of the deceased. It is especially improper, in addressing the jury in a murder case, for the prosecuting attorney to make reference to his knowledge of the good qualities of the deceased where there is no evidence in the record bearing upon his character. . . . A prosecutor should never inject into his argument evidence not introduced at the trial." People v. Dukes, 12 Ill.2d 334, 341, 146 N.E.2d 14, 17–18 (1957).

[84] "A lawyer should not ignore known customs or practice of the Bar or of a particular Court, even when the law permits, without giving timely notice to the opposing counsel." ABA Canon 25.

[85] The provisions of Sections (A), (B), (C), and (D) of this Disciplinary Rule incorporate the fair trial-free press standards which apply to lawyers as adopted by the ABA House of Delegates, Feb. 19, 1968, upon the recommendation of the Fair Trial and Free Press Advisory Committee of the ABA Special Committee on Minimum Standards for the Administration of Criminal Justice.

Cf. ABA Canon 20; see generally ABA Advisory Committee on Fair Trial and Free Press, Standards Relating to Fair Trial and Free Press (1966).

"From the cases coming here we note that unfair and prejudicial news comment on pending trials has become increasingly prevalent. Due process requires that the accused receive a trial by an impartial jury free from outside influences. Given the pervasiveness of modern communications and the difficulty of effacing prejudicial publicity from the minds of the jurors, the trial courts must take strong measures to ensure that the balance is never weighed against the accused. And appellate tribunals have the duty to make an independent evaluation of the circumstances. Of course, there is nothing that prescribes the press from reporting events that transpire in the courtroom. But where there is a reasonable likelihood that prejudicial news prior to trial will prevent a fair trial, the judge should continue the case until the threat abates, or transfer it to another county not so permeated with publicity. . . . The courts must take such steps by rule and regulation that will protect their processes from prejudicial outside interferences. Neither prosecutors, counsel for defense, the accused, witnesses, court staff nor enforcement officers coming under the jurisdiction of the court should be permitted to frustrate its function. Collaboration between counsel and the press as to information affecting the fairness of a criminal trial is not only subject to regulation, but is highly censurable and worthy of disciplinary measures." Sheppard v. Maxwell, 384 U.S. 333, 362–63, 16 L.Ed.2d 600, 620, 86 S.Ct. 1507, 1522 (1966).

(1) Information contained in a public record.

(2) That the investigation is in progress.

(3) The general scope of the investigation including a description of the offense and, if permitted by law, the identity of the victim.

(4) A request for assistance in apprehending a suspect or assistance in other matters and the information necessary thereto.

(5) A warning to the public of any dangers.

(B) A lawyer or law firm associated with the prosecution or defense of a criminal matter shall not, from the time of the filing of a complaint, information, or indictment, the issuance of an arrest warrant, or arrest until the commencement of the trial or disposition without trial, make or participate in making an extrajudicial statement that a reasonable person would expect to be disseminated by means of public communication and that relates to:

(1) The character, reputation, or prior criminal record (including arrests, indictments, or other charges of crime) of the accused.

(2) The possibility of a plea of guilty to the offense charged or to a lesser offense.

(3) The existence or contents of any confession, admission, or statement given by the accused or his refusal or failure to make a statement.

(4) The performance or results of any examinations or tests or the refusal or failure of the accused to submit to examinations or tests.

(5) The identity, testimony, or credibility of a prospective witness.

(6) Any opinion as to the guilt or innocence of the accused, the evidence, or the merits of the case.

(C) DR 7-107(B) does not preclude a lawyer during such period from announcing:

(1) The name, age, residence, occupation, and family status of the accused.

(2) If the accused has not been apprehended, any information necessary to aid in his apprehension or to warn the public of any dangers he may present.

(3) A request for assistance in obtaining evidence.

(4) The identity of the victim of the crime.

(5) The fact, time, and place of arrest, resistance, pursuit, and use of weapons.

(6) The identity of investigating and arresting officers or agencies and the length of the investigation.

(7) At the time of seizure, a description of the physical evidence seized, other than a confession, admission, or statement.

(8) The nature, substance, or text of the charge.

(9) Quotations from or references to public records of the court in the case.

(10) The scheduling or result of any step in the judicial proceedings.

(11) That the accused denies the charges made against him.

(D) During the selection of a jury or the trial of a criminal matter, a lawyer or law firm associated with the prosecution or defense of a criminal matter shall not make or participate in making an extra-judicial statement that a reasonable person would expect to be disseminated by means of public communication and that relates to the trial, parties, or issues in the trial or other matters that are reasonably likely to interfere with a fair trial, except that he may quote from or refer without comment to public records of the court in the case.

(E) After the completion of a trial or disposition without trial of a criminal matter and prior to the imposition of sentence, a lawyer or law firm associated with the prosecution or defense shall not make or participate in making an extra-judicial statement that a reasonable person would expect to be disseminated by public communication and that is reasonably likely to affect the imposition of sentence.

(F) The foregoing provisions of DR 7-107 also apply to professional disciplinary proceedings and juvenile disciplinary proceedings when pertinent and consistent with other law applicable to such proceedings.

(G) A lawyer or law firm associated with a civil action shall not during its investigation or litigation make or participate in making an extra-judicial statement, other than a quotation from or reference to public records, that a reasonable person would expect to be disseminated by means of public communication and that relates to:

(1) Evidence regarding the occurrence or transaction involved.

(2) The character, credibility, or criminal record of a party, witness, or prospective witness.

(3) The performance or results of any examinations or tests or the refusal or failure of a party to submit to such.

(4) His opinion as to the merits of the claims or defenses of a party, except as required by law or administrative rule.

(5) Any other matter reasonably likely to interfere with a fair trial of the action.

(H) During the pendency of an administrative proceeding, a lawyer or law firm associated therewith shall not make or participate in making a statement, other than a quotation from or reference to public records, that a reasonable person would expect to be disseminated by means of public communication if it is made outside the official course of the proceeding and relates to:

(1) Evidence regarding the occurrence or transaction involved.

(2) The character, credibility, or criminal record of a party, witness, or prospective witness.

(3) Physical evidence or the performance or results of any examinations or tests or the refusal or failure of a party to submit to such.

(4) His opinion as to the merits of the claims, defenses, or positions of an interested person.

(5) Any other matter reasonably likely to interfere with a fair hearing.

(I) The foregoing provisions of DR 7-107 do not preclude a lawyer from replying to charges of misconduct publicly made against him or from participating in the proceedings of legislative, administrative, or other investigative bodies.

(J) A lawyer shall exercise reasonable care to prevent his employees and associates from making an extra-judicial statement that he would be prohibited from making under DR 7-107.

DR 7-108 Communication With or Investigation of Jurors.

(A) Before the trial of a case a lawyer connected therewith shall not communicate with or cause another to communicate with anyone he knows to be a member of the venire from which the jury will be selected for the trial of the case.

(B) During the trial of a case:

(1) A lawyer connected therewith shall not communicate with or cause another to communicate with any member of the jury.[86]

(2) A lawyer who is not connected therewith shall not communicate with or cause another to communicate with a juror concerning the case.

(C) DR 7-108(A) and (B) do not prohibit a lawyer from communicating with veniremen or jurors in the course of official proceedings.

(D) After discharge of the jury from further consideration of a case with which the lawyer was connected, the lawyer shall not ask questions of or make comments to a member of that jury that are calculated merely to harass or embarrass the juror or to influence his actions in future jury service.[87]

(E) A lawyer shall not conduct or cause, by financial support or otherwise, another to conduct a vexatious or harassing investigation of either a venireman or a juror.

(F) All restrictions imposed by DR 7-108 upon a lawyer also apply to communications with or investigations of members of a family of a venireman or a juror.

(G) A lawyer shall reveal promptly to the court improper conduct by a venireman or a juror, or by another toward a venireman or a juror or a member of his family, of which the lawyer has knowledge.

DR 7-109 Contact With Witnesses.

(A) A lawyer shall not suppress any evidence that he or his client has a legal obligation to reveal or produce.[88]

(B) A lawyer shall not advise or cause a person to secrete himself or to leave the jurisdiction of a tribunal for the purpose of making him unavailable as a witness therein.[89]

(C) A lawyer shall not pay, offer to pay, or acquiesce in the payment of compensation to a witness contingent upon the content of his testimony or the outcome of the case.[90] But a lawyer may advance, guarantee, or acquiesce in the payment of:

(1) Expenses reasonably incurred by a witness in attending or testifying.

(2) Reasonable compensation to a witness for his loss of time in attending or testifying.

(3) A reasonable fee for the professional services of an expert witness.

---

86 See ABA Canon 23.

87 "[I]t would be unethical for a lawyer to harass, entice, induce or exert influence on a juror to obtain his testimony." *ABA Opinion* 319 (1968).

88 See ABA Canon 5.

89 Cf. ABA Canon 5.

"*Rule 15.* . . . A member of the State Bar shall not advise a person, whose testimony could establish or tend to establish a material fact, to avoid service of process, or secrete himself, or otherwise to make his testimony unavailable." Cal.Business and Professions Code § 6076 (West 1962).

90 See In re O'Keefe, 49 Mont. 369, 142 P. 638 (1914).

DR 7–110 Contact With Officials.[91]

(A) A lawyer shall not give or lend any thing of value to a judge, official, or employee of a tribunal, except as permitted by Section C(4) of Canon 5 of the Code of Judicial Conduct, but a lawyer may make a contribution to the campaign fund of a candidate for judicial office in conformity with Section B(2) under Canon 7 of the Code of Judicial Conduct.

(B) In an adversary proceeding, a lawyer shall not communicate, or cause another to communicate, as to the merits of the cause with a judge or an official before whom the proceeding is pending, except:

(1) In the course of official proceedings in the cause.

(2) In writing if he promptly delivers a copy of the writing to opposing counsel or to the adverse party if he is not represented by a lawyer.

(3) Orally upon adequate notice to opposing counsel or to the adverse party if he is not represented by a lawyer.

(4) As otherwise authorized by law, or by Section A(4) under Canon 3 of the Code of Judicial Conduct.[92]

As amended in 1974.

CANON 8

A Lawyer Should Assist in Improving the Legal System

ETHICAL CONSIDERATIONS

EC 8–1 Changes in human affairs and imperfections in human institutions make necessary constant efforts to maintain and improve our legal system.[1] This system should function in a manner that commands public respect and fosters the use of legal remedies to achieve redress of grievances. By reason of education and experience, lawyers are especially qualified to recognize deficiencies in the legal system and to initiate corrective measures therein. Thus they should participate in proposing and supporting legislation and

---

91 Cf. ABA Canon 3.

92 "*Rule 16.* . . . A member of the State Bar shall not, in the absence of opposing counsel, communicate with or argue to a judge or judicial officer except in open court upon the merits of a contested matter pending before such judge or judicial officer; nor shall he, without furnishing opposing counsel with a copy thereof, address a written communication to a judge or judicial officer concerning the merits of a contested matter pending before such judge or judicial officer. This rule shall not apply to ex parte matters." Cal.Business and Professions Code § 6076 (West 1962).

1 ". . . [Another] task of the great lawyer is to do his part individually and as a member of the organized bar to improve his profession, the courts, and the law. As President Theodore Roosevelt aptly put it, 'Every man owes some of his time to the upbuilding of the profession to which he belongs.' Indeed, this obligation is one of the great things which distinguishes a profession from a business. The soundness and the necessity of President Roosevelt's admonition insofar as it relates to the legal profession cannot be doubted. The advances in natural science and technology are so startling and the velocity of change in business and in social life is so great that the law along with the other social sciences, and even human life itself, is in grave danger of being extinguished by new gods of its own invention if it does not awake from its lethargy." Vanderbilt, *The Five Functions of the Lawyer: Service to Clients and the Public,* 40 A.B.A.J. 31, 31–32 (1954).

programs to improve the system,[2] without regard to the general interests or desires of clients or former clients.[3]

EC 8–2 Rules of law are deficient if they are not just, understandable, and responsive to the needs of society. If a lawyer believes that the existence or absence of a rule of law, substantive or procedural, causes or contributes to an unjust result, he should endeavor by lawful means to obtain appropriate change in the law. He should encourage the simplification of laws and the repeal or amendment of laws that are outmoded.[4] Likewise, legal procedures should be improved whenever experience indicates a change is needed.

EC 8–3 The fair administration of justice requires the availability of competent lawyers. Members of the public should be educated to recognize the existence of legal problems and the resultant need for legal services, and should be provided methods for intelligent selection of counsel. Those persons unable to pay for legal services should be provided needed services. Clients and lawyers should not be penalized by undue geographical restraints upon representation in legal matters, and the bar should address itself to improvements in licensing, reciprocity, and admission procedures consistent with the needs of modern commerce.

EC 8–4 Whenever a lawyer seeks legislative or administrative changes, he should identify the capacity in which he appears, whether on behalf of himself, a client, or the public.[5] A lawyer may advocate such changes on behalf of a client even though he does not agree with them. But when a lawyer purports to act on behalf of the public, he should espouse only those changes which he conscientiously believes to be in the public interest.

EC 8–5 Fraudulent, deceptive, or otherwise illegal conduct by a participant in a proceeding before a tribunal or legislative body is inconsistent with fair administration of justice, and it should never be participated in or condoned by lawyers. Unless constrained by his obligation to preserve the confidences and secrets of his client, a lawyer should reveal to appropriate authorities any knowledge he may have of such improper conduct.

EC 8–6 Judges and administrative officials having adjudicatory powers ought to be persons of integrity, competence, and suitable temperament. Generally, lawyers are qualified, by personal observation or investigation, to evaluate the qualifications of persons seeking or being considered for such public offices, and for this reason they have a special responsibility to aid in the selection of only those who are qualified.[6]

---

2 See ABA Cannon 29; Cf. Cheatham, *The Lawyer's Role and Surroundings,* 25 Rocky Mt.L.Rev. 405, 406–07 (1953).

"The lawyer tempted by repose should recall the heavy costs paid by his profession when needed legal reform has to be accomplished through the initiative of public-spirited laymen. Where change must be thrust from without upon an unwilling Bar, the public's least flattering picture of the lawyer seems confirmed. The lawyer concerned for the standing of his profession will, therefore, interest himself actively in the improvement of the law. In doing so he will not only help to maintain confidence in the Bar, but will have the satisfaction of meeting a responsibility inhering in the nature of his calling." *Professional Responsibility: Report of the Joint Conference,* 44 A.B.A.J. 1159, 1217 (1958).

3 See Stayton, *Cum Honore Officium,* 19 Tex.B.J. 765, 766 (1956); *Professional Responsibility: Report of the Joint Conference,* 44 A.B.A.J. 1159, 1162 (1958); and Paul, *The Lawyer as a Tax Adviser,* 25 Rocky Mt.L.Rev. 412, 433–34 (1953).

4 "There are few great figures in the history of the Bar who have not concerned themselves with the reform and improvement of the law. The special obligation of the profession with respect to legal reform rests on considerations too obvious to require enumeration. Certainly it is the lawyer who has both the best chance to know when the law is working badly and the special competence to put it in order." *Professional Responsibility: Report of the Joint Conference,* 44 A.B.A.J. 1159, 1217 (1958).

5 "*Rule 14.* . . . A member of the State Bar shall not communicate with, or appear before, a public officer, board, committee or body, in his professional capacity, without first disclosing that he is an attorney representing interests that may be affected by action of such officer, board, committee or body." Cal.Business and Professions Code § 6076 (West 1962).

6 See ABA Canon 2.

"Lawyers are better able than laymen to appraise accurately the qualifications of candidates for judicial office. It is proper that they should make that appraisal known to the voters in a proper and dignified manner. A lawyer may with propriety endorse a candidate for judicial office and seek like endorsement from other lawyers. But the lawyer who endorses a judicial candidate or seeks that endorsement from other lawyers should be actuated by a sincere belief in the superior qualifications of the candidate for judicial service and not by personal or selfish motives; and a lawyer should not use or attempt to use the power or prestige of the judicial office to secure such endorsement. On the other hand, the

It is the duty of lawyers to endeavor to prevent political considerations from outweighing judicial fitness in the selection of judges. Lawyers should protest earnestly against the appointment or election of those who are unsuited for the bench and should strive to have elected [7] or appointed thereto only those who are willing to forego pursuits, whether of a business, political, or other nature, that may interfere with the free and fair consideration of questions presented for adjudication. Adjudicatory officials, not being wholly free to defend themselves, are entitled to receive the support of the bar against unjust criticism.[8] While a lawyer as a citizen has a right to criticize such officials publicly,[9] he should be certain of the merit of his complaint, use appropriate language, and avoid petty criticisms, for unrestrained and intemperate statements tend to lessen public confidence in our legal system.[10] Criticisms motivated by reasons other than a desire to improve the legal system are not justified.

EC 8–7 Since lawyers are a vital part of the legal system, they should be persons of integrity, of professional skill, and of dedication to the improvement of the system. Thus a lawyer should aid in establishing, as well as enforcing, standards of conduct adequate to protect the public by insuring that those who practice law are qualified to do so.

EC 8–8 Lawyers often serve as legislators or as holders of other public offices. This is highly desirable, as lawyers are uniquely qualified to make significant contributions to the improvement of the legal system. A lawyer who is a public officer, whether full or part-time, should not engage in activities in which his personal or professional interests are or foreseeably may be in conflict with his official duties.[11]

---

lawyer whose endorsement is sought, if he believes the candidate lacks the essential qualifications for the office or believes the opposing candidate is better qualified, should have the courage and moral stamina to refuse the request for endorsement." *ABA Opinion* 189 (1938).

7 "[W]e are of the opinion that, whenever a candidate for judicial office merits the endorsement and support of lawyers, the lawyers may make financial contributions toward the campaign if its cost, when reasonably conducted, exceeds that which the candidate would be expected to bear personally." *ABA Opinion* 226 (1941).

8 See ABA Canon 1.

9 "Citizens have a right under our constitutional system to criticize governmental officials and agencies. Courts are not, and should not be, immune to such criticism." Konigsberg v. State Bar of California, 353 U.S. 252, 269 (1957).

10 "[E]very lawyer, worthy of respect, realizes that public confidence in our courts is the cornerstone of our governmental structure, and will refrain from unjustified attack on the character of the judges, while recognizing the duty to denounce and expose a corrupt or dishonest judge." Kentucky State Bar Ass'n v. Lewis, 282 S.W.2d 321, 326 (Ky.1955).

"We should be the last to deny that Mr. Meeker has the right to uphold the honor of the profession and to expose without fear or favor corrupt or dishonest conduct in the profession, whether the conduct be that of a judge or not. . . . However, this Canon [29] does not permit one to make charges which are false and untrue and unfounded in fact. When one's fancy leads him to make false charges, attacking the character and integrity of others, he does so at his peril. He should not do so without adequate proof of his charges and he is certainly not authorized to make careless, untruthful and vile charges against his professional brethren." In re Meeker, 76 N.M. 354, 364–65, 414 P.2d 862, 869 (1966), appeal dismissed, 385 U.S. 449, 17 L.Ed.2d 510, 87 S.Ct. 613 (1967).

11 "*Opinions 16, 30, 34, 77, 118* and *134* relate to *Canon 6,* and pass on questions concerning the propriety of the conduct of an attorney who is a public officer, in representing private interests adverse to those of the public body which he represents. The principle applied in those opinions is that an attorney holding public office should avoid all conduct which might lead the layman to conclude that the attorney is utilizing his public position to further his professional success or personal interests." *ABA Opinion* 192 (1939).

"The next question is whether a lawyer-member of a legislative body may appear as counsel or co-counsel at hearings before a zoning board of appeals, or similar tribunal, created by the legislative group of which he is a member. We are of the opinion that he may practice before fact-finding officers, hearing bodies and commissioners, since under our views he may appear as counsel in the courts where his municipality is a party. Decisions made at such hearings are usually subject to administrative review by the courts upon the record there made. It would be inconsistent to say that a lawyer-member of a legislative body could not participate in a hearing at which the record is made, but could appear thereafter when the cause is heard by the courts on administrative review. This is subject to an important exception. He should not appear as counsel where the matter is subject to review by the legislative body of which he is a member. . . . We are of the opinion that where a lawyer does so appear there would be conflict of interests between his duty as an advocate for his client on the one hand and the obligation to his governmental unit on the other." In re Becker, 16 Ill.2d 488, 494–95, 158 N.E.2d 753, 756–57 (1959).

Cf. *ABA Opinions* 186 (1938), 136 (1935), 118 (1934), and 77 (1932).

EC 8-9 The advancement of our legal system is of vital importance in maintaining the rule of law and in facilitating orderly changes; therefore, lawyers should encourage, and should aid in making, needed changes and improvements.

DISCIPLINARY RULES

DR 8-101 Action as a Public Official.

(A) A lawyer who holds public office shall not:

(1) Use his public position to obtain, or attempt to obtain, a special advantage in legislative matters for himself or for a client under circumstances where he knows or it is obvious that such action is not in the public interest.

(2) Use his public position to influence, or attempt to influence, a tribunal to act in favor of himself or of a client.

(3) Accept any thing of value from any person when the lawyer knows or it is obvious that the offer is for the purpose of influencing his action as a public official.

DR 8-102 Statements Concerning Judges and Other Adjudicatory Officers.[12]

(A) A lawyer shall not knowingly make false statements of fact concerning the qualifications of a candidate for election or appointment to a judicial office.

(B) A lawyer shall not knowingly make false accusations against a judge or other adjudicatory officer.

DR 8-103 Lawyer Candidate for Judicial Office.

(A) A lawyer who is a candidate for judicial office shall comply with the applicable provisions of Canon 7 of the Code of Judicial Conduct.

Added in 1974.

CANON 9

A Lawyer Should Avoid Even the Appearance of Professional Impropriety

ETHICAL CONSIDERATIONS

EC 9-1 Continuation of the American concept that we are to be governed by rules of law requires that the people have faith that justice can be obtained through our legal system.[1] A lawyer should promote public confidence in our system and in the legal profession.[2]

EC 9-2 Public confidence in law and lawyers may be eroded by irresponsible or improper conduct of a lawyer. On occasion, ethical conduct of a lawyer may appear to laymen to be unethical. In order to avoid misunderstandings and hence to maintain confidence, a lawyer should fully and promptly inform his client of material developments in the matters being handled for the client. While a lawyer should guard against otherwise proper conduct that has a tendency to diminish public confidence in the legal system or in the legal profession, his duty to clients or to the public should never be subordinate merely because the full

---

12 Cf. ABA Canons 1 and 2.

1 "Integrity is the very breath of justice. Confidence in our law, our courts, and in the administration of justice is our supreme interest. No practice must be permitted to prevail which invites towards the administration of justice a doubt or distrust of its integrity." Erwin M. Jennings Co. v. DiGenova, 107 Conn. 491, 499, 141 A. 866, 868 (1928).

2 "A lawyer should never be reluctant or too proud to answer unjustified criticism of his profession, of himself, or of his brother lawyer. He should guard the reputation of his profession and of his brothers as zealously as he guards his own." Rochelle and Payne, *The Struggle for Public Understanding,* 25 Texas B.J. 109, 162 (1962).

discharge of his obligation may be misunderstood or may tend to subject him or the legal profession to criticism. When explicit ethical guidance does not exist, a lawyer should determine his conduct by acting in a manner that promotes public confidence in the integrity and efficiency of the legal system and the legal profession.[3]

EC 9–3 After a lawyer leaves judicial office or other public employment, he should not accept employment in connection with any matter in which he had substantial responsibility prior to his leaving, since to accept employment would give the appearance of impropriety even if none exists.[4]

EC 9–4 Because the very essence of the legal system is to provide procedures by which matters can be presented in an impartial manner so that they may be decided solely upon the merits, any statement or suggestion by a lawyer that he can or would attempt to circumvent those procedures is detrimental to the legal system and tends to undermine public confidence in it.

EC 9–5 Separation of the funds of a client from those of his lawyer not only serves to protect the client but also avoids even the appearance of impropriety, and therefore commingling of such funds should be avoided.

EC 9–6 Every lawyer owes a solemn duty to uphold the integrity and honor of his profession; to encourage respect for the law and for the courts and the judges thereof; to observe the Code of Professional Responsibility; to act as a member of a learned profession, one dedicated to public service; to cooperate with his brother lawyers in supporting the organized bar through the devoting of his time, efforts, and financial support as his professional standing and ability reasonably permit; to conduct himself so as to reflect credit on the legal profession and to inspire the confidence, respect, and trust of his clients and of the public; and to strive to avoid not only professional impropriety but also the appearance of impropriety.[5]

EC 9–7 A lawyer has an obligation to the public to participate in collective efforts of the bar to reimburse persons who have lost money or property as a result of the misappropriation or defalcation of another lawyer, and contribution to a clients' security fund is an acceptable method of meeting this obligation.

DISCIPLINARY RULES

DR 9–101 Avoiding Even the Appearance of Impropriety.[6]

(A) A lawyer shall not accept private employment in a matter upon the merits of which he has acted in a judicial capacity.[7]

---

[3] See ABA Canon 29.

[4] See ABA Canon 36.

[5] "As said in Opinion 49 of the Committee on Professional Ethics and Grievances of the American Bar Association, page 134: 'An attorney should not only avoid impropriety but should avoid the appearance of impropriety.' " State ex rel. Nebraska State Bar Ass'n v. Richards, 165 Neb. 80, 93, 84 N.W.2d 136, 145 (1957).

"It would also be preferable that such contribution [to the campaign of a candidate for judicial office] be made to a campaign committee rather than to the candidate personally. In so doing, possible appearances of impropriety would be reduced to a minimum." *ABA Opinion* 226 (1941).

"The lawyer assumes high duties, and has imposed upon him grave responsibilities. He may be the means of much good or much mischief. Interests of vast magnitude are entrusted to him; confidence is reposed in him; life, liberty, character and property should be protected by him. He should guard, with jealous watchfulness, his own reputation, as well as that of his profession." People ex rel. Cutler v. Ford, 54 Ill. 520, 522 (1870), and also quoted in State Board of Law Examiners v. Sheldon, 43 Wyo. 522, 526, 7 P.2d 226, 227 (1932).

See *ABA Opinion* 150 (1936).

[6] Cf. Code of Professional Responsibility, EC 5–6.

[7] See *ABA* Canon 36.

"It is the duty of the judge to rule on questions of law and evidence in misdemeanor cases and examinations in felony cases. That duty calls for impartial and uninfluenced judgment, regardless of the effect on those immediately involved or others who may, directly or indirectly, be affected. Discharge of that duty might be greatly interfered with if the judge, in another capacity, were permitted to hold himself out to employment by those who are to be, or who may be, brought to trial in felony cases, even though he did not conduct the examination. His private interests as a lawyer in building up his clientele, his duty as such zealously to espouse the cause of his private clients and to defend against charges of crime

(B) A lawyer shall not accept private employment in a matter in which he had substantial responsibility while he was a public employee.[8]

(C) A lawyer shall not state or imply that he is able to influence improperly or upon irrelevant grounds any tribunal, legislative body,[9] or public official.

DR 9–102 Preserving Identity of Funds and Property of a Client.[10]

(A) All funds of clients paid to a lawyer or law firm, other than advances for costs and expenses, shall be deposited in one or more identifiable bank accounts maintained in the state in which the law office is situated and no funds belonging to the lawyer or law firm shall be deposited therein except as follows:

(1) Funds reasonably sufficient to pay bank charges may be deposited therein.

(2) Funds belonging in part to a client and in part presently or potentially to the lawyer or law firm must be deposited therein, but the portion belonging to the lawyer or law firm may be withdrawn when due unless the right of the lawyer or law firm to receive it is disputed by the client, in which event the disputed portion shall not be withdrawn until the dispute is finally resolved.

(B) A lawyer shall:

(1) Promptly notify a client of the receipt of his funds, securities, or other properties.

---

brought by law-enforcement agencies of which he is a part, might prevent, or even destroy, that unbiased judicial judgment which is so essential in the administration of justice.

"In our opinion, acceptance of a judgeship with the duties of conducting misdemeanor trials, and examinations in felony cases to determine whether those accused should be bound over for trial in a higher court, ethically bars the judge from acting as attorney for the defendants upon such trial, whether they were examined by him or by some other judge. Such a practice would not only diminish public confidence in the administration of justice in both courts, but would produce serious conflict between the private interests of the judge as a lawyer, and of his clients, and his duties as a judge in adjudicating important phases of criminal processes in other cases. The public and private duties would be incompatible. The prestige of the judicial office would be diverted to private benefit, and the judicial office would be demeaned thereby." *ABA Opinion* 242 (1942).

"A lawyer, who has previously occupied a judicial position or acted in a judicial capacity, should refrain from accepting employment in any matter involving the same facts as were involved in any specific question which he acted upon in a judicial capacity and, for the same reasons, should also refrain from accepting any employment which might reasonably appear to involve the same facts." *ABA Opinion* 49 (1931).

See *ABA Opinion* 110 (1934).

8 See *ABA Opinions* 135 (1935) and 134 (1935); cf. ABA Canon 36 and *ABA Opinions* 39 (1931) and 26 (1930). But see *ABA Opinion* 37 (1931).

9 "[A statement by a governmental department or agency with regard to a lawyer resigning from its staff that includes a laudation of his legal ability] carries implications, probably not founded in fact, that the lawyer's acquaintance and previous relations with the personnel of the administrative agencies of the government place him in an advantageous position in practicing before such agencies. So to imply would not only represent what probably is untrue, but would be highly reprehensible." *ABA Opinion* 184 (1938).

10 See ABA Canon 11.

"*Rule 9*. . . . A member of the State Bar shall not commingle the money or other property of a client with his own; and he shall promptly report to the client the receipt by him of all money and other property belonging to such client. Unless the client otherwise directs in writing, he shall promptly deposit his client's funds in a bank or trust company . . . in a bank account separate from his own account and clearly designated as 'Clients' Funds Account' or 'Trust Funds Account' or words of similar import. Unless the client otherwise directs in writing, securities of a client in bearer form shall be kept by the attorney in a safe deposit box at a bank or trust company, . . . which safe deposit box shall be clearly designated as 'Client's Account' or 'Trust Account' or words of similar import, and be separate from the attorney's own safe deposit box." Cal.Business and Professions Code § 6076 (West 1962).

"[C]ommingling is committed when a client's money is intermingled with that of his attorney and its separate identity lost so that it may be used for the attorney's personal expenses or subjected to claims of his creditors. . . . The rule against commingling was adopted to provide against the probability in some cases, the possibility in many cases, and the danger in all cases that such commingling will result in the loss of clients' money." Black v. State Bar, 57 Cal.2d 219, 225–26, 368 P.2d 118, 122, 18 Cal.Rptr. 518, 522 (1962).

(2) Identify and label securities and properties of a client promptly upon receipt and place them in a safe deposit box or other place of safekeeping as soon as practicable.

(3) Maintain complete records of all funds, securities, and other properties of a client coming into the possession of the lawyer and render appropriate accounts to his client regarding them.

(4) Promptly pay or deliver to the client as requested by a client the funds, securities, or other properties in the possession of the lawyer which the client is entitled to receive.

DEFINITIONS*

As used in the Disciplinary Rules of the Code of Professional Responsibility:

(1) "Differing interests" include every interest that will adversely affect either the judgment or the loyalty of a lawyer to a client, whether it be a conflicting, inconsistent, diverse, or other interest.

(2) "Law firm" includes a professional legal corporation.

(3) "Person" includes a corporation, an association, a trust, a partnership, and any other organization or legal entity.

(4) "Professional legal corporation" means a corporation, or an association treated as a corporation, authorized by law to practice law for profit.

(5) "State" includes the District of Columbia, Puerto Rico, and other federal territories and possessions.

(6) "Tribunal" includes all courts and all other adjudicatory bodies.

(7) "A Bar association" includes a bar association of specialists as referred to in DR 2-105(A)(1) or (3).

(8) "Qualified legal assistance organization" means an office or organization of one of the four types listed in DR 2-103(D)(1)-(4), inclusive that meets all the requirements thereof.

As amended in 1974.

* "Confidence" and "secret" are defined in DR 4-101(A).

INDEX TO ABA MODEL CODE

A

B

C

D

E

F

G

H

Q

R

S

AMERICAN BAR ASSOCIATION CANONS OF PROFESSIONAL ETHICS

As amended until 1969.

[The ABA adopted 32 Canons of Professional Ethics at its thirty-first annual meeting on August 27, 1908. Between 1908 and 1969, the ABA added Canons 33 through 47. Although the Canons were in effect for 61 years, the general aspirational approach of the Canons proved to be outmoded to regulate the conduct of lawyers in the 1950s and 1960s. The Canons were superseded in 1969 by the Model Code of Professional Responsibility. Ed.]

CANONS OF PROFESSIONAL ETHICS

Preamble.

In America, where the stability of Courts and of all departments of government rests upon the approval of the people, it is peculiarly essential that the system for establishing and dispensing Justice be developed to a high point of efficiency and so maintained that the public shall have absolute confidence in the integrity and impartiality of its administration. The future of the Republic, to a great extent, depends upon our maintenance of Justice pure and unsullied. It cannot be so maintained unless the conduct and the motives of the members of our profession are such as to merit the approval of all just men.

No code or set of rules can be framed, which will particularize all the duties of the lawyer in the varying phases of litigation or in all the relations of professional life. The following canons of ethics are adopted by the American Bar Association as a general guide, yet the enumeration of particular duties should not be construed as a denial of the existence of others equally imperative, though not specifically mentioned.

CANON 1

The Duty of the Lawyer to the Courts

It is the duty of the lawyer to maintain towards the Courts a respectful attitude, not for the sake of the temporary incumbent of the judicial office, but for the maintenance of its supreme importance. Judges, not being wholly free to defend themselves, are peculiarly entitled to receive the support of the Bar against unjust criticism and clamor. Whenever there is proper ground for serious complaint of a judicial officer, it is the right and duty of the lawyer to submit his grievances to the proper authorities. In such cases, but not otherwise, such charges should be encouraged and the person making them should be protected.

CANON 2

The Selection of Judges

It is the duty of the Bar to endeavor to prevent political considerations from outweighing judicial fitness in the selections of Judges. It should protest earnestly and actively against the appointment or election of those who are unsuitable for the Bench; and it should strive to have elevated thereto only those willing to forego other employments, whether of a business, political or other character, which may embarrass their free and fair consideration of questions before them for decision. The aspiration of lawyers for judicial position should be governed by an impartial estimate of their ability to add honor to the office and not by a desire for the distinction the position may bring to themselves.

CANON 3

Attempts to Exert Personal Influence on the Court

Marked attention and unusual hospitality on the part of a lawyer to a Judge, uncalled for by the personal relations of the parties, subject both the Judge and the lawyer to misconstructions of motive and should be avoided. A lawyer should not communicate or argue privately with the Judge as to the merits of a pending cause, and he deserves rebuke and denunciation for any device or attempt to gain from a Judge special personal consideration or favor. A self-respecting independence in the discharge of professional duty, without denial or diminution of the courtesy and respect due the Judge's station, is the only proper foundation for cordial personal and official relations between Bench and Bar.

CANON 4

When Counsel for an Indigent Prisoner

A lawyer assigned as counsel for an indigent prisoner ought not to ask to be excused for any trivial reason, and should always exert his best efforts on his behalf.

CANON 5

The Defense or Prosecution of Those Accused of Crime

It is the right of the lawyer to undertake the defense of a person accused of crime, regardless of his personal opinion as to the guilt of the accused; otherwise innocent persons, victims only of suspicious circumstances, might be denied proper defense. Having undertaken such defense, the lawyer is bound, by all fair and honorable means, to present every defense that the law of the land permits, to the end that no person may be deprived of life or liberty, but by due process of law.

The primary duty of a lawyer engaged in public prosecution is not to convict, but to see that justice is done. The suppression of facts or the secreting of witnesses capable of establishing the innocence of the accused is highly reprehensible.

CANON 6

Adverse Influences and Conflicting Interests

It is the duty of a lawyer at the time of retainer to disclose to the client all the circumstances of his relations to the parties, and any interest in or connection with the controversy, which might influence the client in the selection of counsel.

It is unprofessional to represent conflicting interests, except by express consent of all concerned given after a full disclosure of the facts. Within the meaning of this canon, a lawyer represents conflicting interests when, in behalf of one client, it is his duty to contend for that which duty to another client requires him to oppose.

The obligation to represent the client with undivided fidelity and not to divulge his secrets or confidences forbids also the subsequent acceptance of retainers or employment from others in matters adversely affecting any interest of the client with respect to which confidence has been reposed.

CANON 7

Professional Colleagues and Conflicts of Opinion

A client's proffer of assistance of additional counsel should not be regarded as evidence of want of confidence, but the matter should be left to the determination of the client. A lawyer should decline association as colleague if it is objectionable to the original counsel, but if the lawyer first retained is relieved, another may come into the case.

When lawyers jointly associated in a cause cannot agree as to any matter vital to the interest of the client, the conflict of opinion should be frankly stated to him for his final determination. His decision should be accepted unless the nature of the difference makes it impracticable for the lawyer whose judgment has been overruled to cooperate effectively. In this event it is his duty to ask the client to relieve him.

Efforts, direct or indirect, in any way to encroach upon the professional employment of another lawyer, are unworthy of those who should be brethren at the Bar; but, nevertheless, it is the right of any lawyer, without fear or favor, to give proper advice to those seeking relief against unfaithful or neglectful counsel, generally after communication with the lawyer of whom the complaint is made.

CANON 8

Advising Upon the Merits of a Client's Cause

A lawyer should endeavor to obtain full knowledge of his client's cause before advising thereon, and he is bound to give a candid opinion of the merits and probable result of pending or contemplated litigation. The miscarriages to which justice is subject, by reason of surprises and disappointments in evidence and witnesses, and through mistakes of juries and errors of Courts, even though only occasional, admonish lawyers to beware of bold and confident assurances to clients, especially where the employment may depend upon such assurance. Whenever the controversy will admit of fair adjustment, the client should be advised to avoid or to end the litigation.

CANON 9

Negotiations With Opposite Party

A lawyer should not in any way communicate upon the subject of controversy with a party represented by counsel; much less should he undertake to negotiate or compromise the matter with him, but should deal only with his counsel. It is incumbent upon the lawyer most particularly to avoid everything that may tend to mislead a party not represented by counsel, and he should not undertake to advise him as to the law.

CANON 10

Acquiring Interest in Litigation

The lawyer should not purchase any interest in the subject matter of the litigation which he is conducting.

CANON 11

Dealing With Trust Property

The lawyer should refrain from any action whereby for his personal benefit or gain he abuses or takes advantage of the confidence reposed in him by his client.

Money of the client or collected for the client or other trust property coming into the possession of the lawyer should be reported and accounted for promptly, and should not under any circumstances be commingled with his own or be used by him.

CANON 12

Fixing the Amount of the Fee

In fixing fees, lawyers should avoid charges which overestimate their advice and services, as well as those which undervalue them. A client's ability to pay cannot justify a charge in excess of the value of the service, though his poverty may require a less charge, or even none at all. The reasonable requests of brother lawyers, and of their widows and orphans without ample means, should receive special and kindly consideration.

In determining the amount of the fee, it is proper to consider: (1) the time and labor required, the novelty and difficulty of the questions involved and the skill requisite properly to conduct the cause; (2) whether the acceptance of employment in the particular case will preclude the lawyer's appearance for others in cases likely to arise out of the transaction, and in which there is a reasonable expectation that otherwise he would be employed, or will involve the loss of other employment while employed in the particular case or antagonisms with other clients; (3) the customary charges of the Bar for similar services; (4) the amount involved in the controversy and the benefits resulting to the client from the services; (5) the contingency or the certainty of the compensation; and (6) the character of the employment, whether casual or for an established and constant client. No one of these considerations in itself is controlling. They are mere guides in ascertaining the real value of the service.

In determining the customary charges of the Bar for similar services, it is proper for a lawyer to consider a schedule of minimum fees adopted by a Bar Association, but no lawyer should permit himself to be controlled thereby or to follow it as his sole guide in determining the amount of his fee.

In fixing fees it should never be forgotten that the profession is a branch of the administration of justice and not a mere money-getting trade.

CANON 13

Contingent Fees

A contract for a contingent fee, where sanctioned by law, should be reasonable under all the circumstances of the case, including the risk and uncertainty of the compensation, but should always be subject to the supervision of a court, as to its reasonableness.

CANON 14

Suing a Client for a Fee

Controversies with clients concerning compensation are to be avoided by the lawyer so far as shall be compatible with his self-respect and with his right to receive reasonable recompense for his services; and lawsuits with clients should be resorted to only to prevent injustice, imposition or fraud.

CANON 15

How Far a Lawyer May Go in Supporting a Client's Cause

Nothing operates more certainly to create or to foster popular prejudice against lawyers as a class, and to deprive the profession of that full measure of public esteem and confidence which belongs to the proper discharge of its duties than does the false claim, often set up by the unscrupulous in defense of questionable transactions, that it is the duty of the lawyer to do whatever may enable him to succeed in winning his client's cause.

It is improper for a lawyer to assert in argument his personal belief in his client's innocence or in the justice of his cause.

The lawyer owes "entire devotion to the interest of the client, warm zeal in the maintenance and defense of his rights and the exertion of his utmost learning and ability," to the end that nothing be taken or be withheld from him, save by the rules of law, legally applied. No fear of judicial disfavor or public unpopularity should restrain him from the full discharge of his duty. In the judicial forum the client is entitled to the benefit of any and every remedy and defense that is authorized by the law of the land, and he may expect his lawyer to assert every such remedy or defense. But it is steadfastly to be borne in mind that the great trust of the lawyer is to be performed within and not without the bounds of the law. The office of attorney does not permit, much less does it demand of him for any client, violation of law or any manner of fraud or chicane. He must obey his own conscience and not that of his client.

CANON 16

Restraining Clients From Improprieties

A lawyer should use his best efforts to restrain and to prevent his clients from doing those things which the lawyer himself ought not to do, particularly with reference to their conduct towards Courts, judicial officers, jurors, witnesses and suitors. If a client persists in such wrongdoing the lawyer should terminate their relation.

CANON 17

Ill-Feeling and Personalities Between Advocates

Clients, not lawyers, are the litigants. Whatever may be the ill-feeling existing between clients, it should not be allowed to influence counsel in their conduct and demeanor toward each other or toward suitors in the case. All personalities between counsel should be scrupulously avoided. In the trial of a cause it is indecent to allude to the personal history or the personal peculiarities and idiosyncrasies of counsel on the other side. Personal colloquies between counsel which cause delay and promote unseemly wrangling should also be carefully avoided.

CANON 18

Treatment of Witnesses and Litigants

A lawyer should always treat adverse witnesses and suitors with fairness and due consideration, and he should never minister to the malevolence or prejudices of a client in the trial or conduct of a cause. The client cannot be made the keeper of the lawyer's conscience in professional matters. He has no right to demand that his counsel shall abuse the opposite party or indulge in offensive personalities. Improper speech is not excusable on the ground that it is what the client would say if speaking in his own behalf.

CANON 19

Appearance of Lawyer as Witness for His Client

When a lawyer is a witness for his client, except as to merely formal matters, such as the attestation or custody of an instrument and the like, he should leave the trial of the case to other counsel. Except when essential to the ends of justice, a lawyer should avoid testifying in court in behalf of his client.

CANON 20

Newspaper Discussion of Pending Litigation

Newspaper publications by a lawyer as to pending or anticipated litigation may interfere with a fair trial in the Courts and otherwise prejudice the due administration of justice. Generally they are to be condemned. If the extreme circumstances of a particular case justify a statement to the public, it is unprofessional to make it anonymously. An *ex parte* reference to the facts should not go beyond quotation from the records and papers on file in the court; but even in extreme cases it is better to avoid any *ex parte* statement.

CANON 21

Punctuality and Expedition

It is the duty of the lawyer not only to his client, but also to the Courts and to the public to be punctual in attendance, and to be concise and direct in the trial and disposition of causes.

CANON 22

Candor and Fairness

The conduct of the lawyer before the Court and with other lawyers should be characterized by candor and fairness.

It is not candid or fair for the lawyer knowingly to misquote the contents of a paper, the testimony of a witness, the language or the argument of opposing counsel, or the language of a decision of a textbook; or with knowledge of its invalidity, to cite as authority a decision that has been overruled, or a statute that has been repealed; or in argument to assert as a fact that which has not been proved, or in those jurisdictions where a side has the opening and closing arguments to mislead his opponent by concealing or withholding positions in his opening argument upon which his side then intends to rely.

It is unprofessional and dishonorable to deal other than candidly with the facts in taking the statements of witnesses, in drawing affidavits and other documents, and in the presentation of causes.

A lawyer should not offer evidence which he knows the Court should reject, in order to get the same before the jury by argument for its admissibility, nor should he address to the Judge arguments upon any point not properly calling for determination by him. Neither should he introduce into an argument, addressed to the court, remarks or statements intended to influence the jury or bystanders.

These and all kindred practices are unprofessional and unworthy of an officer of the law charged, as is the lawyer, with the duty of aiding in the administration of justice.

CANON 23

Attitude Toward Jury

All attempts to curry favor with juries by fawning, flattery or pretended solicitude for their personal comfort are unprofessional. Suggestions of counsel, looking to the comfort or convenience of jurors, and propositions to dispense with argument, should be made to the Court out of the jury's hearing. A lawyer must never converse privately with jurors about the case; and both before and during the trial he should avoid communicating with them, even as to matters foreign to the cause.

CANON 24

Right of Lawyer to Control the Incidents of the Trial

As to incidental matters pending the trial, not affecting the merits of the cause, or working substantial prejudice to the rights of the client, such as forcing the opposite lawyer to trial when he is under affliction or bereavement; forcing the trial on a particular day to the injury of the opposite lawyer when no harm will result from a trial at a different time; agreeing to an extension of time for signing a bill of exceptions, cross interrogatories and the like, the lawyer must be allowed to judge. In such matters no client has a right to demand that his counsel shall be illiberal, or that he do anything therein repugnant to his own sense of honor and propriety.

CANON 25

Taking Technical Advantage of Opposite Counsel; Agreements With Him

A lawyer should not ignore known customs or practice of the Bar or of a particular Court, even when the law permits, without giving timely notice to the opposing counsel. As far as possible, important agreements, affecting the rights of clients, should be reduced to writing; but it is dishonorable to avoid performance of an agreement fairly made because it is not reduced to writing, as required by rules of Court.

CANON 26

Professional Advocacy Other Than Before Courts

A lawyer openly, and in his true character may render professional services before legislative or other bodies, regarding proposed legislation and in advocacy of claims before departments of government, upon the same principles of ethics which justify his appearance before the Courts; but it is unprofessional for a lawyer so engaged to conceal his attorneyship, or to employ secret personal solicitations, or to use means other than those addressed to the reason and understanding, to influence action.

CANON 27

Advertising, Direct or Indirect

It is unprofessional to solicit professional employment by circulars, advertisements, through toutors or by personal communications or interviews not warranted by personal relations. Indirect advertisements for professional employment such as furnishing or inspiring newspaper comments, or procuring his photograph to be published in connection with causes in which the lawyer has been or is engaged or concerning the manner of their conduct, the magnitude of the interest involved, the importance of the lawyer's position, and all other like self-laudation, offend the traditions and lower the tone of our profession and are reprehensible; but the customary use of simple professional cards is not improper.

Publication in reputable law lists in a manner consistent with the standards of conduct imposed by these canons of brief biographical and informative data is permissible. Such data must not be misleading and may include only a statement of the lawyer's name and the names of his professional associates; addresses, telephone numbers, cable addresses; branches of the profession practiced; date and place of birth and admission to the bar; schools attended; with dates of graduation, degrees and other educational distinctions; public or quasi-public offices; posts of honor; legal authorships; legal teaching positions; memberships and offices in bar associations and committees thereof, in legal and scientific societies and legal fraternities; foreign language ability; the fact of listings in other reputable law lists; the names and addresses of references; and, with their written consent, the names of clients regularly represented. A certificate of compliance with the Rules and Standards issued by the Standing Committee on Law Lists may be treated as evidence that such list is reputable.

It is not improper for a lawyer who is admitted to practice as a proctor in admiralty to use that designation on his letterhead or shingle or for a lawyer who has complied with the statutory requirements of admission to practice before the patent office, to so use the designation "patent attorney" or "patent lawyer" or "trademark attorney" or "trademark lawyer" or any combination of those terms.

CANON 28

Stirring Up Litigation, Directly or Through Agents

It is unprofessional for a lawyer to volunteer advice to bring a lawsuit, except in rare cases where ties of blood, relationship or trust make it his duty to do so. Stirring up strife and litigation is not only unprofessional, but it is indictable at common law. It is disreputable to hunt up defects in titles or other causes of action and inform thereof in order to be employed to bring suit or collect judgment, or to breed litigation by seeking out those with claims for personal injuries or those having any other grounds of action in order to secure them as clients, or to employ agents or runners for like purposes, or to pay or reward, directly or indirectly, those who bring or influence the bringing of such cases to his office, or to remunerate policemen, court or prison officials, physicians, hospital *attachés* or others who may succeed, under the guise of giving disinterested friendly advice, in influencing the criminal, the sick and the injured, the ignorant or others, to seek his professional services. A duty to the public and to the profession devolves upon every member of the Bar having knowledge of such practices upon the part of any practitioner immediately to inform thereof, to the end that the offender may be disbarred.

CANON 29

Upholding the Honor of the Profession

Lawyers should expose without fear or favor before the proper tribunals corrupt or dishonest conduct in the profession, and should accept without hesitation employment against a member of the Bar who has wronged his client. The counsel upon the trial of a cause in which perjury has been committed owe it to the profession and to the public to bring the matter to the knowledge of the prosecuting authorities. The lawyer should aid in guarding the Bar against the admission to the profession of candidates unfit or unqualified because deficient in either moral character or education. He should strive at all times to uphold the honor and to maintain the dignity of the profession and to improve not only the law but the administration of justice.

CANON 30

Justifiable and Unjustifiable Litigations

The lawyer must decline to conduct a civil cause or to make a defense when convinced that it is intended merely to harass or to injure the opposite party or to work oppression or wrong. But otherwise it is his right, and, having accepted retainer, it becomes his duty to insist upon the judgment of the Court as to the legal merits of his client's claim. His appearance in Court should be deemed equivalent to an assertion on his honor that in his opinion his client's case is one proper for judicial determination.

CANON 31

Responsibility for Litigation

No lawyer is obliged to act either as adviser or advocate for every person who may wish to become his client. He has the right to decline employment. Every lawyer upon his own responsibility must decide what employment he will accept as counsel, what causes he will bring into Court for plaintiffs, what cases he will contest in Court for defendants. The responsibility for advising as to questionable transactions, for bringing questionable suits, for urging questionable defenses, is the lawyer's responsibility. He cannot escape it by urging as an excuse that he is only following his client's instructions.

CANON 32

The Lawyer's Duty in Its Last Analysis

No client, corporate or individual, however powerful, nor any cause, civil or political, however important, is entitled to receive nor should any lawyer render any service or advice involving disloyalty to the law whose ministers we are, or disrespect of the judicial office, which we are bound to uphold, or corruption of any person or persons exercising a public office or private trust, or deception or betrayal of the public. When rendering any such improper service or advice, the lawyer invites and merits stern and just condemnation. Correspondingly, he advances the honor of his profession and the best interests of his client when he renders service or gives advice tending to impress upon the client and his undertaking exact compliance with the strictest principles of moral law. He must also observe and advise his client to observe the statute law, though until a statute shall have been construed and interpreted by competent adjudication, he is free and is entitled to advise as to its validity and as to what he conscientiously believes to be its just meaning and extent. But above all a lawyer will find his highest honor in a deserved reputation for fidelity to private trust and to public duty, as an honest man and as a patriotic and loyal citizen.

CANON 33

Partnerships—Names

Partnerships among lawyers for the practice of their profession are very common and are not to be condemned. In the formation of partnerships and the use of partnership names care should be taken not to violate any law, custom, or rule of court locally applicable. Where partnerships are formed between lawyers who are not all admitted to practice in the courts of the state, care should be taken to avoid any misleading name or representation which would create a false impression as to the professional position or privileges of the member not locally admitted. In the formation of partnerships for the practice of law, no person should be admitted or held out as a practitioner or member who is not a member of the legal profession duly authorized to practice, and amenable to professional discipline. In the selection and use of a firm name, no false, misleading, assumed or trade name should be used. The continued use of the name of a deceased or former partner, when permissible by local custom, is not unethical, but care should be taken that no imposition or deception is practiced through this use. When a member of the firm, on becoming a judge, is precluded from practicing law, his name should not be continued in the firm name.

Partnerships between lawyers and members of other professions or non-professional persons should not be formed or permitted where any part of the partnership's employment consists of the practice of law.

CANON 34

Division of Fees

No division of fees for legal services is proper, except with another lawyer, based upon a division of service or responsibility.

CANON 35

Intermediaries

The professional services of a lawyer should not be controlled or exploited by any lay agency, personal or corporate, which intervenes between client and lawyer. A lawyer's responsibilities and qualifications are individual. He should avoid all relations which direct the performance of his duties by or in the interest of such intermediary. A lawyer's relation to his client should be personal, and the responsibility should be direct to the client. Charitable societies rendering aid to the indigents are not deemed such intermediaries.

A lawyer may accept employment from any organization, such as an association, club or trade organization, to render legal services in any matter in which the organization, as an entity, is interested, but this employment should not include the rendering of legal services to the members of such an organization in respect to their individual affairs.

CANON 36

Retirement From Judicial Position or Public Employment

A lawyer should not accept employment as an advocate in any matter upon the merits of which he has previously acted in a judicial capacity.

A lawyer, having once held public office or having been in the public employ, should not after his retirement accept employment in connection with any matter which he has investigated or passed upon while in such office or employ.

CANON 37

Confidences of a Client

It is the duty of a lawyer to preserve his client's confidences. This duty outlasts the lawyer's employment, and extends as well to his employees; and neither of them should accept employment which involves or may involve the disclosure or use of these confidences, either for the private advantage of the lawyer or his employees or to the disadvantage of the client, without his knowledge and consent, and even though there are other available sources of such information. A lawyer should not continue employment when he discovers that this obligation prevents the performance of his full duty to his former or to his new client.

If a lawyer is accused by his client, he is not precluded from disclosing the truth in respect to the accusation. The announced intention of a client to commit a crime is not included within the confidences which he is bound to respect. He may properly make such disclosures as may be necessary to prevent the act or protect those against whom it is threatened.

CANON 38

Compensation, Commissions and Rebates

A lawyer should accept no compensation, commissions, rebates or other advantages from others without the knowledge and consent of his client after full disclosure.

CANON 39

Witnesses

A lawyer may properly interview any witness or prospective witness for the opposing side in any civil or criminal action without the consent of opposing counsel or party. In doing so, however, he should scrupulously avoid any suggestion calculated to induce the witness to suppress or deviate from the truth, or in any degree to affect his free and untrammeled conduct when appearing at the trial or on the witness stand.

CANON 40

Newspapers

A lawyer may with propriety write articles for publications in which he gives information upon the law; but he should not accept employment from such publications to advise inquirers in respect to their individual rights.

CANON 41

Discovery of Imposition and Deception

When a lawyer discovers that some fraud or deception has been practiced, which has unjustly imposed upon the court or a party, he should endeavor to rectify it; at first by advising his client, and if his client refuses to forego the advantage thus unjustly gained, he should promptly inform the injured person or his counsel, so that they may take appropriate steps.

CANON 42

Expenses of Litigation

A lawyer may not properly agree with a client that the lawyer shall pay or bear the expenses of litigation; he may in good faith advance expenses as a matter of convenience, but subject to reimbursement.

CANON 43

Approved Law Lists

It shall be improper for a lawyer to permit his name to be published in a law list the conduct, management or contents of which are calculated or likely to deceive or injure the public or the profession, or to lower the dignity or standing of the profession.

CANON 44

Withdrawal From Employment as Attorney or Counsel

The right of an attorney or counsel to withdraw from employment, once assumed, arises only from good cause. Even the desire or consent of the client is not always sufficient. The lawyer should not throw up the unfinished task to the detriment of his client except for reasons of honor or self-respect. If the client insists upon an unjust or immoral course in the conduct of his case, or if he persists over the attorney's remonstrance in presenting frivolous defenses, or if he deliberately disregards an agreement or obligation as to fees or expenses, the lawyer may be warranted in withdrawing on due notice to the client, allowing him time to employ another lawyer. So also when a lawyer discovers that his client has no case and the client is determined to continue it; or even if the lawyer finds himself incapable of conducting the case effectively. Sundry other instances may arise in which withdrawal is to be justified. Upon withdrawing from a case after a retainer has been paid, the attorney should refund such part of the retainer as has not been clearly earned.

CANON 45

Specialists

The canons of the American Bar Association apply to all branches of the legal profession; specialists in particular branches are not to be considered as exempt from the application of these principles.

CANON 46

Notice to Local Lawyers

A lawyer available to act as an associate of other lawyers in a particular branch of the law or legal service may send to local lawyers only and publish in his local legal journal, a brief and dignified announcement of his availability to serve other lawyers in connection therewith. The announcement should be in a form which does not constitute a statement or representation of special experience or expertise.

CANON 47

Aiding the Unauthorized Practice of Law

No lawyer shall permit his professional services, or his name, to be used in aid of, or to make possible, the unauthorized practice of law by any lay agency, personal or corporate.

SELECTED STANDARDS ON PROFESSIONALISM AND COURTESY

TABLE OF CONTENTS

ABA REPORT OF COMMISSION ON PROFESSIONALISM (1986)

(Selected sections)

[The report has been approved for distribution by the House of Delegates of the American Bar Association. However, the views expressed are those of the Commission on Professionalism. They have not been approved by the House of Delegates or the Board of Governors and, accordingly, should not be construed as representing the policy of the Association. Ed.]

* * *

III. THE MEANING OF PROFESSIONALISM

"Professionalism" is an elastic concept the meaning and application of which are hard to pin down. That is perhaps as it should be. The term has a rich, long-standing heritage, and any single definition runs the risk of being too confining.

Yet the term is so important to lawyers that at least a working definition seems essential. Lawyers are proud of being part of one of the "historic" or "learned" professions, along with medicine and the clergy, which have been seen as professions through many centuries.

When he was asked to define a profession, Dean Roscoe Pound of Harvard Law School said:

> The term refers to a group . . . pursuing a learned art as a common calling in the spirit of public service—no less a public service because it may incidentally be a means of livelihood. Pursuit of the learned art in the spirit of a public service is the primary purpose.

The rhetoric may be dated, but the Commission believes the spirit of Dean Pound's definition stands the test of time. The practice of law "in the spirit of a public service" can and ought to be the hallmark of the legal profession.

More recently, others have identified some common elements which distinguish a profession from other occupations. Commission member Professor Eliot Freidson of New York University defines our profession as:

> An occupation whose members have special privileges, such as exclusive licensing, that are justified by the following assumptions:
>
> 1. That its practice requires substantial intellectual training and the use of complex judgments.
> 2. That since clients cannot adequately evaluate the quality of the service, they must trust those they consult.

3. That the client's trust presupposes that the practitioner's self-interest is overbalanced by devotion to serving both the client's interest and the public good, and

4. That the occupation is self-regulating—that is, organized in such a way as to assure the public and the courts that its members are competent, do not violate their client's trust, and transcend their own self-interest.

Again, the Commission suggests that this list of elements is useful in thinking through the issues which follow.

Some may argue on the basis of the cases previously discussed that the legal profession is no longer "special." They might say that lawyers should treat their ideals as archaic, construe the rules of professional conduct as narrowly as possible, and try only to maximize their incomes. The Commission disagrees. Moreover, the testimony we have heard and the surveys we have examined indicate that the public wants the legal profession to maintain its long-held professional ideals. Indeed, the public should expect no less.

We have earlier described the diversity of the Bar, both in terms of demographics and areas of practice. One can properly ask whether any common ideas of professionalism can suffice for such a varied institution. We believe they can. While one must always be conscious of the variety within the legal profession, more unites than separates us.

* * *

The suggestions and conclusions which follow are grouped by the role to be played by each segment of the Bar. In discussing the practicing Bar, we want it to be clear that we are including in that category all lawyers—whether litigators or non-litigators, whether sole practitioners, members or employees of firms, government lawyers or lawyers employed by corporations, educational institutions or other entities.

It is our hope that the recommendations which follow will not be unobserved aspirations, but will represent concrete ways in which lawyers can inspire a rebirth of respect and confidence in themselves, in the services they provide and in the legal system itself. We believe that much can be done. Taken individually, the proposals may not appear substantial, but in the aggregate we believe they can have a significant impact. However, to be effective, they must have the support not only of every part of the legal community, but also of the citizens of this country—the public whose interests lawyers are to serve.

We first present a summary of our recommendations, and then a discussion of each.

IV. SUMMARY OF RECOMMENDATIONS

A. LAW SCHOOLS

1. Law schools should give continuing attention to the form and content of their courses in ethics and professionalism. They should weave ethical and professional issues into courses in both substantive and procedural fields. They should give serious consideration to supplementing courses in ethics and professionalism with a required summer reading list for entering students and with a film or videotape on ethics, along the lines discussed later in this report.

2. Law schools should expose students to promising new methods of dealing with legal problems. Thus, for example, consideration should be given to instruction in such matters as alternative methods of dispute resolution and processes of negotiation.

3. Deans and faculties of law schools should keep in mind that the law school experience provides a student's first exposure to the profession, and that professors inevitably serve as important role models for students. Therefore, the highest standards of ethics and professionalism should be adhered to within law schools.

4. Law schools should adopt codes of student conduct, possibly based on the Model Rules of Professional Conduct. They should report convictions of serious infractions of law school rules to the Character and Fitness Committees, or their equivalent, of states in which the student applies for admission to the Bar.

5. Law schools should retain high admission standards in the face of declining applications and should not lower their standards for graduation.

B. PRACTICING BAR AND BAR ASSOCIATIONS

1. Law firms should help their newly-admitted associates to face the practical and ethical issues which inevitably arise in practice. This can be done in a variety of ways, and small firms or sole practitioners should work together to sponsor programs to facilitate such training. Local bar associations and law schools should assist in such efforts.

2. In order to assure greater competence of practicing lawyers, continuing legal education courses should be strengthened and made mandatory. Where practical, some form of examination in courses taken should be required.

3. The Commission recommends that the American Bar Association prepare a series of six to eight films or videotapes dealing with ethical and professional issues. The tapes should effectively present a wide range of such issues and should use the Socratic approach so effectively used in the Columbia University Media & Society Seminar programs. If feasible, at least one such tape should be designed especially for use in law schools. The tapes also should be made available to state and local bar associations for use in mandatory continuing legal education programs.

4. False, fraudulent or misleading advertising is not constitutionally protected and should be referred to disciplinary authorities for action against offending lawyers. Appropriate measures short of disciplinary action should be considered. Such measures could include requiring an advertisement to contain warnings or disclaimers.

5. The Bar should place increasing emphasis on the role of lawyers as officers of the court, or more broadly, as officers of the system of justice. Lawyers should exercise independent judgment as to how to pursue legal matters. They have a duty to make the system of justice work properly. Ideally, clients should recognize this duty and appreciate the importance to society of maintaining the system of justice.

6. The Bar should study the issue of the participation of law firms and individual lawyers in business activities, certainly where either actual or potential conflicts of interest may be involved.

7. When not representing clients before legislative bodies, lawyers should put aside self-interest and should support legislation that is in the public interest. In addition, the Bar should urge legislative bodies to consider the consequences of proposed legislation on the courts. All too frequently, such legislation, when enacted, inundates the courts with cases never contemplated by the drafters.

8. Fees are a source of misunderstanding between many lawyers and their clients. Further, the amount of fees charged by lawyers in some instances results in bitter criticism of the Bar. The Commission suggests:

a. Fee arrangements between lawyers and their clients should be in writing, where feasible.

b. If, at the end of a lawyer's services in any matter, the client believes that the fee charged was inappropriate, the client should be able to have the matter reviewed by an impartial fee review committee, possibly appointed by the state Supreme Court. All such committees or entities should include lay members.

9. Lawyers and judges should report to the appropriate disciplinary committee or prosecuting attorney any serious misconduct on the part of other lawyers and judges which they believe would support a complaint for discipline or criminal charges.

10. Bar associations should be constantly alert to seek improvements in the system of justice. This should embrace such activities as supporting an expanded use of alternative methods of dispute resolution.

C. JUDGES

1. Trial judges should take a more active role in the conduct of litigation. They should see that cases advance promptly, fairly and without abuse. Granting increased authority to judges runs the risk of arbitrary behavior on their part, but reviewing courts should provide whatever counterbalance is needed.

2. Judges should impose sanctions for abuse of the litigation process. Currently, the Federal Rules of Civil Procedure permit the imposition of sanctions for such abuses, and increasing use is being made of the sanctions to penalize the lawyer or the client, or both. In many state systems, the Supreme Courts have not promulgated such rules. State Supreme Courts should adopt rules similar to Rule 11 of the Federal Rules, so that authority to act is clearly given to trial judges.

3. Merit selection should be the means by which judges are chosen. The Commission believes that a bench of the quality that merit selection can provide is essential to improve our system of justice.

4. State disciplinary agencies under the control of state supreme courts are, in general, insufficiently funded and staffed. They now cannot do much more than deal with charges of theft, neglect or the commission of a felony. Adequate funding should be made available to the disciplinary agencies, enabling them to do a thorough and competent job in pursuing the full range of offenses which occur.

5. State supreme courts control admission to the Bar. They often charge character and fitness committees or their equivalent with the responsibility of reviewing the qualifications of applicants. Adequate funding and authority should be provided to such committees so that they can do a thorough job of investigation.

D. IN GENERAL

All segments of the Bar should:

1. Preserve and develop within the profession integrity, competence, fairness, independence, courage and a devotion to the public interest.
2. Resolve to abide by higher standards of conduct than the minimum required by the Code of Professional Responsibility and the Model Rules of Professional Conduct.
3. Increase the participation of lawyers in *pro bono* activities and help lawyers recognize their obligation to participate.
4. Resist the temptation to make the acquisition of wealth a primary goal of law practice.
5. Encourage innovative methods which simplify and make less expensive the rendering of legal services.
6. Educate the public about legal processes and the legal system.
7. Resolve to employ all the organizational resources necessary in order to assure that the legal profession is effectively self-regulating.

* * *

ABA LAWYER'S CREED OF PROFESSIONALISM (1988)

On August 9th, 1988, the American Bar Association House of Delegates adopted the following resolutions regarding so-called "Codes of Courtesy."

PROFESSIONALISM AND COURTESY

BE IT RESOLVED that the American Bar Association recommends to state and local bar associations that they encourage their members to accept as a guide for their individual conduct, and to comply with, a lawyer's creed of professionalism.

BE IT FURTHER RESOLVED that nothing contained in such a creed shall be deemed to supersede or in any way amend the Model Rules of Professional Conduct or other disciplinary codes, alter existing standards of conduct against which lawyer negligence might be judged or become a basis for the imposition of civil penalty of any kind.

Following is a proposed example of "A Lawyer's Creed of Professionalism."

Preamble

As a lawyer I must strive to make our system of justice work fairly and efficiently. In order to carry out that responsibility, not only will I comply with the letter and spirit of the disciplinary standards applicable to all lawyers, but I will also conduct myself in accordance with the following Creed of Professionalism when dealing with my client, opposing parties, their counsel, the courts and the general public.

A. With respect to my client:

1. I will be loyal and committed to my client's cause, but I will not permit that loyalty and commitment to interfere with my ability to provide my client with objective and independent advice;
2. I will endeavor to achieve my client's lawful objectives in business transactions and in litigation as expeditiously and economically as possible;
3. In appropriate cases, I will counsel my client with respect to mediation, arbitration and other alternative methods of resolving disputes;
4. I will advise my client against pursuing litigation (or any other course of action) that is without merit and against insisting on tactics which are intended to delay resolution of the matter or to harass or drain the financial resources of the opposing party;
5. I will advise my client that civility and courtesy are not to be equated with weakness;
6. While I must abide by my client's decision concerning the objectives of the representation, I nevertheless will counsel my client that a willingness to initiate or engage in settlement discussions is consistent with zealous and effective representation.

B. With respect to opposing parties and their counsel:

1. I will endeavor to be courteous and civil, both in oral and in written communications;
2. I will not knowingly make statements of fact or of law that are untrue;
3. In litigation proceedings I will agree to reasonable requests for extensions of time or for waiver of procedural formalities when the legitimate interests of my client will not be adversely affected;
4. I will endeavor to consult with opposing counsel before scheduling depositions and meetings and before re-scheduling hearings, and I will cooperate with opposing counsel when scheduling changes are requested;
5. I will refrain from utilizing litigation or any other course of conduct to harass the opposing party;
6. I will refrain from engaging in excessive and abusive discovery, and I will comply with all reasonable discovery requests;
7. I will refrain from utilizing delaying tactics;

8. In depositions and other proceedings, and in negotiations, I will conduct myself with dignity, avoid making groundless objections and refrain from engaging in acts of rudeness or disrespect;

9. I will not serve motions and pleadings on the other party, or his counsel, at such a time or in such a manner as will unfairly limit the other party's opportunity to respond;

10. In business transactions I will not quarrel over matters of form or style, but will concentrate on matters of substance and content;

11. I will clearly identify, for other counsel or parties, all changes that I have made in documents submitted to me for review.

C. With respect to the courts and other tribunals:

1. I will be a vigorous and zealous advocate on behalf of my client, while recognizing, as an officer of the court, that excessive zeal may be detrimental to my client's interests as well as to the proper functioning of our system of justice;

2. Where consistent with my client's interests, I will communicate with opposing counsel in an effort to avoid litigation and to resolve litigation that has actually commenced;

3. I will voluntarily withdraw claims or defenses when it becomes apparent that they do not have merit or are superfluous;

4. I will refrain from filing frivolous motions;

5. I will make every effort to agree with other counsel, as early as possible, on a voluntary exchange of information and on a plan for discovery;

6. I will attempt to resolve, by agreement, my objections to matters contained in my opponent's pleadings and discovery requests;

7. When scheduled hearings or depositions have to be cancelled, I will notify opposing counsel, and, if appropriate, the court (or other tribunal) as early as possible;

8. Before dates for hearings or trials are set—or, if that is not feasible, immediately after such dates have been set—I will attempt to verify the availability of key participants and witnesses so that I can promptly notify the court (or other tribunal) and opposing counsel of any likely problem in that regard;

9. In civil matters, I will stipulate to facts as to which there is no genuine dispute;

10. I will endeavor to be punctual in attending court hearings, conferences and depositions;

11. I will at all times be candid with the court.

D. With respect to the public and to our system of justice:

1. I will remember that, in addition to commitment to my client's cause, my responsibilities as a lawyer include a devotion to the public good;

2. I will endeavor to keep myself current in the areas in which I practice and, when necessary, will associate with, or refer my client to, counsel knowledgeable in another field of practice;

3. I will be mindful of the fact that, as a member of a self-regulating profession, it is incumbent on me to report violations by fellow lawyers of any disciplinary rule;

4. I will be mindful of the need to protect the image of the legal profession in the eyes of the public and will be so guided when considering methods and contents of advertising;

5. I will be mindful that the law is a learned profession and that among its desirable goals are devotion to public service, improvement of administration of justice, and the contribution of uncompensated time and civic influence on behalf of those persons who cannot afford adequate legal assistance.

ABA LAWYER'S PLEDGE OF PROFESSIONALISM (1988)

I will remember that the practice of law is first and foremost a profession, and I will subordinate business concerns to professionalism concerns.

I will encourage respect for the law and our legal system through my words and actions.

I will remember my responsibilities to serve as an officer of the court and protector of individual rights.

I will contribute time and resources to public service, public education, charitable, and *pro bono* activities in my community.

I will work with the other participants in the legal system, including judges, opposing counsel and those whose practices are different from mine, to make our legal system more accessible and responsive.

I will resolve matters expeditiously and without unnecessary expense.

I will resolve disputes through negotiation whenever possible.

I will keep my clients well-informed and involved in making the decisions that affect them.

I will continue to expand my knowledge of the law.

I will achieve and maintain proficiency in my practice.

I will be courteous to those with whom I come into contact during the course of my work.

I will honor the spirit and intent, as well as the requirements, of the applicable rules or code of professional conduct for my jurisdiction, and will encourage others to do the same.

ABA ASPIRATIONAL GOALS ON LAWYER ADVERTISING (1988)

Preamble

During the past decade, the courts have sought to define the nature and extent of permissible advertising by lawyers. In a series of decisions, the U.S. Supreme Court has held that lawyer advertising which is not false or misleading is commercial speech entitled to protection under the First Amendment of the U.S. Constitution.

Pending further clarification by the courts, some advertising practices exist which may be detrimental. Some forms of advertising may adversely affect public perceptions about the justice system itself. For example, empirical evidence suggests that undignified advertising can detract from the public's confidence in the legal profession and respect for the justice system.

Under present case law, the matter of dignity is widely believed to be so subjective as to be beyond the scope of constitutionally permitted regulation. Nevertheless, it seems entirely proper for the organized bar to suggest non-binding aspirational goals urging lawyers who wish to advertise to do so in a dignified manner. Although only aspirational, such goals must be scrupulously sensitive to fundamental constitutional rights of lawyers and the needs of the public.

It is the role and responsibility of lawyers to provide legal services to the public. It has been demonstrated by responsible studies that people sometimes do not receive needed legal services, either because they are unaware of available services, don't understand how they can benefit from those services or don't understand how to obtain them. Therefore, it is also the legal profession's responsibility to inform the public about the availability of legal services and how to obtain and use them.

Advertising is one of many methods by which lawyers can inform the public about legal services. Although most people find a lawyer through word-of-mouth networks of family, friends and work associates, when properly done, advertising can help people to better understand the legal services available to them and how to obtain those services.

When properly done, advertising can also be a productive way for lawyers to build and maintain their client bases. Advertising and other forms of marketing can enable lawyers to attain efficiencies of scale which may help make legal services more affordable. As the Supreme Court pointed out in *Bates v. State Bar of Arizona,* 433 U.S. 350, 377 (1977), it is "entirely possible that advertising will serve to reduce, not advance, the cost of legal services to the consumer."

Lawyers are at all times officers of the court, and as such, they have a special obligation to assure that their conduct conforms to the highest ideals of the legal profession. Thus, lawyers who advertise should be mindful not only of the effect their advertising may have on their own professional image but also of the effect it may have on the public's overall perception of the judicial system.

If lawyer advertising avoids false, misleading or deceptive representations, or coercive or misleading solicitation, it advances the goal of bringing needed legal services to more people than are now being served.

However, when advertising though not false, misleading or deceptive degenerates into undignified and unprofessional presentations, the public is not served, the lawyer who advertised does not benefit and the image of the judicial system may be harmed.

Accordingly, lawyer advertising should exemplify the inherent dignity and professionalism of the legal community. Dignified lawyer advertising tends to inspire public confidence in the professional competence and ability of lawyers and portrays the commitment of lawyers to serve clients' legal needs in accordance with the ethics and public service tradition of a learned profession.

Lawyer advertising is a key facet of the marketing and delivery of legal services to the public. The professional conduct rules for lawyers adopted by the states regulate some aspects of lawyer advertising, but they also leave lawyers much latitude to decide how to advertise. The following Aspirational Goals are presented in an effort to suggest how lawyers can achieve the beneficial goals of advertising while minimizing or eliminating altogether its negative implications.

These aspirational goals are not intended to establish mandatory requirements which might form the basis for disciplinary enforcement. Rules of Professional Conduct and Disciplinary Rules of Codes of Professional Responsibility in effect in all jurisdictions establish the standards which all lawyers who advertise must meet. Rather, these aspirational goals are intended to provide suggested objectives which all lawyers who engage in advertising their services should be encouraged to achieve in order that lawyer advertising may be more effective and reflect the professionalism of the legal community.

Aspirational Goals

1. Lawyer advertising should encourage and support the public's confidence in the individual lawyer's competence and integrity as well as the commitment of the legal profession to serve the public's legal needs in the tradition of the law as a learned profession.

2. Since advertising may be the only contact many people have with lawyers, advertising by lawyers should help the public understand its legal rights and the judicial process and should uphold the dignity of the legal profession.

3. While "dignity" and "good taste" are terms open to subjective interpretation, lawyers should consider that advertising which reflects the ideals stated in these Aspirational Goals is likely to be dignified and suitable to the profession.

4. Since advertising must be truthful and accurate, and not false or misleading, lawyers should realize that ambiguous or confusing advertising can be misleading.

5. Particular care should be taken in describing fees and costs in advertisements. If an advertisement states a specific fee for a particular service, it should make clear whether or not all problems of that type can be handled for that specific fee. Similar care should be taken in describing the lawyer's areas of practice.

6. Lawyers should consider that the use of inappropriately dramatic music, unseemly slogans, hawkish spokespersons, premium offers, slapstick routines or outlandish settings in advertising does not instill confidence in the lawyer or the legal profession and undermines the serious purpose of legal services and the judicial system.

7. Advertising developed with a clear identification of its potential audience is more likely to be understandable, respectful and appropriate to that audience, and, therefore, more effective. Lawyers should consider using advertising and marketing professionals to assist in identifying and reaching an appropriate audience.

8. How advertising conveys its message is as important as the message itself. Again, lawyers should consider using professional consultants to help them develop and present a clear message to the audience in an effective and appropriate way.

9. Lawyers should design their advertising to attract legal matters which they are competent to handle.

10. Lawyers should be concerned with making legal services more affordable to the public. Lawyer advertising may be designed to build up client bases so that efficiencies of scale may be achieved that will translate into more affordable legal services.

THE TEXAS LAWYER'S CREED— A MANDATE FOR PROFESSIONALISM (1989)

Promulgated by the Supreme Court of Texas and the Texas Court of Criminal Appeals (1989)

I am a lawyer; I am entrusted by the People of Texas to preserve and improve our legal system. I am licensed by the Supreme Court of Texas. I must therefore abide by the Texas Disciplinary Rules of Professional Conduct, but I know that Professionalism requires more than merely avoiding the violation of laws and rules. I am committed to this Creed for no other reason than it is right.

I. OUR LEGAL SYSTEM

A lawyer owes to the administration of justice personal dignity, integrity, and independence. A lawyer should always adhere to the highest principles of professionalism.

1. I am passionately proud of my profession. Therefore, "My word is my bond."

2. I am responsible to assure that all persons have access to competent representation regardless of wealth or position in life.

3. I commit myself to an adequate and effective pro bono program.

4. I am obligated to educate my clients, the public, and other lawyers regarding the spirit and letter of this Creed.

5. I will always be conscious of my duty to the judicial system.

II. LAWYER TO CLIENT

A lawyer owes to a client allegiance, learning, skill, and industry. A lawyer shall employ all appropriate means to protect and advance the client's legitimate rights, claims, and objectives. A lawyer shall not be deterred by any real or imagined fear of judicial disfavor or public unpopularity, nor be influenced by mere self-interest.

1. I will advise my client of the contents of this Creed when undertaking representation.

2. I will endeavor to achieve my client's lawful objectives in legal transactions and in litigation as quickly and economically as possible.

3. I will be loyal and committed to my client's lawful objectives, but I will not permit that loyalty and commitment to interfere with my duty to provide objective and independent advice.

4. I will advise my client that civility and courtesy are expected and are not a sign of weakness.

5. I will advise my client of proper and expected behavior.

6. I will treat adverse parties and witnesses with fairness and due consideration. A client has no right to demand that I abuse anyone or indulge in any offensive conduct.

7. I will advise my client that we will not pursue conduct which is intended primarily to harass or drain the financial resources of the opposing party.

8. I will advise my client that we will not pursue tactics which are intended primarily for delay.

9. I will advise my client that we will not pursue any course of action which is without merit.

10. I will advise my client that I reserve the right to determine whether to grant accommodations to opposing counsel in all matters that do not adversely affect my client's lawful objectives. A client has no right to instruct me to refuse reasonable requests made by other counsel.

11. I will advise my client regarding the availability of mediation, arbitration, and other alternative methods of resolving and settling disputes.

III. LAWYER TO LAWYER

A lawyer owes to opposing counsel, in the conduct of legal transactions and the pursuit of litigation, courtesy, candor, cooperation, and scrupulous observance of all agreements and mutual understandings. Ill feelings between clients shall not influence a lawyer's conduct, attitude, or demeanor toward opposing counsel. A lawyer shall not engage in unprofessional conduct in retaliation against other unprofessional conduct.

1. I will be courteous, civil, and prompt in oral and written communications.

2. I will not quarrel over matters of form or style, but I will concentrate on matters of substance.

3. I will identify for other counsel or parties all changes I have made in documents submitted for review.

4. I will attempt to prepare documents which correctly reflect the agreement of the parties. I will not include provisions which have not been agreed upon or omit provisions which are necessary to reflect the agreement of the parties.

5. I will notify opposing counsel, and, if appropriate, the Court or other persons, as soon as practicable, when hearings, depositions, meetings, conferences or closings are cancelled.

6. I will agree to reasonable requests for extensions of time and for waiver of procedural formalities, provided legitimate objectives of my client will not be adversely affected.

7. I will not serve motions or pleadings in any manner that unfairly limits another party's opportunity to respond.

8. I will attempt to resolve by agreement my objections to matters contained in pleadings and discovery requests and responses.

9. I can disagree without being disagreeable. I recognize that effective representation does not require antagonistic or obnoxious behavior. I will neither encourage nor knowingly permit my client or anyone under my control to do anything which would be unethical or improper if done by me.

10. I will not, without good cause, attribute bad motives or unethical conduct to opposing counsel nor bring the profession into disrepute by unfounded accusations of impropriety. I will avoid disparaging personal remarks or acrimony towards opposing counsel, parties and witnesses. I will not be influenced by any ill feeling between clients. I will abstain from any allusion to personal peculiarities or idiosyncrasies of opposing counsel.

11. I will not take advantage, by causing any default or dismissal to be rendered, when I know the identity of an opposing counsel, without first inquiring about that counsel's intention to proceed.

12. I will promptly submit orders to the Court. I will deliver copies to opposing counsel before or contemporaneously with submission to the Court. I will promptly approve the form of orders which accurately reflect the substance of the rulings of the Court.

13. I will not attempt to gain an unfair advantage by sending the Court or its staff correspondence or copies of correspondence.

14. I will not arbitrarily schedule a deposition, Court appearance, or hearing until a good faith effort has been made to schedule it by agreement.

15. I will readily stipulate to undisputed facts in order to avoid needless costs or inconvenience for any party.

16. I will refrain from excessive and abusive discovery.

17. I will comply with all reasonable discovery requests. I will not resist discovery requests which are not objectionable. I will not make objections nor give instructions to a witness for the purpose of delaying or obstructing the discovery process. I will encourage witnesses to respond to all deposition questions which are reasonably understandable. I will neither encourage nor permit my witness to quibble about words where their meaning is reasonably clear.

18. I will not seek Court intervention to obtain discovery which is clearly improper and not discoverable.

19. I will not seek sanctions or disqualification unless it is necessary for protection of my client's lawful objectives or is fully justified by the circumstances.

IV. LAWYER AND JUDGE

Lawyers and judges owe each other respect, diligence, candor, punctuality, and protection against unjust and improper criticism and attack. Lawyers and judges are equally responsible to protect the dignity and independence of the Court and the profession.

1. I will always recognize that the position of judge is the symbol of both the judicial system and administration of justice. I will refrain from conduct that degrades this symbol.

2. I will conduct myself in Court in a professional manner and demonstrate my respect for the Court and the law.

3. I will treat counsel, opposing parties, the Court, and members of the Court staff with courtesy and civility.

4. I will be punctual.

5. I will not engage in any conduct which offends the dignity and decorum of proceedings.

6. I will not knowingly misrepresent, mischaracterize, misquote or miscite facts or authorities to gain an advantage.

7. I will respect the rulings of the Court.

8. I will give the issues in controversy deliberate, impartial and studied analysis and consideration.

9. I will be considerate of the time constraints and pressures imposed upon the Court, Court staff and counsel in efforts to administer justice and resolve disputes.

PART TWO

CODES OF JUDICIAL CONDUCT

TABLE OF CONTENTS

Introduction

As in the case of regulating lawyers' conduct, the ABA has sought to provide standards for regulating judicial conduct. In 1924, the ABA adopted the Canons of Judicial Ethics. During the 1960s, the federal Judicial Conference of the United States developed standards for federal judges. Soon after the ABA adopted the Model Code of Professional Responsibility, the ABA appointed a commission to produce a revised code of conduct for judges. The resulting document is the 1972 Code of Judicial Conduct. In 1990, the ABA replaced the 1972 Code with a new Code of Judicial Conduct. The unabridged edition of this supplement contains the 1990 Code of Judicial Conduct in part eight.

At the February 2007 ABA meeting, the House of Delegates approved a complete revision to the Code of Judicial Conduct. The new code is patterned after the rules and comment approach of the Model Rules. Of course, the MPRE will continue to test the 1990 version of the CJC until at least 2008. And, it will take several years for a majority of the states to consider and adopt revisions based upon the new judicial code.

In March 2008, the Judicial Conference of the United States approved the Rules for Judicial-Conduct and Judicial-Disability Proceedings. These rules represent the first binding standards for the discipline of Federal Judges on grounds of misconduct disability. The Judicial Conference amended these rules in 2015.

AMERICAN BAR ASSOCIATION
MODEL CODE OF JUDICIAL CONDUCT (2016)

Adopted by the House of Delegates at the February 2008 meeting of the ABA.
Amended for housekeeping revisions in 2009.

Also amended in August 2010.

TABLE OF CONTENTS

CANON 3

A JUDGE SHALL CONDUCT THE JUDGE'S PERSONAL AND EXTRAJUDICIAL ACTIVITIES TO MINIMIZE THE RISK OF CONFLICT WITH THE OBLIGATIONS OF JUDICIAL OFFICE.

CANON 4

A JUDGE OR CANDIDATE FOR JUDICIAL OFFICE SHALL NOT ENGAGE IN POLITICAL OR CAMPAIGN ACTIVITY THAT IS INCONSISTENT WITH THE INDEPENDENCE, INTEGRITY, OR IMPARTIALITY OF THE JUDICIARY

ABA MODEL CODE OF JUDICIAL CONDUCT (2016)

PREAMBLE

[1] An independent, fair and impartial judiciary is indispensable to our system of justice. The United States legal system is based upon the principle that an independent, impartial, and competent judiciary, composed of men and women of integrity, will interpret and apply the law that governs our society. Thus, the judiciary plays a central role in preserving the principles of justice and the rule of law. Inherent in all the Rules contained in this Code are the precepts that judges, individually and collectively, must respect and honor the judicial office as a public trust and strive to maintain and enhance confidence in the legal system.

[2] Judges should maintain the dignity of judicial office at all times, and avoid both impropriety and the appearance of impropriety in their professional and personal lives. They should aspire at all times to conduct that ensures the greatest possible public confidence in their independence, impartiality, integrity, and competence.

[3] The Model Code of Judicial Conduct establishes standards for the ethical conduct of judges and judicial candidates. It is not intended as an exhaustive guide for the conduct of judges and judicial candidates, who are governed in their judicial and personal conduct by general ethical standards as well as by the Code. The Code is intended, however, to provide guidance and assist judges in maintaining the highest standards of judicial and personal conduct, and to provide a basis for regulating their conduct through disciplinary agencies.

PREAMBLE—REPORTER'S EXPLANATION OF CHANGES†

EXPLANATION OF BLACK LETTER

1. The 1990 Preamble has been essentially dissected, with the objective of describing the general purpose and rationale of the Code in the Preamble, and moving to a new "Scope" section the specific explanation of how the Rules are intended to operate. This approach parallels that taken in the ABA Model Rules of Professional Conduct, whose general format the proposed Rules and Comments also follow.

2. The 1990 Code Preamble language discussing the "degree of discipline to be imposed" in the course of enforcing the Code's provisions has been deleted completely.

3. New language has been added to emphasize that, at all times, judges should avoid both impropriety and the appearance of impropriety in their professional and personal lives and that they should aspire to conduct that ensures the greatest possible public confidence in their independence, integrity, impartiality, and competence.

4. Other changes in language are solely stylistic.

SCOPE

[1] The Model Code of Judicial Conduct consists of four Canons, numbered Rules under each Canon, and Comments that generally follow and explain each Rule. Scope and Terminology sections provide

† The "Reporters' Explanations of Changes" have not been approved by the ABA Joint Commission to Evaluate the Model Code of Judicial Conduct. They have been drafted by the Commission's Reporters, based on the proceedings and record of the Commission, solely to inform the ABA House of Delegates about each of the proposed amendments to the Model Code prior to their being considered at the ABA 2007 Midyear Meeting. THEY ARE NOT TO BE ADOPTED AS PART OF THE MODEL CODE.

additional guidance in interpreting and applying the Code. An Application section establishes when the various Rules apply to a judge or judicial candidate.

[2] The Canons state overarching principles of judicial ethics that all judges must observe. Although a judge may be disciplined only for violating a Rule, the Canons provide important guidance in interpreting the Rules. Where a Rule contains a permissive term, such as "may" or "should," the conduct being addressed is committed to the personal and professional discretion of the judge or candidate in question, and no disciplinary action should be taken for action or inaction within the bounds of such discretion.

[3] The Comments that accompany the Rules serve two functions. First, they provide guidance regarding the purpose, meaning, and proper application of the Rules. They contain explanatory material and, in some instances, provide examples of permitted or prohibited conduct. Comments neither add to nor subtract from the binding obligations set forth in the Rules. Therefore, when a Comment contains the term "must," it does not mean that the Comment itself is binding or enforceable; it signifies that the Rule in question, properly understood, is obligatory as to the conduct at issue.

[4] Second, the Comments identify aspirational goals for judges. To implement fully the principles of this Code as articulated in the Canons, judges should strive to exceed the standards of conduct established by the Rules, holding themselves to the highest ethical standards and seeking to achieve those aspirational goals, thereby enhancing the dignity of the judicial office.

[5] The Rules of the Model Code of Judicial Conduct are rules of reason that should be applied consistent with constitutional requirements, statutes, other court rules, and decisional law, and with due regard for all relevant circumstances. The Rules should not be interpreted to impinge upon the essential independence of judges in making judicial decisions.

[6] Although the black letter of the Rules is binding and enforceable, it is not contemplated that every transgression will result in the imposition of discipline. Whether discipline should be imposed should be determined through a reasonable and reasoned application of the Rules, and should depend upon factors such as the seriousness of the transgression, the facts and circumstances that existed at the time of the transgression, the extent of any pattern of improper activity, whether there have been previous violations, and the effect of the improper activity upon the judicial system or others.

[7] The Code is not designed or intended as a basis for civil or criminal liability. Neither is it intended to be the basis for litigants to seek collateral remedies against each other or to obtain tactical advantages in proceedings before a court.

SCOPE—REPORTER'S EXPLANATION OF CHANGES†

EXPLANATION OF BLACK LETTER

This new Scope section contains the concepts in the 1990 Preamble that explain how the various parts of the Rules are intended to operate. The Scope section indicates that judges may be disciplined only for violating a Rule. With regard to the Canons, or Rule headings, the Scope section explains that the Canons are overarching principles that provide important guidance in interpreting the rules.

TERMINOLOGY

The first time any term listed below is used in a Rule in its defined sense, it is followed by an asterisk (*).

† The "Reporters' Explanations of Changes" have not been approved by the ABA Joint Commission to Evaluate the Model Code of Judicial Conduct. They have been drafted by the Commission's Reporters, based on the proceedings and record of the Commission, solely to inform the ABA House of Delegates about each of the proposed amendments to the Model Code prior to their being considered at the ABA 2007 Midyear Meeting. THEY ARE NOT TO BE ADOPTED AS PART OF THE MODEL CODE.

"Aggregate," in relation to contributions for a candidate, means not only contributions in cash or in kind made directly to a candidate's campaign committee, but also all contributions made indirectly with the understanding that they will be used to support the election of a candidate or to oppose the election of the candidate's opponent. See Rules 2.11 and 4.4.

"Appropriate authority" means the authority having responsibility for initiation of disciplinary process in connection with the violation to be reported. See Rules 2.14 and 2.15.

"Contribution" means both financial and in-kind contributions, such as goods, professional or volunteer services, advertising, and other types of assistance, which, if obtained by the recipient otherwise, would require a financial expenditure. See Rules 2.11, 2.13, 3.7, 4.1, and 4.4.

"De minimis," in the context of interests pertaining to disqualification of a judge, means an insignificant interest that could not raise a reasonable question regarding the judge's impartiality. See Rule 2.11.

"Domestic partner" means a person with whom another person maintains a household and an intimate relationship, other than a person to whom he or she is legally married. See Rules 2.11, 2.13, 3.13, and 3.14.

"Economic interest" means ownership of more than a de minimis legal or equitable interest. Except for situations in which the judge participates in the management of such a legal or equitable interest, or the interest could be substantially affected by the outcome of a proceeding before a judge, it does not include:

(1) an interest in the individual holdings within a mutual or common investment fund;

(2) an interest in securities held by an educational, religious, charitable, fraternal, or civic organization in which the judge or the judge's spouse, domestic partner, parent, or child serves as a director, an officer, an advisor, or other participant;

(3) a deposit in a financial institution or deposits or proprietary interests the judge may maintain as a member of a mutual savings association or credit union, or similar proprietary interests; or

(4) an interest in the issuer of government securities held by the judge.

See Rules 1.3 and 2.11.

"Fiduciary" includes relationships such as executor, administrator, trustee, or guardian. See Rules 2.11, 3.2, and 3.8.

"Impartial," "impartiality," and **"impartially"** mean absence of bias or prejudice in favor of, or against, particular parties or classes of parties, as well as maintenance of an open mind in considering issues that may come before a judge. See Canons 1, 2, and 4, and Rules 1.2, 2.2, 2.10, 2.11, 2.13, 3.1, 3.12, 3.13, 4.1, and 4.2.

"Impending matter" is a matter that is imminent or expected to occur in the near future. See Rules 2.9, 2.10, 3.13, and 4.1.

"Impropriety" includes conduct that violates the law, court rules, or provisions of this Code, and conduct that undermines a judge's independence, integrity, or impartiality. See Canon 1 and Rule 1.2.

"Independence" means a judge's freedom from influence or controls other than those established by law. See Canons 1 and 4, and Rules 1.2, 3.1, 3.12, 3.13, and 4.2.

"Integrity" means probity, fairness, honesty, uprightness, and soundness of character. See Canon 1 and Rule 1.2.

"Judicial candidate" means any person, including a sitting judge, who is seeking selection for or retention in judicial office by election or appointment. A person becomes a candidate for judicial office as soon as he or she makes a public announcement of candidacy, declares or files as a candidate with the election or appointment authority, authorizes or, where permitted, engages in solicitation or acceptance of contributions or support, or is nominated for election or appointment to office. See Rules 2.11, 4.1, 4.2, and 4.4.

"Knowingly," "knowledge," "known," and **"knows"** mean actual knowledge of the fact in question. A person's knowledge may be inferred from circumstances. See Rules 2.11, 2.13, 2.15, 2.16, 3.6, and 4.1.

"Law" encompasses court rules as well as statutes, constitutional provisions, and decisional law. See Rules 1.1, 2.1, 2.2, 2.6, 2.7, 2.9, 3.1, 3.4, 3.9, 3.12, 3.13, 3.14, 3.15, 4.1, 4.2, 4.4, and 4.5.

"Member of the candidate's family" means a spouse, domestic partner, child, grandchild, parent, grandparent, or other relative or person with whom the candidate maintains a close familial relationship.

"Member of the judge's family" means a spouse, domestic partner, child, grandchild, parent, grandparent, or other relative or person with whom the judge maintains a close familial relationship. See Rules 3.7, 3.8, 3.10, and 3.11.

"Member of a judge's family residing in the judge's household" means any relative of a judge by blood or marriage, or a person treated by a judge as a member of the judge's family, who resides in the judge's household. See Rules 2.11 and 3.13.

"Nonpublic information" means information that is not available to the public. Nonpublic information may include, but is not limited to, information that is sealed by statute or court order or impounded or communicated in camera, and information offered in grand jury proceedings, presentencing reports, dependency cases, or psychiatric reports. See Rule 3.5.

"Pending matter" is a matter that has commenced. A matter continues to be pending through any appellate process until final disposition. See Rules 2.9, 2.10, 3.13, and 4.1.

"Personally solicit" means a direct request made by a judge or a judicial candidate for financial support or in-kind services, whether made by letter, telephone, or any other means of communication. See Rule 4.1.

"Political organization" means a political party or other group sponsored by or affiliated with a political party or candidate, the principal purpose of which is to further the election or appointment of candidates for political office. For purposes of this Code, the term does not include a judicial candidate's campaign committee created as authorized by Rule 4.4. See Rules 4.1 and 4.2.

"Public election" includes primary and general elections, partisan elections, nonpartisan elections, and retention elections. See Rules 4.2 and 4.4.

"Third degree of relationship" includes the following persons: great-grandparent, grandparent, parent, uncle, aunt, brother, sister, child, grandchild, great-grandchild, nephew, and niece. See Rule 2.11.

TERMINOLOGY—REPORTER'S EXPLANATION OF CHANGES†

EXPLANATION OF BLACK LETTER

1. The Commission proposes to change the use of asterisks to indicate defined terms, employing them in a Rule only where the defined term is used for the first time. Several commentators observed that the use of asterisks each time a frequently-appearing defined term occurred was more interruptive than useful to the reader.

2. Apart from the addition of "domestic partner" to the definitions of "Member of the candidate's family" and "Member of the judge's family," the following terms are defined in a manner essentially identical to the way they are defined in the 1990 Code (any differences are intended to be purely stylistic):

Aggregate

Appropriate authority

Economic interest

Fiduciary

† The "Reporters' Explanations of Changes" have not been approved by the ABA Joint Commission to Evaluate the Model Code of Judicial Conduct. They have been drafted by the Commission's Reporters, based on the proceedings and record of the Commission, solely to inform the ABA House of Delegates about each of the proposed amendments to the Model Code prior to their being considered at the ABA 2007 Midyear Meeting. THEY ARE NOT TO BE ADOPTED AS PART OF THE MODEL CODE.

Knowingly, knowledge, known, or knows

Law

Member of the candidate's family

Member of the judge's family

Member of the judge's family residing in the judge's household

Nonpublic information

Public election

Third degree of relationship

3. The following terms are no longer contained in the Terminology Section:

"Continuing part-time judge," on the theory that the provision applicable to continuing part-time judges in the Application Section provides a definition already.

"Court personnel," which in the 1990 Code was not, in fact, a definition, but a statement that the term did not include lawyers in a proceeding before the judge. The Commission believed this was too evident to need statement, and otherwise believed that the term "court personnel" is clear enough that it does not need definition. The term "court personnel" has been replaced with "court staff, court officials, and others subject to the judge's direction and control."

"Periodic part-time judge" (on the same theory as applied to "continuing part-time judge"; see above)

"Pro tempore part-time judge" (same reason as above)

"Require," which the Commission believed is easily understood.

The following definitions have been modified:

"De minimis" is defined specifically in the context of "interests pertaining to the disqualification of a judge," because it is only in Rule 2.11 ("Disqualification") that the Commission believes a precise definition of the term need be applied.

"Judicial candidate" is similar to the 1990 Code's term "candidate." The phrase "including a sitting judge" has been added for clarification. The language stating that the term "candidate" applies to a judge who is seeking a non-judicial office has been deleted, consistent with the reformulation of the term being defined.

"Political organization" has been expanded to include the qualifying language "sponsored by or affiliated with a political party or candidate," the principal purpose of which is to further the election or appointment of candidates for political office. In addition, language has been added to clarify that the term is not meant to include a judicial candidate's own campaign committee.

4. The following new defined terms have been added:

"Domestic partner," on the theory that now commonplace "non-traditional" relationships that exist outside marriage are deserving of treatment equal to that afforded marital relationships in evaluating their potential conflict-of-interest implications under the Rules.

"Impartiality," because it is a fundamental goal of the judicial system, and additionally because it has become a defined term in recent decisional law with respect to political activity of judges.

"Impending matter," in order to set temporal limits on the phrase.

"Impropriety," because of its fundamental importance as a concept underlying the importance of appearances created by judges.

"Independence," as a fundamental concept underlying the justice system.

"Integrity," for the same reason as above.

"Pending matter," so as to set temporal limits on the phrase and create greater certainty in the application of the Code's restrictions on judicial speech.

2016 MODEL CODE

Application

The Application section establishes when the various Rules apply to a judge or judicial candidate.

I. Applicability of This Code

(A) The provisions of the Code apply to all full-time judges. Parts II through V of this section identify provisions that apply to four categories of part-time judges only while they are serving as judges, and provisions that do not apply to part-time judges at any time. All other Rules are therefore applicable to part-time judges at all times. The four categories of judicial service in other than a full-time capacity are necessarily defined in general terms because of the widely varying forms of judicial service. Canon 4 applies to judicial candidates.

(B) A judge, within the meaning of this Code, is anyone who is authorized to perform judicial functions, including an officer such as a justice of the peace, magistrate, court commissioner, special master, referee, or member of the administrative law judiciary.[1]

Comment

[1] The Rules in this Code have been formulated to address the ethical obligations of any person who serves a judicial function, and are premised upon the supposition that a uniform system of ethical principles should apply to all those authorized to perform judicial functions.

[2] The determination of which category and, accordingly, which specific Rules apply to an individual judicial officer, depends upon the facts of the particular judicial service.

[3] In recent years many jurisdictions have created what are often called "problem solving" courts, in which judges are authorized by court rules to act in nontraditional ways. For example, judges presiding in drug courts and monitoring the progress of participants in those courts' programs may be authorized and even encouraged to communicate directly with social workers, probation officers, and others outside the context of their usual judicial role as independent decision makers on issues of fact and law. When local rules specifically authorize conduct not otherwise permitted under these Rules, they take precedence over the provisions set forth in the Code. Nevertheless, judges serving on "problem solving" courts shall comply with this Code except to the extent local rules provide and permit otherwise.

Application—Reporter's Explanation of Changes†

EXPLANATION OF BLACK LETTER

1. The Commission is proposing a more user-friendly Application section as an alternative to the current version, which is complex and difficult with which to work. The most significant substantive change brings within the definition of "judges" justices of the peace, hearing officers, and "members of the administrative law judiciary."

[1] Each jurisdiction should consider the characteristics of particular positions within the administrative law judiciary in adopting, adapting, applying, and enforcing the Code for the administrative law judiciary. *See, e.g.*, Model Code of Judicial Conduct for Federal Administrative Law Judges (1989) and Model Code of Judicial Conduct for State Administrative Law Judges (1995). Both Model Codes are endorsed by the ABA National Conference of Administrative Law Judiciary.

† The "Reporters' Explanations of Changes" have not been approved by the ABA Joint Commission to Evaluate the Model Code of Judicial Conduct. They have been drafted by the Commission's Reporters, based on the proceedings and record of the Commission, solely to inform the ABA House of Delegates about each of the proposed amendments to the Model Code prior to their being considered at the ABA 2007 Midyear Meeting. THEY ARE NOT TO BE ADOPTED AS PART OF THE MODEL CODE.

2. The title of Part I, "Applicability of This Code," is clearer and simpler than the title in the 1990 Code. No change in substance is intended.

3. Part I (A) has been revised to make clear which provisions of the Code apply to certain categories of judges or judicial candidates. This is a stylistic change and does not change the substance of the provision. The Commission placed in Part I (A) the sentence, "the four categories of judicial service in other than full-time capacity are necessarily defined in general terms because of the widely varying forms of judicial service," which had been included in Commentary to Section A of the Application Section in the 1990 Code.

4. In Part I (B) of the revised Application, "justice of the peace" and "member of the administrative judiciary" are included as judges "within the meaning of this Code." The application of the Rules to the administrative law judiciary is consistent with policy adopted by the ABA House of Delegates in Report 101B (2001), which provided that members of the administrative law judiciary should be accountable under appropriate ethical standards adapted from the Code in light of the unique characteristics of particular positions in the administrative law judiciary. The rationale for applying the Rules to justices of the peace and members of the administrative law judiciary derives from the fact that they perform essentially the same function as a trial judge hearing a case without a jury.

5. To facilitate easier recognition of the subject matter of the many Rules cited throughout the Application section, parentheticals have been added with the names of each rule cited, eliminating the need to search through the entire Code. This approach is consistent with the format used when citing Rules throughout the rest of the Code.

6. A footnote reference has been revised to state that each jurisdiction "should consider the characteristics of particular members of the administrative law judiciary positions in adopting, adapting, applying and enforcing the Rules for the administrative law judiciary. See, e.g., Model Code of Judicial Conduct for Federal Administrative Law Judges (1989) (endorsed by the National Conference of Administrative Law Judges in February 1989)." The Commission deleted the language that alluded to the executive branch of government in order to avoid difficulties associated with separation of powers issues.

7. The phrase "for service" was added to Part II to explain more fully the meaning of a judge's being "subject to recall." No substantive change is intended.

8. In Parts III, IV and V, the definitions of the various types of part-time judges have been introduced into the text, and deleted from the "Terminology" section of the Code, consistent with the Commission's decision to place terminology within the body of a Rule when that is the only time that it appears.

9. Sections I(D)(2) and I(E)(2) of the 1990 Code were deleted in acknowledgement that this code is not meant to reach the conduct of lawyers, but that of judges. The situations described in both provisions arise under and are to be decided according to the Model Rules of Professional Conduct for lawyers.

10. Part VI, "Time for Compliance," has not changed in substance. Taken directly from Section F of the 1990 Code's Application section, it acknowledges the need to allow new judges to continue to serve as fiduciaries or in a business relationship for a period of up to one year in order to avoid hardship or serious adverse consequences to the beneficiaries of the fiduciary relationship.

EXPLANATION OF COMMENTS

PART I

[1] A new introductory Comment has been added to highlight the fact that it is desirable to have a uniform system of ethical principles that applies to all individuals serving a judicial function.

[2] This Comment clarifies that the category associated with a judicial officer depends on the judicial service.

[3] This new Comment confirms the propriety of using nontraditional methods in "problem solving" courts, such as drug and domestic violence courts, where they are permitted by law, including court rules.

II. Retired Judge Subject to Recall

A retired judge subject to recall for service, who by law is not permitted to practice law, is not required to comply:

(A) with Rule 3.9 (Service as Arbitrator or Mediator), except while serving as a judge

(B) at any time with Rule 3.8(A) (Appointments to Fiduciary Positions).

Comment

[1] For the purposes of this section, as long as a retired judge is subject to being recalled for service, the judge is considered to "perform judicial functions."

III. Continuing Part-Time Judge

A judge who serves repeatedly on a part-time basis by election or under a continuing appointment, including a retired judge subject to recall who is permitted to practice law ("continuing part-time judge"),

(A) is not required to comply:

(1) with Rule 4.1 (Political and Campaign Activities of Judges and Judicial Candidates in General) (A)(1) through (7), except while serving as a judge; or

(2) at any time with Rules 3.4 (Appointments to Governmental Positions), 3.8(A) (Appointments to Fiduciary Positions), 3.9 (Service as Arbitrator or Mediator), 3.10 (Practice of Law), and 3.11(B) (Financial, Business, or Remunerative Activities); and*

(B) shall not practice law in the court on which the judge serves or in any court subject to the appellate jurisdiction of the court on which the judge serves, and shall not act as a lawyer in a proceeding in which the judge has served as a judge or in any other proceeding related thereto.

Comment

[1] When a person who has been a continuing part-time judge is no longer a continuing part-time judge, including a retired judge no longer subject to recall, that person may act as a lawyer in a proceeding in which he or she has served as a judge or in any other proceeding related thereto only with the informed consent of all parties, and pursuant to any applicable Model Rules of Professional Conduct. An adopting jurisdiction should substitute a reference to its applicable rule.

IV. Periodic Part-Time Judge

A periodic part-time judge who serves or expects to serve repeatedly on a part-time basis, but under a separate appointment for each limited period of service or for each matter,

(A) is not required to comply:

(1) with Rule 4.1 (Political and Campaign Activities of Judges and Judicial Candidates in General) (A)(1) through (7), except while serving as a judge; or

(2) at any time with Rules 3.4 (Appointments to Governmental Positions), 3.8(A) (Appointments to Fiduciary Positions), 3.9 (Service as Arbitrator or Mediator), 3.10 (Practice of Law), and 3.11(B) (Financial, Business, or Remunerative Activities); and*

---

* Ed. Note: In August 2010, the ABA House of Delegated Amended III(A) to clarify the rules applicable to continuing part-time judges.

* Ed. Note: In August 2010, the ABA House of Delegates amended IV(A) to clarify the application of the rules to periodic part-time judges.

(B) shall not practice law in the court on which the judge serves or in any court subject to the appellate jurisdiction of the court on which the judge serves, and shall not act as a lawyer in a proceeding in which the judge has served as a judge or in any other proceeding related thereto.

V. PRO TEMPORE PART-TIME JUDGE

A pro tempore part-time judge who serves or expects to serve once or only sporadically on a part-time basis under a separate appointment for each period of service or for each case heard is not required to comply:

(A) except while serving as a judge, with Rules 2.4 (External Influences on Judicial Conduct), 3.2 (Appearances before Governmental Bodies and Consultation with Government Officials), and 4.1 (Political and Campaign Activities of Judges and Judicial Candidates in General) (A)(1) through (7); or

(B) at any time with Rules 3.4 (Appointments to Governmental Positions), 3.8(A) (Appointments to Fiduciary Positions), 3.9 (Service as Arbitrator or Mediator), 3.10 (Practice of Law), and 3.11(B) (Financial, Business, or Remunerative Activities).**

VI. TIME FOR COMPLIANCE

A person to whom this Code becomes applicable shall comply immediately with its provisions, except that those judges to whom Rules 3.8 (Appointments to Fiduciary Positions) and 3.11 (Financial, Business, or Remunerative Activities) apply shall comply with those Rules as soon as reasonably possible, but in no event later than one year after the Code becomes applicable to the judge.

Comment

[1] If serving as a fiduciary when selected as judge, a new judge may, notwithstanding the prohibitions in Rule 3.8, continue to serve as fiduciary, but only for that period of time necessary to avoid serious adverse consequences to the beneficiaries of the fiduciary relationship and in no event longer than one year. Similarly, if engaged at the time of judicial selection in a business activity, a new judge may, notwithstanding the prohibitions in Rule 3.11, continue in that activity for a reasonable period but in no event longer than one year.

CANON 1

A JUDGE SHALL UPHOLD AND PROMOTE THE INDEPENDENCE, INTEGRITY, AND IMPARTIALITY OF THE JUDICIARY, AND SHALL AVOID IMPROPRIETY AND THE APPEARANCE OF IMPROPRIETY.

CANON 1—REPORTER'S EXPLANATION OF CHANGES†

1990 MODEL CODE COMPARISON

Canon 1 is a combination of Canons 1 and 2.

** Ed. Note: In August 2010, the ABA House of Delegates amended (A) and (B) to clarify the application of the rules to pro tempore part-time judges.

† The "Reporters' Explanations of Changes" have not been approved by the ABA Joint Commission to Evaluate the Model Code of Judicial Conduct. They have been drafted by the Commission's Reporters, based on the proceedings and record of the Commission, solely to inform the ABA House of Delegates about each of the proposed amendments to the

2016 MODEL CODE

EXPLANATION OF BLACK LETTER

1. Canon 1 combines most of the subject matter of Canons 1 and 2 in the 1990 Code, addressing both the obligation of judges to uphold the independence, integrity, and impartiality of the judiciary and the obligation to avoid impropriety and its appearance. The admonishment that judges avoid not only impropriety but also its appearance is in the text of Canon 1 and in Rule 1.2.

The decision to combine Canons 1 and 2 in the 1990 Code into a single Canon was based on the premise that they are directed toward essentially the same end: to articulate a limited number of general, overarching principles that should govern a judge's conduct. Former Canons 1 and 2 were inextricably linked: avoiding "impropriety and the appearance of impropriety" in former Canon 2 was instrumental to upholding "the independence and integrity of the judiciary" in former Canon 1. Moreover, the former Code blurred the distinction between its Canons 1 and 2 by including in Canon 2A a duty to act in a manner that "promotes public confidence in the integrity and impartiality of the judiciary," which essentially paraphrased Canon 1's directive to "uphold the integrity and independence of the judiciary." Although one could argue that former Canon 1 was concerned with protecting independence and integrity in fact, while former Canon 2 concentrated upon protecting appearances and public perception, the overlap between them was so great that in the Commission's view preserving the two as discrete Canons was unnecessarily confusing. Accordingly, the two Canons have been combined to underscore the instrumental relationship between them, and thereby reinforce the importance of both.

2. Addition of "promote" to Canon 1

As an overarching objective, the Commission deemed it desirable to speak in terms of an ethical duty to promote as well as uphold judicial independence, integrity and impartiality.

3. "Appearance of impropriety" standard

At the center of the Commission's deliberations over Canon 1 was the "appearance of impropriety." The discussions reflected two competing tensions. On the one hand, a primary purpose of the Code is to advise and inspire judges to adhere to the highest standards of ethical conduct. To preserve public confidence in the courts, it is not enough that judges avoid actual improprieties; they must avoid the appearance of impropriety as well. On the other hand, another purpose of the Rules is to serve as the basis for discipline. To discipline judges for appearing to act improperly—even if they did not act improperly in fact—was considered by some commentators to raise due process issues because of the potential vagueness of the term "impropriety."

To address the concern that a duty to avoid the appearance of impropriety was too vague to be independently enforceable, the Commission's preliminary draft included a comment to the effect that ordinarily, when judges are disciplined for violating their duty to avoid the appearance of impropriety, it is in combination with other, more specific rule violations that give rise to the appearance problem. When the preliminary draft was circulated for public comment in June 2005, that comment was criticized widely for, among other things, diluting the "appearance of impropriety" standard unnecessarily.

Of additional concern was the preliminary draft's deletion of former Canon 2A's directive that "a judge shall . . . act at all times in a manner that promotes public confidence in the integrity and impartiality of the judiciary" (the "act at all times" clause), which had been a rule through which the appearance of impropriety was commonly enforced.

The Commission deleted the offending draft Comment, and restored the "act at all times clause." The Commission had in the interim considered retaining the appearance of impropriety language only in the Canon, and, as a precaution against it being used as a disciplinary standard, included a statement in the Scope Section that the Canons could themselves be enforced only when some Rule was violated. Urgings from legal organizations and the judiciary led the Commission to accept an amendment, during debate in the House of Delegates, that reinstated the obligation of a judge to avoid impropriety and the appearance of impropriety as black letter Rule 1.2. With an enforceable rule thus "on the books," any objections to the non-enforceability of the Canons were withdrawn, and the Scope provision was retained.

Model Code prior to their being considered at the ABA 2007 Midyear Meeting. THEY ARE NOT TO BE ADOPTED AS PART OF THE MODEL CODE.

4. Use of "independence, integrity, and impartiality"

In the prior Code, "impartiality" did not appear in the titles of Canons 1 or 2, even though it did appear in underlying sections, such as Canon 2A. In the Commission's view, independence, integrity, and impartiality are overarching, fundamental values that the Rules promote, which warrant mention in the title of Canon 1. The term "impartiality" has been added to integrity and independence throughout the Rules, and the Rules have been revised throughout to preserve consistency.

The importance of judicial independence, integrity, and impartiality is underscored by the recurrence of the phrase throughout the Rules. Although it was used in earlier Codes as well, the Commission took pains to ensure that the three terms appear together wherever appropriate, and in the same sequence whenever they are employed.

RULE 1.1 Compliance With the Law

A judge shall comply with the law,* including the Code of Judicial Conduct.

RULE 1.1—REPORTER'S EXPLANATION OF CHANGES†

1990 MODEL CODE COMPARISON

The Rule is the first clause of Canon 2A, combined with a statement from the Commentary to Canon 1A.

EXPLANATION OF BLACK LETTER

1. Creation of a new rule

This Rule reproduces the first clause of former Canon 2A. The former Canon linked the duty to respect and comply with the law to the duty to act at all times in a manner that promoted public confidence in the independence, integrity, and impartiality of the judiciary, which the Commission regarded as distinct and discrete concepts. To be sure, the judge who does not comply with the law diminishes public confidence in judges, but the "act at all times" clause encompasses a far broader range of conduct that deserved to be singled out and articulated at the front of the Canon. The reference to a judge's duty to "respect" the law was deleted because it was believed to be both impossible to define and unnecessary.

2. Addition of "including the Code of Judicial Conduct"

The Commission wanted to leave no room for doubt that the scope of "law" within the meaning of this rule, applies to the Rules themselves.

3. Canon 1A's pronouncement that a judge "should participate in establishing, maintaining and enforcing high standards of conduct" has been revised and moved to the Preamble. The Commission concluded that such hortatory language should not be confused with enforceable standards and that to avoid such confusion, it should not appear in black letter Rules.

EXPLANATION OF COMMENTS

The Commentary to Canon 1A was deleted as unnecessary. Integrity and independence, which were discussed in the deleted comment, are defined terms in the revised Terminology Section.

---

† The "Reporters' Explanations of Changes" have not been approved by the ABA Joint Commission to Evaluate the Model Code of Judicial Conduct. They have been drafted by the Commission's Reporters, based on the proceedings and record of the Commission, solely to inform the ABA House of Delegates about each of the proposed amendments to the Model Code prior to their being considered at the ABA 2007 Midyear Meeting. THEY ARE NOT TO BE ADOPTED AS PART OF THE MODEL CODE.

RULE 1.2 Promoting Confidence in the Judiciary

A judge shall act at all times in a manner that promotes public confidence in the independence,* integrity,* and impartiality* of the judiciary, and shall avoid impropriety and the appearance of impropriety.

Comment

[1] Public confidence in the judiciary is eroded by improper conduct and conduct that creates the appearance of impropriety. This principle applies to both the professional and personal conduct of a judge.

[2] A judge should expect to be the subject of public scrutiny that might be viewed as burdensome if applied to other citizens, and must accept the restrictions imposed by the Code.

[3] Conduct that compromises or appears to compromise the independence, integrity, and impartiality of a judge undermines public confidence in the judiciary. Because it is not practicable to list all such conduct, the Rule is necessarily cast in general terms.

[4] Judges should participate in activities that promote ethical conduct among judges and lawyers, support professionalism within the judiciary and the legal profession, and promote access to justice for all.

[5] Actual improprieties include violations of law, court rules or provisions of this Code. The test for appearance of impropriety is whether the conduct would create in reasonable minds a perception that the judge violated this Code or engaged in other conduct that reflects adversely on the judge's honesty, impartiality, temperament, or fitness to serve as a judge.

[6] A judge should initiate and participate in community outreach activities for the purpose of promoting public understanding of and confidence in the administration of justice._ In conducting such activities, the judge must act in a manner consistent with this Code.

RULE 1.2—REPORTER'S EXPLANATION OF CHANGES†

1990 MODEL CODE COMPARISON

The Rule is Canon 2A.

Comment [1] is based upon the first two sentences of Commentary to Canon 2A, with the first sentence of the second paragraph of Commentary to Canon 2A inserted as a second sentence.

Comment [2] is taken from the first paragraph of Commentary to Canon 2A.

Comment [3] is taken from the first two paragraphs of Commentary to Canon 2A.

The third paragraph of Commentary to Canon 2A was deleted.

Comment [4] is new.

Comment [5] is a reformulation of the second paragraph of Commentary to Canon 2A.

Comment [6] is new.

EXPLANATION OF BLACK LETTER

<u>Creation of a new rule</u>

The first clause of Rule 1.2 is taken from Canon 2. This language was formerly included in the text of Canon 2A and is now a free-standing rule, for reasons explained above in the general discussion of Canon 1.

† The "Reporters' Explanations of Changes" have not been approved by the ABA Joint Commission to Evaluate the Model Code of Judicial Conduct. They have been drafted by the Commission's Reporters, based on the proceedings and record of the Commission, solely to inform the ABA House of Delegates about each of the proposed amendments to the Model Code prior to their being considered at the ABA 2007 Midyear Meeting. THEY ARE NOT TO BE ADOPTED AS PART OF THE MODEL CODE.

The second clause, directing judges to avoid impropriety and the appearance of impropriety was added at the urging of the judiciary and others, to make creating an "appearance of impropriety" an independent basis for discipline.

EXPLANATION OF COMMENTS

[1], [2], [3] The substance of Comments [1], [2], and [3] is derived from Commentary to former Canon 2A. Language from the former Commentary that was deemed self-evident, redundant, or otherwise unnecessary was deleted.

[4] Comment [4] is new. The Commission heard from a number of witnesses who underscored the importance of encouraging judges to promote professionalism among lawyers and judges—to make it clear that doing so was a part of their jobs. Although it was never suggested that judges be subject to discipline for failing to undertake such activities, the Commission agreed that judges should strive to promote professionalism and access to justice and that the aspirational objectives of the Code were well served by including this Comment.

[5] Comment [5] is derived from commentary accompanying Canon 2A of the 1990 Code. It modifies the former commentary's "test" for the appearance of impropriety by stating that an appearance problem arises from the perception that the judge either violated the Code or engaged in other conduct that reflects adversely on the judge's honesty, impartiality, temperament or fitness.

[6] Comment [6] is new, and is designed to encourage judges to participate in community outreach activity. Existing ABA policy encourages judges to engage in such activity as a means to promote public confidence in the courts.

RULE 1.3 Avoiding Abuse of the Prestige of Judicial Office

A judge shall not abuse the prestige of judicial office to advance the personal or economic interests* of the judge or others, or allow others to do so.

Comment

[1] It is improper for a judge to use or attempt to use his or her position to gain personal advantage or deferential treatment of any kind. For example, it would be improper for a judge to allude to his or her judicial status to gain favorable treatment in encounters with traffic officials. Similarly, a judge must not use judicial letterhead to gain an advantage in conducting his or her personal business.

[2] A judge may provide a reference or recommendation for an individual based upon the judge's personal knowledge. The judge may use official letterhead if the judge indicates that the reference is personal and if there is no likelihood that the use of the letterhead would reasonably be perceived as an attempt to exert pressure by reason of the judicial office.

[3] Judges may participate in the process of judicial selection by cooperating with appointing authorities and screening committees, and by responding to inquiries from such entities concerning the professional qualifications of a person being considered for judicial office.

[4] Special considerations arise when judges write or contribute to publications of for-profit entities, whether related or unrelated to the law. A judge shall not permit anyone associated with the publication of such materials to exploit the judge's office in a manner that violates this Rule or other applicable law. In contracts for publication of a judge's writing, the judge shall retain sufficient control over the advertising to avoid such exploitation.

RULE 1.3—REPORTER'S EXPLANATION OF CHANGES†

1990 MODEL CODE COMPARISON:

The Rule and its Comment come from Canon 2B and its Commentary.

EXPLANATION OF BLACK LETTER

1. Creation of separate Rule on abusing prestige of office

This Rule was segregated from former Canon 2B for treatment as a stand-alone Rule because it relates directly to a judge's personal conduct. Former Canon 2B's prohibition on a judge allowing family, social, and political relationships to influence judicial conduct and its prohibition on a judge conveying or allowing others to convey the impression that other persons are in a position to influence the judge related directly to a judge's judicial decision-making responsibilities. For that reason, these provisions belonged more logically in proposed Canon 2. Former Canon 2B's limitation on a judge serving as a character witness, on the other hand, related to a judge's personal conduct and has been moved to Rule 3.3.

2. Substitution of "abuse" for "lend"

The term "abuse" has been substituted for "lend." In the Commission's view, the term "lend" created unnecessary confusion. For example, a judge who wrote a letter of recommendation for a law clerk "lent" the prestige of the judge's office to the recommendation, and some judges told the Commission that they declined to write letters on their clerks' behalf as a consequence. In the Commission's view, however, the problem that Rule 1.3 seeks to address is more accurately characterized as "abuse" of the office.

3. Addition of "economic" interests

Although a judge's "personal" interests might commonly be thought to include "economic" interests, the Commission wanted to avoid any possibility of confusion, and thus made it clear that a judge may not abuse the prestige of office to advance either.

4. Addition of prohibition on others' abuse

The Rule has been revised to prohibit judges from allowing others to abuse the prestige of the judge's office to advance the judge's or others' personal or economic interests. In the Commission's view, judges should not be permitted to look the other way if friends or relatives seek to trade on the judge's position to benefit themselves or others. "Personal" replaced "private" for stylistic reasons not intended to change substantive meaning.

EXPLANATION OF COMMENTS

[1] This Comment elaborates on the core objective underlying the Rule by making plain that a judge should not use his or her position as a judge to gain personal advantage in business or daily life. The last sentence was changed to limit the admonition that a judge should not use his or her judicial letterhead for personal business to situations in which the use of letterhead could "gain advantage." There are times when a judge might draft a personal note on stationery that includes the judge's title that could not conceivably enable the judge to "gain advantage," as, for example, when the judge corresponds with a long-time acquaintance who is well aware of the judge's position. Material from the 1990 comment regarded as too general to be helpful was deleted.

[2] The Commission was in accord that judges should be permitted to use their titles and office letterheads when writing references for people with respect to whom the judge's experience as a judge was relevant. The prohibition on abusing the prestige of judicial office to advance the interests of another is intended to prevent inappropriate exploitation of judges' positions, and there is nothing inappropriate about judges identifying themselves as such when judicial experience is germane to the recommendation. The Comment thus clarifies that a judge may write letters on the basis of a judge's experience on the job (e.g., law clerks)

† The "Reporters' Explanations of Changes" have not been approved by the ABA Joint Commission to Evaluate the Model Code of Judicial Conduct. They have been drafted by the Commission's Reporters, based on the proceedings and record of the Commission, solely to inform the ABA House of Delegates about each of the proposed amendments to the Model Code prior to their being considered at the ABA 2007 Midyear Meeting. THEY ARE NOT TO BE ADOPTED AS PART OF THE MODEL CODE.

or general expertise in the law (e.g., a neighbor applying for admission to law school). This Comment does not admonish judges to avoid writing letters of reference on behalf of someone with respect to whom the judge's status as a judge is irrelevant, rather, it merely advises judges to consider whether their position as a judge might be perceived as exerting pressure by reason of their office and to refrain if it would.

[3] Changes were stylistic and not intended to change substantive meaning.

[4] Deleted material was redundant of the text and otherwise not illuminating.

CANON 2

A JUDGE SHALL PERFORM THE DUTIES OF JUDICIAL OFFICE IMPARTIALLY, COMPETENTLY, AND DILIGENTLY.

CANON 2—REPORTER'S EXPLANATION OF CHANGES†

1990 MODEL CODE COMPARISON

The Canon is former Canon 3.

Canon 2 addresses solely the judge's professional duties as a judge, which constitute part of Canon 3 in the 1990 Code.

EXPLANATION OF BLACK LETTER

Discussion of Canon

This Canon is at the heart of the Rules, in that it governs core judicial functions. It bears emphasis, however, that the judicial function has changed over time and logically reaches such matters as administration, discipline, and some forms of outreach. Judicial activities or conduct, therefore, are not limited to the adjudication of cases, but are intended to reach the broader duties of judicial office. Thus, this Canon on the duties of judicial office includes rules governing judicial discipline, administration, and reporting.

The element of "competence" was added to the Canon in recognition of the importance that competence plays in a judge's discharge of his or her duties.

RULE 2.1 Giving Precedence to the Duties of Judicial Office

The duties of judicial office, as prescribed by law,* shall take precedence over all of a judge's personal and extrajudicial activities.

Comment

[1] To ensure that judges are available to fulfill their judicial duties, judges must conduct their personal and extrajudicial activities to minimize the risk of conflicts that would result in frequent disqualification. See Canon 3.

† The "Reporters' Explanations of Changes" have not been approved by the ABA Joint Commission to Evaluate the Model Code of Judicial Conduct. They have been drafted by the Commission's Reporters, based on the proceedings and record of the Commission, solely to inform the ABA House of Delegates about each of the proposed amendments to the Model Code prior to their being considered at the ABA 2007 Midyear Meeting. THEY ARE NOT TO BE ADOPTED AS PART OF THE MODEL CODE.

[2] Although it is not a duty of judicial office unless prescribed by law, judges are encouraged to participate in activities that promote public understanding of and confidence in the justice system.

RULE 2.1—REPORTER'S EXPLANATION OF CHANGES†

1990 MODEL CODE COMPARISON

The Canon is Canon 3A.

The Comment is new.

EXPLANATION OF BLACK LETTER

1. Deletion of heading

2. Change "judicial duties" to "duties of judicial office"

The wording was changed to emphasize that its application goes beyond adjudicative functions to reach the broader scope of responsibilities that accompany the judicial office.

3. Addition of "shall"

The Commission wanted to make clear that this rule was doing more than making the descriptive point that judicial functions do take precedence; by inserting the term "shall," the Code clearly imposes an ethical duty on judges to give priority to the duties of judicial office.

4. Replace "all the judge's other activities" with "all of a judge's personal and extrajudicial activities"

This change was made to avoid confusion. Judges should give priority to their judicial duties, broadly defined to reach not only adjudication but also the other duties of judicial office (such as administration and discipline), and the Commission wanted to be clear that the matters of secondary importance were limited to personal and extrajudicial activities.

5. Deletion of third sentence

This sentence was deleted as unnecessary.

EXPLANATION OF COMMENTS

[1] New Comment

This Comment has been added to highlight the relationship between Canon 2 and Canon 3: because judges must disqualify themselves from cases in which they have a conflict of interest, they must conduct their extrajudicial activities in ways that minimize their need to disqualify themselves.

[2] New Comment

This comment has been added, along with Comment 6 to Rule 1.2, to underscore the value of judicial outreach. Although undertaking activities that encourage public understanding of and confidence in the justice system is not a duty of judicial office per se, such activities promote public confidence in the courts and to that extent facilitate the courts' mission.

RULE 2.2 Impartiality and Fairness

A judge shall uphold and apply the law,* and shall perform all duties of judicial office fairly and impartially.*

Comment

[1] To ensure impartiality and fairness to all parties, a judge must be objective and open-minded.

[2] Although each judge comes to the bench with a unique background and personal philosophy, a judge must interpret and apply the law without regard to whether the judge approves or disapproves of the law in question.

[3] When applying and interpreting the law, a judge sometimes may make good-faith errors of fact or law. Errors of this kind do not violate this Rule.

[4] It is not a violation of this Rule for a judge to make reasonable accommodations to ensure pro se litigants the opportunity to have their matters fairly heard.

RULE 2.2—REPORTER'S EXPLANATION OF CHANGES†

1990 MODEL CODE COMPARISON

The Rule is the first half of the first sentence of Canon 3B(2).

Comments [1]–[4] are new.

EXPLANATION OF BLACK LETTER

New Rule on upholding the law

This Rule is taken from the first half of the first sentence of Canon 3B(2), which spoke in terms of judges being "faithful" to the law. In its stead, the Commission substituted the phrase "uphold and apply the law." In the Commission's view, "fidelity" lacked clear meaning; the essential point was and remains that judges should interpret and apply the law as they understand it to be written, and the Rule has been revised to make that point more clearly.

Although there is some similarity between this Rule and Rule 1.1, their purposes are fundamentally different. Whereas Rule 1.1 addresses the judge's duty to comply with the law, this Rule directs the judge to follow the rule of law when deciding cases. The duty to follow the law is inextricably linked to a corresponding duty to be fair and impartial. Although the duty to decide cases with impartiality was implicit in numerous provisions in the former Code, it was not stated explicitly. This Rule corrects that oversight and does so by linking the judge's obligation to decide cases with impartiality to a corresponding duty to apply the law.

EXPLANATION OF COMMENTS

[1] This new Comment defines impartiality with reference to the two definitions of impartiality accepted by the Supreme Court in *Republican Party of Minnesota v. White*, lack of bias toward a participant in the judicial process, and open-mindedness.

[2] Comments [2] and [3] were inserted to underscore the distinction between the judge whose honest understanding of the law is influenced by upbringing, education, and life experience, which is neither avoidable nor improper, and the judge who disregards the law.

[3] Comment [3] underscores the point that judges sometime commit good faith errors of fact or law, which does not violate this rule. Rather, the rule is directed at judges who deliberately or repeatedly disregard court orders or other clear requirements of law.

[4] Throughout the life of the Commission, some witnesses urged the Commission to create special rules enabling judges to assist pro se litigants, while others urged the Commission to disregard calls for such rules. This Comment makes clear that judges do not compromise their impartiality when they make reasonable accommodations to pro se litigants who may be completely unfamiliar with the legal system and the litigation process. To the contrary, by leveling the playing field, such judges ensure that pro se litigants

† The "Reporters' Explanations of Changes" have not been approved by the ABA Joint Commission to Evaluate the Model Code of Judicial Conduct. They have been drafted by the Commission's Reporters, based on the proceedings and record of the Commission, solely to inform the ABA House of Delegates about each of the proposed amendments to the Model Code prior to their being considered at the ABA 2007 Midyear Meeting. THEY ARE NOT TO BE ADOPTED AS PART OF THE MODEL CODE.

receive the fair hearing to which they are entitled. On the other hand, judges should resist unreasonable demands for assistance that might give an unrepresented party an unfair advantage.

RULE 2.3 Bias, Prejudice, and Harassment

(A) A judge shall perform the duties of judicial office, including administrative duties, without bias or prejudice.

(B) A judge shall not, in the performance of judicial duties, by words or conduct manifest bias or prejudice, or engage in harassment, including but not limited to bias, prejudice, or harassment based upon race, sex, gender, religion, national origin, ethnicity, disability, age, sexual orientation, marital status, socioeconomic status, or political affiliation, and shall not permit court staff, court officials, or others subject to the judge's direction and control to do so.

(C) A judge shall require lawyers in proceedings before the court to refrain from manifesting bias or prejudice, or engaging in harassment, based upon attributes including but not limited to race, sex, gender, religion, national origin, ethnicity, disability, age, sexual orientation, marital status, socioeconomic status, or political affiliation, against parties, witnesses, lawyers, or others.

(D) The restrictions of paragraphs (B) and (C) do not preclude judges or lawyers from making legitimate reference to the listed factors, or similar factors, when they are relevant to an issue in a proceeding.

Comment

[1] A judge who manifests bias or prejudice in a proceeding impairs the fairness of the proceeding and brings the judiciary into disrepute.

[2] Examples of manifestations of bias or prejudice include but are not limited to epithets; slurs; demeaning nicknames; negative stereotyping; attempted humor based upon stereotypes; threatening, intimidating, or hostile acts; suggestions of connections between race, ethnicity, or nationality and crime; and irrelevant references to personal characteristics. Even facial expressions and body language can convey to parties and lawyers in the proceeding, jurors, the media, and others an appearance of bias or prejudice. A judge must avoid conduct that may reasonably be perceived as prejudiced or biased.

[3] Harassment, as referred to in paragraphs (B) and (C), is verbal or physical conduct that denigrates or shows hostility or aversion toward a person on bases such as race, sex, gender, religion, national origin, ethnicity, disability, age, sexual orientation, marital status, socioeconomic status, or political affiliation.

[4] Sexual harassment includes but is not limited to sexual advances, requests for sexual favors, and other verbal or physical conduct of a sexual nature that is unwelcome.

RULE 2.3—REPORTER'S EXPLANATION OF CHANGES†

1990 MODEL CODE COMPARISON

Paragraph (A) is taken from the first sentence of Canon 3B(5).

Paragraph (B) is taken from the second sentence of Canon 3B(5).

† The "Reporters' Explanations of Changes" have not been approved by the ABA Joint Commission to Evaluate the Model Code of Judicial Conduct. They have been drafted by the Commission's Reporters, based on the proceedings and record of the Commission, solely to inform the ABA House of Delegates about each of the proposed amendments to the Model Code prior to their being considered at the ABA 2007 Midyear Meeting. THEY ARE NOT TO BE ADOPTED AS PART OF THE MODEL CODE.

Paragraph (C) is taken from Canon 3B(6).

Paragraph (D) is taken from Canon 3B(6).

Comment [1] is the second sentence of the second paragraph of Commentary to Canon 3B(5).

Comment [2] is the third and fourth sentences of the second paragraph of Commentary to Canon 3B(5).

Comments [3] and [4] are new.

The first paragraph of Commentary to Canon 3B(5) was deleted.

EXPLANATION OF BLACK LETTER

1. Paragraphs (B) and (C): Addition of "harassment"

Canon 3B(5) required judges to avoid bias and prejudice, but included nothing in the black letter about harassment, which it relegated to a discussion in the Commentary, limited to sexual harassment. The Commission agreed that harassment was a form of bias or prejudice that the Rules proscribed but wanted to expand it beyond sexual harassment to reach other forms of harassment as well, for which reason it deleted the term "sexual" from the Commentary in an early draft. Witnesses, however, argued that the proposed change could be construed to have an unintended consequence. By deleting the reference to "sexual" harassment per se, the change could be construed as deleting sexual harassment from the range of behaviors barred by the Rules, or at least diminishing its significance. The Commission remained of the view that harassment—including but not limited to sexual harassment—should be proscribed by the Rules. It was, however, persuaded both that sexual harassment deserved special mention, given the significance of the problem, and that harassment per se was sufficiently distinct from bias and prejudice to deserve separate mention in the black letter of the Rule.

2. Paragraphs (B) and (C): Additions to list of factors upon which bias, prejudice, or harassment can be based

Although the Rule prohibits bias, prejudice, or harassment on any basis, it includes an illustrative list, to which four new items were added: gender ("sex" is a term of art employed in sex discrimination statutes, but may not capture bias, prejudice, or harassment against trans-gendered individuals); ethnicity (which the Commission regarded as distinct from national origin; for example, in the case of an Arab-Canadian, discrimination on the basis of Arab ancestry would relate to ethnicity, while discrimination based on Canadian derivation would relate to national origin); marital status (the Commission was made aware of instances in which judges had berated a party for cohabiting or having a child outside of wedlock); and political affiliation (as, for example, when a judge displays animus toward plaintiffs affiliated with a particular political party).

3. Paragraph (D): Legitimate reference to listed factors

When a case before the judge raises issues of bias or prejudice, the judge must be in a position to discuss such issues without fear of violating this rule, for which reason an exception has been created in the text. The substance of this provision formerly was in Canon 3B(6).

EXPLANATION OF COMMENTS

The first paragraph of Commentary to Canon 3B(5) was deleted given the new black letter provision prohibiting harassment and new Comments [2]–[4].

[1] Comment [1] is the second sentence of the second paragraph of Commentary to Canon 3B(5), but with the phrase "on any basis" deleted. The phrase "or prejudice" was added to reach not only favoritism or opposition by a judge to an idea, which is the more common understanding of "bias," but also specially favoring or opposing individuals, which is generally contemplated by the term "prejudice."

[2] The new language was added after several witnesses urged the Commission to provide some illustrations of bias and to better inform judges of what bias entails and what some of the most common bias-related problems are. The list is explicitly non-exclusive and self-explanatory. The last two sentences

are taken from the second paragraph of the comment to Canon 3B(5). The terms "in addition to oral communication" and "judicial" were deleted as excess language.

The term "behavior" was replaced with "conduct" in the last sentence for consistency with the rest of the Rules. The last sentence now instructs judges to avoid conduct that may be perceived as "prejudiced or biased" in order to be more comprehensive and consistent with the thrust of the Rule. The addition of the term "reasonably" in the last sentence is consistent with Title VII jurisprudence, which separates the merely vulgar from the deeply offensive.

[3] This new Comment defines harassment and underscores that the prohibition in the black letter includes, but is not limited to, sexual harassment.

[4] This new Comment separately elaborates on the meaning of "sexual harassment." Although the Rule forbids all forms of harassment, witnesses before the Commission were emphatic about the need to single out sexual harassment for special mention, given the nature, extent, and history of the problem.

RULE 2.4 External Influences on Judicial Conduct

(A) A judge shall not be swayed by public clamor or fear of criticism.

(B) A judge shall not permit family, social, political, financial, or other interests or relationships to influence the judge's judicial conduct or judgment.

(C) A judge shall not convey or permit others to convey the impression that any person or organization is in a position to influence the judge.

Comment

[1] An independent judiciary requires that judges decide cases according to the law and facts, without regard to whether particular laws or litigants are popular or unpopular with the public, the media, government officials, or the judge's friends or family. Confidence in the judiciary is eroded if judicial decision making is perceived to be subject to inappropriate outside influences.

RULE 2.4—REPORTER'S EXPLANATION OF CHANGES†

1990 MODEL CODE COMPARISON

Paragraph (A) is the second sentence of Canon 3B(2).

Paragraph (B) is the first sentence of Canon 2B.

Paragraph (C) is the second half of the second sentence of Canon 2B.

Comment [1] is new.

EXPLANATION OF BLACK LETTER

1. Paragraph (B): Addition of "financial"

   Paragraph (B) is the first sentence of Canon 2B.

   "Financial" relationships were added to the list on influences that judges should avoid. Although the pre-existing rule referred to "other" relationships, the Commission regarded financial relationships as important enough to warrant separate mention.

† The "Reporters' Explanations of Changes" have not been approved by the ABA Joint Commission to Evaluate the Model Code of Judicial Conduct. They have been drafted by the Commission's Reporters, based on the proceedings and record of the Commission, solely to inform the ABA House of Delegates about each of the proposed amendments to the Model Code prior to their being considered at the ABA 2007 Midyear Meeting. THEY ARE NOT TO BE ADOPTED AS PART OF THE MODEL CODE.

2. Paragraph (C): Expansion of scope of Rule

The scope of the Rule was expanded slightly. As previously drafted, the Rule forbade a judge from permitting others to convey the impression that "they," meaning the "others," were in a position to influence the judge. As a technical matter, that prohibition did not reach the situation in which "others" conveyed the impression that a third person was in a position to influence the judge, and the change has been made to cover that scenario.

The Commission felt that the term "special," modifying position, was at best a redundancy and at worst added confusion by creating the impression that there might be persons who are in a position to influence the court.

EXPLANATION OF COMMENTS

[1] Comment [1] is new.

This new Comment is intended to underscore the general purpose underlying paragraphs (A) and (B) by linking the duty not to be swayed by the public, friends, or family to the judge's primary obligation to follow the law and facts impartially.

RULE 2.5 Competence, Diligence, and Cooperation

(A) A judge shall perform judicial and administrative duties, competently and diligently.

(B) A judge shall cooperate with other judges and court officials in the administration of court business.

Comment

[1] Competence in the performance of judicial duties requires the legal knowledge, skill, thoroughness, and preparation reasonably necessary to perform a judge's responsibilities of judicial office.

[2] A judge should seek the necessary docket time, court staff, expertise, and resources to discharge all adjudicative and administrative responsibilities.

[3] Prompt disposition of the court's business requires a judge to devote adequate time to judicial duties, to be punctual in attending court and expeditious in determining matters under submission, and to take reasonable measures to ensure that court officials, litigants, and their lawyers cooperate with the judge to that end.

[4] In disposing of matters promptly and efficiently, a judge must demonstrate due regard for the rights of parties to be heard and to have issues resolved without unnecessary cost or delay. A judge should monitor and supervise cases in ways that reduce or eliminate dilatory practices, avoidable delays, and unnecessary costs.

RULE 2.5—REPORTER'S EXPLANATION OF CHANGES†

1990 MODEL CODE COMPARISON

Part A is taken from Canons 3B(2) and 3C(1). Part B is the second half of Canon 3C(1).

† "Reporters' Explanations of Changes" have not been approved by the ABA Joint Commission to Evaluate the Model Code of Judicial Conduct. They have been drafted by the Commission's Reporters, based on the proceedings and record of the Commission, solely to inform the ABA House of Delegates about each of the proposed amendments to the Model Code prior to their being considered at the ABA 2007 Midyear Meeting. THEY ARE NOT TO BE ADOPTED AS PART OF THE MODEL CODE.

Comments [1] and [2] are new.

Comment [3] is the second paragraph of Commentary to Canon 3B(8).

Comment [4] is the first three sentences of Commentary to 3B(8).

EXPLANATION OF BLACK LETTER

1. New Rule combining duties of competence and diligence

This Rule governs competence, formerly governed by Canon 3B(2), and diligence, formerly governed by Canon 3C and makes the requirements applicable to both adjudicative and administrative duties of a judge. The duty of competence is analogous to a lawyer's professional duty of competence, while the duty to apply the law is discussed elsewhere (the term "fidelity" is no longer used). Corresponding Commentary was moved accordingly. The phrasing was changed from passive to active voice for stylistic reasons.

2. Expansion of Rule

The black letter Rule was clarified to make plain that the duty at issue was one of diligence, and expanded slightly to extend the duty of diligence to all judicial duties and not just "judicial matters," which is generally understood to be limited to case adjudication.

3. Change Rule standard

The obligation to cooperate with others in judicial administration was upgraded from hortatory to mandatory. Efficient and effective administration is a duty of the judicial office, the proper execution of which necessitates cooperation among the judges of the court.

EXPLANATION OF COMMENTS

[1] Comment [1] was added simply to define competence and underscore its fundamental importance in relation to core judicial functions.

[2] New Comment [2] was added to emphasize that the duty to perform judicial and administrative duties competently and diligently requires judges to devote time to proper time management and use of court resources and personnel.

RULE 2.6 Ensuring the Right to Be Heard

(A) A judge shall accord to every person who has a legal interest in a proceeding, or that person's lawyer, the right to be heard according to law.*

(B) A judge may encourage parties to a proceeding and their lawyers to settle matters in dispute but shall not act in a manner that coerces any party into settlement.

Comment

[1] The right to be heard is an essential component of a fair and impartial system of justice. Substantive rights of litigants can be protected only if procedures protecting the right to be heard are observed.

[2] The judge plays an important role in overseeing the settlement of disputes, but should be careful that efforts to further settlement do not undermine any party's right to be heard according to law. The judge should keep in mind the effect that the judge's participation in settlement discussions may have, not only on the judge's own views of the case, but also on the perceptions of the lawyers and the parties if the case remains with the judge after settlement efforts are unsuccessful. Among the factors that a judge should consider when deciding upon an appropriate settlement practice for a case are (1) whether the parties have requested or voluntarily consented to a certain level of participation by the judge in settlement discussions, (2) whether the parties and their counsel are relatively sophisticated in legal matters, (3) whether the case will be tried by the judge or a jury, (4) whether the parties participate with their counsel in settlement discussions, (5) whether any parties are unrepresented by counsel, and (6) whether the matter is civil or criminal.

[3] Judges must be mindful of the effect settlement discussions can have, not only on their objectivity and impartiality, but also on the appearance of their objectivity and impartiality. Despite a judge's best efforts, there may be instances when information obtained during settlement discussions could influence a judge's decision making during trial, and, in such instances, the judge should consider whether disqualification may be appropriate. See Rule 2.11(A)(1).

RULE 2.6—REPORTER'S EXPLANATION OF CHANGES†

1990 MODEL CODE COMPARISON

Paragraph A of the Rule is 3B(7),

Paragraph B of the Rule is 3B(8) commentary.

Comments [1], [2], and [3] are new.

EXPLANATION OF BLACK LETTER

1. Paragraph (B): New paragraph on settlements

This new paragraph was added in recognition of the fact that out-of-court settlement is a commonly used method of case resolution. It is important for judges to remember that a litigant's right to be heard can inadvertently be impaired by a judge who is overzealous in encouraging an out-of-court resolution. Accordingly, the Rule draws a line between encouraging settlement, which is permitted, and coercing settlement, which is not. The Commission heard testimony from some witnesses who went further, urging the adoption of rules that would prohibit judges from presiding at trial over cases with respect to which they had previously conducted settlement negotiations that ultimately were unsuccessful. Although several members of the Commission agreed that, as a general matter, it was the better practice for judges not to try cases they had attempted to settle given the risk that statements the judge made during settlement negotiations might later be construed as lack of impartiality, the Commission declined to adopt such a rule. The Commission ultimately concluded that such an issue was better left for rules of practice and procedure than ethics.

EXPLANATION OF COMMENTS

[1] New Comment [1] emphasizes what is implicit in the Rule, that judges' duties include ensuring that those entitled have their day in court. In so doing, the Comment underscores the relationship between substantive and procedural justice, i.e. that protection of substantive rights depends in part on respecting procedural rights to be heard.

[2] New Comment [2] provides judges with guidance in conducting settlement talks. It undertakes to sensitize judges to concerns that can arise when they lead settlement discussions and to advise judges on what factors to take into account when deciding how to oversee settlement.

[3] New Comment [3] underscores the point that sometimes events transpiring during settlement talks may bias judges toward a party or create an appearance of bias that necessitates disqualification.

---

† The "Reporters' Explanations of Changes" have not been approved by the ABA Joint Commission to Evaluate the Model Code of Judicial Conduct. They have been drafted by the Commission's Reporters, based on the proceedings and record of the Commission, solely to inform the ABA House of Delegates about each of the proposed amendments to the Model Code prior to their being considered at the ABA 2007 Midyear Meeting. THEY ARE NOT TO BE ADOPTED AS PART OF THE MODEL CODE.

RULE 2.7 Responsibility to Decide

A judge shall hear and decide matters assigned to the judge, except when disqualification is required by Rule 2.11 or other law.*

Comment

[1] Judges must be available to decide the matters that come before the court. Although there are times when disqualification is necessary to protect the rights of litigants and preserve public confidence in the independence, integrity, and impartiality of the judiciary, judges must be available to decide matters that come before the courts. Unwarranted disqualification may bring public disfavor to the court and to the judge personally. The dignity of the court, the judge's respect for fulfillment of judicial duties, and a proper concern for the burdens that may be imposed upon the judge's colleagues require that a judge not use disqualification to avoid cases that present difficult, controversial, or unpopular issues.

RULE 2.7—REPORTER'S EXPLANATION OF CHANGES†

1990 MODEL CODE COMPARISON

The Rule is Canon 3B(1).

Comment [1] is new.

EXPLANATION OF BLACK LETTER

Clarification of instances requiring disqualification

1. The Rule is Canon 3B(1), with a slight modification to cross-reference the disqualification rule explicitly and to acknowledge that in some instances disqualification may be required by other law.

EXPLANATION OF COMMENTS

[1] New Comment [1] was added to emphasize that although disqualification remains an important and at times essential option for a judge, it should not be misused as a tool to avoid deciding cases that the judge may regard as unpleasant or unpopular. The effective administration of justice depends on judges remaining available to hear the cases that parties file, and this Comment is intended to remind judges of that concern when they approach issues of disqualification.

RULE 2.8 Decorum, Demeanor, and Communication With Jurors

(A) A judge shall require order and decorum in proceedings before the court.

(B) A judge shall be patient, dignified, and courteous to litigants, jurors, witnesses, lawyers, court staff, court officials, and others with whom the judge deals in an official capacity, and shall require similar conduct of lawyers, court staff, court officials, and others subject to the judge's direction and control.

(C) A judge shall not commend or criticize jurors for their verdict other than in a court order or opinion in a proceeding.

† The "Reporters' Explanations of Changes" have not been approved by the ABA Joint Commission to Evaluate the Model Code of Judicial Conduct. They have been drafted by the Commission's Reporters, based on the proceedings and record of the Commission, solely to inform the ABA House of Delegates about each of the proposed amendments to the Model Code prior to their being considered at the ABA 2007 Midyear Meeting. THEY ARE NOT TO BE ADOPTED AS PART OF THE MODEL CODE.

Comment

[1] The duty to hear all proceedings with patience and courtesy is not inconsistent with the duty imposed in Rule 2.5 to dispose promptly of the business of the court. Judges can be efficient and businesslike while being patient and deliberate.

[2] Commending or criticizing jurors for their verdict may imply a judicial expectation in future cases and may impair a juror's ability to be fair and impartial in a subsequent case.

[3] A judge who is not otherwise prohibited by law from doing so may meet with jurors who choose to remain after trial but should be careful not to discuss the merits of the case.

RULE 2.8—REPORTER'S EXPLANATION OF CHANGES†

1990 MODEL CODE COMPARISON

Paragraph (A) is Canon 3B(3).

Paragraph (B) is Canon 3B(4).

Paragraph (C) is the first sentence of Canon 3B(11).

Comment [1] is the Commentary to Canon 3B(4).

Comment [2] is the Commentary to Canon 3B(11).

Comment [3] is new.

EXPLANATION OF BLACK LETTER

1. Paragraph (B): Extension of duty of courtesy

Paragraph (B) is Canon 3B(4), modified to extend the duty of courtesy to court staff, where episodes of abusive behavior occasionally have arisen. "Court officials" was added to be consistent with the list used later in the same paragraph.

2. Paragraph (C): Expressing appreciation to jurors

The Commission moved discussion permitting judges to express appreciation to jurors from the black letter Rule to the Comment on the grounds that it was advice not needed in the black letter.

EXPLANATION OF COMMENTS

[3] New Comment [3] was added in light of the growing recognition that judicial outreach is a valued part of the judicial role and includes outreach to jurors. The Comment makes clear that judges can commend jurors for their service and that the prohibition on judges commending or criticizing the jury for their verdict does not foreclose other communications between judges and jurors. To the contrary, the Commission saw value in creating an opportunity for the judge to learn more about the jury's experience, as long as the merits of the case were not discussed.

---

† The "Reporters' Explanations of Changes" have not been approved by the ABA Joint Commission to Evaluate the Model Code of Judicial Conduct. They have been drafted by the Commission's Reporters, based on the proceedings and record of the Commission, solely to inform the ABA House of Delegates about each of the proposed amendments to the Model Code prior to their being considered at the ABA 2007 Midyear Meeting. THEY ARE NOT TO BE ADOPTED AS PART OF THE MODEL CODE.

RULE 2.9 Ex Parte Communications

(A) A judge shall not initiate, permit, or consider ex parte communications, or consider other communications made to the judge outside the presence of the parties or their lawyers, concerning a pending* or impending matter,* except as follows:

(1) When circumstances require it, ex parte communication for scheduling, administrative, or emergency purposes, which does not address substantive matters, is permitted, provided:

(a) the judge reasonably believes that no party will gain a procedural, substantive, or tactical advantage as a result of the ex parte communication; and

(b) the judge makes provision promptly to notify all other parties of the substance of the ex parte communication, and gives the parties an opportunity to respond.

(2) A judge may obtain the written advice of a disinterested expert on the law applicable to a proceeding before the judge, if the judge gives advance notice to the parties of the person to be consulted and the subject matter of the advice to be solicited, and affords the parties a reasonable opportunity to object and respond to the notice and to the advice received.

(3) A judge may consult with court staff and court officials whose functions are to aid the judge in carrying out the judge's adjudicative responsibilities, or with other judges, provided the judge makes reasonable efforts to avoid receiving factual information that is not part of the record, and does not abrogate the responsibility personally to decide the matter.

(4) A judge may, with the consent of the parties, confer separately with the parties and their lawyers in an effort to settle matters pending before the judge.

(5) A judge may initiate, permit, or consider any ex parte communication when expressly authorized by law* to do so.

(B) If a judge inadvertently receives an unauthorized ex parte communication bearing upon the substance of a matter, the judge shall make provision promptly to notify the parties of the substance of the communication and provide the parties with an opportunity to respond.

(C) A judge shall not investigate facts in a matter independently, and shall consider only the evidence presented and any facts that may properly be judicially noticed.

(D) A judge shall make reasonable efforts, including providing appropriate supervision, to ensure that this Rule is not violated by court staff, court officials, and others subject to the judge's direction and control.

Comment

[1] To the extent reasonably possible, all parties or their lawyers shall be included in communications with a judge.

[2] Whenever the presence of a party or notice to a party is required by this Rule, it is the party's lawyer, or if the party is unrepresented, the party, who is to be present or to whom notice is to be given.

[3] The proscription against communications concerning a proceeding includes communications with lawyers, law teachers, and other persons who are not participants in the proceeding, except to the limited extent permitted by this Rule.

[4] A judge may initiate, permit, or consider ex parte communications expressly authorized by law, such as when serving on therapeutic or problem-solving courts, mental health courts, or drug courts. In this

capacity, judges may assume a more interactive role with parties, treatment providers, probation officers, social workers, and others.

[5] A judge may consult with other judges on pending matters, but must avoid ex parte discussions of a case with judges who have previously been disqualified from hearing the matter, and with judges who have appellate jurisdiction over the matter.

[6] The prohibition against a judge investigating the facts in a matter extends to information available in all mediums, including electronic.

[7] A judge may consult ethics advisory committees, outside counsel, or legal experts concerning the judge's compliance with this Code. Such consultations are not subject to the restrictions of paragraph (A)(2).

RULE 2.9—REPORTER'S EXPLANATION OF CHANGES†

1990 MODEL CODE COMPARISON

Paragraph (A) is the second sentence of Canon 3B(7).

Paragraph (A)(1) is Canon 3B(7)(a).

Paragraph (A)(1)(a) is Canon 3B(7)(a)(i).

Paragraph (A)(1)(b) is Canon 3B(7)(a)(ii).

Paragraph (A)(2) is a modified version of Canon 3B(7)(b).

Paragraph (A)(3) is Canon 3B(7)(c).

Paragraph (A)(4) is Canon 3B(7)(d).

Paragraph (A)(5) is Canon 3B(7)(e).

Paragraph (B) is new.

Paragraph (C) is paragraph 6 of the Commentary to Canon 3B(7).

Paragraph (D) is from the eighth paragraph of Commentary to Canon 3B(7).

Comment [1] is the second paragraph of Commentary to Canon 3B(7).

Comment [2] is the third paragraph of Commentary to Canon 3B(7).

Comment [3] is the first paragraph of Commentary to Canon 3B(7).

Comments [4]–[7] are new.

The fourth, fifth, seventh and ninth paragraphs of Commentary to Canon 3B(7) were deleted.

EXPLANATION OF BLACK LETTER

1. "Issues on the merits" was deleted as duplicative; the Rule's exclusion of "substantive matters" from the scope of permissible ex parte communications would necessarily subsume all "issues on the merits." Replacing "authorized" with "permitted" is stylistic and does not change the substance of the provision.

2. Paragraph (A)(1)(a): Addition of "substantive"

"Substantive" was added in recognition of the fact that a scheduling, administrative, or emergency ex parte communication that is unrelated to substantive matters per se could nonetheless, in some instances, enable a party to gain an inappropriate advantage related to the substance or merits of the case.

---

† The "Reporters' Explanations of Changes" have not been approved by the ABA Joint Commission to Evaluate the Model Code of Judicial Conduct. They have been drafted by the Commission's Reporters, based on the proceedings and record of the Commission, solely to inform the ABA House of Delegates about each of the proposed amendments to the Model Code prior to their being considered at the ABA 2007 Midyear Meeting. THEY ARE NOT TO BE ADOPTED AS PART OF THE MODEL CODE.

3. Paragraph (A)(1)(b): Addition of delegation

Paragraph (A)(1)(b) is Canon 3B(7)(a)(ii), but revised to add the notion that a judge may delegate the notification obligation to others.

4. Paragraph (A)(2): Addition of requirement of advance notice

Paragraph (A)(2) is Canon 3B(7)(b), but modified to add the requirement of advance notice. Under the 1990 Code, a judge could consult with an outside legal expert ex parte before notifying the parties. If such a consultation was problematic for reasons that had not occurred to the judge, post-consultation notification to the parties would come too late to prevent the problem from arising. As revised, the Rule requires the judge to notify the parties before the ex parte contact is made.

5. Paragraph (A)(3): Addition of limitation on consultation

Paragraph (A)(3) is a modified version of Canon 3B(7)(c). The permissibility of a judge's consultation on a case with other court personnel was qualified to include the common sense limitations that the judge must not relinquish ultimate responsibility for deciding the case and, in the course of such consultation, should be careful not to acquire improper factual information.

6. Paragraph (B): Creation of new paragraph on inadvertent communications

New Paragraph (B) addresses an issue not covered by the 1990 Code. In situations where a judge inadvertently receives an unauthorized ex parte communication, the new Rule directs the judge to notify all the other parties of the substance of the communication and give them an opportunity to respond. In an age when misdirected faxes and email are common, the need for some provision to deal with inadvertent disclosures of ex parte information impressed the Commission as necessary.

7. Paragraph (C): Creation of new paragraph prohibiting investigation

In the Commission's view, former Commentary prohibiting a judge from undertaking independent factual investigations was largely unsupported by the Rule itself and warranted inclusion as part of the Rule. Moreover, the judge's duty to consider only the evidence presented is a defining feature of the judge's role in an adversarial system and warrants explicit mention in the black letter. The term "must" was replaced with "shall," both for consistency and to make clear that compliance with the proscription is absolute. Specific acknowledgement of the category of evidence or facts that are judicially noticed was considered a beneficial clarification, and was therefore added to this paragraph.

8. Paragraph (D): Creation of new paragraph on avoiding communication through staff

Paragraph (D) was moved to the black letter from the eighth paragraph of Commentary to Canon 3B(7). In the Commission's view, a judge's duty to take steps to avoid violating the Rule against ex parte communications through staff could not be inferred from the black letter of the former Rule.

EXPLANATION OF COMMENTS

[3] Comment [3] is the first paragraph of Commentary to Canon 3B(7), with the addition of "by this Rule," a revision made for stylistic reasons and not intended to change substantive meaning.

[4] New comment dealing with problem-solving and therapeutic courts

The Commission heard a great deal of testimony about therapeutic or problem-solving courts. In these non-traditional courts that hear matters on an increasingly broad array of issues ranging from drugs to juvenile justice, domestic relations, and crime, judges communicate with parties, service providers (such as social workers), and others in ways that can be in tension with traditional rules governing ex parte communications. Several witnesses thus urged the Commission to create special rules for such courts. The Commission was reluctant to do so because therapeutic courts were too many and varied for the Commission to devise rules of general applicability. Instead, the Commission drafted this new Comment, which calls special attention to the exception for ex parte communications authorized by law and notes that this exception enables individual jurisdictions to devise special rules for their therapeutic courts.

[5] New comment regarding judge-to-judge consultations

New Comment [5] was added to clarify that while a judge may consult with other judges about a case, the judge should not consult with judges who have been disqualified from hearing the case. If, for whatever reason, a judge is disqualified from hearing a given matter, it would defeat the purpose of the disqualification rules to permit another judge to confer with the disqualified colleague. In addition, the Comment clarifies that a judge should not consult on a matter with any judge having appellate jurisdiction over the matter.

[6] New Comment containing prohibition against independently investigating facts.

Given the ease with which factual investigation can now be accomplished via electronic databases and the Internet, the risk that a judge or the judge's staff could inadvertently violate Rules 2.9(B) and (C) has heightened considerably. The need for vigilance on the part of judges has increased accordingly.

[7] New Comment regarding judges seeking ex parte guidance regarding compliance with Rules

The Commission wanted to make clear that judges may seek ex parte guidance concerning their compliance with the Code without violating this Rule. Judges routinely consult ethics advisory committees, counsel and outside experts concerning their obligations under the Code in a given context. Because such consultations are not problematic, New Comment [7] was added accordingly.

Deletion of the fourth, fifth, seventh and ninth paragraphs of Commentary to Canon 3B(7)

The Commission deleted the reference to requests for amicus briefs in the fourth paragraph of Canon 3B(7) Commentary as being "often desirable procedures," because it is not an ethical concern.

The fifth paragraph of Canon 3(B)(7) Commentary concerning clearly acceptable purposes for ex parte communications was deleted because it is redundant of the black letter Rule.

The Commission decided to delete Commentary language in the seventh paragraph of Canon 3B(7) authorizing a judge to request that a party submit proposed findings of fact and conclusions of law as long as the other party was given an opportunity to respond to the submission. In the Commission's view, the permissibility of the practice was so free from doubt as to render the Comment unnecessary.

The Commission deleted the ninth paragraph of Canon 3B(7) Commentary. The subject matter, keeping records of communications, is an administrative, rather than an ethical matter.

RULE 2.10 Judicial Statements on Pending and Impending Cases

(A) A judge shall not make any public statement that might reasonably be expected to affect the outcome or impair the fairness of a matter pending* or impending* in any court, or make any nonpublic statement that might substantially interfere with a fair trial or hearing.

(B) A judge shall not, in connection with cases, controversies, or issues that are likely to come before the court, make pledges, promises, or commitments that are inconsistent with the impartial* performance of the adjudicative duties of judicial office.

(C) A judge shall require court staff, court officials, and others subject to the judge's direction and control to refrain from making statements that the judge would be prohibited from making by paragraphs (A) and (B).

(D) Notwithstanding the restrictions in paragraph (A), a judge may make public statements in the course of official duties, may explain court procedures, and may comment on any proceeding in which the judge is a litigant in a personal capacity.

(E) Subject to the requirements of paragraph (A), a judge may respond directly or through a third party to allegations in the media or elsewhere concerning the judge's conduct in a matter.

Comment

[1] This Rule's restrictions on judicial speech are essential to the maintenance of the independence, integrity, and impartiality of the judiciary.

[2] This Rule does not prohibit a judge from commenting on proceedings in which the judge is a litigant in a personal capacity, or represents a *client* as permitted by these Rules. In cases in which the judge is a litigant in an official capacity, such as a writ of mandamus, the judge must not comment publicly.

[3] Depending upon the circumstances, the judge should consider whether it may be preferable for a third party, rather than the judge, to respond or issue statements in connection with allegations concerning the judge's conduct in a matter.

RULE 2.10—REPORTER'S EXPLANATION OF CHANGES†

1990 MODEL CODE COMPARISON

Paragraph (A) is the first sentence of Canon 3B(9).

Paragraph (B) is Canon 3B(10).

Paragraph (C) is the second sentence of Canon 3B(9).

Paragraph (D) is the third and fourth sentences of Canon 3B(9).

Paragraph (E) is new.

Comment [1] is the first sentence of the Commentary to Canon 3B(10).

Comment [2] is new.

Comment [3] is the fifth through seventh sentences of the Commentary to Canon 3B(10).

EXPLANATION OF BLACK LETTER

1. <u>Paragraphs (A) and (C): Separation of former Canon</u>

Former Canon 3B(9) was subdivided into two separate subsections (addressing the judge's statements and the statements of staff, court officers, and others). Paragraph (A) is the first sentence of Canon 3B(9), but was reworded to improve clarity.

In Paragraph (C), the phrase "court personnel" was replaced with "court staff, court officials and others" to broaden the judge's duty to prohibit others from making inappropriate comment on pending and impending cases to include all persons within the judge's control regardless of whether such persons technically qualified as court personnel.

2. In Paragraph (B), "judicial" was inserted before "office" for clarity.

3. <u>Paragraph (E): Adding language concerning responding to media</u>

Judges are justifiably reluctant to speak about pending cases. However, the Commission wanted to make clear that when a judge's conduct is called into question, the judge may respond as long as the response will not affect the fairness of the proceeding.

EXPLANATION OF COMMENTS

<u>Deletion of reference to Model Rules of Professional Conduct</u>

In the Commentary to Canon 3B(10), the cross-reference to the Model Rules of Professional Conduct was deleted as unnecessary.

---

† The "Reporters' Explanations of Changes" have not been approved by the ABA Joint Commission to Evaluate the Model Code of Judicial Conduct. They have been drafted by the Commission's Reporters, based on the proceedings and record of the Commission, solely to inform the ABA House of Delegates about each of the proposed amendments to the Model Code prior to their being considered at the ABA 2007 Midyear Meeting. THEY ARE NOT TO BE ADOPTED AS PART OF THE MODEL CODE.

Substance of Canon 3B(11) and its Commentary moved

The Commission moved Canon 3B(11) and its Commentary, relating to judges commending or criticizing jurors, to Rule 2.8, the Rule devoted to judicial decorum, demeanor, and communication with jurors.

The definitions of "pending" and "impending" in Commentary to Canon 3B(10) were moved to Terminology.

Comment [2] suggests that it may be appropriate in some instances for statements that explain or defend the role or action of a judge in a particular matter to be made by a third person, rather than by the judge. This suggestion reflects a preference for keeping to a minimum the extent to which judges discuss cases directly with the media.

RULE 2.11 Disqualification

(A) A judge shall disqualify himself or herself in any proceeding in which the judge's impartiality* might reasonably be questioned, including but not limited to the following circumstances:

(1) The judge has a personal bias or prejudice concerning a party or a party's lawyer, or personal knowledge* of facts that are in dispute in the proceeding.

(2) The judge knows* that the judge, the judge's spouse or domestic partner,* or a person within the third degree of relationship* to either of them, or the spouse or domestic partner of such a person is:

(a) a party to the proceeding, or an officer, director, general partner, managing member, or trustee of a party;

(b) acting as a lawyer in the proceeding;

(c) a person who has more than a de minimis* interest that could be substantially affected by the proceeding; or

(d) likely to be a material witness in the proceeding.

(3) The judge knows that he or she, individually or as a fiduciary,* or the judge's spouse, domestic partner, parent, or child, or any other member of the judge's family residing in the judge's household,* has an economic interest* in the subject matter in controversy or is a party to the proceeding.

(4) The judge knows or learns by means of a timely motion that a party, a party's lawyer, or the law firm of a party's lawyer has within the previous [insert number] year[s] made aggregate* contributions* to the judge's campaign in an amount that [is greater than $[insert amount] for an individual or $[insert amount] for an entity] [is reasonable and appropriate for an individual or an entity].

(5) The judge, while a judge or a judicial candidate,* has made a public statement, other than in a court proceeding, judicial decision, or opinion, that commits or appears to commit the judge to reach a particular result or rule in a particular way in the proceeding or controversy.

(6) The judge:

(a) served as a lawyer in the matter in controversy, or was associated with a lawyer who participated substantially as a lawyer in the matter during such association;

(b) served in governmental employment, and in such capacity participated personally and substantially as a lawyer or public official concerning the proceeding, or has publicly expressed in such capacity an opinion concerning the merits of the particular matter in controversy;

(c) was a material witness concerning the matter; or

(d) previously presided as a judge over the matter in another court.

(B) A judge shall keep informed about the judge's personal and fiduciary economic interests, and make a reasonable effort to keep informed about the personal economic interests of the judge's spouse or domestic partner and minor children residing in the judge's household.

(C) A judge subject to disqualification under this Rule, other than for bias or prejudice under paragraph (A)(1), may disclose on the record the basis of the judge's disqualification and may ask the parties and their lawyers to consider, outside the presence of the judge and court personnel, whether to waive disqualification. If, following the disclosure, the parties and lawyers agree, without participation by the judge or court personnel, that the judge should not be disqualified, the judge may participate in the proceeding. The agreement shall be incorporated into the record of the proceeding.

Comment

[1] Under this Rule, a judge is disqualified whenever the judge's impartiality might reasonably be questioned, regardless of whether any of the specific provisions of paragraphs (A)(1) through (6) apply. In many jurisdictions, the term "recusal" is used interchangeably with the term "disqualification."

[2] A judge's obligation not to hear or decide matters in which disqualification is required applies regardless of whether a motion to disqualify is filed.

[3] The rule of necessity may override the rule of disqualification. For example, a judge might be required to participate in judicial review of a judicial salary statute, or might be the only judge available in a matter requiring immediate judicial action, such as a hearing on probable cause or a temporary restraining order. In matters that require immediate action, the judge must disclose on the record the basis for possible disqualification and make reasonable efforts to transfer the matter to another judge as soon as practicable.

[4] The fact that a lawyer in a proceeding is affiliated with a law firm with which a relative of the judge is affiliated does not itself disqualify the judge. If, however, the judge's impartiality might reasonably be questioned under paragraph (A), or the relative is known by the judge to have an interest in the law firm that could be substantially affected by the proceeding under paragraph (A)(2)(c), the judge's disqualification is required.

[5] A judge should disclose on the record information that the judge believes the parties or their lawyers might reasonably consider relevant to a possible motion for disqualification, even if the judge believes there is no basis for disqualification.

[6] "Economic interest," as set forth in the Terminology section, means ownership of more than a de minimis legal or equitable interest. Except for situations in which a judge participates in the management of such a legal or equitable interest, or the interest could be substantially affected by the outcome of a proceeding before a judge, it does not include:

(1) an interest in the individual holdings within a mutual or common investment fund;

(2) an interest in securities held by an educational, religious, charitable, fraternal, or civic organization in which the judge or the judge's spouse, domestic partner, parent, or child serves as a director, officer, advisor, or other participant;

(3) a deposit in a financial institution or deposits or proprietary interests the judge may maintain as a member of a mutual savings association or credit union, or similar proprietary interests; or

(4) an interest in the issuer of government securities held by the judge.

RULE 2.11—REPORTER'S EXPLANATION OF CHANGES†

1990 MODEL CODE COMPARISON

Paragraph (A) is Canon 3E(1).

Paragraph (A)(1) is Canon 3E(1)(a).

Paragraph (A)(2) is Canon 3E(1)(d).

Paragraph (A)(2)(a) is Canon 3E(1)(d)(i).

Paragraph (A)(2)(b) is Canon 3E(1)(d)(ii).

Paragraph (A)(2)(c) is Canon 3E(1)(d)(iii).

Paragraph (A)(2)(d) is Canon 3E(1)(d)(iv).

Paragraph (A)(3) is Canon 3E(1)(c).

Paragraph (A)(4) is Canon 3E(1)(e).

Paragraph (A)(5) combines Canons 3E(1)(f), 3E(1)(f)(i), and 3E(1)(f)(ii).

Paragraph (A)(6) is the first two words of Canon 3E(1)(b).

Paragraph (A)(6)(a) is the remainder of the first half of Canon 3E(1)(b).

Paragraph (A)(6)(b) is the Commentary to Canon 3E(1)(b).

Paragraph (A)(6)(c) is the second half of Canon 3E(1)(b).

Paragraph (A)(6)(d) is new.

Paragraph (B) is Canon 3E(2).

Paragraph (C) is Canon 3F.

Comment [1] is the first paragraph of Commentary to Canon 3E(1).

Comment [2] is new.

Comment [3] is the third paragraph of Commentary to Canon 3E(1).

Comment [4] is the Commentary to Canon 3E(1)(f).

Comment [5] is the second paragraph of Commentary to Cannon 3E(1).

Comment [6] is new.

The Commentary to Canon 3F was deleted, as being largely redundant of the black letter and otherwise administrative, rather than ethical, in its recommendations.

EXPLANATION OF BLACK LETTER

Most changes to this Rule and its accompanying Comment are stylistic and structural rather than substantive. Only substantive changes are addressed below.

1. <u>Paragraphs (A)(2), (A)(3), and (B): Addition of "domestic partner"</u>

"Domestic partner" was added to treat domestic partners comparably to spouses for purposes of evaluating economic conflicts.

† The "Reporters' Explanations of Changes" have not been approved by the ABA Joint Commission to Evaluate the Model Code of Judicial Conduct. They have been drafted by the Commission's Reporters, based on the proceedings and record of the Commission, solely to inform the ABA House of Delegates about each of the proposed amendments to the Model Code prior to their being considered at the ABA 2007 Midyear Meeting. THEY ARE NOT TO BE ADOPTED AS PART OF THE MODEL CODE.

2. Paragraph (A)(2)(a): Addition of "general partner, managing member"

These additions were made to ensure completeness of the list.

3. In Paragraph (A)(2)(d), "to the judge's knowledge", which is included in former Canon 3E (1) (d) (iv), was deleted as unnecessary.

4. Paragraph (A)(6)(b): New paragraph on government lawyers

Paragraph (A)(6)(b) makes explicit in the black letter what former Canon 3E(1)(b) stated only in Commentary. Judges must not sit on cases concerning matters with which they were involved as government lawyers, for the same reason that they must not sit on cases concerning matters in which they were involved as lawyers, and the Rule has been revised to so state.

5. Paragraph A(6)(d): New paragraph on judges sitting on cases they previously heard:

Trial judges sometimes sit by designation on courts of appeal, and vice versa. Such judges should not hear cases over which they presided in a different court, and this Rule makes that clear. This Rule, however, leaves unaffected the propriety of a judge who decided a case on a panel of an appellate court participating in the rehearing of the case en banc with that same court.

EXPLANATION OF COMMENTS

[2] New Comment [2] was added to clarify that the disqualification rules apply regardless of whether a motion to disqualify has been filed. The terms "recusal" and "disqualification" have been defined in different and sometimes inconsistent ways to apply where judges act on their own initiative or pursuant to a motion by a party. This Comment is intended to render such distinctions irrelevant here.

[6] New Comment [6] was added to elaborate on the meaning of "economic interest." Although the term is separately defined in the Terminology section, it is important enough to bear recapitulation here.

RULE 2.12 Supervisory Duties

(A) A judge shall require court staff, court officials, and others subject to the judge's direction and control to act in a manner consistent with the judge's obligations under this Code.

(B) A judge with supervisory authority for the performance of other judges shall take reasonable measures to ensure that those judges properly discharge their judicial responsibilities, including the prompt disposition of matters before them.

Comment

[1] A judge is responsible for his or her own conduct and for the conduct of others, such as staff, when those persons are acting at the judge's direction or control. A judge may not direct court personnel to engage in conduct on the judge's behalf or as the judge's representative when such conduct would violate the Code if undertaken by the judge.

[2] Public confidence in the judicial system depends upon timely justice. To promote the efficient administration of justice, a judge with supervisory authority must take the steps needed to ensure that judges under his or her supervision administer their workloads promptly.

RULE 2.12—REPORTER'S EXPLANATION OF CHANGES†

1990 MODEL CODE COMPARISON

The Rule is Canon 3C(2) and (3).

† The "Reporters' Explanations of Changes" have not been approved by the ABA Joint Commission to Evaluate the Model Code of Judicial Conduct. They have been drafted by the Commission's Reporters, based on the proceedings and

Comments [1] and [2] are new.

EXPLANATION OF BLACK LETTER

1. Canons 3C(2) and (3) combined

   Canons 3C(2) and (3) were combined under a general rubric, "Supervisory Duties."

2. Revision to Court staff standards

   Rule 2.12(A) was reworded to reflect a more comprehensive understanding of the standards of conduct required of court personnel. Judges must insist that court staff and officials act in a manner consistent with all of a judge's obligations under the Code and not simply those previously enumerated in Canon 3C(2) relating to diligence, fidelity, and lack of bias or prejudice.

3. Proper discharge of judicial responsibilities of subordinate judges

   The Commission reordered the provision to emphasize the importance of the obligation of the supervisory judge to ensure the prompt discharge of judicial responsibilities over all matters.

EXPLANATION OF COMMENTS

[1] New Comment [1] was added to emphasize the critical position judicial staff occupy in the justice system—not only in terms of their relevance to the administration of justice but also in terms of their role in preserving public confidence in the system as a whole. The Comment explains the black letter to underscore that a judge must never direct staff within his or her control to engage in conduct that would violate the Code if undertaken by the judge.

[2] New Comment [2] was added to underscore that public confidence in the courts depends on judges with supervisory authority taking the steps needed to ensure that judges under their supervision administer their workloads both properly and expeditiously.

RULE 2.13 Administrative Appointments

(A) In making administrative appointments, a judge:

(1) shall exercise the power of appointment impartially* and on the basis of merit; and

(2) shall avoid nepotism, favoritism, and unnecessary appointments.

(B) A judge shall not appoint a lawyer to a position if the judge either knows* that the lawyer, or the lawyer's spouse or domestic partner,* has contributed more than $[insert amount] within the prior [insert number] year[s] to the judge's election campaign, or learns of such a contribution* by means of a timely motion by a party or other person properly interested in the matter, unless:

(1) the position is substantially uncompensated;

(2) the lawyer has been selected in rotation from a list of qualified and available lawyers compiled without regard to their having made political contributions; or

(3) the judge or another presiding or administrative judge affirmatively finds that no other lawyer is willing, competent, and able to accept the position.

(C) A judge shall not approve compensation of appointees beyond the fair value of services rendered.

---

record of the Commission, solely to inform the ABA House of Delegates about each of the proposed amendments to the Model Code prior to their being considered at the ABA 2007 Midyear Meeting. THEY ARE NOT TO BE ADOPTED AS PART OF THE MODEL CODE.

Comment

[1] Appointees of a judge include assigned counsel, officials such as referees, commissioners, special masters, receivers, and guardians, and personnel such as clerks, secretaries, and bailiffs. Consent by the parties to an appointment or an award of compensation does not relieve the judge of the obligation prescribed by paragraph (A).

[2] Unless otherwise defined by law, nepotism is the appointment or hiring of any relative within the third degree of relationship of either the judge or the judge's spouse or domestic partner, or the spouse or domestic partner of such relative.

[3] The rule against making administrative appointments of lawyers who have contributed in excess of a specified dollar amount to a judge's election campaign includes an exception for positions that are substantially uncompensated, such as those for which the lawyer's compensation is limited to reimbursement for out-of-pocket expenses.

RULE 2.13—REPORTER'S EXPLANATION OF CHANGES†

1990 MODEL CODE COMPARISON

Paragraph (A) is taken from Canon 3C(4).

Paragraph (B) is taken from Canon 3C(5).

Paragraph (B)(1) is Canon 3C(5)(a).

Paragraph (B)(2) is Canon 3C(5)(b).

Paragraph (B)(3) is Canon 3C(5)(c).

Paragraph (C) is Canon 3C(4).

Comment [1] is the Commentary to Canon 3C.

Comments [2] and [3] are new.

EXPLANATION OF BLACK LETTER

1. Paragraph (A): Movement of "unnecessary appointments"

The first sentence of former Canon 3C(4) was folded into the Rule for largely stylistic reasons not intended to change substantive meaning.

2. Paragraph (B): Addition of "spouse or domestic partner"

The proscription against the appointment of a lawyer who has contributed a defined amount to the judge's election campaign is extended to the spouse or domestic partner of the lawyer.

EXPLANATION OF COMMENTS

[2] The black letter directs judges to avoid nepotism, and new Comment [2] was added simply to add clarity to the meaning of nepotism with a conventional definition.

[3] The black letter prohibits a judge from awarding appointments to contributors who have given more than a specified amount to the judge's election campaign but creates an exception for "substantially uncompensated" positions. This new Comment clarifies the meaning of "substantially uncompensated" to reach positions in which the appointee is merely reimbursed for out-of-pocket expenses.

† The "Reporters' Explanations of Changes" have not been approved by the ABA Joint Commission to Evaluate the Model Code of Judicial Conduct. They have been drafted by the Commission's Reporters, based on the proceedings and record of the Commission, solely to inform the ABA House of Delegates about each of the proposed amendments to the Model Code prior to their being considered at the ABA 2007 Midyear Meeting. THEY ARE NOT TO BE ADOPTED AS PART OF THE MODEL CODE.

RULE 2.14 Disability and Impairment

A judge having a reasonable belief that the performance of a lawyer or another judge is impaired by drugs or alcohol, or by a mental, emotional, or physical condition, shall take appropriate action, which may include a confidential referral to a lawyer or judicial assistance program.

Comment

[1] "Appropriate action" means action intended and reasonably likely to help the judge or lawyer in question address the problem and prevent harm to the justice system. Depending upon the circumstances, appropriate action may include but is not limited to speaking directly to the impaired person, notifying an individual with supervisory responsibility over the impaired person, or making a referral to an assistance program.

[2] Taking or initiating corrective action by way of referral to an assistance program may satisfy a judge's responsibility under this Rule. Assistance programs have many approaches for offering help to impaired judges and lawyers, such as intervention, counseling, or referral to appropriate health care professionals. Depending upon the gravity of the conduct that has come to the judge's attention, however, the judge may be required to take other action, such as reporting the impaired judge or lawyer to the appropriate authority, agency, or body. See Rule 2.15.

RULE 2.14—REPORTER'S EXPLANATION OF CHANGES†

1990 MODEL CODE COMPARISON

The Rule and Comment are new.

EXPLANATION OF BLACK LETTER

Creation of new Rule on impairment

This is a new Rule, governing a difficult and extremely important issue. Impairment can undermine judicial competence, diligence, and demeanor specifically, and public confidence in the courts generally. The Rule imposes a mandatory obligation to take appropriate action when a judge learns of a colleague's impairment. The objective of this provision is to guide and encourage judges to address impairment problems when they arise.

EXPLANATION OF COMMENTS

[1] This Comment was added to define "appropriate action." There was some concern that disagreement could arise over whether a particular action taken in response to knowledge of impairment was sufficient. This Comment takes a functional approach, by asking whether the action taken would be reasonably likely to rectify the problem.

[2] The Commission was alert to the need for sensitivity when dealing with impairment problems and was careful not to prescribe specific action in response to specific evidence of impairment. Often, referral to a lawyer or judicial assistance referral program may be the most appropriate course, but the Commission recognized that different circumstances may warrant different responses.

† "Reporters' Explanations of Changes" have not been approved by the ABA Joint Commission to Evaluate the Model Code of Judicial Conduct. They have been drafted by the Commission's Reporters, based on the proceedings and record of the Commission, solely to inform the ABA House of Delegates about each of the proposed amendments to the Model Code prior to their being considered at the ABA 2007 Midyear Meeting. THEY ARE NOT TO BE ADOPTED AS PART OF THE MODEL CODE.

RULE 2.15 Responding to Judicial and Lawyer Misconduct

(A) A judge having knowledge* that another judge has committed a violation of this Code that raises a substantial question regarding the judge's honesty, trustworthiness, or fitness as a judge in other respects shall inform the appropriate authority.*

(B) A judge having knowledge that a lawyer has committed a violation of the Rules of Professional Conduct that raises a substantial question regarding the lawyer's honesty, trustworthiness, or fitness as a lawyer in other respects shall inform the appropriate authority.

(C) A judge who receives information indicating a substantial likelihood that another judge has committed a violation of this Code shall take appropriate action.

(D) A judge who receives information indicating a substantial likelihood that a lawyer has committed a violation of the Rules of Professional Conduct shall take appropriate action.

Comment

[1] Taking action to address known misconduct is a judge's obligation. Paragraphs (A) and (B) impose an obligation on the judge to report to the appropriate disciplinary authority the known misconduct of another judge or a lawyer that raises a substantial question regarding the honesty, trustworthiness, or fitness of that judge or lawyer. Ignoring or denying known misconduct among one's judicial colleagues or members of the legal profession undermines a judge's responsibility to participate in efforts to ensure public respect for the justice system. This Rule limits the reporting obligation to those offenses that an independent judiciary must vigorously endeavor to prevent.

[2] A judge who does not have actual knowledge that another judge or a lawyer may have committed misconduct, but receives information indicating a substantial likelihood of such misconduct, is required to take appropriate action under paragraphs (C) and (D). Appropriate action may include, but is not limited to, communicating directly with the judge who may have violated this Code, communicating with a supervising judge, or reporting the suspected violation to the appropriate authority or other agency or body. Similarly, actions to be taken in response to information indicating that a lawyer has committed a violation of the Rules of Professional Conduct may include but are not limited to communicating directly with the lawyer who may have committed the violation, or reporting the suspected violation to the appropriate authority or other agency or body.

RULE 2.15—REPORTER'S EXPLANATION OF CHANGES†

1990 MODEL CODE COMPARISON

Paragraph (A) is the second sentence of Canon 3D(1).

Paragraph (B) is the second sentence of Canon 3D(2).

Paragraph (C) is the first sentence of Canon 3D(1).

Paragraph (D) is the first sentence of Canon 3D(2).

Comment [1] is new.

† The "Reporters' Explanations of Changes" have not been approved by the ABA Joint Commission to Evaluate the Model Code of Judicial Conduct. They have been drafted by the Commission's Reporters, based on the proceedings and record of the Commission, solely to inform the ABA House of Delegates about each of the proposed amendments to the Model Code prior to their being considered at the ABA 2007 Midyear Meeting. THEY ARE NOT TO BE ADOPTED AS PART OF THE MODEL CODE.

Most of Comment [2] is new. The second sentence of the Comment is the Commentary to Canon 3D.

Canon 3D(3) was deleted.

EXPLANATION OF BLACK LETTER

Rules regulating the response to lawyer and judicial misconduct were consolidated to reflect closely related concepts.

1. Paragraph (A): Change to parallel Rule 8.3

The Rule was reworded to parallel the lawyer reporting obligations in Rule 8.3 of the Model Rules of Professional Conduct to require reporting to the "appropriate authority" whenever the judge has knowledge of another judge's violation of the Code that raises a substantial question as to the judge's "honesty, trustworthiness, or fitness as a judge in other respects."

2. Paragraphs (B) and (D): Language changes

Changes were made to parallel the obligations by judges to address the misconduct of lawyers.

3. Paragraph (C): Change in duty

Former Canon 3(D)(1) was revised to state that when a judge receives information indicating a substantial likelihood that another judge has violated the Rules, the judge receiving such information shall—no longer should—take "appropriate action." In the Commission's view, in situations where the judge does not "know" but receives information making it substantially likely that another judge has violated the Rules, the judge receiving such information shall take action. The appropriate action would vary with the circumstances. In some instances, it could involve talking to the judge in question or in other instances, taking steps to verify the information received and report it to the appropriate authorities.

4. Deletion of Canon 3D(3)

Former Canon 3D(3) declared that the acts of a judge in the discharge of disciplinary responsibilities were absolutely privileged. Although there was no opposition to the concept that judges should be immune from suit in such situations, the Commission concluded that such a provision was inappropriate for the Model Code of Judicial Conduct. Neither the ABA nor an adopting court is in a position to grant or deny judicial immunity in the context of judicial conduct standards. Accordingly, Canon 3D(3) was viewed as a generalized statement of support for judicial immunity, which, in the Commission's view, was not appropriate for the Code.

EXPLANATION OF COMMENTS

[1] Language was added to underscore the relationship between reporting serious misconduct of judges and lawyers and the judge's responsibility to preserve public confidence in the courts.

[2] Commentary concerning "appropriate action" in response to judicial and lawyer misconduct is consistent with the Commentary in former Canon 3D.

RULE 2.16 Cooperation With Disciplinary Authorities

(A) A judge shall cooperate and be candid and honest with judicial and lawyer disciplinary agencies.

(B) A judge shall not retaliate, directly or indirectly, against a person known* or suspected to have assisted or cooperated with an investigation of a judge or a lawyer.

Comment

[1] Cooperation with investigations and proceedings of judicial and lawyer discipline agencies, as required in paragraph (A), instills confidence in judges' commitment to the integrity of the judicial system and the protection of the public.

RULE 2.16—REPORTER'S EXPLANATION OF CHANGES†

1990 MODEL CODE COMPARISON

The Rule and its Comments are new.

EXPLANATION OF BLACK LETTER

Creation of new Rule

Several witnesses noted that disciplinary authorities often struggle to gain the cooperation of targeted judges in disciplinary matters and the cooperation of judges in lawyer disciplinary proceedings. In the Commission's view, the need for a judge's cooperation in the disciplinary process is paramount. Moreover, for a judge to retaliate against a person for cooperating in disciplinary proceedings against him or her would be patently unethical. This Rule thus serves to address an important omission in the former Code.

CANON 3

A JUDGE SHALL CONDUCT THE JUDGE'S PERSONAL AND EXTRAJUDICIAL ACTIVITIES TO MINIMIZE THE RISK OF CONFLICT WITH THE OBLIGATIONS OF JUDICIAL OFFICE.

CANON 3—REPORTER'S EXPLANATION OF CHANGES†

1990 MODEL CODE COMPARISON

This renumbered Canon 3 is drawn almost exclusively from Canon 4 of the 1990 Code. However, some material involving the "personal" activities of a judge has been repositioned to this Canon from Canon 2 of the 1990 Code.

EXPLANATION OF BLACK LETTER

1. Expanded the reach of this Canon to include "personal" as well as "extrajudicial" activities.

Some activities governed by this Canon, such as accepting gifts or participating in private clubs, are "extrajudicial" in the sense that they are not part of a judge's official duties, yet they are less formal and less public than participating in a seminar or accepting an award. Accordingly, the Commission added the word "personal" to the Canon title to make it more accurate and more complete.

2. Replaced "conflict with judicial obligations" with "conflict with the obligations of judicial office."

No significant substantive change is intended. The substituted phrase is used as a reminder that judges have a variety of duties—including administrative duties—that go with the judicial *office*.

---

† The "Reporters' Explanations of Changes" have not been approved by the ABA Joint Commission to Evaluate the Model Code of Judicial Conduct. They have been drafted by the Commission's Reporters, based on the proceedings and record of the Commission, solely to inform the ABA House of Delegates about each of the proposed amendments to the Model Code prior to their being considered at the ABA 2007 Midyear Meeting. THEY ARE NOT TO BE ADOPTED AS PART OF THE MODEL CODE.

† The "Reporters' Explanations of Changes" have not been approved by the ABA Joint Commission to Evaluate the Model Code of Judicial Conduct. They have been drafted by the Commission's Reporters, based on the proceedings and record of the Commission, solely to inform the ABA House of Delegates about each of the proposed amendments to the Model Code prior to their being considered at the ABA 2007 Midyear Meeting. THEY ARE NOT TO BE ADOPTED AS PART OF THE MODEL CODE.

RULE 3.1 Extrajudicial Activities in General

A judge may engage in extrajudicial activities, except as prohibited by law* or this Code. However, when engaging in extrajudicial activities, a judge shall not:

(A) participate in activities that will interfere with the proper performance of the judge's judicial duties;

(B) participate in activities that will lead to frequent disqualification of the judge;

(C) participate in activities that would appear to a reasonable person to undermine the judge's independence,* integrity,* or impartiality;*

(D) engage in conduct that would appear to a reasonable person to be coercive; or

(E) make use of court premises, staff, stationery, equipment, or other resources, except for incidental use for activities that concern the law, the legal system, or the administration of justice, or unless such additional use is permitted by law.

Comment

[1] To the extent that time permits, and judicial independence and impartiality are not compromised, judges are encouraged to engage in appropriate extrajudicial activities. Judges are uniquely qualified to engage in extrajudicial activities that concern the law, the legal system, and the administration of justice, such as by speaking, writing, teaching, or participating in scholarly research projects. In addition, judges are permitted and encouraged to engage in educational, religious, charitable, fraternal or civic extrajudicial activities not conducted for profit, even when the activities do not involve the law. See Rule 3.7.

[2] Participation in both law-related and other extrajudicial activities helps integrate judges into their communities, and furthers public understanding of and respect for courts and the judicial system.

[3] Discriminatory actions and expressions of bias or prejudice by a judge, even outside the judge's official or judicial actions, are likely to appear to a reasonable person to call into question the judge's integrity and impartiality. Examples include jokes or other remarks that demean individuals based upon their race, sex, gender, religion, national origin, ethnicity, disability, age, sexual orientation, or socioeconomic status. For the same reason, a judge's extrajudicial activities must not be conducted in connection or affiliation with an organization that practices invidious discrimination. See Rule 3.6.

[4] While engaged in permitted extrajudicial activities, judges must not coerce others or take action that would reasonably be perceived as coercive. For example, depending upon the circumstances, a judge's solicitation of contributions or memberships for an organization, even as permitted by Rule 3.7(A), might create the risk that the person solicited would feel obligated to respond favorably, or would do so to curry favor with the judge.

RULE 3.1—REPORTER'S EXPLANATION OF CHANGES†

1990 MODEL CODE COMPARISON

To the extent that Rule 3.1 serves as a general list of restrictions upon a judge's participation in extrajudicial activities, it is chiefly derived from Canon 4A. However, the new set of restrictions is somewhat different, as it focuses attention more sharply upon interference with the independence, integrity, and impartiality of judges.

† The "Reporters' Explanations of Changes" have not been approved by the ABA Joint Commission to Evaluate the Model Code of Judicial Conduct. They have been drafted by the Commission's Reporters, based on the proceedings and record of the Commission, solely to inform the ABA House of Delegates about each of the proposed amendments to the Model Code prior to their being considered at the ABA 2007 Midyear Meeting. THEY ARE NOT TO BE ADOPTED AS PART OF THE MODEL CODE.

Rule 3.1(A) is essentially the same as Canon 4A(3).

Rule 3.1(B) is new, but is derived from Canon 4A(3), but contains more specific content. See Rule 3.1(A).

Rule 3.1(C) is based upon Canon 4A(1), but with expanded coverage and revised language.

Rule 3.1(D) is new.

Rule 3.1(E) is new, but has some overlap with aspects of Canon 2B ("lend the prestige of judicial office to advance the private interests of the judge or others").

Comment [1] is derived from the first paragraph of the Commentary following Canon 4B, although the subject matter of Canon 4B, Avocational Activities, is not addressed separately.

Comment [2] is based upon the first paragraph of the Commentary following Canon 4A.

Comment [3] is the second paragraph of the Commentary to 4A.

Comment [4] is new.

EXPLANATION OF BLACK LETTER

1. Rule 3.1, lead-in is restructured to permit extrajudicial activities generally, but subject to the listed prohibitions.

The restrictions set forth in Rule 3.1 are generally applicable to all of Canon 3, and are frequently cross-referenced in other Rules within Canon 3.

2. Rule 3.1(A) added the italicized words in "interfere with the proper performance of *the judge's* judicial duties."

3. Rule 3.1(B) is newly added as a specific instance of the prohibition contained in Rule 3.1(A).

One way to interfere with the proper performance of judicial duties is to become involved in extrajudicial activities that will lead to frequent disqualification.

No substantive change is intended.

4. Rule 3.1(C) substituted the phrase "would appear to a reasonable person to undermine" for "cast reasonable doubt on," and broadened coverage from "act impartially" to "the judge's independence, integrity, or impartiality."

The Commission decided that the words "cast reasonable doubt on" are too closely associated with the criminal law, and did not accurately express the proper level of certainty required. The substitute wording makes the standard turn upon the thought processes of a "reasonable person," which is a familiar standard in the law generally and also suggestive of the "might reasonably be questioned" language of 28 U.S.C. § 455. Concern with impairment of a judge's independence, integrity, and impartiality, rather than impartiality alone, is a theme that is prevalent in the Rules.

5. Rule 3.1(D) added a new provision to guard against overt or subtle efforts by a judge to coerce others into participating in extrajudicial activities favored by the judge.

The Commission heard testimony suggesting that coercion of this kind can be a significant problem in small communities with only one judge or a small number of judges, and a small number of lawyers who need to maintain good relations with the judiciary.

6. Rule 3.1(E) added a new prohibition against using court facilities and other resources for a judge's extrajudicial activities, but with an exception for incidental use in connection with a law-related event.

The rationale for the general restriction is that favoring a particular charity or other extrajudicial event by providing access to facilities that are closed to others is an abuse of the prestige of judicial office; see Rule 1.3. The rationale for the exception, however, is that certain activities, such as opening a real courtroom for use in a moot court competition or using a court's conference room for a meeting of a bar association task force that includes the judge, are not abuses of judicial office.

EXPLANATION OF COMMENTS

[1] This Comment was reworded to confirm the special role that judges can play in engaging in extrajudicial activities that involve the law, the legal system, and the administration of justice, but also to approve participation in activities that are *not* law-related, as long as they are undertaken in connection with not-for-profit organizations.

In both instances, the sense of the Comment is to be somewhat more encouraging than was the 1990 Code, so that judges will reach out to the communities of which they are a part, and avoid isolating themselves.

Specific examples in the 1990 Code, both in black letter (avocational activities such as speaking and writing) and in the Commentary (improving criminal and juvenile justice and expressing opposition to the persecution of lawyers and judges in other countries), were removed as unnecessarily restrictive or of insufficiently general application.

[2] This Comment focuses on the positive value of judges being integrated into the activity of the community. The first paragraph of Comment to Canon 4A had addressed that notion implicitly, but spoke in terms of judges not becoming isolated from the communities in which they live.

No substantive change is intended.

[3] This Comment is modified from the second paragraph of the Commentary following Canon 4A.

The cross-reference to Section 2C in the 1990 Code was to the provision on discriminatory organizations, although the Commentary did not make that sufficiently clear. The provision regarding discriminatory organizations has been repositioned to Canon 3; accordingly, the cross-reference is to Rule 3.6.

[4] New Comment [4] fleshes out the intention of Rule 3.1(D), which is also new.

RULE 3.2 Appearances Before Governmental Bodies and Consultation With Government Officials

A judge shall not appear voluntarily at a public hearing before, or otherwise consult with, an executive or a legislative body or official, except:

(A) in connection with matters concerning the law, the legal system, or the administration of justice;

(B) in connection with matters about which the judge acquired knowledge or expertise in the course of the judge's judicial duties; or

(C) when the judge is acting pro se in a matter involving the judge's legal or economic interests, or when the judge is acting in a fiduciary* capacity.

Comment

[1] Judges possess special expertise in matters of law, the legal system, and the administration of justice, and may properly share that expertise with governmental bodies and executive or legislative branch officials.

[2] In appearing before governmental bodies or consulting with government officials, judges must be mindful that they remain subject to other provisions of this Code, such as Rule 1.3, prohibiting judges from using the prestige of office to advance their own or others' interests, Rule 2.10, governing public comment on pending and impending matters, and Rule 3.1(C), prohibiting judges from engaging in extrajudicial activities that would appear to a reasonable person to undermine the judge's independence, integrity, or impartiality.

[3] In general, it would be an unnecessary and unfair burden to prohibit judges from appearing before governmental bodies or consulting with government officials on matters that are likely to affect them as private citizens, such as zoning proposals affecting their real property. In engaging in such activities,

however, judges must not refer to their judicial positions, and must otherwise exercise caution to avoid using the prestige of judicial office.

RULE 3.2—REPORTER'S EXPLANATION OF CHANGES†

1990 MODEL CODE COMPARISON

Rule 3.2 is derived from Canon 4C(1). Minor revisions and additions have been made.

Rule 3.2(A) is essentially the same as the middle clause of Canon 4C(1).

Rule 3.2(B) is new.

Rule 3.2(C) is essentially the same as the last clause of Canon 4C(1), but with some minor modifications.

All the Comments are new; Canon 4C(1) had no substantive Commentary.

EXPLANATION OF BLACK LETTER

1. Rule 3.2 lead-in: added the word "voluntarily."

This was a minor but necessary addition, to make clear that judges who are formally summoned to appear before various governmental bodies may not refuse to appear on the ground that it would be "unethical" to do so.

2. Rule 3.2(A): no substantive change is intended.

3. Rule 3.2(B): a new paragraph.

This provision was added to reflect the growing recognition that in the course of carrying out their judicial duties, judges often gain expertise and special insight into legal and social problems and matters of public policy. The point of this provision is to establish that judges are permitted to share this information with other governmental bodies and officials.

4. Rule 3.2(C): modified existing language.

Rule 3.2(C) substituted "the judge's legal or economic interests" for "the judge's interests," and extended the exception to situations in which a judge is "acting in a fiduciary capacity."

EXPLANATION OF COMMENTS

[1] New Comment [1] simply explains the rationale of Rule 3.2(A) and, implicitly, of Rule 3.2(B).

[2] New Comment [2] serves as a reminder that even when it is permissible under Rules 3.2(A) or 3.2(B) for a judge voluntarily to consult with other governmental branch personnel, the judge remains subject to other restrictions of this Code, some of which are given as examples.

[3] New Comment [3] more narrowly describes the types of interests judges may address in their appearances before or consultations with government bodies. Under the original language, the Commission believed a judge might act pro se in connection with any political or social matter that "interested" the judge, which would allow the exception to swallow the rule. Without resorting to legalistic definitions of legally protected interests sufficient to justify formal intervention, the Comment distinguishes between matters that affect judges directly as private citizens and more general causes.

---

† The "Reporters' Explanations of Changes" have not been approved by the ABA Joint Commission to Evaluate the Model Code of Judicial Conduct. They have been drafted by the Commission's Reporters, based on the proceedings and record of the Commission, solely to inform the ABA House of Delegates about each of the proposed amendments to the Model Code prior to their being considered at the ABA 2007 Midyear Meeting. THEY ARE NOT TO BE ADOPTED AS PART OF THE MODEL CODE.

RULE 3.3 Testifying as a Character Witness

A judge shall not testify as a character witness in a judicial, administrative, or other adjudicatory proceeding or otherwise vouch for the character of a person in a legal proceeding, except when duly summoned.

Comment

[1] A judge who, without being subpoenaed, testifies as a character witness abuses the prestige of judicial office to advance the interests of another. See Rule 1.3. Except in unusual circumstances where the demands of justice require, a judge should discourage a party from requiring the judge to testify as a character witness.

RULE 3.3—REPORTER'S EXPLANATION OF CHANGES†

1990 MODEL CODE COMPARISON

Rule 3.3 is derived from the last sentence of Canon 2B.

Comment [1] is based upon the last paragraph of the Commentary to Canon 2B.

EXPLANATION OF BLACK LETTER

1. Rule 3.3: substituted the phrase "except when duly summoned" for "testify voluntarily," and added the phrase "otherwise vouch for the character of a person in a legal proceeding." New language, specifying that the Rule applies in all forms of "adjudicatory proceedings," was also added.

Regarding the first revision, similar language ("properly summoned") appeared in the Commentary in the 1990 Code; thus, no substantive change was intended. The Commission added the language about "vouching" because testimony under oath is not the only mode in which judges might abuse the prestige of judicial office when the character of a person is in issue in a legal proceeding.

The remaining addition, "in a judicial, administrative, or other adjudicatory proceeding," is simply a reminder that Rule 3.3 is not limited to civil or criminal trials in courts, but applies whenever testimony is taken on a formal record.

EXPLANATION OF COMMENTS

[1] This Comment is the last sentence of the Commentary to Canon 2B.

Although the Rule permits testifying as a character witness upon receipt of a subpoena or other process, it has always been understood that judges should not encourage a party to issue a sham subpoena for what is in fact voluntary testimony. The Comment goes a step further and suggests that judges should actively discourage parties from compelling their testimony as character witnesses.

RULE 3.4 Appointments to Governmental Positions

A judge shall not accept appointment to a governmental committee, board, commission, or other governmental position, unless it is one that concerns the law, the legal system, or the administration of justice.

† The "Reporters' Explanations of Changes" have not been approved by the ABA Joint Commission to Evaluate the Model Code of Judicial Conduct. They have been drafted by the Commission's Reporters, based on the proceedings and record of the Commission, solely to inform the ABA House of Delegates about each of the proposed amendments to the Model Code prior to their being considered at the ABA 2007 Midyear Meeting. THEY ARE NOT TO BE ADOPTED AS PART OF THE MODEL CODE.

Comment

[1] Rule 3.4 implicitly acknowledges the value of judges accepting appointments to entities that concern the law, the legal system, or the administration of justice. Even in such instances, however, a judge should assess the appropriateness of accepting an appointment, paying particular attention to the subject matter of the appointment and the availability and allocation of judicial resources, including the judge's time commitments, and giving due regard to the requirements of the independence and impartiality of the judiciary.

[2] A judge may represent his or her country, state, or locality on ceremonial occasions or in connection with historical, educational, or cultural activities. Such representation does not constitute acceptance of a government position.

RULE 3.4—REPORTER'S EXPLANATION OF CHANGES†

1990 MODEL CODE COMPARISON

Rule 3.4 is derived from the first sentence of Canon 4C(2). It has been recast and simplified.

Comment [1] is based upon the first paragraph of the Commentary to Canon 4C(2), but again reworded and simplified. The second paragraph of the Commentary to Canon 4C(2) was deleted as unnecessary and somewhat confusing.

Comment [2] has been moved into the Comments from the last sentence of the black letter of Canon 4C(2).

EXPLANATION OF BLACK LETTER

1. Rule 3.4: add the word "board" to the list of governmental entities for completeness.

As has been done throughout the revised Code, "improvement in the law," has been changed to "concerns the law," because what constitutes an "improvement" is almost always debatable.

EXPLANATION OF COMMENTS

[1] The Commentary to Canon 4C(2) was modified by removing language that was merely repetitive of the black letter text, and by deleting as infelicitous the reference to the need to "protect" the courts from controversy.

Comment [1] as revised more clearly reflects the point that service on governmental bodies should not be allowed to distract judges from their judicial duties or otherwise compromise their independence, impartiality, or integrity.

[2] New Comment [2] was moved from the black letter text of Canon 4C(2) of the 1990 Code.

In the Commission's view, the provision was of insufficiently general applicability to warrant treatment in the text.

RULE 3.5 Use of Nonpublic Information

A judge shall not intentionally disclose or use nonpublic information* acquired in a judicial capacity for any purpose unrelated to the judge's judicial duties.

† The "Reporters' Explanations of Changes" have not been approved by the ABA Joint Commission to Evaluate the Model Code of Judicial Conduct. They have been drafted by the Commission's Reporters, based on the proceedings and record of the Commission, solely to inform the ABA House of Delegates about each of the proposed amendments to the Model Code prior to their being considered at the ABA 2007 Midyear Meeting. THEY ARE NOT TO BE ADOPTED AS PART OF THE MODEL CODE.

Comment

[1] In the course of performing judicial duties, a judge may acquire information of commercial or other value that is unavailable to the public. The judge must not reveal or use such information for personal gain or for any purpose unrelated to his or her judicial duties.

[2] This rule is not intended, however, to affect a judge's ability to act on information as necessary to protect the health or safety of the judge or a member of a judge's family, court personnel, or other judicial officers if consistent with other provisions of this Code.

RULE 3.5—REPORTER'S EXPLANATION OF CHANGES†

1990 MODEL CODE COMPARISON

Rule 3.5 is based upon Canon 3B(12), with minor revisions, including addition of the word "intentionally" in the first line of the black letter text.

Comments [1] and [2] are new.

EXPLANATION OF BLACK LETTER

1. Rule 3.5 includes element of "intentional" conduct:

In the 1990 Code, this provision, Canon 3B(12) was found in the Canon on the performance of *judicial* duties. It was repositioned to Canon 3 on personal and extrajudicial activity, because it is a form of misuse of judicial office for personal gain or advantage. The word "intentionally" was added so as not to impose discipline for mere carelessness.

EXPLANATION OF COMMENTS

[1] New Comment [1] provides a link between using nonpublic information for personal advantage and abuse of judicial office.

[2] New Comment [2] recognizes the unfortunate reality that physical violence has become more common than formerly in and around the courts. If a judge learns of nonpublic information that constitutes a credible threat of violence against court personnel or family members, this Comment contemplates that the judge may take protective measures on the basis of that information.

RULE 3.6 Affiliation With Discriminatory Organizations

(A) A judge shall not hold membership in any organization that practices invidious discrimination on the basis of race, sex, gender, religion, national origin, ethnicity, or sexual orientation.

(B) A judge shall not use the benefits or facilities of an organization if the judge knows* or should know that the organization practices invidious discrimination on one or more of the bases identified in paragraph (A). A judge's attendance at an event in a facility of an organization that the judge is not permitted to join is not a violation of this Rule when the judge's attendance is an isolated event that could not reasonably be perceived as an endorsement of the organization's practices.

† The "Reporters' Explanations of Changes" have not been approved by the ABA Joint Commission to Evaluate the Model Code of Judicial Conduct. They have been drafted by the Commission's Reporters, based on the proceedings and record of the Commission, solely to inform the ABA House of Delegates about each of the proposed amendments to the Model Code prior to their being considered at the ABA 2007 Midyear Meeting. THEY ARE NOT TO BE ADOPTED AS PART OF THE MODEL CODE.

Comment

[1] A judge's public manifestation of approval of invidious discrimination on any basis gives rise to the appearance of impropriety and diminishes public confidence in the integrity and impartiality of the judiciary. A judge's membership in an organization that practices invidious discrimination creates the perception that the judge's impartiality is impaired.

[2] An organization is generally said to discriminate invidiously if it arbitrarily excludes from membership on the basis of race, sex, gender, religion, national origin, ethnicity, or sexual orientation persons who would otherwise be eligible for admission. Whether an organization practices invidious discrimination is a complex question to which judges should be attentive. The answer cannot be determined from a mere examination of an organization's current membership rolls, but rather, depends upon how the organization selects members, as well as other relevant factors, such as whether the organization is dedicated to the preservation of religious, ethnic, or cultural values of legitimate common interest to its members, or whether it is an intimate, purely private organization whose membership limitations could not constitutionally be prohibited.

[3] When a judge learns that an organization to which the judge belongs engages in invidious discrimination, the judge must resign immediately from the organization.

[4] A judge's membership in a religious organization as a lawful exercise of the freedom of religion is not a violation of this Rule.

[5] This Rule does not apply to national or state military service.

RULE 3.6—REPORTER'S EXPLANATION OF CHANGES†

1990 MODEL CODE COMPARISON

Rule 3.6 is based upon Canon 2C of the 1990 Code and its extensive Commentary. The Commentary was revised substantially, including some substantive changes. Some aspects of the Commentary in the 1990 Code were reworked and moved to the black letter text of Rule 3.6(B).

EXPLANATION OF BLACK LETTER

1. Rule 3.6(A) text is similar to Canon 2C of the 1990 Code.

It does expand the list of prohibited bases of invidious discrimination by adding gender, ethnicity, and sexual orientation.

2. Rule 3.6(B) derives chiefly from the last paragraph of the Commentary to Canon 2C of the 1990 Code, revised to change its focus, and then moved to the black letter text because of its practical importance.

The former Commentary permitted a judge who was already a member of an organization that engaged in invidious discrimination to remain a member for up to one year, if during that year the judge took steps to change the organization's policy. Rule 3.6(B) instead focuses upon the extent to which the judge actually *uses* the benefits or facilities provided by the organization. Building upon ideas found earlier in the Commentary to Canon 2C, the new Rule effectively provides that a judge cannot be the *initiating party* in scheduling an event or taking advantage of the facilities, but is permitted to attend an isolated event that has been scheduled or arranged by someone else, as long as it is clear that merely attending cannot reasonably be seen as an endorsement of the organization and its policies. A hypothetical that informed the Commission's deliberations concerned a wedding reception held at a discriminatory club that the judge could not join according to Rule 3.6(A): the judge could not schedule his or her *own* child's reception at the club, but could attend the reception of a friend or relative's child.

---

† The "Reporters' Explanations of Changes" have not been approved by the ABA Joint Commission to Evaluate the Model Code of Judicial Conduct. They have been drafted by the Commission's Reporters, based on the proceedings and record of the Commission, solely to inform the ABA House of Delegates about each of the proposed amendments to the Model Code prior to their being considered at the ABA 2007 Midyear Meeting. THEY ARE NOT TO BE ADOPTED AS PART OF THE MODEL CODE.

Because Rule 3.6(B) does not allow any active engagement with an organization that practices invidious discrimination, the one-year "grace period" to try to effect change has been eliminated. The Commission concluded that any active involvement would constitute too much of an endorsement of the organization; even good-faith behind-the-scene activities would not sufficiently negate the public's perception of bias.

See Comment [3], which confirms that the lack of any black letter exception regarding membership means that a judge must resign immediately upon learning of the organization's practices.

EXPLANATION OF COMMENTS

[1] This Comment blends the first sentence of the Commentary to Canon 2C of the 1990 Code with language found in the long second paragraph of that Commentary. Revised in part for style and in part for more completeness, the new Comment stresses that support for invidious discrimination generally, and especially through participation in organizations engaging in it, calls into question a judge's integrity and impartiality, and creates an appearance of impropriety.

[2] Based closely upon the first paragraph of the Commentary to Canon 2C, this Comment provides guidelines—but no hard-and-fast rules—to help determine when an organization engages in invidious discrimination, thus falling under the ban of Rule 3.6(A). The key test is a functional one: whether an excluded applicant (not possessing one of the listed characteristics) *would otherwise be eligible for admission to membership*. In addition, the Comment explains that certain organizations practicing some forms of discrimination cannot be said to be practicing *invidious* or *improper* discrimination, either because the discrimination is based upon rationales that are not socially harmful, or because the members of the organization have a constitutional right to associate without governmental interference.

Although the Commission received a large number of submissions arguing that a particular organization either did or did not practice invidious discrimination, it determined not to cast any judgments in stone. Policies of an organization might change over time, as might the constitutional standard for judging whether an organization is sufficiently "private" to be immune from governmental regulation of its membership policies.

[3] New Comment [3] replaces Commentary in the 1990 Code suggesting that as an alternative to resigning, a judge might instead remain with the organization for up to one year, while attempting to effect change from within. The Commission chose not to add such language to the text of Rule 3.6. Thus, Comment [3] requires immediate resignation to comply with Rule 3.6(A).

[4] The tenor of New Comment [4] was implicit in the Commentary to Canon 2C of the 1990 Code. Comment [4] makes clear that while many religious organizations engage in some forms of discrimination, and some religious organizations may engage in some invidious discrimination, participation by a judge in any bona fide religious organization cannot be prohibited or punished by governmental authorities because of the constitutional guarantee of the free exercise of religion.

[5] New Comment [5] was adopted by the Commission after receiving considerable commentary and after considerable debate. Like religious organizations, military organizations often engage in discrimination and sometimes engage in discrimination that would be found to be invidious in other contexts. The Commission concluded, however, that the practical difficulties involved in enforcing a ban on holding membership in military organizations, and the necessity for uniform rules across the military services, justified an interpretation that service in state and national military organizations does not violate this Rule.

RULE 3.7 Participation in Educational, Religious, Charitable, Fraternal, or Civic Organizations and Activities

(A) Subject to the requirements of Rule 3.1, a judge may participate in activities sponsored by organizations or governmental entities concerned with the law, the legal system, or the administration of justice, and those sponsored by or on behalf of educational, religious, charitable, fraternal, or civic organizations not conducted for profit, including but not limited to the following activities:

(1) assisting such an organization or entity in planning related to fund-raising, and participating in the management and investment of the organization's or entity's funds;

(2) soliciting* contributions* for such an organization or entity, but only from members of the judge's family,* or from judges over whom the judge does not exercise supervisory or appellate authority;

(3) soliciting membership for such an organization or entity, even though the membership dues or fees generated may be used to support the objectives of the organization or entity, but only if the organization or entity is concerned with the law, the legal system, or the administration of justice;

(4) appearing or speaking at, receiving an award or other recognition at, being featured on the program of, and permitting his or her title to be used in connection with an event of such an organization or entity, but if the event serves a fund-raising purpose, the judge may participate only if the event concerns the law, the legal system, or the administration of justice;

(5) making recommendations to such a public or private fund-granting organization or entity in connection with its programs and activities, but only if the organization or entity is concerned with the law, the legal system, or the administration of justice; and

(6) serving as an officer, director, trustee, or nonlegal advisor of such an organization or entity, unless it is likely that the organization or entity:

(a) will be engaged in proceedings that would ordinarily come before the judge; or

(b) will frequently be engaged in adversary proceedings in the court of which the judge is a member, or in any court subject to the appellate jurisdiction of the court of which the judge is a member.

(B) A judge may encourage lawyers to provide pro bono publico legal services.

Comment

[1] The activities permitted by paragraph (A) generally include those sponsored by or undertaken on behalf of public or private not-for-profit educational institutions, and other not-for-profit organizations, including law-related, charitable, and other organizations.

[2] Even for law-related organizations, a judge should consider whether the membership and purposes of the organization, or the nature of the judge's participation in or association with the organization, would conflict with the judge's obligation to refrain from activities that reflect adversely upon a judge's independence, integrity, and impartiality.

[3] Mere attendance at an event, whether or not the event serves a fund-raising purpose, does not constitute a violation of paragraph 4(A). It is also generally permissible for a judge to serve as an usher or a food server or preparer, or to perform similar functions, at fund-raising events sponsored by educational, religious, charitable, fraternal, or civic organizations. Such activities are not solicitation and do not present an element of coercion or abuse the prestige of judicial office.

[4] Identification of a judge's position in educational, religious, charitable, fraternal, or civic organizations on letterhead used for fund-raising or membership solicitation does not violate this Rule. The letterhead may list the judge's title or judicial office if comparable designations are used for other persons.

[5] In addition to appointing lawyers to serve as counsel for indigent parties in individual cases, a judge may promote broader access to justice by encouraging lawyers to participate in pro bono publico legal services, if in doing so the judge does not employ coercion, or abuse the prestige of judicial office. Such encouragement may take many forms, including providing lists of available programs, training lawyers to

do pro bono publico legal work, and participating in events recognizing lawyers who have done pro bono publico work.

RULE 3.7—REPORTER'S EXPLANATION OF CHANGES†

1990 MODEL CODE COMPARISON

Rule 3.7(A) and its Comments are based upon Canon 4C(3) and its subparagraphs and their Commentary. The 1990 Code has been thoroughly reorganized in the proposed Code, making line-by-line comparison difficult. Virtually all the concepts in Canon 4C(3) have been retained, although some have been made more expansive or more restrictive.

The specific reference in Rule 3.7(B) to pro bono publico legal services is new.

EXPLANATION OF BLACK LETTER

1. Rule 3.7(A) was expanded.

The lead-in to Paragraph (A) added "[s]ubject to the requirements of Rule 3.1," and included law-related public and private organizations and entities, as well as most nonprofit organizations, even if not law-related, within the reach of this paragraph; eliminated specific reference to service as an officer, director, or nonlegal advisor, and placed discussion of those specific situations in the subparagraphs.

This provision is integral to the reorganization of the material on participation in extrajudicial activities, and of Canon 3 generally. Canon 4C(3) of the 1990 Code referred at the outset to service as an officer or a director of various not-for-profit organizations, and then used several subparagraphs to deal with activities in which such officers or directors engaged. The lead-in to Rule 3.7(A) establishes its coverage of essentially the same organizations—public and private, law related and not law related—but then deals in the following subparagraphs with *all* activities related to those organizations, *including* service as an officer or a director.

The opening phrase, "[s]ubject to the requirements of Rule 3.1," is not greatly different in meaning from "subject to the other requirements of this Code," which appeared at the end of Canon 4C(3). Organizationally, however, the specific cross-reference in the proposed Code focuses attention upon particular problems closely associated with extrajudicial and personal activities—such as coercion, undue influence, or interference with the primacy of judicial duties—which is why they were gathered together in a single Rule at the beginning of Canon 3.

2. Rule 3.7(A)(1): repositioned, but substantially the same as the first clause of Canon 4C(3)(b)(i) of the 1990 Code.

The difference, however, as explained above in connection with the lead-in to Rule 3.7(A), is that the 1990 Code allowed these activities (assistance in planning fund-raising and management and investment of an organization's funds) *only* in connection with service as an officer, director, trustee, or nonlegal advisor, or the somewhat nebulous "as a member or otherwise." In the proposed Code, these activities are permissible without more, if participation in the activities of the organization or entity itself is permissible.

3. Rule 3.7(A)(2): substantially the same as the second clause of Canon 4C(3)(b)(i), except added soliciting funds from family members as permissible activity.

The repositioning of this provision into one of the subparagraphs of Rule 3.7(A) has the same significance as described above: it will apply to all judges who engage in this form of extrajudicial activity, not just those who serve as officers, directors, and the like. Judges were already permitted by the 1990 Code to solicit contributions for charities from judges over whom they did not exercise supervisory or appellate authority, because the element of coercion is largely missing, and there is little likelihood that the judge making the

† "Reporters' Explanations of Changes" have not been approved by the ABA Joint Commission to Evaluate the Model Code of Judicial Conduct. They have been drafted by the Commission's Reporters, based on the proceedings and record of the Commission, solely to inform the ABA House of Delegates about each of the proposed amendments to the Model Code prior to their being considered at the ABA 2007 Midyear Meeting. THEY ARE NOT TO BE ADOPTED AS PART OF THE MODEL CODE.

contribution would be perceived as attempting to influence the judge making the solicitation. The same rationales support extending permission to judges to solicit this kind of contribution from their own family members.

4. Rule 3.7(A)(3): based upon some aspects of Canon 4C(3)(b)(iii), but with other elements added or deleted or repositioned elsewhere in Canon 3.

The basic idea of prohibiting a judge from soliciting membership in an organization where charging membership dues is essentially a fund-raising device is retained. The rationale is essentially the same as that in the 1990 Code: the risk that persons contacted will feel coerced into joining, or will attempt to curry favor with a sitting judge by joining.

In the proposed Code, however, it is not necessary to advert specifically to the element of coercion—that is covered by the cross-reference to Rule 3.1. Beyond this, the Commission decided to limit the permission granted to solicit membership to membership in law-related organizations—one of several places in Canon 3 where this line is drawn. It was felt that solicitation of membership in a law-related organization, such as a bar association or moot court society, would be perceived as more natural or more appropriate than soliciting membership in a fine arts society or the American Red Cross. This perception is related, at least indirectly, to the thematic requirement of avoiding abuse of the prestige of judicial office. A person who loves opera or is a dedicated member of an environmental protection organization, and who also happens to be a judge, should not use that position as an added reason for someone else to join the cause. On the other hand, it is not inappropriate for judges to use their positions as leaders in the legal community to increase membership in law-related organizations.

5. Rule 3.7(A)(4): a new provision for the Model Code of Judicial Conduct, based upon Commentary to Canons 5B(2) and 5B(3) of the Code of Conduct for United States Judges, and reversing the thrust of Commentary to Canon 4C(3)(b).

The Code of Conduct for United States Judges provides that as a general matter, judges may *not* participate in the fund-raising activities of charitable and other civic organizations other than by attending, which is similar to Commentary in the 1990 Code. In context, however, the federal provision appears to be limited to non-law-related organizations and activities. The Commission adopted the same general stance in Rule 3.7(A)(4), but made the implicit exception explicit: a judge *is* permitted to be a featured speaker or participant at an event that has a fund-raising purpose, *but only if the organization or entity is a law-related one*. The rationale for making this distinction is the same as that for Rule 3.7(A)(3).

6. Rule 3.7(A)(5): essentially the same as Canon 4C(3)(b)(ii) of the 1990 Code.

The one exception is that the authority to make recommendations to fund-granting organizations and entities is not limited to officers, directors, and others directly associated with the organization or entity. This is consistent with the revised organization of Canon 3 generally, and Rule 3.7 specifically, as noted above in connection with the lead-in to Rule 3.7(A) and Rule 3.7(A)(1).

7. Rule 3.7(A)(6): essentially identical to Canon 4C(3)(a) of the 1990 Code.

In the 1990 Code, there was some redundancy between this provision and Canon 4C(3) itself. The main paragraph already dealt generally with service as officer, director, and the like, while subparagraph (a) dealt with restrictions on such service. Rule 3.7(A)(6) makes no substantive change in the combined effect of those two provisions, but makes explicit that service is allowed in both private organizations and public entities, *whether or not they are law related*, as long as the two caveats are satisfied.

Unlike situations in which a judge is soliciting funds or members, participating as an officer or a director does not present the dangers of coercion or abuse of the prestige of judicial office; accordingly, neither the 1990 Code nor the proposed Code differentiate in this area along that axis.

8. Rule 3.7(B): a new provision, encouraging judges to provide leadership in increasing *pro bono publico* lawyering in their respective jurisdictions.

This provision is consistent with the thrust of Rule 3.7(A). It was placed in a separate paragraph because paragraph (A) deals with a large variety of organizations and entities, with varied goals and programs, whereas paragraph (B) refers to specific activities, whether or not conducted in connection with a particular organization or entity.

EXPLANATION OF COMMENTS

[1] New Comment [1] clarifies that the restructuring of Rule 3.7(A) was intended to make it applicable to all public and private not-for-profit organizations and entities. Previously, there was some confusion about the status of public and private universities, including their law schools (which are obviously law-related). Thus, it is permissible, for example, for a judge to serve as a trustee of a private university (rather than merely its law school), as long as it is not conducted for profit.

[2] This Comment is derived from Commentary to Canon 4C(3) of the 1990 Code, but it has been thoroughly revised to provide more clarity. The revised Comment serves as a reminder that participation in law-related activities is permitted more often than is participation in non-law-related activities, *but that even in connection with the former*, other requirements of the proposed Code may counsel caution or even abstention from the activity. Obvious examples include participating in activities sponsored by organizations that practice invidious discrimination, or serving as the president of a major university (the time commitment associated with the latter making it impossible for a judge to attend to judicial duties).

[3] New Comment [3] is designed to provide a safe harbor for certain minor and noncoercive activities undertaken in connection with an organization's or entity's fund-raising efforts. When a judge donates time to serve food or serve as an usher or other facilitator at an event, the dangers associated with direct solicitation of funds are not present. It is not logical to assume that someone will make a larger donation, merely because a judge is tending the barbeque pit at a charity picnic.

The Commission stopped short, however, of giving as specific examples situations involving the handling of money, such as when a judge serves as ticket-taker or cashier (at a charity bingo night, for example, or a charity auction). At the same time, these activities were not specifically excluded, either. Whether such activities are appropriate depends upon analysis of the overall event, and the significance of the judge's participation. As long as there is no coercion—even subtle and unstated coercion—and as long as the judge's position as a judge is not being exploited, the activity is permissible.

[4] This Comment is based upon parts of the second paragraph of the Commentary to Canon 4C(3)(b) of the 1990 Code, but simplified. Letterhead including a judge's name and position, even when used for fund-raising or membership solicitation purposes, is not coercive and does not abuse the prestige of judicial office, as long as the judge is identified in the same way as other persons on the letterhead. It must be assumed, of course, that the judge's service in some official position in the organization or entity is itself appropriate under other provisions of Rules 3.7 and 3.1.

[5] New Comment [5], responsive to new Rule 3.7(B), makes clear that judges may encourage lawyers to engage in *pro bono publico* service generally, quite apart from situations in which judges may appoint counsel for indigent parties in individual cases. Although the Joint Commission assumed that participation in organizations that promote *pro bono publico* legal services would generally be permissible under rule 3.7(A), it wanted to stress the importance of such service by including a specific provision on this topic.

RULE 3.8 Appointments to Fiduciary Positions

(A) A judge shall not accept appointment to serve in a fiduciary* position, such as executor, administrator, trustee, guardian, attorney in fact, or other personal representative, except for the estate, trust, or person of a member of the judge's family,* and then only if such service will not interfere with the proper performance of judicial duties.

(B) A judge shall not serve in a fiduciary position if the judge as fiduciary will likely be engaged in proceedings that would ordinarily come before the judge, or if the estate, trust, or ward becomes involved in adversary proceedings in the court on which the judge serves, or one under its appellate jurisdiction.

(C) A judge acting in a fiduciary capacity shall be subject to the same restrictions on engaging in financial activities that apply to a judge personally.

(D) If a person who is serving in a fiduciary position becomes a judge, he or she must comply with this Rule as soon as reasonably practicable, but in no event later than [one year] after becoming a judge.

Comment

[1] A judge should recognize that other restrictions imposed by this Code may conflict with a judge's obligations as a fiduciary; in such circumstances, a judge should resign as fiduciary. For example, serving as a fiduciary might require frequent disqualification of a judge under Rule 2.11 because a judge is deemed to have an economic interest in shares of stock held by a trust if the amount of stock held is more than de minimis.

RULE 3.8—REPORTER'S EXPLANATION OF CHANGES†

1990 MODEL CODE COMPARISON

Rule 3.8(A) is essentially identical to Canon 4E(1), with only minor stylistic revisions.

Rule 3.8(B) is essentially identical to Canon 4E(2), also with only minor revisions.

Rule 3.8(C) bears the same relationship to Canon 4E(3).

Rule 3.8(D) is based upon the first paragraph of the Commentary to Canon 4E, but states more directly the time for compliance with the Rule.

Comment [1] is similar to the second paragraph of Commentary to Canon 4E, but recast.

EXPLANATION OF BLACK LETTER

1. Rule 3.8(A): changed the phrase "A judge shall not serve" to "A judge shall not accept appointment to."

No significant substantive change is intended. The new language suggests more of a choice on the judge's part—a choice that must be rejected, except in the case of family members.

2. Rule 3.8(B): changed the phrase "shall not serve as a fiduciary" to "shall not serve in a fiduciary position."

No substantive change is intended, except that serving in a fiduciary *position* connotes a formal appointment and acceptance, as in Rule 3.8(A).

3. Rule 3.8(C): changed the phrase "the same restrictions that apply" to "shall be subject to the same restrictions."

The change is stylistic only.

4. Rule 3.8(D): is new to the black letter text.

It states when a newly elected or appointed judge, who is *already* serving in a fiduciary capacity, must comply with this Rule. The suggested outer limit is one year, but jurisdictions may choose some other time limit.

EXPLANATION OF COMMENTS

[1] This is a slight recasting of the second paragraph of the 1990 Commentary. The Comment serves as a reminder that in addition to the restrictions set forth in Rule 3.8, other provisions of the proposed Code may implicate the permissibility of serving in a fiduciary capacity. For example, if serving as a fiduciary (even for a family member, which is generally permitted) would cause the judge frequently to be disqualified under Rule 2.11, the judge must resign as fiduciary to avoid violation of Rule 3.1(B).

† The "Reporters' Explanations of Changes" have not been approved by the ABA Joint Commission to Evaluate the Model Code of Judicial Conduct. They have been drafted by the Commission's Reporters, based on the proceedings and record of the Commission, solely to inform the ABA House of Delegates about each of the proposed amendments to the Model Code prior to their being considered at the ABA 2007 Midyear Meeting. THEY ARE NOT TO BE ADOPTED AS PART OF THE MODEL CODE.

RULE 3.9 Service as Arbitrator or Mediator

A judge shall not act as an arbitrator or a mediator or perform other judicial functions apart from the judge's official duties unless expressly authorized by law.*

Comment

[1] This Rule does not prohibit a judge from participating in arbitration, mediation, or settlement conferences performed as part of assigned judicial duties. Rendering dispute resolution services apart from those duties, whether or not for economic gain, is prohibited unless it is expressly authorized by law.

RULE 3.9—REPORTER'S EXPLANATION OF CHANGES†

1990 MODEL CODE COMPARISON

Rule 3.9 is based upon Canon 4F, slightly recast.

Comment [1] is the same as the Commentary to Canon 4F, except that an additional sentence was added.

EXPLANATION OF BLACK LETTER

1. Rule 3.9: changed the phrase "in a private capacity" to "apart from the judge's official duties," and slightly revised the text in other respects.

The only substantive change was made in recognition of the fact that a judge could be called upon to provide dispute resolution services *for another governmental entity*. Thus, the phase "in a private capacity" was deemed to be too narrow.

EXPLANATION OF COMMENTS

[1] The first sentence of this Comment is carried forward from the 1990 Commentary. The second sentence explains that the prohibition extends to judges going outside their regular judicial duties to assist in dispute resolution, whether or not for economic gain, unless doing so is expressly authorized by law, such as by court rule.

The Commission heard testimony and received comments on this issue. Some objected that allowing judges to participate in private "rent-a-judge" programs for economic gain would allow judges to trade on their status as judges, thus abusing the prestige of judicial office. Others expressed concern that allowing judges to routinely perform extrajudicial "judicial" services, even without compensation, could create public confusion about the role of the judiciary as an independent branch of the government, thus diminishing respect for the judicial system. Still others were concerned that extrajudicial participation even in *pro bono publico* mediation and arbitration could distract judges from their primary obligations.

Several judges stated their support for permitting judges to provide alternative dispute resolution services to other court systems or to private parties, but without compensation. In their view, this would provide an important public service to the community, demystify the law, and integrate judges into the community as Canon 3 encourages.

The Commission continued the proscription of Canon 4F of the 1990 Code that all such activities are prohibited, whether or not compensation is involved, but that courts or jurisdictions could authorize such activities as conditions warrant.

† The "Reporters' Explanations of Changes" have not been approved by the ABA Joint Commission to Evaluate the Model Code of Judicial Conduct. They have been drafted by the Commission's Reporters, based on the proceedings and record of the Commission, solely to inform the ABA House of Delegates about each of the proposed amendments to the Model Code prior to their being considered at the ABA 2007 Midyear Meeting. THEY ARE NOT TO BE ADOPTED AS PART OF THE MODEL CODE.

RULE 3.10 Practice of Law

A judge shall not practice law. A judge may act pro se and may, without compensation, give legal advice to and draft or review documents for a member of the judge's family,* but is prohibited from serving as the family member's lawyer in any forum.

Comment

[1] A judge may act pro se in all legal matters, including matters involving litigation and matters involving appearances before or other dealings with governmental bodies. A judge must not use the prestige of office to advance the judge's personal or family interests. See Rule 1.3.

RULE 3.10—REPORTER'S EXPLANATION OF CHANGES†

1990 MODEL CODE COMPARISON

Rule 3.10 is essentially identical to Canon 4G, with language based upon the second paragraph of Commentary to 4G added as black letter text.

Comment [1] is based upon the first paragraph of the Commentary to Canon 4G.

EXPLANATION OF BLACK LETTER

1. <u>Rule 3.10: blended the two sentences of Canon 4G into one.</u>

2. <u>Commentary from the 1990 Code interpreting Canon 4G as prohibiting a judge from representing a family member has been added to the black letter.</u>

The prohibition against "representing a family member in any court" is a narrower restriction than was "acting as an advocate or negotiator . . . in a legal matter." The Commission took the view that in some informal settings, such as a dispute in a neighborhood association or a purely private and minor commercial dispute, a judge may serve as an "advocate" for a family member without becoming his or her lawyer and thus practicing law in violation of Rule 3.10.

EXPLANATION OF COMMENTS

[1] The first paragraph of the Commentary to Canon 4G was revised slightly and recast. "A judge must not abuse the prestige of office to advance" was replaced with "A judge must not use the prestige of office to advance." No substantive change is intended.

RULE 3.11 Financial, Business, or Remunerative Activities

(A) A judge may hold and manage investments of the judge and members of the judge's family.*

(B) A judge shall not serve as an officer, director, manager, general partner, advisor, or employee of any business entity except that a judge may manage or participate in:

(1) a business closely held by the judge or members of the judge's family; or

† The "Reporters' Explanations of Changes" have not been approved by the ABA Joint Commission to Evaluate the Model Code of Judicial Conduct. They have been drafted by the Commission's Reporters, based on the proceedings and record of the Commission, solely to inform the ABA House of Delegates about each of the proposed amendments to the Model Code prior to their being considered at the ABA 2007 Midyear Meeting. THEY ARE NOT TO BE ADOPTED AS PART OF THE MODEL CODE.

(2) a business entity primarily engaged in investment of the financial resources of the judge or members of the judge's family.

(C) A judge shall not engage in financial activities permitted under paragraphs (A) and (B) if they will:

(1) interfere with the proper performance of judicial duties;

(2) lead to frequent disqualification of the judge;

(3) involve the judge in frequent transactions or continuing business relationships with lawyers or other persons likely to come before the court on which the judge serves; or

(4) result in violation of other provisions of this Code.

Comment

[1] Judges are generally permitted to engage in financial activities, including managing real estate and other investments for themselves or for members of their families. Participation in these activities, like participation in other extrajudicial activities, is subject to the requirements of this Code. For example, it would be improper for a judge to spend so much time on business activities that it interferes with the performance of judicial duties. See Rule 2.1. Similarly, it would be improper for a judge to use his or her official title or appear in judicial robes in business advertising, or to conduct his or her business or financial affairs in such a way that disqualification is frequently required. See Rules 1.3 and 2.11.

[2] As soon as practicable without serious financial detriment, the judge must divest himself or herself of investments and other financial interests that might require frequent disqualification or otherwise violate this Rule.

RULE 3.11—REPORTER'S EXPLANATION OF CHANGES†

1990 MODEL CODE COMPARISON

Rule 3.11(A) is derived from Canon 4D(2), excluding the last two clauses.

Rule 3.11(B) is essentially the same as Canon 4D(3).

Rule 3.11(C) combines some new provisions with elements of Canon 4D(1)(b) and Canon 4D(4).

Comment [1] is largely new, but incorporates several aspects of the Commentary to Canon 4D.

Comment [2] is derived from the black letter text of Canon 4D(4).

EXPLANATION OF BLACK LETTER

1. Rule 3.11(A): retained the core language of Canon 4D(2), but deleted the lead-in phrase "subject to the requirements of this Code," as well as the references to "real estate" holdings and "other remunerative activities."

Rule 3.11 represents a reorganization of most of the material governing extrajudicial financial activities found in Canon 4D of the 1990 Code, except for the gift-related provisions in Canon 4D(5).

In Rule 3.11(A), the initial "subject to the requirements of this Code" was deleted as no longer necessary, in light of Rule 3.11(C)(4), as well as Comment [1]. The reference to "real estate" was deemed too specific for inclusion in the black letter text, and moved to Comment [1] as an example of the kinds of investments that

† The "Reporters' Explanations of Changes" have not been approved by the ABA Joint Commission to Evaluate the Model Code of Judicial Conduct. They have been drafted by the Commission's Reporters, based on the proceedings and record of the Commission, solely to inform the ABA House of Delegates about each of the proposed amendments to the Model Code prior to their being considered at the ABA 2007 Midyear Meeting. THEY ARE NOT TO BE ADOPTED AS PART OF THE MODEL CODE.

a judge might hold or manage. The last clause, "engage in other remunerative activity," was removed as far too broad, and thus inconsistent with other aspects of Rule 3.11. For example, the remunerative activity of being a director or employee of a for-profit business entity is prohibited by Rule 3.11(B), unless the business is closely held by the judge or the judge's family.

2. Rule 3.11(B) is identical to Canon 4D(3) of the 1990 Code, except that the caveat "subject to the requirements of this Code" was eliminated as unnecessary, for the reasons stated immediately above.

The Commission discussed the substantive point of Rule 3.11(B), which is to prohibit judges from engaging in off-bench remunerative activity, except in the case of closely held family businesses, including the investment of financial resources. This exception has been criticized as inconsistent with the rationale for the basic prohibition, and as unfair to judges who do not have family businesses.

Two alternatives were considered, but not adopted. First, it would have been possible to allow judges broadly to engage in remunerative extrajudicial activities, as long as they did not interfere with the performance of judicial duties, lead to frequent disqualification, or otherwise violate the prohibitions found in Rule 3.11(C). The other possibility would have been to eliminate the family business exception and to require all judges to divest themselves of any interests in the family business when ascending the bench. The Commission elected to maintain the status quo of the 1990 Code as a reasonable middle ground.

3. Rule 3.11(C) is a new provision that gathers in one place some of the caveats about extrajudicial financial activities found throughout Canon 4D of the 1990 Code, while adding additional caveats.

These caveats are meant to apply as restrictions on otherwise permissible activities. The specific language of Rule 3.11(C)(1) is taken from the fourth paragraph of the Commentary to Canon 4D(1); the concept is also drawn in part from the second paragraph of the Commentary to Canon 4D(3): otherwise appropriate business activities (falling within the family business exception) would become improper if "participation requires significant time away from judicial duties."

Rule 3.11(C)(2) is a paraphrase of Canon 4D(4), which requires a judge to minimize the number of cases in which the judge is disqualified. The phraseology used in the proposed Code, "will lead to frequent disqualification of the judge," is used elsewhere in the Code—most significantly for present purposes in Rule 3.1(B).

Rule 3.11(C)(3) is taken from Canon 4D(1)(b), and Rule 3.11(C)(4) is a catchall that makes some other caveats found in Canon 4D unnecessary. For example, the Canon 4D(1)(a) provision, "may reasonably be perceived to exploit the judge's judicial position," was not retained in the proposed Code, because of the prohibition against abusing the prestige of judicial office already found in Rule 1.3.

EXPLANATION OF COMMENTS

[1] New Comment [1] restates the rationale of several of the provisions gathered into Rule 3.11(C), giving some practical examples.

[2] New Comment [2] is essentially the same as the black letter text of Canon 4D(4).

RULE 3.12 Compensation for Extrajudicial Activities

A judge may accept reasonable compensation for extrajudicial activities permitted by this Code or other law* unless such acceptance would appear to a reasonable person to undermine the judge's independence,* integrity,* or impartiality.*

Comment

[1] A judge is permitted to accept honoraria, stipends, fees, wages, salaries, royalties, or other compensation for speaking, teaching, writing, and other extrajudicial activities, provided the compensation is reasonable and commensurate with the task performed. The judge should be mindful, however, that judicial duties must take precedence over other activities. See Rule 2.1.

[2] Compensation derived from extrajudicial activities may be subject to public reporting. See Rule 3.15.

RULE 3.12—REPORTER'S EXPLANATION OF CHANGES†

1990 MODEL CODE COMPARISON

Rule 3.12 is based upon Canon 4H(1), but only as it relates to compensation, not reimbursement of expenses associated with extrajudicial activities. (Reimbursement is governed by Rule 3.14 in the proposed Code.)

Comment [1] is based upon the black letter text of Canon 4H(1)(a) and some aspects of the Commentary to Canon 4H, but substantially revised.

Comment [2] is new, and serves as a cross-reference to the public reporting provisions of the proposed Code. (Public reporting was addressed in Canon 4H(2), but in connection with compensation only, not reimbursement of expenses. Rule 3.15 addresses all forms of public reporting—compensation, gifts, other things of value, reimbursement of expenses, and waivers of fees.)

EXPLANATION OF BLACK LETTER

1. Rule 3.12: removed references to reimbursement of expenses, and substituted "reasonable compensation" for "shall not exceed for a person who is not a judge would receive for the same activity"; replaced the phrase "give the appearance of influencing the judge's performance of judicial duties or otherwise give the appearance of impropriety" with "would appear to a reasonable person to undermine the judge's independence, integrity, or impartiality."

The Joint Commission completely reorganized the material on compensation, reimbursement for expenses, acceptance of gifts and the like, and public reporting of all these. After the reorganization, Rule 3.12 deals only with compensation for permissible extrajudicial activities. Public reporting of the compensation received, as well as all other reporting, is governed by Rule 3.15.

The language measuring the reasonableness of compensation by what a non-judge would receive was deleted as unsound: if a judge were to be compensated for teaching a law school course on judicial ethics, or giving a lecture on evidentiary rulings, for example, the judge's services would in fact likely be more valuable than those of a non-judge. On the other hand, it was recognized that significant overcompensation could be a mask for an improper gift or an attempt to influence the judge's conduct in office. Accordingly, the language in Canon 4H(1) about appearances was replaced by the language used throughout Canon 3 of the proposed Code: "would appear to a reasonable person to undermine the judge's independence, integrity, or impartiality."

EXPLANATION OF COMMENTS

[1] New Comment [1] is based in part upon some of the language in Canon 4H of the 1990 Code and Rule 3.12 of the proposed Code.

[2] New Comment [2] makes a cross-reference to the public reporting requirement. Some aspects of public reporting were treated in Canon 4H(2), but now all are treated in Rule 3.15.

---

† The "Reporters' Explanations of Changes" have not been approved by the ABA Joint Commission to Evaluate the Model Code of Judicial Conduct. They have been drafted by the Commission's Reporters, based on the proceedings and record of the Commission, solely to inform the ABA House of Delegates about each of the proposed amendments to the Model Code prior to their being considered at the ABA 2007 Midyear Meeting. THEY ARE NOT TO BE ADOPTED AS PART OF THE MODEL CODE.

RULE 3.13 Acceptance and Reporting of Gifts, Loans, Bequests, Benefits, or Other Things of Value

(A) A judge shall not accept any gifts, loans, bequests, benefits, or other things of value, if acceptance is prohibited by law* or would appear to a reasonable person to undermine the judge's independence,* integrity,* or impartiality.*

(B) Unless otherwise prohibited by law, or by paragraph (A), a judge may accept the following without publicly reporting such acceptance:

(1) items with little intrinsic value, such as plaques, certificates, trophies, and greeting cards;

(2) gifts, loans, bequests, benefits, or other things of value from friends, relatives, or other persons, including lawyers, whose appearance or interest in a proceeding pending* or impending* before the judge would in any event require disqualification of the judge under Rule 2.11;

(3) ordinary social hospitality;

(4) commercial or financial opportunities and benefits, including special pricing and discounts, and loans from lending institutions in their regular course of business, if the same opportunities and benefits or loans are made available on the same terms to similarly situated persons who are not judges;

(5) rewards and prizes given to competitors or participants in random drawings, contests, or other events that are open to persons who are not judges;

(6) scholarships, fellowships, and similar benefits or awards, if they are available to similarly situated persons who are not judges, based upon the same terms and criteria;

(7) books, magazines, journals, audiovisual materials, and other resource materials supplied by publishers on a complimentary basis for official use; or

(8) gifts, awards, or benefits associated with the business, profession, or other separate activity of a spouse, a domestic partner,* or other family member of a judge residing in the judge's household,* but that incidentally benefit the judge.

(C) Unless otherwise prohibited by law or by paragraph (A), a judge may accept the following items, and must report such acceptance to the extent required by Rule 3.15:

(1) gifts incident to a public testimonial;

(2) invitations to the judge and the judge's spouse, domestic partner, or guest to attend without charge:

(a) an event associated with a bar-related function or other activity relating to the law, the legal system, or the administration of justice; or

(b) an event associated with any of the judge's educational, religious, charitable, fraternal or civic activities permitted by this Code, if the same invitation is offered to nonjudges who are engaged in similar ways in the activity as is the judge; and

(3) gifts, loans, bequests, benefits, or other things of value, if the source is a party or other person, including a lawyer, who has come or is likely to come before the judge, or whose interests have come or are likely to come before the judge.

Comment

[1] Whenever a judge accepts a gift or other thing of value without paying fair market value, there is a risk that the benefit might be viewed as intended to influence the judge's decision in a case. Rule 3.13

imposes restrictions upon the acceptance of such benefits, according to the magnitude of the risk. Paragraph (B) identifies circumstances in which the risk that the acceptance would appear to undermine the judge's independence, integrity, or impartiality is low, and explicitly provides that such items need not be publicly reported. As the value of the benefit or the likelihood that the source of the benefit will appear before the judge increases, the judge is either prohibited under paragraph (A) from accepting the gift, or required under paragraph (C) to publicly report it.

[2] Gift-giving between friends and relatives is a common occurrence, and ordinarily does not create an appearance of impropriety or cause reasonable persons to believe that the judge's independence, integrity, or impartiality has been compromised. In addition, when the appearance of friends or relatives in a case would require the judge's disqualification under Rule 2.11, there would be no opportunity for a gift to influence the judge's decision making. Paragraph (B)(2) places no restrictions upon the ability of a judge to accept gifts or other things of value from friends or relatives under these circumstances, and does not require public reporting.

[3] Businesses and financial institutions frequently make available special pricing, discounts, and other benefits, either in connection with a temporary promotion or for preferred customers, based upon longevity of the relationship, volume of business transacted, and other factors. A judge may freely accept such benefits if they are available to the general public, or if the judge qualifies for the special price or discount according to the same criteria as are applied to persons who are not judges. As an example, loans provided at generally prevailing interest rates are not gifts, but a judge could not accept a loan from a financial institution at below-market interest rates unless the same rate was being made available to the general public for a certain period of time or only to borrowers with specified qualifications that the judge also possesses.

[4] Rule 3.13 applies only to acceptance of gifts or other things of value by a judge. Nonetheless, if a gift or other benefit is given to the judge's spouse, domestic partner, or member of the judge's family residing in the judge's household, it may be viewed as an attempt to evade Rule 3.13 and influence the judge indirectly. Where the gift or benefit is being made primarily to such other persons, and the judge is merely an incidental beneficiary, this concern is reduced. A judge should, however, remind family and household members of the restrictions imposed upon judges, and urge them to take these restrictions into account when making decisions about accepting such gifts or benefits.

[5] Rule 3.13 does not apply to contributions to a judge's campaign for judicial office. Such contributions are governed by other Rules of this Code, including Rules 4.3 and 4.4.

RULE 3.13—REPORTER'S EXPLANATION OF CHANGES†

1990 MODEL CODE COMPARISON

Rule 3.13 is based upon Canon 4D(5), its subsections (a) through (h), and the related Commentary. The Commission thoroughly reorganized this material. In the analysis of the black letter and Comments that follows, the source of the language used in the proposed Code will be identified, where germane.

EXPLANATION OF BLACK LETTER

1. Rule 3.13(A): expanded the universe of coverage to include "other things of value," and linked the overall prohibition of acceptance to what "would appear to a reasonable person to undermine the judge's independence, integrity, or impartiality."

This paragraph has some similarity to Canon 4D(5), but ultimately establishes a different organization and a different mode of analysis. Canon 4D(5) established a general prohibition against a judge accepting gifts or loans or similar items from anyone, but then proceeded to make exceptions in subsections (a) through (h).

† The "Reporters' Explanations of Changes" have not been approved by the ABA Joint Commission to Evaluate the Model Code of Judicial Conduct. They have been drafted by the Commission's Reporters, based on the proceedings and record of the Commission, solely to inform the ABA House of Delegates about each of the proposed amendments to the Model Code prior to their being considered at the ABA 2007 Midyear Meeting. THEY ARE NOT TO BE ADOPTED AS PART OF THE MODEL CODE.

Rule 3.13(A) also begins with a list of gifts and things of value that judges are prohibited from accepting. There are no exceptions. The later provisions in Rule 3.13 permit acceptance of some items, sometimes accompanied by public reporting and sometimes not, but in each instance permission is granted only after it has been determined that acceptance has not already been barred by paragraph (A).

This different relationship between earlier and later provisions within Rule 3.13 is characteristic of the Commission's tiered approach to this subject matter. Paragraph (A) establishes a first tier of situations in which acceptance is not permitted at all; paragraph (B) deals with acceptance of items that are not problematic and do not require the transparency of public reporting; and paragraph (C) deals with the tier of items that do not warrant being banned, but must be reported to maintain the public's confidence in the judiciary.

The dividing line between gifts and other items that cannot be accepted at all and those that may be accepted subject to the requirement of public reporting, is when acceptance "would appear to a reasonable person to undermine the judge's independence, integrity, or impartiality." The language is new, and is used thematically throughout Canon 3. It requires judges to evaluate their conduct as would a "reasonable person" subject to later oversight by disciplinary authorities.

2. Rule 3.13(B): established a "tier" of gifts and other things of value that may be accepted without limitation and without public reporting, drawing several items from the exceptions set forth in the subsections of Canon 4D(5), but with an eye toward classifying them according to the proposed new organizational scheme.

In the 1990 Code, the exceptions to the basic rule were set out serially, without further classification, and—except in the catchall provision of Canon 4D(5)(h)—without adverting to whether public reporting was a condition of acceptance. The Commission has now gathered in Rule 3.13(B) the items that are sufficiently non-threatening to the integrity of the judicial system as to warrant no further regulation.

For example, subparagraphs (4), (5), and (6) deal with situations in which the listed benefits are equally available to similarly situated persons who are not judges, thus allaying any fears that the benefit is being extended to influence the judge's decision-making or to curry favor with the judge. Subparagraph (2) is similar to Canon 4D(5)(e), but clarifies the category. If a person's appearance or interest in a case pending or impending before a particular judge would require the disqualification of the judge, then any gift or favor from that person could not influence the judge—because by definition the judge would no longer be sitting on the case.

3. Rule 3.13(C): establishes the third "tier" of items that may be accepted by a judge. These items, while not causing a reasonable person to believe that the judge's independence, integrity, or impartiality would be undermined, are of sufficient concern that public reporting is required.

Placement of these items in Rule 3.13(C) rather than paragraphs (A) or (B) represents the Commission's assessment of the level of concern that may attend the acceptance of various benefits. In subparagraph (C)(2)(a), for example, the judgment was made that the gift of a free ticket to attend a law-related event must be reported, so that others might be able to assess whether a particular judge had a particularly close association with a particular bar association or organization. On the other hand, if a judge is invited to attend, free of charge, an event sponsored by a non-law-related organization, the judge cannot accept *at all* unless the additional condition of equal treatment is met. If that condition is met, however, then public reporting should be sufficient to allay concerns about possible lack of impartiality. (This distinction between events and organizations that are or are not law-related is another theme that occurs throughout Canon 3.)

Rule 3.13(C)(3) addresses the same issue as Canon 4D(5)(h), but according to a more discriminating analysis. Under the 1990 Code, a judge cannot accept any gift or favor from a lawyer or party who has come or is likely to come before the judge. (The further requirement of publicly reporting items over $150 appears to apply to other gifts, not the above.) If this means to impose a lifetime ban once a lawyer or the lawyer's firm "has appeared" before the judge, it appears to be more stringent than necessary, and unworkable in practice, as a judge's career lengthens.

Under Rule 3.13(C)(3), the proposed rule provides that such gifts may be accepted as long as they are reported—which will give another party in litigation an opportunity to consider whether disqualification of the judge is required. More important, placement of this item in paragraph (C) assumes that the size of a particular gift or other circumstances will not cause a reasonable person to fear that the judge's impartiality will be impaired. If a reasonable person would take that view, then the gift is wholly impermissible to accept, because it will have failed the test of Rule 3.13(A).

EXPLANATION OF COMMENTS

[1] New Comment [1] explains the three-tiered approach and its rationale.

[2] New Comment [2] explains the classification in Rule 3.13 of gifts and other things of value given to a judge. This subject was treated in both Canon 4D(5)(d) (gifts for special occasions) and Canon 4D(5)(e) (judge would be disqualified in any event), but without an explanation of the rationale. Rule 3.13(B)(2) does not distinguish between different types of gifts from this category of donor, and Comment [2] provides the common rationale.

[3] New Comment [3] provides the rationale for and giving a concrete example of the principle that acceptance of benefits and other things of value that are generally available to non-judges on the same basis as they are available to judges causes no ethical concerns; accordingly, these items may be accepted, without public reporting.

[4] This Comment builds on the introductory language of Canon 4D(5) of the 1990 Code. The point is that while a code of judicial ethics cannot directly bind family members and others close to a judge, it is still prudent for a judge to urge such individuals not to put the judge in a difficult position by accepting gifts and benefits that the judge could not, because others might perceive the benefit as intended for the judge, but given indirectly.

Comment [4] also adds discussion of a contrasting scenario, which is new. Rule 3.13(B)(8) states that when a gift or other benefit is given to a family member, because of the family member's business or other activities, and the judge benefits merely incidentally, concern that the judge is being influenced or importuned is no longer reasonable, and those gifts need not be reported by the judge. Comment [4] explains the rationale for this new provision.

[5] This Comment paraphrases the first paragraph of the Commentary following Canon 4D(5). The Comment thus makes clear that gifts, donations, or contributions to a judge's campaign for judicial office are governed entirely by Canon 4, which includes regulation of campaign committees.

RULE 3.14 Reimbursement of Expenses and Waivers of Fees or Charges

(A) Unless otherwise prohibited by Rules 3.1 and 3.13(A) or other law,* a judge may accept reimbursement of necessary and reasonable expenses for travel, food, lodging, or other incidental expenses, or a waiver or partial waiver of fees or charges for registration, tuition, and similar items, from sources other than the judge's employing entity, if the expenses or charges are associated with the judge's participation in extrajudicial activities permitted by this Code.

(B) Reimbursement of expenses for necessary travel, food, lodging, or other incidental expenses shall be limited to the actual costs reasonably incurred by the judge and, when appropriate to the occasion, by the judge's spouse, domestic partner,* or guest.

(C) A judge who accepts reimbursement of expenses or waivers or partial waivers of fees or charges on behalf of the judge or the judge's spouse, domestic partner, or guest shall publicly report such acceptance as required by Rule 3.15.

Comment

[1] Educational, civic, religious, fraternal, and charitable organizations often sponsor meetings, seminars, symposia, dinners, awards ceremonies, and similar events. Judges are encouraged to attend educational programs, as both teachers and participants, in law-related and academic disciplines, in furtherance of their duty to remain competent in the law. Participation in a variety of other extrajudicial activity is also permitted and encouraged by this Code.

[2] Not infrequently, sponsoring organizations invite certain judges to attend seminars or other events on a fee-waived or partial-fee-waived basis, and sometimes include reimbursement for necessary travel, food, lodging, or other incidental expenses. A judge's decision whether to accept reimbursement of expenses or a waiver or partial waiver of fees or charges in connection with these or other extrajudicial activities must be based upon an assessment of all the circumstances. The judge must undertake a reasonable inquiry to obtain the information necessary to make an informed judgment about whether acceptance would be consistent with the requirements of this Code.

[3] A judge must assure himself or herself that acceptance of reimbursement or fee waivers would not appear to a reasonable person to undermine the judge's independence, integrity, or impartiality. The factors that a judge should consider when deciding whether to accept reimbursement or a fee waiver for attendance at a particular activity include:

(a) whether the sponsor is an accredited educational institution or bar association rather than a trade association or a for-profit entity;

(b) whether the funding comes largely from numerous contributors rather than from a single entity and is earmarked for programs with specific content;

(c) whether the content is related or unrelated to the subject matter of litigation pending or impending before the judge, or to matters that are likely to come before the judge;

(d) whether the activity is primarily educational rather than recreational, and whether the costs of the event are reasonable and comparable to those associated with similar events sponsored by the judiciary, bar associations, or similar groups;

(e) whether information concerning the activity and its funding sources is available upon inquiry;

(f) whether the sponsor or source of funding is generally associated with particular parties or interests currently appearing or likely to appear in the judge's court, thus possibly requiring disqualification of the judge under Rule 2.11;

(g) whether differing viewpoints are presented; and

(h) whether a broad range of judicial and nonjudicial participants are invited, whether a large number of participants are invited, and whether the program is designed specifically for judges.

RULE 3.14—REPORTER'S EXPLANATION OF CHANGES†

1990 MODEL CODE COMPARISON

Rule 3.14(A) is derived from Canon 4H(1), except that the provisions relating to compensation have been moved to Rule 3.12. Rule 3.14 addresses reimbursement of expenses and waivers of fees or charges only.

Rule 3.14(B) is essentially identical to Canon 4H(1)(b).

Rule 3.14(C) is new as it relates to public reporting of reimbursements and waivers of charges, but is similar to Canon 4(H)(2), which deals with public reporting of compensation received.

Comments [1] through [3] are new.

† The "Reporters' Explanations of Changes" have not been approved by the ABA Joint Commission to Evaluate the Model Code of Judicial Conduct. They have been drafted by the Commission's Reporters, based on the proceedings and record of the Commission, solely to inform the ABA House of Delegates about each of the proposed amendments to the Model Code prior to their being considered at the ABA 2007 Midyear Meeting. THEY ARE NOT TO BE ADOPTED AS PART OF THE MODEL CODE.

EXPLANATION OF BLACK LETTER

1. Rule 3.14(A) applies to reimbursement of expenses only, rather than both reimbursement and compensation, but adds waivers of fees and charges as equivalent to reimbursement.

By cross-reference to other Rules it requires judges to consider whether attending an event on a fee-waived or expenses-reimbursed basis would require later disqualification or undermine the judge's independence, integrity, or impartiality. Rule 3.14 and its subparagraph (A) are integral to the total reorganization of Canons 4D and 4H of the 1990 Code. Compensation for extrajudicial activity is no longer linked with reimbursement for expenses, but is addressed separately in Rule 3.12. Reimbursement, in turn, is addressed separately in Rule 3.14. (Other aspects of Canon 4D, such as engaging in financial and business activities, and receipt of gifts and other things of value, are covered by Rules 3.11 and 3.13, respectively.)

The Commission recognized that attendance at tuition-waived and expense-paid seminars and similar events has been a matter of public concern and media attention. It heard much testimony and received numerous comments about the need for more transparency regarding both the amount of fees waived or expenses reimbursed and the nature and sponsorship of the event attended on a cost-free or reduced-cost basis. In response, the Commission elected to treat acceptance of such benefits separately from acceptance of gifts and other things of value generally (see Rule 3.13), and to require public reporting of the benefits received together with other public reporting (see Rule 3.15). The Commission concluded that separating reimbursement and waivers for treatment in this way makes Canon 3 more readable and easier to follow. Moreover, treatment in a separate Rule allows more careful attention to be paid to whether the invitation to attend should be accepted at all.

Although Rule 3.14 applies to events other than privately funded educational seminars, much of the testimony and comments received by the Commission focused upon that subject. In the Commission's view, judicial education of all kinds is of great value; it helps keep judges current on recent developments, alerts them to future trends, and exposes them to new ways of thinking about the law. Moreover, there was recognition that judicial budgets may not always be adequate to support educational opportunities for judges. For that reason, Rule 3.14—like Canon 4H(1)—permits judges to accept reimbursement for reasonably necessary expenses associated with otherwise permissible extrajudicial activities, and further permits acceptance of waivers of otherwise applicable fees or charges.

A critical aspect of Canon 4H(1) is that permission to accept benefits in connection with extrajudicial activities is conditioned upon the acceptance not giving the appearance of influencing the judge in the performance of judicial duties and not otherwise creating the appearance of impropriety. Rule 3.14 carries this condition forward, for both reimbursements and waivers of fees and charges, but uses language more in harmony with other parts of Canon 3 and the rest of the Model Code. Thus, by cross-referencing Rules 3.1 and 3.13(A), Rule 3.14(A) makes clear that a judge may not accept the proffered benefits if doing so would appear to a reasonable person to undermine the judge's independence, integrity, or impartiality, or if accepting would, for example, lead to frequent disqualification or otherwise interfere with the proper performance of the judge's judicial duties.

2. Rule 3.14(B) is substantially the same as Canon 4H(1)(b) of the 1990 Code.

The exception is that it applies to both reimbursements and waivers of fees and charges, and applies to an accompanying domestic partner as well as to a spouse or guest.

3. Rule 3.14(C) is similar to the public reporting requirement set out in Canon 4H(2).

The exception is that it applies to reimbursements and waivers rather than compensation. In addition, the actual mechanism for reporting is not contained in Rule 3.14(C) itself; the Rule instead cross-references Rule 3.15, which describes all the public reporting required by various Rules in Canon 3.

EXPLANATION OF COMMENTS

[1] New Comment [1] states the rationale for allowing judges to accept these two forms of benefits, and also making clear that Rule 3.14 can apply to any permissible extrajudicial activity, not just privately funded educational programs.

[2] New Comment [2] focuses attention upon educational programs specifically. Not only must a judge consider whether accepting an invitation to attend on an expenses-paid or fee-waived basis would be proper (under Rules 3.1, 3.13(A), and 3.14(A)), but the judge also has an affirmative duty to make reasonable inquiry into the factors that should inform that decision.

Near the end of its deliberations, the Commission became aware of guidelines newly issued by the Judicial Conference of the United States on this subject. The Guidelines delineate a process for helping judges make the inquiry just noted. Any program that wishes to invite judges to attend on a cost-free basis is required to provide considerable information about funding, sponsorship, and program content in advance, and have this information available to judges receiving an invitation. The Commission thought this "pre-registration" approach had merit, but considered the possibility that it would be more difficult to implement throughout all the state jurisdictions, as opposed to in the single federal jurisdiction for which it was designed. Thus the Commission thought it more prudent to wait until the operation of the federal program could be assessed.

[3] New Comment [3] provides guidance to judges in making the determination required by Rule 3.14(A), as explained in Comment [2]. It is founded on revised Advisory Opinion 67 of the Committee on Codes of Conduct of the Judicial Conference of the United States. The factors identified in Opinion 67 can usefully be employed by each judge who has been issued an invitation to attend a cost-free event and is considering whether to accept.

RULE 3.15 Reporting Requirements

(A) A judge shall publicly report the amount or value of:

(1) compensation received for extrajudicial activities as permitted by Rule 3.12;

(2) gifts and other things of value as permitted by Rule 3.13(C), unless the value of such items, alone or in the aggregate with other items received from the same source in the same calendar year, does not exceed $[insert amount]; and

(3) reimbursement of expenses and waiver of fees or charges permitted by Rule 3.14(A), unless the amount of reimbursement or waiver, alone or in the aggregate with other reimbursements or waivers received from the same source in the same calendar year, does not exceed $[insert amount].

(B) When public reporting is required by paragraph (A), a judge shall report the date, place, and nature of the activity for which the judge received any compensation; the description of any gift, loan, bequest, benefit, or other thing of value accepted; and the source of reimbursement of expenses or waiver or partial waiver of fees or charges.

(C) The public report required by paragraph (A) shall be made at least annually, except that for reimbursement of expenses and waiver or partial waiver of fees or charges, the report shall be made within thirty days following the conclusion of the event or program.

(D) Reports made in compliance with this Rule shall be filed as public documents in the office of the clerk of the court on which the judge serves or other office designated by law,* and, when technically feasible, posted by the court or office personnel on the court's website.

RULE 3.15—REPORTER'S EXPLANATION OF CHANGES†

1990 MODEL CODE COMPARISON

Rule 3.15 is based upon Canon 4H(2). However, consistent with the reorganization of Canon 3, this provision is no longer limited to public reporting of compensation received for extrajudicial activities, but includes public reporting of gifts and other things of value accepted pursuant to Rule 3.13, and reimbursement of expenses and waiver or partial waiver of fees and charges accepted pursuant to Rule 3.14.

Technical matters such as what and where to report, on what schedule, and how the information will become transparent to the general public are derived from Canon 4H(2) as well, but with several modifications.

EXPLANATION OF BLACK LETTER

1. Rule 3.15(A) requires that in addition to reporting compensation received, judges must report gifts and other things of value accepted, as well as reimbursements of expenses and waivers of fees and charges.

It deletes a 1990 Code provision on treatment of a spouse's compensation or income in community property states. An important feature of the reorganization of Canon 3 is the gathering of all the public reporting provisions in one place, now Rule 3.15(A), and then cross-referencing this Rule in the Rules where reportable events are discussed.

This organization has the important side effect of removing discussion of monetary limits (if any) from the earlier Rules, and repositioning it in Rule 3.15(A). Thus, for example, Canon 4D(5)(h) of the 1990 Code, which established a reporting threshold of $150 per item, has been recast and moved to Rule 3.15(A)(2). Instead of establishing a threshold amount for all jurisdictions, which might have to be raised periodically in any event on account of inflation, the Commission required establishment of an annual threshold amount that takes into account aggregation of items from the same source. The actual dollar amount, however, was left for each jurisdiction to supply according to conditions there.

The reminder in the 1990 Code that community property earned by a judge's spouse is not attributable to the judge for purposes of public reporting was deleted as unnecessary: all the substantive provisions in Canon 3 speak of the judge receiving compensation or receiving gifts or reimbursement of expenses.

Canon 4I of the 1990 Code, which required disclosure of a judge's income and assets in some circumstances, is not included in the proposed Code. The Commission concluded that this form of public reporting is already regulated by statute or court rule in most jurisdictions; thus, its inclusion in a Code of Judicial Conduct is unnecessary.

2. Rule 3.15(B) provides a list of what must be reported when reporting is required under paragraph (A).

3. Rule 3.15(C) addresses the frequency of mandatory public reporting.

The requirement of reporting no less frequently than annually is consistent with Canon 4H(2) of the 1990 Code. Reporting in connection with reimbursements and waivers of fees or charges, however, is required within thirty days of the underlying event, not on a calendar-based schedule.

The Commission borrowed this special reporting requirement from the guidelines recently issued by the Judicial Conference of the United States. Such a requirement can be implemented immediately, is responsive to the need for transparency, and should not be overly burdensome to judges. In situations involving reimbursement in particular, a judge will have to gather receipts for submission to the reimbursing entity, which can be used to satisfy the public reporting requirement. With respect to fee waivers, a judge should be able to obtain a statement of what the fees or charges would have been for a person who was not being offered a waiver. As this requirement becomes better known, it is likely that the sponsoring entity granting the waiver will develop this information and provide the requisite statement as a matter of course.

---

† "Reporters' Explanations of Changes" have not been approved by the ABA Joint Commission to Evaluate the Model Code of Judicial Conduct. They have been drafted by the Commission's Reporters, based on the proceedings and record of the Commission, solely to inform the ABA House of Delegates about each of the proposed amendments to the Model Code prior to their being considered at the ABA 2007 Midyear Meeting. THEY ARE NOT TO BE ADOPTED AS PART OF THE MODEL CODE.

4. Rule 3.15(D) directs that the reports required by Rule 3.15 be located in a central place and made accessible to the public to ensure transparency.

It tracks Canon 4H(2), except that it calls for posting on the appropriate website when feasible, to facilitate public access. Ordinarily, it is assumed that such posting will be to the court's official website, and will be done by court personnel according to a uniform format, rather than by each reporting judge individually.

CANON 4

A JUDGE OR CANDIDATE FOR JUDICIAL OFFICE SHALL NOT ENGAGE IN POLITICAL OR CAMPAIGN ACTIVITY THAT IS INCONSISTENT WITH THE INDEPENDENCE, INTEGRITY, OR IMPARTIALITY OF THE JUDICIARY.

CANON 4—REPORTER'S EXPLANATION OF CHANGES†

1990 MODEL CODE COMPARISON

Canon 4 of the proposed Code is derived from Canon 5 of the 1990 Code, as amended in 1997, 1999, and 2003—the last time in response to the decision of the U.S. Supreme Court in *Republican Party of Minnesota v. White*, 536 U.S. 765 (2002). Much of the material in Canon 5 was retained, but was reorganized along several axes. The reorganized Canon 4 differentiates more clearly between sitting judges who are and are not also judicial candidates and nonjudges who become candidates. Canon 4 continues to differentiate between judicial candidates running in public elections and those seeking appointment, and, within the former category, it further differentiates between partisan, nonpartisan, and retention elections.

EXPLANATION OF BLACK LETTER

1. Replaced "shall refrain from" with "shall not engage in."

The new language is less passive and fits more comfortably with the language of the other three Canons.

2. Replaced "political activity" with "political or campaign activity."

This more accurately reflects the actual content of Canon 4. Canon 5 of the 1990 Code also dealt with more than just "political" activity so the new Canon 4 title has been amplified.

3. Replaced "inappropriate activity" with "activity that is inconsistent with the independence, integrity, or impartiality of the judiciary."

The undefined term "inappropriate" was not sufficiently precise. Concern that the independence, integrity, or impartiality of the judiciary (including candidates who aspire to join the judiciary) will be compromised or undermined is a pervasive theme in the proposed Code.

RULE 4.1 Political and Campaign Activities of Judges and Judicial Candidates in General

(A) Except as permitted by law,* or by Rules 4.2, 4.3, and 4.4, a judge or a judicial candidate* shall not:

† The "Reporters' Explanations of Changes" have not been approved by the ABA Joint Commission to Evaluate the Model Code of Judicial Conduct. They have been drafted by the Commission's Reporters, based on the proceedings and record of the Commission, solely to inform the ABA House of Delegates about each of the proposed amendments to the Model Code prior to their being considered at the ABA 2007 Midyear Meeting. THEY ARE NOT TO BE ADOPTED AS PART OF THE MODEL CODE.

(1) act as a leader in, or hold an office in, a political organization;*

(2) make speeches on behalf of a political organization;

(3) publicly endorse or oppose a candidate for any public office;

(4) solicit funds for, pay an assessment to, or make a contribution* to a political organization or a candidate for public office;

(5) attend or purchase tickets for dinners or other events sponsored by a political organization or a candidate for public office;

(6) publicly identify himself or herself as a candidate of a political organization;

(7) seek, accept, or use endorsements from a political organization;

(8) personally solicit* or accept campaign contributions other than through a campaign committee authorized by Rule 4.4;

(9) use or permit the use of campaign contributions for the private benefit of the judge, the candidate, or others;

(10) use court staff, facilities, or other court resources in a campaign for judicial office;

(11) knowingly,* or with reckless disregard for the truth, make any false or misleading statement;

(12) make any statement that would reasonably be expected to affect the outcome or impair the fairness of a matter pending* or impending* in any court; or

(13) in connection with cases, controversies, or issues that are likely to come before the court, make pledges, promises, or commitments that are inconsistent with the impartial* performance of the adjudicative duties of judicial office.

(B) A judge or judicial candidate shall take reasonable measures to ensure that other persons do not undertake, on behalf of the judge or judicial candidate, any activities prohibited under paragraph (A).

Comment

GENERAL CONSIDERATIONS

[1] Even when subject to public election, a judge plays a role different from that of a legislator or executive branch official. Rather than making decisions based upon the expressed views or preferences of the electorate, a judge makes decisions based upon the law and the facts of every case. Therefore, in furtherance of this interest, judges and judicial candidates must, to the greatest extent possible, be free and appear to be free from political influence and political pressure. This Canon imposes narrowly tailored restrictions upon the political and campaign activities of all judges and judicial candidates, taking into account the various methods of selecting judges.

[2] When a person becomes a judicial candidate, this Canon becomes applicable to his or her conduct.

PARTICIPATION IN POLITICAL ACTIVITIES

[3] Public confidence in the independence and impartiality of the judiciary is eroded if judges or judicial candidates are perceived to be subject to political influence. Although judges and judicial candidates may register to vote as members of a political party, they are prohibited by paragraph (A)(1) from assuming leadership roles in political organizations.

[4] Paragraphs (A)(2) and (A)(3) prohibit judges and judicial candidates from making speeches on behalf of political organizations or publicly endorsing or opposing candidates for public office, respectively, to prevent them from abusing the prestige of judicial office to advance the interests of others. See Rule 1.3.

These Rules do not prohibit candidates from campaigning on their own behalf, or from endorsing or opposing candidates for the same judicial office for which they are running. See Rules 4.2(B)(2) and 4.2(B)(3).

[5] Although members of the families of judges and judicial candidates are free to engage in their own political activity, including running for public office, there is no "family exception" to the prohibition in paragraph (A)(3) against a judge or candidate publicly endorsing candidates for public office. A judge or judicial candidate must not become involved in, or publicly associated with, a family member's political activity or campaign for public office. To avoid public misunderstanding, judges and judicial candidates should take, and should urge members of their families to take, reasonable steps to avoid any implication that they endorse any family member's candidacy or other political activity.

[6] Judges and judicial candidates retain the right to participate in the political process as voters in both primary and general elections. For purposes of this Canon, participation in a caucus-type election procedure does not constitute public support for or endorsement of a political organization or candidate, and is not prohibited by paragraphs (A)(2) or (A)(3).

STATEMENTS AND COMMENTS MADE DURING A CAMPAIGN FOR JUDICIAL OFFICE

[7] Judicial candidates must be scrupulously fair and accurate in all statements made by them and by their campaign committees. Paragraph (A)(11) obligates candidates and their committees to refrain from making statements that are false or misleading, or that omit facts necessary to make the communication considered as a whole not materially misleading.

[8] Judicial candidates are sometimes the subject of false, misleading, or unfair allegations made by opposing candidates, third parties, or the media. For example, false or misleading statements might be made regarding the identity, present position, experience, qualifications, or judicial rulings of a candidate. In other situations, false or misleading allegations may be made that bear upon a candidate's integrity or fitness for judicial office. As long as the candidate does not violate paragraphs (A)(11), (A)(12), or (A)(13), the candidate may make a factually accurate public response. In addition, when an independent third party has made unwarranted attacks on a candidate's opponent, the candidate may disavow the attacks, and request the third party to cease and desist.

[9] Subject to paragraph (A)(12), a judicial candidate is permitted to respond directly to false, misleading, or unfair allegations made against him or her during a campaign, although it is preferable for someone else to respond if the allegations relate to a pending case.

[10] Paragraph (A)(12) prohibits judicial candidates from making comments that might impair the fairness of pending or impending judicial proceedings. This provision does not restrict arguments or statements to the court or jury by a lawyer who is a judicial candidate, or rulings, statements, or instructions by a judge that may appropriately affect the outcome of a matter.

PLEDGES, PROMISES, OR COMMITMENTS INCONSISTENT WITH IMPARTIAL PERFORMANCE OF THE ADJUDICATIVE DUTIES OF JUDICIAL OFFICE

[11] The role of a judge is different from that of a legislator or executive branch official, even when the judge is subject to public election. Campaigns for judicial office must be conducted differently from campaigns for other offices. The narrowly drafted restrictions upon political and campaign activities of judicial candidates provided in Canon 4 allow candidates to conduct campaigns that provide voters with sufficient information to permit them to distinguish between candidates and make informed electoral choices.

[12] Paragraph (A)(13) makes applicable to both judges and judicial candidates the prohibition that applies to judges in Rule 2.10(B), relating to pledges, promises, or commitments that are inconsistent with the impartial performance of the adjudicative duties of judicial office.

[13] The making of a pledge, promise, or commitment is not dependent upon, or limited to, the use of any specific words or phrases; instead, the totality of the statement must be examined to determine if a reasonable person would believe that the candidate for judicial office has specifically undertaken to reach a particular result. Pledges, promises, or commitments must be contrasted with statements or announcements of personal views on legal, political, or other issues, which are not prohibited. When making such statements, a judge should acknowledge the overarching judicial obligation to apply and uphold the law, without regard to his or her personal views.

[14] A judicial candidate may make campaign promises related to judicial organization, administration, and court management, such as a promise to dispose of a backlog of cases, start court sessions on time, or avoid favoritism in appointments and hiring. A candidate may also pledge to take action outside the courtroom, such as working toward an improved jury selection system, or advocating for more funds to improve the physical plant and amenities of the courthouse.

[15] Judicial candidates may receive questionnaires or requests for interviews from the media and from issue advocacy or other community organizations that seek to learn their views on disputed or controversial legal or political issues. Paragraph (A)(13) does not specifically address judicial responses to such inquiries. Depending upon the wording and format of such questionnaires, candidates' responses might be viewed as pledges, promises, or commitments to perform the adjudicative duties of office other than in an impartial way. To avoid violating paragraph (A)(13), therefore, candidates who respond to media and other inquiries should also give assurances that they will keep an open mind and will carry out their adjudicative duties faithfully and impartially if elected. Candidates who do not respond may state their reasons for not responding, such as the danger that answering might be perceived by a reasonable person as undermining a successful candidate's independence or impartiality, or that it might lead to frequent disqualification. See Rule 2.11.

Rule 4.1—Reporter's Explanation of Changes†

1990 Model Code Comparison

Rule 4.1(A)(1) is virtually identical to Canon 5A(1)(a).

Rule 4.1(A)(2) is identical to Canon 5A(1)(c).

Rule 4.1(A)(3) is essentially the same as Canon 5A(1)(b).

Rule 4.1(A)(4) is virtually identical to the first clause of Canon 5A(1)(e).

Rule 4.1(A)(5) is closely patterned on the second clause of Canon 5A(1)(e), and includes the concept embodied in Canon 5A(1)(d), which was eliminated.

Rule 4.1(A)(6) is new, but the prohibition it establishes is removed by later Rules in Canon 4 in some situations.

Rule 4.1(A)(7) is new, and is similar to Rule 4.1(A)(6) in terms of its relationship to other Rules in Canon 4.

Rule 4.1(A)(8) is derived from the first two sentences of Canon 5C(2), but employs different terminology and applies only to solicitation of campaign contributions, not "publicly stated support."

Rule 4.1(A)(9) is essentially identical to the last sentence of Canon 5C(2).

Rule 4.1(A)(10) is new, but is a corollary of one aspect of Canon 2B: lending the prestige—here the trappings—of judicial office to advance a judge's interests.

Rule 4.1(A)(11) is based upon Canon 5A(3)(d)(ii), but substantially revised.

Rule 4.1(A)(12) is new to the Canon on political and campaign activity, but is substantially similar to the first sentence of Canon 3B(9).

Rule 4.1(A)(13) is essentially identical to Canon 5A(3)(d)(i).

Rule 4.1 (B) is based upon elements of Canon 5A(3)(a) and Canon 5A(3)(b), which have been combined and recast.

---

† The "Reporters' Explanations of Changes" have not been approved by the ABA Joint Commission to Evaluate the Model Code of Judicial Conduct. They have been drafted by the Commission's Reporters, based on the proceedings and record of the Commission, solely to inform the ABA House of Delegates about each of the proposed amendments to the Model Code prior to their being considered at the ABA 2007 Midyear Meeting. THEY ARE NOT TO BE ADOPTED AS PART OF THE MODEL CODE.

Comment [1] is new.

Comment [2] is based upon Canon 5E, which has been removed from the black letter text.

Comment [3] is new, but includes a principle taken from the first sentence of the Commentary following Canon 5A(1). See also Comment [6].

Comment [4] is new, but includes reference to the principles embodied in Canon 5C(1)(b), substantially reworded.

Comment [5] is new, but is tangentially related to the Commentary following Canon 5A(3)(a).

Comment [6] is based upon the first sentence of the Commentary following Canon 5A(1), but includes fuller treatment.

Comment [7] is a new Comment, but is based upon Canon 5A(3)(d)(ii), which is now embodied in Rule 4.1(A)(11).

Comment [8] is based upon Canon 5A(3)(e), which has been removed from the black letter text; the new Comment is more detailed and covers slightly more ground.

Comment [9] is new, but also is based upon Canon 5A(3)(e).

Comment [10] is new, but is derived from aspects of Canon 3B(9) and following Commentary.

Comment [11] is new.

Comment [12] is new.

Comment [13] is new.

Comment [14] is based upon the fourth sentence of the Commentary following Canon 5A(3)(d), but provides more detailed treatment, with examples.

Comment [15] is loosely based upon the last paragraph of the Commentary following Canon 5C(2), but provides far more detailed discussion.

EXPLANATION OF BLACK LETTER

1. <u>Rule 4.1(A)'s lead-in added cross-references to specific Rules in Canon 4.</u>

This formulation is critical to the reorganization of Canon 4. Rule 4.1(A) sets out a generally applicable set of prohibitions that apply to all sitting judges and to all judicial candidates (including sitting judges seeking to retain current office or to achieve other judicial office). Rule 4.2 (various forms of public elections), Rule 4.3 (appointment to judicial office), and Rule 4.4 (campaign committees) then selectively eliminate these prohibitions, as appropriate to the specific situation.

2. <u>Rule 4.1(A)(4) replaced "political organization or candidate" with "political organization or a candidate for public office."</u>

No substantive change is intended. The Commission wanted to make clear that the prohibition against soliciting funds or making contributions applies to all candidates for public office, not just candidates for judicial office (as is clear in other provisions of both the 1990 Code and the proposed Code).

3. <u>Rule 4.1(A)(5): made several stylistic revisions in the course of blending Canon 5A(1)(d) and the second clause of Canon 5A(1)(e).</u>

No substantive change is intended. The earlier "attend political gatherings" was eliminated, but the word "attend" was added to the blended Rule. "[D]inners or other events" was substituted for "political party dinners or other functions."

4. <u>Rule 4.1(A)(6) adds a prohibition against a candidate self-identifying as a "candidate of" a political organization.</u>

Canon 5C(1)(a)(ii) of the 1990 Code specifically permitted judges subject to public election to identify themselves at any time as political party *members*. This provision has been eliminated in the proposed Code as unnecessary.

The purpose of Rule 4.1(A)(6) is a different one, however. In the organizational scheme of Canon 4, it is necessary first to prohibit for all judges and judicial candidates what is to be prohibited for any. In the later Rules, exceptions are made as appropriate, leaving in place the general prohibitions that are not singled out for exception. For example, in connection with Rule 4.1(A)(6), see Rule 4.2(C)(1): a candidate running in a partisan public election for judicial office must be permitted to communicate to voters the fact that a particular political organization or party nominated him or her. Thus, because an exception to Rule 4.1(A)(6) appears only in Rule 4.2(C)(1), a candidate running in another type of judicial election is still subject to Rule 4.1(A)(6).

5. Rule 4.1(A)(7): added this provision, which broadly prohibits judicial candidates from seeking, accepting, or using endorsements from political organizations.

As with Rule 4.1(A)(6), the full impact of this new Rule can be judged only by ascertaining the situations in which later Rules in Canon 4 make an exception to it.

6. Rule 4.1(A)(8): retained the language "personally solicit . . . campaign contributions," now defined in the Terminology section; deleted the prohibition against personally soliciting "publicly stated support," and retained the provision permitting contributions to be accepted only through a duly established campaign committee.

The prohibition against seeking "support"—at least from political organizations—is covered (and more broadly) in Rule 4.1(A)(7), and was no longer needed in this Rule.

The Commission was urged to change the operative language (and the definition in the Terminology section) to "solicit campaign contributions in person," to focus more clearly upon the immediacy of the situation and the possibility of coercion. By analogy to the rules regulating lawyer advertising and solicitation, a ban on "in-person" solicitation of campaign contributions would *permit* mailings and similar communications, but would continue to forbid both hand-to-hand transfer of funds and live telephone solicitation. If the original broader language was retained, even a simple mailing to friends and neighbors would be prohibited.

The Commission considered the two possibilities through long debate over many meetings. The Commission was aware that several courts have struck down provisions forbidding "personal solicitation" of campaign funds—often in broad language. Ultimately, the Commission adopted the broader prohibition on the theory that the solicitation of campaign funds in the judicial election context could justify restrictions greater than are permitted for lawyer advertising.

7. Rule 4.1(A)(9) replaces "for the private benefit of the candidate or others" (in Canon 5C(2)) with "for the private benefit of the judge, the candidate, or others."

No substantive changed is intended. Rule 4.1(A) applies to both judges who are *not* currently candidates and to all current judicial candidates.

8. Rule 4.1(A)(10), which prohibits use of official resources for a judge's campaign, breaks little new ground.

Although new to the Canon on political and campaign activity, this provision breaks little new ground. Compare Rule 1.3 (abusing the prestige of judicial office) and Rule 3.1(E) (using official resources in connection with extrajudicial activity).

9. Rule 4.1(A)(11) replaces "knowingly misrepresent the identity, qualifications, present position or other fact" (in Canon 5A(3)(d)(ii)) with "knowingly, or with reckless disregard for the truth, make any false or misleading statement."

Although the 1990 Code language was specific, its precise reach was unclear. The new language used in the proposed Code is established in the law of libel and slander.

10. Rule 4.1(A)(12): added this provision that is new material for Canon 4 on political and campaign activity, but that is a reiteration for emphasis of Rule 2.10(A).

This reiteration is helpful because Rule 2.10(A) can apply only to sitting judges.

11. Rule 4.1(A)(13): replaced "with respect to" (in Canon 5(A)(3)(d)(i)) with "in connection with."

This is a stylistic change only. The language is otherwise identical to policy adopted in 2003 in the wake of the decision in *Republican Party of Minnesota v. White*.

To encourage adoption of an appropriately narrow interpretation of the pledges and promises clause, by disciplinary authorities and by judges and candidates assessing their own conduct, the Commission has included several Comments describing the intended reach of Rule 4.1(A)(13). See Comments [11] through [15]. A judge or candidate who announces his or her personal views on a matter that is likely to come before the court does not compromise impartiality unless the announcement demonstrates a closed mind on the subject, or includes a pledge or a promise to rule in a particular way if the matter comes before the court.

12. Rule 4.1(B) combines in a single Rule, and greatly simplifies, most provisions of Canon 5A(3)(a) and Canon 5A(3)(b).

First, it changes the separate treatment of actions of members of a candidate's family and actions of employees and others who are under the control of a candidate to unitary treatment of actions of "other persons"; second, it explains that the judge or candidate is required to take "reasonable measures" to ensure that these other persons do not undertake action on behalf of the judge or candidate that would otherwise be prohibited; and third, it eliminates the injunction to maintain the dignity appropriate to the judicial office during a judicial campaign.

The Commission concluded that "maintaining appropriate dignity" was too subjective a standard for use in a Rule with potential disciplinary consequences.

No significant substantive changes are intended by other adjustments in the Rule. What constitutes a "reasonable measure" will obviously depend upon whether the person who is attempting to act improperly *on behalf of* the judge or candidate is a family member, an employee, or an appointee.

EXPLANATION OF COMMENTS

[1] New Comment [1] in effect serves as a preamble to Canon 4. Two key points are involved: that states have a compelling interest in the quality of their judiciary and in the regularity of the selection process; and that restrictions on political and campaign-related speech must be narrowly tailored and the least restrictive possible, even when serving such a compelling state interest.

[2] The jurisdictional point of this Comment was originally placed in Canon 5E of the 1990 Code. The Commission concluded that treatment in the black letter text was not required, given that this provision does not establish independent standards of conduct. In transferring this material to a Comment, the Commission also significantly reduced its level of detail. Prior references to the jurisdictional situation when a candidate is successful or unsuccessful in obtaining judicial office were eliminated as not properly within the scope of this Code.

[3] New Comment [3] explains how restrictions on political participation of judges and judicial candidates were drawn: mere participation in electoral politics does not warrant a restriction, but assuming a leadership role would call into question the judge's or candidate's independence.

[4] New Comment [4] gathers in one place several provisions of Canon 5C(1) of the 1990 Code, and substantially revises the language. Although judicial candidates generally are not permitted to endorse *other* candidates, to avoid abusing the prestige of judicial office, they are nevertheless permitted to campaign on their own behalf. Moreover, although the pros and cons as a matter of policy seemed to be evenly balanced, the Commission elected to retain the traditional exception that permits campaigning for other *judicial candidates* who are effectively running in the same race.

[5] New Comment [5] serves as a reminder that judges and judicial candidates must avoid abusing the prestige of office when their own family members are involved in politics. Thus, while family members are not and cannot be subject to this Code, the people who *are* subject to it must take reasonable steps to ensure that the public does not receive the impression that a judge or judicial candidate is endorsing a family member's candidacy.

[6] This Comment carries forward Commentary from the 1990 Code, noting that judges and judicial candidates do not forfeit the right to vote, and adds a reminder that this principle applies in both general and primary elections. For jurisdictions that employ caucuses rather than secret ballot voting in primary

elections, the Commission ultimately concluded that even though a caucus participant may take a public stand in favor of a particular candidate, this should not be counted as a prohibited endorsement, because there is no other way to vote or express a preference in such situations.

[8] This Comment carries forward and expands upon the "right to reply" provision originally found in Canon 5A(3)(e) of the 1990 Code. The last sentence, an aspirational standard, was added to stem increased use of negative campaign ads run by independent groups not controlled by a candidate or the candidate's campaign committee.

[10] New Comment [10] is a reminder that Rule 4.1(A)(12) has brought into the political and electoral context the traditional prohibition against making statements that will improperly influence a trial. Compare Rule 2.10(A). The last sentence of Comment [10] serves as an additional reminder that some statements are *designed* to affect the outcome of a trial, and properly so. A lawyer making a closing argument to a jury and a judge instructing that jury are prime examples.

[11] New Comments [11] and [12] introduce the series of Comments explicating "pledges and promises clause," which is carried forward from Canon 5A(3)(d)(i) of the 1990 Code essentially unchanged.

[13] New Comment [13] describes the fundamental difference between "pledges" and "promises," which are prohibited, and "statements or announcements of personal views," which are permitted and constitutionally protected. The key distinction is between personal statements that are truly personal and that *will not interfere with future decision making*, and improper pledges and promises that commit a judge or judicial candidate to decide a future case in a particular way. A prohibited pledge or promise concerns future decision making.

[14] This Comment is based upon Commentary following Canon 5A(3)(d), but is more complete. It makes the important point that pledges and promises regarding *administration* of the judicial system, as opposed to *decision making in actual cases*, is not prohibited.

[15] The constitutional distinction between (1) making pledges and promises about future decision making, and (2) making statements or announcements about personal views, has emerged in recent years as issue advocacy and other citizen groups (as well as the media) have become more affirmative in issuing questionnaires for judicial candidates to answer. The Commission received testimony and commentary on this issue, and deliberated at length. Comment [15] represents the Commission's understanding of how this issue can and must be resolved.

First, citizens are not subject to the Code of Judicial Conduct, and may inquire of judicial candidates their position on issues. Each citizen is entitled to decide what qualities in a judicial candidate will earn that citizen's vote, and all citizens are entitled to applaud or criticize the answers given, or to comment on a candidate's failure or refusal to answer.

Second, judicial candidates who choose to answer the questionnaires cannot be prevented from doing so, as long as their answers take the form of constitutionally protected statements and announcements of personal views, and do not constitute pledges and promises about future decision making.

Third, and critically important, judicial candidates have the right to refuse to answer, with or without giving reasons, or to answer only in formats that are agreeable to them (assuming they comply with Rule 4.1(A)(13)).

Thus, the Commission took no firm stand on the best response to questionnaires of this kind (and explicitly noted in Comment [15] that the black letter text of Rule 4.1(A)(13) does not provide a clear answer, either). But the principles set forth in this Comment and the previous Comments should assist judicial candidates in formulating their positions on judicial campaign speech.

RULE 4.2 Political and Campaign Activities of Judicial Candidates in Public Elections

(A) A judicial candidate* in a partisan, nonpartisan, or retention public election* shall:

(1) act at all times in a manner consistent with the independence,* integrity,* and impartiality* of the judiciary;

(2) comply with all applicable election, election campaign, and election campaign fund-raising laws and regulations of this jurisdiction;

(3) review and approve the content of all campaign statements and materials produced by the candidate or his or her campaign committee, as authorized by Rule 4.4, before their dissemination; and

(4) take reasonable measures to ensure that other persons do not undertake on behalf of the candidate activities, other than those described in Rule 4.4, that the candidate is prohibited from doing by Rule 4.1.

(B) A candidate for elective judicial office may, unless prohibited by law,* and not earlier than [insert amount of time] before the first applicable primary election, caucus, or general or retention election:

(1) establish a campaign committee pursuant to the provisions of Rule 4.4;

(2) speak on behalf of his or her candidacy through any medium, including but not limited to advertisements, websites, or other campaign literature;

(3) publicly endorse or oppose candidates for the same judicial office for which he or she is running;

(4) attend or purchase tickets for dinners or other events sponsored by a political organization* or a candidate for public office;

(5) seek, accept, or use endorsements from any person or organization other than a partisan political organization; and

(6) contribute to a political organization or candidate for public office, but not more than $[insert amount] to any one organization or candidate.

(C) A judicial candidate in a partisan public election may, unless prohibited by law, and not earlier than [insert amount of time] before the first applicable primary election, caucus, or general election:

(1) identify himself or herself as a candidate of a political organization; and

(2) seek, accept, and use endorsements of a political organization.

Comment

[1] Paragraphs (B) and (C) permit judicial candidates in public elections to engage in some political and campaign activities otherwise prohibited by Rule 4.1. Candidates may not engage in these activities earlier than [insert amount of time] before the first applicable electoral event, such as a caucus or a primary election.

[2] Despite paragraphs (B) and (C), judicial candidates for public election remain subject to many of the provisions of Rule 4.1. For example, a candidate continues to be prohibited from soliciting funds for a political organization, knowingly making false or misleading statements during a campaign, or making certain promises, pledges, or commitments related to future adjudicative duties. See Rule 4.1(A), paragraphs (4), (11), and (13).

[3] In partisan public elections for judicial office, a candidate may be nominated by, affiliated with, or otherwise publicly identified or associated with a political organization, including a political party. This

relationship may be maintained throughout the period of the public campaign, and may include use of political party or similar designations on campaign literature and on the ballot.

[4] In nonpartisan public elections or retention elections, paragraph (B)(5) prohibits a candidate from seeking, accepting, or using nominations or endorsements from a partisan political organization.

[5] Judicial candidates are permitted to attend or purchase tickets for dinners and other events sponsored by political organizations.

[6] For purposes of paragraph (B)(3), candidates are considered to be running for the same judicial office if they are competing for a single judgeship or if several judgeships on the same court are to be filled as a result of the election. In endorsing or opposing another candidate for a position on the same court, a judicial candidate must abide by the same rules governing campaign conduct and speech as apply to the candidate's own campaign.

[7] Although judicial candidates in nonpartisan public elections are prohibited from running on a ticket or slate associated with a political organization, they may group themselves into slates or other alliances to conduct their campaigns more effectively. Candidates who have grouped themselves together are considered to be running for the same judicial office if they satisfy the conditions described in Comment [6].

RULE 4.2—REPORTER'S EXPLANATION OF CHANGES†

1990 MODEL CODE COMPARISON

Rule 4.2 is derived from the specific regulation of campaign activity included in Canon 5C, with the exception of provisions concerning campaign committees, which are treated in Rule 4.4. Rule 4.2, in tandem with Rule 4.1, has imposed a logical and tiered organization on this material without making major substantive changes.

The key to understanding the organization of Canon 4 of the proposed Code is to remember that Rule 4.1 applies to all judges (whether or not they are also judicial candidates) and to all judicial candidates (whether or not they are also sitting judges). Rule 4.2 applies only to judicial candidates running in partisan, nonpartisan, or retention public elections. Rule 4.2 adds some restrictions on the activity of judicial candidates that do not appear in Rule 4.1, makes exceptions to some of the restrictions set out in Rule 4.1, and then makes further exceptions that apply only to judicial candidates in partisan elections.

Rule 4.3 applies to the activities of judicial candidates seeking appointive judicial office, but these provisions are relatively straightforward and did not require significant reorganization.

The lead-in to Rule 4.2(A) is similar to that of Canon 5C(1), except that it identifies the three modes of public elections to which this paragraph (and the rest of the Rule) will apply.

Rule 4.2(A)(1) is based upon parts of Canon 5A(3).

Rule 4.2(A)(2) is new as a separate provision, but is consistent with the pervasive statement in the 1990 Code that activities prohibited by law are also prohibited by Canon 5.

Rule 4.2(A)(3) is a new provision, but the requirement that candidates actively take responsibility for campaign literature and other campaign activities is implicit in many provisions of Canon 5 of the 1990 Code.

Rule 4.2(A)(4) is derived from parts of Canon 5A(3)(a)–(c). This material, which governs judicial candidates only, has been repositioned to Rule 4.2.

† The "Reporters' Explanations of Changes" have not been approved by the ABA Joint Commission to Evaluate the Model Code of Judicial Conduct. They have been drafted by the Commission's Reporters, based on the proceedings and record of the Commission, solely to inform the ABA House of Delegates about each of the proposed amendments to the Model Code prior to their being considered at the ABA 2007 Midyear Meeting. THEY ARE NOT TO BE ADOPTED AS PART OF THE MODEL CODE.

The lead-in to Rule 4.2(B) is based upon Canon 5C(1), but with a different disposition of the *timing* of the activities that are permitted for judicial candidates. In addition, Rule 4.2(B), like the rest of Rule 4.2, applies only to candidates, whereas Canon 5C(1) applies to sitting judges as well.

Rule 4.2(B)(1) is based upon the second sentence of Canon 5C(2), except that the timing provided for the establishment of campaign committees is different.

Rule 4.2(B)(2) combines and rewords Canons 5C(1)(b)(i)–(b)(iii).

Rule 4.2(B)(3) is virtually identical to Canon 5C(1)(b)(iv).

Rule 4.2(B)(4) is based upon Canon 5C(1)(a)(i), but reworded for consistency with other Rules in Canon 4 of the proposed Code.

Rule 4.2(B)(5) takes the opposite stance from that found in Canon 5C(2), but with an important caveat. The 1990 Code allows judicial candidates to solicit endorsements—"publicly stated support"—only through campaign committees. The proposed Code permits candidates to solicit such support on their own, but not from partisan political organizations.

Rule 4.2(B)(6) is similar to Canon 5C(1)(a)(iii), but establishes dollar limitations (to be supplied by each jurisdiction) on the contributions that can be made.

Rule 4.2(C) and its two subparagraphs permit only candidates in partisan elections to identify themselves as candidates of political organizations' and to seek such organizations' endorsements. Canon 5(C)(1)(a)(ii) had permitted the first of these two activities for candidates in both partisan and non-partisan elections. The 1990 Code did not advert to the distinction between partisan and nonpartisan or retention elections. In furtherance of the organizational scheme of the proposed Code, Rule 4.2(C) states the additional activities that are permitted only for candidates in partisan public elections.

Comments [1] and [2] explain the relationship of Rule 4.2 to Rule 4.1, which is the core of the new organizational scheme. They also explain that a person becomes a judicial candidate according to the definition in the Terminology section, but that the additional activities in which a candidate may engage depend upon the timing counting back from the primary or election in question. The first sentence of Comment [1] is a revision of Commentary to Canon 5C(1).

Comments [3] and [4] are new; the 1990 Code did not distinguish between partisan, nonpartisan, and retention public elections for judicial office.

Comment [5] is similar to Canon 5C(1)(a)(i), but with the important difference that the provision applies *only* to judicial candidates, *while* they are candidates.

Comments [6] and [7] clarify the intended meaning of Rule 4.2(B)(3), which is based upon Canon 5C(1)(b)(iv), and has some similarity to Canon 5C(5). In both instances, the key is to determine when candidates are running for the *same* judicial office.

EXPLANATION OF BLACK LETTER

1. <u>Rule 4.2(A) lead-in: substituted "a judicial candidate in a partisan, nonpartisan, or retention public election" for "a [judge or] candidate subject to public election."</u>

This is an important element of the reorganization of Canon 4 of the proposed Code. By distinguishing between the three modes of public elections, Rule 4.2(A) sets up the possibility of applying further restrictions and permissive provisions to all three modes or to some designated subset, as required. In Rule 4.2(A), for example, obligations *in addition to those already imposed by Rule 4.1* are imposed upon all three types of candidates.

2. <u>Rule 4.2(A)(1): substituted "act at all times in a manner" for "act in a manner," and deleted the requirement that a candidate "shall maintain the dignity appropriate to judicial office."</u>

The first change is stylistic only. The mandatory duty to "maintain dignity" was deleted because it is too subjective.

3. Rule 4.2(A)(2): added this new broad provision that is consistent with the overarching principle that candidates for judicial office must obey applicable laws and regulations.

Some of the specific regulations regarding campaign finance are separately referenced in Rule 4.4, but Rule 4.2(A)(2) might well apply to restrictions on ballot insignia applicable to nonpartisan elections, for example. Thus, although a candidate in a nonpartisan election is not prevented from stating he or she is a member of a particular party, the candidate is prohibited from stating he or she is "the candidate" of that party, if the election laws do not allow party designations on the ballot. Compare Rule 4.1(A)(6), which prohibits all judges and judicial candidates from such self-designation, and Rule 4.2(C)(1), which allows candidates in *partisan* elections to do so.

4. Rule 4.2(A)(3): added the requirement that judicial candidates personally approve the contents of campaign literature and other materials.

The requirement is implicit in several other provisions of Canon 4. For example, if a candidate is prohibited by Rule 4.1(A)(11) from making false or misleading statements in a campaign, it is almost inevitable that the candidate will have a duty to review campaign materials before they are disseminated under his or her name.

5. Rule 4.2(A)(4): substituted "take reasonable measures to ensure" for "shall prohibit," "shall discourage," and "shall encourage to adhere."

The language of the 1990 Code variously applied to employees and officials serving at the pleasure of the candidate (who can be prohibited), others under the direction and control of the candidate (who can be discouraged), and family members (who can be encouraged to assist the candidate in complying with the Rules). What constitutes a "reasonable measure" depends upon circumstances such as those noted above. Rule 4.2(A)(4), which applies only to judicial candidates, is already covered by Rule 4.1(B), which applies to all judges *and* candidates.

6. Rule 4.2(B) lead-in identifies a time period prior to the relevant primary or election, during which certain activities that would or might otherwise be prohibited by Rule 4.1(A) are permitted.

Although the creation of this time period is not new, its use in this Rule to disconnect the status of *being* a judicial candidate from being permitted to engage in the *activities* of a candidate is an important feature of the reorganization of Canon 4. During its deliberations, the Commission was mindful of the need to establish a time period to ensure that a judge elected to a ten-year term could not immediately announce plans to run for reelection, establish a campaign committee, and raise campaign funds for almost ten full years. With the time period in place, the judge can continue to call himself or herself a candidate for ten years, but can raise campaign funds only after the time period has been satisfied, typically one year before the first primary.

7. Rules 4.2(B)(1), 4.2(B)(2), and 4.2(B)(3): retained provisions allowing candidates to establish campaign committees, speak on their own behalf through various communications media, and endorse (or oppose) candidates running for *the same* judicial office.

These activities have traditionally been allowed, and the Commission did not modify these provisions in any substantive ways. It is important to note that permission is granted to all three types of judicial election candidates to engage in these activities, but only during the stated time period.

8. Rule 4.2(B)(4): specifically permitted what Rule 4.1(A)(5) prohibits for both judges and candidates; the permission applies to all candidates, including candidates running in nonpartisan and retention elections.

This is approximately the same result as would be obtained under the 1990 Code, but in a reorganized format. Under Canon 5A(1), judicial candidates are prohibited from attending events of political organizations, unless otherwise permitted. But Canon 5C(1) permits a candidate to "attend political gatherings" *at any time,* which negates the prescription.

In the proposed Code, Rule 4.1(A)(5) generally prohibits attending such political organization functions—as the first layer. Rule 4.2(B)(4) permits an exception, but only during a candidate's candidacy *and after a specific time.*

9. Rule 4.2(B)(5) provides an important distinction between judicial candidates running in partisan and other types of public judicial elections; the full impact of this paragraph depends on other parts of Rule 4.2, especially Rule 4.2(C).

This provision showcases the tiered approach of the proposed Code. According to Rule 4.1(A)(7), judges and candidates may not seek, accept, or use endorsements from a political organization. Rule 4.2(B)(5) continues this prohibition for *all* public election judicial candidates during the time period, because all are permitted to accept endorsements *only* from organizations that are *not* political organizations.

It is only in Rule 4.2(C)(2) that this restriction is finally removed—but for judicial candidates running in partisan elections *only*.

10. Rule 4.2(B)(6) represents an important compromise that allows all candidates for judicial office to make contributions to political organizations or other candidates for public office, but only during the time period.

Under the Canon 5(C)(1)(a)(iii) of the 1990 Code, a judge who was subject to public election at some later time (perhaps ten years away, as in the previous example) and any candidate running in a public election could make such contributions *at any time*. This included candidates running in nonpartisan and retention elections, because the 1990 Code did not distinguish between different modes of public election. Under Rule 4.2(B)(6), all candidates (including sitting judges who become candidates) may make contributions, even to political organizations, but only during the time period.

11. Rule 4.2(C): stated the two exceptions to the earlier prohibitions that apply *only* to judicial candidates in partisan public elections.

This provision permits identification as a candidate of a political organization and acceptance of endorsements from a political organization.

EXPLANATION OF COMMENTS

New Comments [1] through [7] help explain the relationships between the several paragraphs of Rule 4.2, as well as the relationship of this Rule to other Rules in Canon 4, especially Rule 4.1.

RULE 4.3 Activities of Candidates for Appointive Judicial Office

A candidate for appointment to judicial office may:

(A) communicate with the appointing or confirming authority, including any selection, screening, or nominating commission or similar agency; and

(B) seek endorsements for the appointment from any person or organization other than a partisan political organization.

Comment

[1] When seeking support or endorsement, or when communicating directly with an appointing or confirming authority, a candidate for appointive judicial office must not make any pledges, promises, or commitments that are inconsistent with the impartial performance of the adjudicative duties of the office. See Rule 4.1(A)(13).

RULE 4.3—REPORTER'S EXPLANATION OF CHANGES†

1990 MODEL CODE COMPARISON

Rule 4.3(A) is essentially the same as Canon 5B(2)(a)(i), except that it includes a more expansive list of those whom candidates for appointive judicial office may contact.

† The "Reporters' Explanations of Changes" have not been approved by the ABA Joint Commission to Evaluate the Model Code of Judicial Conduct. They have been drafted by the Commission's Reporters, based on the proceedings and

Rule 4.3(B) is derived from Canon 5B(2)(a)(ii), but it allows candidates to seek endorsements for the appointment from a broader array of persons and organizations.

Comment [1] is new.

EXPLANATION OF BLACK LETTER

1. Rule 4.3(A): added "or confirming authority," and substituted "any selection, screening, or nominating commission or similar agency" for "other agency designated to screen candidates."

The second revision is stylistic only and introduced no substantive change. The Commission added a reference to a "confirming authority," having in mind most obviously the U.S. Senate when sitting to confirm or reject presidential nominations of federal judges. Some state jurisdictions include a similar confirmation process in their overall appointment process, and in those jurisdictions candidates must be allowed to state their qualifications and views to confirming agencies as well as nominating and screening agencies.

2. Rule 4.3(B): greatly relaxed the restrictions on organizations or individuals from whom a candidate for appointive judicial office can seek support for the appointment.

Canon 5B(2)(a) of the 1990 Code limits candidates to seeking support from organizations that "regularly" make recommendations to appointing authorities, and to individuals who have been invited by the appointing (or confirming) authority to provide information.

By eliminating the restriction of obtaining support from only those organizations that regularly make recommendations, the Commission expanded the ability of a candidate to seek endorsement from any person or organization (with the exception of partisan political organizations).

The ability of a candidate to identify his or her own sponsors recognizes the realities in today's world, in which candidates almost universally seek the affirmative support of friends and allies with the appointing authority.

EXPLANATION OF COMMENTS

[1] New Comment [1] serves as a reminder that although candidates for appointive judicial office are not submitting themselves to the voting public, they are submitting themselves to a much smaller "electorate," an appointing authority. It is just as improper in the appointment system to make pledges and promises that are inconsistent with the impartial performance of judicial duties as it is in a campaign for elected office.

RULE 4.4 Campaign Committees

(A) A judicial candidate* subject to public election* may establish a campaign committee to manage and conduct a campaign for the candidate, subject to the provisions of this Code. The candidate is responsible for ensuring that his or her campaign committee complies with applicable provisions of this Code and other applicable law.*

(B) A judicial candidate subject to public election shall direct his or her campaign committee:

(1) to solicit and accept only such campaign contributions* as are reasonable, in any event not to exceed, in the aggregate,* $[insert amount] from any individual or $[insert amount] from any entity or organization;

(2) not to solicit or accept contributions for a candidate's current campaign more than [insert amount of time] before the applicable primary election, caucus, or

record of the Commission, solely to inform the ABA House of Delegates about each of the proposed amendments to the Model Code prior to their being considered at the ABA 2007 Midyear Meeting. THEY ARE NOT TO BE ADOPTED AS PART OF THE MODEL CODE.

general or retention election, nor more than [insert number] days after the last election in which the candidate participated; and

(3) to comply with all applicable statutory requirements for disclosure and divestiture of campaign contributions, and to file with [name of appropriate regulatory authority] a report stating the name, address, occupation, and employer of each person who has made campaign contributions to the committee in an aggregate value exceeding $[insert amount]. The report must be filed within [insert number] days following an election, or within such other period as is provided by law.

Comment

[1] Judicial candidates are prohibited from personally soliciting campaign contributions or personally accepting campaign contributions. See Rule 4.1(A)(8). This Rule recognizes that in many jurisdictions, judicial candidates must raise campaign funds to support their candidacies, and permits candidates, other than candidates for appointive judicial office, to establish campaign committees to solicit and accept reasonable financial contributions or in-kind contributions.

[2] Campaign committees may solicit and accept campaign contributions, manage the expenditure of campaign funds, and generally conduct campaigns. Candidates are responsible for compliance with the requirements of election law and other applicable law, and for the activities of their campaign committees.

[3] At the start of a campaign, the candidate must instruct the campaign committee to solicit or accept only such contributions as are reasonable in amount, appropriate under the circumstances, and in conformity with applicable law. Although lawyers and others who might appear before a successful candidate for judicial office are permitted to make campaign contributions, the candidate should instruct his or her campaign committee to be especially cautious in connection with such contributions, so they do not create grounds for disqualification if the candidate is elected to judicial office. See Rule 2.11.

RULE 4.4—REPORTER'S EXPLANATION OF CHANGES†

1990 MODEL CODE COMPARISON

Rule 4.4(A) combines aspects of the second sentence of Canon 5C(2), part of Canon 5C(4), and some of the Commentary following Canon 5C(2).

Rule 4.4(B)(1) is essentially the same as Canon 5C(3), but also includes an element from Canon 5C(2).

Rule 4.4(B)(2) is essentially the same as the fifth sentence of Canon 5C(2), but with additional language citing compliance with any applicable laws relating to divestiture of campaign funds subsequent to the campaign.

Rule 4.4(B)(3) is based upon Canon 5C(4), but includes an entirely new reference to divestiture of campaign funds.

Comment [1] is based upon the third, fourth, and fifth sentences of the Commentary following Canon 5C(2).

Comment [2] combines aspects of the second sentence of Canon 5C(2) and part of Canon 5C(4).

Comment [3] is partly new, but is based upon aspects of Canon 5C(2) and the following Commentary, plus parts of Canon 5C(4).

† The "Reporters' Explanations of Changes" have not been approved by the ABA Joint Commission to Evaluate the Model Code of Judicial Conduct. They have been drafted by the Commission's Reporters, based on the proceedings and record of the Commission, solely to inform the ABA House of Delegates about each of the proposed amendments to the Model Code prior to their being considered at the ABA 2007 Midyear Meeting. THEY ARE NOT TO BE ADOPTED AS PART OF THE MODEL CODE.

EXPLANATION OF BLACK LETTER

1. Rule 4.4(A) makes explicit that campaign committees are permitted only for candidates subject to public election, deleted reference to "committees of responsible persons," and adds a final sentence stating directly the candidate's responsibility for acts of his or her campaign committee.

The placement of the material on campaign committees within Canon 5C of the 1990 Code made it obvious (if not explicit) that these provisions applied only to candidates for elective judicial office (those "subject to public election"). Because Rule 4.4 stands alone in Canon 4, it was necessary to state the point explicitly.

The direction to establish committees composed only of "responsible persons" seemed unnecessary, and was deleted. The last sentence of Rule 4.4(A) is new in this form, but merely makes explicit what is referred to indirectly or assumed throughout Canon 5C of the 1990 Code.

2. Rule 4.4(B)(1) combines and recasts material from both Canon 5C(2) and Canon 5C(3) of the 1990 Code.

No substantive change is intended. This provision establishes that campaign contributions must be "reasonable" in amount (to avoid a suggestion of undue influence) and in addition are subject to aggregate limits (per campaign) for individuals and organizations, limits which each jurisdiction will set according to its conditions and policy choices.

3. Rule 4.4(B)(2) adds the word "current" before the word "campaign," and leaves the post-election time period for ending campaign solicitation open for variation in each jurisdiction.

These are minor adjustments, but could become significant in some settings. The Joint Commission wanted to make it even clearer than in the 1990 Code that the time window for a campaign committee to solicit funds applies to *each* campaign separately. Thus, Rule 4.4(B)(2) specifies that it applies always to a candidate's *current* campaign. More significantly, to prevent the early buildup of campaign funds, the Commission specified that a specific time restriction should be enacted (to be chosen by each jurisdiction) establishing the point at which contributions may be solicited and accepted. The time for continuing to raise campaign funds after the election to pay off debts of the campaign was left to each state to decide.

4. Rule 4.4(B)(3) adds "or within such other period as is provided by law."

Only a minor substantive changed is intended. The Commission, aware that many jurisdictions already have laws regulating elections, including the reporting of campaign contributions and divestiture of the contributions subsequent to a campaign, did not want to interfere with the operation of these laws. In the 1990 Code, possible obligations under law to divest a campaign of its funds were not addressed.

This paragraph recognizes that many jurisdictions already have provisions in their general election and campaign finance laws regarding disclosure and divestiture of campaign funds, and defers to local choices and existing law (if applicable) in setting the specific details.

EXPLANATION OF COMMENT

Comments [1]–[3] explain the operation and rationale for the black letter text of Rule 4.4, borrowing from and recasting both black letter text and Commentary from the 1990 Code.

The treatment of contributions from *lawyers* in Comment [3] builds upon the treatment given in Canon 5C(2) of the 1990 Code, but goes a step further. Canon 5C(2) merely states that solicitation (by a campaign committee) of such contributions is not prohibited whereas Comment [3] to Rule 4.4 urges special caution in light of the enhanced possibility that significant contributions from lawyers (and parties) who might later come before the judge would be a cause for disqualification of the judge under Rule 2.11.

RULE 4.5 Activities of Judges Who Become Candidates for Nonjudicial Office

(A) Upon becoming a candidate for a nonjudicial elective office, a judge shall resign from judicial office, unless permitted by law* to continue to hold judicial office.

(B) Upon becoming a candidate for a nonjudicial appointive office, a judge is not required to resign from judicial office, provided that the judge complies with the other provisions of this Code.

Comment

[1] In campaigns for nonjudicial elective public office, candidates may make pledges, promises, or commitments related to positions they would take and ways they would act if elected to office. Although appropriate in nonjudicial campaigns, this manner of campaigning is inconsistent with the role of a judge, who must remain fair and impartial to all who come before him or her. The potential for misuse of the judicial office, and the political promises that the judge would be compelled to make in the course of campaigning for nonjudicial elective office, together dictate that a judge who wishes to run for such an office must resign upon becoming a candidate.

[2] The "resign to run" rule set forth in paragraph (A) ensures that a judge cannot use the judicial office to promote his or her candidacy, and prevents post-campaign retaliation from the judge in the event the judge is defeated in the election. When a judge is seeking appointive nonjudicial office, however, the dangers are not sufficient to warrant imposing the "resign to run" rule.

RULE 4.5—REPORTER'S EXPLANATION OF CHANGES†

1990 MODEL CODE COMPARISON

Rule 4.5(A) is derived from Canon 5A(2), but has been simplified and reworded.

Rule 4.5(B) is new, but is implicit in and derived from Canon 5A(2).

Comments [1] and [2] are new.

EXPLANATION OF BLACK LETTER

1. Rule 4.5(A) recasts text, substituting "nonjudicial elective office" for "in a primary or in a general election," and deleting the specific exception for state constitutional conventions.

The Commission retained the "resign-to-run" rule with only minor revisions for style and clarity. Canon 5A(2) of the 1990 Code has always been interpreted to apply to elective nonjudicial offices only; the proposed Rule makes that explicit. The Commission also removed the special exception for judges who campaign for election to a state constitutional convention because of the rarity with which such a situation occurs. The remaining language, "unless permitted by law to continue to hold judicial office" should address such situations.

2. Rule 4.5(B) add a paragraph to clarify what seemed implicit in Canon 5A(2)—that if a judge becomes a candidate for appointment to a nonjudicial office, the judge is not required to resign from judicial office as a general proposition.

The Commission decided to make explicit that the "resign-to-run" rule applies only to nonjudicial elective offices, because it is only there that the dangers justifying the rule (as explained in Comments [1] and [2]) are at their height. In addition, because a sitting judge may become a "candidate" for an appointive non-judicial office—an undefined term in the proposed Code—merely by being considered by an executive branch officer for appointment, the Commission decided it was unwarranted to require automatic resignation. This consideration is especially strong when the executive branch may be considering several nominees for the same position, and when the confirmation process, if any, is both lengthy and of uncertain outcome.

---

† The "Reporters' Explanations of Changes" have not been approved by the ABA Joint Commission to Evaluate the Model Code of Judicial Conduct. They have been drafted by the Commission's Reporters, based on the proceedings and record of the Commission, solely to inform the ABA House of Delegates about each of the proposed amendments to the Model Code prior to their being considered at the ABA 2007 Midyear Meeting. THEY ARE NOT TO BE ADOPTED AS PART OF THE MODEL CODE.

As a fail-safe, the Commission added the reminder that a judge who remains on the bench while a candidate for appointive nonjudicial office must continue to abide by the other provisions of this Code (such as maintaining independence, integrity, and impartiality).

EXPLANATION OF COMMENTS

New Comments [1] and [2] explain the rationale for applying the "resign-to-run" rule to elective nonjudicial offices, but not to appointive ones. The rationale is based chiefly upon the federal decisional law.

RULES OF JUDICIAL CONDUCT AND DISABILITY

[Adopted by the Judicial Conference of the United States on March 11, 2008. Amended September 17, 2015.]

TABLE OF CONTENTS

Preface

These Rules were promulgated by the Judicial Conference of the United States, after public comment, pursuant to 28 U.S.C. §§ 331 and 358, to establish standards and procedures for addressing complaints filed by complainants or identified by chief judges under the Judicial Conduct and Disability Act, 28 U.S.C. §§ 351–364.

ARTICLE I. GENERAL PROVISIONS

1. Scope

These Rules govern proceedings under the Judicial Conduct and Disability Act (the Act), 28 U.S.C. §§ 351–364, to determine whether a covered judge has engaged in conduct prejudicial to the effective and expeditious administration of the business of the courts or is unable to discharge the duties of office because of mental or physical disability.

Commentary on Rule 1

In September 2006, the Judicial Conduct and Disability Act Study Committee ("Breyer Committee"), appointed in 2004 by Chief Justice Rehnquist, presented a report ("Breyer Committee Report"), 239 F.R.D. 116 (Sept. 2006), to Chief Justice Roberts that evaluated implementation of the Judicial Conduct and Disability Act of 1980, 28 U.S.C. §§ 351–364. The Breyer Committee had been formed in response to criticism from the public and Congress regarding the effectiveness of the Act's implementation. The Executive Committee of the Judicial Conference directed its Committee on Judicial Conduct and Disability to consider the Breyer Committee's recommendations and to report on their implementation to the Conference.

The Breyer Committee found that it could not evaluate implementation of the Act without establishing interpretive standards, Breyer Committee Report, 239 F.R.D. at 132, and that a major problem faced by chief judges in implementing the Act was the lack of authoritative interpretive standards. *Id.* at 212–15. The Breyer Committee then established standards to guide its evaluation, some of which were new formulations and some of which were taken from the "Illustrative Rules Governing Complaints of Judicial Misconduct and Disability," discussed below. The principal standards used by the Breyer Committee are in Appendix E of its Report. *Id.* at 238.

Based on the Breyer Committee's findings, the Committee on Judicial Conduct and Disability concluded that there was a need for the Judicial Conference to exercise its power under Section 358 of the Act to fashion standards guiding the various officers and bodies that must exercise responsibility under the Act. To that end, the Committee on Judicial Conduct and Disability proposed rules that were based largely on Appendix E of the Breyer Committee Report and the Illustrative Rules.

The Illustrative Rules were originally prepared in 1986 by the Special Committee of the Conference of Chief Judges of the United States Courts of Appeals, and were subsequently revised and amended, most recently in 2000, by the predecessor to the Committee on Judicial Conduct and Disability. The Illustrative Rules were adopted, with minor variations, by circuit judicial councils, to govern complaints under the Judicial Conduct and Disability Act.

After being submitted for public comment pursuant to 28 U.S.C. § 358(c), the Judicial Conference promulgated the present Rules on March 11, 2008. They were amended on September 17, 2015.

2. Effect and Construction

(a) Generally. These Rules are mandatory; they supersede any conflicting judicial-council rules. Judicial councils may promulgate additional rules to implement the Act as long as those rules do not conflict with these Rules.

(b) Exception. A Rule will not apply if, when performing duties authorized by the Act, a chief judge, a special committee, a judicial council, the Committee on Judicial Conduct and Disability, or the Judicial Conference expressly finds that exceptional circumstances

render application of that Rule in a particular proceeding manifestly unjust or contrary to the purposes of the Act or these Rules.

Commentary on Rule 2

Unlike the Illustrative Rules, these Rules provide mandatory and nationally uniform provisions governing the substantive and procedural aspects of misconduct and disability proceedings under the Act. The mandatory nature of these Rules is authorized by 28 U.S.C. § 358(a) and (c). Judicial councils retain the power to promulgate rules consistent with these Rules. For example, a local rule may authorize the electronic distribution of materials pursuant to Rule 8(b).

Rule 2(b) recognizes that unforeseen and exceptional circumstances may call for a different approach in particular cases.

3. Definitions

(a) Chief Judge. "Chief judge" means the chief judge of a United States court of appeals, of the United States Court of International Trade, or of the United States Court of Federal Claims.

(b) Circuit Clerk. "Circuit clerk" means a clerk of a United States court of appeals, the clerk of the United States Court of International Trade, the clerk of the United States Court of Federal Claims, or the circuit executive of the United States Court of Appeals for the Federal Circuit.

(c) Complaint. A complaint is:

(1) a document that, in accordance with Rule 6, is filed by any person in his or her individual capacity or on behalf of a professional organization; or

(2) information from any source, other than a document described in (c)(1), that gives a chief judge probable cause to believe that a covered judge, as defined in Rule 4, has engaged in misconduct or may have a disability, whether or not the information is framed as or is intended to be an allegation of misconduct or disability.

(d) Court of Appeals, District Court, and District Judge. "Courts of appeals," "district court," and "district judge," where appropriate, include the United States Court of Federal Claims, the United States Court of International Trade, and the judges thereof.

(e) Disability. "Disability" is a temporary or permanent impairment, physical or mental, rendering a judge unable to discharge the duties of the particular judicial office. Examples of disability include substance abuse, the inability to stay awake during court proceedings, or impairment of cognitive abilities that renders the judge unable to function effectively.

(f) Judicial Council and Circuit. "Judicial council" and "circuit," where appropriate, include any courts designated in 28 U.S.C. § 363.

(g) Magistrate Judge. "Magistrate judge," where appropriate, includes a special master appointed by the Court of Federal Claims under 42 U.S.C. § 300aa-12(c).

(h) Misconduct. Cognizable misconduct:

(1) is conduct prejudicial to the effective and expeditious administration of the business of the courts. Misconduct includes, but is not limited to:

(A) using the judge's office to obtain special treatment for friends or relatives;

(B) accepting bribes, gifts, or other personal favors related to the judicial office;

(C) having improper discussions with parties or counsel for one side in a case;

(D) treating litigants, attorneys, or others in a demonstrably egregious and hostile manner;

(E) engaging in partisan political activity or making inappropriately partisan statements;

(F) soliciting funds for organizations; or

(G) retaliating against complainants, witnesses, or others for their participation in this complaint process;

(H) refusing, without good cause shown, to cooperate in the investigation of a complaint under these Rules; or

(I) violating other specific, mandatory standards of judicial conduct, such as those pertaining to restrictions on outside income and requirements for financial disclosure.

(2) is conduct occurring outside the performance of official duties if the conduct might have a prejudicial effect on the administration of the business of the courts, including a substantial and widespread lowering of public confidence in the courts among reasonable people.

(3) does not include:

(A) an allegation that is directly related to the merits of a decision or procedural ruling. An allegation that calls into question the correctness of a judge's ruling, including a failure to recuse, without more, is merits-related. If the decision or ruling is alleged to be the result of an improper motive, *e.g.*, a bribe, ex parte contact, racial or ethnic bias, or improper conduct in rendering a decision or ruling, such as personally derogatory remarks irrelevant to the issues, the complaint is not cognizable to the extent that it attacks the merits.

(B) an allegation about delay in rendering a decision or ruling, unless the allegation concerns an improper motive in delaying a particular decision or habitual delay in a significant number of unrelated cases.

(i) Subject Judge. "Subject judge" means any judge described in Rule 4 who is the subject of a complaint.

Commentary on Rule 3

Rule 3 is derived and adapted from the Breyer Committee Report and the Illustrative Rules.

Unless otherwise specified or the context otherwise indicates, the term "complaint" is used in these Rules to refer both to complaints identified by a chief judge under Rule 5 and to complaints filed by a complainant under Rule 6.

Under the Act, a "complaint" may be filed by "any person" or "identified" by a chief judge. *See* 28 U.S.C. § 351(a), (b). Under Rule 3(c)(1), a complaint may be submitted by a person, in his or her individual capacity, or by a professional organization. Generally, the word "complaint" brings to mind the commencement of an adversary proceeding in which the contending parties are left to present the evidence and legal arguments, and judges play the role of an essentially passive arbiter. The Act, however, establishes an administrative, inquisitorial process. For example, even absent a complaint under Rule 6, chief judges are expected in some circumstances to trigger the process—"identify a complaint," *see* 28 U.S.C. § 351(b) and Rule 5—and conduct an investigation without becoming a party. *See* 28 U.S.C. § 352(a); Breyer Committee Report, 239 F.R.D. at 214; Illustrative Rule 2(j). Even when a complaint is filed by someone other than the chief judge, the complainant lacks many rights that a litigant would have, and the chief judge, instead of being limited to the "four corners of the complaint," must, under Rule 11, proceed as though misconduct or disability has been alleged where the complainant reveals information of misconduct or disability but does not claim it as such. *See* Breyer Committee Report, 239 F.R.D. at 183–84.

An allegation of misconduct or disability filed under Rule 6 is a "complaint," and the Rule so provides in subsection (c)(1). However, both the nature of the process and the use of the term "identify" suggest that the word "complaint" covers more than a document formally triggering the process. The process relies on chief judges considering known information and triggering the process when appropriate. "Identifying" a "complaint," therefore, is best understood as the chief judge's concluding that information known to the judge constitutes probable cause to believe that misconduct occurred or a disability exists, whether or not the information is framed as, or intended to be, an accusation. This definition is codified in subsection (c)(2).

Rule 3(e) relates to disability and provides only the most general definition, recognizing that a fact-specific approach is the only one available. A mental disability could involve cognitive impairment or any psychiatric or psychological condition that renders the judge unable to discharge the duties of office. Such duties may include those that are administrative. If, for example, the judge is a chief judge, the judicial council, fulfilling its obligation under 28 U.S.C. § 332(d)(1) to make "necessary and appropriate orders for the effective and expeditious administration of justice," may find, under 28 U.S.C. § 45(d) or § 136(e), that the judge is "temporarily unable to perform" his or her chief-judge duties. In that event, an appropriate remedy could involve, under Rule 20(b)(1)(D)(vii), temporary reassignment of chief-judge duties to the next judge statutorily eligible to perform them.

The phrase "prejudicial to the effective and expeditious administration of the business of the courts" is not subject to precise definition, and subsection (h)(1) therefore provides some specific examples. Although the Code of Conduct for United States Judges may be informative, its main precepts are highly general; the Code is in many potential applications aspirational rather than a set of disciplinary rules.

Ultimately, the responsibility for determining what constitutes misconduct under the statute is the province of the judicial council of the circuit, subject to such review and limitations as are ordained by the statute and by these Rules.

Even where specific, mandatory rules exist—for example, governing the receipt of gifts by judges, outside earned income, and financial disclosure obligations—the distinction between the misconduct statute and these specific, mandatory rules must be borne in mind. For example, an inadvertent, minor violation of any one of these rules, promptly remedied when called to the attention of the judge, might still be a violation but might not rise to the level of misconduct under the statute. By contrast, a pattern of such violations of the Code might well rise to the level of misconduct.

Under Rule 3(h)(1)(G), a judge's efforts to retaliate against any person for his or her involvement in the complaint process may constitute cognizable misconduct. The Rule makes this explicit in the interest of public confidence in the complaint process.

Rule 3(h)(1)(H) provides that a judge's refusal, without good cause shown, to cooperate in the investigation of a complaint under these Rules may constitute cognizable misconduct. While the exercise of rights under the Fifth Amendment to the Constitution would constitute good cause under Rule 3(h)(1)(H), given the fact-specific nature of the inquiry, it is not possible to otherwise anticipate all circumstances that might also constitute good cause. The Commentary on Rule 13 provides additional discussion regarding Rule 3(h)(1)(H). The Rules contemplate that judicial councils will not consider commencing proceedings under Rule 3(h)(1)(H) except as necessary after other means to acquire the information have been tried or have proven futile.

Rule 3(h)(2) reflects that an allegation can meet the statutory standard even though the judge's alleged conduct did not occur in the course of the performance of official duties. And some conduct in the categories listed under subsection (h)(1), or in categories not listed, might depending on the circumstances amount to "misconduct" under subsection (h)(2), or under both subsection (h)(1) and subsection (h)(2). Also, the Code of Conduct for United States Judges expressly covers a wide range of extra-official activities, and some of these activities may constitute misconduct. For example, allegations that a judge solicited funds for a charity or participated in a partisan political event are cognizable under the Act.

On the other hand, judges are entitled to some leeway in extra-official activities. For example, misconduct may not include a judge being repeatedly and publicly discourteous to a spouse (not including physical abuse) even though this might cause some reasonable people to have diminished confidence in the courts. Rule 3(h)(2) states that conduct of this sort is covered, for example, when it might lead to a "substantial and widespread" lowering of such confidence.

Rule 3(h)(3)(A) tracks the Act, 28 U.S.C. § 352(b)(1)(A)(ii), in excluding from the definition of misconduct allegations "[d]irectly related to the merits of a decision or procedural ruling." This exclusion preserves the independence of judges in the exercise of judicial power by ensuring that the complaint procedure is not used to collaterally attack the substance of a judge's ruling. Any allegation that calls into question the correctness of an official action of a judge—without more—is merits-related. The phrase "decision or procedural ruling" is not limited to rulings issued in deciding Article III cases or controversies. Thus, a complaint challenging the correctness of a chief judge's determination to dismiss a prior misconduct complaint would be properly dismissed as merits-related—in other words, as challenging the substance of the judge's administrative determination to dismiss the complaint—even though it does not concern the judge's rulings in Article III litigation. Similarly, an allegation that a judge had incorrectly declined to approve a Criminal Justice Act voucher is merits-related under this standard.

Conversely, an allegation—however unsupported—that a judge conspired with a prosecutor to make a particular ruling is not merits-related, even though it "relates" to a ruling in a colloquial sense. Such an allegation attacks the propriety of conspiring with the prosecutor and goes beyond a challenge to the correctness—"the merits"—of the ruling itself. An allegation that a judge ruled against the complainant because the complainant is a member of a particular racial or ethnic group, or because the judge dislikes the complainant personally, is also not merits-related. Such an allegation attacks the propriety of arriving at rulings with an illicit or improper motive. Similarly, an allegation that a judge used an inappropriate term to refer to a class of people is not merits-related even if the judge used it on the bench or in an opinion; the correctness of the judge's rulings is not at stake. An allegation that a judge treated litigants or attorneys in a demonstrably egregious and hostile manner while on the bench is also not merits-related.

The existence of an appellate remedy is usually irrelevant to whether an allegation is merits-related. The merits-related ground for dismissal exists to protect judges' independence in making rulings, not to protect or promote the appellate process. A complaint alleging an incorrect ruling is merits-related even though the complainant has no recourse from that ruling. By the same token, an allegation that is otherwise cognizable under the Act should not be dismissed merely because an appellate remedy appears to exist (for example, vacating a ruling that resulted from an improper ex parte communication). However, there may be occasions when appellate and misconduct proceedings overlap, and consideration and disposition of a complaint under these Rules may be properly deferred by the chief judge until the appellate proceedings are concluded in order to avoid, *inter alia*, inconsistent decisions.

Because of the special need to protect judges' independence in deciding what to say in an opinion or ruling, a somewhat different standard applies to determine the merits-relatedness of a non-frivolous allegation that a judge's language in a ruling reflected an improper motive. If the judge's language was relevant to the case at hand—for example, a statement that a claim is legally or factually "frivolous"—then the judge's choice of language is presumptively merits-related and excluded, absent evidence apart from the ruling itself suggesting an improper motive. If, on the other hand, the challenged language does not seem relevant on its face, then an additional inquiry under Rule 11 is necessary.

With regard to Rule 3(h)(3)(B), a complaint of delay in a single case is excluded as merits-related. Such an allegation may be said to challenge the correctness of an official action of the judge—in other words, assigning a low priority to deciding the particular case. But, by the same token, an allegation of a habitual pattern of delay in a significant number of unrelated cases, or an allegation of deliberate delay in a single case arising out of an illicit motive, is not merits-related.

The remaining subsections of Rule 3 provide technical definitions clarifying the application of the Rules to the various kinds of courts covered.

4. Covered Judges

A complaint under these Rules may concern the actions or capacity only of judges of United States courts of appeals, judges of United States district courts, judges of United States bankruptcy courts, United States magistrate judges, and judges of the courts specified in 28 U.S.C. § 363.

Commentary on Rule 4

This Rule tracks the Act. Rule 8(c) and (d) contain provisions as to the handling of complaints against persons not covered by the Act, such as other court personnel, or against both covered judges and noncovered persons.

ARTICLE II. INITIATION OF A COMPLAINT

5. Identification of a Complaint

(a) Identification. When a chief judge has information constituting reasonable grounds for inquiry into whether a covered judge has engaged in misconduct or has a disability, the chief judge may conduct an inquiry, as he or she deems appropriate, into the accuracy of the information even if no related complaint has been filed. A chief judge who finds probable cause to believe that misconduct has occurred or that a disability exists may seek an informal resolution that he or she finds satisfactory. If no informal resolution is achieved or is feasible, the chief judge may identify a complaint and, by written order stating the reasons, begin the review provided in Rule 11. If the evidence of misconduct is clear and convincing and no informal resolution is achieved or is feasible, the chief judge must identify a complaint. A chief judge must not decline to identify a complaint merely because the person making the allegation has not filed a complaint under Rule 6. This Rule is subject to Rule 7.

(b) Submission Not Fully Complying with Rule 6. A legible submission in substantial but not full compliance with Rule 6 must be considered as possible grounds for the identification of a complaint under Rule 5(a).

Commentary on Rule 5

This Rule is adapted from the Breyer Committee Report, 239 F.R.D. at 245–46.

The Act authorizes a chief judge, by written order stating reasons, to identify a complaint and thereby dispense with the filing of a written complaint. *See* 28 U.S.C. § 351(b). Under Rule 5, when a chief judge becomes aware of information constituting reasonable grounds to inquire into possible misconduct or disability on the part of a covered judge, and no formal complaint has been filed, the chief judge has the power in his or her discretion to begin an appropriate inquiry. A chief judge's decision whether to informally seek a resolution and/or to identify a complaint is guided by the results of that inquiry. If the chief judge concludes that there is probable cause to believe that misconduct has occurred or a disability exists, the chief judge may seek an informal resolution, if feasible, and if failing in that, may identify a complaint. Discretion is accorded largely for the reasons police officers and prosecutors have discretion in making arrests or bringing charges. The matter may be trivial and isolated, based on marginal evidence, or otherwise highly unlikely to lead to a misconduct or disability finding. On the other hand, if the inquiry leads the chief judge to conclude that there is clear and convincing evidence of misconduct or a disability, and no satisfactory informal resolution has been achieved or is feasible, the chief judge is required to identify a complaint.

An informal resolution is one agreed to by the subject judge and found satisfactory by the chief judge. Because an informal resolution under Rule 5 reached before a complaint is filed under Rule 6 will generally cause a subsequent Rule 6 complaint alleging the identical matter to be concluded, *see* Rule 11(d), the chief judge must be sure that the resolution is fully appropriate before endorsing it. In doing so, the chief judge must balance the seriousness of the matter against the particular judge's alacrity in addressing the issue.

The availability of this procedure should encourage attempts at swift remedial action before a formal complaint is filed.

When a chief judge identifies a complaint, a written order stating the reasons for the identification must be provided; this begins the process articulated in Rule 11. Rule 11 provides that once a chief judge has identified a complaint, the chief judge, subject to the disqualification provisions of Rule 25, will perform, with respect to that complaint, all functions assigned to the chief judge for the determination of complaints filed by a complainant.

In high-visibility situations, it may be desirable for a chief judge to identify a complaint without first seeking an informal resolution (and then, if the circumstances warrant, dismiss or conclude the identified complaint without appointment of a special committee) in order to assure the public that the allegations have not been ignored.

A chief judge's decision not to identify a complaint under Rule 5 is not appealable and is subject to Rule 3(h)(3)(A), which excludes merits-related complaints from the definition of misconduct.

A chief judge may not decline to identify a complaint solely on the basis that the unfiled allegations could be raised by one or more persons in a filed complaint, but none of these persons has opted to do so.

Subsection (a) concludes by stating that this Rule is "subject to Rule 7." This is intended to establish that only (i) the chief judge of the home circuit of a potential subject judge, or (ii) the chief judge of a circuit in which misconduct is alleged to have occurred in the course of official business while the potential subject judge was sitting by designation, shall have the power or a duty under this Rule to identify a complaint.

Subsection (b) provides that submissions that do not comply with the requirements of Rule 6(d) must be considered under Rule 5(a). For instance, if a complaint has been filed but the form submitted is unsigned, or the truth of the statements therein are not verified in writing under penalty of perjury, then a chief judge must nevertheless consider the allegations as known information and as a possible basis for the identification of a complaint under the process described in Rule 5(a).

6. Filing a Complaint

(a) Form. A complainant may use the form reproduced in the appendix to these Rules or a form designated by the rules of the judicial council in the circuit in which the complaint is filed. A complaint form is also available on each court of appeals' website or may be obtained from the circuit clerk or any district court or bankruptcy court within the circuit. A form is not necessary to file a complaint, but the complaint must be written and must include the information described in (b).

(b) Brief Statement of Facts. A complaint must contain a concise statement that details the specific facts on which the claim of misconduct or disability is based. The statement of facts should include a description of:

(1) what happened;

(2) when and where the relevant events happened;

(3) any information that would help an investigator check the facts; and

(4) for an allegation of disability, any additional facts that form the basis of that allegation.

(c) Legibility. A complaint should be typewritten if possible. If not typewritten, it must be legible. An illegible complaint will be returned to the complainant with a request to resubmit it in legible form. If a resubmitted complaint is still illegible, it will not be accepted for filing.

(d) Complainant's Address and Signature; Verification. The complainant must provide a contact address and sign the complaint. The truth of the statements made in the complaint must be verified in writing under penalty of perjury. If any of these

requirements are not met, the submission will be accepted, but it will be reviewed under only Rule 5(b).

(e) Number of Copies; Envelope Marking. The complainant shall provide the number of copies of the complaint required by local rule. Each copy should be in an envelope marked "Complaint of Misconduct" or "Complaint of Disability." The envelope must not show the name of any subject judge.

Commentary on Rule 6

The Rule is adapted from the Illustrative Rules and is self-explanatory.

7. Where to Initiate Complaints

(a) Where to File. Except as provided in (b),

(1) a complaint against a judge of a United States court of appeals, a United States district court, a United States bankruptcy court, or a United States magistrate judge must be filed with the circuit clerk in the jurisdiction in which the subject judge holds office.

(2) a complaint against a judge of the United States Court of International Trade or the United States Court of Federal Claims must be filed with the respective clerk of that court.

(3) a complaint against a judge of the United States Court of Appeals for the Federal Circuit must be filed with the circuit executive of that court.

(b) Misconduct in Another Circuit; Transfer. If a complaint alleges misconduct in the course of official business while the subject judge was sitting on a court by designation under 28 U.S.C. §§ 291–293 and 294(d), the complaint may be filed or identified with the circuit clerk of that circuit or of the subject judge's home circuit. The proceeding will continue in the circuit of the first-filed or first-identified complaint. The judicial council of the circuit where the complaint was first filed or first identified may transfer the complaint to the subject judge's home circuit or to the circuit where the alleged misconduct occurred, as the case may be.

Commentary on Rule 7

Title 28 U.S.C. § 351 states that complaints are to be filed with "the clerk of the court of appeals for the circuit." However, in many circuits, this role is filled by circuit executives. Accordingly, the term "circuit clerk," as defined in Rule 3(b) and used throughout these Rules, applies to circuit executives.

Section 351 uses the term "the circuit" in a way that suggests that either the home circuit of the subject judge or the circuit in which misconduct is alleged to have occurred is the proper venue for complaints. With an exception for judges sitting by designation, the Rule requires the filing or identification of a misconduct or disability complaint in the circuit in which the judge holds office, largely based on the administrative perspective of the Act. Given the Act's emphasis on the future conduct of the business of the courts, the circuit in which the judge holds office is the appropriate forum because that circuit is likely best able to influence a judge's future behavior in constructive ways.

However, when judges sit by designation, the non-home circuit has a strong interest in redressing misconduct in the course of official business, and where allegations also involve a member of the bar—ex parte contact between an attorney and a judge, for example—it may often be desirable to have the judicial and bar misconduct proceedings take place in the same venue. Rule 7(b), therefore, allows transfer to, or filing or identification of a complaint in, the non-home circuit. The proceeding may be transferred by the judicial council of the filing or identified circuit to the other circuit.

8. Action by Clerk

(a) Receipt of Complaint. Upon receiving a complaint against a judge filed under Rule 6 or identified under Rule 5, the circuit clerk must open a file, assign a docket number according to a uniform numbering scheme promulgated by the Committee on Judicial Conduct and Disability, and acknowledge the complaint's receipt.

(b) Distribution of Copies. The circuit clerk must promptly send copies of a complaint filed under Rule 6 to the chief judge or the judge authorized to act as chief judge under Rule 25(f), and copies of complaints filed under Rule 6 or identified under Rule 5 to each subject judge. The circuit clerk must retain the original complaint. Any further distribution should be as provided by local rule.

(c) Complaint Against Noncovered Person. If the circuit clerk receives a complaint about a person not holding an office described in Rule 4, the clerk must not accept the complaint under these Rules.

(d) Complaint Against Judge and Another Noncovered Person. If the circuit clerk receives a complaint about a judge described in Rule 4 and a person not holding an office described in Rule 4, the clerk must accept the complaint under these Rules only with regard to the judge and must so inform the complainant.

Commentary on Rule 8

This Rule is adapted from the Illustrative Rules and is largely self-explanatory.

The uniform docketing scheme described in subsection (a) should take into account potential problems associated with a complaint that names multiple judges. One solution may be to provide separate docket numbers for each subject judge. Separate docket numbers would help avoid difficulties in tracking cases, particularly if a complaint is dismissed with respect to some, but not all of the named judges.

Complaints against noncovered persons are not to be accepted for processing under these Rules but may, of course, be accepted under other circuit rules or procedures for grievances.

9. Time for Filing or Identifying a Complaint

A complaint may be filed or identified at any time. If the passage of time has made an accurate and fair investigation of a complaint impractical, the complaint must be dismissed under Rule 11(c)(1)(E).

Commentary on Rule 9

This Rule is adapted from the Act, 28 U.S.C. §§ 351, 352(b)(1)(A)(iii), and the Illustrative Rules.

10. Abuse of the Complaint Procedure

(a) Abusive Complaints. A complainant who has filed repetitive, harassing, or frivolous complaints, or has otherwise abused the complaint procedure, may be restricted from filing further complaints. After giving the complainant an opportunity to show cause in writing why his or her right to file further complaints should not be limited, the judicial council may prohibit, restrict, or impose conditions on the complainant's use of the complaint procedure. Upon written request of the complainant, the judicial council may revise or withdraw any prohibition, restriction, or condition previously imposed.

(b) Orchestrated Complaints. When many essentially identical complaints from different complainants are received and appear to be part of an orchestrated campaign, the chief judge may recommend that the judicial council issue a written order instructing the circuit clerk to accept only a certain number of such complaints for filing and to refuse

to accept additional complaints. The circuit clerk must send a copy of any such order to anyone whose complaint was not accepted.

Commentary on Rule 10

This Rule is adapted from the Illustrative Rules.

Rule 10(a) provides a mechanism for a judicial council to restrict the filing of further complaints by a single complainant who has abused the complaint procedure. In some instances, however, the complaint procedure may be abused in a manner for which the remedy provided in Rule 10(a) may not be appropriate. For example, some circuits have been inundated with submissions of dozens or hundreds of essentially identical complaints against the same judge or judges, all submitted by different complainants. In many of these instances, persons with grievances against a particular judge or judges used the Internet or other technology to orchestrate mass complaint-filing campaigns against them. If each complaint submitted as part of such a campaign were accepted for filing and processed according to these Rules, there would be a serious drain on court resources without any benefit to the adjudication of the underlying merits.

A judicial council may, therefore, respond to such mass filings under Rule 10(b) by declining to accept repetitive complaints for filing, regardless of the fact that the complaints are nominally submitted by different complainants. When the first complaint or complaints have been dismissed on the merits, and when further, essentially identical submissions follow, the judicial council may issue a second order noting that these are identical or repetitive complaints, directing the circuit clerk not to accept these complaints or any further such complaints for filing, and directing the clerk to send each putative complainant copies of both orders.

ARTICLE III. REVIEW OF COMPLAINT BY CHIEF JUDGE

11. Chief Judge's Review

(a) Purpose of Chief Judge's Review. When a complaint is identified by the chief judge or is filed, the chief judge must review it unless the chief judge is disqualified under Rule 25. If a complaint contains information constituting evidence of misconduct or disability, but the complainant does not claim it as such, the chief judge must treat the complaint as if it did allege misconduct or disability and give notice to the subject judge. After reviewing a complaint, the chief judge must determine whether it should be:

(1) dismissed;

(2) concluded on the ground that voluntary corrective action has been taken;

(3) concluded because intervening events have made action on the complaint no longer necessary; or

(4) referred to a special committee.

(b) Chief Judge's Inquiry. In determining what action to take under Rule 11(a), the chief judge may conduct a limited inquiry. The chief judge, or a designee, may communicate orally or in writing with the complainant, the subject judge, and any others who may have knowledge of the matter, and may obtain and review transcripts and other relevant documents. In conducting the inquiry, the chief judge must not determine any reasonably disputed issue. Any such determination must be left to a special committee appointed under Rule 11(f) and to the judicial council that considers the committee's report.

(c) Dismissal.

(1) Permissible grounds. A complaint must be dismissed in whole or in part to the extent that the chief judge concludes that the complaint:

(A) alleges conduct that, even if true, is not prejudicial to the effective and expeditious administration of the business of the courts and does not indicate a mental or physical disability resulting in the inability to discharge the duties of judicial office;

(B) is directly related to the merits of a decision or procedural ruling;

(C) is frivolous;

(D) is based on allegations lacking sufficient evidence to raise an inference that misconduct has occurred or that a disability exists;

(E) is based on allegations that are incapable of being established through investigation;

(F) has been filed in the wrong circuit under Rule 7; or

(G) is otherwise not appropriate for consideration under the Act.

(2) Impermissible grounds. A complaint must not be dismissed solely because it repeats allegations of a previously dismissed complaint if it also contains material information not previously considered and does not constitute harassment of the subject judge.

(d) Corrective Action. The chief judge may conclude a complaint proceeding in whole or in part if:

(1) an informal resolution under Rule 5 satisfactory to the chief judge was reached before the complaint was filed under Rule 6; or

(2) the chief judge determines that the subject judge has taken appropriate voluntary corrective action that acknowledges and remedies the problems raised by the complaint.

(e) Intervening Events. The chief judge may conclude a complaint proceeding in whole or in part upon determining that intervening events render some or all of the allegations moot or make remedial action impossible.

(f) Appointment of Special Committee. If some or all of a complaint is not dismissed or concluded, the chief judge must promptly appoint a special committee to investigate the complaint or any relevant portion of it and to make recommendations to the judicial council. Before appointing a special committee, the chief judge must invite the subject judge to respond to the complaint either orally or in writing if the judge was not given an opportunity during the limited inquiry. In the chief judge's discretion, separate complaints may be joined and assigned to a single special committee. Similarly, a single complaint about more than one judge may be severed and more than one special committee appointed.

(g) Notice of Chief Judge's Action; Petition for Review.

(1) When chief judge appoints special committee. If the chief judge appoints a special committee, the chief judge must notify the complainant and the subject judge that the matter has been referred to a committee, notify the complainant of a complainant's rights under Rule 16, and identify the members of the committee. A copy of the order appointing the special committee must be sent to the Committee on Judicial Conduct and Disability.

(2) When chief judge disposes of complaint without appointing special committee. If the chief judge disposes of a complaint under Rule 11(c), (d), or (e), the chief judge must prepare a supporting memorandum that sets forth the reasons for the disposition. If the complaint was initiated by identification under Rule 5, the

memorandum must so indicate. Except as authorized by 28 U.S.C. § 360, the memorandum must not include the name of the complainant or of the subject judge. The order and memoranda incorporated by reference in the order must be promptly sent to the complainant, the subject judge, and the Committee on Judicial Conduct and Disability.

(3) Right to petition for review. If the chief judge disposes of a complaint under Rule 11(c), (d), or (e), the complainant and the subject judge must be notified of the right to petition the judicial council for review of the disposition, as provided in Rule 18. If the chief judge so disposes of a complaint that was identified under Rule 5 or filed by its subject judge, the chief judge must transmit the order and memoranda incorporated by reference in the order to the judicial council for review in accordance with Rule 19. In the event of such a transmission, the subject judge may make a written submission to the judicial council but will have no further right of review except as allowed under Rule 21(b)(1)(B). When a disposition is to be reviewed by the judicial council, the chief judge must promptly transmit all materials obtained in connection with the inquiry under Rule 11(b) to the circuit clerk for transmittal to the council.

(h) Public Availability of Chief Judge's Decision. The chief judge's decision must be made public to the extent, at the time, and in the manner provided in Rule 24.

Commentary on Rule 11

This Rule describes complaint-review actions available either to the chief judge or, where that judge is the subject judge or is otherwise disqualified under Rule 25, to the judge designated under Rule 25(f) to perform the chief judge's duties under these Rules. Subsection (a) of this Rule provides that where a complaint has been filed under Rule 6, the ordinary doctrines of waiver do not apply. The chief judge must identify as a complaint any misconduct or disability issues raised by the factual allegations of the complaint even if the complainant makes no such claim with regard to those issues. For example, an allegation limited to misconduct in fact-finding that mentions periods during a trial when the judge was asleep must be treated as a complaint regarding disability. A formal order giving notice of the expanded scope of the proceeding must be given to the subject judge.

Subsection (b) describes the nature of the chief judge's inquiry. It is based largely on the Breyer Committee Report, 239 F.R.D. at 243–45. The Act states that dismissal is appropriate "when a limited inquiry . . . demonstrates that the allegations in the complaint lack any factual foundation or are conclusively refuted by objective evidence." 28 U.S.C. § 352(b)(1)(B). At the same time, however, Section 352(a) states that "[t]he chief judge shall not undertake to make findings of fact about any matter that is reasonably in dispute." These two statutory standards should be read together so that a matter is not "reasonably" in dispute if a limited inquiry shows that the allegations do not constitute misconduct or disability, that they lack any reliable factual foundation, or that they are conclusively refuted by objective evidence.

In conducting a limited inquiry under subsection (b), the chief judge must avoid determinations of reasonably disputed issues, including reasonably disputed issues as to whether the facts alleged constitute misconduct or disability, which are ordinarily left to the judicial council and its special committee. An allegation of fact is ordinarily not "refuted" simply because the subject judge denies it. The limited inquiry must reveal something more in the way of refutation before it is appropriate to dismiss a complaint that is otherwise cognizable. If it is the complainant's word against the subject judge's—in other words, there is simply no other significant evidence of what happened or of the complainant's unreliability—then there must be a special-committee investigation. Such a credibility issue is a matter "reasonably in dispute" within the meaning of the Act.

However, dismissal following a limited inquiry may occur when a complaint refers to transcripts or to witnesses and the chief judge determines that the transcripts and witnesses all support the subject judge. Breyer Committee Report, 239 F.R.D. at 243. For example, consider a complaint alleging that the subject judge said X, and the complaint mentions, or it is independently clear, that five people may have heard what the judge said. *Id.* The chief judge is told by the subject judge and one witness that the judge did not say X, and the chief judge dismisses the complaint without questioning the other four possible witnesses. *Id.* In this example, the matter remains reasonably in dispute. If all five witnesses say the subject judge did not say X, dismissal is appropriate, but if potential witnesses who are reasonably accessible have not been questioned, then the matter remains reasonably in dispute. *Id.*

Similarly, under subsection (c)(1)(A), if it is clear that the conduct or disability alleged, even if true, is not cognizable under these Rules, the complaint should be dismissed. If that issue is reasonably in dispute, however, dismissal under subsection (c)(1)(A) is inappropriate.

Essentially, the standard articulated in subsection (b) is that used to decide motions for summary judgment pursuant to Fed. R. Civ. P. 56. Genuine issues of material fact are not resolved at the summary judgment stage. A material fact is one that "might affect the outcome of the suit under the governing law," and a dispute is "genuine" if "the evidence is such that a reasonable jury could return a verdict for the nonmoving party." *Anderson v. Liberty Lobby*, 477 U.S. 242, 248 (1986). Similarly, the chief judge may not resolve a genuine issue concerning a material fact or the existence of misconduct or a disability when conducting a limited inquiry pursuant to subsection (b).

Subsection (c) describes the grounds on which a complaint may be dismissed. These are adapted from the Act, 28 U.S.C. § 352(b), and the Breyer Committee Report, 239 F.R.D. at 239–45. Subsection (c)(1)(A) permits dismissal of an allegation that, even if true, does not constitute misconduct or disability under the statutory standard. The proper standards are set out in Rule 3 and discussed in the Commentary on that Rule. Subsection (c)(1)(B) permits dismissal of complaints related to the merits of a decision by a subject judge; this standard is also governed by Rule 3 and its accompanying Commentary.

Subsections (c)(1)(C)–(E) implement the statute by allowing dismissal of complaints that are "frivolous, lacking sufficient evidence to raise an inference that misconduct has occurred, or containing allegations which are incapable of being established through investigation." 28 U.S.C. § 352(b)(1)(A)(iii).

Dismissal of a complaint as "frivolous" under Rule 11(c)(1)(C) will generally occur without any inquiry beyond the face of the complaint. For instance, when the allegations are facially incredible or so lacking in indicia of reliability that no further inquiry is warranted, dismissal under this subsection is appropriate.

A complaint warranting dismissal under Rule 11(c)(1)(D) is illustrated by the following example. Consider a complainant who alleges an impropriety and asserts that he knows of it because it was observed and reported to him by a person who is identified. The subject judge denies that the event occurred. When contacted, the source also denies it. In such a case, the chief judge's proper course of action may turn on whether the source had any role in the allegedly improper conduct. If the complaint was based on a lawyer's statement that he or she had an improper ex parte contact with a judge, the lawyer's denial of the impropriety might not be taken as wholly persuasive, and it would be appropriate to conclude that a real factual issue is raised. On the other hand, if the complaint quoted a disinterested third party and that disinterested party denied that the statement had been made, there would be no value in opening a formal investigation. In such a case, it would be appropriate to dismiss the complaint under Rule 11(c)(1)(D).

Rule 11(c)(1)(E) is intended, among other things, to cover situations when no evidence is offered or identified, or when the only identified source is unavailable.

Breyer Committee Report, 239 F.R.D. at 243. For example, a complaint alleges that an unnamed attorney told the complainant that the subject judge did X. *Id.* The subject judge denies it. The chief judge requests that the complainant (who does not purport to have observed the subject judge do X) identify the unnamed witness, or that the unnamed witness come forward so that the chief judge can learn the unnamed witness's account. *Id.* The complainant responds that he has spoken with the unnamed witness, that the unnamed witness is an attorney who practices in federal court, and that the unnamed witness is unwilling to be identified or to come forward. *Id.* at 243–44. The allegation is then properly dismissed as containing allegations that are incapable of being established through investigation. *Id.*

If, however, the situation involves a reasonable dispute over credibility, the matter should proceed. For example, the complainant alleges an impropriety and alleges that he or she observed it and that there were no other witnesses; the subject judge denies that the event occurred. Unless the complainant's allegations are facially incredible or so lacking indicia of reliability as to warrant dismissal under Rule

11(c)(1)(C), a special committee must be appointed because there is a material factual question that is reasonably in dispute.

Dismissal is also appropriate when a complaint is filed so long after an alleged event that memory loss, death, or changes to unknown residences prevent a proper investigation.

Subsection (c)(2) indicates that the investigative nature of the process prevents the application of claim preclusion principles where new and material evidence becomes available. However, it also recognizes that at some point a renewed investigation may constitute harassment of the subject judge and should not be undertaken, depending of course on the seriousness of the issues and the weight of the new evidence.

Rule 11(d) implements the Act's provision for dismissal if voluntary appropriate corrective action has been taken. It is largely adapted from the Breyer Committee Report, 239 F.R.D. at 244–45. The Act authorizes the chief judge to conclude the complaint proceedings if "appropriate corrective action has been taken." 28 U.S.C. § 352(b)(2). Under the Rule, action taken after a complaint is filed is "appropriate" when it acknowledges and remedies the problem raised by the complaint. Breyer Committee Report, 239 F.R.D. at 244. Because the Act deals with the conduct of judges, the emphasis is on correction of the judicial conduct that was the subject of the complaint. *Id.* Terminating a complaint based on corrective action is premised on the implicit understanding that voluntary self-correction or redress of misconduct or a disability is preferable to sanctions. *Id.* The chief judge may facilitate this process by giving the subject judge an objective view of the appearance of the judicial conduct in question and by suggesting appropriate corrective measures. *Id.* Moreover, when corrective action is taken under Rule 5 satisfactory to the chief judge before a complaint is filed, that informal resolution will be sufficient to conclude a subsequent complaint based on identical conduct.

"Corrective action" must be voluntary action taken by the subject judge. Breyer Committee Report, 239 F.R.D. at 244. A remedial action directed by the chief judge or by an appellate court without the participation of the subject judge in formulating the directive or without the subject judge's subsequent agreement to such action does not constitute the requisite voluntary corrective action. *Id.* Neither the chief judge nor an appellate court has authority under the Act to impose a formal remedy or sanction; only the judicial council can impose a formal remedy or sanction under 28 U.S.C. § 354(a)(2). *Id.* Compliance with a previous judicial-council order may serve as corrective action allowing conclusion of a later complaint about the same behavior. *Id.*

Where a subject judge's conduct has resulted in identifiable, particularized harm to the complainant or another individual, appropriate corrective action should include steps taken by that judge to acknowledge and redress the harm, if possible, such as by an apology, recusal from a case, or a pledge to refrain from similar conduct in the future. *Id.* While the Act is generally forward-looking, any corrective action should, to the extent possible, serve to correct a specific harm to an individual, if such harm can reasonably be remedied. *Id.* In some cases, corrective action may not be "appropriate" to justify conclusion of a complaint unless the complainant or other individual harmed is meaningfully apprised of the nature of the corrective action in the chief judge's order, in a direct communication from the subject judge, or otherwise. *Id.*

Voluntary corrective action should be proportionate to any plausible allegations of misconduct in a complaint. The form of corrective action should also be proportionate to any sanctions that the judicial council might impose under Rule 20(b), such as a private or public reprimand or a change in case assignments. Breyer Committee Report, 239 F.R.D at 244–45. In other words, minor corrective action will not suffice to dispose of a serious matter. *Id.*

Rule 11(e) implements Section 352(b)(2) of the Act, which permits the chief judge to "conclude the proceeding," if "action on the complaint is no longer necessary because of intervening events," such as a resignation from judicial office. Ordinarily, however, stepping down from an administrative post such as chief judge, judicial-council member, or court-committee chair does not constitute an event rendering unnecessary any further action on a complaint alleging judicial misconduct. Breyer Committee Report, 239 F.R.D. at 245. As long as the subject of a complaint performs judicial duties, a complaint alleging judicial misconduct must be addressed. *Id.*

If a complaint is not disposed of pursuant to Rule 11(c), (d), or (e), a special committee must be appointed. Rule 11(f) states that a subject judge must be invited to respond to the complaint before a special committee is appointed, if no earlier response was invited.

Subject judges receive copies of complaints at the same time that they are referred to the chief judge, and they are free to volunteer responses to them. Under Rule 11(b), the chief judge may request a response if it is thought necessary. However, many complaints are clear candidates for dismissal even if their allegations are accepted as true, and there is no need for the subject judge to devote time to a defense.

The Act requires that the order dismissing a complaint or concluding a proceeding contain a statement of reasons and that a copy of the order be sent to the complainant. 28 U.S.C. § 352(b). Rule 24, dealing with availability of information to the public, contemplates that the order will be made public, usually without disclosing the names of the complainant or the subject judge. If desired for administrative purposes, more identifying information can be included in a non-public version of the order.

When a complaint is disposed of by the chief judge, the statutory purposes are best served by providing the complainant with a full, particularized, but concise explanation, giving reasons for the conclusions reached. *See also* Commentary on Rule 24 (dealing with public availability).

Rule 11(g) provides that the complainant and the subject judge must be notified, in the case of a disposition by the chief judge, of the right to petition the judicial council for review. Because an identified complaint has no "complainant" to petition for review, the chief judge's dispositive order on such a complaint will be transmitted to the judicial council for review. The same will apply where a complaint was filed by its subject judge. A copy of the chief judge's order, and memoranda incorporated by reference in the order, disposing of a complaint must be sent by the circuit clerk to the Committee on Judicial Conduct and Disability.

ARTICLE IV. INVESTIGATION AND REPORT BY SPECIAL COMMITTEE

12. Special Committee's Composition

(a) Membership. Except as provided in (e), a special committee appointed under Rule 11(f) must consist of the chief judge and equal numbers of circuit and district judges. These judges may include senior judges. If a complaint is about a district judge, bankruptcy judge, or magistrate judge, then, when possible, the district-judge members of the special committee must be from districts other than the district of the subject judge. For the courts named in 28 U.S.C. § 363, the special committee must be selected from the judges serving on the subject judge's court.

(b) Presiding Officer. When appointing the special committee, the chief judge may serve as the presiding officer or else must designate a committee member as the presiding officer.

(c) Bankruptcy Judge or Magistrate Judge as Adviser. If the subject judge is a bankruptcy judge or magistrate judge, he or she may, within 14 days after being notified of the special committee's appointment, ask the chief judge to designate as a committee adviser another bankruptcy judge or magistrate judge, as the case may be. The chief judge must grant such a request but may otherwise use discretion in naming the adviser. Unless the adviser is a Court of Federal Claims special master appointed under 42 U.S.C. § 300aa-12(c), the adviser must be from a district other than the district of the subject bankruptcy judge or subject magistrate judge. The adviser cannot vote but has the other privileges of a special-committee member.

(d) Provision of Documents. The chief judge must certify to each other member of the special committee and to any adviser copies of the complaint and statement of facts, in whole or relevant part, and any other relevant documents on file.

(e) Continuing Qualification of Special-Committee Member. A member of a special committee may continue to serve on the committee even though the member relinquishes the position of chief judge, active circuit judge, or active district judge, as the case may be, but only if the member continues to hold office under Article III, Section 1, of the Constitution of the United States, or under 28 U.S.C. § 171.

(f) Inability of Special-Committee Member to Complete Service. If a member of a special committee can no longer serve because of death, disability, disqualification, resignation, retirement from office, or other reason, the chief judge must decide whether to appoint a replacement member, either a circuit or district judge as needed under (a). No special committee appointed under these Rules may function with only a single member, and the votes of a two-member committee must be unanimous.

(g) Voting. All actions by a special committee must be by vote of a majority of all members of the committee.

Commentary on Rule 12

This Rule is adapted from the Act and the Illustrative Rules.

Rule 12 leaves the size of a special committee flexible, to be determined on a case-by-case basis. The question the size of a special committee is one that should be weighed with care in view of the potential for consuming the members' time; a large committee should be appointed only if there is a special reason to do so. Rule 12(a) acknowledges the common practice of including senior judges in the membership of a special committee.

Although the Act requires that the chief judge be a member of each special committee, 28 U.S.C. § 353(a)(1), it does not require that the chief judge preside. Accordingly, Rule 12(b) provides that if the chief judge does not preside, he or she must designate another member of the special committee as the presiding officer.

Rule 12(c) provides that the chief judge must appoint a bankruptcy judge or magistrate judge as an adviser to a special committee at the request of a bankruptcy or magistrate subject judge. Subsection (c) also provides that the adviser will have all the privileges of a member of the special committee except a vote. The adviser, therefore, may participate in all deliberations of the special committee, question witnesses at hearings, and write a separate statement to accompany the committee's report to the judicial council.

Rule 12(e) provides that a member of a special committee who remains an Article III judge may continue to serve on the committee even though the member's status otherwise changes. Thus, a special committee that originally consisted of the chief judge and an equal number of circuit and district judges, as required by the law, may continue to function even though changes of status alter that composition. This provision reflects the belief that stability of membership will contribute to the quality of the work of such committees.

Stability of membership is also the principal concern animating Rule 12(f), which deals with the case in which a special committee loses a member before its work is complete. The Rule permits the chief judge to determine whether a replacement member should be appointed. Generally, appointment of a replacement member is desirable in these situations unless the special committee has conducted evidentiary hearings before the vacancy occurs. However, cases may arise in which a special committee is in the late stages of its work, and in which it would be difficult for a new member to play a meaningful role. The Rule also preserves the collegial character of the special-committee process by prohibiting a single surviving member from serving as a committee and by providing that a committee of two surviving members will, in essence, operate under a unanimity rule.

Rule 12(g) provides that actions of a special committee must be by vote of a majority of all the members. All the members of a special committee should participate in committee decisions. In that circumstance, it seems reasonable to require that special-committee decisions be made by a majority of the membership, rather than a majority of some smaller quorum.

13. Conduct of Special-Committee Investigation

(a) Extent and Methods of Special-Committee Investigation. A special committee should determine the appropriate extent and methods of its investigation in light of the allegations of the complaint and its preliminary inquiry. The investigation may include use of appropriate experts or other professionals. If, in the course of the investigation, the special committee has cause to believe that the subject judge may have engaged in misconduct or has a disability that is beyond the scope of the complaint, the committee must refer the new matter to the chief judge for a determination of whether action under Rule 5 or Rule 11 is necessary before the committee's investigation is expanded to include the new matter.

(b) Criminal Conduct. If the special committee's investigation concerns conduct that may be a crime, the committee must consult with the appropriate prosecutorial authorities to the extent permitted by the Act to avoid compromising any criminal investigation. The special committee has final authority over the timing and extent of its investigation and the formulation of its recommendations.

(c) Staff. The special committee may arrange for staff assistance to conduct the investigation. It may use existing staff of the judiciary or may hire special staff through the Director of the Administrative Office of the United States Courts.

(d) Delegation of Subpoena Power; Contempt. The chief judge may delegate the authority to exercise the subpoena powers of the special committee. The judicial council or special committee may institute a contempt proceeding under 28 U.S.C. § 332(d) against anyone who fails to comply with a subpoena.

Commentary on Rule 13

This Rule is adapted from the Illustrative Rules.

Rule 13, as well as Rules 14, 15, and 16, are concerned with the way in which the special committee carries out its mission. They reflect the view that the special committee has two roles that are separated in ordinary litigation. First, the special committee has an investigative role of the kind that is characteristically left to executive branch agencies or discovery by civil litigants. 28 U.S.C. § 353(c). Second, it has a formalized fact-finding and recommendation-of-disposition role that is characteristically left to juries, judges, or arbitrators. *Id.* Rule 13 generally governs the investigative stage. Even though the same body has responsibility for both roles under the Act, it is important to distinguish between them in order to ensure that appropriate rights are afforded at appropriate times to the subject judge.

Rule 13(a) includes a provision making clear that the special committee may choose to consult appropriate experts or other professionals if it determines that such a consultation is warranted. If, for example, the special committee has cause to believe that the subject judge may be unable to discharge all of the duties of office by reason of mental or physical disability, the committee could ask the subject judge to respond to inquiries and, if necessary, request the judge to undergo a medical or psychological examination. In advance of any such examination, the special committee may enter into an agreement with the subject judge as to the scope and use that may be made of the examination results. In addition or in the alternative, the special committee may ask to review existing records, including medical records.

The extent of the subject judge's cooperation in the investigation may be taken into account in the consideration of the underlying complaint. If, for example, the subject judge impedes reasonable efforts to confirm or disconfirm the presence of a disability, the special committee may still consider whether the conduct alleged in the complaint and confirmed in the investigation constitutes disability. The same would be true of a complaint alleging misconduct.

The special committee may also consider whether such a judge might be in violation of his or her duty to cooperate in an investigation under these Rules, a duty rooted not only in the Act's definition of misconduct but also in the Code of Conduct for United States Judges, which emphasizes the need to maintain public confidence in the judiciary, see Canon 2(A) and Canon 1 cmt., and requires judges to "facilitate the performance of the administrative responsibilities of other judges and court personnel," Canon 3(B)(1). If the special committee finds a breach of the duty to cooperate and believes that the breach may amount to misconduct under Rule 3(h)(1)(H), it should determine, under the final sentence of Rule 13(a), whether that possibility should be referred to the chief judge for consideration of action under Rule 5 or Rule 11. See also Commentary on Rule 3.

One of the difficult questions that can arise is the relationship between proceedings under the Act and criminal investigations. Rule 13(b) assigns responsibility for coordination to the special committee in cases in which criminal conduct is suspected, but gives the committee the authority to determine the appropriate pace of its activity in light of any criminal investigation.

Title 28 U.S.C. § 356(a) provides that a special committee will have full subpoena powers as provided in 28 U.S.C. § 332(d). Section 332(d)(1) provides that subpoenas will be issued on behalf of a judicial council by the circuit clerk "at the direction of the chief judge of the circuit or his designee." Rule 13(d) contemplates that, where the chief judge designates someone else as presiding officer of the special committee, the presiding officer also be delegated the authority to direct the circuit clerk to issue subpoenas related to committee proceedings. That is not intended to imply, however, that the decision to use the subpoena power is exercisable by the presiding officer alone. *See* Rule 12(g).

14. Conduct of Special-Committee Hearings

(a) Purpose of Hearings. The special committee may hold hearings to take testimony and receive other evidence, to hear argument, or both. If the special committee is investigating allegations against more than one judge, it may hold joint or separate hearings.

(b) Special-Committee Evidence. Subject to Rule 15, the special committee must obtain material, nonredundant evidence in the form it considers appropriate. In the special committee's discretion, evidence may be obtained by committee members, staff, or both. Witnesses offering testimonial evidence may include the complainant and the subject judge.

(c) Counsel for Witnesses. The subject judge has the right to counsel. The special committee has discretion to decide whether other witnesses may have counsel present when they testify.

(d) Witness Fees. Witness fees must be paid as provided in 28 U.S.C. § 1821.

(e) Oath. All testimony taken at a hearing must be given under oath or affirmation.

(f) Rules of Evidence. The Federal Rules of Evidence do not apply to special-committee hearings.

(g) Record and Transcript. A record and transcript must be made of all hearings.

Commentary on Rule 14

This Rule is adapted from the Act, 28 U.S.C. § 353, and the Illustrative Rules. Rule 14 is concerned with the conduct of fact-finding hearings.

Special-committee hearings will normally be held only after the investigative work has been completed and the committee has concluded that there is sufficient evidence to warrant a formal fact-finding proceeding. Special-committee proceedings are primarily inquisitorial rather than adversarial. Accordingly, the Federal Rules of Evidence do not apply to such hearings. Inevitably, a hearing will have something of an adversary character. Nevertheless, that tendency should be moderated to the extent possible. Even though a proceeding will commonly have investigative and hearing stages, special-committee members should not regard themselves as prosecutors one day and judges the next. Their duty—and that of their staff—is at all times to be impartial seekers of the truth.

Rule 14(b) contemplates that material evidence will be obtained by the special committee and presented in the form of affidavits, live testimony, etc. Staff or others who are organizing the hearings should regard it as their role to present evidence representing the entire picture. With respect to testimonial evidence, the subject judge should normally be called as a special-committee witness. Cases may arise in which the subject judge will not testify voluntarily. In such cases, subpoena powers are available, subject to the normal testimonial privileges. Although Rule 15(c) recognizes the subject judge's statutory right to call witnesses on his or her own behalf, exercise of this right should not usually be necessary.

15. Subject Judge's Rights

(a) Notice.

(1) Generally. The subject judge must receive written notice of:

(A) the appointment of a special committee under Rule 11(f);

(B) the expansion of the scope of an investigation under Rule 13(a);

(C) any hearing under Rule 14, including its purposes, the names of any witnesses the special committee intends to call, and the text of any statements that have been taken from those witnesses.

(2) Suggestion of additional witnesses. The subject judge may suggest additional witnesses to the special committee.

(b) Special-Committee Report. The subject judge must be sent a copy of the special committee's report when it is filed with the judicial council.

(c) Presentation of Evidence. At any hearing held under Rule 14, the subject judge has the right to present evidence, to compel the attendance of witnesses, and to compel the production of documents. At the request of the subject judge, the chief judge or the judge's designee must direct the circuit clerk to issue a subpoena to a witness under 28 U.S.C. § 332(d)(1). The subject judge must be given the opportunity to cross-examine special-committee witnesses, in person or by counsel.

(d) Presentation of Argument. The subject judge may submit written argument to the special committee and must be given a reasonable opportunity to present oral argument at an appropriate stage of the investigation.

(e) Attendance at Hearings. The subject judge has the right to attend any hearing held under Rule 14 and to receive copies of the transcript, of any documents introduced, and of any written arguments submitted by the complainant to the special committee.

(f) Representation by Counsel. The subject judge may choose to be represented by counsel in the exercise of any right enumerated in this Rule. As provided in Rule 20(e), the United States may bear the costs of the representation.

Commentary on Rule 15

This Rule is adapted from the Act and the Illustrative Rules.

The Act states that these Rules must contain provisions requiring that "the judge whose conduct is the subject of a complaint . . . be afforded an opportunity to appear (in person or by counsel) at proceedings conducted by the investigating panel, to present oral and documentary evidence, to compel the attendance of witnesses or the production of documents, to cross-examine witnesses, and to present argument orally or in writing." 28 U.S.C. § 358(b)(2). To implement this provision, Rule 15(e) gives the subject judge the right to attend any hearing held for the purpose of receiving evidence of record or hearing argument under Rule 14.

The Act does not require that the subject judge be permitted to attend all proceedings of the special committee. Accordingly, the Rules do not give a right to attend other proceedings—for example, meetings at which the special committee is engaged in investigative activity, such as interviewing persons to learn whether they ought to be called as witnesses or examining for relevance purposes documents delivered pursuant to a subpoena duces tecum, or meetings in which the committee is deliberating on the evidence or its recommendations.

16. Complainant's Rights in Investigation

(a) Notice. The complainant must receive written notice of the investigation as provided in Rule 11(g)(1). When the special committee's report to the judicial council is filed, the complainant must be notified of the filing. The judicial council may, in its discretion, provide a copy of the report of a special committee to the complainant.

(b) Opportunity to Provide Evidence. If the complainant knows of relevant evidence not already before the special committee, the complainant may briefly explain in writing the basis of that knowledge and the nature of that evidence. If the special committee determines that the complainant has information not already known to the committee that would assist in the committee's investigation, a representative of the committee must interview the complainant.

(c) Presentation of Argument. The complainant may submit written argument to the special committee. In its discretion, the special committee may permit the complainant to offer oral argument.

(d) Representation by Counsel. A complainant may submit written argument through counsel and, if permitted to offer oral argument, may do so through counsel.

(e) Cooperation. In exercising its discretion under this Rule, the special committee may take into account the degree of the complainant's cooperation in preserving the confidentiality of the proceedings, including the identity of the subject judge.

Commentary on Rule 16

This Rule is adapted from the Act and the Illustrative Rules.

In accordance with the view of the process as fundamentally administrative and inquisitorial, these Rules do not give the complainant the rights of a party to litigation and leave the complainant's role largely to the discretion of the special committee. However, Rule 16(b) gives the complainant the prerogative to make a brief written submission showing that he or she is aware of relevant evidence not already known to the special committee. (Such a submission may precede any written or oral argument the complainant provides under Rule 16(c), or it may accompany that argument.) If the special committee determines, independently or from the complainant's submission, that the complainant has information that would assist the committee in its investigation, the complainant must be interviewed by a representative of the committee. Such an interview may be in person or by telephone, and the representative of the special committee may be either a member or staff.

Rule 16 does not contemplate that the complainant will ordinarily be permitted to attend proceedings of the special committee except when testifying or presenting oral argument. A special committee may exercise its discretion to permit the complainant to be present at its proceedings, or to permit the complainant, individually or through counsel, to participate in the examination or cross-examination of witnesses.

The Act authorizes an exception to the normal confidentiality provisions where the judicial council in its discretion provides a copy of the report of the special committee to the complainant and to the subject judge. 28 U.S.C. § 360(a)(1). However, the Rules do not entitle the complainant to a copy of the special committee's report.

In exercising their discretion regarding the role of the complainant, the special committee and the judicial council should protect the confidentiality of the complaint process. As a consequence, subsection (e) provides that the special committee may consider the degree to which a complainant has cooperated in preserving the confidentiality of the proceedings in determining what role beyond the minimum required by these Rules should be given to that complainant.

17. Special-Committee Report

The special committee must file with the judicial council a comprehensive report of its investigation, including findings and recommendations for council action. The report must be accompanied by a statement of the vote by which it was adopted, any separate or dissenting statements of special-committee members, and the record of any hearings held under Rule 14. In addition to being sent to the subject judge under Rule 15(b), a copy of the report and any accompanying statements and documents must be sent to the Committee on Judicial Conduct and Disability.

Commentary on Rule 17

This Rule is adapted from the Illustrative Rules and is self-explanatory. The provision for sending a copy of the special-committee report and accompanying statements and documents to the Committee on Judicial Conduct and Disability was new at the time the Judicial Conference promulgated the Rules for Judicial-Conduct and Judicial-Disability Proceedings in 2008.

ARTICLE V. JUDICIAL-COUNCIL REVIEW

18. Petition for Review of Chief-Judge Disposition Under Rule 11(c), (d), or (e)

(a) Petition for Review. After the chief judge issues an order under Rule 11(c), (d), or (e), the complainant or the subject judge may petition the judicial council of the circuit to review the order. By rules promulgated under 28 U.S.C. § 358, the judicial council may refer a petition for review filed under this Rule to a panel of no fewer than five members of the council, at least two of whom must be district judges.

(b) When to File; Form; Where to File. A petition for review must be filed in the office of the circuit clerk within 42 days after the date of the chief judge's order. The petition for review should be in letter form, addressed to the circuit clerk, and in an envelope marked "Misconduct Petition" or "Disability Petition." The name of the subject judge must not be shown on the envelope. The petition for review should be typewritten or otherwise legible. It should begin with "I hereby petition the judicial council for review of . . . " and state the reasons why the petition should be granted. It must be signed.

(c) Receipt and Distribution of Petition. A circuit clerk who receives a petition for review filed in accordance with this Rule must:

(1) acknowledge its receipt and send a copy to the complainant or subject judge, as the case may be;

(2) promptly distribute to each member of the judicial council, or its relevant panel, except for any member disqualified under Rule 25, or make available in the manner provided by local rule, the following materials:

(A) copies of the complaint;

(B) all materials obtained by the chief judge in connection with the inquiry;

(C) the chief judge's order disposing of the complaint;

(D) any memorandum in support of the chief judge's order;

(E) the petition for review; and

(F) an appropriate ballot; and

(3) send the petition for review to the Committee on Judicial Conduct and Disability. Unless the Committee on Judicial Conduct and Disability requests them, the circuit clerk will not send copies of the materials obtained by the chief judge.

(d) Untimely Petition. The circuit clerk must refuse to accept a petition that is received after the time allowed in (b).

(e) Timely Petition Not in Proper Form. When the circuit clerk receives a petition for review filed within the time allowed but in a form that is improper to a degree that would substantially impair its consideration by the judicial council—such as a document that is ambiguous about whether it is intended to be a petition for review—the circuit clerk must acknowledge its receipt, call the filer's attention to the deficiencies, and give the filer the opportunity to correct the deficiencies within the original time allowed for filing the petition or within 21 days after the date on which a notice of the deficiencies was sent to the complainant, whichever is later. If the deficiencies are corrected within the time allowed, the circuit clerk will proceed according to paragraphs (a) and (c) of this Rule. If the deficiencies are not corrected, the circuit clerk must reject the petition.

Commentary on Rule 18

Rule 18 is adapted largely from the Illustrative Rules.

Subsection (a) permits the subject judge, as well as the complainant, to petition for review of the chief judge's order dismissing a complaint under Rule 11(c), or concluding that appropriate corrective action or intervening events have remedied or mooted the problems raised by the complaint pursuant to Rule 11(d) or (e). Although the subject judge may ostensibly be vindicated by the dismissal or conclusion of a complaint, the chief judge's order may include language disagreeable to the subject judge. For example, an order may dismiss a complaint, but state that the subject judge did in fact engage in misconduct. Accordingly, a subject judge may wish to object to the content of the order and is given the opportunity to petition the judicial council of the circuit for review.

Subsection (b) contains a time limit of 42 days to file a petition for review. It is important to establish a time limit on petitions for review of chief judges' dispositions in order to provide finality to the process. If the complaint requires an investigation, the investigation should proceed; if it does not, the subject judge should know that the matter is closed.

The standards for timely filing under the Federal Rules of Appellate Procedure should be applied to petitions for review. *See* Fed. R. App. P. 25(a)(2)(A), (C).

Rule 18(e) provides for an automatic extension of the time limit imposed under subsection (b) if a person files a petition that is rejected for failure to comply with formal requirements.

19. Judicial-Council Disposition of Petition for Review

(a) Rights of Subject Judge. At any time after a complainant files a petition for review, the subject judge may file a written response with the circuit clerk. The circuit clerk must promptly distribute copies of the response to each member of the judicial council or of the relevant panel, unless that member is disqualified under Rule 25. Copies must also be distributed to the chief judge, to the complainant, and to the Committee on Judicial Conduct and Disability. The subject judge must not otherwise communicate with individual judicial-council members about the matter. The subject judge must be given copies of any communications to the judicial council from the complainant.

(b) Judicial-Council Action. After considering a petition for review and the materials before it, the judicial council may:

(1) affirm the chief judge's disposition by denying the petition;

(2) return the matter to the chief judge with directions to conduct a further inquiry under Rule 11(b) or to identify a complaint under Rule 5;

(3) return the matter to the chief judge with directions to appoint a special committee under Rule 11(f); or

(4) in exceptional circumstances, take other appropriate action.

(c) Notice of Judicial-Council Decision. Copies of the judicial council's order, together with memoranda incorporated by reference in the order and separate concurring or dissenting statements, must be given to the complainant, the subject judge, and the Committee on Judicial Conduct and Disability.

(d) Memorandum of Judicial-Council Decision. If the judicial council's order affirms the chief judge's disposition, a supporting memorandum must be prepared only if the council concludes that there is a need to supplement the chief judge's explanation. A memorandum supporting a judicial-council order must not include the name of the complainant or the subject judge.

(e) Review of Judicial-Council Decision. If the judicial council's decision is adverse to the petitioner, and if no member of the council dissented, the complainant must be notified that he or she has no right to seek review of the decision. If there was a dissent, the petitioner must be informed that he or she can file a petition for review under Rule 21(b).

(f) Public Availability of Judicial-Council Decision. Materials related to the judicial council's decision must be made public to the extent, at the time, and in the manner set forth in Rule 24.

Commentary on Rule 19

This Rule is adapted largely from the Act and is self-explanatory.

The judicial council should ordinarily review the decision of the chief judge on the merits, treating the petition for review for all practical purposes as an appeal. The judicial council may respond to a petition for review by affirming the chief judge's order, remanding the matter, or, in exceptional cases, taking other appropriate action. A petition for review of a judicial council's decision may be filed under Rule 21(b) in any matter in which one or more members of the council dissented from the order.

20. Judicial-Council Action Following Appointment of Special Committee

(a) Subject Judge's Rights. Within 21 days after the filing of the report of a special committee, the subject judge may send a written response to the members of the judicial council. The subject judge must also be given an opportunity to present argument, personally or through counsel, written or oral, as determined by the judicial council. The subject judge must not otherwise communicate with judicial-council members about the matter.

(b) Judicial-Council Action.

(1) Discretionary actions. Subject to the subject judge's rights set forth in subsection (a), the judicial council may:

(A) dismiss the complaint because:

(i) even if the claim is true, the claimed conduct is not conduct prejudicial to the effective and expeditious administration of the business of the courts and does not indicate a mental or physical disability resulting in inability to discharge the duties of office;

(ii) the complaint is directly related to the merits of a decision or procedural ruling;

(iii) the facts on which the complaint is based have not been established; or

(iv) the complaint is otherwise not appropriate for consideration under 28 U.S.C. §§ 351–364.

(B) conclude the proceeding because appropriate corrective action has been taken or intervening events have made the proceeding unnecessary.

(C) refer the complaint to the Judicial Conference with the judicial council's recommendations for action.

(D) take remedial action to ensure the effective and expeditious administration of the business of the courts, including:

(i) censuring or reprimanding the subject judge, either by private communication or by public announcement;

(ii) ordering that no new cases be assigned to the subject judge for a limited, fixed period;

(iii) in the case of a magistrate judge, ordering the chief judge of the district court to take action specified by the council, including the initiation of removal proceedings under 28 U.S.C. § 631(i) or 42 U.S.C. § 300aa-12(c)(2);

(iv) in the case of a bankruptcy judge, removing the judge from office under 28 U.S.C. § 152(e);

(v) in the case of a circuit or district judge, requesting the judge to retire voluntarily with the provision (if necessary) that ordinary length-of-service requirements be waived;

(vi) in the case of a circuit or district judge who is eligible to retire but does not do so, certifying the disability of the judge under 28 U.S.C. § 372(b) so that an additional judge may be appointed; and

(vii) in the case of a circuit chief judge or district chief judge, finding that the judge is temporarily unable to perform chief-judge duties, with the result that those duties devolve to the next eligible judge in accordance with 28 U.S.C. § 45(d) or § 136(e).

(E) take any combination of actions described in (b)(1)(A)-(D) of this Rule that is within its power.

(2) Mandatory actions. A judicial council must refer a complaint to the Judicial Conference if the council determines that a circuit judge or district judge may have engaged in conduct that:

(A) might constitute ground for impeachment; or

(B) in the interest of justice, is not amenable to resolution by the judicial council.

(c) Inadequate Basis for Decision. If the judicial council finds that a special committee's report, recommendations, and record provide an inadequate basis for decision, it may return the matter to the committee for further investigation and a new report, or it may conduct further investigation. If the judicial council decides to conduct further investigation, the subject judge must be given adequate prior notice in writing of that decision and of the general scope and purpose of the additional investigation. The judicial council's conduct of the additional investigation must generally accord with the

procedures and powers set forth in Rules 13 through 16 for the conduct of an investigation by a special committee.

(d) Judicial-Council Vote. Judicial-council action must be taken by a majority of those members of the council who are not disqualified. A decision to remove a bankruptcy judge from office requires a majority vote of all the members of the judicial council.

(e) Recommendation for Fee Reimbursement. If the complaint has been finally dismissed or concluded under (b)(1)(A) or (B) of this Rule, and if the subject judge so requests, the judicial council may recommend that the Director of the Administrative Office use funds appropriated to the judiciary to reimburse the judge for reasonable expenses incurred during the investigation, when those expenses would not have been incurred but for the requirements of the Act and these Rules. Reasonable expenses include attorneys' fees and expenses related to a successful defense or prosecution of a proceeding under Rule 21(a) or (b).

(f) Judicial-Council Order. Judicial-council action must be by written order. Unless the judicial council finds that extraordinary reasons would make it contrary to the interests of justice, the order must be accompanied by a memorandum setting forth the factual determinations on which it is based and the reasons for the council action. Such a memorandum may incorporate all or part of any underlying special-committee report. If the complaint was initiated by identification under Rule 5, the memorandum must so indicate. The order and memoranda incorporated by reference in the order must be provided to the complainant, the subject judge, and the Committee on Judicial Conduct and Disability. The complainant and the subject judge must be notified of any right to review of the judicial council's decision as provided in Rule 21(b). If the complaint was identified under Rule 5 or filed by its subject judge, the judicial council must transmit the order and memoranda incorporated by reference in the order to the Committee on Judicial Conduct and Disability for review in accordance with Rule 21. In the event of such a transmission, the subject judge may make a written submission to the Committee on Judicial Conduct and Disability but will have no further right of review.

Commentary on Rule 20

This Rule is largely adapted from the Illustrative Rules.

Rule 20(a) provides that within 21 days after the filing of the report of a special committee, the subject judge may address a written response to all of the members of the judicial council. The subject judge must also be given an opportunity to present argument to the judicial council, personally or through counsel, or both, at the direction of the council. Whether that argument is written or oral would be for the judicial council to determine. The subject judge may not otherwise communicate with judicial-council members about the matter.

Rule 20(b)(1)(D) recites the remedial actions enumerated in 28 U.S.C. § 354(a)(2) while making clear that this list is not exhaustive. A judicial council may consider lesser remedies. Some remedies may be unique to senior judges, whose caseloads can be modified by agreement or through statutory designation and certification processes.

Under 28 U.S.C. §§ 45(d) and 136(e), which provide for succession where "a chief judge is temporarily unable to perform his duties as such," the determination whether such an inability exists is not expressly reserved to the chief judge. Nor, indeed, is it assigned to any particular judge or court-governance body. Clearly, however, a chief judge's inability to function as chief could implicate "the effective and expeditious administration of justice," which the judicial council of the circuit must, under 28 U.S.C. § 332(d)(1), "make all necessary and appropriate orders" to secure. For this reason, such reassignment is among a judicial council's remedial options, as subsection (b)(1)(D)(vii) makes clear. Consistent with 28 U.S.C. §§ 45(d) and 136(e), however, any reassignment of chief-judge duties must not outlast the subject judge's inability to perform them. Nor can such reassignment result in any extension of the subject judge's term as chief judge.

Rule 20(c) provides that if the judicial council decides to conduct an additional investigation, the subject judge must be given adequate prior notice in writing of that decision and of the general scope and purpose of the additional investigation. The conduct of the investigation will be generally in accordance with the procedures set forth in Rules 13 through 16 for the conduct of an investigation by a special committee. However, if hearings are held, the judicial council may limit testimony or the presentation of evidence to avoid unnecessary repetition of testimony and evidence before the special committee.

Rule 20(d) provides that judicial-council action must be taken by a majority of those members of the council who are not disqualified, except that a decision to remove a bankruptcy judge from office requires a majority of all the members of the council as required by 28 U.S.C. § 152(e). However, it is inappropriate to apply a similar rule to the less severe actions that a judicial council may take under the Act. If some members of the judicial council are disqualified in the matter, their disqualification should not be given the effect of a vote against council action.

With regard to Rule 20(e), the judicial council, on the request of the subject judge, may recommend to the Director of the Administrative Office that the subject judge be reimbursed for reasonable expenses incurred, including attorneys' fees. The judicial council has the authority to recommend such reimbursement where, after investigation by a special committee, the complaint has been finally dismissed or concluded under subsection (b)(1)(A) or (B) of this Rule. It is contemplated that such reimbursement may be provided for the successful prosecution or defense of a proceeding under Rule 21(a) or (b), in other words, one that results in a Rule 20(b)(1)(A) or (B) dismissal or conclusion.

Rule 20(f) requires that judicial-council action be by order and, normally, that it be supported with a memorandum of factual determinations and reasons. Notice of the action must be given to the complainant and the subject judge, and must include notice of any right to petition for review of the judicial council's decision under Rule 21(b). Because an identified complaint has no "complainant" to petition for review, a judicial council's dispositive order on an identified complaint on which a special committee has been appointed must be transmitted to the Committee on Judicial Conduct and Disability for review. The same will apply where a complaint was filed by its subject judge.

ARTICLE VI. REVIEW BY COMMITTEE ON JUDICIAL CONDUCT AND DISABILITY

21. Committee on Judicial Conduct and Disability

(a) Committee Review. The Committee on Judicial Conduct and Disability, consisting of seven members, considers and disposes of all petitions for review under (b) of this Rule, in conformity with the Committee's jurisdictional statement. Its review of judicial-council orders is for errors of law, clear errors of fact, or abuse of discretion. Its disposition of petitions for review is ordinarily final. The Judicial Conference may, in its sole discretion, review any such Committee decision, but a complainant or subject judge does not have a right to this review.

(b) Reviewable Matters.

(1) Upon petition. A complainant or subject judge may petition the Committee for review of a judicial-council order entered in accordance with:

(A) Rule 20(b)(1)(A), (B), (D), or (E); or

(B) Rule 19(b)(1) or (4) if one or more members of the judicial council dissented from the order.

(2) Upon Committee's initiative. At its initiative and in its sole discretion, the Committee may review any judicial-council order entered under Rule 19(b)(1) or (4), but only to determine whether a special committee should be appointed. Before undertaking the review, the Committee must invite that judicial council to explain why it believes the appointment of a special committee is unnecessary, unless the

reasons are clearly stated in the council's order denying the petition for review. If the Committee believes that it would benefit from a submission by the subject judge, it may issue an appropriate request. If the Committee determines that a special committee should be appointed, the Committee must issue a written decision giving its reasons.

(c) Committee Vote. Any member of the Committee from the same circuit as the subject judge is disqualified from considering or voting on a petition for review related to that subject judge. Committee decisions under (b) of this Rule must be by majority vote of the qualified Committee members. Those members hearing the petition for review should serve in that capacity until final disposition of the petition, whether or not their term of committee membership has ended. If only six members are qualified to consider a petition for review, the Chief Justice shall select an additional judge to join the qualified members to consider the petition. If four or fewer members are qualified to consider a petition for review, the Chief Justice shall select a panel of five judges, including the qualified Committee members, to consider it.

(d) Additional Investigation. Except in extraordinary circumstances, the Committee will not conduct an additional investigation. The Committee may return the matter to the judicial council with directions to undertake an additional investigation. If the Committee conducts an additional investigation, it will exercise the powers of the Judicial Conference under 28 U.S.C. § 331.

(e) Oral Argument; Personal Appearance. There is ordinarily no oral argument or personal appearance before the Committee. In its discretion, the Committee may permit written submissions.

(f) Committee Decision. A Committee decision under this Rule must be transmitted promptly to the Judicial Conference. Other distribution will be by the Administrative Office at the direction of the Committee chair.

(g) Finality. All orders of the Judicial Conference or of the Committee (when the Conference does not exercise its power of review) are final.

Commentary on Rule 21

This Rule is largely self-explanatory.

Rule 21(a) is intended to clarify that the delegation of power to the Committee on Judicial Conduct and Disability to dispose of petitions for review does not preclude review of such dispositions by the Judicial Conference. However, there is no right to such review in any party.

Rules 21(b)(1)(B) and (b)(2) are intended to fill a jurisdictional gap as to review of a dismissal or a conclusion of a complaint under Rule 19(b)(1) or (4). Where one or more members of a judicial council reviewing a petition have dissented, the complainant or the subject judge has the right to petition for review by the Committee. Under Rule 21(b)(2), the Committee may review such a dismissal or conclusion in its sole discretion, whether or not a dissent occurred, and only as to the appointment of a special committee. Any review under Rule 21(b)(2) will be conducted as soon as practicable after the dismissal or conclusion at issue. No party has a right to such review, and such review will be rare.

Rule 21(c) provides for review only by Committee members from circuits other than that of the subject judge. The Rule provides that every petition for review must be considered and voted on by at least five, and if possible by seven, qualified Committee members to avoid the possibility of tie votes. If six, or four or fewer, members are qualified, the Chief Justice shall appoint other judges to join the qualified members to consider the petition for review. To the extent possible, the judges whom the Chief Justice selects to join the qualified members should be drawn from among former members of the Committee.

Under this Rule, all Committee decisions are final in that they are unreviewable unless the Judicial Conference, in its discretion, decides to review a decision. Committee decisions, however, do not necessarily constitute final action on a complaint for purposes of Rule 24.

22. Procedures for Review

(a) Filing Petition for Review. A petition for review of a judicial-council decision on a reviewable matter, as defined in Rule 21(b)(1), may be filed by sending a brief written statement to the Committee on Judicial Conduct and Disability at JCD_PetitionforReview@ao.uscourts.gov or to:

Judicial Conference Committee on Judicial Conduct and Disability

Attn: Office of General Counsel

Administrative Office of the United States Courts One Columbus Circle, NE

Washington, D.C. 20544

The Administrative Office will send a copy of the petition for review to the complainant or the subject judge, as the case may be.

(b) Form and Contents of Petition. No particular form is required. The petition for review must contain a short statement of the basic facts underlying the complaint, the history of its consideration before the appropriate judicial council, a copy of the council's decision, and the grounds on which the petitioner seeks review. The petition for review must specify the date and docket number of the judicial-council order for which review is sought. The petitioner may attach any documents or correspondence arising in the course of the proceeding before the judicial council or its special committee. A petition for review should not normally exceed 20 pages plus necessary attachments. A petition for review must be signed by the petitioner or his or her attorney.

(c) Time. A petition for review must be submitted within 42 days after the date of the order for which review is sought.

(d) Action on Receipt of Petition. When a petition for review of a judicial-council decision on a reviewable matter, as defined in Rule 21(b)(1), is submitted in accordance with this Rule, the Administrative Office shall acknowledge its receipt, notify the chair of the Committee on Judicial Conduct and Disability, and distribute the petition to the members of the Committee for their deliberation.

Commentary on Rule 22

Rule 22 is self-explanatory.

ARTICLE VII. MISCELLANEOUS RULES

23. Confidentiality

(a) General Rule. The consideration of a complaint by a chief judge, a special committee, a judicial council, or the Committee on Judicial Conduct and Disability is confidential. Information about this consideration must not be disclosed by any judge or employee of the judiciary or by any person who records or transcribes testimony except as allowed by these Rules. A chief judge may disclose the existence of a proceeding under these Rules when necessary or appropriate to maintain public confidence in the judiciary's ability to redress misconduct or disability.

(b) Files. All files related to a complaint must be separately maintained with appropriate security precautions to ensure confidentiality.

(c) Disclosure in Decisions. Except as otherwise provided in Rule 24, written decisions of a chief judge, a judicial council, or the Committee on Judicial Conduct and Disability, and dissenting opinions or separate statements of members of a council or the Committee may contain information and exhibits that the authors consider appropriate for inclusion, and the information and exhibits may be made public.

(d) Availability to Judicial Conference. On request of the Judicial Conference or its Committee on Judicial Conduct and Disability, the circuit clerk must furnish any requested records related to a complaint. For auditing purposes, the circuit clerk must provide access to the Committee on Judicial Conduct and Disability to records of proceedings under the Act at the site where the records are kept.

(e) Availability to District Court. If the judicial council directs the initiation of proceedings for removal of a magistrate judge under Rule 20(b)(1)(D)(iii), the circuit clerk must provide to the chief judge of the district court copies of the report of the special committee and any other documents and records that were before the council at the time of its decision. On request of the chief judge of the district court, the judicial council may authorize release to that chief judge of any other records relating to the investigation.

(f) Impeachment Proceedings. If the Judicial Conference determines that consideration of impeachment may be warranted, it must transmit the record of all relevant proceedings to the Speaker of the House of Representatives.

(g) Subject Judge's Consent. If both the subject judge and the chief judge consent in writing, any materials from the files may be disclosed to any person. In any such disclosure, the chief judge may require that the identity of the complainant, or of witnesses in an investigation conducted under these Rules, not be revealed.

(h) Disclosure in Special Circumstances. The Judicial Conference, its Committee on Judicial Conduct and Disability, or a judicial council may authorize disclosure of information about the consideration of a complaint, including the papers, documents, and transcripts relating to the investigation, to the extent that disclosure is justified by special circumstances and is not prohibited by the Act. Disclosure may be made to judicial researchers engaged in the study or evaluation of experience under the Act and related modes of judicial discipline, but only where the study or evaluation has been specifically approved by the Judicial Conference or by the Committee on Judicial Conduct and Disability. Appropriate steps must be taken to protect the identities of the subject judge, the complainant, and witnesses from public disclosure. Other appropriate safeguards to protect against the dissemination of confidential information may be imposed.

(i) Disclosure of Identity by Subject Judge. Nothing in this Rule precludes the subject judge from acknowledging that he or she is the judge referred to in documents made public under Rule 24.

(j) Assistance and Consultation. Nothing in this Rule prohibits a chief judge, a special committee, a judicial council, or the Judicial Conference or its Committee on Judicial Conduct and Disability, in the performance of any function authorized under the Act or these Rules, from seeking the help of qualified staff or experts or from consulting other judges who may be helpful regarding the performance of that function.

Commentary on Rule 23

Rule 23 was adapted from the Illustrative Rules.

The Act applies a rule of confidentiality to "papers, documents, and records of proceedings related to investigations conducted under this chapter" and states that they may not be disclosed "by any person in any proceeding," with enumerated exceptions. 28 U.S.C. § 360(a). Three questions arise: Who is bound by the confidentiality rule, what proceedings are subject to the rule, and who is within the circle of people who may have access to information without breaching the rule?

With regard to the first question, Rule 23(a) provides that judges, employees of the judiciary, and those persons involved in recording proceedings and preparing transcripts are obliged to respect the confidentiality requirement. This of course includes subject judges who do not consent to identification under Rule 23(i).

With regard to the second question, Rule 23(a) applies the rule of confidentiality broadly to consideration of a complaint at any stage.

With regard to the third question, there is no barrier of confidentiality among a chief judge, a judicial council, the Judicial Conference, and the Committee on Judicial Conduct and Disability. Each may have access to any of the confidential records for use in their consideration of a referred matter, a petition for review, or monitoring the administration of the Act. A district court may have similar access if the judicial council orders the district court to initiate proceedings to remove a magistrate judge from office, and Rule 23(e) so provides.

In extraordinary circumstances, a chief judge may disclose the existence of a proceeding under these Rules. The disclosure of such information in high-visibility or controversial cases is to reassure the public that the judiciary is capable of redressing judicial misconduct or disability. Moreover, the confidentiality requirement does not prevent the chief judge from "communicat[ing] orally or in writing with . . . [persons] who may have knowledge of the matter," as part of a limited inquiry conducted by the chief judge under Rule 11(b).

Rule 23 recognizes that there must be some exceptions to the Act's confidentiality requirement. For example, the Act requires that certain orders and the reasons for them must be made public. 28 U.S.C. § 360(b). Rule 23(c) makes it explicit that written decisions, as well as dissenting opinions and separate statements, may contain references to information that would otherwise be confidential and that such information may be made public. However, subsection (c) is subject to Rule 24(a), which provides the general rule regarding the public availability of decisions. For example, the name of a subject judge cannot be made public in a decision if disclosure of the name is prohibited by that Rule.

The Act makes clear that there is a barrier of confidentiality between the judicial branch and the legislative branch. It provides that material may be disclosed to Congress only if it is believed necessary to an impeachment investigation or trial of a judge. 28 U.S.C. § 360(a)(2). Accordingly, Section 355(b) of the Act requires the Judicial Conference to transmit the record of a proceeding to the House of Representatives if the Conference believes that impeachment of a subject judge may be appropriate. Rule 23(f) implements this requirement.

The Act provides that confidential materials may be disclosed if authorized in writing by the subject judge and by the chief judge. 28 U.S.C. § 360(a)(3). Rule 23(g) implements this requirement. Once the subject judge has consented to the disclosure of confidential materials related to a complaint, the chief judge ordinarily will refuse consent only to the extent necessary to protect the confidentiality interests of the complainant or of witnesses who have testified in investigatory proceedings or who have provided information in response to a limited inquiry undertaken pursuant to Rule 11. It will generally be necessary, therefore, for the chief judge to require that the identities of the complainant or of such witnesses, as well as any identifying information, be shielded in any materials disclosed, except insofar as the chief judge has secured the consent of the complainant or of a particular witness to disclosure, or there is a demonstrated need for disclosure of the information that, in the judgment of the chief judge, outweighs the confidentiality interest of the complainant or of a particular witness (as may be the case where the complainant is delusional or where the complainant or a particular witness has already demonstrated a lack of concern about maintaining the confidentiality of the proceedings).

Rule 23(h) permits disclosure of additional information in circumstances not enumerated. For example, disclosure may be appropriate to permit a prosecution for perjury based on testimony given before a special committee. Another example might involve evidence of criminal conduct by a judge discovered by a special committee.

Subsection (h) also permits the authorization of disclosure of information about the consideration of a complaint, including the papers, documents, and transcripts relating to the investigation, to judicial researchers engaged in the study or evaluation of experience under the Act and related modes of judicial discipline. The Rule envisions disclosure of information from the official record of a complaint proceeding to a limited category of persons for appropriately authorized research purposes only, and with appropriate safeguards to protect individual identities in any published research results. In authorizing disclosure, a judicial council may refuse to release particular materials when such release would be contrary to the interests of justice, or when those materials constitute purely internal communications. The Rule does not envision disclosure of purely internal communications between judges and their colleagues and staff.

Under Rule 23(j), any of the specified judges or entities performing a function authorized under these Rules may seek expert or staff assistance or may consult with other judges who may be helpful regarding performance of that function; the confidentiality requirement does not preclude this. A chief judge, for example, may properly seek the advice and assistance of another judge who the chief judge deems to be in the best position to communicate with the subject judge in an attempt to bring about corrective action. As another example, a new chief judge may wish to confer with a predecessor to learn how similar complaints have been handled. In consulting with other judges, of course, a chief judge should disclose information regarding the complaint only to the extent the chief judge deems necessary under the circumstances.

24. Public Availability of Decisions

(a) General Rule; Specific Cases. When final action has been taken on a complaint and it is no longer subject to review, all orders entered by the chief judge and judicial council, including memoranda incorporated by reference in those orders and any dissenting opinions or separate statements by members of the judicial council, but excluding any orders under Rule 5 or 11(f), must be made public, with the following exceptions:

(1) if the complaint is finally dismissed under Rule 11(c) without the appointment of a special committee, or if it is concluded under Rule 11(d) because of voluntary corrective action, the publicly available materials must not disclose the name of the subject judge without his or her consent.

(2) if the complaint is concluded because of intervening events, or dismissed at any time after a special committee is appointed, the judicial council must determine whether the name of the subject judge should be disclosed.

(3) if the complaint is finally disposed of by a privately communicated censure or reprimand, the publicly available materials must not disclose either the name of the subject judge or the text of the reprimand.

(4) if the complaint is finally disposed of under Rule 20(b)(1)(D) by any action other than private censure or reprimand, the text of the dispositive order must be included in the materials made public, and the name of the subject judge must be disclosed.

(5) the name of the complainant must not be disclosed in materials made public under this Rule unless the chief judge orders disclosure.

(b) Manner of Making Public. The orders described in (a) must be made public by placing them in a publicly accessible file in the office of the circuit clerk and by placing the orders on the court's public website. If the orders appear to have precedential value, the chief judge may cause them to be published. In addition, the Committee on Judicial Conduct and Disability will make available on the judiciary's website, www.uscourts.gov, selected illustrative orders described in paragraph (a), appropriately redacted, to provide additional information to the public on how complaints are addressed under the Act.

(c) Orders of Committee on Judicial Conduct and Disability. Orders of the Committee on Judicial Conduct and Disability constituting final action in a complaint proceeding

arising from a particular circuit will be made available to the public in the office of the circuit clerk of the relevant court of appeals. The Committee on Judicial Conduct and Disability will also make such orders available on the judiciary's website, www.uscourts.gov. When authorized by the Committee on Judicial Conduct and Disability, other orders related to complaint proceedings will similarly be made available.

(d) Complaints Referred to Judicial Conference. If a complaint is referred to the Judicial Conference under Rule 20(b)(1)(C) or 20(b)(2), materials relating to the complaint will be made public only if ordered by the Judicial Conference.

Commentary on Rule 24

Rule 24 is adapted from the Illustrative Rules and the recommendations of the Breyer Committee.

The Act requires the circuits to make available only written orders of a judicial council or the Judicial Conference imposing some form of sanction. 28 U.S.C. § 360(b). The Judicial Conference, however, has long recognized the desirability of public availability of a broader range of orders and other materials. In 1994, the Judicial Conference "urge[d] all circuits and courts covered by the Act to submit to the West Publishing Company, for publication in Federal Reporter 3d, and to Lexis all orders issued pursuant to [the Act] that are deemed by the issuing circuit or court to have significant precedential value to other circuits and courts covered by the Act." Report of the Proceedings of the Judicial Conference of the United States, Mar. 1994, at 28. Following this recommendation, the 2000 revision of the Illustrative Rules contained a public availability provision very similar to Rule 24. In 2002, the Judicial Conference again voted to encourage the circuits "to submit non-routine public orders disposing of complaints of judicial misconduct or disability for publication by on-line and print services." Report of the Proceedings of the Judicial Conference of the United States, Sept. 2002, at 58. The Breyer Committee Report further emphasized that "[p]osting such orders on the judicial branch's public website would not only benefit judges directly, it would also encourage scholarly commentary and analysis of the orders." Breyer Committee Report, 239 F.R.D. at 216. With these considerations in mind, Rule 24 provides for public availability of a wide range of materials.

Rule 24 provides for public availability of orders of a chief judge, a judicial council, and the Committee on Judicial Conduct and Disability, as well as the texts of memoranda incorporated by reference in those orders, together with any dissenting opinions or separate statements by members of the judicial council. No memoranda other than those incorporated by reference in those orders shall be disclosed. However, these orders and memoranda are to be made public only when final action on the complaint has been taken and any right of review has been exhausted. The provision that decisions will be made public only after final action has been taken is designed in part to avoid public disclosure of the existence of pending proceedings. Whether the name of the subject judge is disclosed will then depend on the nature of the final action. If the final action is an order predicated on a finding of misconduct or disability (other than a privately communicated censure or reprimand) the name of the subject judge must be made public. If the final action is dismissal of the complaint, the name of the subject judge must not be disclosed. Rule 24(a)(1) provides that where a proceeding is concluded under Rule 11(d) by the chief judge on the basis of voluntary corrective action, the name of the subject judge must not be disclosed. Shielding the name of the subject judge in this circumstance should encourage informal disposition.

If a complaint is dismissed as moot, or because intervening events have made action on the complaint unnecessary, after appointment of a special committee, Rule 24(a)(2) allows the judicial council to determine whether the subject judge will be identified. In such a case, no final decision has been rendered on the merits, but it may be in the public interest—particularly if a judicial officer resigns in the course of an investigation—to make the identity of the subject judge known.

Once a special committee has been appointed, and a proceeding is concluded by the full judicial council on the basis of a remedial order of the council, Rule 24(a)(4) provides for disclosure of the name of the subject judge.

Rule 24(a)(5) provides that the identity of the complainant will be disclosed only if the chief judge so orders. Identifying the complainant when the subject judge is not identified would increase the likelihood that the identity of the subject judge would become publicly known, thus circumventing the policy of nondisclosure. It may not always be practicable to shield the complainant's identity while making public disclosure of the judicial council's order and supporting memoranda; in some circumstances, moreover, the complainant may consent to public identification.

Rule 24(b) makes clear that circuits must post on their external websites all orders required to be made public under Rule 24(a).

Matters involving orders issued following a special-committee investigation often involve highly sensitive situations, and it is important that judicial councils have every opportunity to reach a correct and just outcome. This would include the ability to reach informal resolution before a subject judge's identity must be released. But there must also come a point of procedural finality. The date of finality—and thus the time at which other safeguards and rules such as the publication requirement are triggered—is the date on which the judicial council issues a Final Order. *See In re Complaint of Judicial Misconduct*, 751 F.3d 611, 617 (2014) (requiring publication of a judicial council order "[e]ven though the period for review had not yet elapsed" and concluding that "the order was a final decision because the Council had adjudicated the matter on the merits after having received a report from a special investigating committee"). As determined in the cited case, modifications of this kind to a final order are subject to review by the Committee on Judicial Conduct and Disability.

25. Disqualification

(a) General Rule. Any judge is disqualified from participating in any proceeding under these Rules if the judge, in his or her discretion, concludes that circumstances warrant disqualification. If a complaint is filed by a judge, that judge is disqualified from participating in any consideration of the complaint except to the extent that these Rules provide for a complainant's participation. A chief judge who has identified a complaint under Rule 5 is not automatically disqualified from considering the complaint.

(b) Subject Judge. A subject judge is disqualified from considering a complaint except to the extent that these Rules provide for participation by a subject judge.

(c) Chief Judge Disqualified from Considering Petition for Review of Chief Judge's Order. If a petition for review of the chief judge's order entered under Rule 11(c), (d), or (e) is filed with the judicial council in accordance with Rule 18, the chief judge is disqualified from participating in the council's consideration of the petition.

(d) Member of Special Committee Not Disqualified. A member of the judicial council who serves on a special committee, including the chief judge, is not disqualified from participating in council consideration of the committee's report.

(e) Subject Judge's Disqualification After Appointment of Special Committee. Upon appointment of a special committee, the subject judge is disqualified from participating in the identification or consideration of any complaint, related or unrelated to the pending matter, under the Act or these Rules. The disqualification continues until all proceedings on the complaint against the subject judge are finally terminated with no further right of review.

(f) Substitute for Disqualified Chief Judge. If the chief judge is disqualified from performing duties that the Act and these Rules assign to a chief judge, those duties must be assigned to the most-senior active circuit judge not disqualified. If all circuit judges in regular active service are disqualified, the judicial council may determine whether to request a transfer under Rule 26, or, in the interest of sound judicial administration, to permit the chief judge to dispose of the complaint on the merits. Members of the judicial council who are named in the complaint may participate in this determination if necessary to obtain a quorum of the council.

(g) Judicial-Council Action When Multiple Judges Disqualified. Notwithstanding any other provision in these Rules to the contrary,

(1) a member of the judicial council who is a subject judge may participate in its disposition if:

(A) participation by one or more subject judges is necessary to obtain a quorum of the judicial council;

(B) the judicial council finds that the lack of a quorum is due to the naming of one or more judges in the complaint for the purpose of disqualifying that judge or those judges, or to the naming of one or more judges based on their participation in a decision excluded from the definition of misconduct under Rule 3(h)(3); and

(C) the judicial council votes that it is necessary, appropriate, and in the interest of sound judicial administration that one or more subject judges be eligible to act.

(2) otherwise disqualified members may participate in votes taken under (g)(1)(B) and (g)(1)(C).

(h) Disqualification of Members of Committee on Judicial Conduct and Disability. No member of the Committee on Judicial Conduct and Disability is disqualified from participating in any proceeding under the Act or these Rules because of consultations with a chief judge, a member of a special committee, or a member of a judicial council about the interpretation or application of the Act or these Rules, unless the member believes that the consultation would prevent fair-minded participation.

Commentary on Rule 25

Rule 25 is adapted from the Illustrative Rules.

Subsection (a) provides the general rule for disqualification. Of course, a judge is not disqualified simply because the subject judge is on the same court. However, this subsection recognizes that there may be cases in which an appearance of bias or prejudice is created by circumstances other than an association with the subject judge as a colleague. For example, a judge may have a familial relationship with a complainant or subject judge. When such circumstances exist, a judge may, in his or her discretion, conclude that disqualification is warranted.

Subsection (e) makes it clear that the disqualification of the subject judge relates only to the subject judge's participation in any proceeding arising under the Act or these Rules. For example, the subject judge cannot initiate complaints by identification, conduct limited inquiries, or choose between dismissal and special-committee investigation as the threshold disposition of a complaint. Likewise, the subject judge cannot participate in any proceeding arising under the Act or these Rules as a member of any special committee, the judicial council of the circuit, the Judicial Conference, or the Committee on Judicial Conduct and Disability. The Illustrative Rule, based on Section 359(a) of the Act, is ambiguous and could be read to disqualify a subject judge from service of any kind on each of the bodies mentioned. This is undoubtedly not the intent of the Act; such a disqualification would be anomalous in light of the Act's allowing a subject judge to continue to decide cases and to continue to exercise the powers of chief circuit or district judge. It would also create a substantial deterrence to the appointment of special committees, particularly where a special committee is needed solely because the chief judge may not decide matters of credibility in his or her review under Rule 11.

While a subject judge is barred by Rule 25(b) from participating in the disposition of the complaint in which he or she is named, Rule 25(e) recognizes that participation in proceedings arising under the Act or these Rules by a judge who is the subject of a special committee investigation may lead to an appearance of self-interest in creating substantive and procedural precedents governing such proceedings. Rule 25(e) bars such participation.

Under the Act, a complaint against the chief judge is to be handled by "that circuit judge in regular active service next senior in date of commission." 28 U.S.C. § 351(c). Rule 25(f) provides that seniority among judges other than the chief judge is to be determined by date of commission, with the result that complaints against the chief judge may be routed to a former chief judge or other judge who was appointed earlier than the chief judge. The Rules do not purport to prescribe who is to preside over meetings of the judicial council. Consequently, where the presiding member of the judicial council is disqualified from participating under these Rules, the order of precedence prescribed by Rule 25(f) for performing "duties that the Act and these Rules assign to a chief judge" does not apply to determine the acting presiding member of the council. That is a matter left to the internal rules or operating practices of each judicial council. In most cases the most senior active circuit judge who is a member of the judicial council and who is not disqualified will preside.

Sometimes a single complaint is filed against a large group of judges. If the normal disqualification rules are observed in such a case, no court of appeals judge can serve as acting chief judge of the circuit, and the judicial council will be without appellate members. Where the complaint is against all circuit and district judges, under normal rules no member of the judicial council can perform the duties assigned to the council under the statute.

A similar problem is created by successive complaints arising out of the same underlying grievance. For example, a complainant files a complaint against a district judge based on alleged misconduct, and the complaint is dismissed by the chief judge under the statute. The complainant may then file a complaint against the chief judge for dismissing the first complaint, and when that complaint is dismissed by the next senior judge, still a third complaint may be filed. The threat is that the complainant will bump down the seniority ladder until, once again, there is no member of the court of appeals who can serve as acting chief judge for the purpose of the next complaint. Similarly, complaints involving the merits of litigation may involve a series of decisions in which many judges participated or in which a rehearing en banc was denied by the court of appeals, and the complaint may name a majority of the judicial council as subject judges.

In recognition that these multiple-judge complaints are virtually always meritless, the judicial council is given discretion to determine: (1) whether it is necessary, appropriate, and in the interest of sound judicial administration to permit the chief judge to dispose of a complaint where it would otherwise be impossible for any active circuit judge in the circuit to act, and (2) whether it is necessary, appropriate, and in the interest of sound judicial administration, after appropriate findings as to need and justification are made, to permit subject judges of the judicial council to participate in the disposition of a petition for review where it would otherwise be impossible to obtain a quorum.

Applying a rule of necessity in these situations is consistent with the appearance of justice. *See, e.g., In re Complaint of Doe*, 2 F.3d 308 (8th Cir. Jud. Council 1993) (invoking the rule of necessity); *In re Complaint of Judicial Misconduct*, No. 91-80464 (9th Cir. Jud. Council 1992) (same). There is no unfairness in permitting the chief judge to dispose of a patently insubstantial complaint that names all active circuit judges in the circuit.

Similarly, there is no unfairness in permitting subject judges, in these circumstances, to participate in the review of the chief judge's dismissal of an insubstantial complaint. The remaining option is to assign the matter to another body. Among other alternatives, the judicial council may request a transfer of the petition under Rule 26. Given the administrative inconvenience and delay involved in these alternatives, it is desirable to request a transfer only if the judicial council determines that the petition for review is substantial enough to warrant such action.

In the unlikely event that a quorum of the judicial council cannot be obtained to consider the report of a special committee, it would normally be necessary to request a transfer under Rule 26.

Rule 25(h) recognizes that the jurisdictional statement of the Committee on Judicial Conduct and Disability contemplates consultation between members of the Committee and judicial participants in proceedings under the Act and these Rules. Such consultation should not automatically preclude participation by a member in that proceeding.

26. Transfer to Another Judicial Council

In exceptional circumstances, a chief judge or a judicial council may ask the Chief Justice to transfer a proceeding based on a complaint identified under Rule 5 or filed under Rule 6 to the judicial council of another circuit. The request for a transfer may be

made at any stage of the proceeding before a reference to the Judicial Conference under Rule 20(b)(1)(C) or 20(b)(2) or a petition for review is filed under Rule 22. Upon receiving such a request, the Chief Justice may refuse the request or select the transferee judicial council, which may then exercise the powers of a judicial council under these Rules.

Commentary on Rule 26

Rule 26 implements the Breyer Committee's recommended use of transfers. Breyer Committee Report, 239 F.R.D. at 214–15.

Rule 26 authorizes the transfer of a complaint proceeding to another judicial council selected by the Chief Justice. Such transfers may be appropriate, for example, in the case of a serious complaint where there are multiple disqualifications among the original judicial council, where the issues are highly visible and a local disposition may weaken public confidence in the process, where internal tensions arising in the council as a result of the complaint render disposition by a less involved council appropriate, or where a complaint calls into question policies or governance of the home court of appeals. The power to effect a transfer is lodged in the Chief Justice to avoid disputes in a judicial council over where to transfer a sensitive matter and to ensure that the transferee council accepts the matter.

Upon receipt of a transferred proceeding, the transferee judicial council shall determine the proper stage at which to begin consideration of the complaint—for example, reference to the transferee chief judge, appointment of a special committee, etc.

27. Withdrawal of Complaint or Petition for Review

(a) Complaint Pending Before Chief Judge. With the chief judge's consent, the complainant may withdraw a complaint that is before the chief judge for a decision under Rule 11. The withdrawal of a complaint will not prevent the chief judge from identifying or having to identify a complaint under Rule 5 based on the withdrawn complaint.

(b) Complaint Pending Before Special Committee or Judicial Council. After a complaint has been referred to the special committee for investigation and before the committee files its report, the complainant may withdraw the complaint only with the consent of both the subject judge and either the special committee or the judicial council.

(c) Petition for Review. A petition for review addressed to the judicial council under Rule 18, or the Committee on Judicial Conduct and Disability under Rule 22, may be withdrawn if no action on the petition has been taken.

Commentary on Rule 27

Rule 27 is adapted from the Illustrative Rules and treats the complaint proceeding, once begun, as a matter of public business rather than as the property of the complainant. Accordingly, the chief judge or the judicial council remains responsible for addressing any complaint under the Act, even a complaint that has been formally withdrawn by the complainant.

Under subsection (a), a complaint pending before the chief judge may be withdrawn if the chief judge consents. Where the complaint clearly lacked merit, the chief judge may accordingly be saved the burden of preparing a formal order and supporting memorandum. However, the chief judge may, or be obligated under Rule 5, to identify a complaint based on allegations in a withdrawn complaint.

If the chief judge appoints a special committee, Rule 27(b) provides that the complaint may be withdrawn only with the consent of both the body before which it is pending (the special committee or the judicial council) and the subject judge. Once a complaint has reached the stage of appointment of a special committee, a resolution of the issues may be necessary to preserve public confidence. Moreover, the subject judge is given the right to insist that the matter be resolved on the merits, thereby eliminating any ambiguity that might remain if the proceeding were terminated by withdrawal of the complaint.

With regard to all petitions for review, Rule 27(c) grants the petitioner unrestricted authority to withdraw the petition. It is thought that the public's interest in the proceeding is adequately protected, because there will necessarily have been a decision by the chief judge and often by the judicial council as well in such a case.

28. Availability of Rules and Forms

These Rules and copies of the complaint form as provided in Rule 6(a) must be available without charge in the office of the circuit clerk of each court of appeals, district court, bankruptcy court, or other federal court whose judges are subject to the Act. Each court must also make these Rules, the complaint form, and complaint-filing instructions available on the court's website, or provide an Internet link to these items on the appropriate court of appeals website or on www.uscourts.gov.

29. Effective Date

These Rules will become effective 30 days after promulgation by the Judicial Conference of the United States.

Appendix to the Rules: Form AO 310 (Complaint of Judicial Misconduct or Disability)

APPENDIX

COMPLAINT FORM

Judicial Council of the ______ Circuit

COMPLAINT OF JUDICIAL MISCONDUCT OR DISABILITY

To begin the complaint process, complete this form and prepare the brief statement of facts described in item 5 (below). The RULES FOR JUDICIAL-CONDUCT AND JUDICIAL-DISABILITY PROCEEDINGS, adopted by the Judicial Conference of the United States, contain information on what to include in a complaint (Rule 6), where to file a complaint (Rule 7), and other important matters. The rules are available in federal court clerks' offices, on individual federal courts' Web sites, and on www.uscourts.gov.

Your complaint (this form and the statement of facts) should be typewritten and must be legible. For the number of copies to file, consult the local rules or clerk's office of the court in which your complaint is required to be filed. Enclose each copy of the complaint in an envelope marked "COMPLAINT OF MISCONDUCT" or "COMPLAINT OF DISABILITY" and submit it to the appropriate clerk of court. **Do not put the name of any judge on the envelope.**

1. Name of Complainant: ______________________

Contact Address: ______________________

Daytime telephone: (   ) ______________________

2. Name(s) of Judge(s): ______________________

Court: ______________________

3. Does this complaint concern the behavior of the judge(s) in a particular lawsuit or lawsuits?

[ ] Yes   [ ] No

If "yes," give the following information about each lawsuit:

Court: ______________________

Case Number: ______________________

Docket number of any appeal to the ________ Circuit: ______________________

Are (were) you a party or lawyer in the lawsuit?

[ ] Party   [ ] Lawyer   [ ] Neither

If you are (were) a party and have (had) a lawyer, give the lawyer's name, address, and telephone number:

____

____

____

4. Have you filed any lawsuits against the judge?

[ ] Yes   [ ] No

If "yes," give the following information about each such lawsuit:

Court: ______________________

Case Number: ______________________

Present status of lawsuit: ______________________

Name, address, and telephone number of your lawyer for the lawsuit against the judge:

____

____

____

Court to which any appeal has been taken in the lawsuit against the judge:

____

Docket number of the appeal: ____________________

Present status of the appeal: ____________________

5. **Brief Statement of Facts.** Attach a brief statement of the specific facts on which the claim of judicial misconduct or disability is based. Include what happened, when and where it happened, and any information that would help an investigator check the facts. If the complaint alleges judicial disability, also include any additional facts that form the basis of that allegation.

6. **Declaration and signature:**

I declare under penalty of perjury that the statements made in this complaint are true and correct to the best of my knowledge.

(Signature) ______________________________ (Date) ________________

PART THREE

RULES OF EVIDENCE AND PROCEDURE THAT AFFECT THE LEGAL PROFESSION

TABLE OF CONTENTS

Introduction

Until recently, most courses and casebooks in professional responsibility focused solely on the ABA's model codes of conduct. However, the law which governs and regulates the conduct of lawyers must go far beyond the ABA's pronouncements. One other source of law which affects lawyers' conduct must include rules of evidence, procedure, and court. This part includes rules of evidence and procedure which affect the practice of law.

SELECTED RULES OF EVIDENCE AND PROCEDURE

FEDERAL RULES OF EVIDENCE FOR UNITED STATES COURTS AND MAGISTRATES

Rule 501. Privilege in General

The common law—as interpreted by United States courts in the light of reason and experience—governs a claim of privilege unless any of the following provides otherwise:

- the United States Constitution;
- a federal statute; or
- rules prescribed by the Supreme Court.

But in a civil case, state law governs privilege regarding a claim or defense for which state law supplies the rule of decision.

Rule 502. Attorney-Client Privilege and Work Product; Limitations on Waiver

The following provisions apply, in the circumstances set out, to disclosure of a communication or information covered by the attorney-client privilege or work-product protection.

(a) Disclosure Made in a Federal Proceeding or to a Federal Office or Agency; Scope of a Waiver.—When the disclosure is made in a federal proceeding or to a federal office or agency and waives the attorney-client privilege or work-product protection, the waiver extends to an undisclosed communication or information in a federal or state proceeding only if:

(1) the waiver is intentional;

(2) the disclosed and undisclosed communications or information concern the same subject matter; and

(3) they ought in fairness to be considered together.

(b) Inadvertent Disclosure.—When made in a federal proceeding or to a federal office or agency, the disclosure does not operate as a waiver in a federal or state proceeding if:

(1) the disclosure is inadvertent;

(2) the holder of the privilege or protection took reasonable steps to prevent disclosure; and

(3) the holder promptly took reasonable steps to rectify the error, including (if applicable) following Fed. R. Civ. P. 26(b)(5)(B).

(c) Disclosure Made in a State Proceeding.—When the disclosure is made in a state proceeding and is not the subject of a state-court order concerning waiver, the disclosure does not operate as a waiver in a federal proceeding if the disclosure:

(1) would not be a waiver under this rule if it had been made in a federal proceeding; or

(2) is not a waiver under the law of the state where the disclosure occurred.

(d) Controlling Effect of a Court Order.—A federal court may order that the privilege or protection is not waived by disclosure connected with the litigation pending before the court—in which event the disclosure is also not a waiver in any other federal or state proceeding.

(e) Controlling Effect of a Party Agreement.—An agreement on the effect of disclosure in a federal proceeding is binding only on the parties to the agreement, unless it is incorporated into a court order.

(f) Controlling Effect of this Rule.—Notwithstanding Rules 101 and 1101, this rule applies to state proceedings and to federal court-annexed and federal court-mandated arbitration proceedings, in the circumstances set out in the rule. And notwithstanding Rule 501, this rule applies even if state law provides the rule of decision.

(g) Definitions.—In this rule:

(1) "attorney-client privilege" means the protection that applicable law provides for confidential attorney-client communications; and

(2) "work-product protection" means the protection that applicable law provides for tangible material (or its intangible equivalent) prepared in anticipation of litigation or for trial.

Explanatory Note on Evidence Rule 502 Prepared by the Judicial Conference Advisory Committee on Evidence Rules (Revised 11/28/2007)

This new rule has two major purposes:

1) It resolves some longstanding disputes in the courts about the effect of certain disclosures of communications or information protected by the attorney-client privilege or as work product—specifically those disputes involving inadvertent disclosure and subject matter waiver.

2) It responds to the widespread complaint that litigation costs necessary to protect against waiver of attorney-client privilege or work product have become prohibitive due to the concern that any disclosure (however innocent or minimal) will operate as a subject matter waiver of all protected communications or information. This concern is especially troubling in cases involving electronic discovery. *See, e.g., Hopson v. City of Baltimore,* 232 F.R.D. 228, 244 (D.Md. 2005) (electronic discovery may encompass "millions of documents" and to insist upon "record-by-record pre-production privilege review, on pain of subject matter waiver, would impose upon parties costs of production that bear no proportionality to what is at stake in the litigation").

The rule seeks to provide a predictable, uniform set of standards under which parties can determine the consequences of a disclosure of a communication or information covered by the attorney-client privilege or work-product protection. Parties to litigation need to know, for example, that if they exchange privileged information pursuant to a confidentiality order, the court's order will be enforceable. Moreover, if a federal court's confidentiality order is not enforceable in a state court then the burdensome costs of privilege review and retention are unlikely to be reduced.

The rule makes no attempt to alter federal or state law on whether a communication or information is protected under the attorney-client privilege or work-product immunity as an initial matter. Moreover, while establishing some exceptions to waiver, the rule does not purport to supplant applicable waiver doctrine generally.

The rule governs only certain waivers by disclosure. Other common-law waiver doctrines may result in a finding of waiver even where there is no disclosure of privileged information or work product. *See, e.g., Nguyen v. Excel Corp.,* 197 F.3d 200 (5th Cir. 1999) (reliance on an advice of counsel defense waives the privilege with respect to attorney-client communications pertinent to that defense); *Ryers v. Burleson,* 100 F.R.D. 436 (D.D.C. 1983) (allegation of lawyer malpractice constituted a waiver of confidential communications under the circumstances). The rule is not intended to displace or modify federal common law concerning waiver of privilege or work product where no disclosure has been made.

Subdivision (a). The rule provides that a voluntary disclosure in a federal proceeding or to a federal office or agency, if a waiver, generally results in a waiver only of the communication or information disclosed; a subject matter waiver (of either privilege or work product) is reserved for those unusual situations in which fairness requires a further disclosure of related, protected information, in order to prevent a selective and misleading presentation of evidence to the disadvantage of the adversary. *See, e.g., In re United Mine Workers of America Employee Benefit Plans Litig.*, 159 F.R.D. 307, 312 (D.D.C. 1994) (waiver of work product limited to materials actually disclosed, because the party did not deliberately disclose documents in an attempt to gain a tactical advantage). Thus, subject matter waiver is limited to situations in which a party intentionally puts protected information into the litigation in a selective, misleading and unfair manner. It follows that an inadvertent disclosure of protected information can never result in a subject matter waiver. *See* Rule 502(b). The rule rejects the result in *In re Sealed Case,* 877 F.2d 976 (D.C.Cir. 1989), which held that inadvertent disclosure of documents during discovery automatically constituted a subject matter waiver.

The language concerning subject matter waiver—"ought in fairness"—is taken from Rule 106, because the animating principle is the same. Under both Rules, a party that makes a selective, misleading presentation that is unfair to the adversary opens itself to a more complete and accurate presentation.

To assure protection and predictability, the rule provides that if a disclosure is made at the federal level, the federal rule on subject matter waiver governs subsequent state court determinations on the scope of the waiver by that disclosure.

Subdivision (b). Courts are in conflict over whether an inadvertent disclosure of a communication or information protected as privileged or work product constitutes a waiver. A few courts find that a disclosure must be intentional to be a waiver. Most courts find a waiver only if the disclosing party acted carelessly in disclosing the communication or information and failed to request its return in a timely manner. And a few courts hold that any inadvertent disclosure of a communication or information protected under the attorney-client privilege or as work product constitutes a waiver without regard to the protections taken to avoid such a disclosure. *See generally Hopson v. City of Baltimore,* 232 F.R.D. 228 (D.Md. 2005), for a discussion of this case law.

The rule opts for the middle ground: inadvertent disclosure of protected communications or information in connection with a federal proceeding or to a federal office or agency does not constitute a waiver if the holder took reasonable steps to prevent disclosure and also promptly took reasonable steps to rectify the error. This position is in accord with the majority view on whether inadvertent disclosure is a waiver.

Cases such as *Lois Sportswear, U.S.A., Inc. v. Levi Strauss & Co.*, 104 F.R.D. 103, 105 (S.D.N.Y. 1985) and *Hartford Fire Ins. Co. v. Garvey*, 109 F.R.D. 323, 332 (N.D.Cal. 1985), set out a multi-factor test for determining whether inadvertent disclosure is a waiver. The stated factors (none of which is dispositive) are the reasonableness of precautions taken, the time taken to rectify the error, the scope of discovery, the extent of disclosure and the overriding issue of fairness. The rule does not explicitly codify that test, because it is really a set of non-determinative guidelines that vary from case to case. The rule is flexible enough to accommodate any of those listed factors. Other considerations bearing on the reasonableness of a producing party's efforts include the number of documents to be reviewed and the time constraints for production. Depending on the circumstances, a party that uses advanced analytical software applications and linguistic tools in screening for privilege and work product may be found to have taken "reasonable steps" to prevent inadvertent disclosure. The implementation of an efficient system of records management before litigation may also be relevant.

The rule does not require the producing party to engage in a post-production review to determine whether any protected communication or information has been produced by mistake. But the rule does require the producing party to follow up on any obvious indications that a protected communication or information has been produced inadvertently.

The rule applies to inadvertent disclosures made to a federal office or agency, including but not limited to an office or agency that is acting in the course of its regulatory, investigative or enforcement authority. The consequences of waiver, and the concomitant costs of pre-production privilege review, can be as great with respect to disclosures to offices and agencies as they are in litigation.

Subdivision (c). Difficult questions can arise when 1) a disclosure of a communication or information protected by the attorney-client privilege or as work product is made in a state proceeding, 2) the communication or information is offered in a subsequent federal proceeding on the ground that the disclosure waived the privilege or protection, and 3) the state and federal laws are in conflict on the question of waiver. The Committee determined that the proper solution for the federal court is to apply the law that is most protective of privilege and work product. If the state law is more protective (such as where the state law is that an inadvertent disclosure can never be a waiver), the holder of the privilege or protection may well have relied on that law when making the disclosure in the state proceeding. Moreover, applying a more restrictive federal law of waiver could impair the state objective of preserving the privilege or work-product protection for disclosures made in state proceedings. On the other hand, if the federal law is more protective, applying the state law of waiver to determine admissibility in federal court is likely to undermine the federal objective of limiting the costs of production.

The rule does not address the enforceability of a state court confidentiality order in a federal proceeding, as that question is covered both by statutory law and principles of federalism and comity. *See* 28 U.S.C. § 1738 (providing that state judicial proceedings "shall have the same full faith and credit in every court within the United States . . . as they have by law or usage in the courts of such State . . . from which they are taken"). *See also Tucker v. Ohtsu Tire & Rubber Co.,* 191 F.R.D. 495, 499 (D.Md. 2000) (noting that a federal court considering the enforceability of a state confidentiality order is "constrained by principles of comity, courtesy, and . . . federalism"). Thus, a state court order finding no waiver in connection with a disclosure made in a state court proceeding is enforceable under existing law in subsequent federal proceedings.

Subdivision (d). Confidentiality orders are becoming increasingly important in limiting the costs of privilege review and retention, especially in cases involving electronic discovery. But the utility of a confidentiality order in reducing discovery costs is substantially diminished if it provides no protection outside the particular litigation in which the order is entered. Parties are unlikely to be able to reduce the costs of pre-production review for privilege and work product if the consequence of disclosure is that the communications or information could be used by non-parties to the litigation.

There is some dispute on whether a confidentiality order entered in one case is enforceable in other proceedings. *See generally Hopson v. City of Baltimore,* 232 F.R.D. 228 (D.Md. 2005), for a discussion of this case law. The rule provides that when a confidentiality order governing the consequences of disclosure in that case is entered in a federal proceeding, its terms are enforceable against non-parties in any federal or state proceeding. For example, the court order may provide for return of documents without waiver irrespective of the care taken by the disclosing party; the rule contemplates enforcement of "claw-back" and "quick peek" arrangements as a way to avoid the excessive costs of pre-production review for privilege and work product. *See Zubulake v. UBS Warburg LLC,* 216 F.R.D. 280, 290 (S.D.N.Y. 2003) (noting that parties may enter into "so-called 'claw-back' agreements that allow the parties to forego privilege review altogether in favor of an agreement to return inadvertently produced privilege documents"). The rule provides a party with a predictable protection from a court order—predictability that is needed to allow the party to plan in advance to limit the prohibitive costs of privilege and work product review and retention.

Under the rule, a confidentiality order is enforceable whether or not it memorializes an agreement among the parties to the litigation. Party agreement should not be a condition of enforceability of a federal court's order.

Under subdivision (d), a federal court may order that disclosure of privileged or protected information "in connection with" a federal proceeding does not result in waiver. But subdivision (d) does not allow the federal court to enter an order determining the waiver effects of a separate disclosure of the same information in other proceedings, state or federal. If a disclosure has been made in a state proceeding (and is not the subject of a state-court order on waiver), then subdivision (d) is inapplicable. Subdivision (c) would govern the federal court's determination whether the state-court disclosure waived the privilege or protection in the federal proceeding.

Subdivision (e). Subdivision (e) codifies the well-established proposition that parties can enter an agreement to limit the effect of waiver by disclosure between or among them. Of course such an agreement can bind only the parties to the agreement. The rule makes clear that if parties want protection against non-parties from a finding of waiver by disclosure, the agreement must be made part of a court order.

Subdivision (f). The protections against waiver provided by Rule 502 must be applicable when protected communications or information disclosed in federal proceedings are subsequently offered in state proceedings. Otherwise the holders of protected communications and information, and their lawyers, could not rely on the protections provided by the Rule, and the goal of limiting costs in discovery would be substantially undermined. Rule 502(f) is intended to resolve any potential tension between the provisions of Rule 502 that apply to state proceedings and the possible limitations on the applicability of the Federal Rules of Evidence otherwise provided by Rules 101 and 1101.

The rule is intended to apply in all federal court proceedings, including court-annexed and court-ordered arbitrations, without regard to any possible limitations of Rules 101 and 1101. This provision is not intended to raise an inference about the applicability of any other rule of evidence in arbitration proceedings more generally.

The costs of discovery can be equally high for state and federal causes of action, and the rule seeks to limit those costs in all federal proceedings, regardless of whether the claim arises under state or federal law. Accordingly, the rule applies to state law causes of action brought in federal court.

Subdivision (g). The rule's coverage is limited to attorney-client privilege and work product. The operation of waiver by disclosure, as applied to other evidentiary privileges, remains a question of federal common law. Nor does the rule purport to apply to the Fifth Amendment privilege against compelled self-incrimination.

The definition of work product "materials" is intended to include both tangible and intangible information. *See In re Cendant Corp. Sec. Litig.*, 343 F.3d 658, 662 (3d Cir. 2003) ("work product protection extends to both tangible and intangible work product").

Rule 605. Judge's Competency as a Witness

The presiding judge may not testify as a witness at the trial. A party need not object to preserve the issue.

APPENDIX OF DELETED RULES OF EVIDENCE

Rule 503. Lawyer-Client Privilege [Not enacted.]

(a) Definitions. As used in this rule:

(1) A "client" is a person, public officer, or corporation, association, or other organization or entity, either public or private, who is rendered professional legal services by a lawyer, or who consults a lawyer with a view to obtaining professional legal services from him.

(2) A "lawyer" is a person authorized, or reasonably believed by the client to be authorized, to practice law in any state or nation.

(3) A "representative of the lawyer" is one employed to assist the lawyer in the rendition of professional services.

(4) A communication is "confidential" if not intended to be disclosed to third persons other than those to whom disclosure is in furtherance of the rendition of professional legal services to the client or those reasonably necessary for the transmission of the communication.

(b) General rule of privilege. A client has a privilege to refuse to disclose and to prevent any other person from disclosing confidential communications made for the purpose of facilitating the rendition of professional legal services to the client, (1) between himself or his representative and his lawyer or his lawyer's representative, or (2) between his lawyer and the lawyer's representative, or (3) by him or his lawyer to a lawyer representing another in a matter of common interest, or (4) between representatives of the client or between the client and a representative of the client, or (5) between lawyers representing the client.

(c) Who may claim the privilege. The privilege may be claimed by the client, his guardian or conservator, the personal representative of a deceased client, or the successor, trustee, or similar representative of a corporation, association, or other organization, whether or not in existence. The person who was the lawyer at the time of the communication may claim the privilege but only on behalf of the client. His authority to do so is presumed in the absence of evidence to the contrary.

(d) Exceptions. There is no privilege under this rule:

(1) Furtherance of crime or fraud. If the services of the lawyer were sought or obtained to enable or aid anyone to commit or plan to commit what the client knew or reasonably should have known to be a crime or fraud; or

(2) Claimants through same deceased client. As to a communication relevant to an issue between parties who claim through the same deceased client, regardless of whether the claims are by testate or intestate succession or by *inter vivos* transaction; or

(3) Breach of duty by lawyer or client. As to a communication relevant to an issue of breach of duty by the lawyer to his client or by the client to his lawyer; or

(4) Document attested by lawyer. As to a communication relevant to an issue concerning an attested document to which the lawyer is an attesting witness; or

(5) Joint clients. As to a communication relevant to a matter of common interest between two or more clients if the communication was made by any of them to a lawyer retained or consulted in common, when offered in an action between any of the clients.

FEDERAL RULES OF CIVIL PROCEDURE

Rule 11. Signing of Pleadings, Motions, and Other Papers; Representations to Court; Sanctions*

(a) Signature. Every pleading, written motion, and other paper must be signed by at least one attorney of record in the attorney's name—or by a party personally if the party is unrepresented. The paper must state the signer's address, e-mail address, and telephone number. Unless a rule or statute specifically states otherwise, a pleading need not be verified or accompanied by an affidavit. The court must strike an unsigned paper unless the omission is promptly corrected after being called to the attorney's or party's attention.

(b) Representations to the Court. By presenting to the court a pleading, written motion, or other paper—whether by signing, filing, submitting, or later advocating it—an attorney or unrepresented party certifies that to the best of the person's knowledge, information, and belief, formed after an inquiry reasonable under the circumstances:

(1) it is not being presented for any improper purpose, such as to harass, cause unnecessary delay, or needlessly increase the cost of litigation;

(2) the claims, defenses, and other legal contentions are warranted by existing law or by a nonfrivolous argument for extending, modifying, or reversing existing law or for establishing new law;

(3) the factual contentions have evidentiary support or, if specifically so identified, will likely have evidentiary support after a reasonable opportunity for further investigation or discovery; and

(4) the denials of factual contentions are warranted on the evidence or, if specifically so identified, are reasonably based on belief or a lack of information.

(c) Sanctions.

(1) ***In General.*** If, after notice and a reasonable opportunity to respond, the court determines that Rule 11(b) has been violated, the court may impose an appropriate sanction on any attorney, law firm, or party that violated the rule or is responsible for the violation. Absent exceptional circumstances, a law firm must be held jointly responsible for a violation committed by its partner, associate, or employee.

(2) ***Motion for Sanctions.*** A motion for sanctions must be made separately from any other motion and must describe the specific conduct that allegedly violates Rule 11(b). The motion must be served under Rule 5, but it must not be filed or be presented to the court if the challenged

---

* [Ed.] This footnote contains the text of Rule 11 prior to the 1993 Amendment.

Every pleading, motion, and other paper of a party represented by an attorney shall be signed by at least one attorney of record in the attorney's individual name, whose address shall be stated. A party who is not represented by an attorney shall sign the party's pleading, motion, or other paper and state the party's address. Except when otherwise specifically provided by rule or statute, pleadings need not be verified or accompanied by affidavit. The rule in equity that the averments of an answer under oath must be overcome by the testimony of two witnesses or of one witness sustained by corroborating circumstances is abolished. The signature of an attorney or party constitutes a certificate by the signer that the signer has read the pleading, motion, or other paper; that to the best of the signer's knowledge, information, and belief formed after reasonable inquiry it is well grounded in fact and is warranted by existing law or a good faith argument for the extension, modification, or reversal of existing law, and that it is not interposed for any improper purpose, such as to harass or to cause unnecessary delay or needless increase in the cost of litigation. If a pleading, motion, or other paper is not signed, it shall be stricken unless it is signed promptly after the omission is called to the attention of the pleader or movant. If a pleading, motion, or other paper is signed in violation of this rule, the court, upon motion or upon its own initiative, shall impose upon the person who signed it, a represented party, or both, an appropriate sanction, which may include an order to pay to the other party or parties the amount of the reasonable expenses incurred because of the filing of the pleading, motion, or other paper, including a reasonable attorney's fee.

paper, claim, defense, contention, or denial is withdrawn or appropriately corrected within 21 days after service or within another time the court sets. If warranted, the court may award to the prevailing party the reasonable expenses, including attorney's fees, incurred for the motion.

(3) ***On the Court's Initiative.*** On its own, the court may order an attorney, law firm, or party to show cause why conduct specifically described in the order has not violated Rule 11(b).

(4) ***Nature of a Sanction.*** A sanction imposed under this rule must be limited to what suffices to deter repetition of the conduct or comparable conduct by others similarly situated. The sanction may include nonmonetary directives; an order to pay a penalty into court; or, if imposed on motion and warranted for effective deterrence, an order directing payment to the movant of part or all of the reasonable attorney's fees and other expenses directly resulting from the violation.

(5) ***Limitations on Monetary Sanctions.*** The court must not impose a monetary sanction:

(A) against a represented party for violating Rule 11(b)(2); or

(B) on its own, unless it issued the show-cause order under Rule 11(c)(3) before voluntary dismissal or settlement of the claims made by or against the party that is, or whose attorneys are, to be sanctioned.

(6) ***Requirements for an Order.*** An order imposing a sanction must describe the sanctioned conduct and explain the basis for the sanction.

(d) Inapplicability to Discovery. This rule does not apply to disclosures and discovery requests, responses, objections, and motions under Rules 26 through 37.

Rule 16. Pretrial Conferences; Scheduling; Management

(a) Purposes of a Pretrial Conference. In any action, the court may order the attorneys and any unrepresented parties to appear for one or more pretrial conferences for such purposes as:

(1) expediting disposition of the action;

(2) establishing early and continuing control so that the case will not be protracted because of lack of management;

(3) discouraging wasteful pretrial activities;

(4) improving the quality of the trial through more thorough preparation; and

(5) facilitating settlement.

(b) Scheduling.

(1) ***Scheduling Order.*** Except in categories of actions exempted by local rule, the district judge—or a magistrate judge when authorized by local rule—must issue a scheduling order:

(A) after receiving the parties' report under Rule 26(f); or

(B) after consulting with the parties' attorneys and any unrepresented parties at a scheduling conference.

(2) ***Time to Issue.*** The judge must issue the scheduling order as soon as practicable, but unless the judge finds good cause for delay, the judge must issue it within the earlier of 90 days after any defendant has been served with the complaint or 60 days after any defendant has appeared.

(3) ***Contents of the Order.***

(A) *Required Contents.* The scheduling order must limit the time to join other parties, amend the pleadings, complete discovery, and file motions.

(B) *Permitted Contents.* The scheduling order may:

(i) modify the timing of disclosures under Rules 26(a) and 26(e)(1);

(ii) modify the extent of discovery;

(iii) provide for disclosure, discovery, or preservation of electronically stored information;

(iv) include any agreements the parties reach for asserting claims of privilege or of protection as trial-preparation material after information is produced, including agreements reached under Federal Rule of Evidence 502;

(v) direct that before moving for an order relating to discovery, the movant must request a conference with the court;

(vi) set dates for pretrial conferences and for trial; and

(vii) include other appropriate matters.

(4) ***Modifying a Schedule.*** A schedule may be modified only for good cause and with the judge's consent.

(c) Attendance and Matters for Consideration at a Pretrial Conference.

(1) ***Attendance.*** A represented party must authorize at least one of its attorneys to make stipulations and admissions about all matters that can reasonably be anticipated for discussion at a pretrial conference. If appropriate, the court may require that a party or its representative be present or reasonably available by other means to consider possible settlement.

(2) ***Matters for Consideration.*** At any pretrial conference, the court may consider and take appropriate action on the following matters:

(A) formulating and simplifying the issues, and eliminating frivolous claims or defenses;

(B) amending the pleadings if necessary or desirable;

(C) obtaining admissions and stipulations about facts and documents to avoid unnecessary proof, and ruling in advance on the admissibility of evidence;

(D) avoiding unnecessary proof and cumulative evidence, and limiting the use of testimony under Federal Rule of Evidence 702;

(E) determining the appropriateness and timing of summary adjudication under Rule 56;

(F) controlling and scheduling discovery, including orders affecting disclosures and discovery under Rule 26 and Rules 29 through 37;

(G) identifying witnesses and documents, scheduling the filing and exchange of any pretrial briefs, and setting dates for further conferences and for trial;

(H) referring matters to a magistrate judge or a master;

(I) settling the case and using special procedures to assist in resolving the dispute when authorized by statute or local rule;

(J) determining the form and content of the pretrial order;

(K) disposing of pending motions;

(L) adopting special procedures for managing potentially difficult or protracted actions that may involve complex issues, multiple parties, difficult legal questions, or unusual proof problems;

(M) ordering a separate trial under Rule 42(b) of a claim, counterclaim, crossclaim, third-party claim, or particular issue;

(N) ordering the presentation of evidence early in the trial on a manageable issue that might, on the evidence, be the basis for a judgment as a matter of law under Rule 50(a) or a judgment on partial findings under Rule 52(c);

(O) establishing a reasonable limit on the time allowed to present evidence; and

(P) facilitating in other ways the just, speedy, and inexpensive disposition of the action.

(d) Pretrial Orders. After any conference under this rule, the court should issue an order reciting the action taken. This order controls the course of the action unless the court modifies it.

(e) Final Pretrial Conference and Orders. The court may hold a final pretrial conference to formulate a trial plan, including a plan to facilitate the admission of evidence. The conference must be held as close to the start of trial as is reasonable, and must be attended by at least one attorney who will conduct the trial for each party and by any unrepresented party. The court may modify the order issued after a final pretrial conference only to prevent manifest injustice.

(f) Sanctions.

(1) ***In General.*** On motion or on its own, the court may issue any just orders, including those authorized by Rule 37(b)(2)(A)(ii)-(vii), if a party or its attorney:

(A) fails to appear at a scheduling or other pretrial conference;

(B) is substantially unprepared to participate—or does not participate in good faith—in the conference; or

(C) fails to obey a scheduling or other pretrial order.

(2) ***Imposing Fees and Costs.*** Instead of or in addition to any other sanction, the court must order the party, its attorney, or both to pay the reasonable expenses—including attorney's fees—incurred because of any noncompliance with this rule, unless the noncompliance was substantially justified or other circumstances make an award of expenses unjust.

Rule 23. Class Actions

(a) Prerequisites. One or more members of a class may sue or be sued as representative parties on behalf of all members only if:

(1) the class is so numerous that joinder of all members is impracticable;

(2) there are questions of law or fact common to the class;

(3) the claims or defenses of the representative parties are typical of the claims or defenses of the class; and

(4) the representative parties will fairly and adequately protect the interests of the class.

(b) Types of Class Actions. A class action may be maintained if Rule 23(a) is satisfied and if:

(1) prosecuting separate actions by or against individual class members would create a risk of:

(A) inconsistent or varying adjudications with respect to individual class members that would establish incompatible standards of conduct for the party opposing the class; or

(B) adjudications with respect to individual class members that, as a practical matter, would be dispositive of the interests of the other members not parties to the individual adjudications or would substantially impair or impede their ability to protect their interests;

(2) the party opposing the class has acted or refused to act on grounds that apply generally to the class, so that final injunctive relief or corresponding declaratory relief is appropriate respecting the class as a whole; or

(3) the court finds that the questions of law or fact common to class members predominate over any questions affecting only individual members, and that a class action is superior to other available methods for fairly and efficiently adjudicating the controversy. The matters pertinent to these findings include:

(A) the class members' interests in individually controlling the prosecution or defense of separate actions;

(B) the extent and nature of any litigation concerning the controversy already begun by or against class members;

(C) the desirability or undesirability of concentrating the litigation of the claims in the particular forum; and

(D) the likely difficulties in managing a class action.

(c) Certification Order; Notice to Class Members; Judgment; Issues Classes; Subclasses.

(1) ***Certification Order.***

(A) *Time to Issue.* At an early practicable time after a person sues or is sued as a class representative, the court must determine by order whether to certify the action as a class action.

(B) *Defining the Class; Appointing Class Counsel.* An order that certifies a class action must define the class and the class claims, issues, or defenses, and must appoint class counsel under Rule 23(g).

(C) *Altering or Amending the Order.* An order that grants or denies class certification may be altered or amended before final judgment.

(2) ***Notice.***

(A) *For (b)(1) or (b)(2) Classes.* For any class certified under Rule 23(b)(1) or (b)(2), the court may direct appropriate notice to the class.

(B) *For (b)(3) Classes.* For any class certified under Rule 23(b)(3), the court must direct to class members the best notice that is practicable under the circumstances, including individual notice to all members who can be identified through reasonable effort. The notice must clearly and concisely state in plain, easily understood language:

(i) the nature of the action;

(ii) the definition of the class certified;

(iii) the class claims, issues, or defenses;

(iv) that a class member may enter an appearance through an attorney if the member so desires;

(v) that the court will exclude from the class any member who requests exclusion;

(vi) the time and manner for requesting exclusion; and

(vii) the binding effect of a class judgment on members under Rule 23(c)(3).

(3) ***Judgment.*** Whether or not favorable to the class, the judgment in a class action must:

(A) for any class certified under Rule 23(b)(1) or (b)(2), include and describe those whom the court finds to be class members; and

(B) for any class certified under Rule 23(b)(3), include and specify or describe those to whom the Rule 23(c)(2) notice was directed, who have not requested exclusion, and whom the court finds to be class members.

(4) ***Particular Issues.*** When appropriate, an action may be brought or maintained as a class action with respect to particular issues.

(5) ***Subclasses.*** When appropriate, a class may be divided into subclasses that are each treated as a class under this rule.

(d) Conducting the Action.

(1) ***In General.*** In conducting an action under this rule, the court may issue orders that:

(A) determine the course of proceedings or prescribe measures to prevent undue repetition or complication in presenting evidence or argument;

(B) require—to protect class members and fairly conduct the action—giving appropriate notice to some or all class members of:

(i) any step in the action;

(ii) the proposed extent of the judgment; or

(iii) the members' opportunity to signify whether they consider the representation fair and adequate, to intervene and present claims or defenses, or to otherwise come into the action;

(C) impose conditions on the representative parties or on intervenors;

(D) require that the pleadings be amended to eliminate allegations about representation of absent persons and that the action proceed accordingly; or

(E) deal with similar procedural matters.

(2) ***Combining and Amending Orders.*** An order under Rule 23(d)(1) may be altered or amended from time to time and may be combined with an order under Rule 16.

(e) Settlement, Voluntary Dismissal, or Compromise. The claims, issues, or defenses of a certified class may be settled, voluntarily dismissed, or compromised only with the court's approval. The following procedures apply to a proposed settlement, voluntary dismissal, or compromise:

(1) The court must direct notice in a reasonable manner to all class members who would be bound by the proposal.

(2) If the proposal would bind class members, the court may approve it only after a hearing and on finding that it is fair, reasonable, and adequate.

(3) The parties seeking approval must file a statement identifying any agreement made in connection with the proposal.

(4) If the class action was previously certified under Rule 23(b)(3), the court may refuse to approve a settlement unless it affords a new opportunity to request exclusion to individual class members who had an earlier opportunity to request exclusion but did not do so.

(5) Any class member may object to the proposal if it requires court approval under this subdivision (e); the objection may be withdrawn only with the court's approval.

(f) Appeals. A court of appeals may permit an appeal from an order granting or denying class-action certification under this rule if a petition for permission to appeal is filed with the circuit clerk within 14 days after the order is entered. An appeal does not stay proceedings in the district court unless the district judge or the court of appeals so orders.

(g) Class Counsel.

(1) ***Appointing Class Counsel.*** Unless a statute provides otherwise, a court that certifies a class must appoint class counsel. In appointing class counsel, the court:

(A) must consider:

(i) the work counsel has done in identifying or investigating potential claims in the action;

(ii) counsel's experience in handling class actions, other complex litigation, and the types of claims asserted in the action;

(iii) counsel's knowledge of the applicable law; and

(iv) the resources that counsel will commit to representing the class;

(B) may consider any other matter pertinent to counsel's ability to fairly and adequately represent the interests of the class;

(C) may order potential class counsel to provide information on any subject pertinent to the appointment and to propose terms for attorney's fees and nontaxable costs;

(D) may include in the appointing order provisions about the award of attorney's fees or nontaxable costs under Rule 23(h); and

(E) may make further orders in connection with the appointment.

(2) ***Standard for Appointing Class Counsel.*** When one applicant seeks appointment as class counsel, the court may appoint that applicant only if the applicant is adequate under Rule 23(g)(1) and (4). If more than one adequate applicant seeks appointment, the court must appoint the applicant best able to represent the interests of the class.

(3) ***Interim Counsel.*** The court may designate interim counsel to act on behalf of a putative class before determining whether to certify the action as a class action.

(4) ***Duty of Class Counsel.*** Class counsel must fairly and adequately represent the interests of the class.

(h) Attorney's Fees and Nontaxable Costs. In a certified class action, the court may award reasonable attorney's fees and nontaxable costs that are authorized by law or by the parties' agreement. The following procedures apply:

(1) A claim for an award must be made by motion under Rule 54(d)(2), subject to the provisions of this subdivision (h), at a time the court sets. Notice of the motion must be served on all parties and, for motions by class counsel, directed to class members in a reasonable manner.

(2) A class member, or a party from whom payment is sought, may object to the motion.

(3) The court may hold a hearing and must find the facts and state its legal conclusions under Rule 52(a).

(4) The court may refer issues related to the amount of the award to a special master or a magistrate judge, as provided in Rule 54(d)(2)(D).

Rule 26. General Provisions Governing Discovery; Duty of Disclosure

(a) Required Disclosures.

(1) ***Initial Disclosure.***

(A) *In General.* Except as exempted by Rule 26(a)(1)(B) or as otherwise stipulated or ordered by the court, a party must, without awaiting a discovery request, provide to the other parties:

(i) the name and, if known, the address and telephone number of each individual likely to have discoverable information—along with the subjects of that information—that the disclosing party may use to support its claims or defenses, unless the use would be solely for impeachment;

(ii) a copy—or a description by category and location—of all documents, electronically stored information, and tangible things that the disclosing party has in its possession, custody, or control and may use to support its claims or defenses, unless the use would be solely for impeachment;

(iii) a computation of each category of damages claimed by the disclosing party—who must also make available for inspection and copying as under Rule 34 the documents or other evidentiary material, unless privileged or protected from disclosure, on which each computation is based, including materials bearing on the nature and extent of injuries suffered; and

(iv) for inspection and copying as under Rule 34, any insurance agreement under which an insurance business may be liable to satisfy all or part of a possible judgment in the action or to indemnify or reimburse for payments made to satisfy the judgment.

(B) *Proceedings Exempt from Initial Disclosure.* The following proceedings are exempt from initial disclosure:

(i) an action for review on an administrative record;

(ii) a forfeiture action in rem arising from a federal statute;

(iii) a petition for habeas corpus or any other proceeding to challenge a criminal conviction or sentence;

(iv) an action brought without an attorney by a person in the custody of the United States, a state, or a state subdivision;

(v) an action to enforce or quash an administrative summons or subpoena;

(vi) an action by the United States to recover benefit payments;

(vii) an action by the United States to collect on a student loan guaranteed by the United States;

(viii) a proceeding ancillary to a proceeding in another court; and

(ix) an action to enforce an arbitration award.

(C) *Time for Initial Disclosures—In General.* A party must make the initial disclosures at or within 14 days after the parties' Rule 26(f) conference unless a different time is set by stipulation or court order, or unless a party objects during the conference that initial disclosures are not appropriate in this action and states the objection in the proposed discovery plan. In ruling on the objection, the court must determine what disclosures, if any, are to be made and must set the time for disclosure.

(D) *Time for Initial Disclosures—For Parties Served or Joined Later.* A party that is first served or otherwise joined after the Rule 26(f) conference must make the initial disclosures within 30 days after being served or joined, unless a different time is set by stipulation or court order.

(E) *Basis for Initial Disclosure; Unacceptable Excuses.* A party must make its initial disclosures based on the information then reasonably available to it. A party is not excused from making its disclosures because it has not fully investigated the case or because it challenges the sufficiency of another party's disclosures or because another party has not made its disclosures.

(2) ***Disclosure of Expert Testimony.***

(A) In General. In addition to the disclosures required by Rule 26(a)(1), a party must disclose to the other parties the identity of any witness it may use at trial to present evidence under Federal Rule of Evidence 702, 703, or 705.

(B) Witnesses Who Must Provide a Written Report. Unless otherwise stipulated or ordered by the court, this disclosure must be accompanied by a written report—prepared and signed by the witness—if the witness is one retained or specially employed to provide expert testimony in the case or one whose duties as the party's employee regularly involve giving expert testimony. The report must contain:

(i) a complete statement of all opinions the witness will express and the basis and reasons for them;

(ii) the facts or data considered by the witness in forming them;

(iii) any exhibits that will be used to summarize or support them;

(iv) the witness's qualifications, including a list of all publications authored in the previous 10 years;

(v) a list of all other cases in which, during the previous 4 years, the witness testified as an expert at trial or by deposition; and

(vi) a statement of the compensation to be paid for the study and testimony in the case.

(C) Witnesses Who Do Not Provide a Written Report. Unless otherwise stipulated or ordered by the court, if the witness is not required to provide a written report, this disclosure must state:

(i) the subject matter on which the witness is expected to present evidence under Federal Rule of Evidence 702, 703, or 705; and

(ii) a summary of the facts and opinions to which the witness is expected to testify.

(D) Time to Disclose Expert Testimony. A party must make these disclosures at the times and in the sequence that the court orders. Absent a stipulation or a court order, the disclosures must be made:

(i) at least 90 days before the date set for trial or for the case to be ready for trial; or

(ii) if the evidence is intended solely to contradict or rebut evidence on the same subject matter identified by another party under Rule 26(a)(2)(B) or (C), within 30 days after the other party's disclosure.

(E) Supplementing the Disclosure. The parties must supplement these disclosures when required under Rule 26(e).

(3) ***Pretrial Disclosures.***

(A) *In General.* In addition to the disclosures required by Rule 26(a)(1) and (2), a party must provide to the other parties and promptly file the following information about the evidence that it may present at trial other than solely for impeachment:

(i) the name and, if not previously provided, the address and telephone number of each witness—separately identifying those the party expects to present and those it may call if the need arises;

(ii) the designation of those witnesses whose testimony the party expects to present by deposition and, if not taken stenographically, a transcript of the pertinent parts of the deposition; and

(iii) an identification of each document or other exhibit, including summaries of other evidence—separately identifying those items the party expects to offer and those it may offer if the need arises.

(B) *Time for Pretrial Disclosures; Objections.* Unless the court orders otherwise, these disclosures must be made at least 30 days before trial. Within 14 days after they are made, unless the court sets a different time, a party may serve and promptly file a list of the following objections: any objections to the use under Rule 32(a) of a deposition designated by another party under Rule 26(a)(3)(A)(ii); and any objection, together with the grounds for it, that may be made to the admissibility of materials identified under Rule 26(a)(3)(A)(iii). An objection not so made—except for one under Federal Rule of Evidence 402 or 403—is waived unless excused by the court for good cause.

(4) ***Form of Disclosures.*** Unless the court orders otherwise, all disclosures under Rule 26(a) must be in writing, signed, and served.

(b) Discovery Scope and Limits.

(1) ***Scope in General.*** Unless otherwise limited by court order, the scope of discovery is as follows: Parties may obtain discovery regarding any nonprivileged matter that is relevant to any party's claim or defense and proportional to the needs of the case, considering the importance of the issues at stake in the action, the amount in controversy, the parties' relative access to relevant information, the parties' resources, the importance of the discovery in resolving the issues, and whether the burden or expense of the proposed discovery outweighs its likely benefit. Information within this scope of discovery need not be admissible in evidence to be discoverable.

(2) ***Limitations on Frequency and Extent.***

(A) *When Permitted.* By order, the court may alter the limits in these rules on the number of depositions and interrogatories or on the length of depositions under Rule 30. By order or local rule, the court may also limit the number of requests under Rule 36.

(B) *Specific Limitations on Electronically Stored Information.* A party need not provide discovery of electronically stored information from sources that the party identifies as not reasonably accessible because of undue burden or cost. On motion to compel discovery or for a protective order, the party from whom discovery is sought must show that the information is not reasonably accessible because of undue burden or cost. If that showing is made, the court may nonetheless order discovery from such sources if the requesting party shows good cause, considering the limitations of Rule 26(b)(2)(C). The court may specify conditions for the discovery.

(C) *When Required.* On motion or on its own, the court must limit the frequency or extent of discovery otherwise allowed by these rules or by local rule if it determines that:

(i) the discovery sought is unreasonably cumulative or duplicative, or can be obtained from some other source that is more convenient, less burdensome, or less expensive;

(ii) the party seeking discovery has had ample opportunity to obtain the information by discovery in the action; or

(iii) the proposed discovery is outside the scope permitted by Rule 26(b)(1).

(3) ***Trial Preparation: Materials.***

(A) *Documents and Tangible Things.* Ordinarily, a party may not discover documents and tangible things that are prepared in anticipation of litigation or for trial by or for another party or its representative (including the other party's attorney, consultant, surety, indemnitor, insurer, or agent). But, subject to Rule 26(b)(4), those materials may be discovered if:

(i) they are otherwise discoverable under Rule 26(b)(1); and

(ii) the party shows that it has substantial need for the materials to prepare its case and cannot, without undue hardship, obtain their substantial equivalent by other means.

(B) *Protection Against Disclosure.* If the court orders discovery of those materials, it must protect against disclosure of the mental impressions, conclusions, opinions, or legal theories of a party's attorney or other representative concerning the litigation.

(C) *Previous Statement.* Any party or other person may, on request and without the required showing, obtain the person's own previous statement about the action or its subject matter. If the request is refused, the person may move for a court order, and Rule 37(a)(5) applies to the award of expenses. A previous statement is either:

(i) a written statement that the person has signed or otherwise adopted or approved; or

(ii) a contemporaneous stenographic, mechanical, electrical, or other recording—or a transcription of it—that recites substantially verbatim the person's oral statement.

(4) ***Trial Preparation: Experts.***

(A) *Deposition of an Expert Who May Testify.* A party may depose any person who has been identified as an expert whose opinions may be presented at trial. If Rule 26(a)(2)(B) requires a report from the expert, the deposition may be conducted only after the report is provided.

(B) *Trial-Preparation Protection for Draft Reports or Disclosures.* Rules 26(b)(3)(A) and (B) protect drafts of any report or disclosure required under Rule 26(a)(2), regardless of the form in which the draft is recorded.

(C) *Trial-Preparation Protection for Communications Between a Party's Attorney and Expert Witnesses.* Rules 26(b)(3)(A) and (B) protect communications between the party's attorney and any witness required to provide a report under Rule 26(a)(2)(B), regardless of the form of the communications, except to the extent that the communications:

(i) relate to compensation for the expert's study or testimony;

(ii) identify facts or data that the party's attorney provided and that the expert considered in forming the opinions to be expressed; or

(iii) identify assumptions that the party's attorney provided and that the expert relied on in forming the opinions to be expressed.

(D) *Expert Employed Only for Trial Preparation.* Ordinarily, a party may not, by interrogatories or deposition, discover facts known or opinions held by an expert who has been retained or specially employed by another party in anticipation of litigation or to prepare for trial and who is not expected to be called as a witness at trial. But a party may do so only:

(i) as provided in Rule 35(b); or

(ii) on showing exceptional circumstances under which it is impracticable for the party to obtain facts or opinions on the same subject by other means.

(E) *Payment.* Unless manifest injustice would result, the court must require that the party seeking discovery:

(i) pay the expert a reasonable fee for time spent in responding to discovery under Rule26(b)(4)(A) or (D); and

(ii) for discovery under (D), also pay the other party a fair portion of the fees and expenses it reasonably incurred in obtaining the expert's facts and opinions.

(5) ***Claiming Privilege or Protecting Trial-Preparation Materials.***

(A) *Information Withheld.* When a party withholds information otherwise discoverable by claiming that the information is privileged or subject to protection as trial-preparation material, the party must:

(i) expressly make the claim; and

(ii) describe the nature of the documents, communications, or tangible things not produced or disclosed—and do so in a manner that, without revealing information itself privileged or protected, will enable other parties to assess the claim.

(B) *Information Produced.* If information produced in discovery is subject to a claim of privilege or of protection as trial-preparation material, the party making the claim may notify any party that received the information of the claim and the basis for it. After being notified, a party must promptly return, sequester, or destroy the specified information and any copies it has; must not use or disclose the information until the claim is resolved; must take reasonable steps to retrieve the information if the party disclosed it before being notified; and may promptly present the information to the court under seal for a determination of the claim. The producing party must preserve the information until the claim is resolved.

(c) Protective Orders.

(1) ***In General.*** A party or any person from whom discovery is sought may move for a protective order in the court where the action is pending—or as an alternative on matters relating to a deposition, in the court for the district where the deposition will be taken. The motion must include a certification that the movant has in good faith conferred or attempted to confer with other affected parties in an effort to resolve the dispute without court action. The court may, for good cause, issue an order to protect a party or person from annoyance, embarrassment, oppression, or undue burden or expense, including one or more of the following:

(A) forbidding the disclosure or discovery;

(B) specifying terms, including time and place or the allocation of expenses, for the disclosure or discovery;

(C) prescribing a discovery method other than the one selected by the party seeking discovery;

(D) forbidding inquiry into certain matters, or limiting the scope of disclosure or discovery to certain matters;

(E) designating the persons who may be present while the discovery is conducted;

(F) requiring that a deposition be sealed and opened only on court order;

(G) requiring that a trade secret or other confidential research, development, or commercial information not be revealed or be revealed only in a specified way; and

(H) requiring that the parties simultaneously file specified documents or information in sealed envelopes, to be opened as the court directs.

(2) ***Ordering Discovery.*** If a motion for a protective order is wholly or partly denied, the court may, on just terms, order that any party or person provide or permit discovery.

(3) ***Awarding Expenses.*** Rule 37(a)(5) applies to the award of expenses.

(d) Timing and Sequence of Discovery.

(1) ***Timing.*** A party may not seek discovery from any source before the parties have conferred as required by Rule 26(f), except in a proceeding exempted from initial disclosure under Rule 26(a)(1)(B), or when authorized by these rules, by stipulation, or by court order.

(2) ***Early Rule 34 Requests.***

(A) Time to Deliver. More than 21 days after the summons and complaint are served on a party, a request under Rule 34 may be delivered:

(i) to that party by any other party, and

(ii) by that party to any plaintiff or to any other party that has been served.

(B) ***When Considered Served.*** The request is considered to have been served at the first Rule 26(f) conference.

(3) ***Sequence.*** Unless the parties stipulate or the court orders otherwise for the parties' and witnesses' convenience and in the interests of justice:

(A) methods of discovery may be used in any sequence; and

(B) discovery by one party does not require any other party to delay its discovery.

(e) Supplementing Disclosures and Responses.

(1) ***In General.*** A party who has made a disclosure under Rule 26(a)—or who has responded to an interrogatory, request for production, or request for admission—must supplement or correct its disclosure or response:

(A) in a timely manner if the party learns that in some material respect the disclosure or response is incomplete or incorrect, and if the additional or corrective information has not otherwise been made known to the other parties during the discovery process or in writing; or

(B) as ordered by the court.

(2) ***Expert Witness.*** For an expert whose report must be disclosed under Rule 26(a)(2)(B), the party's duty to supplement extends both to information included in the report and to information given during the expert's deposition. Any additions or changes to this information must be disclosed by the time the party's pretrial disclosures under Rule 26(a)(3) are due.

(f) Conference of the Parties; Planning for Discovery.

(1) ***Conference Timing.*** Except in a proceeding exempted from initial disclosure under Rule 26(a)(1)(B) or when the court orders otherwise, the parties must confer as soon as practicable—and in any event at least 21 days before a scheduling conference is to be held or a scheduling order is due under Rule 16(b).

(2) ***Conference Content; Parties' Responsibilities.*** In conferring, the parties must consider the nature and basis of their claims and defenses and the possibilities for promptly settling or resolving the case; make or arrange for the disclosures required by Rule 26(a)(1); discuss any issues about preserving discoverable information; and develop a proposed discovery plan. The attorneys of record and all unrepresented parties that have appeared in the case are jointly responsible for arranging the conference, for attempting in good faith to agree on the proposed discovery plan, and for submitting to the court within 14 days after the conference a written report outlining the plan. The court may order the parties or attorneys to attend the conference in person.

(3) ***Discovery Plan.*** A discovery plan must state the parties' views and proposals on:

(A) what changes should be made in the timing, form, or requirement for disclosures under Rule 26(a), including a statement of when initial disclosures were made or will be made;

(B) the subjects on which discovery may be needed, when discovery should be completed, and whether discovery should be conducted in phases or be limited to or focused on particular issues;

(C) any issues about disclosure, discovery, or preservation of electronically stored information, including the form or forms in which it should be produced;

(D) any issues about claims of privilege or of protection as trial-preparation materials, including—if the parties agree on a procedure to assert these claims after production—whether to ask the court to include their agreement in an order under Federal Rule of Evidence 502;

(E) what changes should be made in the limitations on discovery imposed under these rules or by local rule, and what other limitations should be imposed; and

(F) any other orders that the court should issue under Rule 26(c) or under Rule 16(b) and(c).

(4) ***Expedited Schedule.*** If necessary to comply with its expedited schedule for Rule 16(b)conferences, a court may by local rule:

(A) require the parties' conference to occur less than 21 days before the scheduling conference is held or a scheduling order is due under Rule 16(b); and

(B) require the written report outlining the discovery plan to be filed less than 14 days after the parties' conference, or excuse the parties from submitting a written report and permit them to report orally on their discovery plan at the Rule 16(b) conference.

(g) Signing Disclosures and Discovery Requests, Responses, and Objections.

(1) ***Signature Required; Effect of Signature.*** Every disclosure under Rule 26(a)(1) or (a)(3) and every discovery request, response, or objection must be signed by at least one attorney of record in the attorney's own name—or by the party personally, if unrepresented—and must state the signer's address, e-mail address, and telephone number. By signing, an attorney or party certifies that to the best of the person's knowledge, information, and belief formed after a reasonable inquiry:

(A) with respect to a disclosure, it is complete and correct as of the time it is made; and

(B) with respect to a discovery request, response, or objection, it is:

(i) consistent with these rules and warranted by existing law or by a nonfrivolous argument for extending, modifying, or reversing existing law, or for establishing new law;

(ii) not interposed for any improper purpose, such as to harass, cause unnecessary delay, or needlessly increase the cost of litigation; and

(iii) neither unreasonable nor unduly burdensome or expensive, considering the needs of the case, prior discovery in the case, the amount in controversy, and the importance of the issues at stake in the action.

(2) ***Failure to Sign.*** Other parties have no duty to act on an unsigned disclosure, request, response, or objection until it is signed, and the court must strike it unless a signature is promptly supplied after the omission is called to the attorney's or party's attention.

(3) ***Sanction for Improper Certification.*** If a certification violates this rule without substantial justification, the court, on motion or on its own, must impose an appropriate sanction on the signer, the party on whose behalf the signer was acting, or both. The sanction may include an order to pay the reasonable expenses, including attorney's fees, caused by the violation.

Rule 37. Failure to Make or Cooperate in Discovery; Sanctions

(a) Motion for an Order Compelling Disclosure or Discovery.

(1) ***In General*** On notice to other parties and all affected persons, a party may move for an order compelling disclosure or discovery. The motion must include a certification that the movant has in good faith conferred or attempted to confer with the person or party failing to make disclosure or discovery in an effort to obtain it without court action.

(2) ***Appropriate Court.*** A motion for an order to a party must be made in the court where the action is pending. A motion for an order to a nonparty must be made in the court where the discovery is or will be taken.

(3) ***Specific Motions.***

(A) *To Compel Disclosure.* If a party fails to make a disclosure required by Rule 26(a), any other party may move to compel disclosure and for appropriate sanctions.

(B) *To Compel a Discovery Response.* A party seeking discovery may move for an order compelling an answer, designation, production, or inspection. This motion may be made if:

(i) a deponent fails to answer a question asked under Rule 30 or 31;

(ii) a corporation or other entity fails to make a designation under Rule 30(b)(6) or 31(a)(4);

(iii) a party fails to answer an interrogatory submitted under Rule 33; or

(iv) a party fails to produce documents or fails to respond that inspection will be permitted—or fails to permit inspection—as requested under Rule 34.

(C) *Related to a Deposition.* When taking an oral deposition, the party asking a question may complete or adjourn the examination before moving for an order.

(4) ***Evasive or Incomplete Disclosure, Answer, or Response.*** For purposes of this subdivision (a), an evasive or incomplete disclosure, answer, or response must be treated as a failure to disclose, answer, or respond.

(5) ***Payment of Expenses; Protective Orders.***

(A) *If the Motion Is Granted (or Disclosure or Discovery Is Provided After Filing).* If the motion is granted—or if the disclosure or requested discovery is provided after the motion was filed—the court must, after giving an opportunity to be heard, require the party or deponent whose conduct necessitated the motion, the party or attorney advising that conduct, or both to pay the movant's reasonable expenses incurred in making the motion, including attorney's fees. But the court must not order this payment if:

(i) the movant filed the motion before attempting in good faith to obtain the disclosure or discovery without court action;

(ii) the opposing party's nondisclosure, response, or objection was substantially justified; or

(iii) other circumstances make an award of expenses unjust.

(B) *If the Motion Is Denied.* If the motion is denied, the court may issue any protective order authorized under Rule 26(c) and must, after giving an opportunity to be heard, require the movant, the attorney filing the motion, or both to pay the party or deponent who opposed the motion its reasonable expenses incurred in opposing the motion, including attorney's fees. But the court must not order this payment if the motion was substantially justified or other circumstances make an award of expenses unjust.

(C) *If the Motion Is Granted in Part and Denied in Part.* If the motion is granted in part and denied in part, the court may issue any protective order authorized under Rule 26(c) and may, after giving an opportunity to be heard, apportion the reasonable expenses for the motion.

(b) Failure to Comply with a Court Order.

(1) ***Sanctions Sought in the District Where the Deposition Is Taken.*** If the court where the discovery is taken orders a deponent to be sworn or to answer a question and the deponent fails to obey, the failure may be treated as contempt of court. If a deposition-related motion is transferred to the court where the action is pending, and that court orders a deponent to be sworn or to answer a question and the deponent fails to obey, the failure may be treated as contempt of either court where the discovery is taken or the court where the action is pending.

(2) ***Sanctions Sought in the District Where the Action Is Pending.***

(A) *For Not Obeying a Discovery Order.* If a party or a party's officer, director, or managing agent—or a witness designated under Rule 30(b)(6) or 31(a)(4)—fails to obey an order to provide or permit discovery, including an order under Rule 26(f), 35, or 37(a), the court where the action is pending may issue further just orders. They may include the following:

(i) directing that the matters embraced in the order or other designated facts be taken as established for purposes of the action, as the prevailing party claims;

(ii) prohibiting the disobedient party from supporting or opposing designated claims or defenses, or from introducing designated matters in evidence;

(iii) striking pleadings in whole or in part;

(iv) staying further proceedings until the order is obeyed;

(v) dismissing the action or proceeding in whole or in part;

(vi) rendering a default judgment against the disobedient party; or

(vii) treating as contempt of court the failure to obey any order except an order to submit to a physical or mental examination.

(B) *For Not Producing a Person for Examination.* If a party fails to comply with an order under Rule 35(a) requiring it to produce another person for examination, the court may issue any of the orders listed in Rule 37(b)(2)(A)(i)-(vi), unless the disobedient party shows that it cannot produce the other person.

(C) *Payment of Expenses.* Instead of or in addition to the orders above, the court must order the disobedient party, the attorney advising that party, or both to pay the reasonable expenses, including attorney's fees, caused by the failure, unless the failure was substantially justified or other circumstances make an award of expenses unjust.

(c) Failure to Disclose, to Supplement an Earlier Response, or to Admit.

(1) ***Failure to Disclose or Supplement.*** If a party fails to provide information or identify a witness as required by Rule 26(a) or (e), the party is not allowed to use that information or witness to supply evidence on a motion, at a hearing, or at a trial, unless the failure was substantially justified or is harmless. In addition to or instead of this sanction, the court, on motion and after giving an opportunity to be heard:

(A) may order payment of the reasonable expenses, including attorney's fees, caused by the failure;

(B) may inform the jury of the party's failure; and

(C) may impose other appropriate sanctions, including any of the orders listed in Rule 37(b)(2)(A)(i)-(vi).

(2) ***Failure to Admit.*** If a party fails to admit what is requested under Rule 36 and if the requesting party later proves a document to be genuine or the matter true, the requesting party may move that the party who failed to admit pay the reasonable expenses, including attorney's fees, incurred in making that proof. The court must so order unless:

(A) the request was held objectionable under Rule 36(a);

(B) the admission sought was of no substantial importance;

(C) the party failing to admit had a reasonable ground to believe that it might prevail on the matter; or

(D) there was other good reason for the failure to admit.

(d) Party's Failure to Attend Its Own Deposition, Serve Answers to Interrogatories, or Respond to a Request for Inspection.

(1) ***In General.***

(A) *Motion; Grounds for Sanctions.* The court where the action is pending may, on motion, order sanctions if:

(i) a party or a party's officer, director, or managing agent—or a person designated under Rule 30(b)(6) or 31(a)(4)—fails, after being served with proper notice, to appear for that person's deposition; or

(ii) a party, after being properly served with interrogatories under Rule 33 or a request for inspection under Rule 34, fails to serve its answers, objections, or written response.

(B) *Certification.* A motion for sanctions for failing to answer or respond must include a certification that the movant has in good faith conferred or attempted to confer with the party failing to act in an effort to obtain the answer or response without court action.

(2) ***Unacceptable Excuse for Failing to Act.*** A failure described in Rule 37(d)(1)(A) is not excused on the ground that the discovery sought was objectionable, unless the party failing to act has a pending motion for a protective order under Rule 26(c).

(3) ***Types of Sanctions.*** Sanctions may include any of the orders listed in Rule 37(b)(2)(A)(i)–(vi). Instead of or in addition to these sanctions, the court must require the party failing to act, the attorney advising that party, or both to pay the reasonable expenses, including attorney's fees, caused by the failure, unless the failure was substantially justified or other circumstances make an award of expenses unjust.

(e) Failure to Preserve Electronically Stored Information. If electronically stored information that should have been preserved in the anticipation or conduct of litigation is lost because a party failed to take reasonable steps to preserve it, and it cannot be restored or replaced through additional discovery, the court:

(1) upon finding prejudice to another party from loss of the information, may order measures no greater than necessary to cure the prejudice; or

(2) only upon finding that the party acted with the intent to deprive another party of the information's use in the litigation may:

(A) presume that the lost information was unfavorable to the party;

(B) instruct the jury that it may or must presume the information was unfavorable to the party; or

(C) dismiss the action or enter a default judgment.

(f) Failure to Participate in Framing a Discovery Plan. If a party or its attorney fails to participate in good faith in developing and submitting a proposed discovery plan as required by Rule 26(f), the court may, after giving an opportunity to be heard, require that party or attorney to pay to any other party the reasonable expenses, including attorney's fees, caused by the failure.

Rule 60. Relief From Judgment or Order

(a) Corrections Based on Clerical Mistakes; Oversights and Omissions. The court may correct a clerical mistake or a mistake arising from oversight or omission whenever one is found in a judgment, order, or other part of the record. The court may do so on motion or on its own, with or without notice. But after an appeal has been docketed in the appellate court and while it is pending, such a mistake may be corrected only with the appellate court's leave.

(b) Grounds for Relief from a Final Judgment, Order, or Proceeding. On motion and just terms, the court may relieve a party or its legal representative from a final judgment, order, or proceeding for the following reasons:

(1) mistake, inadvertence, surprise, or excusable neglect;

(2) newly discovered evidence that, with reasonable diligence, could not have been discovered in time to move for a new trial under Rule 59(b);

(3) fraud (whether previously called intrinsic or extrinsic), misrepresentation, or misconduct by an opposing party;

(4) the judgment is void;

(5) the judgment has been satisfied, released or discharged; it is based on an earlier judgment that has been reversed or vacated; or applying it prospectively is no longer equitable; or

(6) any other reason that justifies relief.

(c) Timing and Effect of the Motion.

(1) ***Timing.*** A motion under Rule 60(b) must be made within a reasonable time—and for reasons (1), (2), and (3) no more than a year after the entry of the judgment or order or the date of the proceeding.

(2) ***Effect on Finality.*** The motion does not affect the judgment's finality or suspend its operation.

(d) Other Powers to Grant Relief. This rule does not limit a court's power to:

(1) entertain an independent action to relieve a party from a judgment, order, or proceeding;

(2) grant relief under 28 U.S.C. § 1655 to a defendant who was not personally notified of the action; or

(3) set aside a judgment for fraud on the court.

(e) Bills and Writs Abolished. The following are abolished: bills of review, bills in the nature of bills of review, and writs of coram nobis, coram vobis, and audita querela.

Rule 63. Judge's Inability to Proceed

If a judge conducting a hearing or trial is unable to proceed, any other judge may proceed upon certifying familiarity with the record and determining that the case may be completed without prejudice to the parties. In a hearing or a nonjury trial, the successor judge must, at a party's request, recall any witness whose testimony is material and disputed and who is available to testify again without undue burden. The successor judge may also recall any other witness.

Rule 68. Offer of Judgment

(a) Making an Offer; Judgment on an Accepted Offer. At least 14 days before the date set for trial, a party defending against a claim may serve on an opposing party an offer to allow judgment on specified terms, with the costs then accrued. If, within 14 days after being served, the opposing party serves written notice accepting the offer, either party may then file the offer and notice of acceptance, plus proof of service. The clerk must then enter judgment.

(b) Unaccepted Offer. An unaccepted offer is considered withdrawn, but it does not preclude a later offer. Evidence of an unaccepted offer is not admissible except in a proceeding to determine costs.

(c) Offer After Liability Is Determined. When one party's liability to another has been determined but the extent of liability remains to be determined by further proceedings, the party held liable may make an offer of judgment. It must be served within a reasonable time—but at least 14 days—before a hearing to determine the extent of liability.

(d) Paying Costs After an Unaccepted Offer. If the judgment that the offeree finally obtains is not more favorable than the unaccepted offer, the offeree must pay the costs incurred after the offer was made.

FEDERAL RULES OF CRIMINAL PROCEDURE

Rule 44. Right to and Appointment of Counsel

(a) Right to Appointed Counsel. A defendant who is unable to obtain counsel is entitled to have counsel appointed to represent the defendant at every stage of the proceeding from initial appearance through appeal, unless the defendant waives this right.

(b) Appointment Procedure. Federal law and local court rules govern the procedure for implementing the right to counsel.

(c) Inquiry Into Joint Representation.

(1) Joint Representation. Joint representation occurs when:

(A) two or more defendants have been charged jointly under Rule 8(b) or have been joined for trial under Rule 13; and

(B) the defendants are represented by the same counsel, or counsel who are associated in law practice.

(2) Court's Responsibilities in Cases of Joint Representation. The court must promptly inquire about the propriety of joint representation and must personally advise each defendant of the right to the effective assistance of counsel, including separate representation. Unless there is good cause to believe that no conflict of interest is likely to arise, the court must take appropriate measures to protect each defendant's right to counsel.

(As amended Apr. 30, 1979, eff. Dec. 1, 1980; Mar. 9, 1987, eff. Aug. 1, 1987; Apr. 22, 1993, eff. Dec. 1, 1993; Apr. 29, 2002, eff. Dec. 1, 2002.)

FEDERAL RULES OF APPELLATE PROCEDURE

Rule 38. Damages and Costs for Frivolous Appeals

If a court of appeals determines that an appeal is frivolous, it may, after a separately filed motion or notice from the court and reasonable opportunity to respond, award just damages and single or double costs to the appellee.

(As amended Apr. 29, 1994, eff. Dec. 1, 1994; Apr. 24, 1998, eff. Dec. 1, 1998.)

Rule 46. Attorneys

(a) Admission to the Bar.

(1) *Eligibility.* An attorney is eligible for admission to the bar of a court of appeals if that attorney is of good moral and professional character and is admitted to practice before the Supreme Court of the United States, the highest court of a state, another United States court of appeals, or a United States district court (including the district courts for Guam, the Northern Mariana Islands, and the Virgin Islands).

(2) *Application.* An applicant must file an application for admission, on a form approved by the court that contains the applicant's personal statement showing eligibility for membership. The applicant must subscribe to the following oath or affirmation:

"I, _______, do solemnly swear (or affirm) that I will conduct myself as an attorney and counselor of this court, uprightly and according to law; and that I will support the Constitution of the United States.

(3) *Admission Procedures.* On written or oral motion of a member of the court's bar, the court will act on the application. An applicant may be admitted by oral motion in open court. But, unless the court orders otherwise, an applicant need not appear before the court to be admitted. Upon admission, an applicant must pay the clerk the fee prescribed by local rule or court order.

(b) Suspension or Disbarment.

(1) *Standard.* A member of the court's bar is subject to suspension or disbarment by the court if the member:

(A) has been suspended or disbarred from practice in any other court; or

(B) is guilty of conduct unbecoming a member of the court's bar.

(2) *Procedure.* The member must be given an opportunity to show good cause, within the time prescribed by the court, why the member should not be suspended or disbarred.

(3) *Order.* The court must enter an appropriate order after the member responds and a hearing is held, if requested, or after the time prescribed for a response expires, if no response is made.

(c) Discipline. A court of appeals may discipline an attorney who practices before it for conduct unbecoming a member of the bar or for failure to comply with any court rule. First, however, the court must afford the attorney reasonable notice, an opportunity to show cause to the contrary, and, if requested, a hearing.

(Amended Mar. 10, 1986, eff. July 1, 1986; April 24, 1998, eff. Dec. 1, 1998.)

RULES OF THE UNITED STATES SUPREME COURT

PART II. ATTORNEYS AND COUNSELORS

Rule 5. Admission to the Bar

1. To qualify for admission to the Bar of this Court, an applicant must have been admitted to practice in the highest court of a State, Commonwealth, Territory or Possession, or the District of Columbia for a period of at least three years immediately before the date of application; must not have been the subject of any adverse disciplinary action pronounced or in effect during that 3-year period; and must appear to the Court to be of good moral and professional character.

2. Each applicant shall file with the Clerk (1) a certificate from the presiding judge, clerk, or other authorized official of that court evidencing the applicant's admission to practice there and the applicant's current good standing, and (2) a completely executed copy of the form approved by this Court and furnished by the Clerk containing (a) the applicant's personal statement, and (b) the statement of two sponsors endorsing the correctness of the applicant's statement, stating that the applicant possesses all the qualifications required for admission, and affirming that the applicant is of good moral and professional character. Both sponsors must be members of the Bar of this Court who personally know, but are not related to, the applicant.

3. If the documents submitted demonstrate that the applicant possesses the necessary qualifications, and if the applicant has signed the oath or affirmation and paid the required fee, the Clerk will notify the applicant of acceptance by the Court as a member of the Bar and issue a certificate of admission. An applicant who so wishes may be admitted in open court on oral motion by a member of the Bar of this Court, provided that all other requirements for admission have been satisfied.

4. Each applicant shall sign the following oath or affirmation: I, _______, do solemnly swear (or affirm) that as an attorney and as a counselor of this Court, I will conduct myself uprightly and according to law, and that I will support the Constitution of the United States.

5. The fee for admission to the Bar and a certificate bearing the seal of the Court is $200, payable to the United States Supreme Court. The Marshal will deposit such fees in a separate fund to be disbursed by the Marshal at the direction of the Chief Justice for the costs of admissions, for the benefit of the Court and its Bar, and for related purposes.

6. The fee for a duplicate certificate of admission to the Bar bearing the seal of the Court is $15, and the fee for a certificate of good standing is $10, payable to the United States Supreme Court. The proceeds will be maintained by the Marshal as provided in paragraph 5 of this Rule.

Rule 6. Argument Pro Hac Vice

1. An attorney not admitted to practice in the highest court of a State, Commonwealth, Territory or Possession, or the District of Columbia for the requisite three years, but otherwise eligible for admission to practice in this Court under Rule 5.1, may be permitted to argue *pro hac vice.*

2. An attorney qualified to practice in the courts of a foreign state may be permitted to argue *pro hac vice.*

3. Oral argument *pro hac vice* is allowed only on motion of the counsel of record for the party on whose behalf leave is requested. The motion shall state concisely the qualifications of the attorney who is to argue *pro hac vice.* It shall be filed with the Clerk, in the form required by Rule 21, no later than the date on which the respondent's or appellee's brief on the merits is due to be filed, and it shall be accompanied by proof of service as required by Rule 29.

Rule 7. Prohibition Against Practice

No employee of this Court shall practice as an attorney or counselor in any court or before any agency of government while employed by the Court; nor shall any person after leaving such employment participate in any professional capacity in any case pending before this Court or in any case being considered for filing in this Court, until two years have elapsed after separation; nor shall a former employee ever participate in any professional capacity in any case that was pending in this Court during the employee's tenure.

Rule 8. Disbarment and Disciplinary Action

1. Whenever a member of the Bar of this Court has been disbarred or suspended from practice in any court of record, or has engaged in conduct unbecoming a member of the Bar of this Court, the Court will enter an order suspending that member from practice before this Court and affording the member an opportunity to show cause, within 40 days, why a disbarment order should not be entered. Upon response, or if no response is timely filed, the Court will enter an appropriate order.

2. After reasonable notice and an opportunity to show cause why disciplinary action should not be taken, and after a hearing if material facts are in dispute, the Court may take any appropriate disciplinary action against any attorney who is admitted to practice before it for conduct unbecoming a member of the Bar or for failure to comply with these Rules or any Rule or order of the Court.